Red Eagle

Red Eagle

The Army in Polish Politics, 1944–1988

Andrew A. Michta

Hoover Institution Press

Stanford University, Stanford, California

The Hoover Institution on War, Revolution and Peace, founded at
Stanford University in 1919 by the late President Herbert Hoover,
is an interdisciplinary research center for advanced study on
domestic and international affairs in the twentieth century. The
views expressed in its publications are entirely those of the
authors and do not necessarily reflect the views of the staff,
officers, or Board of Overseers of the Hoover Institution.

Hoover Press Publication 386

First printing, 1990
Manufactured in the United States of America
Printed on acid-free paper
96 95 94 93 92 91 90   9 8 7 6 5 4 3 2 1
Library of Congress Cataloging in Publication Data
Michta, Andrew A.
    The Red Eagle.

    Includes bibliographical references.
    1. Poland—Politics and government—1945–1980.
2. Poland—Politics and government—1980–
3. Poland. Polskie Siły Zbrojne. Armia Krajowa—
Political activity. I. Title.
DK4436.M55 1990   943.805   89-19742
ISBN 0-8179-8861-0
ISBN 0-8179-8862-9 (pbk.)

Design by P. Kelley Baker

To Christine

Contents

——— **6** ———

In Control of the Party:
The Army Between the
Ninth Congress and Martial Law   108

——— **7** ———

Jaruzelski's Martial Law   131

——— **8** ———

The Soviet Role
in the Crisis   148

——— **9** ———

Normalization and Beyond,
1982–1988   171

——— **10** ———

Conclusion   204

List of Acronyms Appearing Frequently in Text

AK	Armia Krajowa (Home Army)
AL	Armia Ludowa (People's Army)
CSOP	Centralna Szkoła Oficerów Politycznych (Central School of Political Officers)
FJN	Front Jedności Narodu (Front of National Unity)
FZSMP	Federacja Związków Socjalistycznej Młodzieży Polskiej (Federation of the Unions of Polish Socialist Youth)
GL	Gwardia Ludowa (People's Guard)
GRU	Glavnoye Razvedyvatel'noye Upravleniye (Main Intelligence Administration of the Soviet Armed Forces)
KGB	Komitet Gosudarstvennoy Bezopastnosti (Committee for State Security)
KBW	Korpus Bezpieczeństwa Wewnętrznego (Corps of Internal Security)
KOK	Komitet Obrony Kraju (National Defense Committee)
KOR	Komitet Obrony Robotników (Committee for Workers' Defense)
KRN	Krajowa Rada Narodowa (Home National Council)

LWP	Ludowe Wojsko Polskie (Polish People's Army)
MPA	Main Political Administration
NIK	Najwyższa Izba Kontroli (Supreme Control Commission)
NKVD	Narodnyy Komissariat Vnutrennikh Del (People's Commissariat of Internal Affairs)
OPZZ	Ogólnopolskie Porozumienie Związków Zawodowych (National Association of Trade Unions)
OSWPiZ	Oficerska Szkoła Wojsk Pancernych i Zmechanizowanych (Tank and Armored Infantry Officer School)
OTK	Obrona Terytorialna Kraju (National Territorial Defense)
PAP	Polska Agencja Prasowa (Polish Press Agency)
PKWN	Polski Komitet Wyzwolenia Narodowego (Polish Committee of National Liberation)
POP	Podstawowa Organizacja Partyjna (Basic Party Cell)
PPR	Polska Partia Robotnicza (Polish Workers' Party)
PPS	Polska Partia Socjalistyczna (Polish Socialist Party)
PRON	Patriotyczny Ruch Odrodzenia Narodowego (Patriotic Movement of National Rebirth)
PUWP	Polish United Workers Party
SB	Służba Bezpieczeństwa (Security Police)
Sejm	Polish Parliament
UB	Urząd Bezpieczeństwa (State Security Agency)
UPA	Ukraińska Powstańcza Armia (Ukrainian Resistance Army)
WAP	Wojskowa Akademia Polityczna (Military Political Academy)
WiP	Wolność i Pokój (Freedom and Peace)
WOW	Wojska Obrony Wewnętrznej (Internal Defense Detachments)
WRON	Wojskowa Rada Ocalenia Narodowego (Military Council of National Salvation)
WTO	Warsaw Treaty Organization
ZBoWiD	Związek Bojowników o Wolność i Demokrację (Union of Fighters for Freedom and Democracy)
ZOMO	Zmotoryzowane Odwody Milicji Obywatelskiej (Mechanized Units of the Citizens' Militia)
ZPP	Związek Patriotów Polskich (Union of Polish Patriots)
ZSL	Zjednoczone Stronnictwo Ludowe (United Peasant Party)

Foreword

In only a few instances has the history of the Soviet Union's domination over the countries in Eastern Europe after World War II followed a course as complicated as that of communist rule in Poland. That nation has always considered itself a part of the West; its culture has been defined by a fervent Roman Catholicism and has been symbolized by centuries of opposition to tsarist and communist imperial expansion. Thus Stalin may have been quite serious when he reportedly stated that "trying to impose communism on Poland was like trying to saddle a cow." For their plans to succeed the Soviets initially required a small group of loyal Polish communists; even more importantly, they also needed a large military and police force to suppress all opposition.

The author points out in this timely and incisive study that the takeover in Poland and the continuing hold on political power by the communists cannot be fully understood without an inquiry into the role of the indigenous armed forces. The importance of the military in domestic politics became obvious when martial law was imposed on December 13, 1981, as Gen. Wojciech Jaruzelski and his officers came to the communist party's rescue. In reality, the accession of the army to the highest party and government offices was not as sudden as it might have appeared to the casual observer of the turmoil in Polish politics and the rise of the country's first independent trade union, Solidarity. Exercise of power by Jaruzelski and his entourage is only the most visible aspect of the army's involvement in domestic affairs; it was preceded by several other instances of the army's direct or indirect intervention during crises.

Historically, the army had played a special role in Poland's political life long before the expansion of communist power into Central Europe. As the author explains, the country's history of partitions, insurrections, and defeats has endowed the military with special authority in Polish society. It is against the background of this tradition that the evolution of the Polish People's Army as an actor in communist politics must be analyzed. The communists have repeatedly tried to claim the tradition of the Polish military as a source of their legitimacy. In the aftermath of the declaration and enforcement of martial law, however, this source of legitimacy was ultimately lost to them.

Professor Michta's book lays bare the roots and traces the evolution of the Polish army's involvement in the country's domestic affairs since the Second World War. He places particular emphasis on the events that led to the emergence as political actors of General Jaruzelski and his group of army officers, who became Poland's rulers. Through its detailed and well-documented analysis of the army's role in postwar Polish history, and especially during the 1980–1981 crisis, this study sheds new light on the nature of civil-military relations in Eastern Europe.

Poland's "normalization" during the late 1980s, charted and supervised by Jaruzelski and his senior army officers, ultimately failed to address the country's pressing economic and political problems. Thus today Poland once again finds itself at a crossroads. The economy is in chaos; inflation more than doubled prices during 1988; and the country's foreign debt has surpassed $39 billion. After more than two months of so-called roundtable talks, the regime agreed, among other concessions, to relegalize Solidarity and reform the electoral system to allow for a more open vote. The national elections of June 4 and 18, 1989, resulted in a humiliating defeat for government candidates. After almost a decade of rule by generals and colonels, Poland finds itself in the midst of a deep economic and political crisis that can only be resolved through radical reform of the system. Such reform requires that professional communist party functionaries and the military transfer governmental power to a coalition consisting of Solidarity and other genuine political movements.

Richard F. Staar
Coordinator,
International Studies Program
Hoover Institution

Preface

As this book is going to press, Poland is once again in the forefront of world attention. After more than four months of often agonizing negotiations between the government and opposition forces in Poland, on April 5, 1989, Minister of the Interior Gen. Czesław Kiszczak and Solidarity leader Lech Wałęsa signed a historic compromise agreement that only last year few in the West would have thought possible. After eight years of police repression, the government of Gen. Wojciech Jaruzelski has granted the trade union Solidarity the legal right to organize and operate in the country. Solidarity, whose very existence had been considered a sufficient political threat by the military in 1981 to warrant the declaration of martial law, was again registered with a Polish court. Within less than a decade, the Polish drama has come full circle.

The relegalization of Solidarity is only a part of what appears to be a sweeping change in Poland's politics. The new agreement provides for the creation of a second chamber of parliament (the Senate) and a presidency in place of the current Council of State. The government negotiators have also accepted the opposition's formula on trade-union pluralism; as a result, another independent group, Rural Solidarity, an association of private farmers, has been recognized. The regime has retained control of the Sejm (the lower chamber of the parliament), but it has pledged free elections to the newly established Senate to be held in June, 1989. It has also promised the opposition access to the media, including daily and weekly publications.

The government of the United States hailed the agreement as a seminal change in Poland's domestic affairs and a significant advance on that country's road to greater democracy and badly needed economic change, and has announced its readiness to negotiate economic aid to Poland. The reaction from Western Europe has been equally encouraging. Most important, Soviet reaction to the roundtable accords has been largely positive. In the spirit of Mikhail Gorbachev's policy of *glasnost'* (openness), the Soviet press reported the formation of the Senate and the legalization of Solidarity, while praising the Polish government and the trade union for displaying common sense in reaching the agreement. For now at least, Gorbachev has signaled that he finds the Polish reforms acceptable. However, it is too early to tell whether the same can be said of Polish society.

Solidarity has been an institution in Polish politics for almost nine years. During eight of these it functioned underground as an illegal opposition organization. During that period its leaders built a record of political achievement second to none that is based on belief in the fundamental values of individual freedom and political pluralism. One can only admire the vision and commitment of the opposition activists in their struggle for basic human rights in Poland. In 1989 the Polish government has finally conceded that no matter how strong its repressive apparatus, it needs at least some social cooperation to govern the country. The key question now is whether the proposed changes will endure, and if so, if they will go far enough to start Poland moving in the direction of genuine political and economic reform.

Memphis, Tennessee
May 1989

Acknowledgments

I would like to thank the John M. Olin Foundation and the United States Department of State for their generous financial support throughout this project. Special thanks go to Dr. Richard F. Staar of the Hoover Institution on War, Revolution and Peace who encouraged me in my work and offered his advice on the final revision. Professors Bruce Parrott of the Johns Hopkins School of Advanced International Studies and Vojtech Mastny of Boston University read an early version and made invaluable comments and suggestions.

I am greatly indebted to Tadeusz K. Zachurski of the Radio Free Europe's Polish Section in Washington, D.C.; P. Hartley Walsh of the Library of Congress; Maciej Siekierski of the Hoover Institution's East European Collection; and Andreas Tamberg of Delphic Associates for their assistance in my research. I would also like to thank Margie Rouen, Maria Quironez, and Robert Kunath of the Hoover Institution Library, as well as Ronald Bulatoff of the Hoover Institution Archives, for their tireless patience in helping me locate sources on the Polish army. I am grateful to Vaiva Semion for her careful preparation of the bibliography. Special thanks go to Raymond Meyer of the Hoover Institution Press for his meticulous editing of this book.

Finally, a word of thanks to Professor Donald Abenheim of the U.S. Naval Postgraduate School for long discussions of European military history that helped me to see the Polish army's present in its past.

Introduction

─1────────────────────────

Civil-Military Relations in
Eastern Europe: An Overview

This book describes the military's intervention in Poland's domestic politics from 1944 to the present, with special emphasis on the rise of the officer elite to leadership of the Polish communist party in the 1980s. The imposition of martial law in Poland in 1981 was a clear signal that our assumptions about civilian supremacy over the miliary under communism needed to be revised in order to explain the Polish army's political role during and after the crackdown. Some of the analyses that appeared in the aftermath of martial law called for a radical reassessment of our understanding of communism in Eastern Europe. In one case, it was even suggested that in Poland the "party-state" might already have been replaced by the "army-state."[1] Furthermore, due in part to journalistic reportage on Poland, which in 1981 sought to encapsulate martial-law events in terms easily understood by newspaper readers and the audience of the electronic media, concepts such as "coup d'état" or "military rule"[2] were introduced as shorthand for the Polish military's action.

It is the author's contention that, far from generating a revolution within the Polish party and government, the crisis of 1981 merely brought to the forefront the bureaucratic mechanism already in place. Everything that we know about the dynamics of Soviet-style bureaucracies strongly suggests that they are inherently resistant to fundamental structural modifications; in 1981, during the last years of Brezhnev's conservative leadership, the likelihood of revolutionary systematic change in the Soviet bloc was virtually nil.

Important and insightful as the available studies on Solidarity and martial law are, they have not satisfactorily explained the role of the military in Poland, and the connection between the army's place in Polish politics and the outcome of the 1981 crisis. It is striking that the Polish regime, which during the first sixteen months of Solidarity's existence appeared virtually paralyzed, could in the end rely on the army to come to its defense. Martial law, an elaborate police operation planned and executed by senior Polish officers, dealt a devastating blow to the opposition and restored the structure of the pre-existing system of political power. This book argues that roots of Jaruzelski's action can be found in the 40-year-long history of civil-military relations in Poland. It suggests that the imposition of martial law in 1981 was an extension of the military's traditional involvement in Poland's domestic politics, the pattern of which considerably predated the crisis. Finally, it treats Polish civil-military relations as a product equally of Soviet domination and communist rule, on the one hand, and of the country's military ethos, on the other.

The question of civil-military relations in communist states is by no means new to Western political science, and it has been the subject of vigorous, if inconclusive, debate. A satisfactory answer as to the direction of influence and control, the nature and extent of the vested interests of political and military elites (if, indeed, these ought to be considered separately) in the political system, and the level of institutional interpenetration between the army and the communist party are fundamental to the analysis of communist regimes' strength and stability. In Western scholarship, the discussion of civil-military relations under communism generally follows one (or a combination) of three paradigms: (1) the interest group model (Roman Kolkowicz); (2) the participatory model (Timothy J. Colton); and (3) the historical-institutional model (William E. Odom).

The "interest group" interpretation is built on the premise that in communist states the military functions as a separate political interest group, with a distinctive set of values and goals that differentiates it from the civilian apparat. In this view, the professionalism of the military generates perpetual tension between the army and the party; however, the officers traditionally submit to the apparatchiks' authority, and consequently the army's influence on political decisionmaking at the highest level is limited.[3] Colton's "participatory model" accepts Kolkowicz's argument that the military functions as a clearly defined interest group, but contends that the party refrains from interfering in the army's internal affairs, allows the military a degree of participation in the political decisionmaking process, and ensures that its basic internal, domestic, and foreign-policy objectives are in line with those of the military. Thus, in Colton's interpretation, the Main Political Administration serves the military's interests, rather than being an instrument of civilian party control over the armed forces. In the participatory model, the army is the source of expert advice for politicians and engages in a bargaining process with the party leadership. Using the Soviet case as an example, Colton notes that, as a rule, the military's participation in communist politics has been limited to intramilitary matters, to providing expert advice to the party, while overall the army has refrained from challenging the party's supremacy.[4] Odom's vigorous critique rejects both the "interest group paradigm" and the "participatory model" on the grounds that they assume a cleavage between civilian and military authority in the communist state; drawing upon historical evidence, he argues that such cleavages have never existed. Reviewing the role of civilian-military cooperation in the creation of the Soviet Union, Odom concludes that in the process of that creation the party and the military have forged an alliance based on consensus about their common objectives both domestically and with respect to the country's strategic position in Eastern Europe. Thus, in Odom's view, the army is essentially an administrative arm of the party, and occasional cleavages over policy represent intraparty functional divisions, not a genuine conflict of interests between the army and the party. The civil-military relationship in communist states is by nature symbiotic, the communist military being first and foremost a political institution whose behavior is bureaucratic in character.[5]

It should be pointed out, however, that the three paradigms outlined above (of which Colton's matrix is the most detailed) are best applied to the discussion of civil-military relations in the Soviet Union and the People's Republic of China, that is, to countries characterized by state sovereignty and relative autonomy of the two principal actors. The task becomes more complex when one examines the relationship between the party and the army in Soviet client states of Eastern Europe, where the condition of state sovereignty does not obtain and the autonomy of the elites is seriously limited by Soviet control. A rare case study analysis of civil-military relations in Czechoslovakia was undertaken by Condoleezza Rice in her 1984 book on the evolution of the Czechoslovak army in the context of Soviet-Czechoslovak relations.[6]

As Rice noted, Moscow's policy objectives are a major determinant of civil-military relations in Eastern Europe, and changes in Soviet policy have a discernible impact upon them. Using Kolkowicz's analysis, Rice argues that in Eastern Europe "the party is determined to control the political activity of the military";[7] at the same time, she accepts Colton's premise that, over the years, the East European military has increasingly become a participant in the political process, while its goals and those of the apparatchiks have remained consonant. In the relationship of dominance and dependence characteristic of the Soviet East European empire, the available means of control determine policy options. Rice identifies the Soviet military stationed in Eastern Europe as the locus of Soviet power in relation to satellite military establishments, as well as the direct conduit of Soviet influence in the region.[8] Through bi- and multilateral contacts within the framework of the Warsaw Pact, the Soviets have successfully established a mechanism for strengthening their political control over the satellites and subordinating East European armies to the Soviet Army's general staff.

The Warsaw Pact provides the requisite institutional framework for frequent consultations, military maneuvers, exchange of advisors and military representatives.[9] As this book argues, the Soviets ensure their control over East European militaries through (1) immediate supervision, (2) indoctrination, and (3) personal contacts. The most powerful of the three control methods is immediate supervision exercised through the stationing of troops, through liaison officers detailed to each of the satellites, and through operations of the KGB and Soviet military intelligence on the satellites' territory. Next in the order of importance comes the extensive training program for non-Soviet officers provided by Soviet military and military-political academies. In addition, Moscow has retained the bureaucratic prerogative to approve all promotions in satellite armies to colonel and above.[10] Direct supervision and indoctrination are supplemented by extensive personal contacts between Soviet and East European officers conducted under the banner of "comradeship-in-arms." Friendships forged in the process may prove important political assets in time of crisis, as demonstrated in 1981 by General Jaruzelski's rapport with Marshal Kulikov; conversely, as Czechoslovakia's General Dzúr learned in 1968, their lack may further undercut an East European officer's position in relation to the Soviets. In the case of Poland in 1981, the presence of a direct Soviet "military control channel," and Jaruzelski's reputation as a trusted Soviet friend, were of paramount importance in the choice of a Polish military solution to the crisis.

The Polish Army in Domestic Politics: Between the Past and the Present

An essay by Andrzej Korbonski and Sarah M. Terry traces the evolution of civil-military relations in Poland through four distinct stages. These are: (1) selective co-optation of the military into party structures; (2) political subordination of the military to the party; (3) accommodation between the military and the party; and (4) participation in managing the country.[11] Similar in its method to Rice's study, Korbonski's and Terry's work combines Colton's participation model, Kolkowicz's interest-group paradigm, and some historical material; the authors identify stages in civil-military relations in Poland that correspond roughly to major periods of the country's postwar development. Korbonski and Terry argue that the dichotomy between "political apparatchiks" and "military professionals" is a useful operational distinction applicable to the Polish case (again, the argument is based on Kolkowicz, and indirectly on Samuel Huntington's 1957 analysis of civil-military relations); they conclude that the Polish military has failed to evolve into a "fully emancipated . . . professional fighting force, and its ability to articulate its own interests and demands has remained restricted."[12]

This book contends that the events of 1981 and the so-called normalization of 1982–1986 (officially concluded in July 1986 with the closing of the tenth congress of the Polish communist party) warrant a re-evaluation of Korbonski's and Terry's view of the military's role as an actor separate from the party apparat, and that only gradually increased its participation in the governing of the country. The pattern of "Polish normalization" in the 1980s, which blurred the traditional distinction between civilian and military elites, calls into question (at least as far as senior army and government leaders in Eastern Europe are concerned) the value of the interest-group approach as the framework for analysis.

Besides the essay by Korbonski and Terry, two other important studies of the Polish civil-military relations have been published in the aftermath of martial law in Poland: George Malcher's *Communists in Uniform*, and George Sanford's *Military Rule in Poland*.[13] Malcher's study is strong in its detailed reading of the Polish military press, but its conclusion (Malcher's focus is on the Main Political Administration) does not allow for any differentiation between the military and the civilian apparat. By placing too much emphasis on ideology, Malcher oversimplifies the character of civil-military interpenetration in Poland. Sanford's book, on the other hand, is a general study of Polish politics, rather than an analysis of civil-military relations per se. It covers the crisis, the role of the Catholic Church, the opposition, and the independent trade-union movement; his discussion of civil-military relations is of necessity limited in scope and draws upon Korbonski and Terry for its methodological framework. While an excellent source on Polish society under martial law, Sanford's analysis barely touches upon the issue of Polish military tradition as an influence on the politics of the People's Army.

In addition to Soviet control over armies and communist parties of Eastern Europe, other sources of influence on civil-military relations in the region are each country's history and its national ethos. Among Soviet satellites, Poland is arguably the country where the impact of national tradition is the strongest. This book examines the least-discussed determinant of the interaction between the army and the party in Eastern Europe: the relationship between internationalist ideology and national tradition. It contends that the Polish army, like all modern communist armed forces, has been built on the precepts of communism as well as its own history. Historical evidence demonstrates unequivocally that all communist armies, including the Soviet Army, were created and first staffed chiefly by prerevolutionary officers. Historically, as Odom points out, wherever communists managed to take power, they needed a strong army to consolidate their hold on it; this first "agency of new government" was organized and staffed by members of the prerevolutionary officer corps. Although all communist armies were subsequently purged, the new "proletarian officers" have preserved the key elements of their national ethos bequeathed to them by their teachers. As this book argues, this is particularly true of non-Soviet Warsaw Pact armies, which were created in an "artificially revolutionary" situation brought about and maintained by the presence of the Soviet Army. Among them, the Polish People's Army is arguably the best example of a communist armed force built around a long, very strong, and highly respected national military tradition. While the Soviet system of supervision and control and the bureaucratic mechanism of the communist state are important determinants of civil-military relations in Poland, Polish military tradition has been a major influence in the evolution of the army and its role in the country's politics. Communist indoctrination notwithstanding, the national military tradition has shaped three generations of Polish officers since World War II, and it remains a part of Polish officers' esprit de corps. Without it one cannot account fully for the evolution of Polish-Soviet relations, the pattern of Polish crisis resolution, and, ultimately, for the rise of the military as the leading political elite in the country after 1981.

In Polish history and Polish national mythology,[14] the military tradition is virtually synonymous with national identity. Since 1945, Polish communists have made repeated efforts to claim the military tradition as a means of strengthening and, hopefully, legitimizing their rule. Therefore, except during the last years of Stalinism, the Polish army has never been forced to renounce completely its uniform, ranks, drill, and institutional hierarchy. In effect, the Polish People's Army has attempted to be all thing to all people: an "internationalist" force built upon a nationalist (i.e., patriotic) tradition. Today the Polish officer is taught to take pride both in his country's pre–World War II military past and in his army's achievements under communism. Gen. Wojciech Jaruzelski, the man who has shaped the Polish army over the last twenty years, encapsulated this view of his army's tradition in an address made in 1981 to the graduating class of the Officer School of the Air Defense Forces in Koszalin:

> The people's army is the inheritor of the military achievement of numerous past generations of [Polish] soldiers. In addition, it has developed its own record of achievement over 38 years of struggle, service, and work for Poland.[15]

As Teresa Rakowska-Harmstone points out, this formula, which attempts to blend nationalism and internationalism, defines the character of communist armed forces as "national in form and socialist in content."[16] Because of the constant Soviet pressure for Warsaw Pact integration, the pattern of the Polish People's Army's development has been informed by traditional communist insistence on the party's control of the military. Nevertheless, the degree of successful communist party control over the army is directly related to the strength and cohesion of the party itself. In the Polish case, between 1968 and 1981 the trend was one of general weakening of the party's internal cohesion and, concomitantly, of the growing political assertiveness of the military.

The part of the national heritage that bears directly on Polish civil-military relations under communism is the history of the army's taking "full responsibility for the Commonwealth." This responsibility has been understood as giving the army the task of defending Poland against foreign enemies and also the implicit right to intervene in domestic politics. Because Poland vanished from the map of Europe as a nation-state between 1795 and 1918, the task of rebuilding the republic became, in Polish military history, inextricably intertwined with the soldier's duty to defend the national territory. Until 1918, Poland was to her citizens the shared history, culture, and patriotic cause of her people, rather than a state within clearly defined borders. For the soldiers who fought in the armies of the partitioning powers in World War I, and for those who committed themselves to armed struggle for national liberation in Józef Piłsudski's Polish Legions, the soldier's responsibility to his country became a perpetual commitment.

It was in the name of this concern for the survival of the motherland that Marshal Piłsudski lauched his coup d'état against the elected government in May 1926. In 1981, after 40 years of communist rule and in a fundamentally different political situation, the same rationale was given by General Jaruzelski to justify his action against Solidarity. It is not this author's intention by any means to equate the two military leaders; Piłsudski felt responsible for the state that he had in large measure created, whereas Jaruzelski was an agent of Soviet power. Nevertheless, it is striking that, like Piłsudski in 1926, 75 years later a communist Polish army officer would aspire to present himself to the nation as an ardent Polish patriot. Today, the traditional Polish soldier's role as guardian of the state, albeit attenuated by the Marxist ideology of internationalist proletarian solidarity, has remained a part of the Polish officer's esprit de corps. The military of communist Poland has translated this imperative into a "civic and moral right" to intervene when internal stability is threatened, "to say [to the internal enemy]: 'enough of anarchy and disorder.'"[17]

During the 45 years of the People's Army's existence, Polish soldiers and officers have been told repeatedly that they are responsible not only for the efficient operation of the armed forces, but also for law and order in the country as a whole. Current Polish army regulations, introduced by Jaruzelski in 1977, state explicitly that the soldier is responsible for "preventing others from violating both military procedures and public order, and he is required to assist his superiors as well as government officials in maintaining law and order."[18]

Tradition, however strong, is nevertheless itself subject to gradual change. It would be an obvious mistake simply to equate the ethos of pre-World War II Polish officers with the esprit de corps of the military in communist Poland. While reviewing the powerful influence of Poland's military history upon the character of the People's Army, one should remember that Jaruzelski and his officers are also communist politicians, deeply committed to the existing political system in Poland. Their official pronouncements professing dedication to Marxist-Leninist principles and their allegiance to the Soviet Union indicate that they see no contradiction between, on the one hand, declaring themselves Polish patriots, and on the other hand, stressing their commitment to Marxist "proletarian internationalism."[19]

This apparent contradiction is not necessarily a sign of intentional duplicity. Throughout their careers, Polish officers are trained to serve the communist state. They are expected to be both patriots and internationalists, as these roles are defined according to communist standards. The system of indoctrination the officers are subjected to is directed at forging a mind-set that combines discipline, "progressive elements" of Polish military history, and Marxist-Leninist internationalism. The term used by Polish theoreticians of military education to describe their efforts is "military upbringing" (*wojskowe wychowanie*), which includes: (1) sociopolitical education (*szkolenie społeczno-polityczne*); (2) general army training (*szkolenie ogólnowojskowe*); (3) combat training (*szkolenie bojowe*); and (4) specialized technical training (*szkolenie techniczne*).[20] The first goal defines the communist army's approach to morale building; the remaining three are strictly professional objectives typical of any modern army. The program of "military upbringing," as practiced by the Polish People's Army, aims at turning its officers and men into "dedicated patriots, unquestionably committed to Poland and socialism, and [who prove] their commitment every day through eager service and work."[21] The two themes, Polish patriotism and socialist internationalism, form the core of morale building in the People's Army. The former inevitably draws upon Polish military history; the latter explains Poland's alliance with the other countries of the Eastern bloc in the Warsaw Treaty Organization (WTO) and the communist system in terms of a "progressive socialist ideal."

Today, as a result of military sociopolitical education, Poland's senior officers openly accept the premise that the "army is an all-national institution," as well as the argument that their highest political goal is "socialist [i.e., communist] Poland."[22] One can only speculate whether these are genuine convictions, and if so, to what degree they are determined by indoctrination alone. The preponderance of Soviet power within the East European bloc must be quite obvious to Polish officers, who through their professional contacts are made constantly aware of Moscow's military might. It is impossible to determine for certain whether in 1981 the Polish military acted as defenders of communism in Poland (and thereby protected Soviet geopolitical interests in Eastern Europe) out of personal belief, or because they feared the consequences of disobedience. However, it remains a fact that for the past twenty years, Jaruzelski and his officers have consistently behaved in accordance with the declared principles of socialist internationalism, while explaining their decisions in terms borrowed from Poland's military tradition: the soldier's responsibility to the motherland.

Although, as this book seeks to demonstrate, throughout the postwar period the fundamental political objectives of the People's Army's senior officers (preservation of the existing political system internally and of the Eastern bloc alliance externally) have been virtually identical with those of the civilian elite of the Polish communist party, it would be a mistake to describe the party and army elites in Poland as completely similar. The military officers display certain significant differences that set them apart from the civilian apparat of the Polish United Workers Party (Polska Zjednoczona Partia Robotnicza; PUWP).

First, unlike the apparatchiks, Polish officers have derived their political authority not only from the Soviet Union's dominant position in Eastern Europe, but also from Poland's military tradition, of which they claim to be a part. The army in Poland, especially the officer corps, has enjoyed a measure of respect paralleled in Eastern Europe only by the position of the pre–World War II Hungarian officer corps. The roots of the Polish military ethos reach down through two centuries of the nation's history and are constitutive of the Polish cultural heritage. At least until 1981, one of the Polish military's greatest assets was the officer corps's ability to present the army as the inheritor of the country's heroic military tradition, and thus draw upon traditional respect for the Polish soldier. Polish society, because of the nation's history of frequent wars, defeats, and insurrections, has come to regard the military as the symbol of national survival. Not surprisingly, a public opinion poll taken in Poland in 1981 showed that the army was one of the most highly respected and trusted institutions in Polish society, rated third after Solidarity and the Catholic Church.[23]

The second major difference that until 1981 set apart the civilian PUWP apparat and the Polish military elite was the latter's ability to insulate itself from the periodic crises that had plagued the Polish communists throughout the postwar period. The Poles' consistent unwillingness to take the army to task for its role in the country's politics is striking in the light of available evidence confirming the officers' active role in governing Poland. As this book argues, long before the 1981 imposition of martial law, the army intervened repeatedly to strengthen and consolidate communist power in Poland, and was on several occasions employed directly against the population. Even so, until 1981 the Polish military was never seriously criticized by society. On the contrary, in the 1970s the army's image of an impartial defender of the motherland was strengthened by its displays of professional skill and professed detachment from domestic politics.

The ability to preserve successfully the secrecy of the army's internal politics has been the third major difference between the Polish military and the civilian party apparat, one which proved to be of great value to Jaruzelski during the preparations for the showdown with Solidarity, and which has remained essential to his power today. Protected by the army's traditional insistence on security and classification of sensitive information, until 1981 the officer corps had been virtually immune to the scandals that plagued the PUWP. Even espionage cases that involved army officers, such as the notorious case of Col. Jerzy Pawłowski, the Polish fencing champion who turned foreign agent, were immediately hushed up. As a result, it was relatively easy for the Jaruzelski group to project the desired image of nationalism and patriotism, and at the same time to retain the necessary room to maneuver in party politics. In effect, the military in Poland had been capable of creating a myth of its own fairness and impartiality and had had no need to fear that the actions of particular officers would ever be judged or criticized publicly, as had always been the case whenever a change in top-level leadership took place within the party.

This insulation of the military in communist societies in general has been its major political asset. In the Polish case, Jaruzelski's alleged declaration that the army would not fire on the workers, presumably made in reference to the 1976 food riots, was taken both by political observers and by the general public as a declaration of the general's moral principles, rather than as an expression of a particular political stance during the crisis. In light of the evidence presented in this book, however, it is apparent that in 1976 Jaruzelski refused to expend his political assets by defending the hopelessly ineffective and corrupt Gierek regime simply because such action would have been ill-timed and politically harmful to his position in the party. Stories about Jaruzelski's fierce nationalism, which at the time circulated among the Poles, were more expressions of the nation's traditional beliefs in the army's patriotism than an objective judgment based on facts. Thanks chiefly to Poland's history, until 1981 the Polish army was the only state institution that had managed to retain its prestige in society, despite the periodic crises that shook the country's systemic foundations.

Factual data and a detailed description of events during the Solidarity period provide only a partial explanation of the resolution of the 1981 crisis. The military succeeded in crushing a 10-million-member-strong opposition movement because it took that movement by complete surprise. Despite all the clear warnings that the army might introduce a state of emergency, Solidarity did not believe the military would wage war against the nation. The myth of the Polish soldier and the national insurrectionary tradition, two essential ingredients of the Polish sense of national identity, made such a move inconceivable. As 1981 demonstrated, beliefs and reality were two different things. Therefore, it is important to examine the military's experience in communist Poland. The careers of Jaruzelski and his officers mirror the evolution of the Polish People's Army. Their biographies are also a story of the tortuous evolution of Polish communism, while their prominence after 1981 has its direct roots in the transformation of Poland's internal politics in the 1970s.

Finally, purely bureaucratic factors contributed to the rise of Jaruzelski and his men as the governing political elite in Poland. The "Polish August" was a culmination of the decade-long process of change in the balance of power within the PUWP. At the same time, the 1970s witnessed a rapid modernization of the Polish People's Army, which, under Jaruzelski's tutelage, had been transformed into a well-equipped fighting force led by a well-educated and politically active officer elite with a strong sense of esprit de corps. These were the assets the military translated into growing political influence in Poland, although the army's involvement in the country's crises before the advent of Solidarity was muted and often indirect. Still, the outcomes of the crises in 1970 and 1976 were strongly influenced by Jaruzelski's willingness to throw the army's authority behind one, and to withhold it from another solution. As this book seeks to demonstrate, Jaruzelski's willingness in 1970 to use his regulars on a mass scale against the striking workers of the Baltic coast brought the internal crisis within the party to a head and accelerated the elevation of Edward Gierek to the position of party first secretary; in 1976, the military's unwillingness to back up the regime during the Radom-Ursus riots was instrumental in bringing about the government's hasty retreat in the face of the workers' violent opposition to price rises. The two crises of the 1970s secured for the military a level of political influence that, in 1981, allowed the army elite to move to center stage and effectively assume party leadership. High-ranking officers of the People's Army were appointed to key party and government posts. In this book, the analysis of the process through which the Polish officer corps evolved from a relatively uneducated and amorphous group into the highly cohesive and integrated elite of the 1980s draws upon the People's Army's history, with an emphasis on the careers of the officers who were to play key roles in 1981.

Polish Party Politics

The principal focus of this book is the army's behavior during and after Jaruzelski's imposition of martial law. It is impossible to identify a single cause of the Polish crisis of 1980–1981. The wave of labor unrest in Poland that shook the foundations of the communist state resulted from a confluence of economic and political pressures within Polish society. The mismanagement of the country's economy, starkly demonstrated by a $30 billion debt to the West, was ostensibly a principal cause of the Polish August. Less visible but equally important were the pent-up pressures for political liberalization that had intermittently confronted the government throughout the postwar period, and that came to a head in August 1980. The third, and possibly most important, factor that contributed to the initial success of the workers' revolt was the internal collapse of the ruling Polish United Workers' Party.

Throughout the 1970s, the growing corruption and inefficiency of the party apparatchiks undermined those last vestiges of authority that in 1970 had permitted Edward Gierek to defuse the "December Crisis." As a result, in Poland in 1981, for the first time in the history of a Soviet-bloc state, the military replaced the civilian apparat as the leader of the ruling elite. The change within the PUWP's top leadership was the most dramatic event in the party's history since the communists took power in Poland after World War II. It was also an important event for the Soviet bloc as a whole; for the first time in the history of the Soviet empire, in Poland in 1981 the presumed doctrinal principle of the party's supremacy over the military was shown to have been more an ideological assertion than a reality.

The Polish party that emerged from the 1981 crisis, although structurally unchanged, had undergone a major transformation. The crackdown of December 1981, engineered by Gen. Wojciech Jaruzelski and swiftly executed by the armed and security forces, marked not only the PUWP's return to a more traditional approach to large-scale political dissent, but also an important qualitative change inside the party itself: the military, headed by General Jaruzelski, became overtly the leading political force in Poland. Organizational changes within the structure of the Polish government followed.

If the resolution of the 1981 crisis of itself set a precedent in the history of Soviet-controlled communist parties, even more surprising was the "Polish normalization" of 1982–1986, during which the Soviets not only tolerated, but fully supported the political entrenchment of Jaruzelski's group. This book argues that, in fact, the novelty of the situation was more apparent than real. Jaruzelski and his officers were party politicians as well as soldiers. As politicians, they enjoyed in 1981 a unique advantage over the apparatchiks in that they represented an institution with high national prestige; on the more practical side, they commanded the army and dominated the security forces. In terms of bureaucratic politics, the period between 1981 and 1986 saw personnel changes in the government that strengthened Jaruzelski's power base in the army and the police; however, these changes were not qualitatively different from similar campaigns conducted by previous party leaders who had

relied for support on the "old guard" (Gomułka) or Silesian regional apparatchiks (Gierek). The mechanics of Jaruzelski's "house cleaning" were also
similar to previously used means: the general purged potential opponents and
elevated his trusted cronies to key government and party positions. However,
Jaruzelski's "normalization" introduced several important changes into the
structure of the government. In 1983, Jaruzelski revamped the National
Defense Committee (Komitet Obrony Kraju; KOK) and substantially strengthened the position of chairman of the Council of State relative to that of prime
minister. As discussed in Chapter 9, these changes contributed to an unprecedented concentration of political power in Jaruzelski's hands. With respect to
internal party politics, "normalization" was ultimately a reversion to the early
Stalinist period, when first secretary and chairman of the Council of State
(until 1953 the latter was called president of the Polish People's Republic) were
the most powerful state offices. At the closing of "normalization" in 1986, both
positions were held by Jaruzelski.

"Normalization" within the party and government was not, however,
synonymous with resolving the Polish crisis. In fact, the return to Stalinist
formulas (advocated by Jaruzelski and his cronies) only widened the gap
between the regime and Polish society and ultimately further aggravated the
situation. The two waves of nationwide strikes that shook Poland in 1988 were
a clear reminder that the "normalized" communist party of 1988 was no more
capable of winning over the hearts and minds of the Polish people than it had
been in 1980. Although after "normalization" the PUWP was better able to
repress dissent, it remained incapable of governing the country effectively.

In 1981, it was not immediately obvious to an outside observer that the
manner in which the regime handled the crisis indicated a lasting change
inside Poland's ruling elite. Until the crackdown of December 13, the government compromised, negotiated, and procrastinated. Although a sizeable
amount of information about the civilian party leadership was available, the
Polish military was, for the most part, an enigma both to Western students of
Poland and to the Poles themselves. The secrecy that had surrounded the
affairs of the army throughout the postwar period made it difficult to separate
hard facts from myths and speculation. Since December 1981, enough material has been made public in the West, including the authoritative testimony of
Col. Ryszard J. Kukliński, a defector and a former CIA agent inside the Polish
general staff, who was intimately involved in military planning until November 1981.

Soviet Intervention

This book regards Soviet intervention in Poland as a crucial political factor.
For in 1981, Soviet pressure ultimately dictated the course of events there.

Thus an entire chapter is devoted to Soviet policies toward Poland during the first sixteen months of Solidarity's existence and during the period between the imposition of martial law and its formal suspension, in 1982.

Jaruzelski's action against Solidarity was preceded by detailed preparations. We know today that these plans were closely supervised by, and coordinated with the Soviets. Moscow's repeated demands for a speedy resolution of the crisis were backed up by threats of direct military action. But the plans to use the Polish army and security forces to suppress political opposition in the country took months to prepare; at the same time, a political solution to the crisis was sought, even if only to buy time. Although ultimately successful, martial law was, from the Kremlin's standpoint, a second-best solution compared with the time-tested political means of containing the crisis by temporary concessions to the workers' demands and subsequent crackdown against the opposition. Here again, the experience of the 1970s strongly influenced the course of events in 1981.

Brezhnev had good reason to hesitate in giving his support to the Polish military's plans for action against Solidarity. The decision to rely on Jaruzelski and his entourage was, in the Kremlin's view, potentially much more dangerous than the already-proven political solution. Notwithstanding the obvious doctrinal problems that would be raised by the military's success in destroying Solidarity (the precedent-setting rise of the army to the pinnacle of political power in a communist state simply did not look right), failure meant that a joint WTO military action against Poland would have to be initiated at the time when Solidarity had been fully alerted and was prepared to fight. As reported by Colonel Kukliński, the Soviets made the necessary preparations to ensure that they had the capability to act unilaterally if Jaruzelski's plans failed, but they were visibly anxious to avoid the political damage bloody resistance to their invasion of Poland would cause them worldwide. Since at the time the debate over missile deployment was already under way in Western Europe, Brezhnev knew that an invasion of Poland by the Warsaw Pact would effectively bury détente. This book argues that, although the Soviets twice made preparations to invade, in December 1980 and in March–April 1981, their readiness during the latter period was principally an insurance policy against Jaruzelski's failure that the Kremlin hoped it would not have to rely upon to keep Poland in line. There is no question that by imposing martial law and crushing Solidarity, the Polish military did Soviet bidding; abundant evidence has emerged since 1981 demonstrating the extent of Soviet intervention in Poland's politics during the crisis. There was also nothing surprising in the government's claim that the decision to impose martial law was made autonomously by the Polish authorities. It could only be expected that in a grave national crisis, the army and the party would appeal to the Poles' patriotism. One should also keep in mind that since the 1970s, the Polish military had increasingly become involved in the governing of the country. It was to be expected that Jaruzelski and his officers would view the threat of direct Soviet intervention as a sufficient justification for their action. As the general argued in his speech to the nation on December 13, 1981, the army's goal was to avert a "national catastrophe" and a "civil war."

It is true that in 1981 the Polish army's general staff was uniquely qualified to judge the imminence of Soviet invasion. Since, in addition to direct contacts between the Polish and Soviet communist parties, the mechanisms of Soviet control over Poland include the military channel, in particular, direct Soviet supervision of the Polish army through Marshal Viktor Kulikov's Warsaw Pact command post in Legnica, in western Poland, Jaruzelski knew with great clarity what was at stake, and what moves the Soviets were ready to make. It is clear that from the start Jaruzelski chose not to resist the Soviets openly. Frequent disagreements between the Poles and Soviet liaison officers in Poland (reported by Colonel Kukliński) concerned predominantly the timing of the military operation. This suggests that the Polish military felt strong ties to the existing political system. Kukliński's revelations are a commentary on Jaruzelski's brand of patriotism and on his loyalty to the Soviets; however, they also indicate that in 1981 the military recognized that the organizational structure of the Warsaw Pact largely precluded any concerted resistance by the Polish army if Soviet forces were deployed against it.

Against the "Coup d'État" Argument

This book argues that from Moscow's standpoint, the immediate result of the 1981 crackdown was a compromise solution. On the one hand, it led to the emergence of a qualitatively new phenomenon: an open transfer of political power in a communist state from the civilian apparat to the top-level military establishment; on the other hand, senior Polish military officers acted in the name of the communist party and were allowed to continue governing Poland on the condition that they exercise their authority within the existing Leninist party structures. Hence, as this book argues, despite outward appearances, the change effected in 1981 within the structure of political power in Poland was not a military coup d'état, but a shift of key government posts from one functional group, the civilian apparat, to another, the top-level military elite.

The 1981 restructuring of Poland's ruling elite was the culmination of the long-term process of the gradual erosion of the party's power, paralleled by a steady, if not immediately apparent, consolidation of the officer elite's role in Poland's domestic politics. In 1981 there was no conspiracy inside the Polish armed forces, nor did the generals capture power by overwhelming the existing government. The major difference between Jaruzelski's crackdown and the coups d'état that periodically rock Third World countries lay in the absence of conflict between a legitimate regime (the PUWP regime could never claim to have been legitimately elected) and a military that might have felt threatened by the government's policies, or else whose officer corps was representative of a class challenged by the regime. In 1981, the Polish military had no professional grievances against the PUWP; on the contrary, the 1970s had witnessed rapid modernization of the armed forces and career advancement for People's Army officers.[24] Hence, in the Polish case the action was taken not to alter the political direction of the government, but rather to prop it up against the onslaught of the opposition. This makes the Polish case fundamentally different from, for example, Pinochet's overthrow of the Allende government in Chile.

After the imposition of martial law, the army moved to institutionalize the change by converting emergency martial-law decrees into permanent legislation. This legislation gave the military a decisive voice in the government and granted Jaruzelski the authority to use his troops against the opposition whenever, in his judgment, such action might be warranted. The transition occurred within the framework of the same ideology and the same centralized Stalinist form of government that had previously obtained. Both the old apparatchiks and the new Jaruzelski leadership belonged to the same political tradition and professed similar objectives: maintenance of the communist system domestically and preservation of the WTO alliances internationally. This political creed has been traditionally justified by the PUWP as Poland's *raison d'état*, arising from the country's proximity to, and the nature of its relationship with the Soveit Union. In purely bureaucratic terms, after the PUWP's protracted internal crisis of the 1970s and with Moscow's approval, in 1981 the apparatchiks simply stepped aside.

◆   ◆   ◆

The book is organized as follows. Chapter 2 gives a brief overview of Poland's military tradition, with a particular emphasis on the development of the Insurrectionary Tradition and the formation of the Polish military ethos.

Chapter 3 reviews in detail the creation and the early evolution of the Polish People's Army. Special emphasis is placed on the military's role in the communist takeover in Poland after the war, and on the 1956 Polish October. The chapter concludes with General Jaruzelski's appointment as defense minister in 1968.

Chapter 4 focuses on Jaruzelski's career, including his role during the 1968 invasion of Czechoslovakia. It discusses the maturation process through which, in the 1970s, the Polish military became a major influence in the country's political life. Jaruzelski's behavior during the two crises of that decade is briefly examined.

Chapter 5 discusses the beginnings of the crisis of 1980–1981, the military's hard-line political campaign against Solidarity, and Jaruzelski's early preparations for imposing martial law. The preparations for the introduction of martial law in Poland are considered on two planes. First, their political dimension is examined. This discussion focuses on the extensive political campaign against Solidarity, which indirectly challenged the civilian PUWP leadership's ability to govern. The consistency with which this campaign was conducted suggests that it was a part of a comprehensive, if ad hoc, strategy aimed at reassuring the Kremlin that even though the apparatchiks were incapable of action, the Polish army represented a viable alternative to direct intervention by the WTO. The principal themes of the campaign are reconstructed from articles, speeches, and official statements published in *Wojsko Ludowe* (People's army), the monthly of the Polish Army's Main Political Administration; *Żołnierz Polski* (The soldier of Poland), the army weekly; and *Żołnierz Wolności* (The soldier of freedom), the People's Army's daily newspaper. Here, as well as in the subsequent two chapters, the testimony of Col. Ryszard Kukliński, is weighed against other sources of evidence.

Chapter 6 analyzes the military's behavior between the Ninth Extraordinary PUWP Congress and the imposition of martial law. It traces the pattern of actions through which Jaruzelski took complete control of the PUWP.

Chapter 7 discusses the mechanics of the 1981 crackdown. Special emphasis is placed on Jaruzelski's priorities at the time, that is, the consolidation of the party as the military's primary objective, over and above economic reform.

Chapter 8 traces the evolution of the Soviet attitude to the Polish crisis between 1980 and 1982. The Kremlin's apparent doubts about Jaruzelski immediately after the crackdown and Moscow's gradual acceptance of the general's regime are discussed; Polish-Soviet cooperation before and during the period of martial law is a major topic of the analysis. The succession of Soviet actions will be gleaned from Kukliński's testimony, from the pattern of official visits to Poland immediately prior to the declaration of martial law, and the movements of the Soviet Army. Official statements made by the CPSU Politburo, Soviet press releases, and open messages addressed to the Polish communists serve as an additional insight into the evolution of the Soviet position during the crisis and the process through which the idea of using Poland's army against Solidarity came to fruition.

Chapter 9 looks at Jaruzelski's "normalization program," implemented in Poland between December 1982 and June 1986, as well as the opposition's dramatic challenge to the government in 1988. Finally, the analysis addresses the question of the costs to the institution of the military, both in terms of the army's social prestige and the soldier's morale, of Jaruzelski's role in the Polish drama of the 1980s. The dramatic rise in draft resistance among Polish youth, organized in the independent movement Freedom and Peace, and the first signs of oppositional activities within the armed forces are indications that Poland is in the midst of re-evaluating its traditional understanding of the army's role in society. Although the military regime has failed to gain acceptance in Poland, as demonstrated by the 1987 referendum on economic reform and a wave of strikes that shook Poland during April and May and again in August of 1988, it has nonetheless introduced changes in the government's structure that will determine the distribution of political power in Poland in the 1990s.

Sources of Poland's Military Tradition

— 2

The Military Ethos

Poland's military tradition differs substantially from those of her Eastern bloc neighbors. Between the late eighteenth century, when the country rapidly declined politically and socially, and the re-emergence of Poland as an independent state in 1918, the Polish military ethos evolved around three national themes: the Insurrectionary Tradition, the aristocratic military ideal, and the national myth of the patriotic Polish soldier—the motherland's favorite son. To varying degrees, the three themes have been carried over to the present day and, as part of the People's Army's esprit de corps, have shaped the military's self-image and the civil-military relations in communist Poland.

The Insurrectionary Tradition is the strongest of the three. It has its roots in the last desperate campaigns fought until the Third Partition of the Commonwealth of Poland-Lithuania, which, in 1795, erased the country from the map of Europe. The military commanders of those battles, the most famous of which are Tadeusz Kościuszko and Kazimierz Pułaski, have become national icons, enshrined in Poland's history not only as generals of campaigns past, but also as great patriotic leaders. Such images left indelible marks on the Polish national identity during the Period of Partitions, which lasted from 1795 to 1918. The belief that the nation would rise against the occupying powers and, led by its *naczelnik* (leader), restore the country to its former greatness became an indestructible element of Poland's romantic tradition. This strand of Polish romanticism has survived in present-day Poland. In Polish schools of today, children memorize the patriotic poems of midnineteenth century Polish romantics as great masterpieces of Polish literature. The Polish national anthem still tells of General Dąbrowski, a Polish commander under Napoleon, who will "lead the nation" to freedom and independence. In the Polish national consciousness, the uprisings against the Russians in 1830 and 1864 have remained milestones on the road to independence.

Although prominent in the esprit de corps of the army of the Second Commonwealth,[1] the aristocratic military ideal is the weakest strand in the military ethos of today's People's Army. In interwar Poland, the army ranked among the most respected institutions in the country, and the military profession enjoyed high prestige. To be an officer meant to be one of the best and the brightest, dedicated to one's *naczelnik* and the country. The primacy of one's ultimate allegiance to the leader, rather than to the government, has been a legacy of prepartition Poland. This aspect of the aristocratic military ideal made it possible for Piłsudski to stage a successful military coup d'état in 1926.

Piłsudski's ascendancy between the wars owed even more to the Poles' belief that the army was the guardian of the country's independence. The brief Polish-Soviet war of 1919–1920, as a result of which Poland's eastern borders were extended, made the military custodian of Poland's statehood and, after the 1926 coup, a major political force in civilian life as well. The acceptance by the majority of the Poles of the army's rapidly rising influence was in part due to the belief that the soldier—the defender of the motherland against Bolshevism—was guided in his actions by patriotism and dedication to the country. Between the two world wars, Marshal Józef Piłsudski and his fellow officers transformed the ideals of the Polish Insurrectionary Tradition into the legacy of the army as the sole guardian of the state. This belief was badly shaken by the disasters of the 1939 campaign; nevertheless, in the course of World War II the Poles fought first in allied armies and eventually in two Polish armed forces, one controlled by the prewar government-in-exile, the other subordinated to Polish communists and the Soviet high command.

The power of the Polish military ethos has proved strong enough to leave indelible marks on the new Polish People's Army, created in 1944 under the guidance of the communist government. The new army grew from a small force organized, armed, trained, and outfitted according to the Soviet model into the second largest Warsaw Pact force, which today numbers over 400,000 officers and men.[2] During the more than 40 years since the war, the Polish officers' esprit de corps has evolved into a curious blend of nationalism, dating back to the early Polish insurrections, and Marxist-Leninist orthodoxy. The communist character of the Polish People's Army has been determined by Soviet domination and control. The roots of the nationalism still prominently displayed in the Polish officers' ethos must be sought in Polish military history.

The Army of the Commonwealth of Poland-Lithuania

Poland's military history is replete with wars, insurrections, and campaigns won and lost. Still, with the exception of the reign of the late Jagiellonians and Stefan Bathory (in the late fifteenth and early sixteenth centuries) and the period immediately following King Jan Sobieski's victory over the Turks at Vienna (in late seventeenth century), the Commonwealth of Poland-Lithuania never enjoyed a military preponderance in East-Central Europe commensurate with the country's wealth, size, and population. At the end of the fifteenth century, the Commonwealth was at the peak of its power and, considering the state's vast territories, ranked among the most populous countries of Europe. The country prospered, nourished by territorial expansion to the east and northeast and by a flourishing economy, especially agriculture and the Vistula grain trade.[3] After Poland-Lithuania's power peaked in the midsixteenth century, the Commonwealth fought an increasingly futile rearguard action in an attempt to preserve its integrity and its outmoded political institutions.

Until the Third Partition of Poland in 1795, the Commonwealth's standing army was small. The defense of the Eastern Borderlands was left to private armies of leading aristocratic houses. For a centrally controlled army, Poland-Lithuania relied mainly on the Kwarciani, a small and predominantly mercenary force, and the *levée en masse* of the nobility, in which every *szlachcic* (nobleman) was obliged to serve in time of war. As the country's fortunes declined following a series of defeats during the peasant risings in the Ukraine in the midseventeenth century, an attempt was made to formalize the procedures for creating and maintaining an army sufficient for the country's needs. In 1652, the Commonwealth's armed forces were reorganized; the division of the army into the permanent force, Wojsko Kwarciane, and the supplementary force, Wojsko Suplementowe, was abolished, and a unified army known as Wojsko Komputowe was put in their place. Still, the distinction between "Polish" and "foreign" contingents was retained. The size of the Komput depended on the appropriations voted in each year by the Sejm (Polish parliament) and varied in accordance with the Commonwealth's needs, which were smaller in peacetime, greater during war. Until the mideighteenth century, the Komput numbered between 11 and 33 thousand soldiers.[4]

Only in 1788 did the Great Sejm vote for a standing army of 100,000 men. The legislation provided for the creation of the general staff and the standardization of the size and structure of the armies of Poland-Lithuania. It also established artillery and engineering corps, and authorized funding for two new military academies, the Artillery School in Warsaw and the Engineering

School in Kamieniec, plus a new military school in Wilno.[5] Because of the rapidly deteriorating political situation in the country and the determination of Russia and Prussia to maintain Poland as a client state, these plans were never fully implemented. The army that fought to defend the liberal May Constitution of 1791 was only 70 thousand strong and, for the most part, badly trained, poorly led, and unprepared to face the Russian invasion.[6] Throughout the seventeenth and eighteenth centuries, fearful that any strengthening of the central government would jeopardize its privileges and its "golden Polish freedoms," the nobility resisted the creation of a permanent military force subordinated to the king.[7] As a result, the traditional structure of the Polish military began to change only late in the history of the Polish-Lithuanian Commonwealth. A genuine attempt to create a professional national army was made only by the last Polish king, Stanisław August Poniatowski. The first Polish military academy, the Korpus Kadetów, was founded in 1765. After the first partition of Poland, in 1775, Poniatowski established the Military Department of the Permanent Council in charge of the reorganization and consolidation of Polish armed forces. One of the last royal decrees abolished the long-standing tradition of separate "Polish" and "foreign" contingents within the army. This final legacy of Poniatowski laid the foundations of Poland's national army. Drawing upon the ideas of the Enlightenment, Poniatowski and his group of reformers regarded the army as a force to be subordinated to the king, unified, and trained. Nevertheless, during the final years of the state's independent existence, a pattern of military insubordination to civilian authority remained the rule rather than an exception; this pattern was to be carried over into Poland's mainstream military tradition.

Although the Commonwealth's army often lacked proper equipment and training, the overall quality of its soldiers compensated for organizational weakness. Individual military prowess was viewed by the Polish nobility as the essential trait of a *szlachcic*. The *towarzysz*, or comrade-in-arms, as it was customary to call the nobleman-soldier, with his individual courage, resourcefulness, but also insubordination and rowdiness, epitomized the aristocratic military ideal.[8] The *towarzysz* owed his allegiance to his *hetman*,[9] his general, and his colonel; loyalty to the king often came second. Ultimately, the *hetman* owed his allegiance to the king and the Commonwealth and was supposed to act in the best interest of the country, but such lofty patriotic principles were frequently abandoned, as leading aristocratic houses mutinied against the king's authority to further their own interests.[10]

Insurrections

The Commonwealth of Poland-Lithuania eventually lost its independence with the country's Third Partition by Russia, Prussia, and Austria in 1795.

Still, although the reforms of the Great Four-Year Sejm were never implemented, the national debate that preceded the enactment of the May Constitution of 1791 left an indelible mark on Polish history. The absorption of the liberal ideal of the Enlightenment strengthened the Poles' sense of community with Western Europe, and the growing awareness of the external threat to the very existence of Poland as a sovereign state accelerated the process of the crystallization of national consciousness.[11]

The introduction of the May Constitution also brought to the fore the role of pro-Russian factionalism in Poland's internal politics, which subsequently became a permanent factor in the country's history. The Confederation of Targowica, signed in St. Petersburg by a small group of the empress's Polish protégés (including two *hetmans*) in April of 1792 and announced a month later, declared as its goal the restoration of the status quo ante. The Confederation of Targowica became a justification of the 1792 Russian invasion of Poland and the Second Partition of the country.[12]

The decline of the Commonwealth of Poland-Lithuania marked the emergence of the modern Polish nation. The Rising of 1794, led by *naczelnik* Tadeusz Kościuszko against the Russian intervention, solidified this process. It also began a great Polish romantic myth of national resurrection through armed struggle; to the majority of Poles the soldier had become, by definition, the embodiment of the highest patriotic values.

In its first test during the rising of 1794, the country's newly unified national army fought bravely and lost. The uprising lasted for about a year; after a few victories, the Polish forces were destroyed. Kościuszko was captured and imprisoned; many of the insurrectionists lost their estates; and the reformers' hopes for rapid change were dashed.[13] But the immediate military defeat only reinvigorated the sense of nationalism and dedication to the re-establishment of a sovereign Poland, which the approaching years of foreign tutelage would never succeed in eradicating. Simultaneously, the ethos of the Polish soldier emerged, forged in heroic, though hopeless battle against overwhelming odds.

Kościuszko's military defeat gave birth to the Insurrectionary Tradition that was to become an inseparable part of Poland's military history. Throughout the two hundred years during which Poland did not exist as a state, the Poles had cultivated individual heroism, dedication, and courage as the necessary attributes of the Polish soldier who would liberate his country. The Insurrectionary Tradition nourished a number of nationalist movements, contributed to the shaping and preservation of Polish culture, and became a major force behind two national uprisings. In the nineteenth century, the belief that armed force was the only means of regaining national independence further enhanced the image of the Polish soldier in the eyes of society; yet, during that time, Polish armies existed only intermittently and were always incorporated into the armed forces of the Russian Empire and, briefly under Napoleon, of France.

Sacrifice for the good of the nation was regarded as the principal trait of the Polish soldier. This image, albeit romanticized and often completely sentimental, was strengthened by the extinction of the Dąbrowski Legions (1779–1802), which had been founded with the express aim of liberating Poland through an alliance with France. The legionaries never reached their country. They fought briefly against the Spanish insurrectionists and were later sent to San Domingo to fight the natives. Within a year, most of the soldiers had died of malaria.[14] The pattern repeated itself in the ultimately futile sacrifice of Polish lives for the Napoleonic cause. The Polish veterans of Napoleon's campaigns sweetened the bitterness over the emperor's failure to lead them back to their motherland by adding to the legend of the hero-soldier, stories of gallant, although suicidal, cavalry charges at Samosierra in Spain and the brief liberation of several Polish and Lithuanian provinces.

The Congress Kingdom of 1815–1830, set up by the Russians after Napoleon's defeat, saw the Polish army undergo a major reorganization. The small Polish force established by Tsar Alexander I and directly subordinated to his brother Duke Constantine, the Viceroy of Poland, was based on conscription for twenty years of service, regular drill, and field training, and was led by a professional Polish officer corps. New officers were educated at Szkoła Podchorążych, a military academy in Warsaw, which was to turn them into loyal subjects of Moscow's autocrat. Contrary to the intention of the Russians, the academy soon became a center of Polish nationalism; the November Rising of 1830 was initiated by a group of young cadets from the academy, much to the chagrin of the senior Polish officers loyal to Moscow.[15]

The rising, which eventually became a full-blown Polish-Russian war fought by the two countries' regular armies, lasted for over a year and, once again, after initial successes, ended in defeat for the Polish forces. There followed the Great Emigration, mostly to France, of the veterans fleeing from Russian revenge. Although the November Rising failed to win for Poland her national independence, it added a new ingredient to the Insurrectionary Tradition of the Polish military. Whereas for Kościuszko the sacrifice of blood was a *means* to recreating the Polish state, for the survivors of 1831 clinging to the memories of their struggle, that sacrifice had become an *end in itself*. Because, like the one preceding it, the November Rising was crushed, its survivors sought to find redeeming national values in the tragedy of defeat and in the misery of the repression that followed the insurrection: the Polish Romantic tradition and the myth of the soldier-pilgrim in search of his home were born.[16]

Poland was too exhausted after the war of 1831 to participate fully in the great revolutionary upheaval of 1848. The next period of turmoil occurred in

1863. During the January Rising of 1863, the Poles, faithful to the tradition of sacrifice for the motherland, fought a guerrilla war against the Russians that, from the very start, offered few realistic prospects of victory. The soldier-insurrectionist of 1863 became to his fellow Poles increasingly a symbol of perpetual resistance, regarded as a value in itself. In light of the growing influence of positivism in Poland in the second half of the nineteenth century, an intellectual movement which called for supplanting armed struggle for Polish independence with industrialization and service to the nation, to be a soldier of the January Rising was to be a patriotic idealist. The generation of the Poles that followed was split into Romantics, who continued to believe that armed struggle was the only means to regain national independence, and "positivists," who rejected it in favor of compromise with the occupying powers in the name of economic modernization and "organic work." Even the positivists, however, did not question the patriotic sacrifice of the Polish soldier; rather, they objected to the idea that armed struggle could be an effective road to independence.

Józef Piłsudski: From Insurrectionary Struggle to the Polish State

The January Rising of 1863 collapsed, but the yearnings of the Poles for independence did not subside. In the early 1900s, new elements were added to Polish politics: the growing popularity of socialist ideas and the further polarization within the nationalist camp between those who favored armed struggle and those who opposed it, preferring instead an accommodation with the imperial powers. Early in the century, the national aspirations of the Poles became briefly intertwined with the revolutionary agenda of the time.[17]

The early career of Józef Piłsudski, the man who was to realize the dream of independent Polish statehood, represented such a commingling of nationalist and revolutionary themes.[18] His illegal Polish Socialist Party (PPS) was radicalized into armed struggle against the Russians by the predicament in which the Romanov empire found itself after the outbreak of hostilities with Japan in 1904. Calling for a patriotic war against Moscow, Piłsudski organized in May of the same year the PPS's fighting units (*bojówki*), which mounted a vigorous, albeit largely ineffective, terrorist campaign against the Russians and their Polish collaborators. Piłsudski was convinced that Russia had to be weakened if Poland was to have a chance at independence. Acting on this assumption, he traveled to Tokyo in June–July of 1904 to forge an alliance with Japan and win Japanese backing for the creation of a Polish legion; in return for Japanese assistance, the Poles would provide Tokyo with intelligence about the overall situation in Russia, with special emphasis on Siberia.[19]

Piłsudski's program stood in stark contrast to the vision of Poland's future professed by Roman Dmowski, a nationalist politician intent upon working for a gradual accommodation with the Russian empire. Dmowski and his National Democrats (Endecja) bitterly opposed Piłsudski's prescription for the recreation of the Polish state; this competition would make a strong imprint both on Piłsudski's future political actions and on the military's role in regaining the country's independence.[20] In 1905, as the revolutionary turmoil in the Romanov empire gradually subsided, Dmowski's National Democrats became the only Polish political party to be directly involved in the work of the Russian Duma. However, it had quickly become clear that Nicholas II had never envisaged the Duma as a genuine parliament, and that the hoped-for national autonomy would not be granted to the Poles. As a result, Dmowski's approach to regaining Poland's independence became discredited in the eyes of the majority of his fellow countrymen. Once again, the Poles turned to military struggle as the only possible means for regaining independence. Piłsudski's Military Organization was created in the spirit of the Polish Insurrectionary Tradition.

Piłsudski's political agenda had by then evolved away from his earlier forays into socialist internationalism and toward the unequivocal primacy of Polish national self-determination. In 1908 he moved to Galicja, the Austro-Hungarian partition of Poland, where, with his closest associates, he built the paramilitary Riflemen's Association (Związek Strzelecki). After the outbreak of World War I, the association served as the cornerstone of Piłsudski's Polish Legions.[21] Even more important to Piłsudski's political future was the creation of the Polish Military Organization (Polska Organizacja Wojskowa; POW), which operated as a secret society overseeing the legions, gathering intelligence and organizing terrorist attacks in the Russian partition. The POW continued to exist throughout the war, even after Piłsudski's legions were disbanded following his refusal to swear allegiance to the kaiser.

In 1914, after the German armies had pushed the Russians out of the Polish territories, Piłsudski's position in relation to the National Democrats greatly improved. Dmowski continued diplomatic action with the allies in London and Paris, while Piłsudski's legions fought on the Eastern Front. This was to be of crucial importance for the postwar interpretation of the military's role in the winning back of Poland's independence; since the Germans' control of Poland was virtually unchallenged throughout the war, the legions fought on Polish soil. Piłsudski made it clear to the kaiser's general staff that, although he viewed the Russians as his chief enemies, he was not interested in the future Polish state becoming a German client. In response, the Germans disbanded Piłsudski's legions and put their *naczelnik* in prison.

The legions did not liberate any Polish territory, nor did they manage to be the hoped-for catalyst of a national rising. Their importance, however, to

Piłsudski's political position in the Second Commonwealth was crucial. Although the Polish state was recreated in 1918 chiefly because the occupying powers collapsed, Piłsudski, as the leader of an incessant struggle against the occupiers, was the only man of sufficient moral authority among the Poles to assume the country's leadership. Following his release from the prison in Magdeburg, he arrived in Warsaw on November 10, 1919, and was recognized as chief (*naczelnik*) of the Polish state. After more than a hundred years of struggle, the Insurrectionary Tradition in Poland appeared to have been finally vindicated.

Piłsudski's political victory in 1919 was the necessary precondition for building the military's mystique. The army did, however, play an important and tangible role in the unification of the three partitions into a Polish nation; the hastily created new regiments brought together the separate experiences the Poles had acquired during the years of foreign occupation. The ragtag Polish army, which included small militia and defense units and forces created in France and Russia, plus Polish prisoners of war who had been drafted into the German and Austro-Hungarian armies, was created around the core of Piłsudski's legionnaires. The Army Law of February 1919 made Piłsudski its commander in chief.[22] For its officer corps, the new army drew upon the legionnaires and Polish officers from the armies of the partitioning powers. Some of the top Polish generals of the 1918–1939 interwar period learned their trade serving the tsar or the kaiser. Generals J. Dowbór-Muśnicki, W. Anders, J. K. Rómmel, and L. Żeligowski were former tsarist officers; Generals S. Szeptycki and S. Haller had been in the Prussian service. After joining Piłsudski, they proved to be ardent nationalists despite their past allegiance to foreign powers.[23]

Because of their country's long history of occupation, the Poles saw nothing inherently wrong in the fact that the majority of the officers in the new Polish army had at one time served a foreign government. The fighting that accompanied the birth of the Second Commonwealth, between 1918 and 1920, provided ample opportunity for the military to demonstrate its patriotic devotion to Poland, regardless of its members' past professional experience. The special role of the military as guarantor of Poland's independence in the years of the Second Commonwealth was underscored by the campaigns fought in defense of the country's newly regained and acquired territories. Poland's frontiers were settled as a result of a series of brief campaigns fought either by the regular Polish army or, as was the case in the Poznań region and in Silesia, by insurrectionists supported and supplied by Poland.

The only war to endanger seriously the budding Second Commonwealth was the Polish-Soviet conflict of 1919–1920.[24] The initial Polish advance into the Ukraine, ostensibly made in support of Semen Petlura's Ukrainian Republic, was halted and a quick Soviet counteroffensive threatened to destroy the Polish defenses and overrun the country. At the critical moment in the war, however, the invading Red Army under Tukhachevskii was defeated at the outskirts of Warsaw in a battle that entered into Polish patriotic mythology as the "Miracle on the Vistula." Shortly thereafter the Russians sued for peace, granting Poland the Eastern Borderlands; the peace treaty was signed in Riga in March 1921. Although the war was fought in a succession of relatively brief engagements, the young Bolshevik state and the Second Polish Common-wealth were equally exhausted.

The remarkable career of Piłsudski's legions and the victory in the war with the Soviets reaffirmed the old myths and wove the separate strands of the Insurrectionary Tradition and the military ideal into one. It became an axiom in the Second Commonwealth of 1918–1939 that Poland had regained her independence through the feats of her soldiers—patriotic insurrectionists led by their *naczelnik*, who were ready to risk and sacrifice all to reawaken the nation's conscience. If anyone had been initially skeptical about this glorifica-tion of the military, and indeed quite a few Poles expressed such skepticism, the Polish victory over the Soviet Union in the 1919–1920 war effectively silenced all criticism. The war over frontiers between the terribly weakened infant Bolshevik state and the equally unprepared Polish Commonwealth rose in the eyes of many Poles to the level of a prophecy finally fulfilled. Their military, which had gained the victory, became to the Poles the embodiment of patriotism, of the old-fashioned chivalry of the nobleman, and of the heroism of the soldier-fighter serving his motherland. This perception of the army's role in the resurrection of the state, combined with Piłsudski's tremendous personal prestige, became the principal foundation of army officers' influence in the country's political life in peacetime.

Piłsudski, who had been instrumental in establishing the Second Com-monwealth, retired from public life shortly after the conclusion of the Treaty of Riga. He retained his position of the army's chief inspector, however, and his estate became a focus of the country's political life. To the majority of his countrymen, he remained their *naczelnik*. Piłsudski's retirement proved to be short-lived, for he was soon brought back to power by a military coup d'état, known as the May Coup of 1926. The marshal returned to Warsaw ostensibly to save the country from anarchy, weak government, and incessant political squabbles.

Troops loyal to the elected government put up strong resistance and casualties quickly mounted. Three days of street fighting and aerial bombard-ment cost 379 dead (including 164 civilians) and 920 wounded.[25] Although after the coup Piłsudski did not himself assume the presidency, until his death in 1935 he remained Poland's de facto ruler. With parliamentary institutions in place, Poland maintained a façade of democracy, while in fact for the rest of her interwar existence, the country was a semiauthoritarian state run by the military. Piłsudski and the "colonels" who succeeded him derived their authority from the army's special position in Polish society. The respect that the Poles had for their armed forces and the image of the Polish soldier as the favorite son of the motherland led the majority to believe that the soldier who had risked his life for the motherland could act ultimately only in the country's best interest. This image of the military was the *suprema ratio* for the public acceptance of Piłsudski's 1926 coup d'état, and of the continuous government by the military after the marshal's death in 1935.

The mystique that surrounded the military during the twenty years of the Second Commonwealth was a direct consequence of the particular mixture of leadership and charisma, cunning, and plain good luck that allowed Piłsudski to guide the nation through its early independence. The army took credit for Poland's rise to the status of a European power. Because of her victory over the Soviets in the 1919–1920 war and the apparent strength of her army, Poland came to be seen as a bulwark against Bolshevism. In the international arena, Piłsudski often played great power politics. His activities in this sphere included making plans for a Central European Federation under Poland's aegis and, following Hitler's rise to power, toying with the idea of a preemptive action in conjunction with France against Germany. In the eyes of Polish society, the nation's military prowess and the strength of its armed forces were the primary guarantee of Poland's independence.

World War II:
Defeat and Endurance

The awakening from the dream of power was traumatic. In September 1939, as General Guderian's panzers roamed the countryside and the Soviets closed in from the East, the Polish army proved unable to sustain a prolonged defensive effort. Contrary to all the assurances of readiness issued by Commander in Chief Śmigły-Rydz prior to the invasion, the Polish army was caught unprepared, with inadequate supplies and poor intelligence, and without an implementable defense strategy. By the seventh day of fighting, communications between the Polish high command and the field forces had broken down;[26] in retreat, the Poles put up a heroic fight, hoping for promised help from France and Britain. Despite growing chaos at the level of the general staff, individual Polish armies managed to launch powerful, if ultimately futile, counteroffensives. The fiercest Polish counterstrike was mounted on the Bzura River between September 9 and 18 by Gen. T. Kutrzeba's Army Poznań. Although ultimately unsuccessful, the Battle on the Bzura stalled the German advance long enough to allow Army Warsaw and Army Lublin to regroup and gave the capital time to strengthen its defenses.[27] In keeping with the Polish

Insurrectionary Tradition, the last battle, fought in early October 1939 by General Kleeberg's Polesie Group, became a symbolic statement of endurance and futile heroism. Similarly heroic, if ultimately strategically insignificant, was the defiance of a 100-man-strong garrison at Westerplatte, an outpost on the Baltic Sea that held out for about a week against the German onslaught. After the Soviet invasion of eastern Poland on September 17, 1939, the government, including the commander in chief of the army, sought refuge and was interned in Romania. The Fourth Partition of Poland, agreed upon by the Soviet Union and Germany in August 1939 in a secret protocol of the Ribbentrop-Molotov Non-Aggression Pact, became a fait accompli.

The September 1939 Campaign, as the beginning of the war has come to be known in Polish history, did not weaken the nation's belief in the fighting spirit of its army. Although hopelessly outnumbered, the Polish soldier once again proved himself in battle; it was the politicians who failed the test.[28] To the majority of the Poles, who had known only twenty years of national independence, there was something almost familiar about the new Russian-German occupation. Underground resistance started immediately after the army had laid down its weapons. Before 1939 came to an end, the first guerrilla detachment, led by a cavalry major, had already begun to fight the German occupation forces. Armed resistance was unanimously accepted by the Poles as the only way to regain their country's independence. An underground military organization, the Home Army (Armia Krajowa; AK) led the struggle.[29] Arguments over who was responsible for the September disaster soon subsided in light of the spectacular fiascoes of the French, British, and Soviet defense plans.

The Poles fought in World War II both in the armies of the Western Allies and in the Soviet Army. Immediately after the 1939 defeat, thousands of soldiers, officers, and civilians traveled from Romania, Hungary, and Lithuania to France and England to join the newly formed Polish forces abroad. By May 1940, more than 82,000 officers and men constituted two infantry divisions and two indepedent brigades in the West. The Polish forces in France took part in the French campaign, fought in Norway, in the Champagne, and on the Maginot Line; the remnants of the Second Division crossed into neutral Switzerland. The Carpathian Brigade stationed in Syria crossed into Palestine and thus survived as a fighting unit.[30] The Polish air force in France withdrew to England. During the Battle of Britain, Polish fighter pilots earned the admiration and appreciation of the British for their skill and courage.[31] On the Western front, Poles fought in Africa and northern Europe, and participated in the ill-fated Arnhem airborne operation and the liberation of France and the Low Countries. In May 1944, Polish troops took Monte Cassino, one of the most heavily fortified German positions in Italy, and which blocked the Allies' approach to Rome. The storming of Monte Cassino is to this day a symbol of the Polish soldier's patriotism and self-sacrifice in combat.[32]

By the end of the war there were about 230,000 Polish soldiers under British command, including three infantry divisions, two armored divisions, one airborne and one armored brigade, and sixteen air-force squadrons. In addition, Poles operated twenty ships of the Polish navy under British command. The continuous existence of Poland's armed forces was decisive in maintaining the Polish nation's claim to full-allied status and to the right to independent statehood after victory. In light of the fate that befell the Baltic states after the war, it is evident that the sacrifice of Polish blood ensured the very existence of the Polish state after the conflict had ended. The Soviets knew that the United States and Britain could never accept Poland's direct incorporation into the Soviet Union, Stalin's preferred solution in Estonia, Latvia, and Lithuania.

The initial period of German and Soviet occupation witnessed a determined Polish effort to build an oppositional force on the foundation of the traditional view of Germany and Russia as Poland's two enemies. The situation changed dramatically after the German invasion of the USSR on June 22, 1941, and the emergence of the Grand Alliance. Fearing the consequences of dependence on the Soviet Union, the underground Home Army and its London government-in-exile found it difficult to accommodate themselves to the new realities. In fact, the Poles had good reasons to be wary of the Soviets. The history of Polish-Soviet relations before the war and the Soviet-Nazi cooperation from 1939 to 1941 were well remembered, and the fate of thousands of Poles sent to the gulag after the Soviet invasion in 1939 further strengthened the Polish government's fear and suspicion.[33]

During World War II, the military once again assumed the leadership of the Polish state. The government-in-exile, situated first in Paris, then in London, was led until 1943 by Gen. Władysław Sikorski, a prewar officer famous for his tactical skill during the Polish-Soviet war of 1919–1920 and for his independent political orientation during the reign of the "colonels." Sikorski was initially closely associated with the Piłsudskiites; he was a co-founder of the Riflemen's Association in Lwów and later contributed to the creation of the army of the Second Commonwealth. Sikorski also had some experience in government. As a prominent national political figure, he was appointed Poland's prime minister in 1922 and held that post for a few years. The general's political fortunes declined after Piłsudski's 1926 coup, during which Sikorski chose to support the elected government. In the wake of the political bankruptcy of the "colonels'" regime, all too vividly demonstrated by Poland's military defeat, the general had the best possible political credentials: he was a military man, a patriot, and an opponent of the compromised regime.

After Poland's defeat in 1939, Sikorski made his way to France where, as prime minister of the new government, he organized his country's new army. Within months, however, events proved Sikorski's traditional pro-French orientation untenable. After the fall of France and the German invasion of the Soviet Union, Sikorski made diplomatic overtures to the Soviets. On July 30, 1941, a Polish-Soviet agreement on cooperation was signed; the Poles imprisoned by the Soviets were to be granted immediate amnesty and a Polish army was to be created in the USSR under the command of Gen. Władysław Anders. Although sincere, Sikorski's attempts to improve Polish-Soviet relations were short-lived. The discovery in the Katyn Forest of the mass grave of the Polish officers shot by the Russians in 1940 made a Polish-Soviet partnership—if, in fact, Stalin had ever wanted one—impossible.[34] The Soviets used the public revelation of the Katyn Forest massacre as a pretext for severing diplomatic relations with Sikorski's government. Sikorski himself died in 1943 in a plane crash near Gibraltar.

Although Sikorski altered the traditional formula of Poland's "two enemies" by his opening to the East, to a large degree he fit the pattern of Poland's political generals, in the tradition of the country's struggle for independence. Trying to balance Poland's traditional pro-Western orientation against an opening to Moscow, Sikorski acted on the assumption that an accommodation with the Soviets was necessary if Poland was to re-emerge independent after the war. Furthermore, it was clear to him that only by going directly to Stalin did he stand a chance of saving the thousands of Polish citizens languishing in Soviet prisons and labor camps.[35] Anders's army became a refuge for the Polish citizens deported into the Far Eastern regions of the USSR; for them, joining that army was the only way of escaping the starvation and backbreaking labor of the Soviet camps.[36] Thousands of Poles released from the gulag made their way to Anders's recruitment camp.

The Polish army was neither sufficiently equipped nor trained to constitute an effective fighting force. Anders's soldiers were poorly supplied, lacked adequate food rations and the necessary armaments, and never enjoyed the promised Soviet support. In fact, Stalin never stopped being suspicious of the "London Poles," and the Anders army was treated more like an intruder on Soviet territory than a bona fide ally. The atmosphere of mutual distrust bred tension and conflict, the more so since Anders's recruits had little reason to feel gratitude to the Soviets in view of the treatment they had received in 1939.[37] Fearing that Stalin's goal was to incorporate the Polish soldiers directly into the Soviet Army, Anders was unyielding in his opposition to sending his troops to the front until they were properly trained, supplied, and ready to operate as an army. In 1942, when it became clear that Polish-Soviet differences on this score would not be resolved, the Poles were evacuated to Iran. The Anders army later fought in Africa and Italy under British command.

The Beginnings of the People's Army

The break with the Sikorski government over the Katyn Forest massacre clearly indicated that Stalin no longer needed the good will of the London Poles. In 1943, the Union of Polish Patriots (Związek Patriotów Polskich; ZPP), a Soviet-sponsored organization of Polish communists in the USSR, was permitted by Stalin to undertake the formation of a new army. The recruitment to the First Kościuszko Infantry Division began in May 1943 at Seltse on the Oka River, near Ryazan. The recruits were Polish; most of the officers and NCOs were Russian.[38] The division was formally led by a prewar Polish colonel, Zygmunt Berling, later promoted by Stalin to general. On July 15, 1943, the recruits were sworn in as soldiers subordinated to both Polish and Soviet commands. As had been the case in the nineteenth-century Polish Kingdom, in 1943 a Russian-sponsored and Russian-controlled Polish army became once again a reality. The fact that the Soviet-controlled Polish People's Army (Ludowe Wojsko Polskie) made a contribution to Poland's liberation from German occupation would eventually secure for the new army a modicum of national acceptance. In turn, the military's claim to continue the traditions of the legitimate national army would become an important propaganda asset in the policies of the future communist government.[39]

Gen. Zygmunt Berling, the commander of the Kościuszko Division, had the same legionary background that was so typical of Poland's interwar officer corps. Never a member of the military elite, he nevertheless reached the rank of lieutenant colonel. After the 1939 campaign, Berling was imprisoned by the Soviets, together with thousands of Polish soldiers and officers. Following the Stalin-Sikorski agreement of July 1941 to form a Polish army in the USSR, Berling was released from prison and became chief of staff of the Fifth Infantry Division in the Anders army; later he was demoted by Anders to base commander.[40] Never completely trusted by his fellow officers, who knew of his prewar prosocialist sympathies, Berling chose to remain in the Soviet Union rather than evacuate with the rest of Anders's troops to Iran.[41] By then he was in close contact with leading Moscow Poles, including the head of the Union of Polish Patriots, Wanda Wasilewska. In 1943 he was recommended by the ZPP to Stalin as the best officer to command the Kościuszko Division.

Berling's division retained some characteristics of a national military force. In the end, the Kościuszko Division was organizationally a compromise solution; on the one hand, the Soldier's Oath referred directly to comradeship-in-arms with the Soviets; on the other hand, nationalism rather than internationalist principles reigned supreme among the troops. Because of the role the Soviet Army had played in the 1939 invasion of Poland and the repression during the Soviet occupation, the majority of the soldiers of the Kościuszko

Division were mistrustful of the Soviets, notwithstanding all Wasilewska's efforts to "raise their consciousness."[42]

Because of the strength of the anti-Soviet feeling among the Poles, the Russians agreed to maintain at least the outward appearance that the Kościuszko Division was a thoroughly Polish outfit. The division was dressed in the national uniform and marched under Polish colors. But that was as far as Soviet concessions to Polish nationalism went. As required by the Soviet Army's training methods, Berling's recruits were subjected to political indoctrination in addition to military drill. Conforming to the Soviet pattern, the First Division had its special unit for political control—the nucleus of the future Main Political Administration of the Polish People's Army, headed by Włodzimierz Sokorski, Berling's political officer.

Berling's soldiers used the Soviet drill method, as well as the Soviet platoon, company, battalion, and regiment organization. The two Polish armies that were eventually organized in the USSR operated as an integral part of the Soviet Army. The operations of the Polish forces were coordinated by the Military Council of the Polish Army and the Main Staff for the Formation of the Polish Army in the USSR.[43]

On October 12, 1943, the Kościuszko Division fought its first battle on the Ukrainian front, at Lenino.[44] In August of 1943, the Soviets and the Union of Polish Patriots had already made arrangements for the formation of the First Polish Corps in the USSR; in early April of 1944, the First Polish Corps was transformed into the First Polish Army in the USSR, commanded by General Berling and incorporated into the forces of the First Byelorussian Front. In 1944 that army included an armored brigade, five artillery brigades, and a cavalry brigade.[45] As of March 1944, the First Army numbered about 45,000 members, including 4,400 officers; by August it had grown to over 100,000, with 6,300 officers. By February 1945 the army had between 9,300 and 9,400 officers.[46] The officer corps was thoroughly penetrated by the Soviets. Over 50 percent of Berling's officer corps were Soviet Army officers; over 80 percent of all line officers were Soviets who barely spoke Polish. Almost all command posts, as well as those on regimental, brigade, and division staffs were allocated to Soviet officers. The only two Poles with prewar military service who had been assigned army staff-level positions were Berling himself and one Col. Leon Nałęcz-Bukojemski, commander of the First Artillery Brigade (1 Brygada Artylerii Armat). The Poles had no influence on selection of Soviet officers assigned to serve with the First Army; furthermore, it was not until January 1945 that a formal agreement between the Poles and their Soviet patrons was signed on the procedures governing the service of Soviet officers detailed to the Polish army.

The 1945 Polish-Soviet agreement stipulated that Soviet officers were assigned to the Polish forces only temporarily; that they were exempt from taking the Polish military oath; and that their service in the Polish army would count as part of their service in the Soviet Army. Although the Soviets were formally subordinated to the Polish command, their promotions to colonel and above were still the prerogative of their own government. Finally, if a Soviet officer serving in the Polish army committed a capital crime, he could be tried and convicted only by a Soviet court martial.

The creation of the Polish People's Army (Ludowe Wojsko Polskie) was formally decreed by the Moscow-controlled Home National Council (Krajowa Rada Narodowa; KRN) in July 1944, in Chełm outside Lublin.[47] The KRN decree announced the creation of the Supreme Command, which replaced both the Military Council of the Polish Army in the USSR and the Main Staff for the Formation of the Polish Army in the USSR, and the formation of a regular army based on conscription. It also announced that the new armed forces would combine the regular armies with the underground pro-Moscow People's Army (Armia Ludowa; AL), one of the resistance forces in Poland.[48] The AL had come into being through the reorganization and renaming of the People's Guard (Gwardia Ludowa; GL) in 1944. The Supreme Command was headed by AL-commander Gen. Michał Rola-Żymierski. Berling became Rola-Żymierski's deputy for military affairs, and he retained his position as commander of the First Army. Col. Aleksander Zawadzki was put in charge of political affairs of the First Army and Col. Marian Spychalski became the first chief of the general staff; both men had almost no military experience and won their appointments on the strength of their political credentials as dedicated communists. Both Zawadzki and Spychalski would play important roles in Polish politics after the war.

As early as the summer of 1944, it became clear that the Soviets intended to eliminate the pro-Western Home Army as a factor in postwar Poland. On July 17, in Wilno, the NKVD arrested the entire staff of the Home Army's Wolyńska Division, despite the fact that the pro-London guerrillas were cooperating with the Soviet army during its advance against the German lines. The arrest of the general staff was a harbinger of things to come.[49] Despite Soviet assurances of cooperation, Home Army soldiers were being disarmed and deported en masse into the Soviet Union, and their officers imprisoned.[50] In the Lublin region alone (Lublin was the first seat of the pro-Moscow Polish government), the Home Army underground structure was wiped out by the NKVD through mass arrests.[51]

Berling's career continued to run into snags because of his conflict with the party's political leadership. According to the testimony of Jakub Berman, a prominent communist in the pro-Moscow government and a number-two man in the Polish regime until 1956, Berling and his political officer, Włodzimierz Sokorski, clashed with the ZPP's Hilary Minc and Roman Zambrowski (the latter was also a political officer in the Polish army), and indirectly with

Berman himself, in 1944 in Lublin. Apparently at stake was influence with Stalin and, indirectly, the emerging distribution of political power in Poland. Reportedly at the center of the controversy were two postulates on the future shape of Poland. One, supported among others by Sokorski, proposed a system of "organized democracy" that (according to Berman) would have given the army a considerable voice in shaping the country's political institutions. The ZPP and the party attacked the plan for its "recidivist legionary leanings from the time of Piłsudski,"[52] and countered with their own "postulate number two," drawn up by Minc and Zambrowski, in which "the party and ideology were accorded the decisive role in shaping the future of Poland."[53]

According to Berman, Berling appealed directly to Stalin, but his telegram went unheeded. Apparently the Soviets were the instigators of the conflict in the first place, and Stalin eventually ordered Berling's removal.[54] According to Sokorski, Berling was attacked for his prewar service in the Polish army. The conflict resulted in Berling's ostracism. Reportedly, Wanda Wasilewska, one of the ZPP's founders, refused to even see the general and his officers.[55]

Another problem was the issue of the Warsaw rising of 1944. As the Home Army troops fought a two-month-long desperate battle against the Germans in full view of the Soviet Army and Polish forces positioned across the Vistula, the Russians refused to heed repeated pleas from the Western Allies to come to the city's rescue. In late September 1944, Berling ordered two battalions from the Third Infantry Division to cross the river, followed by units of the Second Infantry Division. After heavy fighting, the rescue effort was easily thwarted by the Germans. It is still unclear how independent Berling's effort to assist the pro-London resistance in Warsaw was. However, the fact that Berling was abruptly relieved of his duties as commander of the First Army in late September of the same year, and replaced by a Soviet-born general, W. Korczyc, suggests that the Warsaw relief operation did not help Berling politically. In its aftermath, Berling's standing with the "Moscow Poles" further deteriorated; nevertheless, his last-ditch attempt to help Warsaw in its hour of need did more for the image of the Polish military than the propaganda campaigns run by the Soviet-controlled Polish Committee for National Liberation (Polski Komitet Wyzwolenia Narodowego; PKWN). Because of Berling's action, the Polish People's Army was gradually accepted by the nation as Polish first, and "people's" (i.e., Soviet-dominated) only because Moscow controlled the country.

Berling's relative eclipse was accompanied by the rise of another politically important military man, Michał Rola-Żymierski.[56] A lawyer and an economist by training, Żymierski had a substantial military career before the war. He was a member of Piłsudski's Riflemen's Association. Between 1911 and 1912, he had fought in the Austrian army, and then joined the Legions and Piłsudski's clandestine Polish Military Organization (Polska Organizacja Wojskowa). In 1918, he was detailed by the Polish high command as a military representative to Silesia to help coordinate the military campaign in support of Poland's claims to the region. During the 1926 coup, Żymierski sided with the elected government and, following Piłsudski's victory, was forced into retirement; until 1938 he lived in self-imposed exile in France. During the German occupation of Poland, Żymierski joined the Moscow-controlled underground and soon rose to become member of the general staff of the People's Guard (GL), the communist-controlled resistance forces. Following the GL's reorganization in 1944, Żymierski was appointed commander of the new resistance force, the People's Army (AL), and member of the underground, communist-dominated Home National Council (KRN), the nucleus of the future Polish government. Next, he was chosen for the post of commander of the Polish People's Army, thus bypassing Berling who became his second in command. In 1945, Żymierski was promoted to marshal and became Poland's minister of defense (1945–1949). Competition between Berling, who came to Poland with the so-called "Moscow communists," and Żymierski, who throughout the war was associated with the Polish underground, shaped the People's Army during the Stalinist period.

The Rise of the Army in Communist Poland

—3—

Fighting Anticommunist Resistance

Following the war, the Polish military found itself in an increasingly delicate situation. Armed resistance against the Soviet-controlled Warsaw government continued for at least two years after the war, presenting the army with the unenviable alternative of either fighting the anticommunist underground, and thus jeopardizing the People's Army's claim to being a national force, or refusing to go into the field, and thus openly defying the Soviets. Reportedly, many Polish soldiers and junior officers sympathized with the anticommunist underground and hated their Russian commanders; desertions were frequent, at times even of entire companies.[1] Still, the army was an important asset in the new government's bid for absolute political power and was used both to fight the opposition and to indoctrinate and terrorize the population.

The imposition of communism in Poland was accompanied by state terror directed against the remnants of the democratic and nationalist forces. The mass arrest of wartime fighters loyal to Poland's London government-in-exile quickly drove back underground those who escaped the NKVD and the forces of the Polish State Security Agency (Urząd Bezpieczeństwa; UB). A bloody civil war followed. In the first two years after the war, during which the communists consolidated their hold on Poland, the People's Army gradually assumed a key role in the struggle against the anticommunist underground. In addition, army regulars enforced the expulsion of the Ukrainian population from Poland's southeastern borderlands—the traditional stronghold of Ukrainian nationalism.

The Lublin government was directly responsible for triggering civil war in Poland. Although the Home Army (AK) was officially dissolved on January 18, 1945, the arrests of wartime members of the AK forced the remaining underground leadership to organize a new oppositional network, Resistance Movement "Independence" (Ruch Oporu "Niepodległość"; R.O.NIE). Despite repression, arrests, and summary sentences (the AK's best wartime commander, Gen. L. Okulicki, was arrested in March of 1945 and tried in Moscow, together with fifteen leaders of Poland's wartime underground), R.O.NIE and its successor organization Freedom and Independence (Wolność i Niepodległość) operated until the end of 1948, although they gradually lost control over their armed detachments in the field.[2]

As opposition to the Lublin government spread, the regime's reliance on regular troops became a necessity. Immediately after the war, the pacification campaign against the anticommunist underground was conducted by NKVD troops, Polish security forces, and the police (Milicja Obywatelska; MO). It soon became obvious, however, that regular Polish army troops would have to be brought in to overwhelm the desperate resistance of the remnants of the pro-London Home Army, Polish Nationalists (Narodowe Siły Zbrojne), and a number of other diverse, loosely organized groups.

Poland's new regime at first hoped to win the campaign against the underground without relying on army regulars. On May 25, 1945, the government established the Corps of Internal Security (Korpus Bezpieczeństwa Wewnętrznego; KBW), patterned after Soviet NKVD units and consisting of carefully selected and indoctrinated soldiers who were considered more loyal than average draftees. By shifting the burden of fighting the resistance to the elite KBW, the government hoped to shield the regular army from a fight that presented soldiers and officers alike with difficult moral choices. However, it soon became apparent that the KBW by itself could not defeat the resistance. After the NKVD troops had been withdrawn late in 1945, the Lublin government had to commit army regulars against the partisans. Before the year was past, three infantry divisions of the regular army had been dispatched to fight the underground forces; they cooperated closely with the KBW, Border Guard units (Wojska Ochrony Pogranicza), and the police (MO). In special cases, the regulars were supported by detachments of the 60,000-member-strong Volunteer Reserves of the People's Militia (Ochotnicza Rezerwa Milicji Obywatelskiej).[3] The extent of this civil war in Poland is best shown by the fact that in just under two weeks, between June 19 and July 1 of 1945, government forces conducted 73 "pacification operations," in which they struck some 300 villages.[4]

From the start, the communist regime clearly distrusted the army. The regular soldier was considered unreliable and was deployed against the underground guerrillas as a solution of last resort.[5] Political commissars were assigned to all units to provide the necessary supervision in the field; they were empowered to countermand the COs' orders if, in their judgment, the situation warranted it. Veterans of the communist underground, led by the AL, presented the Lublin regime with a different problem. Although the partisans who joined the new armed forces shared the ideology of the officer corps of the First and the Second Armies, they were nevertheless "national communists," who could claim that they had fought the Germans on Polish soil throughout the entire occupation. During the early postwar years, political cleavages within the Polish military replicated exactly the conflict within the civilian party apparat. The tensions that surfaced in 1948 between Władysław Gomułka, a "national communist," and Bolesław Bierut, a "Muscovite," spread into the officer corps. In the army, the problem was compounded by the animosity and mistrust among Polish officers of Jewish extraction, Soviet citizens who became officers in the Polish army, and ethnic Poles. The conflict was fueled by a dramatic rise of anti-Semitism in Poland immediately after the war in response to the inordinately high proportion of Polish Jews in the police and security apparat. As the State Security Agency (UB) unleashed a campaign of terror against any form of political opposition, the Poles began to equate all Jews with the hated communist regime.

A small number of officers who returned from the Polish forces in the West chose to join the new army. On the whole, however, when compared with the prewar period, the officer corps was fragmented, and its prestige in society was low, in particular that of the officers commissioned because of their peasant or working-class background. These "proletarian officers" were for the most part uneducated and incompetent; they quickly became a caricature of the then-popular party slogan: "You need no high-school diploma, but only a true desire to become an officer."

A separate group of officers in the People's Army were Home Army veterans and prewar officers who decided to serve under the communists. Between 1945 and 1948 their number grew steadily; prewar officers were being employed to train and organize the new army because of the shortage of "proletarian" cadres. As a result, by the end of the civil war, a substantial portion of the Polish officer corps consisted of prewar officers. While no accurate data on their exact number is available, we know by the regime's own admission that the lack of qualified line commanders was the People's Army's biggest problem from its inception. Although in the final phases of the war, the Lublin government was quite successful in conscripting new recruits for its army, it could not find a sufficient number of trained officers with "proletarian" credentials. As Poland's defense minister Żymierski reported during a meeting of the Polish Committee of National Liberation (PKWN) on September 18, 1944, for each 12,000 recruits the new army had at its disposal only about 960 officers, or less than one officer for 1,200 men.[6]

The regime's efforts to use regular troops against the Polish underground led on occasion to desertions. However, because of the long and tragic history of Polish-Ukrainian conflict, the war against the Ukrainian nationalists did not constitute a morale problem for the People's Army. Among the campaigns fought jointly by the regular army and the KBW forces against the guerrillas of the Ukrainian Resistance Army (Ukraińska Powstańcza Armia; UPA), the most notorious and brutal was the "Vistula" operation of 1947. Wojciech Jaruzelski, then a young lieutenant, participated in the fighting and is said to have distinguished himself during the pacification of Ukrainian villages. The "Vistula" operation, during which the Poles deployed about 20,000 troops against 2,000 Ukrainian guerrillas, was launched in part as a reprisal for the ambush killing of legendary Gen. Karol Świerczewski, one of the leading communist officers who had distinguished himself during the Spanish Civil War.[7]

Political Action Prior to 1949

The problems with officer enlistment and shaky troop morale notwithstanding, the People's Army played an essential role in the seizure of power by Polish communists. In addition to fighting the underground, the army was a powerful instrument of intimidation and political propaganda, especially in the countryside where the network of police outposts was weak. Beginning on December 12, 1946, troops were dispatched to towns and villages as "defense-propaganda" detachments subordinated to Poland's High Command. According to one source, in December 1946 alone, 45,000 soldiers and officers organized and supervised some 25,000 procommunist demonstrations. As part of an effective political intimidation campaign, troops were stationed in villages to prevent the peasants from supporting the underground.[8]

The "defense-propaganda" campaign (*kampania propagandowo-ochronna*) was prepared according to orders drafted by the Ministry of Defense. The deployment of troops in areas known to have supported the opposition not only prevented the partisans from entering the villages, but also made it virtually impossible for those opposition parties that were still permitted to operate legally (such as S. Mikołajczyk's Polish Peasant Party) to campaign for the upcoming referendum and national election. As revealed in the memoirs of one of the officers, who as a young lieutenant took part in the operation, the campaign was meticulously planned and timed.[9] The country was divided into four "operational zones," which were ranked in importance according to the degree of oppositional activities in each area; the campaign was conducted in two phases. During the first phase, platoon-strength units headed by junior officers were sent out, with orders to move randomly from one village to another, so as to maximize surprise and make it difficult for the underground intelligence network to anticipate their next move. Their orders were to enter the village, assist the local party cell in organizing a proregime propaganda meeting, and "correct administrative problems" on the local-government level, for example, investigate a corrupt official, remove supply bottlenecks, and so forth.

During the second phase of the "defense-propaganda campaign," which immediately preceded the 1947 elections to the Sejm, army officers were dispatched to all electoral districts in order to "secure the elections and supervise the vote count."[10] For the duration of the elections, the officers dispatched into the countryside were put in charge of the local police and security forces. On the eve of the voting and on election day, they inspected all polling stations; in some cases, they conducted several unexpected visits to the same village. The presence of the military, police, and security forces at polling stations was a clear message to the voters. Still, the government took no chances; the officers' final task was to stay at the polling stations after the polls had closed to "supervise the vote count." Not surprisingly, as recalled by one officer, the elections were a "decisive blow to the reactionaries."[11] Polish People's Army officers supervised the greatest electoral fraud in Poland's history to date.

In the aftermath of the fraudulent election of 1947, the communists launched an overt terrorist campaign that eventually destroyed the only organized opposition political party, Mikołajczyk's Polish Peasant Party (Polskie Stronnictwo Ludowe). On the orders of the regime, special military tribunals unleashed state terror against the remaining opposition; in 1947, over 6,000 Poles were sentenced by special military judges, some of them to death, on fabricated charges based on confessions extracted under torture.[12] Terror by the security police and summary trials by military tribunals laid the groundwork for the final consolidation of political power by Poland's communist party, the Polish Workers' Party (Polska Partia Robotnicza; PPR).[13] In 1948, the communists eliminated the remainder of the Polish Socialist Party (Polska Partia Socjalistyczna). As a precondition to their merger with the PPR, the socialists were forced to abandon their political platform and repudiate the heritage of the Polish socialist movement. The Polish United Workers' Party (Polska Zjednoczona Partia Robotnicza), created in 1948, was a Soviet-style communist party, on the Leninist model, having a monopoly of power in the country.

Although the military's contribution to communist victory in Poland, both in combatting the resistance and as an agent of state terror, was considerable, the army itself soon fell victim to the terror it had helped to unleash. On October 31, 1944, when prewar officers enlisted in the People's Army numbered only about 4,200 and constituted barely 14 percent of the needed officer corps, the PPR Central Committee issued a directive to remove the "untrustworthy elements from the army, increase vigilance, and create an officer corps from among the young honest [Polish] democrats." In November 1944 the directive was supported by then–PPR secretary Władysław Gomułka.

On August 18, 1945, the party issued "Directives for creating officer cadres of the Polish Army," which divided the prewar officers into two groups: (1) second lieutenants and lieutenants, who were deemed suitable to serve in the People's Army; and (2) officers from the rank of captain through the rank of general, who were deemed unsuitable for the purposes of the new army.[14] While Żymierski and Berling fell into the second category, the directive opened the door to rapid advancement to the officers of Jaruzelski's generation, that is, those who had attended officer schools between 1943 and 1945. Their promotion would be rapid, and a decade later these "first category" officers would become generals, constituting the majority of the People's Army's senior-officer corps.

In 1947, on Soviet orders, the regime moved to reorganize the People's Army according to the Soviet pattern. As was the case in the Soviet Army after the Russian Civil War, this required the removal of all "unreliable" officers, not only the prewar professional cadres, but also AL/GL and AK veterans, and those with a record of service in the West, including those who had fought in the Spanish Civil War. The first postwar purge of the People's Army was initiated in 1947, when several officers from the Pomeranian Military District headquarters in Bydgoszcz were arrested on charges of espionage and cooperation with the anticommunist underground. The purge of the Bydgoszcz officers continued into 1948. Nineteen officers were arrested; of these, seventeen were convicted, one committed suicide, and one died in prison. Eight years later they were all rehabilitated during the 1956 "thaw."[15] In 1948 the military counterintelligence arrested 65 people, mostly army officers, of the Lublin Military District and the Third Infantry Division. They were accused of conspiring against the state;[16] 48 of them drew long prison terms.[17]

The purge of the Bydgoszcz and Lublin officers signaled a major change in civil-military relations in Poland. If until 1947 the PUWP could harbor the illusion that, although ultimately subordinated to the Soviets, it would be allowed to control the People's Army, it was quickly disabused of such "nationalist" notions. Concurrently with the abandoning of all pretense of "people's democracies" in Eastern Europe, Stalin dispatched additional Soviet Army officers to Poland to supervise the Polish army's transformation into a relatively modern force, organized and trained according to the Soviet model, and subjected exclusively to Moscow's authority. This early modernization period, which had begun in earnest in 1949 with the arrival of Marshal K. Rossovskii as Poland's defense minister, lasted until 1956. It was accompanied by brutal purges from the Polish officer corps of those who had served in the prewar Polish army, had fought in the underground resistance, both communist and noncommunist, or had served in the West. As had been the case in Soviet Russia in the late 1920s and early 1930s, the "prerevolutionary" officers who built the Polish People's Army were now considered expendable.

Still, some appearances were maintained. Until 1949, the army was formally entrusted to Gen. Michał Rola-Żymierski, later promoted to Marshal of Poland. Żymierski's rise as minister of defense was paralleled by Berling's relative eclipse; in 1948, Berling was finally removed from his field command and named head of the General Staff Academy in Warsaw. In 1953, Berling was completely pushed aside, being given the post of deputy minister of state farms and deputy minister of agriculture. He held the two posts until 1956.[18] Albeit the army was formally under Żymierski's command until 1949, it was in reality controlled by Soviet officers during his tenure of this position. As Poland's defense minister, Żymierski was a figurehead, and, until the arrival of Marshal Konstantin Rokossovskii in 1949, the Polish army was controlled by two Soviet officers, Generals Korczyc and Popławski.[19] The only senior Polish officer with some influence on military matters was General Świerczewski, a dedicated communist who had fought in the Dąbrowski Brigade during the Spanish Civil War, and in 1944 was commander of the second army of the Polish Forces organized by the ZPP.[20] Świerczewski was assassinated, however, in a UPA ambush in 1947.

Żymierski, whose military career in Piłsudski's Legions was marred by occasional problems with the law, was viewed by Stalin as an opportunist who, albeit useful at the time, could never be trusted. Żymierski's career as Poland's defense minister was brief. Despite his party loyalty and his political maneuvering, after 1949 the marshal's position in the new regime became increasingly precarious, and he eventually became yet another victim of the purge of the Polish officer corps. After the arrival in 1949 of Marshal Konstantin Rokossovskii, Stalin's appointee dispatched to Poland to take over the country's armed forces, Żymierski was relieved of his post as defense minister and became a member of the Council of the State. As the tide of Stalinism in Poland rose and direct Soviet control over the People's Army became a matter of course, the elimination of Żymierski was only a question of time.

Although Żymierski remained to the end a loyal servant of the regime, his past in Piłsudski's Legions and the prewar Polish army, as well as his role as a leader of the Polish, albeit communist, underground during the German occupation made him untrustworthy in Soviet eyes. In 1953, two years after his elevation to the Council of the State, the marshal was purged from the army and imprisoned;[21] his wife was also arrested. Charges against Żymierski were fabricated based on a confession forced from his brother Stanisław, a onetime colonel and Polish Air Force pilot in Great Britain, who signed a statement under torture that he had spied for the French, and that the marshal had been at one time a Gestapo agent.[22] Żymierski was spared a show trial and, possibly, execution because of the turmoil that followed Stalin's death. Still, he remained in prison until 1955, and although he was then released from prison and assigned to work with Polish veterans' organizations, his military career was over.[23]

Rokossovskii's Soldiers: 1949–1956

With the advent of the Cold War, the Soviets moved to consolidate their position in Poland by rapidly increasing the level of political control exercised over the Polish army. Poland was to maintain a strong army, fully subordinated to Moscow, and to contribute to the Soviet defense effort by becoming a producer of a wide variety of basic weapons.[24] In Stalin's eyes, the Poles could never be fully trusted, especially considering the centuries-old Polish-Russian animosity and the Poles' memories of Soviet repression in the early years of the war. Armed resistance against the communist government in Poland only confirmed Stalin's opinion that, unless tight control was maintained, the country would turn against the Soviets. To prevent even the slightest chance of rebellion, Konstantin Rokossovskii, a Soviet officer of Polish origin and a distinguished commander in World War II, was given the rank of Polish marshal and sent to Poland as minister of defense, deputy premier, and a voting member of the PUWP's Politburo. Rokossovskii's task was to ensure a rapid transformation of the Polish People's Army into an exact image of the Soviet Army and to act as Stalin's personal representative in Warsaw.

Shortly after his arrival, Rokossovskii moved the Soviet Army's Polish command post from Legnica to Warsaw. The new Soviet headquarters in Warsaw oversaw the satellite armed forces of Poland and Czechoslovakia. It also coordinated the operations of Soviet divisions stationed in Poland and East Germany. In effect Rokossovskii's Soviet Army Warsaw command became the precursor of the future command post of the Warsaw Pact when it was again moved, in 1956, to Legnica in southwestern Poland.[25]

The change of the Polish army's supreme commander was a clear sign that the Soviets were abandoning all pretense of "people's democracy" in Poland and were moving ahead at full speed to transform the country into an obedient satellite. Moscow's decision to tighten its control over East European armies came against the backdrop of the first Berlin crisis, the growing determination of the United States to contain communist expansion, and Yugoslavia's defection from the Soviet bloc. Within the PUWP the purge of the early 1950s was directed against "right-wing national deviationism," as Poland's president Bolesław Bierut elegantly described Gomułka's insistence that his party should retain a modicum of independence on domestic policy issues. Gomułka's openly expressed misgivings about the role of the Soviet-controlled Communist Information Bureau (Cominform), created in 1948, sealed his fate. Rokossovskii's arrival in Warsaw, in November 1949, came shortly after a series of plenums held from June to September by the PUWP's Central Committee that condemned Gomułka's "national road to communism." Gomułka was denounced for his "national deviations" by, among others, Deputy Defense Minister Gen. Marian Spychalski. Both Spychalski and Gomułka were arrested in 1951.

Rokossovskii replaced the purged Polish officers with his own people. The Polish army between 1949 and 1956 included several thousand Russian officers; some of those brought in after 1949 were Soviets of Polish extraction.[26] Estimates of the total number of Soviet Army officers assigned to Poland under Rokossovskii vary. According to one author, following Rokossovskii's 1949–1950 purge, Soviet officers of every rank constituted about 50 percent of the entire officer corps.[27] Another source estimates that, during Rokossovskii's tenure as Poland's defense minister, roughly 90 percent of the top positions in the Defense Ministry were occupied by Soviet officers, including Gen. Jerzy Bordziłowski, a Soviet officer who became chief of the Polish general staff; Ivan Turkiel, another Soviet general, was commander of the Polish air force.[28] Whatever the actual number of the Soviets assigned to Poland might have been, their presence in key positions assured greater Soviet control over the Poles at the time when the People's Army was being re-equipped with modern weapons. In accordance with Stalin's wishes, between 1949 and 1956 the Polish army became a part of the Soviet-controlled, integrated East European armed forces directly subordinated to the Soviet high command. In effect, during Rokossovskii's tenure as defense minister, the PUWP did not have much influence over its own army.

Under Rokossovskii's tutelage, the Polish People's Army abandoned all remaining pretense of being a national force and underwent a major transformation to conform to the Soviet model. This transformation included adoption of Soviet operational doctrine, tactics, weapons, training and drill methods, and strategy. The modernization program was complemented by a massive political indoctrination campaign; stress was also placed on professional training of the new officer class. To meet the growing demand for officers during Rokossovskii's tenure, the General Staff Academy was supplemented by two new schools: the Military Political Academy and the Military Technical Academy. In 1949 a revised conscription law was passed, which fixed the size of the People's Army at 400,000 officers and men.[29]

The training of new "proletarian" cadres was accompanied by a purge of officers whose loyalty to the new regime could be questioned, in particular AK veterans and those who had served in the West and after 1945 had chosen to return to Poland. With respect to prewar officers, Rokossovskii's purge simply continued the policies already set by the Polish Workers' Party (PPR). The postwar purge of the military was an important, if not the most visible, part of Stalin's blueprint for turning the Polish state into a secure and obedient satellite. If "sovietization" of Poland, including the collectivization of agriculture, were to proceed smoothly, all potential sources of national resistance had to be eliminated. Since, in Poland's history, the army had traditionally been at the center of the nation's struggle for independence, the officer corps of the People's Army was scrutinized with particular care.

The most notorious purge of the military during Rokossovskii's tenure as Poland's defense minister started with the arrest on May 15, 1950, of Gen. Józef Kuropieska. Kuropieska was the first important officer arrested in connection with the TUN case (the acronym is composed of the initial letters of the last names of the three key defendants: Gen. S. Tatar and Cols. M. Utnik and S. Nowicki). Kuropieska, who spent the war in a German POW camp in Woldenberg, had been well known for his leftist sympathies.[30] After the war he volunteered for the People's Army, was quickly promoted (Kuropieska was only a captain when the war had ended), and traveled on an official mission to the West in an attempt to convince the officers of the Anders army to return to Poland. Following his arrest, Kuropieska was accused of being a Western spy and repeatedly tortured in prison. However, because of his steadfast refusal to sign a fabricated confession, Kuropieska's case was treated separately from the TUN group; on July 2, 1952, the general was sentenced to death and spent about 700 days on death row awaiting execution.[31] Kuropieska was eventually rehabilitated in 1956; the sixth volume of the general's memoirs describing his ordeal was cleared for publication in 1988.[32]

The most notorious among the military trials of the Rokossovskii era was the case of Gen. Stanisław Tatar, who had returned home after the war. The trial took place between July 31 and August 13, 1951. Tatar and eight other high-ranking officers (including the commander of the 1947 "Vistula" operation against the Ukrainian underground and a close associate of Marshal Michał Rola-Żymierski, Gen. Stefan Mossor)—the so-called TUN group—were charged with conspiracy to create an underground organization inside the armed forces aimed at overthrowing the government.

General Tatar was a prewar officer, a lecturer in the Higher Military School, and an artillery commander during the 1939 German invasion. Captured by the Germans in 1939, Tatar managed to escape and between 1940 and 1943 was placed in charge of operations within the underground Home Army General Headquarters in Poland. In 1944, Tatar was moved to London, where he became deputy chief of staff for home operations to the commander in chief of the Polish Armed Forces in the West. Tatar returned to Poland in July 1947; shortly thereafter he traveled several times to London and brought back with him the silver and dollar deposits of the Fund of National Defense; the money was transferred to the Warsaw government.[33]

The attack on the military coincided with the campaign against "right-wing nationalist deviation," the purge of East European communist parties in the aftermath of Tito's break with Stalin. The Tatar trial was directed both against the prewar officers and former Home Army resistance fighters, and against the "nationalist faction" of Władysław Gomułka and Marian Spychalski within the Polish communist party. Spychalski, whose brother Józef had fought in the Home Army, was blackmailed into publicly attacking Gomułka for his "national deviationism."[34] Spychalski was arrested on April 17, 1951;[35] he was tortured in prison and forced to testify against Tatar and his codefendants. Tatar's "group of nine" was tried in July and August 1951. Gomułka was arrested in August of the same year.

After two years of brutal interrogation, the TUN group was given sentences ranging from life imprisonment for Tatar and Generals F. Herman, J. Kirchmayer, S. Mossor, to fifteen years in prison for Colonels M. Utnik, S. Nowicki, and M. Jurecki, to twelve years for Major W. Roman, and ten years for Lt. Comdr. Sz. Wacek.[36] Although subsequently all the defendants were rehabilitated by Gomułka (Tatar was released in 1956[37]), at the time the Tatar case dealt a major blow to the Polish officers' esprit de corps and caused further deterioration of their morale. It also demonstrated to both the apparatchiks and the military how easily the Soviets could use them for their own political purposes. Tatar was forced to implicate Gomułka and his "national communists"; among other charges, Gomułka and Spychalski were accused of being financial backers and protectors of Tatar's conspiracy.[38] According to one of the two surviving defendants, Col. Marian Utnik, the Tatar trial was clearly a prelude to a much larger purge within the party.[39] In the words of the prosecutor, the Tatar trial demonstrated "the unity between the conspiracy in the army and this section of party leadership that stooped to right-wing nationalist positions."[40]

Gen. Wacław Komar, the chief quartermaster of the Polish army, was arrested in November of 1952 in Marshal Rokossovskii's office.[41] Komar and two other officers were implicated by Tatar's testimony. Their arrests came at the time of the Slansky trial and Stalin's anti-Semitic "doctors' plot." The Komar group was accused of having had financial dealings with Tatar and of working for Western intelligence agencies; Komar was charged with issuing the order in 1947 to assassinate Gen. Karol Świerczewski, and was also accused of being a long-time agent of the Ukrainian Resistance Army.[42]

Komar chose to defend himself during the interrogation by making up the most fantastic stories and accusing the highest party and government officials, including President B. Bierut, of being members of his conspiracy. Apparently, Komar's "crime" was his participation in the Spanish Civil War, in which he had been commander of the 129th International Brigade.[43] Brutally treated throughout the interrogation, Komar was released in 1955; his hair turned grey as a result of the treatment meted out to him during his two years in prison.[44]

Between 1949 and 1954, hundreds of officers were arrested; of these, 83 were tried directly in connection with the Tatar case between 1950 and 1952. Altogether there were 55 military trials for alleged espionage activities; 37 defendants were given death sentences; 19 were executed.[45] In contrast with the Tatar case, these "ripple-effect trials" (*procesy odpryskowe*) were conducted in strict secrecy; they touched all branches of the Polish armed forces, but struck most severely the general staffs.[46]

The military trials were coordinated by a group of Soviet officers assigned to the Ministry of Defense Main Directorate of Information (Główny Zarząd Informacji Ministerstwa Obrony Narodowej), the Polish counterintelligence service, led by Colonels Dimitrii Voznesienskii (a son-in-law of Gen. Karol Świerczewski), Antoni Skulbaszewski, who for a time was the army's chief prosecutor,[47] and Wilhelm Świątkowski, who chaired the Supreme Military Tribunal. All arrests were sanctioned by the minister of defense Marshal K. Rokossovskii.[48]

The purge was also directed against Poland's "native" communist officers, those who had fought throughout the war in Poland in the Soviet-sponsored resistance (GL and AL), and upon liberation had joined the People's Army. The terror contributed to growing demoralization, especially among young officers.

In political terms, however, the military purge trials under Rokossovskii were a watershed in Polish civil-military relations. The arrests of officers and apparatchiks implicated in the Tatar affair and other military trials were directed against both the PUWP's "nationalist faction" and the Polish "native" officer corps. By means of the purge, Rokossovskii succeeded in placing the army outside the Polish communist party's political control as early as 1951. Throughout his tenure as Poland's defense minister, Rokossovskii took his orders directly from Moscow. All military matters were decided by the Soviet Army's general staff and relayed to Rokossovskii exclusively through Soviet military channels; Bierut and the Polish Politburo were rarely notified about changes taking place in the Polish army, and if so, only after they had already been implemented.[49] As Gomułka would later bitterly complain, the promises given him in 1947 by Stalin and Bulganin that all Soviet military advisors would leave Poland by 1951 were quickly forgotten.[50] The trials demonstrated to Gomułka's "national communists" and to Polish officers with GL and AL histories that only close cooperation between the officers and the apparatchiks could guarantee their survival in the face of relentless Soviet efforts to dominate completely the Polish party and the People's Army.

Alliance with the Party:
The Army During the Polish October of 1956

Change in the structure of the Polish army took place after Stalin's death and the turmoil that followed de-Stalinization. The critical moment of the Polish "thaw" came in June of 1956 during the Poznań riots. At the peak of labor unrest, the army was called in after the local police and KBW had failed to break up the demonstrations and restore order. Commanded by General Popławski, troops of the Nineteenth Armored Division of the Fourth Army Corps, KBW, and police, supported by tanks from the Tank and Armored Infantry Officer School (Oficerska Szkoła Wojsk Pancernych i Zmechanizo-wanych) fought pitched battles with the workers and caused heavy civilian casualties. According to data obtained in 1956 from Poznań hospitals, 51 people died in the fighting, including 3 policemen, one KBW soldier, and one cadet from the tank academy; the remainder were civilian casualties, including 32 workers. In addition, 575 people suffered bullet wounds.[51]

In the ensuing political turmoil, fuelled by the killings and by the subsequent mass arrests and trials of the Poznań workers, the party leadership found itself in a deep crisis. The Poznań riots ultimately contributed to the PUWP's bid to wrest control of the Polish army away from the Soviets. In August 1956, the commander of the KBW was fired and his position given to Gen. Wacław Komar, who had recently been released from jail, and who was a close supporter of Gomułka. Komar was representative of the younger senior officers who had earned their commissions on the battlefield rather than obtaining them through political machinations. This group was most embittered by the extent to which the army had been controlled by Rokossovskii and his Soviet staff.

A few months after the Poznań riots, during the Eighth Plenum of the Central Committee, held October 20–21, the crisis within the PUWP leadership reached a climax. The plenum elected the once-disgraced Gomułka first secretary, reprimanded the hard-line Stalinists, and accepted the position that what Gomułka now called the "Poznań tragedy" was an outburst of justified deep discontent among the working class.[52] Polish officers supporting Gomułka got their first assurances that the army was about to undergo sweeping changes; Rokossovskii was dropped from the Politburo.

The Eighth Plenum was a turning point in Polish-Soviet relations after the war. The PUWP asserted that it had the right to make its own personnel decisions, as demonstrated by Gomułka's return and the defeat of the so-called

Natolin group of hard-line Stalinists. Ultimately, however, in the Polish-Soviet confrontation of 1956, it was the readiness on the part of senior Polish officers to throw their lot in with Gomułka that tipped the scales in his favor. Even though during the seven years of direct Soviet control the Polish army had been thoroughly penetrated by Rokossovskii's men, the Corp of Internal Security (KBW), commanded by General Komar, came out for Gomułka. In the face of troop movements by the Soviet Army towards Warsaw, Komar's KBW units were deployed around Warsaw to demonstrate the Poles' resolve to resist direct Soviet pressure. As Khrushchev stormed unannounced into the Polish Central Committee's extraordinary plenary session, demanding to know "who that Gomułka was," KBW soldiers took defensive positions around Warsaw for the express purpose of defending the capital in case of Soviet military action.[53] It seemed for a brief time that the Soviets would opt for a military solution; their divisions stationed in Poland were put on alert and ordered to move toward the capital.[54] In the city there was talk of organizing a "Workers' Committee for the Defense of Warsaw." Next, rebellion in support of Komar and his KBW troops began to spread to the regular forces, as several Polish commanders prepared to fight the approaching Soviet troops. Tensions rose almost to a breaking point when Adm. Jan Wiśniewski closed off Polish ports to Soviet ships.[55]

The test of force never came. Khrushchev did not want to risk a shooting war in Poland, and, more important, he perceptively assessed Gomułka's commitment to communist ideology. Before coming to Warsaw, Khrushchev had feared that Gomułka, once elected to the post of first secretary, would promote far-reaching reforms, but his meeting with the Polish party leader dispelled his doubts. The Soviets accepted Gomułka as the PUWP's first secretary. More important for the future of civil-military relations in Poland, the army's show of determination to resist a Soviet attack won the PUWP a major political victory. It was now up to the reconstituted Politburo to return the favor, and Gomułka was ready to oblige.

One of Gomułka's key demands to the Russians was the transfer of direct control over the Polish People's Army back into Polish hands. The Polish army was allowed to return to its traditional uniform and insignia. In addition, a status-of-forces agreement between Moscow and Warsaw limited Soviet military presence in Poland to two divisions and shifted the Soviet command post back to Legnica.[56] Soviet officers were sent packing; the only high-ranking Soviet general who remained in the Polish army after 1956 was Chief of the General Staff Bordziłowski. Finally, Polish officers supporting Gomułka got what they wanted most: the removal of Marshal Rokossovskii. In 1956 Rokossovskii was shipped back to Moscow and his place was taken by Gomułka's confidant, Gen. Marian Spychalski.

Komar's decision in 1956 to demonstrate his willingness to fight the

Soviets brought the Polish military one step closer to the heart of internal party politics. After 1956, the military would not resume its prescribed role as a mere instrument for implementing party policies, as had been the case in the early postwar years when pacification campaigns, military tribunals, and "defense-propaganda" operations conducted by the army contributed to communist victory in Poland. The experience of powerlessness in the face of Soviet terror had taught both the officers and the apparatchiks a simple and valuable lesson: they needed each other. But there was another unforeseen result of the 1956 confrontation, one that the party failed to notice at the time. In 1956 the army acquired a qualitatively new influence in internal party politics. By siding with Gomułka and Spychalski against the "Natolin group," and by demonstrating their resolve to fight the approaching Soviet divisions, Komar, Wiśniewski, and Frey-Bielecki influenced the outcome of the struggle for the party's highest job.

The new alliance between the Politburo and the military was best symbolized by the selection of Spychalski, Gomułka's adjutant, as Poland's defense minister. The subsequent appointments to the highest positions in the Ministry of Defense of the officers who had sided with Gomułka's bid for power ensured that those who supported him were amply rewarded, and that the army was controlled by people loyal to the first secretary. Gen. J. Frey-Bielecki replaced Ivan Turkiel as head of the air force. Adm. Jan Wiśniewski, who had kept Soviet ships out of Polish ports, became commander in chief of the navy. Several key posts in the Polish military establishment were given to the veterans of the AL and GL, men whose war experience and political credentials were similar to those of General Komar: Gen. J. Zarzycki became chief of the Main Political Administration; Gen. Z. Duszyński was appointed chief inspector of training; and Gen. J. Fonkowicz took over the Defense Ministry's Department of Personnel. These personnel changes were indicative of an understanding emerging between the apparatchiks and the officers about the "national" character of the Polish People's Army. A "national" Polish army had to be more autonomous in its dealings with the Soviets; as 1956 demonstrated, the only way to achieve this goal was to bring the PUWP and the military closer together. Gomułka and Spychalski hoped that the party would remain a senior partner in this new relationship, but their hope was soon dashed by events.

Spychalski's Failed Reforms

Spychalski's tenure as defense minister lasted over a decade, until 1968, when he was replaced by Gen. Wojciech Jaruzelski. During that time an attempt was made to rebuild the army based on the partnership between the party and the military forged in 1956, and to devise a "Polish socialist defense doctrine." The nature of the new alliance between the officers and the apparatchiks was best represented by the defense minister himself. Spychalski was not a professional soldier, but a politician who had turned his hand to military matters. A socialist before the war, he graduated from Warsaw Polytechnic in 1931 with a degree in architectural engineering. His wartime experience was in the Moscow-directed resistance. In 1942, Spychalski joined the communist Polish Workers' Party (PPR), and became chief of intelligence and counter-intelligence of the GL, and after the creation of the AL, a member of its main staff. A close associate of Gomułka, he was a member of the clandestine Home National Council (Krajowa Rada Narodowa), and represented it at a meeting with Stalin and Wasilewska's ZPP that authorized the creation of the Polish People's Army. In 1944, Spychalski was brought into the officer corps of the new armed forces and eventually appointed chief of the general staff.[57] In 1945, Gomułka elevated him to membership in the PPR Politburo; he was also appointed deputy minister of defense.

Spychalski's political fortunes mirrored those of his patron. After a brief tenure as full member of the PUWP's Politburo following the merger with the Polish Socialist Party (PPS), Spychalski was attacked in 1949 for his "nationalist deviation" and, despite his recantation and his denunciation of Gomułka, was purged and jailed in 1951. He was rehabilitated by the Eighth Plenum of the PUWP's Central Committee and allied himself with Gomułka during the 1956 crisis. In 1956, in the view of Komar and Frey-Bielecki, Spychalski's wartime ties to the AL and GL and his record of postwar imprisonment were important enough assets to make up in part for the general's lack of charisma and combat experience. Nevertheless, throughout his career as Poland's defense minister, the general (promoted to marshal in 1963) never truly succeeded in changing his image of a political appointee who was an architect by profession and unfamiliar with the art of soldiering. His abrasive personality and his mercurial temper contributed further to his unpopularity with the officer corps.[58]

Spychalski by no means commanded the loyalties of all the AL and GL veterans; a sizeable portion of them sided with party hard-liners led by Mieczysław Moczar, himself a GL/AL veteran, and his Union of Fighters for Freedom and Democracy (Związek Bojowników o Wolność i Demokrację; ZBoWiD). In 1948, Moczar condemned Gomułka and his "national road to socialism" and declared his unswerving loyalty to Moscow's policies. Although sidelined during the 1956 crisis, Moczar managed to re-establish himself as a powerful power broker in internal party politics, and by the mid-1960s became capable of strongly challenging Gomułka's leadership of the PUWP. By then Moczar's Stalinism was colored by nationalism and a strong dose of malignant anti-Semitism. In the 1960s, the conflict between Gomułka and Spychalski's group and Moczar's "partisans" was an important factor in Poland's politics; it came to a head during the 1968 ZBoWiD-engineered anti-Zionist campaign.[59] Moczar's machinations chipped away at Spychalski's position and contributed to the failure of the marshal's military reforms.

Spychalski's goal during his tenure as defense minister was to restore the "national" character of Poland's armed forces by reducing the degree of direct Soviet control over the army and strengthening ties between the officers and the apparatchiks. While the Soviets would retain overall supervision, the direct day-to-day management of the army was to go to the Poles. As part of Spychalski's plan, the army emphasized its Polish heritage. Those changes within the Polish army coincided roughly with the creation in 1955 of the Warsaw Pact; Spychalski appeared determined to exploit the opportunity to stake a claim to Poland's special place in the nascent military bloc. In 1958, Gen. Zygmunt Duszyński, Poland's deputy defense minister and chief of the Inspectorate of Training, put forth the concept of a self-contained "Polish Front" within the Warsaw Pact. According to Duszyński's plan, fifteen Polish divisions would be organized in three armies and, as a "front" under a Polish commander, would operate together with Soviet and non-Soviet War-saw Pact forces. According to one source, the Soviets initially accepted Duszyński's proposal and agreed that the Inspectorate of Training would operate as the command skeleton of the "Polish Front."[60]

Another Polish contribution to Warsaw Pact strategy, introduced during Spychalski's tenure as defense minister, was the concept of the "defense of national territory," which was devised by Gen. Bolesław Chocha, one of Poland's most prolific postwar military strategists.[61] The doctrine of National Territorial Defense (Obrona Terytorialna Kraju; OTK) defined its primary goal as the preparation of the country for defending itself against a nuclear attack in the event of war with NATO. Chocha recommended that the preparations include: (1) strong air defense to be conducted by Air Defense Detachments (Wojska Obrony Powietrznej Kraju); and (2) strong civil defense that would include population dispersal and shelter construction. In 1965, special Ter-ritorial Defense units were created within the Polish army; the KBW was renamed Internal Defense Detachments (Wojska Obrony Wewnętrznej; WOW) and control over them transferred from the Interior Ministry to the Ministry of Defense. As Chocha envisioned it, the WOW's task in war would be to protect the "internal front," that is, to fight sabotage, guard railroads and communication lines, and maintain law and order in the rear of the "opera-tional forces."[62]

Political training of the military also underwent a change under Spychalski. Cadets at military academies who wanted to become political officers were now required to meet the regular core-course requirements before they could switch to the political curriculum. The form of the party's immediate intrusion into its increasingly mature and cohesive armed forces changed as well. Gradually, the Main Political Administration (MPA) replaced the primary party and communist youth organizations as the principal means of party supervision. The growing importance of the MPA would eventually undercut Spychalski's efforts to preserve the primacy of the military's loyalty to the Polish communist party as a means of guaranteeing the limited autonomy in internal politics the apparatchiks had won in 1956.

Spychalski's reforms began to founder in less than a decade, chiefly because of direct Soviet pressure on the PUWP and the Polish officer corps. By the mid-1960s the Soviet Army's general staff was increasingly skeptical about the strategic validity of the Polish Front and opted for plans that called for direct incorporation of the fifteen Polish divisions into various Soviet fronts within the framework of the Warsaw Pact's doctrine of "coalition warfare." The plans for blocwide operational integration required a degree of Soviet control over the Polish army comparable to that of the Rokossovskii period, even if the means through which it was to be exercised were to be different. The MPA's role as an outside "channel" to the Soviets was underscored during the 1960–1964 purge of the AL and GL appointees of 1956; in the 1960s, ideological orthodoxy, that is, loyalty to Moscow as defined by the MPA, became again the key criterion for new appointments. Gen. Wojciech Jaruzelski, promoted to chief of the MPA in 1960 and elevated four years later to full membership in the Central Committee, epitomized the new breed of the People's Army officers who were preparing to supersede Spychalski's generation.[63] As MPA chief, Jaruzelski presided over the purge of GL and AL veterans from the officer corps; these forced retirements were a harbinger of the upcoming change. Throughout the 1960s Jaruzelski's influence grew, while Spychalski gradually lost control over military appointments. The appointment in 1965 of Jaruzelski as chief of the Polish general staff coincided with Moscow's renewed insistence on Warsaw Pact integration, in accordance with the principles of the "coalition warfare" strategy. The effective end of Spychalski's control over the army came in 1967 during the purge of senior Polish officers after the Six Day War. As Moczar and his ZBoWiD veterans prepared to launch a frontal assault on Gomułka by stirring up an anti-Semitic campaign inside the PUWP, Polish officers of Jewish origin were summoned to the MPA to sign a loyalty statement condemning Israel's action. Those who refused to sign were summarily dismissed; those who signed were dismissed six months later. In the 1967 purge, 14 generals and about 200 colonels were dismissed.[64]

By the mid-1960s, the Soviets had re-established their influence over the Polish military, which had been lost after Rokossovskii's removal, but their methods were different. Instead of using Soviet officers masquerading as Poles, the Soviets built an extensive network of so-called liaison missions, whose primary responsibility was to supervise day-to-day operations of the Polish army.[65] Polish officers trusted by Moscow were promoted. The notion of the Polish Front was modified; General Duszyński, its primary architect, was dismissed in 1964, the year Jaruzelski joined the PUWP's Central Committee.[66] Spychalski was on his way out, while Jaruzelski and his group of former junior line officers in the Berling army positioned themselves to move to center stage.

The crisis of 1956 and the attempt by Gomułka and Spychalski to forge an alliance between the party and the army brought about changes in Polish civil-military relations that outlived Gomułka's tenure of office. However ephemeral the Polish October proved to be, it raised the army's prestige in Polish society. The Polish-Soviet confrontation of 1956 reawakened in the Polish national consciousness the spirit of defiance that had been a part of the Insurrectionary Tradition. The determination of Komar's troops to resist direct Soviet military intervention was, in the eyes of the Poles, a living proof that their soldiers had never ceased to be Polish patriots. Spychalski's policy of limiting Soviet tutelage over the Polish army, combined with the return of the outward appearances of a national force, further strengthened this general perception. More important, the 1956 crisis made the military into an active, if indirect, participant in party politics on the highest level. The army's role in the upheaval and the period of "re-Polonization" of the armed forces under Spychalski laid the foundations upon which Wojciech Jaruzelski would erect the edifice of his political power in the 1960s, 1970s, and 1980s.

The Army in the 1970s

---4---

Jaruzelski's Military Career

Prior to December 1981, Gen. Wojciech Jaruzelski was to the majority of the Poles an enigmatic personality, hovering in the background of party and state politics. Because of his apparent detachment from the daily affairs of the PUWP and his ostensible preoccupation with the professional aspects of running the army, Jaruzelski enjoyed the respect of the majority of his countrymen. He projected the image of an experienced line officer and a soldier wholly preoccupied with military matters.

Until the events of the Solidarity period thrust him into the spotlight of national affairs, Jaruzelski had been a shadowy, somewhat colorless figure; knowledge of him, his life, his family, and his position within the power elite was based on hearsay rather than solid factual information. Between August 1980 and December 1981, the general was known to the Poles for his reported defiance of Gomułka and the latter's close associate Z. Kliszko when they wanted to use the army against the striking workers during the 1970 riots on the Baltic coast; rumor had it that for this he was placed under house arrest.[1] Although documentary evidence that has come to light in the 1980s (discussed in this chapter) has dispelled the myth of Jaruzelski as a "Polish patriot in 1970," while it was believed, the fabrication gave him the aura of an honest proessional soldier.[2]

Information about Jaruzelski's life is scarce.[3] Brief, obligatory hagiographical notes have appeared periodically in official party and military publications; otherwise his life has never been known to the Poles the way the careers of Spychalski or Moczar were. Born on July 6, 1923, in Kurów near Lublin in eastern Poland, of a landed noble family, Jaruzelski grew up in a home that cultivated Catholic virtues and traditional devotion to the motherland (his father served in the Polish cavalry under Marshal Piłsudski). The young Wojciech received his early education at a provincial Jesuit school; in its emphasis on patriotism and religion, his upbringing was similar to that of other children of the lesser Polish nobility. After the Soviet invasion of Poland, on September 17, 1939, following the German attack from the West, the sixteen-year-old Wojciech and his entire family were forcibly deported to the Soviet interior; reportedly, all except Wojciech perished in the gulag. Between 1939 and 1943, Jaruzelski endured forced labor in the Karaganda mines in Kazakhstan and in forests near the Mongolian and Chinese borders. It was most likely in Karaganda that he first encountered and learned the teachings of Marxism-Leninism. To what degree, however, his decision to join the Soviet-controlled First Polish Army was dictated by his internationalist convictions, and to what extent it was simply a means of saving himself from slow death in the Karaganda mine pits must remain a matter of speculation.

Jaruzelski volunteered for the First Polish Army in 1943. Shortly thereafter he was selected for officer's training and attended a Soviet officer candidate school at Ryazan, near Moscow. Commissioned as an infantry lieutenant in the Fifth Regiment of the Second Infantry Division, he fought in several campaigns on the eastern front, participated in the liberation of Warsaw, the crossing of the Oder, and the storming of German fortifications in Pomerania. He was twice decorated with the Cross of Valor and thrice with the Combat Service Medal for bravery under fire. Between 1945 and 1947, Jaruzelski distinguished himself as a dedicated commander during the fight against the anticommunist and nationalist underground resistance in southwestern Poland, in particular during the "Vistula" operation against the Ukrainian nationalist underground.[4] As the communists moved to consolidate power, Jaruzelski's service record brought him to the attention of his military superiors. At the time senior and middle-level officer positions in the Polish army were filled by Russians or Russians of Polish extraction; according to one estimate, Soviet officers constituted 80 percent of the Polish army's senior officers.[5] Jaruzelski's background, especially his training in a Soviet officers' school and his reputation as an enthusiastic and ambitious young communist, must have been an asset in the eyes of the top brass of the new Polish army.

In 1947, Jaruzelski attended infantry officers' school, and from 1948 to 1951 studied at the General Staff Academy in Warsaw, from which he graduated with distinction. In 1947 he had joined the communist Polish Workers' Party (PPR), the precursor of the PUWP. According to an unconfirmed account, after graduation from the Polish General Staff Academy, Jaruzelski briefly attended the Voroshilov General Staff Academy in Moscow.[6] In 1956, he was promoted to one-star general.[7] Following Spychalski's purge of Soviet officers and advisers from the Polish army in 1956–1957, Jaruzelski became, at 33 years of age, the youngest Polish brigadier general. Between 1957 and 1960, he commanded a motorized infantry division. Promoted to two-star general in 1960, at the height of the military purge of Spychalski's 1956 GL and AL appointees, Jaruzelski became the head of the army's Main Political Administration.[8] A year later, he was elected deputy to the Sejm (Polish parliament).

The 1960s were a period of steady advancement for Jaruzelski and consolidation of his influence in the Polish military establishment. In 1962, he became deputy minister of defense and, in 1965, chief of the general staff. He also advanced steadily within the party bureaucracy. His role as chief of the MPA brought him into close contact with the highest echelons of the party. Because the 1960s were a period of renewed emphasis on political indoctrination of the army, Jaruzelski's position as the trustee of the military's morale and ideological "correctness" made him a powerful broker between the civilian party apparat and the increasingly cohesive officer corps. The renewed emphasis on Warsaw Pact integration and Soviet control over satellite armies was the rationale behind the purge of Spychalski's appointees. Quite likely the proliferation of "nationalist" ideas inside the Polish military establishment, such as Duszyński's concept of the "Polish Front," caused serious concern in the Kremlin. The 1960–1964 purge was facilitated by the fact that, shortly after the 1956 "thaw," Gomułka had turned increasingly to Moscow for support, thus weakening the bond between the officers and the apparatchiks forged during the Polish October. By the mid-1960s, Spychalski had lost most of his political support inside the PUWP, and the young officer elite viewed him increasingly as only a political figurehead.

In 1964, Jaruzelski became a full member of the PUWP's Central Committee—an indication of his standing in the party establishment. His elevation to the position of chief of the general staff, shortly after the removal of the last of Spychalski's AL/GL appointees, was a clear signal that the Soviets had considerable confidence in the loyalty of the relatively young general. Jaruzelski's brilliant miliary career was paralleled by his growing influence in the Central Committee; in late February, the PUWP's Eleventh Plenum selected Jaruzelski as one of the trusted party comrades responsible for the preparation of the upcoming Fifth Party Congress.[9]

The apex of Jaruzelski's military career came in 1968, when he replaced Spychalski as defense minister. As was reported on April 12, 1968, by the Polish army daily *Żołnierz Wolności*, Marshal Spychalski was asked to replace Edward Ochab as chairman of the Council of State; Jaruzelski assumed Spychalski's position. The switch occurred at the height of the anti-Semitic campaign of 1968 and the purge of the party ignited by the student riots in

Warsaw in March of that year.[10] The campaign was masterminded by Mie-czysław Moczar, then Poland's minister of the interior, together with his AL/GL hard-line "partisan" nationalists. Although they did not succeed in push-ing Gomułka out of office, Moczar's intrigues forced a reshuffling of the top party and government officials.

The 1968 crisis was in part caused by Poland's growing economic problems and the increasingly apparent return to ideological orthodoxy. In the mid-1960s, Minister of the Interior Moczar, who was also the chairman of the veterans' organization ZBoWiD, became the leader of a vocal group of former PPR and GL and AL veterans from World War II. These "partisans" charged that Poland's intellectual and political life was rapidly drifting toward "cos-mopolitism," destroying the nation's tradition of patriotism and true "Pol-ishness." Despite the claims by Franciszek Szlachcic, who in 1968 was deputy minister of the interior and Moczar's close friend, that the "partisans" had never been interested in forcing Gomułka out of office, the latter felt suffi-ciently threatened by Moczar to move him from the Ministry of the Interior to the Central Committee and the Politburo; by Szlachcic's own admission, this ostensible promotion, "limited [Moczar's] powers to act."[11]

Attacks on "liberals" and "revisionists" inside the PUWP were by 1968 linked with Moczar's anti-Semitic campaign, which Gomułka initially sup-ported to some extent, and which ultimately forced about twenty thousand Polish Jews to emigrate.[12] The March crisis was followed by a purge of the universities, party, and government administration. In Warsaw alone, between March and May 1968, 483 people were fired, including 365 at the ministry and central-agency levels; thirty people were expelled from the Warsaw party organization, including six ministers and deputy ministers. In Gdańsk voivodship, 77 people were fired; the party organizations of the Łódź and Wrocław voivodships were also purged.[13]

As a result of the recent purge of Spychalski's supporters in the armed forces, most of whom were proponents of the army's greater emancipation from Soviet tutelage, Spychalski lacked, in 1968, a sufficient power base to resist Moczar effectively. The cashiering of Polish-Jewish officers after the Six Day War was yet another blow to the marshal's authority.[14] Spychalski's acceptance of a civilian post signaled a tacit recognition on his part that his military career was over.

The Invasion of Czechoslovakia

The appointment of General Jaruzelski as defense minister coincided with the intensification of the Czechoslovak crisis, and by all indications it was tied to the political turmoil underway in Poland's southern neighbor. In 1968, the

Soviets needed a defense minister in Warsaw who would be both loyal to them and able to control his troops. The session of the Sejm that accepted Jaruzelski's promotion followed immediately upon the CPSU Central Committee plenum of April 9–10, during which the Soviets called emphatically for "strengthening the cohesion of the world communist movement," and for "proletarian-internationalist" struggle against "bourgeois ideas"—an unequivocal indictment of Dubček's "revisionism." In his address to the Central Committee, Brezhnev insinuated for the first time that Moscow might resort to force to resolve the Czechoslovak crisis; as he put it, the CPSU was prepared to do "all that's necessary to strengthen the Socialist Commonwealth in the area of politics, economics, and defense."[15]

Jaruzelski's personal contacts with the Soviet general staff and the WTO Joint High Command, as well as his loyal service during the purge of the Spychalski group, undoubtedly played a role in his elevation to Poland's minister of defense.[16] Even before his appointment was made official, Jaruzelski had participated actively in joint Warsaw Pact consultations on the best response to the Czechoslovak deviation. On March 6, Jaruzelski flew to Bulgaria to attend the meeting in Sofia on the following day of the Warsaw Pact's Consultative Committee, chaired by the pact's commander in chief, Marshal Ivan Yakubovskiy. Among the top military brass that convened in Sofia, Jaruzelski was the only participant without the rank of defense minister.[17] Nevertheless, after the plenary discussions had been completed, he was included in the list of very high military officials of Warsaw Pact forces invited to a private dinner reception given by Bulgaria's Gen. Dobriy Dzhurov in honor of Marshal Yakubovskiy and "fraternal ministers of defense." Dzhurov's reception was an opportunity for the military men to discuss in private the operational details of the "appropriate decisions taken [during the committee's plenary session] on the matters under discussion."[18] The fact that despite his still relatively junior position Jaruzelski participated fully in the meeting in Sofia strongly suggests that his appointment to the position of Poland's defense minister had been decided already in early spring of 1968. As the future minister, he had to be personally involved in the contingency planning with regard to Czechoslovakia. Hence, it would also appear that Soviet plans for a military solution to the "Czechoslovak problem" were being reviewed as early as March 1968.[19]

Jaruzelski justified Brezhnev's trust in him by issuing a strong declaration of his unswerving loyalty to the system. Jaruzelski's first official statement as new defense minister came one day after his appointment, during the last plenary session of the Ministry of Defense chaired by Spychalski. Thanking the marshal for his work, Jaruzelski asked him to convey to Gomułka his personal assurances of the Polish army's loyalty and dedication. "The Armed Forces," said the general, "will always serve the party, the working class, the working masses, the entire nation."[20] All this seemed quite routine, except for Jaruzelski's pledge of loyalty to Gomułka, a message clearly intended to reassure the first secretary and to serve notice to Moczar's "partisans" that Spychalski's departure would not alter significantly the structure of political power inside the party leadership; if only for two years, Jaruzelski threw his support behind Gomułka. Jaruzelski's personal expression of loyalty to the first secretary was undoubtedly encouraged by Moscow, as it would help to maintain stability of leadership in Poland in the face of the Czechoslovak crisis.

Jaruzelski's appointment as Poland's defense minister reflected the Soviet decision to put a trusted group of officers in control of one of the least trusted armies of the Warsaw Pact forces.[21] Since promotion to the level of colonel and above in the Polish army must be approved by the Soviets, Jaruzelski could not have been appointed without a clear understanding of what his first task as Poland's defense minister was going to be, and what was expected of him. The general set about fulfilling his commitment by first bringing into the ministry those army officers on whose personal loyalty he could count. Jaruzelski's promotion was accompanied by reshuffling within the senior Polish officer corps. Gen. Józef Urbanowicz became chief of the Main Political Administration; Gen. Bolesław Chocha was promoted to deputy chief of the general staff; Gen. Tadeusz Tuczapski became chief inspector of training. Commander of the Silesian Military District Gen. E. Molczyk, Jaruzelski's principal competitor for the ministerial position, was "kicked upstairs" to become first deputy chief of the general staff; his place in the Silesian district was taken by Jaruzelski's closest friend, Gen. Florian Siwicki. Siwicki's promotion to Molczyk's former post made him automatically the commander of the Polish task force then being readied for the invasion of Czechoslovakia. Jaruzelski realized that in Soviet eyes the upcoming operation would be an important test of his leadership. By putting his trusted aide in charge of the Polish army units assigned to the invasion force, he could expect that they would perform as planned. Siwicki, Chocha, Tuczapski, Urbanowicz, and Gen. Grzegorz Korczyński, who at the time was inspector of territorial defense, constituted the inner circle of Jaruzelski's closest associates in 1968.

Polish officers were directly involved in the drafting of the invasion plans, and Jaruzelski was briefed about all the details. The command post and the planning staff of the Warsaw Pact contingents readied for the invasion were located in Poland, in Marshal Ivan Yakubovskiy's Legnica headquarters.[22] The actual drafting of the operational plan for the invasion of Czechoslovakia began in April 1968, shortly after the Sofia meeting; Yakubovskiy arrived in Poland on April 19 to confer with senior Polish officers. Jaruzelski, Korczyński, Urbanowicz, Chocha, and Tuczapski awaited the marshal at the Warsaw airport. The presence of Soviet Ambassador to Poland A. Aristov, Gen. D. Zherebin of the WTO Joint Command, and Soviet Military Attaché to Poland

Gen. A. Rodionov was a clear sign that the meeting would concern a political problem of blocwide dimensions; in April of 1968, the only such problem was the Czechoslovak crisis. Having also conferred briefly with Poland's party leaders, the next day Yakubovskiy was on his way back to Moscow to report on the results of the Warsaw talks.[23] A week later, on April 26, Siwicki formally assumed the command of the Silesian Military District.[24]

Since the Soviets did not station troops in Czechoslovakia prior to 1968, the necessary reconnaissance before the invasion was conducted under the cover of joint WTO "staff exercises," which took place on Czechoslovak territory at the end of June. The results were then evaluated by Yakubovskiy's Legnica staff and passed on to individual commanders of the non-Soviet Warsaw Pact invasion forces. Plans for the Polish task force were reviewed and updated in the course of personal contacts between senior Polish and Soviet officers. This was done through routine military communication channels, as well as during official visits. One such official occasion to consult with the Soviets was the August 6 trip to Moscow by Jaruzelski, Korczyński, Urbanowicz, and Chocha to attend Marshal Rokossovskii's funeral. After the ceremony, Jaruzelski and his aides met in conference with Soviet defense minister Marshal Grechko, chief of the Soviet Army's Main Political Administration Gen. Yepishev, and the chief of the Soviet general staff, Shtemenko.[25]

As far as the preparations of his army's invasion force were concerned, Jaruzelski left nothing to chance. He was directly involved in the drafting of the invasion plans as well as in their overall coordination. Jaruzelski was a frequent visitor to Siwicki's headquarters. Between April 26 and 27, he participated in a special session of the Silesian District's Military Council and inspected the district's training grounds. During the visit, he urged his officers to emphasize "ideological training and the strengthening of morale and discipline" of the troops.[26] On the eve of the invasion, he conducted the final on-sight inspection of the Polish task force deployed in southwestern Poland, the designated staging area for the Polish contingent. After the inspection, Jaruzelski met one more time with Siwicki.[27]

Strengthening the army's morale became the main theme of Jaruzelski's speeches immediately prior to the invasion; the general was well aware of the ethical dilemma the upcoming operation would force upon his troops. Without referring directly to the planned operation, he repeatedly hinted in his speeches at the rationale for the Polish army's participation in the invasion of Czechoslovakia. On May 9, addressing a rally in commemoration of the victory over Germany in 1945, Jaruzelski again raised the specter of "German revanchism" (Gomułka's term for alleged West German aspirations to reclaim the territories lost to Poland after the war) and pledged his army's unswerving loyalty to the party. He briefly restated the official accusations against "Israel and its ally West Germany" and insisted that any challenge to the party and socialism was tantamount to undermining Poland's security. "The [Polish] army," asserted the general, "exemplifies socialist democracy. In its function and internal relations it rejects [the principles] that govern bourgeois armies."[28]

Jaruzelski's first official public statement on the role of his troops in the invasion of Czechoslovakia came on September 1, 1968, during the traditional promotion of young officers graduating from Poland's eleven military academies. As could have been expected, Jaruzelski participated in the commencement ceremony in Silesia. In his speech to the Wrocław cadets, he presented the rationale for the WTO actions in Czechoslovakia. "At the order of the people's government," he said, "together with the soldiers of the Soviet Army and other allied nations, the Polish soldier hurried into Czechoslovakia. The experience has shown that our help was necessary, and that it arrived at the right time, when underground, well-organized counterrevolutionary processes were just beginning to surface."[29] The speech contained the two political themes that were to become hallmarks of Jaruzelski's tenure of the post of Poland's defense minister throughout the 1970s: comradeship-in-arms with the Soviet Army and the army's duty to defend communist power.

The Army After 1968

Throughout the Warsaw Pact invasion of Czechoslovakia, Jaruzelski made every effort to maintain his army's morale. On September 1, he announced that the Polish officers who had led the troops into Czechoslovakia would be promoted and awarded the Medal of Merit and the Polonia Restituta Cross;[30] the decorations were presented by Siwicki to his officers in the field.[31] Jaruzelski also rewarded his staff officers. On October 9, in Warsaw, Generals Korczyński and Huszcza presented military decorations to a large group of senior officers from all military districts. A propaganda campaign calling for "letters of support for the Polish soldier in Czechoslovakia" was orchestrated; letters praising the soldiers' efforts were delivered to Siwicki's headquarters in Karlovy Vary and read to the assembled troops. Political supervision of the units was also tightened. During the conference on September 29 of the general staff's Basic Party Cell (Podstawowa Organizacja Partyjna; POP), Jaruzelski emphasized that the army had to remain "faithful to the party and the nation," in order to proudly bring with it to the upcoming Fifth Party Congress the "lessons of recent international events."[32]

Gomułka made it clear that he was pleased with Jaruzelski's performance. The approaching 25th anniversary of the Polish People's Army became an occasion for the party to lavish praise upon the defense minister. Preparations were made for a special concert honoring the army; promotions were generously approved; and service medals awarded to senior staff officers. On October 10, both Jaruzelski and Korczyński were promoted to the rank of three-star general. Urbanowicz, Chocha, Tuczapski, Huszcza, and Molczyk received high decorations.[33] The next day, the military officers were honorary guests at the special gala concert given in their honor in Warsaw's Grand Theater, and attended by the party leadership and a senior Soviet delegation led by Marshals Andrey Grechko and Ivan Yakubovskiy. During the ceremony, Grechko spoke of his "deep satisfaction with the military cooperation and fraternal relations between the Polish People's Army and the Soviet armed forces," and stressed that Polish-Soviet friendship was best exemplified "by the helping hand extended to the Czechoslovak nation in the name of defending socialism."[34] The ceremony ended with a 24-gun salute and a review of the guard.

Personal thanks to Jaruzelski from the CPSU Politburo and the Soviet general staff were delivered on October 12, during a private ceremony hosted at the Soviet mission by Ambassador Aristov, Grechko, and Yakubovskiy. In recognition of their service, Jaruzelski, Korczyński, Urbanowicz, Chocha, Tuczapski, Siwicki, and Molczyk were presented with the Order of Lenin. The officers who planned the operation of the Polish forces participating in the invasion of Czechoslovakia were thus honored for their "service in World War II and their contribution to the development of fraternal ties between the Polish and Soviet forces."[35]

Units of the Polish military contingent in Czechoslovakia began to return home on October 24 and, predictably, their arrival was greeted by official optimism.[36] On Jaruzelski's orders, the Polish general staff organized a seminar devoted to the evaluation of "Operation Danube," as the invasion of Czechoslovakia was code-named by the Warsaw Pact. The session was attended by senior Soviet officers from Legnica, and its participants pronounced the operation a resounding success.[37] Displays of official optimism notwithstanding, however, the Polish task force did not always perform according to plan, and field officers spoke privately of morale problems. Reportedly, fraternization between Polish soldiers and Czech civilians during the country's occupation prompted Jaruzelski to withdraw his troops earlier than planned. The invasion also had a negative effect on the army's standing in Polish society. The dramatic decline in the number of applications to military academies following the invasion was a clear indication of the decline in the army's prestige after 1968—a direct aftereffect of the invasion.[38] Although the high-ranking officers went out of their way to present the invasion of Poland's southern neighbor to the military's rank and file as an act of friendship and assistance, the whole affair, coming so closely on the heels of the repression of student dissent in March 1968, was a serious blow to the army's reputation. The majority of the Poles found the use of their soldiers to secure Soviet imperial objectives distasteful, and propaganda could not substitute for facts.[39]

If the army's image suffered after the intervention in Czechoslovakia, Jaruzelski's personal fortunes soared. Jaruzelski's overall credible performance during the invasion demonstrated to the Kremlin his loyalty and thus vastly improved his political position. In 1968, the general proved to the Soviets that he could control his army, and if necessary would not hesitate to use it for purely political ends. Moscow's appreciation of Jaruzelski's services made him an influential man at home. His appointment as Poland's minister of defense coincided with the celebrations of the 25th anniversary of the Polish People's Army and the preparations for the Fifth Congress of the PUWP, held in Warsaw from November 11 to 16, 1968. Reflecting the military's newly acquired status, the Fifth Congress elected Jaruzelski and Korczyński to full membership in the party's Central Committee; Chocha, Tuczapski, Siwicki, and Urbanowicz became candidate members of the Central Committee.[40]

Jaruzelski's growing influence as a politician was complemented by his credentials as a professional soldier. The general's appointment as defense minister and his successful performance during the Czechoslovak invasion came on the eve of the reform of the Warsaw Pact structure that heralded a shift in the Soviet view of the role of the non-Soviet WTO forces. The pact reforms, introduced in 1969, shifted the emphasis from the previous strategy of maintaining the non-Soviet WTO armies as a supplementary force, to the policy of fully integrating the East European operational armies into Soviet war plans. The changes were announced after the 1969 Budapest meeting of the pact's Political Consultative Committee. The reforms (1) created the Committee of Defense Ministers as the highest consultative body of the WTO; (2) reconstituted the WTO Joint High Command; (3) set up a Permanent Staff under the Joint High Command; (4) established the Military Council, charged with planning and quality control, as well as (5) the Technical Committee on Science and Technology responsible for the WTO member states' overall effort in military research and development; and, finally (6) adopted a new statute for the Joint Armed Forces, whereby a non-Soviet WTO deputy defense minister became automatically a deputy commander in chief of the WTO Joint Command.[41] The reforms increased Soviet control over the non-Soviet armies of the Warsaw Pact. With respect to Poland, they destroyed the remnants of Spychalski's plan for a national-communist Polish army, as demonstrated by the fate of General Duszyński's "national front."

The end of the 1960s saw a gradual reassertion of Moscow's control over its satellites in matters of military strategy. In Poland, renewed Soviet emphasis on the operational unity of the WTO led to a dramatic shift in the strategy of the People's Army. Duszyński's idea that the WTO should have different fronts—a line of attack or defense against the NATO forces conducted by the several non-Soviet armies led by East European generals, but subordinated to the Soviet Supreme High Command—was modified to ensure a higher level of coordination within the Warsaw Pact. Rather than strengthening the national control of the Polish forces, as Duszyński had envisioned it, Jaruzelski worked for the army's greater integration into the WTO structure. He accepted the premise that, in case of war, the Polish Front would be merged with Soviet operational forces. In addition, Poland's territorial defense would become part of the total mobilization of the pact's rear, and would complement the Polish army's operational integration into the Soviet-commanded front. These changes called for a greater degree of coordination of WTO operations, an even greater penetration of the Polish officer corps by liaison officers from the Soviet Army, and direct links between the Polish defense minister and the commander in chief of the Warsaw Pact forces.[42]

Jaruzelski made no effort to use his influence and the improvements in his army to recover the modicum of independence from Soviet control that the Polish army had enjoyed under Spychalski in the late 1950s. On the contrary, as suggested by the dramatic increase in WTO joint military maneuvers involving the Polish army, he acted on the assumption that the greater skill of the Polish soldier would contribute to the strength of the Warsaw Pact as a whole, and that the fifteen Polish divisions were an integral part of the Warsaw Pact operational forces.[43] As Jaruzelski had demonstrated in 1968, he was ready to use his troops to defend communist power in Poland and elsewhere in the bloc. The first opportunity to translate his words into action presented itself two years after his promotion to defense minister.

Myth and Reality: Jaruzelski in the 1970 Crisis

In December 1970, Polish soldiers were used to suppress a wave of violent strikes on the Baltic coast. The "Polish December" swept the Gomułka regime from power and led to the political ascendancy of Edward Gierek and his allegedly more "technocratic" apparatchiks. The immediate cause of the strikes was an announcement of a sharp increase in food prices; in fact, the eruption was a culmination of growing social discontent caused by Poland's economic stagnation, declining living standards, and political repression after the 1968 student riots.

The army's role in 1970 has been subject to distortions of fact brought about in part by the military's fervent desire to minimize its responsibility for the bloodshed, as well as Polish society's unwillingness to accept that Polish soldiers could become an obedient tool in the hands of the regime. It is a matter of record, however (the army's subsequent denials notwithstanding), that Jaruzelski and his men were very much involved in the 1970 crackdown. The same group of Polish officers who had performed so well in the invasion of Czechoslovakia was called upon to deal with the 1970 crisis.

The Gdańsk pacification operation was managed by a five-man "Gdańsk task force" headed by Gen. Grzegorz Korczyński, then deputy minister of defense. Korczyński's team was empowered by the Politburo to command all army and police forces dispatched to the area; the Politburo meeting that took the decision to use the army against the workers was attended by Defense Minister Jaruzelski. All operational plans for Korczyński's team were drafted by Gen. Bolesław Chocha, who had been sent to Gdańsk to assess the situation and gather current data on the fighting.[44] The troops ordered to the coast by Jaruzelski totaled about 25,000. They included 13,000 army regulars dispatched to Gdańsk and 12,000 sent to Szczecin; Jaruzelski deployed additional forces around Cracow, Poznań, Wrocław, and Warsaw, to be ready to occupy these key industrial centers if strikes spread throughout the country. During the riots on the Baltic coast, the army participated directly in some 100 operations against the strikers; the total force directly involved in the repression included 61,000 army troops, 1,700 tanks, 1,750 armored personnel carriers, transport aircraft, helicopters, and a number of naval vessels.[45]

More important, the army was sent out against the strikers from the very first day of the confrontation. When news of the Gdańsk rebellion arrived in Warsaw, about 150 soldiers were immediately dispatched to garrison the Gdańsk Regional Party headquarters; it appears that this rapid-response unit had been dispatched to Gdańsk *before* the Politburo had considered all its options.[46] Next, at Gomułka's and Premier Cyrankiewicz's request, Jaruzelski ordered army helicopters to drop tear gas on the crowd surrounding the building.[47] The decision to use live ammunition against the strikers was taken on December 15, 1970, by Gomułka and his associates, including Prime Minister J. Cyrankiewicz, Chairman of the Council of State M. Spychalski, ZBoWiD chairman M. Moczar, and Politburo Member Stanisław Kania;[48] the actual order to fire at demonstrators was issued to the army by Defense Minister Jaruzelski. The only restriction imposed on the use of firearms against civilians was the instruction to fire a warning salvo into the air first, to be followed by another salvo aimed at the pavement; after that the soldiers fired directly into the crowd. Bullets from the second salvo ricocheting off the pavement had wreaked havoc among the marchers even before the officers gave the order to fire directly at the demonstrators.[49]

As the 1970 crisis threatened to escalate into a nationwide general strike, the Soviets withdrew their support from Gomułka. The Gierek regime stepped in to pacify the workers with a combination of rolled-back food prices, promises of rapid improvements in the living standards, and high-sounding appeals to the Poles' patriotism.[50] The new governmental team held a series of meetings at striking plants, pleading for calm and a speedy return to work. During one such meeting with striking Szczecin workers, on January 24, 1971, Defense Minister Jaruzelski admitted that the army was being used to quell the riots, but he tried to minimize his troops' involvement in the fighting.[51] Still, the casualty figures and the number of civilians treated for bullet wounds were staggering; the unrest cost 44 dead and 1,164 wounded.[52] Strikes spread from Gdańsk to neighboring Gdynia and Szczecin; on December 17, the day that has gone down in Polish history as "Black Thursday in Gdynia," the army opened fire with machine guns on the civilians, killing and wounding dozens of them. Finally, in a development curiously foreshadowing events ten years later during the Solidarity crisis, on December 17 the government also decided to impose a state of emergency in the entire coastal region and to militarize all harbors; announcements of the new regulations were printed to be posted the next day. By December 18, Gdańsk was full of rumors that all plants, including shipyards, would be taken over by the army.[53] The dramatic climax of the crisis came with the sudden removal of Gomułka. The new team, headed by Silesia's powerful regional party secretary, Edward Gierek, chose to compromise with the strikers; the state of emergency decrees were shelved.

For Jaruzelski the compromise came not a day too soon. The army's involvement in the 1970 killing of striking shipyard workers had led to the most severe crisis of his soldiers' morale up to that time, especially among the young conscripts. The full scope of the problem was not revealed until 1981, when *Tygodnik Solidarność*, the weekly of the independent trade union Solidarity, ran a series of eyewitness accounts and memoirs written by the draftees who had been deployed in 1970 against the Gdańsk workers.[54] During the crisis, there reportedly occurred individual instances of soldiers disobeying orders. According to unconfirmed rumors, mechanics at the Babie Doły helicopter base refused to service the aircraft used in attacks against civilians. In another alleged incidence of a breakdown in military discipline, a twenty-man-strong army unit clashed with the police.[55] In some cases, when ordered to shoot at the strikers, draftees disobeyed the order.[56]

After 1970, Jaruzelski desperately tried to limit the damage done to the army's morale and image. During the January meeting at the Warski Shipyard mentioned earlier, the general insisted that he personally "felt compelled to explain what had happened" and asked the workers to be indulgent when examining the army's action. "Do you wish, comrades, workers, and friends," pleaded Jaruzelski, "to have an army that would install or change the government? Do you want [in Poland], as in Latin America or Africa, to have a government of colonels and generals? Do you want [an army] that would overthrow this government whenever it disliked a particular decision of this legally elected [party] leadership? No! Our soldier will always defend our people's government. Together with you he will defend the party!"[57]

There are reasons to believe that Jaruzelski was genuinely frightened by the devastating effect the use of his troops against the civilian population had on his army's morale. Considering Poland's place in the key Warsaw Pact Northern Tier (consisting of Poland, Czechoslovakia, and East Germany), reported instances of insubordination and the demoralizing effect that the shedding of civilian blood had on army morale were viewed with utmost concern by both the Poles and the WTO Command. Hence Jaruzelski's primary goal as Poland's defense minister in the aftermath of the events of 1970 was to shield the army from the consequences of its involvement in the suppression of the riots. It was in Jaruzelski's interest as the commander of the army to reach a resolution of the crisis as quickly as possible; otherwise he risked compromising the operational readiness of his forces. Even if Jaruzelski felt no particular personal loyalty to Gierek, the imperative need to end the strikes almost automatically made him a supporter of the Silesian boss and his compromise plan. Gierek appreciated the army's support; on December 20, 1970, Jaruzelski was elevated to candidate member of Gierek's Politburo.

Jaruzelski's support for Gierek in 1970 appeared genuine because the new boss's methods of managing the crisis through political means guaranteed that the army would be allowed to return to its barracks.[58] The alternative, that is, continuing support for Gomułka, who wanted to subdue the strikes by overwhelming force, meant that his soldiers would become embroiled in the crisis, with all that such involvement portended for their morale and discipline. By mid-December, Jaruzelski wanted more than anything to pull his troops out of the fighting. Finally, there was the Soviet factor to consider. Jaruzelski's decision to withdraw support from Gomułka was undoubtedly cleared with the Soviet military and sanctioned by Brezhnev.[59] For the Russians, the continuing use of Polish soldiers against civilians was fraught with the imminent danger that another key Northern Tier, non-Soviet Warsaw Pact army would thereby be rendered operationally useless. Coming only two years after the disintegration of the Czechoslovak army in the aftermath of the 1968 invasion, such a state of the Polish army would have seriously weakened the Warsaw Pact position in Central Europe.[60] In the end, Brezhnev's personal dislike of Gomułka must have also played a role in the latter's removal.[61]

Jaruzelski's major political success after 1970 was his deflecting of the blame for the killing of civilians away from the army. Surprisingly, this did not require much effort on his part. All the facts notwithstanding, the majority of the Poles simply believed that their army could not have fired on them because they could not accept the idea that the Polish soldier would ever allow himself to be turned into a tool of internal communist repression. Stories widely circulating in Warsaw in 1971 alleged that the men dressed in army fatigues who had been seen shooting at the strikers were police in stolen (sic!) army uniforms masquerading as soldiers. Jaruzelski's reputation was further strengthened by a rumor spread in Warsaw, according to which the general allegedly had defied Gomułka and Kliszko and refused to let his troops be used in their bloody affair. If, at a later stage of the crisis, Jaruzelski did indeed voice strong concern over the political ramifications of the fighting in Gdańsk, there is no evidence that he denied the regime the use of his soldiers. Still, the Poles widely interpreted the general's withdrawal of support from the despised Gomułka regime as a sign of his patriotic dedication to the nation. By 1971, Jaruzelski was being depicted as a patriotic Polish soldier. After 1970, Polish society's traditional belief in the army as the defender of the country's independence, and hence a deterrent to Soviet invasion, was reinforced. Because of the quick political resolution of the subsequent crisis in 1976, this image of the People's Army survived until 1981 and was central to the outcome of Jaruzelski's confrontation with Solidarity.

A Political Solution: The Unrest of 1976

Poland's investment boom of the early 1970s, fueled by Western credit, peaked around 1975. The country's indebtedness to the West and the growing inflationary pressures, coupled with low productivity and industrial inefficiency, led to economic stagnation. At the same time, the boom of the first half of the decade raised social expectations of steady improvements in living standards and of greater supplies of food and consumer goods. As the recession in the West reduced further the market for Poland's industrial output, food and raw materials again became the country's principal exports; beginning in 1975, the Gierek government had to borrow from Western banks just to service its debt and make grain purchases abroad.[62]

As in 1970, the immediate cause of the wave of labor unrest in 1976 was an announcement of price rises, issued on June 25. Anticipating trouble, Gierek let his prime minister, Piotr Jaroszewicz, present the planned price increases to the Sejm. The workers' reaction was instantaneous. Violence erupted in the city of Radom; the Ursus tractor factory outside Warsaw and the Płock Petrochemical Plant went on strike.[63] Before the wave of labor unrest gathered momentum, the regime panicked and rescinded the price increases. Within 24 hours of the announcement of price hikes, the visibly shaken prime minister went back on television to inform the nation that no changes would be made until after a "broad consultation with the working class." The regime then moved to limit the damage to its prestige. Beginning on June 28, mass meetings and demonstrations of support for Gierek's policies were orchestrated in major Polish cities, including Warsaw and Katowice.[64] On July 2, Gierek resurfaced in Upper Silesia, his traditional power base, amidst a carefully orchestrated show of support from the coal miners, but the chorus of praise for Poland's party boss rang hollow. Once the crisis had been defused, the secret police moved swiftly to punish participants in the strike. Those involved in the Radom and Ursus protests were arrested, interrogated, beaten, and fired from their jobs.[65]

In 1976 the army stayed in its barracks. According to a story circulated in Poland after the confrontation, when asked for the military's help, stiff-lipped Jaruzelski allegedly informed Gierek that "Polish soldiers would never fire at Polish workers."[66] Whether the story is true or not, it is clear that the 1976 crisis did not escalate to the point where a direct intervention of the armed forces was needed to restore order. Charges by small detachments of police, as in Płock, sufficed to disperse the crowds. If Jaruzelski made the declaration quoted above, it did not necessarily express (as the Poles again chose to interpret it at the time) the general's fiery patriotism. In the Poland of 1976, simple political calculation dictated that Jaruzelski should refrain from any involvement in the crisis. By the mid-1970s, Gierek's power base had been seriously eroded by the country's rapidly accelerating economic decline. Jaruzelski, who had already been promoted to full membership in the Politburo in 1971, doubtlessly observed the growing disarray among Gierek's lieutenants.

More important, the general's personal loyalty to Gierek was, from the beginning, questionable at best.[67] According to one source, by the mid-1970s only Edward Babiuch and Jerzy Łukaszewicz, both Politburo members, remained loyal to Gierek, while the members of that body, including Jan Szydlak, Stanisław Kania, Kazimierz Barcikowski, Andrzej Werblan, Józef Kempa, and even Zdzisław Grudzień, one of Gierek's closest associates from Silesia, opposed him. Gierek's contradictory policies of concessions to the workers' economic demands, on the one hand, and on the other hand the so-called economic maneuver of the late 1970s, which was to limit Poland's borrowing from the West by terminating unfinished capital investment projects, were justifiably regarded by most as a recipe for disaster. Reportedly, several members of the Polish Politburo, including Józef Pińkowski, Poland's future premier, and Stefan Olszowski, a leading hard-liner in the Central Committee, did not hide their hostility to and contempt for Gierek.[68] In this situation, it would have been political folly for Jaruzelski to throw his authority behind a weak and ineffective regime.

Brezhnev's opinion of Gierek mattered most in Jaruzelski's political calculations. For his run-away borrowing that made Poland ever more dependent on the West, Gierek was increasingly in trouble with Moscow. The renewed emphasis on ideological orthodoxy after the 1976 crisis, which culminated in the introduction into Poland's constitution of a clause expressly binding the country to the Soviet Union, was intended by Gierek to reassure Brezhnev of his regime's loyalty.[69] But as the inflationary spiral caused by the government's fiscal policy started to eat away at the population's living standards, and Poland sank deeper and deeper into debt, Jaruzelski could see that Gierek's days as Poland's party boss were numbered, regardless of the concessions the first secretary was willing to offer the Soviets. If Poland's postwar history taught one anything, it was that another crisis would inevitably sweep Gierek and his cronies from power.

Most important for the army's noninvolvement in the 1976 crisis was the government's decision at the outset to deal with the crisis through political means alone. Gierek's decision to limit the use of force to the absolute minimum was strongly influenced by the international situation. Concern over Poland's reputation in Western Europe and her relations with the countries of the CMEA made it imperative to search for a political resolution of the crisis. The eruptions in Radom and Ursus came less than two weeks after Gierek's widely acclaimed visit to West Germany, which the government heralded as a symbol of "new thinking" in Europe. The trip fulfilled Gierek's aspirations to become the Soviet bloc's senior statesman. As East-West détente was beginning to falter, Gierek hoped that rapprochement with the Federal Republic of Germany would help Warsaw position itself as a power broker in Europe.[70] On the practical side, the topics of his talks with Helmut Schmidt included the question of additional West German loans to Poland. A bloody crackdown in Poland would have seriously damaged Gierek's image of a technocrat, which he had striven to project in the West, and an outcry in the West over brutal repression in Poland might have induced the country's creditors to refuse Gierek the badly needed new loans.

In terms of Gierek's standing with the Soviets, his position was further complicated by the upcoming Berlin conference of communist and workers' parties, hosted by the East Germans between June 28 and 30, 1976. In Moscow's calculations, Poland's internal affairs would inevitably figure importantly in the "correlation of forces" between the East and West. Brezhnev would not have forgiven his Polish satrap if his clumsiness had weakened the Soviet position in Europe and undermined his already fragile détente with the West. A political settlement of the dispute, followed by a quiet crackdown against the opposition after the crisis had been defused, was for Gierek the least dangerous course of action. Undoubtedly, the Soviets made Brezhnev's wishes known to the PUWP leadership, and the Polish boss hastened to oblige; Gierek's Berlin meeting with Brezhnev on June 29 was once again "cordial" and conducted in an "atmosphere of complete and mutual understanding."[71]

At no point, then, during the 1976 strikes in Ursus and Radom did there arise even a remote possibility that soldiers would have to be deployed against the workers. Throughout the crisis the army conducted its business as usual; this business included such routine matters as the commissioning of officers at various military academies and Jaruzelski's meeting with a new commander in chief of the Polish U.N. Peace Keeping Contingent.[72] However, there was an unmistakable signal that something was badly amiss inside the Politburo. In contrast to the crises of 1968 and 1970, the chorus of support for Gierek's policies did not even once include a declaration of Jaruzelski's personal loyalty to the beleaguered first secretary. We will probably never know for certain if Gierek refrained from using force to smash Solidarity in 1980 because he had learned in 1976 that the army was no longer behind him.

Jaruzelski's Men

The 1970s witnessed a steady increase in the levels of party membership among Polish officers, reflecting the overall trend in all non-Soviet Warsaw Pact forces. By 1975, party membership among the Polish army officers reached 85 percent of the corps, with 100 percent party membership of the senior officers (colonels and above).[73] However, direct participation of the military in governmental and party bodies remained low. The participation of the military as full members of the PUWP Central Committee, which in 1954 was 9.1 percent (seven members), declined drastically following Spychalski's appointment as defense minister and reached its all-time low of 2.2 percent in 1968. Jaruzelski's appointment was followed by only a small rise in the numbers of the officers with full-membership seats on the Central Committee: in 1971 this percentage rose to 2.6 percent; in 1975, to 2.7 percent.[74] The subsequent fluctuation in the percentages of military membership in the PUWP Central Committee was statistically insignificant, until its dramatic rise after the introduction of martial law in 1981.

However, the relatively low and steady level of the military's membership in the Central Committee in the 1970s does not reflect the army's rising influence in the country's domestic politics. A better gauge of Jaruzelski's role in Poland's internal affairs in the 1970s is the growing importance of the military's behavior in Poland's successive political crises. Whereas in 1970 the party leadership had been able to order the deployment of troops against the striking shipyard workers in Gdańsk, six years later Jaruzelski was already politically strong enough to forestall any such request by declaring that the army would not participate in the suppression of the 1976 unrest in Radom and Ursus. Further, the moderate level of the military's formal political participation at the level of the Central Committee in the 1970s does not account for the growth of Soviet confidence in Jaruzelski, which was due, rather, to his reassuring performance during the invasion of Czechoslovakia and the flexibility he displayed during the 1970 crisis. Above all else, Jaruzelski's power base was the new Polish officer corps, which had finally come of age in the 1970s.

The boom of the 1970s and the modernization of the People's Army had a strong influence on the Polish officers' esprit de corps. Jaruzelski was appointed

Poland's defense minister at the time when the army was in the process of maturation, and when its officers were acquiring a new sense of professional pride resulting from better education and training, as well as from the acquisition of modern Soviet weapons. Specialized military academies offered young Poles an opportunity to earn engineering and medical degrees in addition to their commission, and a chance subsequently to partake of a number of economic privileges, including good pay, better-stocked army shops, and free housing. The number of officers with diplomas of higher education almost tripled during the 1970s, rising from 35 percent in 1971 to 90 percent in 1982.[75] By the end of the decade, out of some 340,000 soldiers and officers in Jaruzelski's army, about 150,000 were military professionals.[76] Finally, the introduction of new military technology, including MiG-23 aircraft, T-62 and T-72 medium tanks, and SA-6 surface-to-air missiles,[77] went a long way in transforming the People's Army into a modern fighting force, in keeping with the requirements of the Warsaw Pact's 1969 reform.

The army watched as the Gierek regime faltered in the late 1970s, and the PUWP found itself increasingly in disarray. Since by the end of the decade Gierek could not even discipline his Politburo cronies (exiling his opponent Stefan Olszowski to the Polish embassy in East Berlin was Gierek's only important bureaucratic victory after 1976), Jaruzelski's control over the armed forces was accepted as a matter of course. Even if some apparatchiks took notice of the general's growing influence, it is quite likely that the confusion inside the apparat's leadership ensured that no effective countermeasures would be taken. State-sponsored organizations did not fare much better than the party. Mieczysław Moczar's AL/GL "partisans" from ZBoWiD, who had almost succeeded in overthrowing Gomułka in 1968, lost most of their influence in the 1970s. In 1972 Jaruzelski was appointed deputy chairman of ZBoWiD after Moczar had been ejected from the Politburo.

As a full member of the Politburo, Jaruzelski took part in all major government decisions, influenced policy, and witnessed the increasingly bitter power struggle between Gierek and Stefan Olszowski, a strong critic of Gierek.[78] While the general was privy to all Politburo deliberations, the apparatchiks were effectively prevented from interfering with the army's internal politics. Although all military appointments were nominally the domain of Stanisław Kania, at the time the Central Committee's secretary for security and military affairs, in reality decisions affecting the army were made by Jaruzelski and, after direct consultations with his Soviet superiors, presented to Kania for rubber-stamp approval.[79] Rather than listening to Kania, Jaruzelski took his counsel from his brother officers. By 1976, Generals Florian Siwicki and Czesław Kiszczak had become Jaruzelski's two most trusted aides. Siwicki and Kiszczak would later play key roles in the crackdown against

Solidarity. Brought into the Politburo in 1981, the two have remained Jaruzelski's key political allies.[80]

The bond between Jaruzelski and his adjutants goes back to World War II. Siwicki and Kiszczak had at least some combat experience with the First Army. Like Jaruzelski, Siwicki graduated from the Infantry Officers School in Ryazan and attended the Soviet Voroshilov General Staff Academy. After the war he fought the anticommunist resistance and held several command posts. In 1963, Siwicki was appointed chief of staff of the Silesian Military District, and five years later, contemporaneously with Jaruzelski's elevation to Poland's defense minister, he was promoted to its commanding officer. Shortly thereafter, Siwicki led the Polish invasion force into Czechoslovakia. In 1971 Jaruzelski promoted him to first deputy chief of the general staff; two years later, Siwicki rose to chief of the general staff and deputy defense minister.

Kiszczak's combat experience was only partly in the First Army, which he joined in 1945. Official Polish sources mention that during the war he fought in the underground movement against the Germans, but no affiliation with a particular group is given.[81] Kiszczak's postwar career was chiefly in military intelligence. From 1972 to 1979, he was chief of Military Intelligence and deputy chief of the general staff.

Other important generals in Jaruzelski's entourage who rose with him in the 1970s include Gen. T. Tuczapski, in charge of territorial defense; Gen. J. Baryła, chief of the Main Political Administration; Gen. W. Oliwa, commander of the Warsaw Military District; and Adm. L. Janczyszyn, commander in chief of the navy. Although they were not as close to Jaruzelski as Siwicki and Kiszczak, they proved loyal and were useful to him during the 1980 crisis. Jaruzelski had ample time to ensure that those among his officers who were not bound to him by friendship and years of service together, would nevertheless feel obligated to him for advancing their careers. Among the members of Jaruzelski's Military Council of National Salvation (Wojskowa Rada Ocalenia Narodowego; WRON), appointed on December 13, 1981, as the martial law government of Poland, 50 percent of the officers with the rank of general owed their promotion to this station to Jaruzelski.[82] Except for Molczyk, those promoted before Jaruzelski's tenure as defense minister, such as Adm. L. Janczyszyn, Gen. F. Siwicki, and Gen. W. Oliwa, had either a background of political work, and thus had collaborated with Jaruzelski during his MPA years, or a background of security work, and thus must have worked closely with Kiszczak. In addition to Jaruzelski, five other members of the Military Council (Siwicki, Tuczapski, Molczyk, Janczyszyn, and Oliwa) were veterans of the First Army; they probably knew Jaruzelski from the World War II period or from the postwar campaign against the anticommunist resistance.[83] Jaruzelski could also count on Siwicki's four deputies: Gen. T. Hupałowski, Gen. J. Skalski,

Gen. A. Jasiński, and Gen. M. Dachowski.[84] In the 1980s, these men would assume key positions in the Ministry of Defense.

The only potentially serious challenger to Jaruzelski's authority in the 1970s was Gen. Eugeniusz Molczyk, chief inspector of training and the Polish liaison officer to the Warsaw Pact Joint High Command. Owing to his access to Kulikov, Molczyk was able to bypass Jaruzelski and reportedly functioned as a Soviet watchdog and a channel for additional Soviet pressure inside Poland's Defense Ministry.[85] Molczyk's most loyal supporter was Gen. Włodzimierz Sawczuk, a onetime MPA chief whom Jaruzelski replaced in 1980 with his confidante, General Baryła. Molczyk, who was deputy defense minister and chief inspector of training, was considered a Stalinist and a strong challenger to Jaruzelski's supremacy in the officer corps.[86] He was eventually dismissed from all his posts and forcibly retired in 1986.

Jaruzelski's Ties to the Main Political Administration

However strong Jaruzelski's control over his staff and line officers was, he could never have translated it into national political influence without the assistance of the People's Army's Main Political Administration. The MPA's duties cut across a broad spectrum of political activities, both in the army and in civilian life. In the words of General Siwicki, they include "responsibility for party political work in the armed forces, for strengthening troop morale and discipline, as well as for cooperation with organs of state administration and social organizations in the realm of propaganda, cultural activities, and the upbringing of Poland's youth."[87] With respect to its internal responsibilities, the Polish MPA's duties do not differ from those of Soviet political officers (*zampolits*);[88] however, the MPA's role as a channel to civilian organizations and its regular contact with regional and local party organizations make it an important tool for gathering information on changes within the civilian apparat and for influencing party politics.

The head of the People's Army's Main Political Administration becomes automatically a deputy defense minister. It appears that in the Polish army, the movement between regular commands, party and governmental appointments, and the MPA is more common than in the Soviet army; this pattern was initiated by Jaruzelski in the 1960s and has endured to this day. Jaruzelski, having served as a line officer, as MPA chief, and on various governmental and party bodies is the most obvious, although not unique, example of this pattern. Gen. Józef Urbanowicz, one of Jaruzelski's close associates who headed the MPA from 1965 to 1971, retained his portfolio as deputy defense minister after

1971. At the height of the 1981 crisis, Urbanowicz was brought into the PUWP Central Committee as a full member.[89] In 1986, MPA chief Gen. J. Baryła was elected to the Politburo, and his army post was taken over by Gen. Tadeusz Szaciło. Another example is Gen. Jan Czapla, who was chief of the MPA from 1971 to 1972; Czapla was subsequently appointed deputy minister of education in place of Gen. Zygmunt Huszcza, who became chairman of the League of National Defense (Liga Obrony Kraju), a paramilitary organization for civil defense training in Poland.[90]

The replacement of Gen. Włodzimierz Sawczuk, Molczyk's crony, with Gen. Józef Baryła, one of Jaruzelski's own men, ensured that in the 1980s the MPA would be in "friendly hands." Having been himself an MPA chief from 1960 to 1965, Jaruzelski fully appreciated the importance of being able to control the army's principal political agency. If run by a loyal officer, the MPA would give him access to regional and local party organizations, while shielding the army from unwanted intrusion into its affairs by civilian apparatchiks.

The MPA connection may even play a role in party appointments at the highest levels. For example, there is circumstantial evidence that the MPA was instrumental in the appointment in 1972 of Stanisław Kania as the Central Committee secretary in charge of Poland's armed forces. Kania, who was himself a graduate of the MPA's Central School for Political Officers in Łódź, was considered in the PUWP a friend of the military.[91]

During Jaruzelski's tenure as defense minister, the army's political organ was assured a steady stream of young political officers, graduates of the political curriculum of higher officer schools, of the MPA's Central School for Political Officers (Centralna Szkoła Oficerów Politycznych) in Łódź, and of the Military Political Academy (Wojskowa Akademia Polityczna) in Warsaw.[92] In the 1970s, the influence of political officers went far enough beyond the realm of strictly military matters to prompt the issuing by the Central Committee's secretariat of "Guidelines on closer ties between, on the one hand, party authorities and army commanders, and on the other hand, army political organization."[93] The guidelines contained regulations for political military propaganda directed at prospective draftees and prescriptions for the army's cooperation with the Federation of the Unions of Polish Socialist Youth (Federacja Związków Socjalistycznej Młodzieży Polskiej)—an umbrella organization for the communist youth movement in Poland—and for its cooperation with factory and local party organizations, including exchange of information on political and economic matters. The guidelines encouraged reciprocity between the party apparat and the armed forces, and thus were an indirect admission that the civil-military partnership forged in 1956 had, with the passage of time, become lopsided in favor of the army.

By the end of the decade, the People's Army had become Jaruzelski's unquestioned political power base. The senior military positions, including that of the MPA chief, were for the most part staffed with his appointees. When the party found itself bogged down in intractable economic problems and displayed weakness and indecision in the crisis of 1976, the officer corps's cohesion was in sharp contrast with the chaos and corruption of Gierek's inner circle. Jaruzelski's stiff military demeanor, his aloofness, stress on military discipline and "clean living" (upon his appointment as defense minister, it was reported that he gave up the ministerial villa for a modest apartment) earned him high marks among his brother officers. To the majority of the Poles he remained an unknown quantity, a low-key general who was considered a professional soldier rather than a politician. Faced with the challenge of the 1980–1981 crisis, Jaruzelski could count on his high standing with the Soviets, the loyalty of his officers, and the authority he enjoyed among his countrymen as a soldier standing in Poland's military tradition.

In Defense of the Party:

Jaruzelski's Tactics
Through the Bydgoszcz Crisis

—5—

Fragmentation of the Party

The severity of the 1980 crisis in Poland came as a surprise to Western observers, and quite likely to the majority of the Poles themselves. Although Poland's political situation was frequently described as volatile, nobody could have expected that the wave of labor unrest on the Baltic coast would this time lead to the party's official recognition of an independent trade union. Still, Gierek and his entourage tried to deal with the problem in the time-tested fashion of the 1970s: temporary concessions to the strikers, to be followed by swift repression.

In the confusion that followed the signing of the Gdańsk-Jastrzębie "Social Accords," which marked the beginning of Solidarity, and the several reshufflings of the top party elite, the military consistently maintained that the continued existence of the trade union would be acceptable only if the limits of Solidarity's authority under the control of the PUWP were clearly delineated. Jaruzelski and his MPA publicists spoke out for a political solution to the crisis, but one that would ensure party supremacy over the independent trade-union movement.

The creation of Solidarity challenged the Polish United Workers' Party on two levels. On the one hand, the union emerged as an alternative to the party's monopoly of power; on the other, because Solidarity temporarily forced the PUWP to retreat, its creation accelerated the decomposition of the party caused by the widespread corruption and political bankruptcy of the Gierek regime. By attempting to force the PUWP to alter the traditional ground of its claim to legitimacy (the party's assertion that it was the vanguard of the revolutionary proletariat), and by trying to make the communists accept social consensus based on a social contract as the precondition of any agreement, the union became a powerful force behind the internal fragmentation of the party hierarchy. From the Politburo's point of view, the problem of Solidarity's existence became both the problem of the party's control over society and the question of the leadership's ability to maintain cohesion of the party rank and file.[1]

Following the signing of the Gdańsk Accords between the government and Solidarity on August 31, 1980, the PUWP entered its most severe crisis to that time. The regime was being challenged not only by the striking workers, but also by growing discontent within the ruling PUWP elite caused by Gierek's inept policies. Opposition to Gierek within the PUWP brought together a loose coalition of party dignitaries, including Stefan Olszowski, whom Gierek had exiled in March 1980 to the post of Poland's ambassador to the German Democratic Republic; Kazimierz Barcikowski, former editor in chief of *Życie Partii*; Tadeusz Grabski, a hard-line Central Committee secretary; ZBoWiD's chairman Mieczysław Moczar, the notorious leader of the ex-GL/AL "partisans" and the chairman of the Supreme Control Commission, who in 1970 became Gierek's avowed enemy after the latter had rejected his nomination for the chairman of the Council of State;[2] and Wojciech Jaruzelski, Poland's defense minister. As Gierek later complained to Jaruzelski in a letter of November 1982, even though he had agreed, in the Politburo session of August 18, to capitulate to his opponents' demands for the purge of his most trusted associates and for Olszowski's return, these far-reaching concessions failed to mend the rift within the Politburo.[3] After the removal of his supporters, Gierek became, by the end of August, Poland's leader in name only. The Fourth Central Committee Plenum of August 24 fired E. Babiuch, J. Łukaszewicz, J. Szydlak, T. Wrzaszczyk, T. Pyka, and Z. Żandarowski—in effect, Gierek lost his entire power base within the Politburo. Stefan Olszowski, Gierek's principal rival in the 1970s, returned triumphantly from his East German exile to reclaim his Politburo seat. Premier Józef Pińkowski was made full Politburo member, while three new deputy members, J. Waszczuk, E. Wojtaszek, and A. Żabinski, were co-opted to replace Gierek's cronies.[4] Together with the first secretary, former prime minister Jaroszewicz, and Katowice Regional Party Secretary Z. Grudzień, those purged (the so-called list of nine) were blamed by the Central Committee for the economic and political crisis.

Only five days after the cabinet changes, on September 5, Gierek was ousted and replaced by Stanisław Kania, a nondescript party apparatchik whose most impressive credentials were his relative obscurity and his lack of visible affiliation with the inner circle of Gierek's associates. Kania and Jaruzelski had known each other and worked together for at least a decade. It is unclear if Jaruzelski's influence was instrumental in Kania's appointment in 1972 as Central Committee secretary in charge in Poland's armed forces; according to one observer, that is precisely what happened.[5] Other apparatchiks added to Kania's Politburo included Kazimierz Barcikowski and Andrzej Żabinski, while Tadeusz Grabski was named Central Committee secretary and Poland's deputy premier;[6] Barcikowski also became a member of the Council of State.

Although in August 1980 the attention of the world was focused on the unprecedented rise of an independent trade-union movement in Poland, an even more important political drama was taking place inside the PUWP Politburo. Those early days of turmoil within the PUWP Politburo determined the course of future events and weighed heavily on the government's handling of the crisis. Never before since the Polish October of 1956 had the party leadership been so badly shaken. What was worse, Gierek's ouster did not lead to an orderly transition of authority to another coalition of apparatchiks, as had been the case after Gomułka's resignation in 1970. Stefan Olszowski would have been a natural candidate for the post of first secretary, but he had been forced to accept a diplomatic post in East Germany in the last year of Gierek's term in office, and his prolonged absence from Warsaw had prevented him from building a coalition of supporters within the Central Committee. On the other hand, the scope of the August purge of the Politburo left the other apparatchiks in a position not much better than that of Olszowski after his return from Berlin. The Politburo was fragmented and had not yet produced a leader supported by the majority. In effect, Kania's selection was an expedient; he was a transitional candidate chosen for his record of being a solid bureaucrat who had made few friends, but even fewer enemies.

We may never know to what degree political paralysis within the top party leadership influenced the regime's decision to reconcile itself initially to Solidarity's existence. Subsequent wrangling between the party and the trade union reflected continuing confusion within the Politburo caused mainly by the lack of strong leadership. In addition to fighting Solidarity, the apparatchiks fought one another, jockeying for position and trying to build up their influence in the Politburo. Among others, Mieczysław Moczar, the old "partisan" of 1968, once again moved to the forefront by using his position as chairman of the PUWP's Supreme Control Commission to charge Gierek with corruption in a letter addressed to the Central Committee.[7] The old policeman was positioning himself for his last political comeback.[8]

The August-September purge of the "list of nine" was completed in December of 1980, when the Seventh Plenum of the Central Committee stripped Gierek and Jaroszewicz of their parliamentary immunity, expelled both from the Central Committee, and initiated proceedings to remove them from the party. Nonetheless, Kania failed to build majority support for his leadership. The remaining Gierek appointees to the Politburo, W. Kruczek, A. Karkoszka, S. Kowalczyk, and A. Werblan were replaced by Olszowski's hard-line adjutant Tadeusz Grabski, ZBoWiD's "nationalist" Mieczysław Moczar, and Tadeusz Fiszbach, a liberal chairman of the Gdańsk regional party committee identified with Kania's policies of compromise and negotiation.[9] The three effectively canceled each other out.

The membership of the new Politburo testified to Kania's inability to consolidate his position within the party by appointing people loyal to him personally. As a result, during his tenure as first secretary, the PUWP never spoke with one voice, and the often conflicting positions of various party leaders only raised the level of tension, increased Solidarity's mistrust of the government, and further undermined Kania's authority. Like all revolutionary turmoil, the Polish crisis of 1980–1981 came about in part as a result of the government's fragmentation and weakness; since Solidarity could not replace the PUWP as the ruling party, the deadlock continued to deepen until the regime overcame its internal cleavages and regained the initiative.

At the core of the growing crisis within the PUWP lay Kania's inability to control the country by administrative means. As tension mounted, the workers' movement spread from the Gdańsk area to the rest of Poland; Solidarity membership eventually reached the ten-million mark. The beleaguered Politburo came under an increasing barrage of criticism not only from the opposition, but also from middle-level and local party apparatchiks who demanded a reassessment of past policies. Leadership change as a part of political crisis management, a measure which had been tried in the past, was the party's instinctive reaction to the challenge; this time, however, the new leader failed to consolidate his hold on the Politburo, and turmoil within the government continued unabated.

As the crisis worsened, it became clear that the stewardship of Stanisław Kania was a holding action, rather than a solution to the problem presented to the PUWP by the paralysis within the Politburo and by Solidarity's very existence. Kania's year-long rule, until October 18, 1981 had neither the authority of its own nor the mandate necessary to build a strong power base inside the Central Committee, to reinvigorate the badly shaken apparat, and to confront the union.[10] His attempts to re-establish the party's internal cohesion and to maintain the apparat's control over the rank and file were at best only partially successful. Although the Politburo eventually managed to contain the rank-and-file pressure for democratization of the party, dissent and morale problems within the PUWP persisted until Jaruzelski's 1981 purge following the imposition of martial law.

In Search of a Leader

The government's initial hopes that Solidarity could be brought under its control were quickly dashed. A strong warning signal that the union would not allow itself to be outmaneuvered by bureaucratic tricks came during the September-October registration crisis, when the regime attempted to alter Solidarity's statutes to reflect the "leading role of the party." In the ensuing confrontation, Kania gave in; the union became a de facto opposition political party. The registration of Solidarity was a watershed in the crisis; it nullified the Politburo's strategy agreed upon in August by the "joint party-government staff." As Kania struggled in public to negotiate and renegotiate yet another agreement with Solidarity, Soviet pressure on the PUWP to put an end to the crisis increased dramatically.[11] The Polish Politburo began frantically searching for another solution.

Kania's inability to deal swiftly with the opposition, the growing disarray of the party's rank and file, Soviet pressure for action, and the consolidation of Solidarity's position in the country deepened the cleavages within the Politburo. The two leading hard-liners, Stefan Olszowski and Tadeusz Grabski, pushed for tough action and a showdown with the union. Their views were in keeping with Moscow's insistence on immediate action, and their call for an early confrontation enjoyed some support from the military, in particular from Gen. Eugeniusz Molczyk, deputy minister of defense and chief inspector of training. Molczyk, who was considered by the majority of Polish officers a dedicated Stalinist, wielded sufficient influence in Moscow to make his pressure felt.[12] Increasingly concerned with the ineffectiveness of Kania's approach, by late November the Soviets had begun drafting contingency plans for an invasion of Poland. Urged by Molczyk to throw the army openly behind the government, Jaruzelski hesitated and played for time. On the one hand, he endorsed Kania's calls for a political resolution to the crisis; on the other hand, the Main Political Administration, led by his aide Gen. Józef Baryła, lashed out against Solidarity, accusing the union of preparing counterrevolution.[13] Keeping all his options open at this stage, Jaruzelski negotiated vigorously with Moscow through its two Warsaw Pact intermediaries, commander in chief Marshal Viktor Kulikov and his assistant, the Soviet chief liaison officer in Poland, Gen. Afanasiy Shcheglov.

The idea of building the core of a new PUWP leadership around Jaruzelski was probably first raised two weeks after the signing of the Gdańsk/Jastrzębie "Social Accords," during the meeting on September 12 between Jaruzelski and Kulikov in Magdeburg, East Germany.[14] The conclusion of the Warsaw Pact maneuvers in East Germany, which brought together all Eastern bloc defense ministers, was a perfect opportunity to consult with the Soviets without interference from the apparatchiks. When, two months later, Kania failed to hold firm against the opposition, this time allowing the registration of the Independent Student Union and the organizational drive for Rural Solidarity, the Soviets must have been strengthened in their view that the PUWP Politburo was incapable of bringing forth a strong leader by itself. Kulikov's intervention was judged necessary.

The Polish army retained its cohesion and discipline, and remained the only government-controlled organization to enjoy a high degree of trust from Polish society;[15] hence the sudden interest in Jaruzelski as a potential party leader. The Soviets began seriously to consider Jaruzelski as a possible leader of Poland in late November 1980.[16] Those discussions were conducted through Warsaw Pact military channels, in order to guarantee their complete secrecy.[17] In a series of meetings, Jaruzelski, Kulikov, and Shcheglov assessed the feasibility of using the Polish army and security forces to suppress Solidarity and agreed on the plans' principal objectives. Still, at this stage a direct Warsaw Pact action against Poland appeared to be the only option immediately available to Moscow.

In light of the fact that direct military action against Poland was the most costly and least desirable solution to the crisis, Soviet preparations for an invasion of Poland in late November and early December of 1980[18] was a sign that Brezhnev had all but given up on Kania, but had not yet accepted the idea of building a new Politburo around Jaruzelski. We will probably never know whether the suggestion to try an occupation of Poland by the Polish army and security forces was first put forth by the Poles themselves, the Soviet military, or the CPSU Politburo. However, at the time the Soviets would undoubtedly welcome any plan that would spare them the political cost of an invasion, while restoring "normality" in Poland. Despite the Soviet determination to bring Poland back under control—through direct invasion, if necessary— Brezhnev and his generals fully appreciated the incalculable risks and potential political costs of a Soviet military action against Poland. The PUWP Politburo had even more at stake in preventing a Warsaw Pact invasion. From the Polish party's point of view, a Soviet occupation would effectively void the 1956 Polish-Soviet compromise, which granted the PUWP the prerogative to micromanage its domestic affairs without open Soviet intervention. If the Soviets decided that they had no choice but to invade, the current Polish communist elite would become, at best, politically irrelevant. Nationalism also played a role, however. One should never underestimate the fact that communist regimes in Eastern Europe, no matter how subservient to Moscow, have a sense of national identity. In the Polish context, in particular, throughout the postwar years communists were forced to reconcile the requirements of "internationalism" with the fierce patriotism of the Poles. Regarded from this perspective, a Polish communist general who opted for internal repression as an alternative to a Soviet invasion (however convoluted and qualified his rationale might be) was choosing a "lesser evil" and, in his own eyes, acting the way a true patriot should act.[19] The Poles could prevent the invasion only by convincing Brezhnev that the PUWP could produce a credible, strong leader. In late 1980 this goal still appeared unattainable.

The Martial Law Option:
The Early Plans

Kania's initial expectations, shared by the Soviets, that personnel changes would suffice to overcome the momentum of the strike and prevent the independent labor union from coming into being were soon dashed. The growing fragmentation of the PUWP, combined with the disastrous state of the economy, and the realization that the locus of political power had shifted from the party to Solidarity, induced the Polish regime to explore other options. As had been the case during previous crises, the party turned to the military for help.

Planning for the imposition of martial law if that step were judged necessary began early, in mid-August of 1980. Shortly after the strikes began, Jaruzelski issued a directive to the general staff to draft the requisite preliminary plans in cooperation with the Interior Ministry, headed at the time by Gen. Mirosław Milewski.[20] On August 24, as the Fourth Plenum called for negotiations with the striking workers, the so-called Joint Party-Government Guidance Staff (similar to the Gdańsk Task Force of 1970) was set up. It was headed by Prime Minister J. Pińkowski and included K. Barcikowski, S. Olszowski, Deputy Premier M. Jagielski (who was then dispatched to negotiate with Gdańsk workers), T. Grabski, Minister of the Interior Milewski, and Defense Minister Jaruzelski. Initially, the plan called for signing a non-binding general agreement with the workers to end the strikes and gain time, so that an effective long-term solution to the crisis could be found. Next the Politburo planned to rely on administrative measures, including selective police terror, to regain control of the situation; martial law was envisioned as a measure of last resort.[21]

The Polish general staff started drafting plans for imposing martial law on October 22, 1980, two days before the expected Warsaw court ruling on Solidarity's registration. On that day Jaruzelski issued a high-priority order to his senior staff officers directing them to prepare plans for the declaration of martial law. Gen. Florian Siwicki was put in charge of the planning process. The actual plans were drafted by a group of officers belonging to the Polish general staff; the group included four deputy chiefs of staff and several staff officers. The very core of this planning staff consisted of nine senior army officers. They worked closely with the Ministry of the Interior, the Central

Committee's Propaganda Department, the Main Political Administration, and the Secretariat of the National Defense Committee (Komitet Obrony Kraju; KOK), a supervisory governmental-military body in charge of overall defense planning. The KOK secretariat drafted the requisite martial-law legislation.[22]

By November 1980 the preliminary plan was ready; it was reviewed by a special session of the KOK, chaired by Premier Pińkowski. The general outline presented by the Ministry of Defense recommended: (1) that declaration of martial law be preceded by a partial mobilization of the army, to include the calling up of 250 thousand reserves; (2) a modification of military-draft legislation to induct into the army all eligible students and recent university graduates;[23] (3) militarization of all plants and industrial enterprises; and (4) a preventive draft of about one million men into Civil Defense units. Fearing that direct participation of the army in the crushing of the revolt, as in 1970, would undermine the soldiers' morale, Jaruzelski tried to limit his troops' role to policing the cities and the countryside. The KOK recommended that actual attacks on industrial plants and crowd dispersal should be carried out by special ZOMO[24] riot police troops of the Ministry of the Interior; the army would provide support and supply the ZOMO with additional weapons and ammunition.[25]

The November session of the KOK approved the plans and authorized further work on the project; however, it also determined that the existing conditions precluded immediate implementation of the plans. The search for a political solution, strongly supported by Kania, was still considered the preferred way out of the crisis. More important, the imposition of martial law required meticulous preparations. Since the military and the security forces needed time to gather intelligence, train their forces, and coordinate the entire operation, for the time being the army limited its attack on Solidarity to a propaganda campaign.

Ideological Campaign Against Solidarity

The military's hard-line position toward Solidarity was put forth in a series of articles, theoretical essays, and official statements printed in army publications. This propaganda campaign had two objectives. The immediate goal was to accuse the union of fomenting counterrevolution in Poland; indirectly, it distanced the military from the deadlocked Politburo leadership.

From the first day of the crisis, the military manifested its hostility toward Solidarity. Within weeks after the signing of the Gdańsk agreement, the Main Political Administration, headed by Jaruzelski's protégé, Gen. Józef Baryła, launched an attack against Solidarity in *Wojsko Ludowe* (The people's army), the MPA's official journal and the most authoritative political publication of the Polish armed forces.[26] By relying on the MPA in 1980, rather than speaking out himself, Jaruzelski retained the political flexibility required by his increasingly central position in the government; at the same time, he could take credit with both the Soviet and Polish party hard-liners for forcefully challenging the opposition.

In its attacks on Solidarity, *Wojsko Ludowe* was joined by *Żołnierz Wolności* (The soldier of freedom), the army daily, and *Żołnierz Polski* (The soldier of Poland), the army's weekly magazine. The military's position, although on the surface not very different from that of hard-line civilian party bureaucrats, was marked by an exceptional consistency throughout the crisis period. In contrast with the constant vacillations of Kania's Politburo, which engaged in an endless tug of war with Solidarity, the army's declared approach to the crisis represented a remarkably coherent strategy.

A clear definition of the military's position in the crisis came on the heels of the Gdańsk Agreements. In September, 1980, barely a month after the popular upheaval on the Baltic coast, *Wojsko Ludowe* ran an article defining the limits of acceptable concessions to Solidarity and warning the opposition not to press its luck. The lead article, entitled "Silne państwo w interesie demokracji" (A strong state is in the interest of democracy), argued that the principles of socialism, the "socialist essence," had to be preserved in Poland. The "socialist state," argued the author, "preserves its essence when it continues as the apparatus of centralized power for overcoming relatively permanent, nonantagonistic contradictions..., when it protects the nation from counter-revolution exported from abroad...."[27] The line of confrontation with the labor union, spelled out by the MPA, was reaffirmed by Jaruzelski. During his brief and, overall, conciliatory speech at the closing of the Sixth Plenary Session of the PUWP Central Committee, on September 5, 1980, the general introduced a theme that would be a part of the military's approach to the crisis until the imposition of martial law in December 1981. While voicing his support for a political settlement of the conflict, Jaruzelski stated in his speech that it was the party's duty to rise to the challenge and confront the labor union. Restating the military's view of the crisis, the general accused the Politburo of weakness, timidity, and indecisiveness. "Comrades!" said Jaruzelski,

> It seems to me that timing, speed, and, of course, firmness are all the most crucial components of our most immediate actions. The congress we are waiting for [the Ninth Congress of the PUWP] will meet our expectations provided that the present Sixth Plenary Session sets us in motion and initiates another important stage in the process of closing party ranks. The present course of events cannot be waited through.[28]

Although on the surface this call for party unity appeared to be little more than a loyal expression of concern on the part of Polish communists in uniform, it soon developed into an indirect challenge to the PUWP civilian party apparat. In the same speech, Jaruzelski pressed the apparatchiks to decide whether they were still able to lead:

> Those who do not feel strong enough for the task, those who have scruples or fears, who for some reason feel that their hands are tied, should all draw the appropriate conclusion and ask to be placed in the second echelon. In the first line there must remain only those who are decisive and have strong convictions; and such people are the [PUWP] majority.[29]

The military's apparent resolve to deal firmly with Solidarity contrasted starkly with Kania's constant hesitation. Addressing the same Sixth Plenum, Kania argued that only by appeasing the workers' demands could peace and social order be restored. Kania reminded the Politburo that:

> [the party's] approach to the strikes [in August] was patience and dialogue with the workers conducted by party comrades. As a result, we have reached agreements with the workers' representatives and we will make sure that those agreements are fulfilled. . . . A political solution to the deep crisis we find ourselves in will become in and of itself a valuable political and moral capital.[30]

There is no doubt that Jaruzelski's calls in early September for strengthening the party expressed his genuine concern. His consultations with Kulikov and Shcheglov must have made it clear to him that the Soviets increasingly saw their options in Poland as a simple alternative: either the Polish communists would take charge, or Warsaw Pact armies would do it for them. Being privy both to the internal workings of the Warsaw government and the opinions of Soviet liaison officers, Jaruzelski understood better than anyone else in the Polish government how rapidly the situation was deteriorating. By taking a hard-line position on Solidarity, Jaruzelski's MPA hoped to instill a sense of urgency into the Polish party leadership, and to reassure the Soviets of the army's loyalty. Ironically, Baryła's thunderous condemnation of Solidarity had yet another result. The army's propaganda campaign, ostensibly aimed at building up support for the party, in fact underscored the apparatchiks' inability to govern. Each time Baryła's journals and newspapers called in vain for the PUWP to unite, Kania's weakness and his Politburo's confusion became all the more apparent.

As the military staunchly maintained that no compromise with the opposition was possible, the contrast between the army's declarations and the party's actions appeared almost intentional. Col. Jerzy Muszyński, in an article entitled "Polish Dissidents of 1980," published in *Wojsko Ludowe* in December 1980, argued that the elimination of political pluralism was a necessary precondition of socialism in Poland. "In socialism," wrote Muszyński, "there is no place for political opposition, whereas the fall of socialism—despite its present difficulties—is out of the question."[31] And yet Kania not only tolerated the presence of just such "political opposition" in the form of Solidarity; he also continued to negotiate with the union. Intentionally or not, in the final analysis the MPA's 1980–1981 ideological campaign against Solidarity further discredited the Kania leadership. The ideological zeal of army spokesmen underscored the contrast between the military and the corrupt party bureaucrats. On the one hand, the civilian apparat was in retreat before the onslaught of the pent-up anger and bitterness of the majority of the Polish population; on the other, the military was offering the Soviets an alternative political position on Solidarity: one of firmness and uncompromising confrontation. Each approach was a distinct policy choice.

The Main Political Administration's criticism of the civilian party apparat became progressively harsher. Three months into the crisis, as the threat of Soviet invasion appeared imminent, Baryła accused the apparatchiks of being unable to rectify the political situation in the country. The criticism insinuated that the PUWP was not only failing to govern the country, but could not even maintain ideological cohesion among its own rank and file. Baryła fired off his charges at the Seventh Plenary Session of the PUWP Central Committee, on December 2, 1980:

> It seems to me that the opportunities presented by the Sixth [previous] Plenum have been wasted. The party has not taken the offensive in the realm of propaganda and direct party action. That is why I have concluded that the present plenary session can fulfill the hopes of the party [rank and file] and of the entire society only on the condition that the party [leadership] will manage to lead, and that its decisions and resolutions will immediately become a weapon of direct, consistent, and active struggle. We are disturbed by the fact that many [party] people and many units within our party have acted as if they had lost the sense of their historical and political rationale, as if they were shy or even ashamed and helpless. This situation cannot be tolerated much longer.[32]

Baryła went on to call for the party to be ready for an all-out confrontation with Solidarity:

> We must realize that the time has come for an all-out political battle with the opponents of the system and with irresponsible extremists for the direction of renewal in our country. The entire party must be ready for this battle; it

should face this struggle united and organizationally strong, acting on the battle-tested principles of democratic centralism. During the war [World War II] years when the situation required the most effort, the call would go out: "Communists forward!" Today this call is more pertinent than ever.[33]

This indictment of the party leadership put Kania on the defensive. During the Seventh Plenum, he admitted that the political results of government action were mixed, but argued that his primary concern had been the disastrous performance of the Polish economy. As he tried to explain, politically:

our principal efforts have concentrated on the implementation of the commitments and agreements that we accepted on the authority of the Fifth Plenum and signed with the workers' representatives. Therefore, the government has approved pay raises for the workers and higher bonus payments for large families.[34]

Justifying his taking a soft line with Solidarity, Kania indicated that his objective was to protect the party rank and file from the aftermath of the revelations about corruption inside Gierek's regime. Kania also pointed out that the majority in the party appeared to favor an agreement with Solidarity. "Since the July-August crisis," he pointedly reminded the plenum, "the majority of the rank and file has chosen the path of accommodation and renewal."[35]

The Threat of Soviet Invasion and the Polish Solution

The first week of December 1980 was a watershed in the Polish crisis. As yet unconvinced that the Polish army was capable of dealing with Solidarity by itself, and suspicious that Kania was playing a double game, the Soviets set invasion plans in motion. In a step reminiscent of the preparations for the 1968 invasion of Czechoslovakia, the Soviets sought to ensure that the Polish army would remain in its barracks before they ordered their troops into Poland. In a series of meetings, Kulikov attempted to browbeat Jaruzelski into accepting Soviet invasion timetables as a fait accompli. This led to tense and often stormy exchanges. Nonetheless, by December 1 it appeared that, even if Jaruzelski was still not giving in to Soviet demands, at least he had recognized the inevitable. On that day he dispatched to Moscow Gen. Tadeusz Hupałowski, first deputy chief of the general staff, with his adjutant Col. Franciszek Puchała, to attend a briefing on Soviet invasion plans and bring back maps showing the Soviet Army's invasion routes.

The Soviet plan called for using the SOYUZ-80 joint Warsaw Pact maneuvers as a cover for introducing into Poland three Soviet armies, totaling fifteen divisions, plus a non-Soviet Warsaw Pact task force consisting of one East German and two Czechoslovak divisions. The Russian forces would occupy eastern and central Poland; the Czechs and East Germans would control the southern and western areas of the country. The eighteen Warsaw Pact divisions in Poland would be supported by a complete naval blockade of Polish ports by the Soviet and East German Baltic fleets. In response to the Polish plea for a face-saving device, the Soviets agreed, after protracted negotiations, to include four Polish divisions in the Warsaw Pact occupation forces, but only after the Soviet, East German, and Czechoslovak units had completed their deployment. It was agreed that the fifth and eleventh Polish armored divisions would be attached to the Czech task force, and the fourth and twelfth Polish mechanized divisions to the German contingent. The target date for full invasion readiness was set as December 8, 1980.[36]

The apparent imminence of Soviet military action against Poland had an almost paralyzing effect on the Polish army and the Kania regime. The Polish general staff was convinced that in light of the internal situation in the country, this "fraternal assistance" would lead to disaster, and might even end with an armed national uprising. Soviet insistence on using German forces to occupy Poland was considered a blatant disregard of the country's history and an insult to the nation's pride. While Jaruzelski and his staff tried to reason with Kulikov, the apparatchiks became frantic. On December 4, the Central Committee issued a dramatic appeal, pleading for calm and cooperation as the "nation's fate was hanging in the balance."[37] On December 3, urged by Gen. Eugeniusz Molczyk, who had just returned from a Bucharest meeting of Warsaw Pact defense ministers, and by Gen. Florian Siwicki, Jaruzelski made one final effort to stem the tide of events. He agreed with his staff that he should plead with the Soviets to call off the invasion; in return he would offer to use his army to occupy the country and destroy Solidarity.

The Polish martial-law plan was presented by Jaruzelski to the summit meeting of the Warsaw Pact in Moscow on December 5. The Polish delegation, led by Kania and Premier Pińkowski, who were called in to account for their failures, also included Stefan Olszowski, Kazimierz Barcikowski, and Poland's foreign minister, Józef Czyrek. Gen. Mirosław Milewski, Poland's minister of the interior, represented the police and security forces. The Poles conferred with the entire Soviet *verkhushka*, including General Secretary Leonid Brezhnev, Premier Nikolai Tikhonov, "chief ideologist" Mikhail Suslov, Soviet Foreign Minister Andrey Gromyko, KGB chief Yuriy Andropov, and Defense Minister Marshal Dmitriy Ustinov.[38] Jaruzelski's arguments ultimately carried the day. Although the Soviets insisted on several changes in the plan, the draft of Jaruzelski's martial law was accepted. At five minutes to midnight, a national tragedy was averted.

According to the plan, the Polish army would be deployed to "defend socialism in Poland," once Polish society had been exhausted by the crisis.[39] The arguments presented by Jaruzelski, combined with the pressure from the West, including President Carter's personal message to Brezhnev calling on the Soviets to refrain from intervention in Poland, finally convinced Moscow that the Polish plan was worth considering. The Soviet invasion orders were suspended, and Jaruzelski was authorized to complete the preparations to implement martial law at the earliest possible date. Soviet behavior during subsequent months suggests that by "earliest possible date" they meant spring of 1981.[40]

As the events revealed, Kania's policies of compromise were by then no longer acceptable to Brezhnev. Whether the contrast between the army's and the Politburo's approach to the opposition had been intentional or not, it made a predictable impression on the audience in the Kremlin. The sharp contrast between the position of noncompromise assumed by the military and the apparatchiks' indecisiveness presented the Soviets with a clear choice almost from the start. The military's unwaveringly hostile position toward Solidarity during the remainder of 1980 allayed Soviet fears and was probably an important factor in the Soviets' decision in December 1980 to shelve their invasion plans.[41] Having been assured by Jaruzelski that the Polish army stood ready to crush Solidarity if Kania's maneuvering failed, Brezhnev was willing to wait while the plans for the imposition of martial law were being refined.

This stay of execution did not mean, however, that Soviet pressure on the Poles would ease. Until the declaration of martial law, secret Polish-Soviet negotiations took place in the midst of growing Soviet impatience and re-peated calls for action. Still, Moscow grudgingly accepted Jaruzelski's argu-ment that only the Poles themselves could fully appreciate the complexity of the internal situation, and thus they should be allowed to determine where and when to strike.[42] Only a man of Jaruzelski's standing with Brezhnev and with his record of service in Czechoslovakia in 1968 and in Poland in 1970 could persuade the Soviet leader that his advice should be heeded. Ultimately, the tug of war between Jaruzelski and Kulikov over timing had far-reaching consequences for Polish-Soviet relations. Jaruzelski's insistence on having the last word on where and when his troops would strike reaffirmed the fundamen-tal principle of Polish-Soviet relations established by the 1956 Gomułka-Khrushchev compromise: the PUWP would guarantee Soviet interests in Poland, but how the Poles would go about doing so would be left in large part to them.

The Second Draft
of the Martial-Law Plan

On December 10, 1981, Jaruzelski ordered the team set up within the Polish general staff to update the plans it had made and to develop specific task assignments for the different armed services and for the security apparatus. Minister of the Interior Mirosław Milewski detailed his deputy, Gen. Bogusław Stachura, to be the principal coordinator of the planning within the ministry and a liaison officer between his ministry and the Ministry of Defense. Stachura set up a coordinating staff inside the Ministry of the Interior, which supervised the work of all the departments, the police, and the special security forces.

Milewski's tasks included infiltrating security police agents and informers into Solidarity and other newly established independent organizations, to gather information identifying the union's activists, and to draw up lists of "enemies of the state," who would be arrested when martial law was declared. The list prepared by the Ministry of the Interior contained over four thousand names of opposition leaders; the 240 of these deemed most dangerous were placed under 24-hour police surveillance.[43]

Work on martial-law plans by the Ministry of Defense was conducted in parallel with similar preparations by the security police and other agencies. The drafting of martial-law decrees was assigned to the secretary of the National Defense Committee (Komitet Obrony Kraju; KOK), Deputy Defense Minister Gen. Tadeusz Tuczapski. Tuczapski's team prepared all martial-law legislation, including the announcement of martial law and specific regulations to be issued by the Council of Ministers. In addition, a propaganda campaign was readied in cooperation with a special representative of the PUWP's Central Committee. The Ministry of Defense categorized all key plants and industrial enterprises into groups according to their importance and thus the order in which they would be taken over by the army. This part of the planning process was coordinated by Deputy Chief of the General Staff for Organization Gen. Antoni Jasiński.[44] Under Jasiński's direction, procedures for the takeover of civil administration by army commissars were spelled out in detail. The particulars of troop deployment during martial law were outlined by Col. Franciszek Puchała, the officer who, in late November, had been dispatched with Gen. Hupałowski to Moscow to study Soviet invasion plans and then briefed Jaruzelski on Soviet intentions.[45] Finally, the responsibility for martial-law preparations in four key industrial ministries was assigned to selected general staff officers: Gen. Leon Kołatkowski was put in charge of the Ministry of Communications; Col. Piotr Panasiuk, the Ministry of Power and Atomic Energy; Col. Jerzy Budrewicz, the Ministry of Transport; and Col. Tadeusz Antoniuk, the Ministry of Foreign Trade and Services.[46]

It soon became apparent that the planning process in the Ministry of Defense was being slowed down not only by the need for utmost secrecy, but also by insufficient coordination with the parallel preparations underway in the Ministry of the Interior. Consultations between General Milewski of the Ministry of the Interior and Gen. Florian Siwicki, Poland's chief of the general staff, were infrequent and on several occasions ended in bitter arguments between the two officers over the particulars of the plan. The differences between the military and the police concerned the rules of engagement for army troops if confronted by civilian demonstrators, the timing of the entire operation, and the precise legal basis for the planned mass arrests of opposition activists.[47]

It is unclear whether the animosity between Siwicki and Milewski was caused by the traditional institutional rivalry between the army and the police, or if the friction was mainly due to their personalities. Subsequent events suggest, though, that Jaruzelski had never counted Milewski among his trusted supporters, and that Milewski knew it. Milewski's arguments with Siwicki were only a harbinger of things to come, as Milewski would continue to challenge Jaruzelski's authority through the period of martial law and beyond. In 1980–1981 Milewski was a "bureaucrat on the outside," who played high-stakes internal party politics, his hopes for office and influence spurred by the chaos prevalent in Kania's Politburo. As the authority of First Secretary Kania and Premier Pińkowski crumbled (Pińkowski was formally Milewski's boss, but was too weak to do anything), Milewski operated with virtually no outside supervision. Moreover, during the crisis Milewski's ministry was the only government agency, other than the Ministry of Defense, that had remained fully mobilized and ready for action against the trade union, even if by themselves the police were too weak to win. Hence, in 1981 Milewski became an important wielder of influence in the PUWP's internal politics.

Milewski was in a dilemma. On the one hand, the Polish police lacked the resources to occupy the country without the army's logistical capability, manpower, and heavy equipment; on the other hand, Milewski's political power after martial law would depend largely on his role in the plans' execution. In effect, by arguing with Siwicki over his agency's institutional prerogatives during the time martial law was in force, Milewski was staking his claim to political influence in the country after the new regime had taken over.

The conflict between Siwicki and Milewski was ended by Jaruzelski's executive fiat after the general had become, in mid-February 1981, Poland's new prime minister and thus Milewski's immediate superior. Jaruzelski's first internal directive as premier was to order the joint conducting of a war game by the Ministry of the Interior and the Ministry of Defense in order that the two ministries might iron out their differences and coordinate their roles in the implementation of the existing martial-law plans under his personal supervision.[48] Nothing could have been more indicative of the extent of the rift between the army and the police in 1981.

Jaruzelski as Prime Minister

In February 1981, when the government was fighting off the demands for registration of Rural Solidarity, Premier Pińkowski was fired and Jaruzelski was appointed in his place. The general assumed the premiership in an atmosphere of increasing chaos in the country and the ever-louder expressions of Soviet displeasure with the situation in Poland. Although Soviet troop movements in and around Poland in December of 1980 gradually subsided,[49] the union's demands for a five-day work week, and Rural Solidarity's drive for registration kept tensions high. A nationwide general strike was a real possibility.

The Eighth Plenum of the Central Committee, which met to consider Jaruzelski's nomination for the office of premier, made its decision on February 10, 1981. Jaruzelski's appointment was given strong support both by the hardliners (Grabski was particularly outspoken in his attacks on the opposition during the meeting) and by Kania, although the value of the latter's backing was by then questionable at best. While holding the new post, Jaruzelski would remain Poland's defense minister. The twofold nature of the responsibilities concomitant of this dual appointment was emphasized in the general's order to the army of February 11, 1981:

> Soldiers:
>
> Being appointed to lead the government, I remain with you because I shall keep my previous military appointment. Under these grave circumstances and in this difficult situation, just as before, we will continue to serve in the same line of battle, aware of our responsibility for the fate of our people's state.[50]

As reported by *Trybuna Ludu* of February 12, in his speech recommending Jaruzelski's appointment, Kania stressed the general's excellent reputation and the authority he would command as commander in chief of the Polish army. The plenum also selected Mieczysław Rakowski, editor in chief of *Polityka* (the party weekly), to the post of deputy prime minister. He was probably Jaruzelski's personal choice; judging from Rakowski's subsequent actions, his loyalty to the general was beyond reproach.

Jaruzelski's appointment brought about a brief but perceptible change in the country's political climate. The opposition hoped it would be able to do business with the new prime minister, whose reputation was that of a conscientious and efficient public servant; Solidarity expressed its readiness to open a new dialogue with the government. The Soviets also appeared reassured, if for entirely different reasons. The February issue of *Wojsko Ludowe* ran the headline: "We Will Defend Socialism. The Party Must Pull Itself Together." Brezhnev and Premier Tikhonov cabled Jaruzelski their congratulations and expressed confidence in his talents and experience.[51]

Clearly, Jaruzelski's promotion to premier had Soviet approval. Problems with Milewski notwithstanding, in order to impose martial law Jaruzelski needed direct executive authority over all branches of the government. Most important, the appointment made Jaruzelski automatically chairman of the National Defense Committee (KOK), which had been the principal coordinator of martial law planning since August 1980. Whether it had been the Soviets' intention or not, Jaruzelski's new appointment placed Kania in an increasingly untenable position. Having served under Gierek as the Central Committee's watchdog over the army, Kania must have known all too well that Jaruzelski, who throughout the 1970s had dealt directly with Moscow and had acted independently of the apparat,[52] would effectively circumvent his authority as first secretary. The elevation of Jaruzelski to premier effectively neutralized Kania in the Politburo probably as early as February 1981. Kania's personal recommendation of Jaruzelski had the added benefit of dispelling suspicion on the part of Solidarity that a change in policy was taking place.

If Jaruzelski was in fact grateful to Kania, he never showed it. Kania's willingness to seek an accommodation with Jaruzelski even at the expense of his own position did little to rein in Baryła's propagandists and ease tension. In February 1981, following Jaruzelski's appointment as prime minister and his call for a moratorium on strikes, the official political military line shifted perceptibly away from the criticism of the party's past mistakes and attacked the opposition with renewed vigor. Jaruzelski's rise to the position of prime minister was the first outward sign that the military was moving to assume a greater role in managing the crisis; *Wojsko Ludowe* greeted Jaruzelski's appointment to the premiership with the headline: "We Will Defend Socialism. The Party Must Pull Itself Together."[53]

Within the army, Jaruzelski made it clear to his officers that the maintenance of the army's morale was the highest of his list of priorities. The party's current weakness and the army's resultant responsibility for preserving Poland's position in the Soviet bloc became central themes of a newly drafted directive issued by Baryła to his political officers. A published evaluation of the army's political work in the Silesian Military District, bearing the title "Taking the Offensive," concluded that the time had come to strengthen the army's political apparat in preparation for the approaching confrontation with the opposition. The lines had been drawn; the report from the Silesian district for the first time expressly referred to Solidarity as a threat to the very existence of the Polish nation-state.[54] As the army defined it, "renewal" could only mean full restoration of the communist party and its leadership role in society.[55]

In his first speech after his appointment, Jaruzelski presented to the Sejm his government's program. His message was one of stern warning to Solidarity. "Evil and politically hostile forces have been threatening our vital alliances and the very survival of our economy," the general asserted. As a soldier, he viewed his new post as an opportunity to render service to his country, and as a reaffirmation of the soldier's duty to protect the fatherland. Then came a warning to the opposition:

> Socialism has been the systemic foundation of our national and state existence for over 37 years. Therefore, attempts to destabilize the system amount to an attack against our home; they create frightful threats to our fatherland.[56]

Although Jaruzelski reassured the representatives of the Sejm that "renewal" (as Kania's policy of liberalization in Poland had come to be known) would continue, he also declared that the government would always remain strong enough and ready to block counterrevolution. In the end, Jaruzelski demanded that peaceful work be resumed; the most important of his government program's ten points was a call for a 90-day moratorium on strikes. Poland needed, as the general put it, "three months of peaceful and productive work." One cannot say for sure whether Jaruzelski's negotiations with Solidarity and calls for calm were only a smoke screen, or if he still hoped for a political victory. If he did, he nevertheless proceeded full speed ahead with the preparations for martial law.

A week after his appointment, on February 16, 1981, Jaruzelski presided over a martial-law war game, conducted jointly by the Ministry of Defense and the Ministry of the Interior. The game was conducted in Warsaw between February 16 and 20, in one of the conference halls of the OTK Inspectorate; it was directed by Siwicki and Milewski and attended by the 45 most trusted senior officers from both ministries, plus two representatives of the Central Committee's propaganda department. In order to guarantee complete secrecy, no official minutes of the proceedings were kept, only four officers were authorized to take brief notes, and all participants were required to sign a secrecy agreement.[57] On February 20, the two teams drew up a series of recommendations based on the results of the exercise and presented them to Jaruzelski. The report emphasized that (1) in order for martial law (whose key component was codenamed "Operation Spring") to succeed, complete surprise had to be achieved, and therefore the army would have to move without proper authorization from the Sejm; (2) the best time for action would be late Saturday night or early Sunday morning, when most of the plants were closed; (3) mass arrests of opposition activists should take place 12–6 hours prior to the formal announcement of martial law in order to strip Solidarity of its leadership at the crucial moment in the confrontation; and (4) plants would be stormed by squads of ZOMO riot police, while the army would surround and patrol the cities, police the countryside, provide logistical support, break Poland's contact with the outside world, and block communications among different plants and regions of the country. On March 2, Jaruzelski flew to Moscow with a Polish delegation to the 26th CPSU Congress;[58] he carried with him a copy of the report "On the State's Preparedness for the Introduction of Martial Law."

Needless to say, Jaruzelski's report was not the only source of information on the feasibility of martial law in Poland that was available to Brezhnev. Mistrusting the Poles as usual, the CPSU Politburo had ordered a concurrent independent assessment of the martial-law option. Assigned to the Warsaw Pact Legnica command, the task was supervised personally by Marshal Kulikov and executed by his adjutant Shcheglov with the assistance of eighteen senior Soviet officers of the Warsaw Pact Joint High Command headquarters. On the eve of the Eighth Plenum, the Shcheglov group toured all Polish military districts and principal installations, ostensibly to check the Polish army's readiness for the upcoming Warsaw Pact maneuvers. In reality, the Soviet officers gathered intelligence on the morale and discipline of Polish army commanders, and made little effort to hide it. In one instance, Shcheglov reportedly bluntly asked a group of Polish officers what they would do if they were ordered to move in on striking workers and force them out of a plant.[59] Shcheglov's findings were summarized and passed on to Moscow through the Warsaw Pact channel of command. The data was collated with the Polish report.

On March 3, during a break in the proceedings of the Soviet party congress, Jaruzelski met with Soviet premier Nikolay Tikhonov and presented him with a copy of the Polish martial-law plan.[60] Jaruzelski's preliminary study and the results of the joint war game of the Polish army and security forces must have been corroborated by Kulikov's report. On March 4, the Polish delegation to the 26th CPSU Congress was received in the Kremlin by Brezhnev, Andropov, Ustinov, Tikhonov, Gromyko, and Suslov. The TASS communiqué on the meeting expressed the Soviets' complete confidence that the "Polish communists had at their disposal the means and the determination to reverse the course of events and liquidate the dangers threatening Poland's socialist achievements."[61] Jaruzelski's martial-law plans were given the green light.

The First Martial-Law Deadline: March 1981

On March 5, the Poles returned from Moscow to an ever more complicated domestic situation. The requested 90-day period of tranquility had not materialized. Furthermore, Soviet pressure on the PUWP did not subside, and the meetings between Kulikov and Jaruzelski again became stormy.[62] Although Jaruzelski de facto committed himself to Operation Spring, he continued to insist that the Poles themselves should decide on the exact timing of the action. This view apparently never sat well with Kulikov, who did not attempt to conceal his growing impatience with the situation.

It also soon became clear that, although the Soviets accepted Jaruzelski's plan, they had not abandoned invasion as a solution of last resort. Soviet preparations continued under the guise of the SOYUZ-81 Warsaw Pact Maneuvers, scheduled to begin on March 16 and involving 150,000 troops, of which some 30,000 would operate on Polish territory. Soviet reconnaissance groups began arriving in Poland as early as February 14; the Soviet Army teams appeared more interested in the country's central airports, national communication centers, and key industrial regions than in the Polish army's training grounds. Kulikov insisted that the Soviet Army units scheduled to participate in the exercises should be deployed in forests adjacent to large industrial and population centers.[63] The message was unmistakable: the Russians were preparing for an invasion in case Jaruzelski hesitated or his plan failed.

Yet there was a fundamental difference between the invasion threat of December 1980 and Soviet military preparations in the spring of 1981. Although some of his officers were being kept in the dark about Kulikov's intentions, judging from Jaruzelski's behavior, he must have known the Soviet plan. Rather than being concerned about Kulikov's actions, Jaruzelski and Siwicki went out of their way to assist the Soviet teams. Their apparent calm and willingness to cooperate, which had been totally absent in 1980, suggest that SOYUZ-81 had been cleared with Poland's defense minister. In his assistance to Kulikov's men, Jaruzelski went so far as to turn over to the Russians the blueprints of selected buildings in various Polish cities that might serve as Soviet military posts after the invasion.[64] The apparent calm with which Jaruzelski and Siwicki regarded all these preparations could only have one explanation: they were convinced that the Soviets were not preparing to move until the Poles had had the chance to implement the plan accepted by Moscow in early March. Another bit of circumstantial evidence supports this conclusion, namely, the striking coincidence between the beginning of the preparations for SOYUZ-81 on February 14 and the official announcement on February 12 that Jaruzelski had been appointed prime minister. It appears that Jaruzelski's promotion, Operation Spring, and Kulikov's SOYUZ-81 backup invasion plan were all parts of one and the same policy decision.

In effect, SOYUZ-81 was an integral part of the Polish martial-law plan, a sort of Soviet "insurance policy" in Poland to be called upon in an emergency. If Jaruzelski's imposition of martial law failed and a national uprising broke out in Poland, thirty thousand Soviet soldiers would have already been positioned within Poland, and over 120,000 of them would be poised around Poland's borders. With SOYUZ-81 underway, Kulikov would have the option to react instantly to a Polish uprising, before Solidarity succeeded in consolidating its government and was, possibly, joined by deserting units of the Polish army.

There were other indications that the deadline for declaring martial law had been set for late March 1981. In the last three weeks before the Bydgoszcz crisis, caused by a police attack on Solidarity activists, Baryła's propaganda campaign became especially vicious, charging that unless things returned quickly to normal the country faced an unprecedented disaster; nine months later the same argumentation would be used by Jaruzelski as his rationale for finally cracking down on Solidarity. In February, as the groundwork for SOYUZ-81 was being laid, Polish army propagandists had already started describing the situation in the gravest of terms. In a marked shift in Baryła's campaign, military publications emphasized the threat the turmoil in Poland presented to the alliance of the countries in the Soviet bloc. *Żołnierz Polski* ran a strongly worded editorial decrying the political direction the country had taken. Stanisław Dymek, the author of the attack, gravely reminded his readers that "socialist Poland constitutes an important link in the defensive alliance of the socialist states—the Warsaw Treaty Organization. Our [i.e., Poland's] security depends upon the strength and durability of this alliance."[65] Three weeks later, the weekly ran another editorial that, with the benefit of hindsight, could be interpreted as a declaration of the army's readiness to step in with force. The piece in *Żołnierz Polski* asserted that the army stood ready to defend communism in Poland:

> Another feature of our army is its deep patriotism and its devotion to the cause of socialism. It stems from the deep understanding that only Poland as a socialist state, joined in the alliance with the Soviet Union and other members of the Warsaw Pact, can remain an independent and free country, a country within secure borders.[66]

In addition to attacks by Baryła's publicists, there were tangible signs that the government was getting tough on Solidarity. Police harassment of opposition activists, accusations that the union had intentionally sabotaged all chances for compromise, indictments handed down against dissidents—all raised tensions and created an ever-widening sense of a profound national malaise; martial-law planners considered such a preparatory propaganda barrage essential to the success of their operation. Nine months later, essentially the same government policy of confrontation with Solidarity would generate a similar atmosphere of perpetual crisis and hopelessness in the country.

In the spring of 1981, immediately after the Polish government had returned from Moscow, police repression was markedly stepped up.[67] On

March 4 and 5, Adam Michnik and Jacek Kuroń, two leading activists of the Committee for Workers' Defense (Komitet Obrony Robotników; KOR), were arrested, charged with slandering the Polish People's Republic, and then released. Next the four founding members of the Confederation of Independent Poland (Konfederacja Polski Niepodległej) were indicted for "acts directed against the state," a charge that carried with it the death penalty. On March 10 another opposition figure, 82-year-old Antoni Pajdak of the delegalized Polish Socialist Party, was attacked by undercover police agents and beaten unconscious. The government also steadfastly resisted the pressure from the peasants for registration of Rural Solidarity, which, although its official status had not yet been confirmed in courts, held its first congress in Poznań on March 9. In Łódź, a stalemate over the right of the local Solidarity chapter to organize in hospitals escalated to a full-blown crisis because local police sabotaged the negotiations. Although the first meeting between Jaruzelski and Solidarity leader Wałęsa, on March 10, was judged successful and businesslike, police harassment of the opposition continued unabated.

As scheduled, SOYUZ-81 began on March 16. On the same day, in what appears an unlikely coincidence, Tadeusz Grabski announced that local party officials responsible for the repression of the 1976 strike in Radom had been cleared of all charges and released. Predictably, the provocative announcement led to protest action by Solidarity's Radom chapter. Three days later, on March 19, the Poles learned that a meeting in Bydgoszcz between Solidarity activists and members of the regional council had been broken up by a squad of uniformed police thugs. If the government had intended to raise tensions by the police action in Bydgoszcz as a prelude to declaration of martial law, the affair proved a costly miscalculation. The workers were outraged at this display of police brutality, and Solidarity responded with a nationwide mobilization for a general strike. If, however, the Bydgoszcz incident was an independent operation by Poland's security police, Jaruzelski found himself facing a mess that threatened to undermine his entire plan.

The Bydgoszcz Crisis:
An Aborted Crackdown

The Bydgoszcz crisis was the first instance since the creation of Solidarity when police force was openly used against the union. A number of Solidarity activists were hurt in the confrontation; three of them, including Jan Rulewski, one of the union's regional leaders, were hospitalized.[68]

The Bydgoszcz confrontation took place against the background of a bureaucratic tug of war over the registration of the farmers' independent trade union, Rural Solidarity. Denying that there were sufficient legal grounds for registering the new union, the government claimed that the existing "agricultural circles" (village cooperatives run by the state) sufficiently represented peasant interests. On the other hand, Rural Solidarity organizers insisted that they were entitled to the same rights as had been extended to industrial workers. The dispute had begun in early February 1981 and continued into March without much promise of an early resolution. Frustrated in their efforts to have their petition reviewed by local government officials, on March 12 the peasant leaders approached the Bydgoszcz chapter of Solidarity and asked for help. Two days later, on March 14, Solidarity in Bydgoszcz learned that large numbers of riot police had arrived in town. On March 16, the peasants conducted a sit-in at the local headquarters of the proregime United Peasant Party. The protest action appeared to have worked; on March 18, the Regional People's Council in Bydgoszcz invited six representatives of the peasant activists to present their grievances.

As requested, the farmers' representatives and several Solidarity activists, led by Rulewski, showed up at the meeting on March 19 of the Bydgoszcz People's Council to outline their demands. Their case was placed last on the meeting's agenda, as "other business." With three items left to be discussed, Council Chairman Edward Berger unexpectedly announced that the session was being adjourned. The union activists, furious over what they saw as another bureaucratic trick, insisted that the proceedings continue and, with the support of several councilmen who remained in the hall, drafted a resolution to that effect. At this point a detachment of uniformed police and several plainclothesmen entered the hall, demanded that the activists leave the building, and then charged them with truncheons. Several of the Solidarity activists were severely beaten and left unconscious.

Within hours of the police attack, rumors had spread throughout the country that Rulewski was dead. In order to calm the workers, Solidarity widely circulated a photograph of the Bydgoszcz leader, taken in the emergency room, which showed him alive, although severely beaten and bruised. State-run television added fuel to the fire by presenting a distorted version of the events and blaming Solidarity for the confrontation. Government propagandists began depicting Rulewski as an ex-criminal; some insinuated that his father had been a *Volksdeutscher* during the war and had collaborated with the Germans.[69] The whole affair looked increasingly like a planned provocation.

Solidarity members were furious and tensions immediately mounted, with the union threatening a general strike if those responsible for the violence went unpunished. On March 27 a four-hour nationwide warning strike was held, and preparation for a general strike gained momentum. Solidarity appeared organized, determined, and ready to fight. In the face of the nation's unity, the government began frantically searching for a compromise. This was not, however, what the Soviets had apparently been told to expect.

Shortly before the warning strike of March 27, Marshal Kulikov consulted with the Soviet Army's chief of operations, who flew to Legnica to meet him, and announced on March 24 that SOYUZ-81 would not end on March 25 as scheduled. Instead, the maneuvers were being extended indefinitely.[70] Next, on March 27, a high-level fact-finding Soviet delegation arrived in Warsaw. Led by Marshal Kulikov, the group included 30 senior officials from the KGB, the Soviet Defense Ministry, and Gosplan; the KGB team included Chairman Andropov's deputy. The Soviets met several times individually with Jaruzelski and Kania, reviewed the Polish martial-law plan, and suggested several changes, but in the end did not insist on immediate action.[71] Apparently, they concluded that in view of the current situation, Jaruzelski had to postpone the introduction of martial law, which then would proceed as planned after the Bydgoszcz crisis had been neutralized. On March 28, the Ninth Central Committee Plenum issued a declaration calling for negotiation and a peaceful resolution of the confrontation. After a feverishly-paced negotiating session, Solidarity's Lech Wałęsa and Deputy Premier Mieczysław Rakowski reached a compromise; the general strike was called off. The crisis reached its dénouement the next day, when the trade union's rank and file confronted Wałęsa, during the meeting of Solidarity's National Commission on April 1, over the undemocratic procedures employed in his negotiations with the government.

Different interpretations circulated at the time as to who bore the responsibility for the Bydgoszcz affair. The blame for the beating of Solidarity activists was finally pinned on Stefan Olszowski and Tadeusz Grabski, two Politburo hard-liners. Stories of the stormy Central Committee plenum of March 28, during which the two were almost voted out of the Politburo, appeared to confirm their guilt; from today's perspective Grabski's and Olszowski's involvement in the affair seems established beyond a reasonable doubt. It remains unclear, however, how Grabski and Olszowski by themselves could mobilize the police apparatus to serve their goals. Also, there remains the question of Jaruzelski's role in the crisis.

The commonly accepted explanation that Bydgoszcz was a "try on" of sorts for martial law, a "reconnaissance in force," is unconvincing.[72] Seasoned politicians of Jaruzelski's mold who play for the highest political stakes (and the martial-law plan was a gamble despite all the meticulous preparation) simply do not risk "dress rehearsals," which could escalate beyond anyone's ability to control them and wreck the entire plan. Having carefully laid the groundwork in the form of Baryła's propaganda campaign, and aware of Kulikov's watchful eye, Jaruzelski could have been doing only one thing: proceeding with the implementation of Operation Spring. The presence of a large contingent of the Soviet Army on Polish soil, as part of SOYUZ-81, meant that any miscalculation could end in disaster. If at any point the Soviets had decided that Jaruzelski's operation had failed, they were prepared to move on their own, and that meant a Warsaw Pact occupation of Poland. In short, there could be no "try on"; the deadline was set and the operation was already in motion until someone's rash miscalculation turned the carefully laid-out plan into shambles. Only one man other than Jaruzelski could have sent the police to Bydgoszcz and ordered them to break up the meeting. That man was Poland's minister of the interior, Gen. Mirosław Milewski.

It may very well be that the stormy Central Committee plenum was an attempt by Milewski, Grabski, and Olszowski to win Soviet backing by ending Jaruzelski's seemingly interminable procrastination. Since even Polish general staff officers had been kept in the dark about the significance of SOYUZ-81 and Jaruzelski's real intentions, it appears quite likely that Milewski and the two apparatchiks were also ignorant of the full scope of the unfolding events. In fact, considered separately from Operation Spring and the whole martial-law plan, SOYUZ-81 looked indeed like a preparation for an invasion. By triggering a confrontation with the opposition, Milewski might have hoped to force Jaruzelski's hand; that is probably why Grabski and Olszowski argued so heatedly for an all-out strike against Solidarity. They knew that once successfully implemented, martial law would almost certainly guarantee Jaruzelski and his cronies a position of influence from which to bid for the highest party offices; correlatively, those left outside Jaruzelski's circle stood little chance of retaining political power. This bode ill for Milewski in particular, who after clashes with Siwicki had had to submit to Jaruzelski's authority on matters of martial-law planning. Grabski and Olszowski must have also seen the writing on the wall.

The Ninth Extraordinary Party Congress was approaching and, considering the gathering of pressures for internal liberalization in the party, it was likely that the two men would be eliminated as serious contenders for the party leadership. In fact, after the ninth congress Grabski was dropped from the Politburo, and Olszowski had no choice but to align himself with Jaruzelski as a junior partner. If, however, in the spring of 1981, Milewski and company could have forced the army to suppress the union, their position would have been secured. They could have claimed some credit with Moscow for eliminating the labor movement and re-establishing orthodoxy among the PUWP's rank and file. They would have also demonstrated to the Kremlin that Jaruzelski's caution might have been unwarranted, and possibly based on motives other than those of a true communist. In short, they would have retained a fighting chance in the contest for the top party post.

Had martial law been imposed in March, Milewski, whose action would have triggered the final confrontation, and Grabski and Olszowski, who would have rallied the party against the opposition, would have all remained important players in Poland's politics, even if Jaruzelski became first secretary. They could have reasonably hoped that, once order had been re-established, the

Kremlin might have been inclined to choose one of them for the country's leader. After all, Moscow's reliance on Jaruzelski, an army man despite his political credentials, was a second-best solution and was agreed on only after the Soviets had become convinced that they could not rely on the apparat to resolve the crisis.[73] With the benefit of hindsight, the bitter recriminations made during the plenum look like a desperate attempt by Milewski, Grabski, and Olszowski to force Jaruzelski into a political partnership. In that sense, it was an attempt to stave off the military's takeover of the party.

The alternative faced by Jaruzelski was clear: either yield to the pressure, and thus give the "troika" an opportunity to claim credit for suppressing Solidarity, or stop the entire operation until the crisis had been defused, he had consolidated his hold on the PUWP, and he had built the core of a new leadership group. The latter meant waiting until after the Ninth Congress. Most important, however, Milewski's provocation meant that had Jaruzelski chosen to follow through with the plan in March, he would have been moving against the union at its highest level of readiness. Doing that would have been sheer madness, and Jaruzelski made sure that Kulikov and his fact-finding task force got the message.

Jaruzelski arrived at the meeting of the Central Committee fully prepared to take on his opponents; the decisive March 28 plenum, during which the confrontation between Grabski and Olszowski, on the one side, and Jaruzelski and Kiszczak on the other took place, was preceded by a Politburo meeting on March 22, thus immediately after Jaruzelski's visit with Kulikov[74] and after the meeting with the Soviet reconnaissance team. Jaruzelski attended that meeting of the Politburo. By the time he faced Grabski and Olszowski, he probably already knew that the Soviets would neither pressure him to continue the operation, nor themselves seriously threaten to invade.

Next came the task of pacifying the population. The army propagandists' harsh tones of only weeks before were replaced by conciliatory pleas for calm. On March 29, 1981, when tensions were at their highest, *Żołnierz Polski* spoke of the government's readiness to cooperate with the union and decried the showdown. Col. Jan Ignaczak, permanent member of the weekly's editorial board and one of Baryła's prominent publicists, wrote in his editorial:

> The Prime Minister has kept his soldier's word of honor that he would do everything in his power to help all of us see as soon as possible the light at the end of the tunnel in which our country finds itself at present.
>
> And now, as we have covered one third of our path, again the country is being threatened with the gravest danger since August of last year, the danger of social unrest, destabilization and anarchy. It is most unfortunate that new tensions, occasioned by Bydgoszcz, arise while the Warsaw Pact maneuvers, this test of our allied credibility, are taking place.
>
> The latest events have placed on today's agenda with utmost urgency the

question of our nation's direction, of the direction of the country. The answer to this question will determine the fate of all of us, the fate of our families, of our nation.[75]

The government's defeat in the Bydgoszcz crisis was a setback to the martial-law planners. However, in terms of internal party politics, Jaruzelski scored a moderate victory. Although humiliated by Solidarity, the general could point out to the Politburo that his reasoning had carried the day with the Soviets. He would also make certain that there would be no more surprises from within the Politburo. After Bydgoszcz, Jaruzelski alone would make all key decisions and issue orders to act. General Milewski retained his position as minister of the interior only until the critical Ninth Party Congress in July. On August 1, at Jaruzelski's request, the Sejm accepted Milewski's resignation and installed Gen. Czesław Kiszczak, Jaruzelski's confidante, in Milewski's place.[76]

The Bydgoszcz confrontation marked a watershed in the Polish crisis. It was Solidarity's last chance for a showdown with the government for which the union's rank and file was fully mobilized. Had Solidarity responded with a general strike and unyielding demands for punishment of those responsible for the violence, it would have been a clear indication to Moscow that Jaruzelski was not strong enough to contain the crisis by himself. The Soviets would then have had to decide whether the PUWP was hopelessly beyond repair and an invasion by them was therefore necessary, or whether Kania, Grabski, Olszowski, or some other apparatchik ought to be given a chance to negotiate a compromise political solution to the crisis, one which would have to include real concessions to the union's demands. Had the Soviets chosen the latter route, Solidarity might have achieved the seemingly impossible: its survival as a legal opposition party in a communist state. Paradoxically, the unwillingness of Solidarity's leadership to risk the general strike in March made Jaruzelski's imposition of martial law a certainty in December.

In Control of the Party:

The Army Between the Ninth Congress and Martial Law

6

Deepening of the Crisis

The period between the Bydgoszcz confrontation in late March and the Ninth PUWP Congress in July was unquestionably a difficult time for the government. Because Jaruzelski had been forced to comromise with his opponents, he emerged from the showdown over the events in Bydgoszcz politically weakened, both in his dealings with Solidarity and in his negotiations with Moscow. Although Brezhnev had accepted the general's advice in March, Jaruzelski's failure to meet the presumed deadline for martial law did nothing to increase Moscow's confidence in the Polish plan.

There was more than ample evidence that Poland was rapidly sinking into chaos. Although the "Paris Club" discussions of the Polish debt crisis led to the loan-rescheduling agreement of April 27 that granted Poland a four-year grace period on debt repayment, the relief package was a drop in the bucket of the country's needs. In the first quarter of 1981, Poland's "realized" (sold) production declined by 10.2 percent relative to the same period in the preceding year; total loss of output during the first quarter was put by the government at 85 billion złotys, while wages in the same period rose on average by 21 percent relative to 1980. In addition, Poland's terms of trade badly deteriorated, both with the West and with CMEA countries; by the end of April, 1981, Poland's trade deficit with the West stood at roughly one billion exchange złotys, while its trade deficit with CMEA reached 1.3 billion.[1] Inflation ran rampant; the country suffered periodic fuel and electric power shortages; and a substantial portion of its industry was either idle or worked at substantially reduced capacity because of the lack of imported raw materials. The rationing system for basic goods could barely ensure that the minimum of the population's needs was met. Angry public outbursts, wildcat strikes, and so-called hunger marches became ever more frequent occurrences in Polish cities and villages.

The deepening economic crisis further undermined the PUWP's ability to control the population. Calls for change could be heard with increased frequency from all sectors of Polish society. The government finally gave in to the union's demand to be permitted its own independent newspaper; on April 3 the first issue of *Tygodnik Solidarność* (Solidarity weekly) appeared in newsstands. Solidarity continued to press for the promised new law on censorship. In late April, teachers held their first congress outside government supervision, calling for a thorough overhaul of the educational curriculum in Polish schools; similar pressure came from university students. In late May 1981, a wave of demonstrations by university students swept across Poland, demanding a revision of the curriculum, release of political prisoners, and democratic government. Even the Sejm, which in the past had been derided by government critics as a "rubber-stamp parliament," displayed an unprecedented assertiveness. Its chamber became a forum for serious and often acrimonious debates about the country's economic and political future. In a surprising development, in late May the deputies delivered a stunning blow to the regime by rejecting, after a heated debate, Jaruzelski's report on the government's plan to stabilize the economy.[2]

More dangerous from Jaruzelski's standpoint was the growing ferment within communist organizations. Between April 23 and 28, the Federation of the Unions of Polish Socialist Youth (Federacja Związków Socjalistycznej Młodzieży Polskiej; FZSMP), an umbrella organization operating in schools, factories, and in the armed forces, held its third national congress. The conference called for far-reaching procedural reforms and introduced secret ballot procedures for the election of the new leadership. The FZSMP congress was attended by top-level party officials, including Kania, Barcikowski, Grabski, and Olszowski, plus several government ministers. The apparatchiks got an earful of often bitter accusations from the floor, and were bluntly told that their past undemocratic practices were responsible for the federation's weakness. The newly elected FZSMP chairman, Jaskiernia, vowed to work for change in the federation's relationship with the party, so that the FZSMP would never again be treated as the "party's kindergarten." The apparatchiks could see all too well that the Polish communist-youth movement was a shambles; between 1980 and 1981 the FZSMP lost over one third of its membership.[3]

There was turmoil in the party itself. The rank and file called for reform and for greater internal democracy. From Jaruzelski's point of view, the pressure for structural changes within the party, which became particularly strong after the confrontation over the events in Bydgoszcz, was the most dangerous aspect of the crisis. It was a given that the Soviets would not tolerate meaningful party reform; any substantial deviation from the Soviet model meant trouble. The Soviets made their position clear by conducting military communications exercises on the eve of the PUWP's Tenth Plenum, which was to take up the issue of the upcoming Ninth Congress.[4]

During the Central Committee plenum of April 29–30, the Politburo finally set the date of the congress for July 14, 1981. It also approved new rules for selecting congressional delegates; the change was a compromise between the traditional electoral-commission system and the intraparty democracy wanted by the rank and file. The new rules retained the key provision that principal delegates would be chosen by the electoral commission; however, no limits would be placed on the number of nominations for additional delegates, and these could be elected by secret ballot. In effect, the Politburo would still control the process, while partially mollifying the disgruntled rank and file. The pretense that the party was truly reforming itself was further strengthened by the co-optation into the Politburo of G. Gabryś and Z. Wroński; the two were industrial workers and had never belonged to the PUWP political establishment.[5] After the Ninth Congress they would be quietly let go.

Kania's keynote address to the Tenth Plenum reaffirmed the PUWP's commitment to the Soviet model. The first secretary went a long way to reaffirm the party's leadership role, maintaining that he was determined to preserve the existing party structure, its hierarchy, and the power distribution among its different branches. In a message intended to allay Moscow's fears and reassure Brezhnev that the PUWP would not drift into Czechoslovak-style reforms, Kania emphatically repeated that all changes within the party would be initiated and approved by the party leadership.[6]

All this political posturing was ultimately of secondary importance. Most of all, Jaruzelski needed time to regroup after the near fiasco of the March operation, and to gather intelligence on Solidarity's strength in different regions of the country. He needed also an easing of the Soviets' pressure for action, so that he could redeploy his forces and launch another propaganda campaign to prepare the nation as much as possible for the shock that the imposition of martial law would cause.[7] The Tenth Plenum prevented serious party reform from taking place. Furthermore, if the haggling over party procedure would draw the people's attention away from his preparations for introducing martial law, Jaruzelski welcomed the debate.

Assurances for Moscow

Extending unqualified support to Jaruzelski's group presented a problem to Brezhnev for several reasons. In the light of the Soviet Politburo's insistence at home on the subordination of the army to the party's authority, the precedent-setting nature of the prospective replacement of the Polish civilian party apparat by professional military men, even though those men were dedicated communists, was simply an awkward proposition. A more important reason for Moscow's continued uneasiness about Jaruzelski was the Polish army's record of relative independence during previous crises, and consequently the dangerous unpredictability of the situation. In communist Poland, the military had intervened in the country's politics several times before, and not always in ways palatable to the Soviets. The 1956 involvement of Komar, Frey-Bielecki, and Wiśniewski in the leadership crisis, when the army openly joined Gomułka in defiance of Khrushchev's wishes, could not be viewed in Moscow as a reassuring precedent.[8] That was ultimately the reason why throughout the crisis the Soviets worked in parallel to the Polish military, preparing their own plans for intervention, should Jaruzelski prove in the end to be untrustworthy. That was the purpose behind the SOYUZ-81 maneuvers, and the often menacing movements of Kulikov's troops, which did not cease until the middle of April.[9]

In view of Soviet apprehension, Jaruzelski initiated an elaborate propaganda campaign stressing Polish-Soviet brotherhood-in-arms, the permanence of the Soviet bloc, and the fidelity of the Polish military to the principles of Marxism-Leninism. Once again, Baryła's publicists moved to the forefront. The campaign began in April, shortly after the Bydgoszcz confrontation. *Wojsko Ludowe* commemorated the 36th anniversary of the Polish-Soviet Treaty of Friendship and Mutual Assistance by stressing the Polish army's loyalty to Moscow. "Friendship With The Soviet Union Is The Guarantee Of Our Security,"[10] read the title of the front page editorial in the journal's April issue. The May issue ran a lengthy essay, by Col. Ireneusz Ruszkiewicz, commemorating the 26th anniversary of the WTO. Ruszkiewicz reiterated Poland's commitment to the alliance and warned that if the crisis continued, it would put into question the country's ability to meet fully its obligations to its allies. "To say," wrote Ruszkiewicz,

> that during this period [the past several months] the country's ability to provide for its defense has been seriously endangered would be simply to recognize the existing, highly disturbing state of affairs... The weakening, even if only temporary, of our defense readiness, has a negative impact on the strength and defensive capabilities of the entire coalition.[11]

In agreement with the Soviet view, the article conceded that the crisis had gone beyond Poland's political and economic problems and had started to undermine Soviet security in Europe. Still, Ruszkiewicz emphasized the Polish army's determination to stem the tide of counterrevolution. He and other army propagandists reaffirmed Polish-Soviet "unity of views" on the nature of the crisis and the need to find a speedy resolution. What made Jaruzelski's position diametrically different from that of Dubček in 1968 was that he consistently declared himself in agreement with Brezhnev's assessment of the situation; the differences were only over the timing of action. Thus, the general provided the sine qua non of the Kremlin's dealings with its satellites: a personal guarantee from a loyal East European leader that Soviet interests would be protected.

In early April, Jaruzelski had an opportunity personally to carry to the Kremlin his assurances of loyalty. On the night of April 3, Jaruzelski and Kania flew secretly to Moscow to brief Brezhnev on the situation in Poland in the aftermath of Bydgoszcz, and to present their revised plans for dealing with the crisis; the two were back in Warsaw the next morning.[12] It appears that Jaruzelski was able to convince the ailing Soviet leader that his contingency plans would work if given another chance; on April 7, during a speech to the Czechoslovak party congress in Prague, Brezhnev announced that SOYUZ-81 had ended. The general secretary failed to mention, however, that after the maneuver, a group of 47 senior Soviet officers from the SOYUZ-81 command staff had been detailed as "observers" to Poland and flown into Warsaw to review the draft of the Polish martial-law plans; the group was installed in Soviet army barracks in Legnica and became the core of Marshal Kulikov's Warsaw Pact staff assigned to monitor the crisis.[13] On April 18, at the Soviet Headquarters of the Warsaw Pact, Kulikov held a briefing for about 80 Soviet general staff officers, during which he announced that (on Warsaw's request) they would be sent to Poland to assist the Polish communists in their struggle. This group of Soviets was later joined by officers from other Warsaw Pact armies and, on April 24 and 25, shipped to Legnica. From April 25 until the introduction of martial law, the Soviets maintained a staff of up to 130 officers dedicated exclusively to Jaruzelski's operation. They monitored the situation in Poland and filed daily reports with their leaders in Moscow.[14]

Jaruzelski cooperated fully with the Soviet team and was obviously well aware of the ultimate purpose of the Legnica staff. Nevertheless, he insisted in his talks with Kulikov that, as far as the timing of the operation was concerned, the Soviets would have to defer to his judgment. Whatever the logic that guided him, throughout the tense months of the crisis Jaruzelski would struggle hopelessly to remain both a loyal communist and a Polish soldier-patriot.[15]

Preparations for the Ninth PUWP Congress

The Ninth Extraordinary Party Congress, scheduled for July 14–20, 1981, would become a landmark in the Polish military's rise to power. After the Bydgoszcz disaster, Jaruzelski had to make sure that the pressures for liberalization of party structures would not result in a lasting weakening of the Politburo's central authority. There was a danger that if the party itself moved to alter its organizational principles or elected a reformist leadership, the Soviets would feel compelled to act militarily against Poland regardless of the general's assurances and the agreed-upon plans.

The main lesson of Bydgoszcz was that, to avoid similar trouble in the future, Jaruzelski needed to ensure his personal control of key party and government posts. Even if before the Bydgoszcz crisis his intentions had been to act in the "shadow" of the Politburo, the near-disaster brought about by Milewski and his cronies demonstrated how dangerous continuing disarray at the top of the party hierarchy was to the martial-law operation. After Bydgoszcz, Jaruzelski had to make sure that he controlled the party.

As the date of the Ninth Extraordinary Party Congress neared, the PUWP readied itself for an impending purge and consolidation of its leadership. The debate: "Party and Socialist Values," about the "crisis of confidence" inside the party was begun in the March issue of the political monthly *Życie Partii* (Party life). The focus of the discussion was the reconstruction of the party's strength and the role of ideology in the struggle against Solidarity. For Jaruzelski, the upcoming congress was to be the test of his ability to prevent the rank-and-file reform movement for "horizontal structures," or greater democracy, from altering the PUWP's organizational hierarchy. If the general was to succeed in retaining Moscow's support, he had to make sure that the party would close ranks behind him; "democratic centralism" in party life had to be preserved as the foundation of the PUWP's "socialist renewal."

The army contributed to the precongress debate with a two-pronged campaign. Through hard-line statements by army ideologues, printed regularly in military publications, Jaruzelski's entourage assured the hard-liners, the Soviets, and East European "fraternal" parties that the general's regime was tough, and that he himself was a principled communist. At the same time, as prime minister, Jaruzelski was a partner of Kania, who was considered a moderate by the Poles. Jaruzelski made sure that his repeated calls for "national accord and reconciliation" would strengthen his popularity in Poland and help calm down the population after the Bydgoszcz drama.

As the debates over voting procedures, the party statutes, and ideology continued, Jaruzelski maneuvered to forestall any serious opposition to his increasing hold on the government. The congress would decide the makeup of the future Politburo; in this respect, the danger facing the general was that the drive for internal party democracy might alter the balance of forces within the Central Committee in favor of genuine party reformers, such as Gdańsk's party secretary, Fiszbach. Hence, Jaruzelski's primary goal during the congress would be to rally the party behind the current leadership and to rein in the reformers.

In anticipation of the arguments among the congress delegates, *Wojsko*

Ludowe published a series of position articles by prominent army ideologues, under the general heading "What I Expect of the 9th Congress." The military press called for strength and the closing of party ranks. Brig. Gen. Norbert Michta,[16] a well-known army theorist of Marxism-Leninism and president of the Higher School of the Social Sciences, started the precongress debate in *Wojsko Ludowe* with a blistering attack on the reformers. "I believe," wrote General Michta, "that the Ninth Extraordinary PUWP Congress ought to state clearly and without any ambiguities that socialist renewal in Poland means a return to the theory and practice of Marxist-Leninist norms in party life and in the manner in which the party governs and exercises power."[17] Michta laid the blame for the party's weakness on the reformers:

> Let us face the truth: by "renewal" many party comrades understand their own hidden desires to transform the PUWP into a Western-style social-democratic party, and they pay no attention to the fact that Solidarity is trying to tear down the [political] structure built by people's power and turn trade-unionism into the dominant political force in the country.[18]

For Solidarity Michta had nothing but contempt. As he pointed out, ideas about future "duality of power" in Poland were a dangerous fantasy. Michta's charges were seconded by Col. Hipolit Grzegorczyk of the Military Technical Academy. Grzegorczyk insinuated that the reformers were giving in to Solidarity's pressure to take Poland out of the Warsaw Pact:

> I expect that the party will clearly and unequivocally restate that our independence is founded on our socialist fraternal alliance, which has been so viciously and relentlessly attacked by the internal and external enemies of our motherland. Furthermore, I expect that the party will teach a lesson to those who manipulate the policies of renewal to push the party towards social-democratic factionalism. I expect the congress to demonstrate that the crisis that has gripped the party does not affect our socialist ideal.[19]

Other army publications followed suit. Stanisław Dymek of *Żołnierz Polski* seconded Grzegorczyk's charges in his June 7 editorial "The State Is Not A Servant." [20] The same issue brought the announcement of a new method of police work being tried in Poland. In the future, joint patrols of the regular police (MO) and the military police would become routine in the government's effort to maintain law and order in the country.

The Kremlin sent a message that it would view the Ninth Congress as an important test of the Polish Politburo's leadership skills. Moscow's position was outlined in a letter of June 5 to the PUWP Central Committee. The Soviets criticized Kania and Jaruzelski for not living up to their expectations and for not reversing the course of events in Poland.[21] The letter was also a warning that reform within the PUWP would be viewed by the Kremlin as a setback to its interests in Poland.

Until the Ninth Congress Jaruzelski steered a moderate course. Although his principal objective was to meet Moscow's expectations by staving off party reform, he was aware that hard-line apparatchiks could still derail the martial-law operation by forcing upon the government another premature confrontation with Solidarity. Having failed to forge an alliance with Jaruzelski during the Bydgoszcz crisis, Grabski and Olszowski might try a last-ditch attempt to fight him from the congress floor. In order to prevent such action, Jaruzelski threw his support behind Kania's re-election. During the Ninth Congress, Kania would be treated by Jaruzelski as an ally whom the general ostensibly supported, even though available evidence suggests that in June Jaruzelski was already determined to use Kania's "political compromise" approach to Solidarity only as a smoke screen for his martial-law preparations. On June 19, during a meeting of the National Defense Committee, Jaruzelski spoke unequivocally in favor of martial law, although he conceded that after Bydgoszcz another delay was unavoidable.[22]

The Ninth Congress:
A Victory for the General

The Ninth Extraordinary PUWP Congress opened in Warsaw on July 14, 1981, and lasted for almost a week, through July 20. In terms of genuine party reform, the assembly produced little of substance, despite the fact that electoral procedures became more open. However, from Jaruzelski's point of view the congress was an unqualified success. First, no changes were introduced into the PUWP structure that would weaken the position of the first secretary and warrant Soviet charges of revisionism. Second, both Kania and Jaruzelski were re-elected and retained the necessary controlling majorities in the Politburo and the Central Committee. Since Kania had probably been marked already for removal in February (whether or not he knew about it is another matter), Jaruzelski automatically became the principal contender for the first-secretaryship.[23] Finally, the Grabski/Olszowski faction ceased to count as a potential political threat to the general. Grabski was dropped from the Central Committee altogether, while Olszowski, a man famous for his bureaucratic survival skills, had no other choice but to accept Jaruzelski's leadership. In return, Olszowski retained his seat on the Politburo.[24] The electoral victory strengthened Jaruzelski's position in the party. Working with Kania remained politically expedient because it guaranteed leadership continuity. Since Kania was generally considered a moderate, his stewardship mollified the rank-and-file reformers and would give Jaruzelski the time to set the martial-law operation in motion.

The elections brought Jaruzelski another important prerequisite of his future government. After the congress, he acquired a solid power base within the PUWP Central Committee by introducing into it additional high-level army officers. The newly elected Central Committee included: Gen. Cz. Kiszczak, chief of Military Police and Counterintelligence, who subsequently replaced M. Milewski as Poland's minister of internal affairs; Gen. F. Siwicki, chief of the general staff and Jaruzelski's closest adjutant; Gen. J. Urbanowicz, deputy minister of defense and one-time chief of the MPA; Gen. E. Molczyk, deputy defense minister in charge of training; Gen. M. Obiedziński, deputy defense minister and the quartermaster of the Polish army; Gen. K. Stec, chief of the Wrocław District Military Staff; and Aleksander Pajko, identified only as "officer of the Polish People's Army."[25] In addition, the new Central Committee included Z. Messner, an economist, and J. Czyrek, Poland's foreign minister, both of whom were close to Jaruzelski and remained in the government after the introduction of martial law in 1981. Both Czyrek and Messner would accompany Jaruzelski on his first visit to Moscow after martial law had been imposed, in March 1982.[26]

All personnel changes were made while keeping watch for any sign of Soviet disapproval, and during the congress Jaruzelski emphatically pledged his loyalty to Moscow. The general's address to the congress became his political manifesto:

> Most important, we will remain a trustworthy and trusting member of the alliance. Our alliance with the Soviet Union and our participation in the socialist, antiwar coalition of the WTO and our further contribution to the common strength of the joint armed forces of the alliance, have been and will remain the foundation of our defensive military doctrine. . . . We value the most Polish-Soviet comradeship-in-arms. . . . In today's difficult times, our armed forces have not been shaken up, have maintained their cohesion and discipline, and are always ready to defend the socialist motherland. The army is a great force; when need arises, it is ready to serve the nation also in peacetime. The party has trusted the army and has appreciated the army's attitude [to the crisis].[27]

In his speech, Jaruzelski also warned the opposition that there were clear limits to the government's willingness to tolerate unrest. Should Solidarity ever go beyond those limits, Jaruzelski announced, the "authorities would be forced to carry out their constitutional duties with determination, in order to prevent a national catastrophe."[28] As was the case during the Sixth Plenum, Jaruzelski's declaration was seconded by his MPA chief. Baryła announced once again the army's unyielding opposition to the trade union's activities. Declaring that the army was "ready to defend socialism the same way it would defend the nation's independence," he pointed out that the opposition's objective was to break the Polish-Soviet alliance. Baryła stated:

> We have indicated on numerous occasions that we will never accept any action that endangers our *raison d'état*, the foundations of our socialist political system, and the hard-won right to national sovereignty. From this very rostrum I wish to stress once more that no one can expect indulgence from us when he agitates against our system, against the party, against our alliances, in particular against our alliance with the Soviet Union and our mutual comradeship-in-arms. For us, the task of strengthening this alliance is a soldierly duty.[29]

Another victory for Jaruzelski, and a sign of his considerable political skill, was his ability to ascribe past problems to causes other than inherent weaknesses of the party structure. The "mistakes" had been committed by the former leaders who had betrayed the "socialist ideal." Gierek's ouster from the party and an announcement of several pending investigations of Poland's corrupt apparatchiks were the extent of the Politburo's concession to the reformers' demands; two years later, during "normalization" after the declaration of martial law, the investigation of Gierek would be quietly dropped.

The introduction of the secret ballot was the only meaningful procedural change brought about by the Ninth Congress, but even this concession was watered down. Although Kania ran against Barcikowski and was elected through direct vote cast by all delegates, the Politburo was then constituted in the traditional fashion from among the Central Committee members. Furthermore, in keeping with established party practice, special working groups set up to study various aspects of Poland's renewal worked in closed sessions, and their recommendations emphasized the need for "implementing fully the existing statutes," rather than redrafting them."[30]

The congress was different from the previous national party gatherings in that it allowed the participants to express their often conflicting views on Poland's past and future. With reference to the former, the rank and file turned in a sweeping vote of nonconfidence in the party leadership. Only three Politburo members and two Central Committee secretaries were re-elected.[31] The government fared just as poorly; from among the ministers, only five (counting Jaruzelski) were elected to the Central Committee.[32] In a surprising development, 40 of the newly elected 270 Central Committee members were also members of Solidarity, including one Zofia Grzyb, who was both a Solidarity member and a full member of the Politburo.[33] Harsh criticism of Kania was also launched from the party's conservative wing; hard-line full

Politburo Member Albin Siwak blamed Kania for tolerating "disrespect for law and order," but that was the extent of the challenge.[34]

The Ninth Extraordinary PUWP Congress was a critical juncture on Jaruzelski's road to power. By re-electing Kania and Jaruzelski, the delegates rejected the hard-line apparatchiks of the Grabski/Olszowski brand. Although Olszowski remained in the Politburo, he was no longer accounted a possible future party leader.[35] The atmosphere that prevailed during the meetings, including militancy on the part of some newly elected Central Committee members, and the insistence by the rank and file that the party should become more open to criticism from below, were a clear indication that a reintroduction of ideological orthodoxy by traditional means had few chances of success. The "Olszowski/Grabski option," that is, the return to normality in Poland through hard-line policies, enjoyed little support in the party. This did not mean, however, that the PUWP resigned itself to seeking an accommodation with Solidarity; on this score the congress was billed as the "turning point on the road to the reconstruction of the party's power."[36]

The militancy of the apparatchiks aside, the Ninth Congress demonstrated that the PUWP was neither capable of the consensus necessary for a lasting accommodation with the union, nor strong and determined enough to fight the opposition. On the positive side, as far as Jaruzelski was concerned, the congress showed the Soviets that the Polish government was able to block party reformers and preserve the basic Leninist structure of the organization. Despite the stormy debates on the congress floor, ultimately all the candidates elected to the Politburo and the Central Committee were nominated by Kania. Jaruzelski spoke harshly against the opposition and warned that counterrevolution would not be tolerated. In the months immediately ahead, he would demonstrate that his government was ready to take the offensive in dealing with the opposition. The Ninth Extraordinary Congress preserved the basic party structure and retained the existing hierarchy of power. The shell of the martial-law government remained intact.

After the congress, Kania's and Jaruzelski's roads parted. Kania's insistence on seeking a political solution to the conflict with Solidarity at all costs became stronger after his re-election by popular vote to the first-secretaryship; on the other hand, Jaruzelski had all but given up on the negotiations and was mainly concerned with building his own coalition inside the Politburo, with an eye to replacing Kania as party leader. The first casualty of Jaruzelski's energetic cleanup of the government after the congress was Milewski. Although Milewski retained his post on the Central Committee, on August 1 he was replaced as minister of the interior by Gen. Czesław Kiszczak, one of Jaruzelski's trusted adjutants.

Government on the Offensive

The outcome of the Ninth PUWP Congress left the Soviets with three options: (1) supporting Kania in the hope that he would deal with the crisis in a manner similar to Gierek's solution to the 1970 upheaval, that is, granting temporary concessions to the union to gain time, and pursuing later the policy of co-optation and eventual destruction of the worker's movement;[37] (2) supporting Jaruzelski and his plan of using the Polish army to crush the opposition; and (3) ordering Warsaw Pact military action. Had a political solution been possible, it would have undoubtedly been the Soviets' preferred choice.[38] Regardless of how promising Jaruzelski's plan might have been, it was an untried and precedent-setting solution that carried with it far more risks than did a political solution. However, it became clear that Solidarity would not be destroyed by bureaucratic maneuvering, and Kania's visit to Brezhnev's Crimean retreat on August 14 was greeted with a luke-warm TASS communiqué that only asserted that "the Soviet Union stood solidly behind Poland and all those forces that would fight for socialism in Poland." Brezhnev's stick was complemented by a carrot; Moscow announced that it would extend additional economic aid to Poland and defer the country's debt payments for five years.[39] The Soviets would help economically, but they also wanted to see results.

Jaruzelski's work after the congress focused on planning for the introduction of martial law. During the three months between the party meeting and his appointment as first secretary, the general built an infrastructure of trusted associates within the government. On the opening day of the July 30–August 1 session of the Sejm, Jaruzelski pushed through Milewski's resignation from the post of interior minister and replaced him with Gen. Czesław Kiszczak. In order to justify Milewski's removal, Jaruzelski used the excuse that the change was simply routine because Milewski's Politburo and Central Committee's functions conflicted with his government job. Such lofty bureaucratic principles notwithstanding, three months later Jaruzelski would himself assume the position of first secretary in addition to his premiership and his post of defense minister, thus demonstrating that, in reality, Milewski had simply been fired. Another boost for Jaruzelski's power base in the government was the appointment of General Hupałowski as minister of administration, local economy, and environment in place of Józef Kempa, an old-time Gierek apparatchik; this change was also approved by the July–August session of the Sejm.[40] By the end of August, Jaruzelski's government included four army officers of the rank of general, of whom two were in key positions: Kiszczak as minister of the interior, and Jaruzelski as premier and minister of defense.

Personnel changes inside the government were followed by a new "get tough" policy with regard to the opposition. This time repression did not fall short of confronting Solidarity directly. During the meeting of the Presidium of the Government before the Second Central Committee Plenum of August 11–12, Jaruzelski launched his first strong public attack against the "Solidarity extremists," who were behind the street demonstrations in Warsaw. Referring to the demands made by their participants for freeing political prisoners, the general denounced the demonstration as illegal and asserted that the government would move in to stop such actions in the future.[41] The Second Plenum supported Jaruzelski's views. The communiqué released after the session denounced the "extremists" and called upon all party members in Solidarity to resist calls for public demonstrations. The governmental press urged the union to accept the regime's solution to the crisis, including the limitations of the union's power and its subordination to the PUWP.

Increasingly excluded, Kania tried to regain control of the situation. In keeping with the Ninth Congress's call for the removal of compromised functionaries, Kania launched a campaign to overhaul the regional party apparat. The purge resulted in the replacement of almost half of all voivodship party first secretaries.[42] If Kania appeared preoccupied with winning back the trust of the rank and file, his colleagues clearly had other concerns. During the Second Plenum, Kania was shown how increasingly out of touch with the Politburo's goals his moderate course had become. During the discussion some 30 speakers, led by Barcikowski, took the stand to restate Jaruzelski's charges against the "Solidarity extremists" and demand, as hard-liner Siwak put it, an "end to anarchy and disorder." Overwhelmed, Kania joined in with his comrades' call for "law and order," but did not follow up his declaration with action.

Preparations for declaring martial law proceeded at full speed, and at the end of the summer of 1981 the regime was not even camouflaging very much its preparations for a showdown, or its contacts with the Soviet staff, at times going so far as to make official announcements of Kulikov's alleged "visits." For example, on August 9, 1981, the government released a communiqué about Kulikov's visit to Warsaw. Next, on August 31, there followed a news release reporting the arrival of the chief of the Main Political Administration of the Soviet Army and Navy, Gen. A. Yepishev. During the ZAPAD-81 maneuvers of September 4–12, conducted in the Byelorussian and Baltic regions, Jaruzelski traveled to meet with the Soviet staff supervising the war games, ostensibly in his capacity as an official Polish observer.[43]

Kania was finally confronted by Jaruzelski on September 13, during a special meeting of the National Defense Committee (Komitet Obrony Kraju; KOK). In what might have been a last-ditch effort to shift the responsibility for the declaration of martial law from the army to the civilian party apparat, Jaruzelski and his advisors, including Kiszczak, Hupałowski, and Siwicki, pressured Kania to initiate the operation. The meeting was meticulously prepared and attended by key officers from the general staff and the security apparat. Three days prior to the meeting of the KOK, on September 10, the general staff consulted with the Ministry of Internal Affairs to agree on the joint report that would be presented to the first secretary, as well as the line of argument to be used to force Kania's hand. Kania once again held firm, and insisted during the meeting that, if given a chance, a political solution could still be achieved.[44]

Kania's refusal to accept the responsibility for the imposition of martial law effectively excluded him from the planning of the operation and marked the beginning of his rapid political decline. Determined to push ahead with the martial-law operation despite the first secretary's objections, Jaruzelski, shortly after the meeting of the KOK, ordered on his own the Defense Ministry to restructure itself in accordance with the operational requirements of war planning. Under the new directive, the so-called Operations Directorate of the General Staff was set up; it would constitute the core of the new administration after the imposition of martial law.[45] By mid-September, as the army began to move to center stage to confront Solidarity, the apparatchiks' ability to govern finally crumbled.

On September 22, following the first session of the Solidarity National Congress and the threatening letter from the Kremlin to Kania, charging that the Polish communists were tolerating counterrevolution, Jaruzelski called on the Warsaw Pact chief of the general staff, Gen. A. Gribkov. Also in September, Adm. L. Janczyszyn, commander in chief of the Polish navy and a close associate of Jaruzelski, conferred with Rear Adm. I. F. Alikov, a member of the USSR Defense Council.[46] In addition to maintaining its liaison with Kulikov's staff of 47 permanent "observers" stationed in Legnica, the Jaruzelski group established continuous contact with the Soviet military attaché in Warsaw, Major Gen. Aleksandr Khomiyenko and his deputy, Col. Aleksandr Tishchenko, both of whom had been assigned to supervise the Polish army.[47] In the flurry of activity preceding the declaration of martial law, Jaruzelski was frequently visited by Kulikov's adjutant, Gen. Afanasiy Shcheglov, his deputy, Lt. Gen. Vladimir Sharygin, as well as another senior Soviet officer stationed in Poland, Gen. Grigoriy Bezsmertniy. As the deadline for the operation neared, daily consultations between Polish and Soviet army officers became virtually routine.[48]

Closing Off the Political Solution

The period of Kania's ascendancy after the Ninth Congress was short-lived, and his inability to control the events was exposed with glaring clarity by the first session of the Solidarity National Congress, which convened in Gdańsk between September 5 and 10. With one stroke, the union meeting destroyed Kania's hopes of using the formula of "workers' self-management" to re-establish at least a semblance of the government's former authority and to reassure the Soviets of his ability to govern Poland. In a resolution accepted almost unanimously by the Solidarity delegates, the government's bill for workers' self-management was rejected out of hand. The union demanded a national referendum on the issue.[49] A much more serious dent in Kania's prestige was caused by the "Message to the Peoples of Eastern Europe," a resolution passed unanimously by the delegates, which called for an independent workers' movement to be organized throughout the Soviet bloc.[50] Moscow and her East European satellites reacted to the "Message" with fury. Two days after the conclusion of the first session of the congress, the CPSU instructed its ambassador to Poland, Boris Aristov, to deliver to Kania a threatening message; the Soviet accusations were immediately published in the Polish press.

The angry Soviet outburst constituted an unequivocal indictment of Kania and his handling of the crisis. Pointing to the repeated attempts on their part to galvanize the Polish party leadership into action against Solidarity, the Kremlin accused the PUWP of breaking promises to stop the "anti-Soviet campaign in Poland." "On numerous occasions," wrote the Soviets,

> we have pointed out to the PUWP leadership and the Polish government that a wave of anti-Sovietism is rising in Poland. We talked about it during our meetings in Moscow in March, in Warsaw in April; with complete frankness we wrote about it in the letter from CC CPSU of June 5, and we talked about it also during our August meeting at the Crimea. . . . The Central Committee of the CPSU and the Soviet government believe that any further indulgence of anti-Sovietism in Poland will do tremendous harm to Polish-Soviet relations. . . . We expect that the party leadership and Poland's government will take immediate action to stop the vicious anti-Soviet campaign.[51]

The barrage of propaganda coming out of Moscow, Prague, and East Berlin accused the PUWP and the beleaguered Kania of tolerating counterrevolution in Poland. In a similar vein, the Polish army's *Żołnierz Wolności* denounced the "Message" in a fiery article entitled "Against Poland's *Raison d'État*."[52] Frightened, Kania's Politburo responded to Soviet accusations with an open declaration that, for the first time, contained an implied threat to use force against Solidarity. "We will defend socialism," read the statement, "the way one would defend Poland's national independence. For this defense the state will use all means required by the situation."[53]

Throughout the controversy over the first session of the Solidarity National Congress, Jaruzelski did little to call attention to himself, while expressing his unswerving dedication to the Kremlin. A few days prior to the opening of the Gdańsk meeting, during his speech to the newly commissioned officers at the Koszalin Military School, the general recapitulated his views on the situation in the country. Stressing the patriotic heritage of the Polish army, Jaruzelski argued that to preserve this tradition the army might be forced to act. In Jaruzelski's view, the army "had a civic duty and a moral obligation to say [to the leaders of Solidarity]: 'enough of this madness.'" He emphasized that, if need be, the army would face down the opposition to prevent it from destroying socialism in Poland. Then came a direct warning to Solidarity that the upcoming second session of the trade-union congress would be regarded as indicative of the union's intentions, and that if Solidarity chose "confrontation rather than cooperation, the consequences of such a decision would be grave."[54] Two weeks after Jaruzelski's Koszalin speech, Stanisław Dymek of *Żołnierz Polski* ran an editorial denouncing the first session of the Solidarity congress as a "show put on by the opposition"; the article blasted the "Message" as an unacceptable interference in the internal affairs of other WTO states.[55] Baryła's publicists were unanimous in their condemnation of the Gdańsk gathering. The army declared its firm commitment to defend communism in Poland.

In October, a new voice was injected into the chorus of the army propaganda condemning the union and demanding action against it. Apparently, after Milewski's departure the police shared with the military a remarkable unity of views on the situation in the country. Brig. Gen. Władysław Pożoga, deputy minister of internal affairs, presented the secret police's position on the crisis in his article in the October issue of *Wojsko Ludowe*. Pożoga's statement, written ostensibly to commemorate the approaching anniversary of the Polish armed forces, the police, and the security apparatus, emphasized in terms borrowed from Jaruzelski his agency's readiness to defend the system. Declaring that the police and the security forces were ready to fight for socialism in Poland, Pożoga accused the opposition of being responsible for the growing infiltration of the country by foreign agents. "We are faced today," wrote Pożoga, "with the fact of the openly coordinated activities of the imperialist spy centers and the domestic antisocialist forces."[56] In effect, in Pożoga's view, Solidarity activists were spies.[57]

At the time of Jaruzelski's address in Koszalin, the preparations for the introduction of martial law were already in motion. By the end of September, the Ministry of Defense had completed the changeover to the wartime command structure. Additional officers of the Ministry of the Interior were assigned to the Operational Command, and secure communication lines established. During October and November, the Ministry of the Interior and the Central Committee Propaganda Department drafted alternate strategies for propaganda campaigns to justify martial law, including the fabrication of evidence that Solidarity was manipulated by Western intelligence centers.

The final decision that the crackdown would begin on December 13 was taken on (or shortly after) October 31.[58]

The second session of the Solidarity National Congress, held between September 26 and October 7, lent urgency to the government's preparations for the crackdown. The increase of rank-and-file support for the union's more militant leaders, shown by the only 55 percent of the vote garnered by Wałęsa in his bid for chairmanship,[59] was a sign that the government's procrastination on the issue of workers' self-management had radicalized the union. It became clear that the compromise version of the self-management law, agreed to by Wałęsa and Deputy Premier M. Rakowski and passed by the Sejm, failed to meet the expectations of Solidarity's rank and file, and in fact was not what Kania had wanted either. In Kania's view, the proposed workers' self-management structure undercut the *nomenklatura* system and was far too independent to be used as a means for regaining control in the country. For most of Solidarity's members, though it did not go far enough in granting the workers a voice in managerial appointments.

In another new development during the second session of the Solidarity congress, the issue of Poland's excessive military spending was raised. For the first time in the history of communist Poland, the army's budget was singled out as the target of potential reductions. Even if the threat of curtailing the country's defense expenditures was remote, the very fact that the army's finances were being openly debated defied the traditional immunity of military affairs to any outside criticism. By raising the issue of military spending, Solidarity indicated that, if necessary, it would not hesitate to challenge the army. Solidarity's direct criticism of military budgets and its increasingly ambivalent attitude toward the Warsaw Pact probably helped increase cohesion within the Polish officer corps and provided the Soviets with additional assurance that Polish generals would act in unison to suppress the opposition.

In the meantime, Kania made his last desperate effort to regain authority. On October 4, the government announced sharp increases in the prices of tobacco and certain foodstuffs. Solidarity responded immediately with a series of wildcat strikes, and Kania capitulated; eleven days later the rollback of the raised prices was announced. The October crisis was probably caused by political maneuvering inside the Politburo, rather than by sheer bureaucratic incompetence. It is possible that the October 4 price hike was engineered by Jaruzelski to test Kania's resolve, raise tensions, and secure for himself the necessary justification to remove Kania from office.[60] The decision to raise prices without any consultation with the union, announced less than a month after the Solidarity congress had demanded consultation on running the country's economy, was too provocative to be merely an economic expedient. The drama in which the government was once again forced to retreat looked very much like a political ploy intended to discredit Kania in the eyes of his own Politburo.

Jaruzelski Takes Over the Party

The remnants of Kania's political influence faded and the weakness of his leadership was again exposed in the October confrontation with the union. Jaruzelski's position as the only man who could unite the party for the struggle with the labor union became unchallengeable. On October 14, *Życie Partii* ran an article entitled "Born of the Party's Ideals," written by one of Baryła's propagandists, Brig. Gen. Władysław Honkisz. He described the Polish army as a staunch defender of socialism and Polish soldiers as "soldiers of the revolution," and expressed the military's readiness to take matters into its own hands, even if this might appear rash to some party people. While conceding that the party had always been the ideological and political leader of the army, Honkisz asserted that, under the present circumstances, the military establishment was the only state institution untouched by ideological decay. "It is the proof of the effectiveness of our political indoctrination," wrote Honkisz, "that today, during the crisis, the soldiers maintain unity and discipline. Unquestionably, the army today is the dominant stabilizing element of the country's political life."[61]

Honkisz's assessment was quite accurate. Since the majority of the draftees on active duty had been called up before August 1980, and therefore had been shielded from the turmoil in the country, the likelihood of a rebellion against their commanding officers was small indeed. One of Jaruzelski's chief objectives while struggling for control of the party was to ensure that the army would remain free of Solidarity's ideals.

Preparations for the imposition of martial law, set in motion immediately after the KOK meeting on September 13, entered their final phase after Jaruzelski's formal assumption of the office of first secretary.[62] On October 17, *Żołnierz Wolności* announced that the Council of Ministers had decided to extend military service by two months. The decision was presented as a move needed to shore up the bankrupt economy. The decree kept in the ranks of the army those draftees who had never directly participated in the independent trade-union movement. In light of subsequent events, the end of the two-month extension coincided with the deadline for the imposition of martial law.

On October 18, Kania was voted out of the Politburo and announced his resignation. Considering the timing of Jaruzelski's order to extend the service time of his troops, it is likely that the Soviets had approved the decision to remove Kania a few days prior to the announcement.[63] With Kania's removal, Jaruzelski added the position of the PUWP first secretary to his premiership and to the portfolio of defense minister. In his acceptance speech to the Fourth Plenum of the PUWP Central Committee, Jaruzelski briefly sketched out the direction of his future action:

> First of all, I feel that the party is sending me to fulfill a new task, to work under extremely difficult conditions. I am aware that presently there is a strong expectation that the situation will change, that it will improve, that the party will go on the offensive and strengthen the socialist state.[64]

Concluding, Jaruzelski noted that although the government had never pushed for confrontation, there would be no more retreats. He declared that the time had come for the party to awaken and act.

Jaruzelski's speech to the Fourth Plenum was seconded by his minister of the interior, Gen. Czesław Kiszczak.[65] Pointing to the two sessions of the Solidarity congress as proof, Kiszczak argued that the union had abandoned the road of negotiated compromise, had become a de facto opposition party, and was preparing to seize power in Poland. Kiszczak asserted:

> Lawlessness has reached a new high in Poland, and it cannot be tolerated any longer. . . . The party can retreat no further. The motherland is in the gravest of dangers, and this situation requires that extraordinary measures be taken; it requires party, political, and other necessary action to lead the nation out of the sociopolitical and economic crisis. [This can be done] under the appropriate conditions of law and order.[66]

The Fourth Central Committee Plenum also marked the final recognition of Jaruzelski's leadership by the onetime principal contender for the position of party leader, Olszowski, who paid homage to the general in his keynote address. Thereafter, Olszowski would become one of the most active proponents of the policies of the new regime during the time of martial law. Olszowski's speech was made in recognition that a new center of political power was about to emerge in the PUWP.

On October 19, immediately after his appointment as first secretary, Jaruzelski convened a meeting of the Military Council of the Polish Ministry of Defense to discuss his short-term strategy.[67] It was during the meeting of October 19 that the final procedural decisions were made and key party leaders were informed of the martial-law deadline. In addition to Colonel Kukliński's testimony, this is confirmed by an apparent indiscretion committed by the Politburo's Albin Siwak, who during a visit with government-controlled trade-unionists in Krosno, in southern Poland, boasted that Jaruzelski and Kiszczak had set up a special six-man Committee of National Salvation that supervised the preparations by special army and police units to crush Solidarity. According to Siwak's remarks, the deadline for military action was in two months.[68]

In late October, the Ministry of Internal Affairs completed the final preparations for an extensive propaganda campaign that (as in March, before the events in Bydgoszcz) would blame Solidarity for Poland's economic and political crisis. Attacks on the union in governmental media intensified, preparing the way for ex post facto justification of the imposition of martial law. The central theme of the campaign was the claim that Solidarity had been "hijacked by extremists," an argument that subsequently would find its way into the government's official explanation of the December crackdown.[69]

Last Two Months Before the Crackdown

Once the decision to attack had been taken, Jaruzelski wasted no time preparing for a showdown with Solidarity. On October 23, the government announced that small army units had been ordered to move into the countryside to supervise food distribution; on October 27, *Żołnierz Wolności* reported the first results of the operation. Each group, consisting of four to five soldiers and a professional officer or warrant officer, was directed by a voivodship (regional) military staff and relied on the logistics of the military districts. According to Col. Jan Kwissa, one of the district chiefs of staff, only those soldiers who had been in the army for two years and whose service had been extended by the additional two months by Jaruzelski's decree were selected for the program.[70] Those seasoned draftees were ordered to "establish links" with local youth organizations; each group was also instructed to contact the local chapters of the veterans' organization (Związek Bojowników o Wolność i Demokrację; ZBoWiD) as well as the Clubs of Reserve Officers attached to the paramilitary League of National Defense (Liga Obrony Kraju). As a result, each small unit, while ostensibly supervising food distribution, was in a position to activate an elaborate intelligence gathering network, and thereby collect information on the situation in the countryside, possible sources of opposition to the planned military action, the leading opposition activists, and the degree of support enjoyed by the labor union in each district.[71]

Based on the information supplied by the paramilitary organizations, as well as the data collected on its own, each army detachment could move quickly to liquidate the emerging bottlenecks in the supply system. In this respect, the small units also served an important propaganda purpose; they showed the army as willing to help relieve the gravest supply problems and stamp out corruption. Last but not least, the small units gave the Poles a foretaste of the military as an administrator, and the projected image was one of order, efficiency, and equitable distribution of goods. What was not readily apparent then was that the small units were well positioned to gather information on virtually every local administrative organ and every local party cell; this information would prove invaluable to Jaruzelski during the first months of martial law.

The decision to dispatch the small army units into the countryside was accompanied by the government's repeated demands that strikes should cease immediately. Calls for discipline and steady work were issued with growing urgency during the last two months before the crackdown; these would later be used by the government as proof that action was taken only when all else had failed. The trade union's activity was being increasingly presented as a direct assault upon the Polish *raison d'état*. "The Abuse of the Right to Strike Equals Social Suicide" ran the headline in *Żołnierz Wolności* on October 28, after a one-hour nationwide warning strike staged by Solidarity.[72] The day following the strike, Jaruzelski convened the Fifth Plenum of the Central Committee, during which he lashed out at the strike organizers, accusing them of "tearing Poland apart."[73] The plenum unanimously accepted his recommendation of Gen. Florian Siwicki, chief of the general staff, for the position of alternate member of the Politburo.

November brought about an ever-greater heightening of tensions. *Wojsko Ludowe* ran a sharply worded editorial accusing Solidarity of breaking agreements with the government, of attempting to dictate the terms for national accord, and of forcing its will upon the Sejm and upon the entire nation. According to the journal, Solidarity was acting against Poland's most vital national interests and contrary to the fundamental class interests of the Polish worker. This time Baryła made no offer of compromise.[74]

Throughout the last two months before the imposition of martial law, the government actively engaged in consultations with the Soviets. In Budapest, on October 28, a meeting of the WTO Military Council took place that provided an opportunity for the Poles to brief their allies on the situation. Between November 3 and 4, an official Polish party delegation participated in a conference in Moscow on ideological and international questions, organized for selected Soviet-bloc Central Committee secretaries. In addition, close contacts between the Soviet and Polish military were maintained during the joint Polish-Soviet military maneuvers organized in the Silesian military district in early November. Again, on November 24, the government officially announced that the commander in chief of the WTO, Marshal Kulikov, and the WTO chief of staff, Gen. A. Gribkov, had arrived in Warsaw; in reality, they had remained stationed in Legnica throughout the crisis. While in Warsaw, Kulikov met again with Siwicki and Molczyk; Gen. Afanasiy Shcheglov, the liaison officer in Poland of the WTO Joint High Command, was also present. During those sessions, held just weeks before the crackdown, last minute technical problems were resolved.

By late November, both Jaruzelski and the Soviets were committed to the December deadline. Thanks to the intelligence-gathering operations of the small army units, Jaruzelski and Siwicki were able to present to their Soviet visitors an assessment of the mood in the countryside and to evaluate the likelihood of local resistance there. Just prior to the Kulikov-Gribkov visit, on November 19, Jaruzelski announced that the small army units would be withdrawn from the countryside. The urban population was the next target of the army reconnaissance operation; on November 23, small army detachments were sent out to towns and cities.

As a final prelude to martial law, the relentless anti-Solidarity propaganda campaign, launched in October, was stepped up. November was marked by the constant flow of articles in the military publications reaffirming Poland's commitment to the Warsaw Pact alliance. Each November issue of *Żołnierz Polski* carried an editorial stressing the Polish army's dedication to the maintenance of the bloc's defenses. The issue of November 1 brought S. Dymek's article "*Raison dÉtat*—Polish Arguments," which emphasized the country's commitment to the WTO and accused Solidarity of attempting to turn Poland into a neutral state.[75] On November 8, Colonel Ignaczak of the weekly's editorial board attacked the growing anti-Sovietism in Poland and remarked that, if matters were to come to a head, "Poland had reliable and trustworthy friends who would aid her whenever the need might arise."[76] On November 22, Jan Budziński declared in another article that the state would oppose with full force any attacks on the Polish-Soviet alliance.[77] The insistence with which the military accused the union of attempting to take Poland out of the Warsaw Pact was intended to impress on Polish society that if things did not improve quickly, a Soviet invasion might again become inevitable. In fact, after the crackdown, the argument that martial law was a "lesser evil" would become the official explanation of the military's action.[78] By questioning the size of military budgets during the Solidarity congress, the union lent some credence to the general's statements that the union threatened the nation's security commitments, even though Solidarity's political agenda never included Poland's withdrawal from the pact.

The "party offensive" called for by the military since the very first day of Solidarity's existence was finally beginning to materialize. About a week after Kulikov's return to Legnica, the government supplemented words with a sudden display of force. On December 2, the police landed by helicopter on the roof of the Warsaw Fire Fighters' Academy and broke up a week-long occupational strike by the cadets. The police action in Warsaw threw the union into a deeply divisive debate over the measures to be taken in response to this use of force by the government, the first since the Bydgoszcz crisis. Tensions mounted rapidly, and Jaruzelski made no effort to relax them. On the contrary, on December 7 Radio Warsaw broadcast an edited tape recording of a closed meeting of Solidarity's leadership during which Wałęsa predicted an all-out confrontation with the government in the near future, and during which other leaders seemed to encourage the overthrow of the communist government in Poland.

In response to the broadcast, which the union quite rightly viewed as a provocation, Solidarity's national commission convened in Gdańsk on December 11 and 12. After a stormy debate, the commission endorsed the plan for a general strike on December 17, called for a referendum on the present political system, and demanded free parliamentary elections. Before the regional Solidarity organizations had time to respond, on the night of December 12–13, General Jaruzelski deployed the army and the security forces throughout the country and readied himself for the morning's announcement that Poland had been placed under martial law.

Jaruzelski's Martial Law

7

The Crackdown

At 6:00 A.M. on December 13, 1981, General Jaruzelski announced that a "state of war" had been declared to exist in Poland, and that the declaration was binding as of midnight of December 12. In his address to the nation he quoted article 33, paragraph 2, of the Polish constitution as legal justification of his decision. Announcing the imposition of martial law, Jaruzelski was careful to present his move as a necessary, albeit painful, solution to the crisis. The address attempted to balance appeals to Polish patriotism with strong invocations of the theme of "proletarian internationalism."

As set forth in the martial-law plan, the military wanted to convince their fellow countrypeople that the Polish soldier-patriot had been compelled to act to save the nation from fratricidal conflict; Jaruzelski pointedly ended his address to the nation by declaiming, "Not yet lost is Poland as long as we live," the opening lines of the national anthem and an expression of patriotic defiance throughout the country's history. On the other hand, with an eye on the Soviets and other East European states, the general emphasized that the military's action was being conducted in the name and under the auspices of the PUWP. "Despite some mistakes that were committed," said Jaruzelski in his address to the nation, "and despite the bitter losses that we have suffered, the party has remained an active and creative force in the process of historical change."[1] These references to the party and communism notwithstanding, the thrust of the speech was to appeal to the Poles' nationalism rather than to the precepts of Marxism-Leninism: Jaruzelski called upon his countrymen to "prove themselves worthy of Poland." In the months to come, until it became clear that resistance to martial law had been broken, appeals to patriotism would be a major theme of the military's campaign to rebuild the government's authority.

In his address announcing the imposition of martial law, Jaruzelski introduced sweeping police measures, including the suspension of all existing unions and organizations, the disconnection of telephone and telex communications, prohibition of all but religious gatherings, restrictions on travel, and the imposition of a curfew. The operation of government troops and the police deployed against Solidarity, as well as the functioning of government administration would be centrally supervised by the National Defense Committee (KOK), which relied on a network of regional and local defense committees set up by military officers and principal local administrators. In addition, the martial-law decree established the so-called Military Council of National Salvation (Wojskowa Rada Ocalenia Narodowego; WRON), which functioned as a principal decisionmaking body for the duration of the state of war. Among its twenty members, there were several highly trusted associates of Jaruzelski— the general's "shadow cabinet." The first seven listed in *Trybuna Ludu* on December 14 were the most influential military men in the country: Generals Florian Siwicki, Czesław Kiszczak, Tadeusz Hupałowski, Czesław Piotrowski, Józef Baryła, and Eugeniusz Molczyk, and Adm. Ludwik Janczyszyn.[2] With the exception of Molczyk, whom Jaruzelski distrusted, and who was eventually retired, this group would remain Jaruzelski's principal power base throughout the first year of martial law, until the general had completed the purge of the PUWP apparat and brought to the fore apparatchiks personally loyal to him. In the course of the purge, all but a few of the appointees chosen by the rank and file during the drive for party democracy at the Ninth Extraordinary Congress would be removed.

Tactics Employed Against the Strikers

Jaruzelski's immediate objective was to destroy Solidarity. Judging from the speed and precision with which the military used force and intimidation to break the union's will to resist, it became clear to the Poles that the action had been planned months in advance, despite the government's protestations that the state of war was a hastily improvised measure.[3] A barrage of official decrees barring all gatherings, except for church attendance, imposing a curfew, and announcing harsh penalties for acts of resistance to martial law pointed to a carefully thought-out plan. Since Solidarity's strength came from the coordinated collective action of its regional chapters, Jaruzelski moved to isolate the areas of potential resistance from one another. The army's intelligence and communications network proved invaluable for this task; after commercial telex and telephone service had been cut, only the military knew the true state of affairs. All of Solidarity's communication lines were severed; its offices taken over by the police; and its leaders arrested. Factories were militarized and placed under the direct control of military commissars; civil rights were suspended, and all but two official newspapers, the party's *Trybuna Ludu* and the army's *Żołnierz Wolności*, were closed down. Special plenipotentiary military commissars (*Pełnomocnicy-Komisarze Wojskowi*) were dispatched to every administrative unit in the country, at both the regional and local levels.[4] To project an image of impartiality, the military announced that Gierek and Jaroszewicz had been taken into custody, pending an investigation of their mismanagement of Poland's economy. Incessant appeals were made to the Poles' patriotism.[5]

As planned during the martial-law war game, troops were deployed in cities to intimidate the public by demonstrating the army's overwhelming presence. WRON dealt with desperate acts of resistance in a systematic and uniform manner. When, on December 14, strikes broke out in Łódź, Cracow, Warsaw, Wrocław, and Gdynia-Gdańsk, as well as in several Silesian coal mines, the ZOMO security forces and army units were immediately brought in to suppress them. In each case, the pacification methods were virtually the same: the army surrounded the striking factory and, if necessary, used tanks to smash the gates. Next the ZOMO launched a frontal assault and quickly routed the workers. During the initial weeks of martial law, this pattern was repeated with only minor modifications. The key to Jaruzelski's success was the regime's monopoly of information on the situation in Poland and the use of the secure lines of the army's communications network. Within a month it became apparent that Solidarity had been beaten.

Rebuilding the Party: The Purge

Police measures employed against the strikes were only one, albeit essential, part of Jaruzelski's plan. After the immediate objective of destroying Solidarity's ability to mobilize the nation to resist had been attained, a greater and much more complex task faced the new regime. Jaruzelski had to accommodate the party and government apparat to the new realities of military rule.

What mattered at least as much as the success in suppressing the union was the shape of the basic political institutions in the country and the distribution of power that would emerge from the turbulence of martial law. Here the political agenda of the military included two major goals: first in order of priority, to reinvigorate the PUWP, a key Soviet demand,[6] and hence to insure that the Jaruzelski group would be able to hold on to power after the emergency measures had been lifted; second, to resuscitate, or at least stabilize, Poland's economy to prevent another eruption of labor unrest, and thus to neutralize the opposition.

The first task, rebuilding the PUWP, was essential if Jaruzelski was to win Soviet acquiescence in the military's long-term political influence in Poland. By the same token, although the revival of the country's economy did play a part in the initial policies of the Jaruzelski regime, securing continuing Soviet approval of his government by far outweighed the imperatives of economic reconstruction. This is borne out by the absence of significant economic legislation following the crackdown, which can be only partially explained by the overall chaos in the Polish economy. The Law Against Parasitism, passed by the Sejm on October 25, 1982, which made it illegal for able-bodied men to avoid employment, could hardly be considered more than another police measure.[7]

At least during the first twelve months of martial law, the military was more concerned about consolidating its political power than about restructuring the economy. For any effective economic reform in Poland would require some degree of decentralization of the cumbersome management structure. In turn, such an assault on the existing administrative apparatus would further aggravate the chaos within the party, deepen the crisis, and make Jaruzelski appear in Soviet eyes as politically ineffective as his predecessor. Therefore, instead of a genuine economic reform, Jaruzelski opted for a reshuffling of the *nomenklatura*. For WRON to remain in power, the military had to prove to the Soviets that, in addition to being reliable policemen in an emergency, they could reclaim the political ground lost by the PUWP during the sixteen months of Solidarity's activity.

From the very beginning, Jaruzelski made it abundantly clear that the emergence of the military communist elite in Poland as the new power center did not spell out the demise of the PUWP. If it were to last, the new regime had to be based on the power of the party, as the Soviets would accept the military's continuing ascendancy only with the party as the guarantor of Moscow's interests in Poland. Soviet insistence on the necessity of resurrecting the PUWP, expressed repeatedly throughout the Solidarity period, was a clear indication that the only way to power in Poland acceptable to Moscow led through the party. Consequently, inasmuch as the crackdown against Solidarity was an opportunity for the military to rise to political prominence, WRON would remain in charge only on the condition of winning complete control of the PUWP on terms acceptable to the Soviets; senior officers could not transgress the boundaries of political behavior prescribed for senior party apparatchiks in their dealings with the CPSU.

It may seem on the surface that the task of controlling the party required the least ingenuity and effort on Jaruzelski's part. The PUWP leadership was weak and exhausted by the strenuous sixteen months of incessant challenge from Solidarity, and Jaruzelski had begun introducing his cronies into the Politburo several months before the crackdown. The factional squabbles inside the Politburo, leading first to the destruction of the Grabski/Olszowski coalition in March, 1981, and later to the eclipse of the Kania leadership, had further undermined the PUWP's cohesion.[8] During the sixteen months of turmoil in Poland, the party rank and file had become demoralized by the revelations of corruption at the highest level and by the repeated reshuffling of the apparat, not to mention the strength of the independent union movement.

The turmoil inside the PUWP was mainly a result of the crisis of confidence in the Politburo, openly expressed by the rank and file. Shaken by the fall of the Gierek regime and by Kania's constant vacillations, the party was ready to welcome a strong leader who would restore its prestige and influence. The corruption of high officials figured prominently in the list of complaints made repeatedly by the rank and file during the crisis of 1980–1981. Jaruzelski promised both to weed out corrupt officials and to re-establish a strong sense of leadership. By restoring the rank and file's self-confidence, Jaruzelski hoped to build a power base at the local and regional level, which would in turn strengthen his control over the Central Committee. He insisted that Central Committee officials become directly involved in the work of the Basic Party Cells (Podstawowa Organizacja Partyjna; POP), the smallest grass-roots party organization in every factory, school, and collective farm, and that they become directly accountable to the rank and file.[9]

The removal of party officials reluctant to support Jaruzelski was done the "old-fashioned way" and did not require any special planning on the general's part. In fact, the ongoing purge of the party, initiated during the conflict with Solidarity ostensibly to force out unreliable and corrupt officials, needed only to be redirected to serve Jaruzelski's purpose. Three days after the imposition of martial law, on December 16, WRON reaffirmed the regime's commitment to continue the intraparty reform and purge. "It is not the Council's purpose," read WRON's official statement, "to return to the conditions that existed prior to August 1980. . . Compromised, corrupt, indolent people, as well as those who do not understand the new [political] situation will have no right to return to the country's political life."[10] The purge of the party was complemented by a thorough overhauling of the entire state administration. Also on December 16, WRON ordered the government to initiate an extensive "verification" of its officials and functionaries. Based on the intelligence gathered by the small army units, Jaruzelski ordered a sweeping purge of regional and local administrations.

The military government was well prepared to move quickly against the entrenched *nomenklatura* because of its direct control of the elaborate security and military intelligence network in the country. The decision of December 16 to dismiss a number of local bureaucrats revealed that the officers deployed in the countryside prior to martial law, ostensibly to supervise the distribution of goods, had gathered the information needed by WRON to purge quickly the entire local party and government bureaucracy.[11] Judging from the swiftness of the purge, the military must have processed the information and determined who would be removed long before December 13. Although the small units spent less time in cities than in villages, the existence of a better state-security network in urban areas, and the higher visibility of town and city party officials, compensated for the brevity of the reconnaissance. Furthermore, as a rule the Politburo had been much more familiar with party secretaries at the city and voivodship level simply because of the former's greater involvement in the work of the Central Committee.

In part, the purge of the local party apparatus continued the review process initiated under Kania's stewardship. The pressure from the conflict with Solidarity allowed the party to remove quickly those local officials who were most directly associated with the Gierek regime; as a result, very early in the crisis, the party was purged of the apparatchiks detested most by Polish society. The vacated positions were then filled by appointees selected by Jaruzelski and Kania. Kania's weakness and the defeat of the Grabski/Olszowski faction meant that although Jaruzelski was not yet the PUWP's first secretary, he had a decisive voice in the making of those appointments. As pointed out by Ryszard Łukasiewicz, deputy director of the Central Committee's Organizational Department, the political campaign leading to the Ninth Extraordinary PUWP Congress was an opportunity to purge the local and regional party apparat. The purge was conducted in 80 percent of all voivodship (regional) party committees and over 65 percent of city, town, county, and factory party organizations. By the time the military took over, about 50 percent of the first secretaries of the Basic Party Cells were new apparatchiks appointed on the eve of the Ninth Congress.[12]

Jaruzelski's purge was directed against the apparatchiks from the Gierek period who had survived the earlier purge by Kania, and against some of Kania's appointees, whom the general considered too weak or too prounion. Immediately after the crackdown of December 13, 349 secretaries of local and city organizations were dismissed, in addition to 307 secretaries at the factory level and 2,091 secretaries of the POPs. Over 1,800 members of the voivodship, town, and village committees were recalled, and all party control commissions were thoroughly purged. The Central Committee's apparat itself had about 250 of its professional staffers replaced.[13]

The most significant aspect of the purge ordered by Jaruzelski was the replacement of over 53 percent of the professional party cadres; out of the eleven thousand of the party's professional staff, six thousand were summarily dismissed. According to official government statistics, following the imposition of martial law over 440 administrators from the top administrative apparat were replaced; they included several acting deputy premiers, voivodship governors, editors in chief of several national journals, and television and radio producers. The entire local state apparat was purged, which resulted in the firing of over 200 mayors and local village administrators, plus over 650 general managers of leading factories and industrial enterprises.[14] However, this radical housecleaning backfired; because of the lack of qualified replacements, several regional and local party organizations were left without the badly needed professional apparat. Two years later, the organizational weakness induced by the purge would prove damaging to the implementation of Jaruzelski's economic program.

Rebuilding the Party: Nationalism and Ideology

The Jaruzelski regime acted on the assumption that if it was to remain in power, it had to resuscitate the party. The PUWP could not hope to regain credibility by bringing about a dramatic improvement of the country's economic situation; Poland's economy would not sustain another Gierek-style investment boom, while sources of foreign credit had all but dried up. The country was effectively bankrupt, and Western bankers were not eager to pour good money after bad. Only if Poland undertook fundamental economic reforms, might it again receive investments or loans from Western sources. Thrown upon his own resources, Jaruzelski opted instead for an ideological campaign to "whip the party into shape" by enforcing discipline and restoring the rank and file's confidence in the leadership.

The campaign was begun by *Wojsko Ludowe* in January 1982, and was picked up by all major newspapers and magazines. Col. Józef Borgosz, a prominent Marxist-Leninist theoretician, outlined the new strategy in an essay, "Against Total Negation," which blended communism and Polish nationalism.[15] In his quest to reconcile communism with Poland's national tradition, Borgosz saw no contradiction between the nation's aspirations to independence and communist doctrine. Instead, Borgosz blamed the errors of judgment of the past party leadership for the crisis of confidence in Marxism's relevance to Poland's historical experience and in its ability to solve the nation's problems.

The rather ponderous and often vacuous essay made for boring reading; yet it contained an important message. The military insisted (as Borgosz argued) that since there had never been any contradiction between Poland's historical experience and communist dogma, the 1980–1981 crisis was simply an accident and an aberration brought about by Gierek's inept leadership. Whether or not the military privately believed this assertion is another matter; in public, Jaruzelski found it politically expedient to view the crisis as the product of mistakes committed by individuals, rather than an organic, systemic ill of Polish communism. This interpretation of Poland's problems coincided with the Soviet view that Solidarity had been brought about by Gierek's "voluntarism."[16] Having expressed a "unity of views" with Moscow on the root causes of the crisis, the military would then insist that the PUWP could overcome its weakness by strengthening party discipline and purging its apparat of Gierek's appointees. Since, as Borgosz ponderously explained, the nation's tradition and communism were naturally symbiotic, the workers' growing distrust of the party was all Gierek's fault. He wrote:

> Those mistakes and the straying from the ideological principles on the part of the former [Gierek] leadership played into the hands of those who view the PUWP as "alien" or "antinational"; past errors led to serious crises, including the most severe among them, the August crisis. . . . Those mistakes were the source of the slander that the PUWP was alien or antination. They also led to a deep social disappointment vis-à-vis the party, which played directly into the hands of all kinds of adversaries of socialism in Poland.[17]

On the surface, the argument seemed to be yet another reiteration of the familiar accusations; upon careful reading, though, it suggested that Jaruzelski would not hesitate to appeal to nationalism to reinvigorate the party and legitimize his government. In their stress on the "nonantagonistic relations between Marxism-Leninism and Polish history," Baryła's publicists implied that where communist ideology was discredited, the nation's patriotic tradition would suffice to earn the government social acceptance and respect. In turn, this would lay the foundations for national reconciliation. In his address during the session of WRON on March 11, 1982, the general outlined his "policy of inclusion," one that embraced all Poles and was based on national solidarity rather than party affiliation:

> The nation's *raison d'état* is only one. Those who respect the constitution, respect our alliances, and the party's leading role in society are with us, can be with us. . . . There are no societies in the world where all agree on everything. What we want now is to define the broadest possible platform for reconciliation with the majority of society. . . . This platform already exists: it consists of the highest interests of our socialist state and the good of the nation.[18]

To draw upon nationalism, however, meant coming to terms with Marxist-Leninist theory. In Jaruzelski's case, this traditional dilemma facing all communist reformers was turned upside down. The question was not to what degree national autonomy would be compatible with "proletarian internationalism," as it had been in the case of Dubček in the Czechoslovakia of 1968. For Jaruzelski, the problem was how to justify the military's claim to represent Poland's genuine national aspirations, and simultaneously to reassert the PUWP's control over the nation; the two goals were ultimately irreconcilable. As his record showed, in the final analysis the general came out on the side of communism rather than that of national self-determination for his people. However, since communism in Poland was bankrupt in 1981–1982, Jaruzelski chose to emphasize nationalism out of the simple realization that communist ideology had failed to take root in his homeland, and that the party was badly shaken by the sixteen-month-long de facto duality of power in Poland.

Although reliance on patriotic images to rally the population around the regime was for the most part a propaganda ploy, it nevertheless became a tough balancing act. If taken to its logical conclusion, Jaruzelski's call for national unity as the unity of the "entire Polish nation"[19] meant repudiating communism. Hence, once the immediate national emergency had passed, in 1983, the pendulum of Baryła's propaganda would again swing back toward "proletarian internationalism." The first year of martial law would demonstrate that, all else aside, a marriage between communist ideology and Polish nationalism was impossible precisely because of the oft-repeated Polish *raison d'état*. There were no indications that the Soviets at any time seriously entertained the idea of permitting Jaruzelski to build "national communism" in Poland. If Jaruzelski's party wanted to appeal to the nationalism of the Poles to gain legitimacy, it was even more pressed to reassure Brezhnev that despite its nationalist trappings, it had remained an elite communist organization. This consideration was the ultimate reason for Jaruzelski's obvious half-heartedness in pushing the "nationalist line" and his renewed emphasis on the importance of ideology characteristic of his martial-law speeches. When *Życie Partii*, a biweekly of the PUWP Central Committee, resumed publication in March 1982, it did so with the express purpose of leading the campaign to purge the party and restore ideological orthodoxy. According to the journal's editorial "declaration of principles," this task could be accomplished only in one way:

> Among the urgent tasks facing us today, the most urgent one is the strengthening of the ideological and organizational unity of the PUWP, its consolidation based on a firm return to Leninist principles in party life.[20]

Another half-hearted attempt to reconcile Polish nationalism with the precepts of communism was made by the already mentioned Brig. Gen. Norbert Michta. Michta's contribution was restricted to tinkering with slogans; he suggested that the Ninth Congress of the PUWP had forged a new alliance among Polish workers, peasants, and soldiers that was embodied in the current membership of the Central Committee.[21] However, as there were plenty of signs that things were returning to the old familiar pattern of party control, no one, other than the authors of these intricate theories, took such reasoning seriously.

The Seventh Plenum that took place in March 1982 officially sanctioned the military's move against Solidarity and called for the reconstruction of the party along the lines of ideological "renewal." The army would play a prominent role in the transformation of the party, as stated in the declaration adopted by the plenum:

> The Central Committee fully supports the decisions of the Military Council of National Salvation [WRON]. The Central Committee accepts the decisions of the Politburo associated with the imposition of martial law. . . . The Polish People's Army has done its duty, has prevented a national catastrophe; the Central Committee thanks the soldiers for their ideological commitment, their discipline, and their high level of civic consciousness. The Central Committee also thanks the police and the security service for faithfully doing their job.[22]

The Seventh Plenum launched a nationwide internal party debate over the immediate goals of the PUWP and the direction of the party's long-term evolution. An "Ideological Declaration of the PUWP Central Committee's Program" was presented in a draft form and later disseminated to party cells throughout the country. Entitled "What Are We Fighting For, Where Are We Heading?" the declaration demanded, without mincing words, that the PUWP repay the debt it had incurred to the army in 1981:

> The army guards Poland's sovereignty and the inviolability of her frontiers. It is the party's patriotic duty to strengthen and support the army in every way.[23]

During the Seventh Plenum, Jaruzelski also called emphatically for a change in the style of party work that would recreate the spirit of activism lost in the complacency of the Gierek era:

> It is imperative that a new style of party work be found. When we say that the party is the same but different, it can't be just another slogan. It must mean that the party will be more effective, better. . . . Each one of us must take stock of his accomplishments and determine whether he has done everything in his power to reach, in the present situation of the ongoing struggle for the hearts and minds of the people, the best possible results.[24]

In keeping with the "ideological renewal," the publication of the declaration coincided with the March announcement of a nationwide competition for the best essay, memoir, or article on the role of ideology. Entitled "The Return to the Source," the contest was sponsored by *Życie Partii* and the Książka i Wiedza publishers, and its goal was to encourage rank-and-file party members to reflect on how the PUWP might "return to the source of 'the party spirit' (*partyjność*)."[25]

Jaruzelski's initial willingness to allow nationalism to come close to displacing "proletarian internationalism" in his new government's bid for popular acceptance went farther than Władysław Gomułka's "Polish road to socialism," a slogan he promulgated in 1956. If he hoped to be regarded as anything but a Soviet stooge, Jaruzelski had to stress his ties to Polish nationalism, even if the patriotic talk was only a political expedient. After the 1981 crackdown, the call for the national unity of all Poles was the only remaining potential foundation for national reconciliation. But Jaruzelski's chances of success were slim. In 1956, Gomułka had led a reinvigorated party and an army victorious in a war of nerves with the Soviets; in 1981, the PUWP was wrecked, and the army had become a tool of political repression. By asserting that Polish nationalism was not in contradiction with Marxism-Leninism, Jaruzelski hoped to challenge the opposition on its own territory. As the traditional embodiment of Poland's past, the military was uniquely suited to appeal to the Poles' nationalism; Jaruzelski probably expected that such appeals would help him and the party gain the upper hand. He would soon learn, however, that such calculations were due to a gross oversight: the Poles respected the army only so long as they believed the soldier to be loyal to his nation. After 1981, once it had become apparent that Jaruzelski's officers did not share the Poles' dream of political emancipation, the military's mystique all but vanished.[26]

Rebuilding the PUWP's morale was thus a formidable task. Although the military's move against Solidarity restored some self-confidence to the rank and file, the demonstration of force was only the first step to regaining the party's authority in the country. The most pressing problem of the day, the ever-declining party membership, especially among Poland's youth, was proof enough that the PUWP had to act quickly. The problem had become so severe that it was openly addressed by Ryszard Łukasiewicz, deputy director of the Central Committee's Organizational Department, in his assessment of the cadre policy published in the March 1982 issue of *Życie Partii*. In a surprisingly sober admission of failure, Łukasiewicz announced that since July 1981 the PUWP had lost over 550 thousand members. Based on the figures available in February 1982, the party's members then numbered 2,597,204; it lost about 20 percent of its membership in six months.[27] Łukasiewicz tried not to sound too pessimistic and claimed that, taken out of context, these figures were misleading:

Compared to the entire post-August [1980] period, when the decline of the membership was "one-sided" [i.e., individual resignations], after the 13th of December there has been taking place in the party a planned process of purging its ranks conducted by the basic party cells [POPs] and various commissions and institutions of party control. As a result of this campaign, we have expelled in the past two months over 85 thousand people from the PUWP ranks, and in addition 12 thousand were expelled as a result of disciplinary action. If one compares these figures with the fact that in February and May of 1981, party cards were being turned in at the rate of about 28 thousand per month and that it was a "one-sided" phenomenon, the present situation has a new political meaning to it. It is a result of a conscious effort [on the part of the leadership] to strengthen the party, to leave behind those who proved to be passive or ideologically weak, opportunistic or undeserving of the name of a party member.[28]

Łukasiewicz's argument that the decline in membership was a sign of the party's health, allegedly proving the thoroughness of the PUWP's purge of itself, was intended to reassure the rank and file and the local apparat that the rapidly shrinking membership not only did not spell disaster, but was in fact a sign of the party's recovery. To any unbiased observer, however, the figures were a vivid proof of how acute the morale problem in the PUWP had become, and no amount of official optimism could hide the truth.

By the end of 1982, Jaruzelski's hopes that party discipline and internal "renewal" might help to recreate the PUWP's authority in the country had been dashed. The purge that followed the imposition of martial law consolidated the general's grip on the apparat, but it failed to reverse the deepening demoralization of the rank and file. The First All-Nation Party Conference on Ideology and Theory, which took place in Warsaw on April 2 and 3, 1982, turned out to be singularly vacuous and demonstrated once again that Polish communism was bankrupt. The lengthy proceedings, opened by Jaruzelski and concluded by Stefan Olszowski, produced their share of ponderous declarations and promises that the party would rise again, stronger than before.[29] This ideological debate would continue until the Tenth Party Congress in 1986.

As the end of the first year of military rule in Poland approached, it had become apparent that no meaningful systemic reforms would be introduced in the near future. As envisioned by Jaruzelski, change was mainly one of style over substance. Clarion calls to search for new ideological solutions that would put the PUWP in the vanguard of the debate about the nation's future yielded no magic formula; ultimately, the military's brief experimentation with Marxist theory ended with a renewed stress on party discipline, duty, and obedience. The quest to imbue the apparatchiks with these soldierly virtues was strengthened by another bureaucratic reshuffling.

In sum, the rebuilding of the party—the centerpiece of Jaruzelski's "normalization program"—would take longer than the general had expected. The institutional overhauling of the PUWP apparat, however thorough, would not suffice to re-establish party discipline, while personnel changes were also only half of the answer. Jaruzelski's tinkering with Polish communism, a supremely delicate task in view of the traditional Soviet distrust of ideological reformers, yielded mixed results. If it had not been Jaruzelski's intention to tailor Polish Marxism-Leninism to the country's military tradition and its patriotic values, he at least tolerated some small alterations. At the same time, Jaruzelski worked to strengthen his position in the Central Committee and the Politburo. In January, Gen. Czesław Kiszczak was elevated to the Politburo as deputy member. In July, Politburo Member Stefan Olszowski, a one-time challenger to Jaruzelski, was eased out of the Central Committee's secretariat, while in October Olszowski's erstwhile associate Grabski was shipped off to the Polish embassy in East Berlin.[30]

After a year of martial law, Jaruzelski operated increasingly in the traditional party environment and according to the rules applicable to other Polish apparatchiks. The military could no longer rely on its pre-1981 authority in Polish society; having shown themselves to be committed supporters of communism, Jaruzelski and his officers had forfeited their historical heritage. Once played, the trump card of Polish nationalism could no longer help the army legitimize its rule.[31]

Ideology vs. Economics: Jaruzelski's 1982 Recovery Program

The purge of the local party and administrative apparat, and the abortive campaign of ideological renewal, revealed Jaruzelski's conviction that the crisis in Poland was at least as much ideological as it was economic. The regime's conception of an organic interrelationship between ideology and economics, albeit nothing new in Marxist-Leninist theory, was important to Jaruzelski's recovery program in a special way. Since according to the officially accepted interpretation of events, the 1980 labor unrest and the emergence of Solidarity were caused by "voluntarism of power,"[32] that is, the growing separation between Gierek's professed long-term communist goals and the increasingly makeshift approach to everyday problems, one needed an ideological commitment to overcome the economic crisis.

This view of the causes of the Polish crisis was not necessarily an exercise in self-delusion. It was precipitated by the coincidence of the party's decline with the time when the army was undergoing its most rapid modernization and was becoming a modern force. As the apparatchiks fell into ever-greater disarray, the military, with Soviet assistance, transformed the People's Army into the best trained, best organized, and best equipped army in Poland's postwar history. To people like Jaruzelski, Kiszczak, Baryła, and Siwicki, who remembered the meager origins of communist Poland's armed forces, the army's subsequent growth was a source of pride; the army's pride in its professional achievement was shown in several of Jaruzelski's speeches.[33] In contrast, the decay and waste of the civilian party apparat must have presented to Jaruzelski a truly abhorrent picture.

A decade-long modernization of the Polish armed forces in the 1970s reinforced in yet another way the military's belief that the root causes of the collapse of the party and the economy were ideological. By the mid-1970s, the army was the only large state-controlled institution that had retained continuous emphasis on indoctrination and ideology as an integral part of its daily operations, career advancement, and professional training. Consequently, the "military party," that is, the professional officer corps whose members were also members of the PUWP, was much more hard-line on matters of ideology than the apparatchiks.[34]

This ideological commitment on the part of the military was further strengthened by a sense of superiority in relation to the civilian authority, an attitude characteristic of all tightly controlled elite military or paramilitary organizations. Frequent displays of incompetence and corruption by Gierek and his cronies only reinforced the military's stereotype of the civilian official; Jaruzelski's penchant for "clean living" added to his contempt for the corrupt apparatchiks. The outrage with which the majority of high-level army officers greeted the emergence of free trade unions and the government's inability to defuse the crisis were probably genuine. From this perspective, the purge of the party and the government immediately after the imposition of martial law in Poland was more than simply a matter of bureaucratic expediency; it was suggestive of a deeply held belief on the part of the military that if the party could recapture its past ideological vitality, an equally strong economic recovery would follow.

WRON's martial-law decrees demonstrate the military's "ideological" approach to the complexities of Poland's economic quagmire. They also bear witness to the new regime's lack of administrative experience and the often-naive belief of the soldier that clearly formulated orders and discipline would always have the intended effect. The militarization of Poland's factories and the presence of army commissars at managerial posts were to reverse Poland's economic decline; systemic weaknesses were to be overcome by uncorrupted, principled individuals. Paradoxically, the underlying premise of this approach was that Poland needed not less but more centrally imposed economic decisionmaking.

At first, the military moved energetically to implement its solution to Poland's economic ills. A WRON decree issued three days after the crackdown ordered a purge of the entire administrative apparatus on all levels. The decree announced the immediate dismissal of "persons incapable of managing particular elements of the economy and of state administration, as well as those who have used their positions for personal gain."[35] How the criteria for judging a manager "incapable of managing" were defined was never revealed. The campaign resulted in the wholesale firing of managers, which only further aggravated the country's economic difficulties.

On December 17, the decree was followed by another WRON resolution that directed the government to adjust the system of economic management to the martial-law regulations. The next day, December 18, the generals issued a communiqué in which they asserted that, despite the difficulties in the distribution of goods and the interruptions of the power supply in some regions of the country, overall industry had already improved its productivity due to markedly better work discipline and the reduction of absenteeism. Finally, instead of planning an agrarian reform, in particular a program that would facilitate the peasants' access to badly needed farm machinery and livestock feed, on December 20 WRON called upon the farmers to increase production, while assuring them that Poland's industrial output had become stabilized.[36] Leaving aside the absurdity of any economic analysis based on a week-long sample, the communiqué was clumsy propaganda and an expression of the soldier's belief that "where there is discipline there must be results." Simplistic solutions to the country's economic problems were attempted throughout the first twelve months of martial law, all of them equally futile; still, the general insisted that the "economy had been shaken into motion."[37]

In fairness, one should point out that during much of 1981–1982, Jaruzelski was in no position to deal effectively with the economy. Although Solidarity was crushed, it did not concede defeat. As WRON's optimistic statement of December 20 was being issued, some 1,300 miners held the Piast coal mine in Tychy near Katowice, and strikes were under way in the Huta Katowice Steelworks and in the Anna Coal Mines. Serious labor unrest continued until the end of the month, even though in each case the government managed to break the opposition by direct armed assaults on the striking factories. As labor strife continued and Poland's economy sank ever lower, the early optimism of the Jaruzelski regime was replaced by words of caution and warnings that the recovery would be slow and painful. In effect, the government admitted that administration by decree had failed to solve the economic crisis when it announced, on December 27, two weeks after the imposition of martial law, that meat and butter rations would again be cut, the reduction being in effect during January 1982.

In the face of continuing resistance, politics took primacy over economics. The institution of loyalty oaths required of all state employees, announced by WRON's Gen. Michał Janiszewski, was a de facto precondition for employment. It would assure Poland's leaders that only trusted and dedicated people would have influence in the country's economic life. The emphasis on work discipline, similar to that required of the Polish soldier, was another component of Jaruzelski's blueprint for Poland's economic recovery; it seemed closer to a set of police measures than to economic planning.

With the state the largest single employer in the country, the militarization of the economy meant the militarization of the entire society. On December 28, the Economic Committee of the Council of Ministers reviewed a new WRON directive requiring that everyone between the ages of 18 and 25 who was not employed or attending school be forced to work; the new regulation remained in effect throughout the period of martial law.[38] The work-discipline campaign, vaguely reminiscent of a similar policy tried by Gomułka in the late 1960s, had predictably meager results. Poland's industrial output declined further, while unrest continued despite the severity of the government's countermeasures. Compared to the average for 1978, by 1982 Poland's net domestic product had declined by 25 percent. Furthermore, despite the forced-labor legislation, industrial employment in 1982 declined by 7 percent relative to 1980; Polish industry employed 300,000 fewer workers.[39]

In the end, Jaruzelski's recovery program during the time of martial law was limited to price increases and further centrally directed manipulation of the economy. The general apparently hoped that by purging the local administrative apparatus, rooting out corruption, and instituting strict work discipline, the economy could be stabilized, or at least its rate of decline slowed. When hopes for a quick economic recovery were dashed, the generals focused all their efforts on the reconstruction of the PUWP and winning Soviet approval for their tenure of power.

In the final analysis, Jaruzelski's economic-recovery plan during the period of martial law did not go beyond the reshuffling of the nomenklatura and militarization of factories. Tighter control and harsh penalties for disobedience helped to slow down the rate of economic decline, but those measures fell far short of the badly needed structural reform. Poland's national income fell between 1980 and 1981 by 13.3 percent; the downward trend continued in 1982.[40] In the face of economic sanctions imposed by the United States and the unavailability of new Western credits, Poland did not have sufficient hard-currency reserves to service her over-30 billion-dollar debt.[41] In the future, Jaruzelski would repeatedly resort to severe price rises to reduce shortages of consumer goods, but the side effect of such action would be an inevitable decline in the living standards of the Poles, and further estrangement of Polish society from its government.

Although it was naive of Jaruzelski to expect that the country's economic performance would meet his expectation of a "recovery by decree and orders," it remains an open question whether the military could have tried another approach during its first year in power. Since Jaruzelski's primary concern was reconstituting the PUWP, and since any real economic reform would have retarded this process, he probably saw no other option but to streamline the existing economic mechanism and consolidate his regime's political position in the country. It is also true that the sheer dilettantism of army commissars contributed to the failure of Jaruzelski's economic policies in 1982; faced with the complexity of Poland's economic problems, they simply did not know any other way but to apply to economic administration the methods learned in the barracks.

On balance, in terms of internal government and party politics and the restructuring of the state apparat, Jaruzelski had, by the end of 1982, some modest accomplishments to show. By removing some of the old and compromised apparatchiks, the general could hope to gain a modicum of acceptance among his fellow Poles. Nevertheless, because of the complete estrangement of Polish society from the PUWP, this "psychological dividend" would be considerably smaller than it had been in 1956 when Gomułka came to power, or in 1970 when Gierek assumed the party leadership. The nation's continued resistance, marked in the first year of martial law by frequent public demonstrations, the wide circulation of underground publications, and Solidarity's continued existence underground were proof that Jaruzelski's "normalization" still had a long road to travel.

The Soviet Role
in the Crisis

—8—————————————————————————

Its Three Phases

Since the end of World War II, Soviet political influence has been a permanent factor in Polish civil-military relations. Thus Moscow's policies toward Poland in 1980–1981 determined to a large degree the final outcome of the crisis and set the stage for Jaruzelski's "normalization" after the imposition of martial law. The current makeup of the Polish regime and the nature of Polish-Soviet relations have their roots in Soviet policy decisions taken between 1980 and 1981 and during the critical first year of martial law. An analysis of Soviet policies during the crisis, and the rationale behind them, will provide a background for the subsequent discussion of the politics of Polish "normalization."

By 1980, the Kremlin was well aware of the military's special role in Poland. The importance of the army in the resolution of crises in Poland was driven home by General Komar's demonstration of resolve to fight the Soviet Army in 1956, and by Jaruzelski's ability to influence Poland's politics in 1970 and 1976 by either granting or withholding the army's support for a particular party leader. Jaruzelski's alleged reluctance to use his troops against the strikers in 1970 could only strengthen those perceptions.[1]

The Soviet approach to the Polish crisis during the sixteen months of Solidarity's legal existence in 1980–1981 went through three stages:

    1. August 1980–mid-December 1980: isolation of Poland and serious preparations for a Warsaw Pact military intervention;

2. December 1980–October 1981: a two-track policy, consisting in, on the one hand, urging Secretary Kania to search for a political solution, and, on the other hand, accepting Jaruzelski's martial-law option and preparing for Operation Spring (during the Bydgoszcz crisis, the Soviets were ready to deploy their forces in support of Jaruzelski's martial-law operation, but the ensuing confusion threatened to bring about a large-scale Soviet invasion);

3. October 1981–December 13 1981: Kania's resignation marked the full endorsement by the Soviets of Jaruzelski's plans for imposing martial law; at this stage, in a major shift in policy, the Soviets relied on Jaruzelski to build a leadership group (the Soviets' decision as to whether he should be supported as Poland's leader after the introduction of martial law was taken in 1982).

Soviet Expectations at the Beginning of the Crisis

The scope and duration of the 1980–1981 Polish crisis were unprecedented, even though throughout the 1970s Poland had earned a dubious reputation in Moscow as the most unruly of the USSR's satellites. The Gierek government was brought to power in 1970 following a wave of labor unrest on the Baltic coast; 1976 witnessed mass worker protests around Warsaw and in the city of Radom in response to the government's announcement of substantial price increases for basic foodstuffs. The 1976 confrontation, which ended in the government's backing down from its initial position, was followed by waves of repression against the strike participants. It also gave birth to a strong dissident movement in Poland, headed by such organizations as the Committee for Workers' Defense (KOR), the Movement for the Defense of Human and Civil Rights (Ruch Obrony Praw Człowieka i Obywatela), and the Confederation of Independent Poland (Konfederacja Polski Niepodległej). Regular underground publications and educational courses organized outside the state's control ("flying universities") became permanent features of Poland's political landscape.

From the point of view of the Soviets, however, Gierek dealt successfully with the recurrent crises. Each case of mass unrest in Poland was effectively checked by temporary government concessions and increased food supplies to the troubled areas; repression then swiftly followed. Throughout the 1970s, it appeared that the PUWP had remained firmly in control of the country's political life and that the opposition, although growing in numbers, was too disorganized and fragmented to seriously challenge Soviet interests in Poland.

The pattern of unrest in Poland, beginning with the first eruption in 1956, established an important principle for the Soviet approach to recurring Polish crises: the PUWP could be relied upon to defuse every political confrontation, without requesting direct Soviet intervention. The marked Soviet hesitancy to intervene in 1956 and Brezhnev's willingness to leave the 1970 and 1976 crises to the Poles themselves expressed Moscow's belief that, in the light of the traditional Polish hostility toward the Russians, overt Soviet involvement was fraught with grave risks and unpredictable consequences. Stalin's notorious quip that trying to impose communism on Poland was like trying to saddle a cow, was not lost on his successors. Hence Moscow judged it best to leave finding a solution to the crises of 1968, 1970, and 1976 to the Poles themselves.

In this light, it appears that the Kremlin at first did not become greatly concerned about the Polish situation. That is probably why the last visit of Edward Gierek to the Crimea, in July and August of 1980, was reported in *Pravda* with routine pronouncements restating that the policies of the PUWP's leadership remained in complete agreement with the general line of the CPSU. There was no reason for Brezhnev to look at the wave of strikes on the Baltic coast in July 1980 as something other than a case of the unruly Poles taking to the streets only to be pacified by a combination of indulgence and firmness on the part of their own government. The initial silence of the Soviet media on the Polish crisis suggests that the Russians first adopted a wait-and-see attitude, even if the rapidity with which the Polish events unfolded was surprising and their pattern unfamiliar. Reportedly, the Soviets themselves were experiencing labor unrest at home and hence wanted to prohibit all news of the strikes in Poland.[2]

The first mention by the Soviets of trouble in Poland came on August 20 in a brief note issued by TASS describing "work stoppages" in Gdańsk; *Pravda* reported Gierek's address to the nation calling for an immediate return to work. The article emphasized Gierek's concern that the stoppages were being used by "forces hostile to Poland's national interests," and concluded the commentary with a quote from Gierek pledging Poland's unyielding commitment to the Socialist Commonwealth.[3]

On August 22, the Soviets followed up with an editorial commentary. *Pravda* reviewed an article in the official PUWP daily *Trybuna Ludu* that called for a greater work effort and self-discipline among the Poles as the solution to the country's economic difficulties. The efforts of the miners in Polish Lower Silesia (Gierek's traditional power base) were praised, and the above-plan coal production touted as a sign of the miners' support for the government. The article's upbeat tone suggested that, at least at this point, the Kremlin was not much alarmed. It still appeared that all the "ingredients" of the past Polish crises were present: eruption of the workers' discontent in strikes, promises of better food supplies and pay raises, and a demonstration of Gierek's support in the southern mining region. In this respect, the labor unrest of 1980 was almost a carbon copy of the 1976 confrontation in Warsaw and Radom.

The remainder of the week saw no official Soviet reporting of the situation in Poland.[4] On August 31, *Pravda* published a brief note about the Fifth PUWP Central Committee Plenum held the day before under the chairmanship of Gierek; it made special mention of the report given to the Central Committee by Politburo Member Stanisław Kania. It was probably then, however, that the new leadership was being formed, and that Kania and Jaruzelski's first assurances that "counterrevolutionary forces in Poland would be destroyed by internal political and administrative means" were extended to Brezhnev.[5] Kukliński's testimony suggests that, although Kania was officially appointed the PUWP's first secretary on September 5, he had already assumed command at the end of August. This is confirmed by an authoritative commentary in *Pravda* on the Polish situation signed by A. Petrov[6] and published on September 1. Petrov's article, entitled "Intrigues of the Enemies of Socialist Poland," charged that the unrest in Gdańsk was being used by Poland's enemies. Petrov made a distinction between "just demands," that is, demands for better economic conditions, and "demands that threaten the [Polish] state's interests," namely the ongoing political debate. The commentary was an indirect indictment of the Gierek leadership's past economic policies, and an indication of Soviet willingness to support his government, provided he would be able to confine the protest to the sphere of "just demands."[7] This conditionality of Brezhnev's support of Gierek undoubtedly further undermined the latter's standing in the Polish Politburo. Gierek himself later admitted in a note to Jaruzelski that after the purge of the "list of nine" he was no longer in control of the Politburo.[8]

Kania's arrival on Poland's political scene must have looked to Moscow like a logical development in a Polish-style political crisis. Experience had taught the Russians that every major disruption in Poland had to be accompanied by a shake-up within the PUWP, and the Kremlin's objective was to fill the top PUWP post with an apparatchik both unquestionably loyal to Moscow and acceptable to the Poles. Kania, whose work within the Politburo and the Central Committee had focused on the country's internal affairs—he had headed Poland's internal security apparatus and supervised the army—was well suited for the job. One the one hand, the Poles were unlikely to associate him with the excesses of Gierek's economic program; on the other hand, his credentials as the country's top policeman were impressive. Last but not least, because of his relatively obscure position in the party hierarchy, choosing Kania would not antagonize such prominent apparatchiks as Grabski, Olszowski, and Moczar, all busy positioning themselves to lead the party.

Most likely, Kania was a compromise candidate chosen by the Poles and thought acceptable to Brezhnev, rather than an appointee directly selected by the Soviets; this explains the curious discrepancy between the time of Kania's appointment and Moscow's announcement of the change. Although Kania assumed leadership of the PUWP on September 5, the news of his appointment was not officially released in the Soviet Union until September 7.

Although Brezhnev might have had doubts about the man himself, he clearly believed that the change of leadership should suffice to put an end to the unrest. Thus, on the day of Kania's appointment, September 5, TASS announced that the situation in Poland was "being gradually normalized," and that both *Trybuna Ludu* and *Żołnierz Wolności* had spoken of a "national moral unity" already emerging in Poland.[9] Soviet optimism was strengthened by the decision taken during the Fourth Plenum of the PUWP's Central Committee to begin drafting contingency plans for an internal crackdown.[10] On September 7, all major Soviet newspapers ran Kania's biography and the text of Brezhnev's congratulatory telegram to the new Polish regime. The telegram expressed Brezhnev's unqualified support for the new first secretary as a trusted comrade whose entire life had been devoted to the strengthening of Polish-Soviet friendship. The CPSU's Politburo expressed its deep conviction that the Polish party would overcome its present temporary difficulties; in time-honored fashion, Gierek's departure was attributed to illness.[11]

Soviet press coverage of the events in Poland immediately following Kania's arrival on the scene was marked by a rather clumsy effort to give the reader an impression that things in fraternal Poland were basically back to normal, and that, as far as the PUWP was concerned, it was business as usual. TASS and *Pravda* ran several items on Kania's meeting with the party cadres of Warsaw, on the Sejm's closing its working session, and on Kania's address to the Sixth Plenum of the PUWP's Central Committee, in which he described past mistakes and called for solving the present difficulties. On September 10, in its section "Fraternal Parties," *Pravda* printed an extensive desctiption of Kania's meeting with the Gdańsk PUWP's *aktiv*, the central core of its active members. The account concluded that the situation in Poland had improved dramatically as compared with the strike period.

The propaganda campaign aside, the Soviets appeared anxious for direct confirmation that the Polish crisis was being successfully managed. Only five days after Kania's appointment, on September 10, they summoned to Moscow a high-level Polish delegation, headed by Deputy Premier Mieczysław Jagielski. It was becoming obvious by September that bureaucratic tricks had failed to break up the union.[12] Still, Moscow reiterated its support for Kania, blamed the West for unrest in Poland, and pledged additional economic help. A TASS commentary of September 13, entitled "For Unity and Cooperation," praised the new prime minister's assertion that Poland would continue to regard the fraternal Soviet Union as a major economic partner, always remembering the traditionally strong political connections between the two countries. TASS commented that "the importance of the Polish-Soviet fraternal relations always became obvious in times of need." Poland could count on help from the Socialist Commonwealth.[13]

On the surface, the "Polish crisis" appeared to have unfolded in a rather routine fashion: the old PUWP leadership had been deposed; a new regime had come to power; and Moscow had pledged badly needed economic help in order to mollify the disgruntled Polish consumer. Although the Gdańsk-Jastrzębie agreements establishing the worker's right to form independent trade unions had been signed, there still seemed to be time to neutralize Solidarity. The Soviets knew that in the past newly appointed PUWP chiefs had felt compelled to experiment with workers' self-management (both Gomułka and Gierek tolerated briefly the existence of such bodies), and that in each case the workers' councils were quickly infiltrated by government agents and destroyed. The agreement to create Solidarity, although in itself a dangerous precedent, was treated by the Soviets as a tactical move taken by the PUWP to gain time to gather its strength for a counteroffensive. An ominous indication that this time the crisis would not be resolved according to the old formula came on the heels of the deadlock over the court registration of the new union.

On September 24, Solidarity's attempt to register with the Warsaw court, a procedure required by Polish law, ran into snags, but the union refused to retreat. As far as Brezhnev was concerned, Kania's failure to block the registration of Solidarity meant that the "Polish crisis pattern" had been broken. The Soviets were faced with a qualitatively new situation and acted with extreme caution. Between September 19 and October 4, there was a virtual blackout on news from Poland; while the confrontation between Solidarity and the government was intensifying, the Soviet reader was being treated to extensive editorials on the first joint Soviet-Cuban space flight. Throughout the critical two weeks, *Pravda* published only three items on Poland. Two of them were the announcement on September 26 of the trial of L. Moczulski, leader of the illegal Confederation of Independent Poland (Konfederacja Polski Niepodległej), and the three-line announcement on October 2 of the upcoming plenum of the PUWP's Central Committee. The third dispatch from Poland came on October 3, the day Solidarity organized a nationwide one-hour warning strike in protest against government tampering with the registration procedures; the Soviet dispatch announced the opening in Poland of the Tenth International Chopin Piano Competition.

After the conciliatory speech by Polish prime minister Pińkowski in the aftermath of the warning strike, the Soviets decided that things had gone too far. In a move intended to evaluate directly the situation in Poland, the Warsaw Pact foreign ministers convened a meeting in Warsaw. Kania had to answer some tough questions from his Warsaw Pact guests, but was himself excluded from subsequent discussions. On October 21, *Pravda* reported that Gromyko had later informed the Polish first secretary of the results of the proceedings. The Soviet minister's demand that the Polish government hold firm was then relayed by Kania to his Central Committee associates, who convened after Gromyko's departure. Jaruzelski read correctly the signs of the impending Soviet action; as the foreign ministers' meeting adjourned, the Polish general staff hurried to complete the preliminary version of the martial-law plan.[14] On October 24, the Warsaw District Court refused to register Solidarity unless its charter included a clause expressly recognizing the leading role in Poland of the PUWP. For its part, Solidarity demanded that the charter be accepted unaltered and set the November 12 deadline for a general strike if the issue had not been satisfactorily resolved by then.

The confrontation over the registration procedures, which was partially a result of Gromyko's ultimatum to Kania during the meeting of the foreign ministers in Warsaw, suggests that the Soviets had underestimated the extent of the party's weakness caused by a decade of corruption under Gierek. Impatient with the increasingly protracted nature of the Polish crisis, and the apparent inability of the PUWP to contain it, the Soviets forced Kania into a confrontation with Solidarity by urging him to stand firm on the issue of the union's registration. This blunder further aggravated the situation, revealed Kania's weakness, and convinced the Soviets that the only option available to them was an invasion of Poland by Warsaw Pact armies.

From Cordon Sanitaire to Plans of Invasion

A change in the Soviet position with respect to the Polish events came at the end of October, after Kania's failure to bloc Solidarity's registration. Soviet hopes for a speedy resolution to the crisis were dashed, and other East Europeans were moved to isolate Poland and pressure Kania to deal firmly with the trade union. On October 29, the German Democratic Republic imposed severe restrictions on travel to and from Poland. Honecker's action suggested that, in the opinion of other Warsaw Pact states, the crisis had reached bloc wide proportions. The East German move was soon followed by similar travel restrictions imposed by Czechoslovakia.

Soviet pressure on the Poles also increased. On October 30, Kania and Prime Minister Józef Pińkowski were summoned to Moscow. Although after the visit Brezhnev reiterated the Kremlin's assertion that the Polish comrades would be able to solve the crisis themselves, the very abruptness of Kania's October trip and the treatment he received in Moscow indicated that he was being held personally responsible for the escalation of the crisis. Upon their arrival in the Soviet capital, Kania and Pińkowski were met by Brezhnev, Tikhonov, Gromyko, and Rusakov; however, they were sent back to Poland only a few hours later without much concern for the customary communist protocol. Although on October 31, *Pravda* published a front page account of the visit, quoting Brezhnev's statement expressing the "conviction of Soviet communists that the communists and workers of fraternal Poland would overcome the difficulties," there were other signs of growing tension between Brezhnev and the Poles.[15] *Pravda's* official optimism was undermined by a terse TASS statement accusing the West of meddling in Poland's internal affairs and supporting counterrevolution there.

The period between Kania's and Pińkowski's visit to Moscow and the ruling of the Polish Supreme Court on November 10 that Solidarity's statutes could stand without reference to the leading role of the party, was a time of a major contest of wills between the new PUWP leadership and the independent trade union; in the end the party lost. On November 2, *Pravda* published an extensive commentary on the reaction in the Polish press to the Polish leaders' Moscow visit, emphasizing that the central theme of the day was to "reaffirm the vitality of Soviet-Polish relations," and to "strengthen the ties between the CPSU and the PUWP," both of which tasks were the responsibility of the PUWP. The article also stressed the need in Polish-Soviet relations for ideological unity and identity of views, an indication that, in Moscow's opinion, a solution to the Polish crisis could not include systemic experimentation.[16] Following the *Pravda* article of November 2, direct Soviet official reportage of the Polish crisis stopped, and news from Poland was reduced to the standard fare of brief TASS releases, such as a couple of lines on Kania's meeting with the Vietnamese foreign minister.

By November, the Soviets had essentially given up on Kania and decided that a Warsaw Pact invasion of Poland was the only way to resolve the crisis. They also began looking for another group within the Polish Politburo to take over after the invasion.[17] Since Jaruzelski continued to press for a "Polish solution" to the crisis, he was an unlikely candidate for the job. The Soviets needed a Pole who would be loyal to Moscow and also have a base of support in the army and the security forces. Unexpectedly, during the registration crisis Moscow began to pay special attention to Mieczysław Moczar, a hard-liner, an old Gierek opponent, and the chief instigator of the 1968 anti-Zionist campaign in Poland.

Moczar, a Stalinist in the 1950s and a "nationalist communist" in the 1960s, suffered a series of political setbacks during the Gierek regime. Nevertheless, he managed to retain the chairmanship of the Union of Fighters for Freedom and Democracy (Związek Bojowników o Wolność i Demokrację; ZBoWiD), the national organization of Polish war veterans. ZBoWiD had traditionally cooperated closely with the People's Army, and a number of army commanders and communist underground resistance leaders were prominent members. It was an indication of ZBoWiD's political strength that even at the apogee of his power, in the early 1970s, Gierek was unable to fire Moczar from his ZBoWiD job and the chairmanship of the party's Supreme Control Commission (Najwyższa Izba Kontroli; NIK). The ease with which Moczar re-emerged as a political figure after Gierek's removal suggests that, in the 1970s, ZBoWiD's connection to the army had given the old partisan a much greater influence in Polish politics than had commonly been assumed at the time. In addition, Moczar was a former head of Poland's security police, and retained considerable contacts inside the Ministry of the Interior.

On November 5, at the height of the controversy over the registration of Solidarity, TASS reported with evident approval and at great length on the plenary meeting in Warsaw of ZBoWiD's national committee, which unanimously re-elected Moczar to the organization's chairmanship. TASS carried excerpts from Moczar's acceptance speech in which he attacked "anti-socialist elements" for "interfering with the process of normalization" in Poland. "Those who want to benefit from Poland's crisis," said Moczar, "will be stopped."

Moczar's was the first statement quoted in the Soviet press that spoke openly of the "Polish crisis." It was also the strongest warning to date to the opposition that counterrevolution would be crushed; its unequivocal endorsement by TASS indicated that Brezhnev shared Moczar's views.[18] To drive the message home, on November 9, the day before the critical decision by the Polish Supreme Court, TASS reported joint Polish-Soviet maneuvers inside Poland. In the Soviet plan, the entry of Warsaw Pact troops into Poland would be followed immediately by the formation of a new hard-line Polish regime;[19] Moczar's sudden political prominence could only be an indication that he was being seriously considered for the job.

Moczar probably had no influence with Jaruzelski, even though the general was deputy chairman of ZBoWiD and, consequently, well-versed in the organization's internal politics. Moczar's position was strong as long as Jaruzelski continued to object strenuously to the timing of the planned direct Warsaw Pact invasion. In late 1980, the Soviets simply refused to consider Jaruzelski's proposals; his negotiating sessions with Kulikov brought him to the verge of complete emotional exhaustion.[20] Whatever fears or moral dilemmas prompted Jaruzelski to argue against the invasion, Moczar appeared to have no such ethical concerns and pushed his advantage with Moscow to the limit.

The role played by ZBoWiD in the unraveling of the Polish crisis remains partially a mystery, but it appears that the Soviets at least considered building around Moczar the core of a leadership to be constituted after the invasion. One cannot tell for certain how serious Brezhnev's support for Moczar's candidacy to lead the new government was. However, Moczar's complete disappearance from Poland's political spotlight after martial law was declared supports the argument that the Soviet press paid him special attention because at the height of the crisis he was a serious contender for the highest party post. Months after the crisis over the registration of Solidarity, during the critical days of October 1981, when Jaruzelski rose to the position of the PUWP's first secretary, ZBoWiD would resurface once again. As reported by TASS and the Polish newspaper *Rzeczpospolita*,[21] on October 10, 1981, just one week before Jaruzelski's appointment, the general chaired a meeting of ZBoWiD activists. In its report on the meeting, TASS asserted that a "decisive moment" had been reached in the crisis in Poland.[22] Once the Bydgoszcz crisis had blown over, Moczar once again vanished from sight. In all likelihood, Moczar was kept in reserve by the Soviets throughout the Polish crisis, to be used in case Jaruzelski failed, and invasion plans had to be implemented.

Meanwhile, in the fall of 1980 the Soviets turned up the heat as a prelude to their invasion of Poland. On November 11, *Pravda* published a TASS commentary on a *Trybuna Ludu* article entitled "The Decisive Factor," written by Poland's foreign minister M. Dobrosielski. Emphasizing the gravity of the situation in Poland, TASS pointedly quoted Dobrosielski as saying: "We don't have very much time and our capabilities are limited. Still the problems we face today can be solved. We must quickly develop a program and, within the framework of our political system, create political/social/economic relations of the kind that would once and for all eliminate the sources of crises in Poland."[23] The TASS commentary singled out Solidarity as the major disruptive force and the proponent of counterrevolution in Poland.

As the so-called "Narożniak affair," the case of a Solidarity printer arrested for allegedly disclosing state secrets and subsequently released because of strike pressure from the trade union, unfolded, the Soviets emphatically called for Moczar's hard-line approach to dealing with the opposition. TASS dispatches of November 21 and November 23 prominently featured Moczar's speeches made to the plenary session of ZBoWiD and to the Sejm at the closing of its parliamentary session. Moczar was quoted as saying that the crisis called for a purge of the party (a prelude to the change of leadership) and a decisive stand against the opposition. The TASS report followed Moczar's remarks with excerpts from a speech by Gen. W. Oliwa, commander of the Warsaw military district, who declared the People's Army's readiness and determination to defend socialism in Poland.[24] In effect, during the Sejm session two opposite conceptions of resolving the crisis were presented: direct Soviet invasion and, possibly, installation of Moczar in the post of first secretary of the PUWP, and internal military and police action. In the TASS report, both speeches preceded Premier Pińkowski's address to the Sejm; at the time, Pińkowski was Kania's closest lieutenant.

It appears that the Soviet decision to invade Poland in the winter of 1980 was to large degree precipitated by concerns about the USSR's strategic position relative to NATO. The Soviets set the date for the invasion on December 8.[25] For the first time since the beginning of the crisis, the threat of a strike by Polish railroad and transportation workers, as part of the general strike, placed the Kremlin in a situation in which its defense posture in Europe would be in jeopardy. The railroad workers' strike would paralyze the lines of communication across Poland, a vital link to Soviet troops in East Germany. On November 25, TASS warned the Poles in an unequivocal manner: "It is believed here that the threat of a general strike in the transportation sector, which has been announced by Solidarity trade union, will affect Poland's vital national interests, including national defense."[26] Moscow decided to move.

Once the decision to invade had been made, the Soviets did not mince words. During the last days of November, Soviet divisions in the northern and western districts of the USSR and in East Germany were placed on high alert. Reserves were called up, and additional equipment was issued to approximately 30 Soviet Army divisions.[27] East German and Czechoslovak forces were also fully mobilized and poised on Poland's frontiers. Reportedly, military hospitals were readied in the Ukraine and Byelorussia.[28] On December 1, Gen. Tadeusz Hupałowski was summoned to Moscow to be briefed on the invasion's operational details, which he then relayed to the Polish general staff. Using SOYUZ-80 as a cover, Moscow intended to send into Poland three Soviet armies (15 divisions), plus two Czechoslovak divisions and one East German division.[29]

Clearly, in late November and early December, Moscow thought there could be no internal Polish solution to the crisis and, hence, considered a WTO invasion the only available course of action. Kania's inability to stand up to Solidarity during the November confrontation over the union's registration must have demonstrated to the Soviets that the PUWP was much weaker than they had originally thought; the "Naroźniak affair" did nothing to dispel those fears. The biggest blow to Kania's credibility with the Soviets was his inability to block Solidarity's preparations for a general strike. As suggested by Romuald Spasowski, then Poland's ambassador to the United States, the Soviets considered the Polish communists' ability to prevent a nationwide strike the litmus test of Kania's ability to govern.[30] In late November, it became obvious that Kania's leadership could not guarantee that transportation and communication lines linking the Soviet Union with its divisions in East Germany would be kept open.

The invasion plan was shelved because Jaruzelski and his officers succeeded in convincing Moscow that they were capable of doing the job by themselves after all. Realizing the gravity of the situation, the Central Committee of the PUWP issued on December 3 a dramatic appeal to the nation, calling for calm and warning that the nation's future was in danger. TASS reported the PUWP's appeal, but still maintained that "there were counterrevolutionaries in Poland."[31] Shortly thereafter, an unannounced meeting of the WTO leaders was held in Moscow; they had been called together to coordinate the invasion plans. The meeting was a watershed in the preparations for the invasion; it was then that the scales were tipped against it. What mattered most with respect to future developments in Poland was General Jaruzelski's presentation of the Polish plan for solving the crisis. It appears that, after the meetings, the Russians regarded Kania as a figurehead, and supported him more to provide a smoke screen for Jaruzelski than out of conviction that the first secretary would be able to find an acceptable political solution to the crisis.[32] Thus, after the meeting, Kania was urged to persevere in his efforts to defuse the crisis. *Krasnaya Zvezda* reported with lukewarm approval Kania's address to the PUWP's Central Committee, in which he promised to "act more decisively."[33] The invasion plans having been put in storage, Soviet interest in Moczar immediately dropped, and news about the "old partisan" all but vanished from the Soviet press.

The Soviets abandoned those plans for the time being because the potential costs of such action were judged higher than previously expected. The assessment of the potential damage to Moscow's standing in world opinion, in particular that of Europe, at the time when the Soviets were attempting to split NATO over the issue of missile deployment in Europe played an important part in Brezhnev's decision to give the Polish military a chance to find a resolution to the crisis. In making its decision, the Kremlin had to consider the impact an invasion of Poland would have on the already strained Soviet-American relationship. Throughout November, Washington made every effort to convey to the Soviets the sense of gravity with which it would view military action against Poland. The warnings from the Carter administration were seconded by a strongly worded declaration by the participants in the EEC summit meeting in Luxembourg. The West's unanimous opposition to direct Soviet action against Poland was best expressed by West Germany's Helmut Schmidt, who flatly stated that "détente could not survive another Afghanistan."[34] Possibly, Brezhnev also feared that an invasion of Poland would precipitate direct military cooperation between the United States and China.[35] Of course, it is unlikely that the West's warnings were by themselves a sufficient deterrent to prevent Moscow from invading Poland. However, they reinforced the view that the planned action would be too costly; on balance, the danger of a bloodbath in Poland, the prospect of having to maintain the bankrupt Polish economy and to police the state, and the damage to Moscow's political standing in the West, all contributed to the decision to postpone the invasion. Considering the political price they would have had to pay, the Soviets were eager to look for another solution to the crisis. The invasion plans had been shelved after the meeting of the WTO leaders in Moscow on December 5, and the Kremlin pressured Kania to pursue a two-track policy: consolidating the

PUWP, on the one hand, while, on the other, using his negotiations with Solidarity as a cover for preparations to impose martial law.

Keeping Both Options Open

The Soviet decision to use the Polish military against Solidarity did not mean abandoning altogether the search for a political solution to the crisis. Although the Kremlin did not hold much hope that the Kania/Pińkowski team would accomplish the task, it continued to pressure Kania to harden his approach to Solidarity. The Soviets worked both through the military channel, by relying on Marshal Kulikov, and through regular contacts between Polish and Soviet apparatchiks. On January 13, Marshal V. Kulikov met in Warsaw with Kania and Pińkowski.[36] Jaruzelski was present, and so were the chief of staff of the WTO forces and the Soviet chief liaison representative to the Polish People's Army. On the Polish side, Jaruzelski was assisted by Gen. F. Siwicki, the Polish chief of staff, and Gen. E. Molczyk, chief inspector of training and the Polish liaison officer to the Warsaw Pact Joint High Command. Concurrently, L. Zamyatin, chief of the CPSU Central Committee's International Information Department paid a week-long visit to Poland, between January 13 and 20.[37]

In a move that would bring Poland one step closer to martial law, on February 9 Pińkowski was replaced by Jaruzelski as Poland's prime minister. The Soviets made it clear that they expected the new prime minister to pursue a policy of firmness in dealing with the opposition; Jaruzelski quickly obliged. *Pravda* reported with approval that Poland's Procuracy had ordered an investigation of J. Kuroń and A. Michnik, two leaders of KOR, and that action against others who threatened normalization in Poland was pending.[38] On February 11, TASS carried a speech by Grabski to the Eighth Plenum of the PUWP's Central Committee; TASS reiterated Grabski's charges that anarchy was becoming commonplace in Poland. The article warned that the opposition's ultimate objective was "duality of political power in Poland,"[39] and that the Polish party leadership's efforts to stem the tide of the opposition's growing power had been largely ineffective.[40] Still, the Kremlin stopped short of denouncing Kania; TASS emphasized that Comrade Kania was determined to make Poland again a "reliable power within the Socialist Commonwealth."[41]

Brezhnev's criticism of the situation in Poland, delivered during the CPSU's Twenty-sixth Congress (February–March 1981), was unequivocal. Charging that counterrevolution was in the making there, Brezhnev thundered that all "fraternal states" would, if need be, come to the rescue of "Poland's socialist gains."[42] Equally harsh criticism of the Poles during the Twenty-sixth Congress came from Cuba's Castro and Vietnam's LeDuan.[43]

When his turn came to speak, Kania pleaded his case in a now familiar way. "Our party has chosen the road of political solution to the social conflict [in Poland]," said Kania. He assured the congress that "counterrevolutionary forces [in Poland] would be stopped" as soon as the party had been strengthened.[44] He argued that his leadership had enough will power to fight, and pleaded for understanding while the PUWP "gathered its strength and ability to be active again."[45]

While Kania was defending his policies of compromise with Solidarity in the congress hall, in private Jaruzelski presented Soviet premier Tikhonov with a copy of his martial law plan.[46] On March 4, one day after the Twenty-sixth CPSU Congress was officially closed, Kania and Jaruzelski were summoned to Moscow for a meeting with Brezhnev. Reported by TASS and published on the front page of *Pravda*, the postmeeting communiqué asserted that "the Socialist Commonwealth cannot be broken and its defense is the duty not only of individual member states, but of the entire coalition,"[47] a veiled threat that the Brezhnev Doctrine could still be invoked with regard to Poland. The inclusion in the talks of B. Aristov, the Soviet ambassador to Poland, was a painful reminder to Kania that his information on the situation in Poland was not going to be taken at face value.

Jaruzelski and Soviet defense minister Marshal D. Ustinov discussed with Brezhnev the details of the Polish plan. Jaruzelski insisted that an additional delay was necessary to permit completion of the preparations, but the Soviets pushed for action already in the spring. They were ready to deploy their own forces in and around Poland to demonstrate support for the general and, should he encounter problems, become active participants in the operation. During the Moscow negotiations, the Soviets forced Jaruzelski to plan that SOYUZ-81 maneuvers would begin on March 16 and involve 150,000 Soviet Army troops, of which 30,000 would be moved immediately into Poland.[48] Kulikov was put in charge of the whole operation, with the authority to activate the Soviet "insurance policy" in the event of Jaruzelski's failure. Moscow expected Operation Spring to begin sometime in April.[49]

Kania's grip on the situation in Poland became progressively weaker, as shown by growing unrest at universities, wildcat strikes, and the opening in Poznań, on March 9, of the first congress of still-unofficial Rural Solidarity, in defiance of the party's refusal to grant it recognition. Soviet accusations in the press and TASS releases charging that counterrevolutionary activities funded by the West were taking place in Poland again became louder.[50] On March 18, on the eve of the Bydgoszcz crisis, Marshal V. Kulikov dropped in on Kania and Jaruzelski to brief them on the progress of SOYUZ-81. On March 19, after the Bydgoszcz crisis had erupted, *Pravda* reported on the meeting, commenting that the "army's role in the defense of socialism was stressed." *Pravda* also stated that several senior Soviet officers had been present during the discussion;[51]

these were probably the eighteen Soviet generals dispatched by Marshal Ustinov in February to assist Kulikov.[52]

Although Milewski's provocation in Bydgoszcz had rendered Jaruzelski's plan impracticable, the Soviets were of the opinion that the operation should proceed all the same. On March 22, *Krasnaya Zvezda* ran a front page article on the comradeship-in-arms between the Soviet and Polish armies, stressing the sacrifice of 600,000 Soviet lives to free Poland from German occupation and bring socialism to that country.[53] On March 24, TASS issued a sharply worded communiqué which unequivocally charged that the occurrences in Bydgoszcz had been caused by Solidarity. March 25 brought a report in *Krasnaya Zvezda* on the beginning of joint Polish-Soviet training operations under the umbrella of the SOYUZ-81 military maneuvers.[54] On March 27, *Pravda* described the situation in Poland as "extremely tense," and charged that Solidarity had broken its 90-day strike-moratorium agreement with the government (no such agreement had ever been reached), and that the counter-revolutionaries working inside Solidarity were both "antisocialist" and "anti-Polish." As proof that counterrevolution was in the making in Poland, *Pravda* pointed to the "provocative literature flooding the country."[55] Once again Moczar's ZBoWiD entered the picture; *Pravda* reported that a special ZBoWiD meeting had been called.

On March 27, Solidarity held a four-hour warning strike. On the same day the Soviets sent an on-site inspection team to Poland.[56] The next day TASS reported the strike and reprinted from the Polish army daily *Żołnierz Wolności* the charges that Solidarity was being used by Western imperialists and counter-revolutionaries. On March 28 *Pravda* accused the AFL-CIO and "American Polonia," an organization of Polish Americans, of meddling in Poland's internal affairs by supplying money and the photocopying and printing equipment used to produce subversive Solidarity publications.[57]

In the meantime, Kania tried to defuse the crisis. The statement issued after the March 22 session of the Politburo called for calm. During the Central Committee's decisive Ninth Plenum, Kania argued in favor of a compromise; this pitted him against Grabski and Olszowski, who accused him of tolerating Solidarity as an "alternative power" in the country.[58] On March 30, a last minute compromise was negotiated between Wałęsa and Deputy Prime Minister Rakowski; the general strike was called off.[59]

The TASS dispatch from Poland of March 30 talked of the highest level of tension in the country and claimed that KOR was in charge of strike preparations. On the same day, *Pravda* printed a fabricated story that Highway E-7, which runs North/South through Poland, had been blocked by counterrevolutionaries between the villages of Łączna and Suchedniów near Kielce, in southern Poland. Western intelligence again reported Soviet troop movements around Poland. Kania's willingness to compromise was greeted by the Soviet press with anger; the *Pravda* report of the compromise was limited to a note that the plenum had taken place, that 44 speeches had been made, and that Kania had closed the meeting. TASS continued to insist that Bydgoszcz was a "Western provocation" and lashed out against U.S. Secretary of State Haig and Defense Secretary Weinberger for expressing concern about the Polish situation.[60] An even harsher tone towards the events in Poland was taken on April 2 in a *Pravda* commentary entitled "Anti-Socialist Gathering," which described an allegedly "counterrevolutionary meeting at Warsaw University" as an "anti-Soviet gathering" and a proof that counterrevolutionary forces were increasingly in control in Poland. *Pravda* insinuated that some of the speakers at the meeting had argued that, in the final analysis, fascism was superior to communism.[61] Charges against KOR and against Solidarity extremists (in particular J. Rulewski) continued in the Soviet press. Increasingly, reflecting Moscow's growing preference for the hard-line approach of Baryła's propagandists, TASS began using *Żołnierz Wolności*, the Polish army's daily, as its main source of information on the crisis instead of the Polish Press Agency or *Trybuna Ludu*, the PUWP's official newspaper.

The Soviets were dismayed and visibly angry that their advice to continue the operation was not heeded. SOYUZ-81 ran for four days and it appeared that the Soviets might decide to act unilaterally after all; the critical period was between April 3 and 7. On the evening of April 3, Kania and Jaruzelski were summoned to Moscow to appear before Brezhnev and account for what had gone wrong. Simultaneously, the Soviets redeployed from Czechoslovakia to Poland 32 Mi-6 helicopters and ferried in large military transports, ten AN-12 aircraft.[62] Although on April 7, after his meeting with the Poles, Brezhnev formally announced in Prague the end of SOYUZ-81, the airlift into Poland continued.[63] In all likelihood, however, this demonstration of force was intended primarily for Jaruzelski and his generals. Although the martial-law operation had been postponed, Kulikov was adamant that the Poles must make a firm commitment in writing to a new deadline. Jaruzelski resisted, but probably gave in by mid-April; the Soviet airlift ceased.[64]

As far as Moscow was concerned, Kania was finished after the Bydgoszcz crisis. The Soviets probably would already have pushed for his removal after the compromise with Solidarity on March 30, had it not been for the realization that a rank-and-file reform movement was growing inside the PUWP. To assess the situation, M. Suslov, Moscow's "chief ideologist," together with N. Rusakov, the CPSU secretary in charge of Soviet relations with Eastern bloc countries, paid an unannounced visit to Warsaw on April 23. On April 26, *Pravda* attacked the rank-and-file reformers for trying to change the principles of party organization by introducing "horizontal structures," which would give greater autonomy in decisionmaking to the lower levels of the party hierarchy. By weakening the Politburo's control over the rank and file, the introduction of the principle of "horizontal structures" would directly defy the Soviet dogma of "democratic centralism." On July 3, Gromyko paid a visit to Warsaw, which had been announced a week in advance, for further consultations with the Poles and an on-site assessment of the situation. Considering that Gromyko's previous visit with Kania, in October 1980, had been instrumental in the PUWP's attempt to stand firm on the issue of Solidarity's registration by the courts, it is probable that Gromyko brought with him another stern warning to Kania and Jaruzelski not to experiment with the organizational structure of the Polish party.

The opening of the Ninth PUWP Extraordinary Congress in Warsaw, on July 14, was given prominent coverage in the Soviet media. *Pravda* ran a front page account of the proceedings, together with the announcement that V. Grishin, a member of the CPSU's Politburo, was representing the Soviet party at the congress. It is unclear why Brezhnev himself did not attend; the reasons could have been both his poor health and his displeasure with Kania's leadership. Grishin brought with him an expression of Moscow's dismay over the situation in Poland. Addressing the Polish congress, Grishin passed a blunt message on to the reformers. "The experience of the communist movement has shown," said Grishin, "that the party can be effective only when democracy is accompanied by discipline, when the party displays unity in word and in deed."[65] For Kania and the Polish Politburo, Grishin had another simple piece of advice: counterrevolution could be defeated only after the party had regained its cohesion and its willingess to fight.[66]

July 20–21 brought extensive Soviet reportage of Jaruzelski's address to the congress. *Pravda* emphasized that the general had stressed the importance of Soviet help to Poland's economic recovery and declared the army's commitment to defend socialism in Poland.[67] The report of the closing of the Ninth Congress included a brief note about a private meeting between Grishin, Kania, and Jaruzelski, immediately following the official closing ceremony.

The Soviet pressure on Kania and Jaruzelski not to experiment with structural party reform was successful. The Ninth Extraordinary PUWP Congress added some new faces to the Central Committee, reshuffled the apparat, and permitted the airing of pent-up frustration by the rank and file, but in the final analysis yielded, as one observer put it, "extraordinarily few results."[68] The Soviets were pleased. On July 22, the day of Poland's communist holiday, Brezhnev and Tikhonov sent a warm congratulatory cable to Kania, Jaruzelski, and Chairman of the Council of the State H. Jabłoński. TASS reported that the newly elected Polish Central Committee had been introduced to the representatives of the communist parties present at the congress and had received "fraternal greetings"; for the first time since the beginning of the crisis the Poles had done what had been expected of them. Jaruzelski's assurances to Moscow gained new credibility.

Following the congress, Jaruzelski was featured ever more prominently in the Soviet press, in particular in a TASS report on the meeting in early August, chaired by the general, of the Polish National Defense Committee and on his involvement in the process of managing the Polish economy, which was by this time critically disrupted. Private talks between Jaruzelski and high-level Soviet military men continued. As reported by the Polish Press Agency and TASS, in early September Jaruzelski met with Marshal Ustinov and with the chief of the Soviet Army's Main Political Administration, Gen. A. Yepishev. This apparent improvement in Polish-Soviet relations was disrupted by the echoes of the First Solidarity Congress.

Soviet reaction to Solidarity's national meeting of delegates, which opened in Gdańsk on September 5, was one of anger and downright condemnation. The *cause célèbre* was the union's notorious "Message to the Working People of Eastern Europe." The Soviets delivered an official demarche to the Polish government, protesting Solidarity's interference in the internal affairs of other countries.[69] On October 13, *Pravda* published an article signed by A. Petrov (an indication that it was an official Soviet view) accusing Kania of weakness in dealing with counterrevolution and charging that the ultimate objective of Solidarity was political control of the country.[70] The Soviets demanded action; in response, the Polish party issued a statement reaffirming its commitment to the Socialist Commonwealth and asking Solidarity for restraint. On September 16, the statement was broadcast on Polish radio together with excerpts from the Soviet official protest note. Six days later, Jaruzelski was visited by the Warsaw Pact Forces' chief of staff, General Gribkov, who vented Soviet displeasure and inquired about the state of martial law preparations.

Support for Jaruzelski's Group

On October 18, Kania received a vote of no-confidence and submitted his official resignation to the Fourth Plenum of the PUWP's Central Committee. On October 19, *Pravda* announced that Jaruzelski had become Poland's new first secretary. A day later, it printed the plenum's resolution and Jaruzelski's address to the Polish Central Committee. The general's customary brief biography followed.

If the two months of Jaruzelski's tenure as first secretary before the imposition of martial law were marked by growing tension, it was partly because Jaruzelski assumed from the beginning a hard-line position toward the opposition's demands.[71] Still, the Soviets remained wary till the end. Their experience with the Polish military had taught them that even the Polish army's most dedicated communists could behave unpredictably. In order to remind Jaruzelski that if he failed, the Warsaw Pact stood ready to help, Moscow continued its barrage against "counterrevolutionaries masquerading as trade unionists" and expressed approval for Jaruzelski's unwillingness to compromise. On October 26, TASS asserted that talks with the union made no sense as long as the wave of strikes continued.[72] On October 30, reporting on the conclusion of the Fifth PUWP Central Committee Plenum on the preceding day, *Pravda* stressed Jaruzelski's warning to the opposition that "only socialism and the party can guarantee Poland's independence" and restated his call to the "realistically thinking elements in Solidarity to stop the strikes." The same commentary reported that Gen. F. Siwicki had been brought into the ruling Politburo as a candidate member.[73] On November 1, TASS carried Jaruzelski's now-famous speech to the Sejm in which he attacked the "extremists in Solidarity."

The Soviets did not comment openly on the summit meeting on November 4 between Jaruzelski, Primate Glemp, and Wałęsa, nor did they express an opinion of Jaruzelski's proposal, made on November 9, to create a special seven-member Front of National Accord that would include a representative of Solidarity. It appears likely, as one author suggests, that Moscow's silence on these subjects indicated its private disapproval of Jaruzelski's initiatives.[74] Publicly the Soviets remained restrained, probably because of Jaruzelski's assurances that the creation of the front was nothing but another tactical move. Since in the past Moscow had reacted violently to any indication of a power-sharing agreement with Solidarity, its silence on a subject as sensitive as a germinal coalition government suggests that the Soviets had ironclad assurances from Jaruzelski that his maneuvering was only intended to put Solidarity off guard. More indicative of Jaruzelski's true intentions was a cable to Brezhnev and Tikhonov sent by the general, congratulating the Soviet leaders on the anniversary of the October Revolution. In his message, Jaruzelski expressed optimism that a speedy resolution of the crisis was approaching, despite the machinations of the "reactionary forces."[75]

The end of November and the beginning of December were marked by a rapid heightening of tension.[76] On November 25, possibly earlier, Marshal Kulikov arrived in Warsaw for consultations with Jaruzelski.[77] Following the meeting with Kulikov, who probably remained in Poland until the imposition of martial law,[78] Jaruzelski addressed the PUWP on November 29, demanding an end to the strikes, and declaring that otherwise a "state of war" would become imminent.[79]

The Soviets continued building their propaganda case against Solidarity to the last minute. On December 9, *Pravda* reprinted a *Rudé právo* article entitled "Program for Counterrevolution," describing an alleged clandestine Solidarity meeting held in Radom in preparation for a confrontation with the government. On December 10, *Pravda* ran a fabricated story accusing Solidarity of training storm troopers to fight the government. On December 11, Solidarity's national commission convened in Gdańsk to decide whether to endorse the call for a general strike issued by the Warsaw regional chapter. Moscow's rejoinder was brief: Solidarity had already called for a counter-revolutionary uprising in Poland.[80] That same night Jaruzelski's forces went into action.

The first Soviet report on the introduction of martial law in Poland was published on December 14, on the front page of *Pravda*; Jaruzelski's speech to the nation was also carried in full. The delay seemed to indicate that Moscow hesitated to throw its full support behind Jaruzelski, until it had become clear that the military operation was proceeding as planned, and that the Polish general had not in the end tried some unexpected move. Clearly, even while assisting the Polish army in the crackdown, the Soviets distrusted the Poles. On December 15, in a brief TASS communiqué, the Kremlin expressed the official support of the "Soviet government and the Soviet people" for the measures taken in Poland. Special note was taken of Jaruzelski's declaration that the "Polish-Soviet alliance was and would remain the cornerstone of the Polish national interest, the guarantee of Poland's frontier; Poland would remain the permanent link of the Warsaw Pact." TASS reported that vigilance among Poland's armed forces continued.[81] Subsequently, the majority of situation reports from Poland were simply restatements of official communiqués published by *Żołnierz Wolności*.

Endorsement of the Blueprint for "Normalization"

Jaruzelski's victory over Solidarity by no means led to Moscow's immediate acceptance of him after the crackdown as Poland's first secretary. Although Solidarity was quickly overpowered, the plans for "normalization" after the introduction of martial law required Soviet approval. While these decisions were being made, resistance to the Polish regime flared up intermittently. *Pravda* and *Izvestiya* ran TASS crisis reports under the heading "K polozheniyu v Polshe" (The situation in Poland); *Krasnaya Zvezda* charged that NATO, in particular the United States and West Germany, and even the People's Republic of China were stirring up trouble in Poland.[82] *Pravda* followed on December 25 with charges of CIA involvement in Poland.[83]

The last spark of resistance to Jaruzelski, an occupation of a Silesian coal mine, was extinguished on December 28. Repression (including stiff prison terms for those arrested during strikes), the curfew, military patrols, and constant security checks continued. Nonetheless, the regime demonstrated its growing confidence that the opposition had been crushed by restoring telephone communications within towns and cities on January 10; they were, however, subject to wiretaps and interruptions. A month later, on February 10, with the exception of Gdańsk, long-distance phone service was also restored in Poland. On February 28, the eve of Jaruzelski's first of the two crucial visits to Moscow during 1982, the government announced that over 2,500 prisoners had been released.[84] The next day Jaruzelski flew to Moscow to outline his "normalization" plan and lobby for Soviet approval.

Jaruzelski's visit to Moscow on March 1, 1982, was announced in all central Soviet newspapers with the same TASS release. The communiqué was accompanied by Jaruzelski's picture and contained the general's official biography, identical to the one published after his appointment as Poland's party chief in October of 1981. The announcement stated rather cautiously that "the Soviet people, welcoming the Polish delegation . . . expressed confidence that the visit would be an opportunity to strengthen further the friendship, unity, and cooperation between the USSR and People's Poland."[85] This was a welcome more appropriate for a revolutionary leader of a Third World "progressive" regime than for the head of "fraternal Poland."

The outcome of the meeting would determine whether Jaruzelski was worthy of continued Soviet support, and whether his blueprint for "normalization" would win Brezhnev's backing. The Soviets were also going to thank the man who had solved their problem in Poland. To underscore the importance of the talks, the welcoming party that met the Poles at the Vnukovo Airport included the CPSU's top brass: Brezhnev, Tikhonov, Andropov, Gromyko, Chernenko, Ustinov, and Rusakov. On the Polish side, Jaruzelski's entourage included Deputy Premier P. Malinowski; Deputy Premier E. Kowalczyk; Foreign Minister J. Czyrek; Politburo member and first secretary of the Katowice voivodship, Z. Messner; Gen. Florian Siwicki, Jaruzelski's close associate and a member of the Politburo; Central Committee Secretary M. Woźniak; Deputy Prime Minister for Economic Affairs J. Obodowski; and Poland's ambassador to the Soviet Union, K. Olszewski. The ceremony was complete, with the review of the guards and a parade in honor of the general.[86]

Several hours of official discussions followed. Whatever Jaruzelski had to say to the Soviet Politburo must have been reassuring, because TASS reportage on the event had a radically warmer tone than its earlier reports on the general. According to the news agency, the talks were conducted "in a friendly and cordial manner and demonstrated the permanence of the fraternal union between Poland and the Soviet Union."[87] The general and his entourage were treated to an official dinner with Brezhnev and his colleagues.

The speeches given during the reception by Brezhnev and Jaruzelski suggest that, if the Soviets had at first felt uncomfortable with the idea of having Jaruzelski, a military man, in charge in Poland, those doubts were now largely gone. "We have accepted with complete understanding," said Brezhnev toasting Jaruzelski, "the information given us about the national solution chosen by our friends in order to defend the people's power, to lower tensions, and to lead the country out of the painfully deep crisis. These are timely measures."[88] In Soviet parlance, Jaruzelski's "normalization" scheme had won Brezhnev's blessing. Next followed Brezhnev's approval of Jaruzelski as a fellow communist: "Had the communists [in Poland] yielded to the counterrevolution, the fate of Poland, the stability of Europe, and even the world would have been threatened."[89]

Jaruzelski was clearly delighted. He thanked Brezhnev and his comrades for the warm reception. "This reception means a lot to me," said the general, "as this is my first trip abroad as first secretary." He also thanked his Moscow colleagues for "meeting our decisions, taken to consolidate the party, with understanding and for extending your trust to us."[90] By "decisions" Jaruzelski meant the set of policies that would constitute the basis for Poland's "normalization" after the introduction of martial law.

The next day, Jaruzelski had a private consultation with Brezhnev and Tikhonov, followed by the issuing of a joint Polish-Soviet communiqué that reaffirmed both sides' "complete unity of views and full commitment to further strengthen their fraternal relations."[91] The Poles were taken back to the airport and bade farewell with all the pomp and circumstance dictated by diplomatic protocol. It was Jaruzelski's moment of triumph; he had won unqualified Soviet approval as Poland's leader.

Jaruzelski visited Moscow once again in 1982, on August 16, but that visit was quite routine. *Pravda* and *Izvestiya* ran a front page account of the "friendly visit" by the general to Brezhnev's Crimean retreat.[92] The picture accompanying the release showed Jaruzelski, this time in civilian clothes, with Brezhnev, Chernenko, and Gromyko. As TASS reported, Jaruzelski had informed the Soviets of the "gradual positive change taking place in Poland," which was best demonstrated by the PUWP's ability "to strengthen its ties to the working class and lead the national renewal dear to all Polish patriots."[93] The message was that Jaruzelski had lived up to his commitment to govern through the party, and that "normalization was proceeding according to plan." As reported by TASS, "L. I. Brezhnev and W. Jaruzelski acknowledged with pleasure that in all aspects the relations between the Soviet Union and the Polish People's Republic were being strengthened according to the principles of socialist internationalism, equality, respect for each other's sovereignty, and friendly assistance, as agreed upon during the previous March meeting."[94]

Despite the precedent this decision had created, the Soviets chose, after some hesitation, to accept Jaruzelski and his government as yet another "fraternal government" in Eastern Europe. The military background of the new Polish first secretary, as well as that of his closest assistants, were played down; at no point in Soviet reports of the 1982 visits was Jaruzelski or his closest associate, Gen. Florian Siwicki, who accompanied him on the March trip, referred to as defense minister, or chief of the Polish general staff, or even as "general." Apparently, Jaruzelski's credentials as a loyal communist, who had assisted Moscow in the invasion of Czechoslovakia in 1968 and in 1981 had defended Soviet strategic interests in Poland, were sufficiently strong to outweigh whatever objections the Kremlin might have had to his military background.

Normalization
and Beyond,
1982–1988

— 9

Expectations and Reality

The destruction of Solidarity as an organization capable of coordinating mass-scale national resistance to the government was accomplished de facto during the first year of military rule. Through ruthless application of force, Jaruzelski succeeded in containing strikes and breaking up demonstrations. In a display of the regime's self-confidence, the Council of State announced on December 19, 1982, that martial law would be suspended on December 31. The decision was viewed as the litmus test of the government's overall control of the situation and a prelude to the complete lifting of the state of war. It also marked the beginning of the regime's "political normalization" campaign.

Jaruzelski's "political normalization" had four basic goals: (1) the reconstruction of the PUWP and the rebuilding of the governmental apparat; (2) fragmenting and defeating the remaining opposition forces; (3) arresting the country's economic decline; and (4) breaking out from the international isolation imposed on Poland after the 1981 crackdown.

The four years of "normalization," between 1982 and 1986, were characterized by increased activism on the part of the regime. Jaruzelski's program was implemented through a series of ideological campaigns, periodic price increases, debt-rescheduling negotiations, and a continuing crackdown on the opposition. Polish "normalization" after 1982 was also marked by important political changes. The preparatory state during which were laid the legal foundations for the new policies that guaranteed the government the powers to intervene at will in the lives of all citizens, lasted until the formal lifting of martial law on July 22, 1983. During that period new legislation was introduced, and several shell organizations were set up that were intended to serve as instruments of the regime's control over the population; the most prominent among them was the Patriotic Movement of National Rebirth (Patriotyczny Ruch Odrodzenia Narodowego; PRON). Concurrently, the government continued to work for the reconstruction of the party and the state bureaucracy. This stage of the "normalization process" lasted until the Sejm elections of 1985, and was characterized by considerable internal party strife. The most severe crisis inside the government occurred in October 1984 over the police murder of a pro-Solidarity priest, Father Jerzy Popiełuszko.

Since Jaruzelski considered ideological renewal essential to the party's political rebirth, during the "normalization" period the PUWP worked intermittently on a new ideological party platform. The effort was highlighted by a national party conference devoted to the party's leadership role; this "ideological renewal" culminated in the Tenth PUWP Congress, held in June of 1986. Bureaucratic politics also figured prominently in Jaruzelski's plans for rebuilding the party. Purges of Jaruzelski's opponents and potential challengers continued throughout the "normalization" period. The PUWP was subjected to several reshufflings, and the government underwent important structural changes.

Jaruzelski's "normalization campaign" officially ended with the Tenth PUWP Congress in 1986. The congress was billed by the regime as a symbol of the party's victory over the opposition, as well as evidence of the PUWP's ability to overcome internal divisions and re-establish its leadership role in Polish society. The grass-roots reforms of the Ninth Congress were reversed. Nevertheless, even though Jaruzelski succeeded in controlling the party, his government's claims that it had re-established its authority were repudiated by the 1987 rejection of his economic program in a nationwide referendum, and by a wave of strikes that followed in 1988. But the 1987 economic reform lay beyond the scope of Jaruzelski's "normalization campaign"; after the Tenth Congress, the party was again able to function.

The concentration on party politics at the expense of the country's economic health would prove to be an immense political blunder. Soon after the Tenth Congress had heralded Jaruzelski as Poland's undisputed leader, social discontent reached the boiling point. The situation was made worse by a series of clumsy economic half-measures, billed as the "Second Stage of the Economic Reform," which resulted in a dramatic decline of the standard of living and a 60 percent inflation between 1986 and 1988.[1] In 1988, Poland was rocked by two waves of strikes, the first in April-May and the second in August, which ultimately led to the resignation of Premier Z. Messner's entire cabinet—an event without precedent in the Soviet bloc. In addition, Jaruzelski had to grapple with the deterioration of his army's morale and a rapidly growing draft-resistance movement among Polish youth. By 1989, when the dust had settled, even though the general had retained a firm grip on the party and the government, the two were becoming increasingly irrelevant in a society exhausted by the protracted economic crisis and desperate for change. Among the calls for reform and the rescinding of Solidarity's proscription, it became obvious that "normalization" had solved none of the nation's problems; on August 31, 1988, Interior Minister Kiszczak invited "private citizen" Lech Wałęsa to participate in a roundtable discussion between the government and the opposition on Poland's economic and political future. Soon afterward the cabinet of Premier Messner was replaced by a new government headed by Mieczysław Rakowski, Jaruzelski's tough deputy prime minister during the period of martial law. Eight years after the introduction of martial law, Jaruzelski would have to choose between his often-repeated conviction that only the PUWP had the right to make policy decisions and the realization that in order to avoid another powerful eruption of popular discontent, his regime needed a modicum of cooperation with the opposition.

The New Laws

The immediate success of martial law was unquestionable. The labor union was crushed and resistance quickly contained by a skillfully executed series of assaults by the ZOMO and selected army units. When the Council of State issued a decree on December 31, 1982, which suspended the emergency decree, a new Law on Trade Unions passed by the Sejm had already been enacted. Among some 70 new legislative acts passed by the Sejm that defined the framework of Jaruzelski's "normalization," this one was arguably the most important. Approved on October 8, 1982,[2] it delegated the responsiblity for new trade-union registration to regional (voivodship) courts, thereby ensuring regional fragmentation of any future trade-union movement. National organization of trade-union activities—a source of Solidarity's strength in the past— was prohibited. The new legislation preserved the right to strike, but strikes would be permitted only as a means of last resort in rectifying general working conditions. Strikes were not allowed in connection with wage demands and would be tolerated only after an obligatory seven-day period of arbitration had elapsed. No trade-union activity would be permitted for police, teachers, firemen, or workers employed in plants classified by the Ministry of Internal Affairs as important to national security. Penalties for breaking the new law would be mandatory imprisonment for one year, a fine of 50,000 złotys, and the suspension of civil rights.[3] In addition, the government was authorized in a special law of October 26, 1982, to direct those currently not holding a job to perform compulsory public service.[4] Additional laws strengthened the government's central controls. For example, the Law on the Protection of State and Official Secrets, enacted on December 14, 1982, or the laws on the National Council of Culture and on Higher Education, passed on May 4, 1982, led to further strengthening of the regime's control of the flow of information in Poland.

Another important piece of legislation drafted during the first year of martial law was the Special Emergency Powers Act, passed by the Sejm as a precondition for the lifting of martial law. The new bill gave Jaruzelski the power to militarize industrial plants and place their employees under the authority of army commissars, if the government deemed such action necessary for maintaining order in the country. The Emergency Powers Act also granted the government the right to detain for an indefinite period of time anyone whose activities were judged contrary to the interests of state security. To ensure control over the flow of information, the government was empowered to outlaw at any time the publication, distribution, and possession of any printed material it considered hostile to its interests. In short, the Special Emergency Powers Act institutionalized the key provisions of martial law and granted the military the legal authority to resort to martial law at any time.[5]

By 1983 it had become clear that the extensive police powers exercised by the regime under martial law, and subsequently written into law, would constitute the ultimate guarantee of the effectiveness of Jaruzelski's "normalization" program. During 1982 alone, more than 50 major pieces of legislation were introduced to strengthen the government's powers to control society and repress dissent.[6] As martial law was being suspended in December of 1982, a new decree of December 18 replaced the initial "state of war" declaration with the Law on Special Legal Regulations for the Period of Suspended Martial Law.[7] While doing away with the sweeping internment regulations of 1981, the new law nevertheless retained the key provisions of the bill, giving the military and security forces the extended mandate to continue running the country. The laws of December 1981 and December 1982, as well as the decree of July 14, 1983, which stipulated that the bill suspending martial law would be replaced upon the lifting of the state of war by a new general piece of legislation (called the Law on Special Legal Regulations for the Period of Overcoming the Socioeconomic Crisis), kept in place the Military Council of National Salvation (WRON), Jaruzelski's de facto cabinet.

Legislative change called for by Jaruzelski's "normalization" program also affected the country's constitution. Two days prior to the lifting of martial law, on July 20, 1983, the Sejm passed four constitutional amendments.[8] One of Jaruzelski's proposals for change in the basic law made the Patriotic Movement of National Rebirth (PRON) a new, constitutionally sanctioned umbrella organization that replaced the defunct Front of National Unity (Front Jedności

Narodu; FJN). PRON's stated goal was to unite Poland's three officially recognized political parties, the PUWP, the United Peasant Party (Zjednoczone Stronnictwo Ludowe; ZSL), and the Democratic Party (Stronnictwo Demokratyczne; SD), in an effort to re-establish a dialogue between the government and Polish society. Jaruzelski's second constitutional amendment reflected the general's ideological creed; it stressed the classless nature of the Polish state and declared that the party's goal was to fulfill the aspirations of the proletariat. Another 1983 constitutional amendment concerned land ownership. While it confirmed the government's guarantees of private land ownership by the peasants, it contained a clause emphasizing the need for further "socialist transformation" of the Polish countryside. The fourth constitutional amendment gave Jaruzelski the power to resort to martial law at any time. It empowered the legislature or the Council of State to declare a state of war in case of "external aggression" or "internal threat."[9] The full importance of this provision would become obvious only in 1985, after the administrative restructuring that shifted the executive powers of government away from the premier and his Council of Ministers to the chairman of the Council of State. In 1985, Jaruzelski would resign from the office of prime minister and assume the chairmanship of the Council of State; in effect, in 1983 he had already arranged for a constitutional carte blanche for himself to impose martial law whenever he judged it appropriate.

The legal framework envisaged by the military and enacted by the Sejm prior to the lifting of martial law restored the badly damaged mechanism of central governmental controls and gave the regime the necessary tools to crack down on the opposition after the state of war had formally been lifted. The very number of new laws and regulations passed by the Sejm on Jaruzelski's initiative was indicative of the character of the new regime and its methods of governing; it revealed a military mind-set applied to civilian administration. As in army barracks, the military insisted on the meticulous spelling out of rules and "standard operating procedures" for the members of Polish society and of its government. Jaruzelski and his generals apparently believed, on the basis of their professional experience, that once the rules had been spelled out, the mechanism of the state and its administrative agencies would function as intended. In this light, one should not treat merely as a smoke screen Jaruzelski's often-repeated arguments that arrested opposition leaders were being punished because they had violated the law, or that the government was committed to maintaining order and enforcing the rules. In fact, the flurry of legislative activity, the frequent reports by Jaruzelski and his ministers to the Sejm, and the reiteration of the theme of "socialist legality" were all part of the soldier's belief that the only way to deal with administrative chaos was through a consistent application of clearly spelled-out regulations and the punishment of those who disobeyed orders.

Regime Consolidation

Among the four tasks facing Jaruzelski in 1982, the consolidation of the party and government, and the re-establishing of the PUWP's "leading role" in Poland continued to have the highest priority. The Jaruzelski regime spared no effort in tackling the daunting task of rebuilding the party and re-establishing a functioning government, with or without social acceptance. Less urgent, but equally important, was the reanimation of Poland's communist youth movement, which had been shattered during the Solidarity period, and which Jaruzelski rightly regarded as essential to the party's future.

During the period between the suspension of martial law on December 31, 1982, and the formal lifting of the state of emergency on July 22, 1983, Jaruzelski conducted a thorough purge of the central and local party apparat and of all government agencies. In February 1983, a sweeping review of the party rolls was initiated, aimed at "closing the party ranks" and purging the PUWP of untrustworthy members.[10] The "verification process" was made even more complicated by the dwindling membership and the apathy of the rank and file. According to figures released by the government, in the three years since the Eighth PUWP Congress, held in February 1980, the party had lost over 820,000 members, or one-third of its total membership.[11] More important, the greatest exodus from the PUWP was that of the industrial workers, the very class the party claimed to represent. For example, in Bielsko Biała, a major industrial town, workers' resignations constituted almost 62 percent of the total number; many of those were 15–20-year party veterans, and 4 percent of those had been in the party since its creation in 1948. It was estimated that the decline in membership would continue for some time at a rate of 20,000 per month.[12]

The decision to initiate a massive purge as a precondition for re-establishing the PUWP's cohesion was an integral part of the planning for the suspension of martial law. It was made on December 18, 1982, during a special session of the Politburo; the announcement that martial law would be suspended by the end of the year came a day later.[13] During the meeting, the Politburo emphasized that in order for the party to consolidate its position, it was imperative that the members should work through the channels of party bureaucracy. In cases where local party organizations at the plant level (POPs) were deemed beyond repair, that is, where they had been taken over by the rank-and-file proponents of "horizontal structures" after the Ninth Congress, Jaruzelski ordered that they should be immediately disbanded.[14] In order to rebuild the POPs and increase the Central Committee's control over local and regional party organizations, special political workers were dispatched to some 200 industrial plants on March 22. In addition, Jaruzelski instituted a practice of frequently summoning local party activists to Warsaw to attend meetings with selected Politburo members and report to the first secretary on the situation in the countryside.

The extent to which the military had come to play a pivotal role in Poland's political life was demonstrated by the importance of the Armed Forces Inspectorate in the purge of 1982–1983. In most cases, party control commissions charged with the implementation of the "verification process" conducted their investigations of individual PUWP members in close cooperation with senior army officers from the Inspectorate. In addition, the Inspectorate was authorized to conduct its own independent investigations of party apparatchiks, of which about 200 were completed by the end of 1982.[15]

Indoctrination was considered a key to the party's ability to renew itself. The verification campaign notwithstanding, the PUWP was unable to overcome the apathy of its members or to attract fresh blood to replenish its ranks. In fact, while the party lost roughly one third of its membership between 1980 and 1982, by its own admission in 1982 it had been able to recruit only 6,500 new candidate members during that same period; furthermore, workers constituted a clear minority among the new recruits.[16] Hence, late 1982 and early 1983 witnessed a special effort on the part of the regime to step up the ideological training of the party *aktiv*. Intensive seminars on Marxism-Leninism were organized at the Central Committee's Higher School of Social Science in Warsaw and at various party schools and training facilities, including evening schools for party cadres. In addition, select party members were sent to the Soviet Union for specialized advanced training in organizational work. A number of meetings, including Politburo sessions and plenums of the Central Committee, were devoted almost exclusively to questions of ideology. For example, the Politburo session of February 15, 1983, reviewed the proposed amendments to the PUWP's ideological party platform, entitled "What Are We Fighting For, Where Are We Heading?" which had been proposed in March 1982 as a basis for the PUWP's renewal.[17]

The argument that the root cause of Poland's problems consisted solely in the party's weakness became the accepted dogma among Jaruzelski's men. This interpretation of the crisis deflected all criticism from the political system itself, and allowed the regime to pin the blame for the developments and occurrences of 1980–1981 on the "past mistakes of the Gierek leadership." It also agreed with official Soviet views on the subject. During a plenum of the CPSU's Central Committee in June 1983, the new Soviet general secretary, Yuriy Andropov, confirmed Jaruzelski's contention that Poland's problems were caused by the "weakening of the party's leadership role." Some responsibility for the crisis was also laid at the door of "Western imperialists," whom Foreign Minister Andrey Gromyko accused of "unacceptable interference in Poland's internal affairs."[18]

The goal of re-establishing the PUWP's "leadership role" became a *sine qua non* of the normalization process. Jaruzelski's incessant emphasis on party discipline and the responsibility of government officials for their performance led on occasion to rather comical results. For example, in January 1983 the general decreed that over 3,000 senior managers and key state officials from 27 ministries and government agencies would be required to take a written test to demonstrate their familiarity with the current economic program.[19] Since only 50 percent of the participants received the grade of "B" or above, the regime declared the results void and announced another series of tests to be administered in April, to allow the cadres ample time to study the intricacies of the subject.

Jaruzelski was determined to ensure his control over key government agencies before martial law was formally lifted. During a session of the Sejm in late March 1983, the old-time Mieczysław Moczar, who during the crisis appeared to have been the Soviets' choice for first secretary, was removed from his position as chairman of the Supreme Control Commission. His place was taken by Jaruzelski's trusted supporter and martial-law planner Gen. Tadeusz Hupałowski. Hupałowski's former position as minister of administration, local economy, and environmental protection was taken over by another associate of Jaruzelski, Gen. Włodzimerz Oliwa of the Warsaw Military District.[20] During the period when Solidarity was legal, Oliwa had distinguished himself as a vociferous critic of the labor union and a proponent of a hard-line approach in dealing with the opposition. Finally, on Jaruzelski's recommendation, Col. Mirosław Wojciechowski, Poland's former military attaché to Stockholm and head of Interpress, the agency that handles contacts with foreign journalists, was put in charge of the Committee for Radio and Television (Komitet Radia i Telewizji), an agency attached to the Council of Ministers and responsible for the supervision of all broadcasting in Poland.[21] By appointing Wojciechowski to head KRiTV, Jaruzelski made one of his trusted military men the overseer of all information and propaganda disseminated in the country.

The session of the Sejm that confirmed these personnel changes was addressed by Gen. Czesław Kiszczak, Poland's minister of the interior, who reported on the successes of the government's action against the strikers, reaffirmed the regime's commitment to use all forces at its disposal against the opposition, and put the official count of civilian casualties from the clashes during the early months of martial law at 15 dead and 36 wounded, most of them victims of gunshot wounds.[22]

While the party and government "house cleaning" proceeded, Jaruzelski made a pronounced effort to open up a new channel of dialogue with the nation through his Patriotic Movement of National Rebirth (PRON). PRON was formally established by the PUWP, the United Peasant Party, and the Democratic Party on July 22, 1982. Its first congress was held from May 7 to 9,

1983, as part of the government's propaganda campaign preceding the formal lifting of martial law. The PRON congress appointed a 400-member National Council (Rada Krajowa) and an 11-member Presidium. It also elected an executive committee consisting of 60 members and an 80-member Financial Control Commission (Komisja Kontroli Finansowej).[23] Throughout the normalization phase, PRON attempted, albeit with limited success, to attract members from a broad spectrum of Polish society that included workers, intelligentsia, artists, peasants, and artisans. The military was represented in the National Council by eleven senior officers, led by Jaruzelski himself. While generally unsuccessful as a forum for negotiation between the government and the nation, PRON's May congress was an important step toward initiating a series of constitutional amendments, among them one that gave constitutional sanction to the movement to draft a new law regulating election to the Sejm. As a result of the new law, PRON replaced the Front of National Unity (FJN) as the principal organizer of elections in Poland.

Jaruzelski's program of re-establishing the PUWP's complete control over the government and administrative agencies was successfully completed by 1986. As reported by the party's weekly *Polityka*, by 1986 out of 444 appointees in the central administration 94.3 percent were party members, 2.6 percent were members of the politically affiliated United Peasant Party (ZSL) and the Democratic Party (SD), and only 3.1 percent were not party members; 83 percent of all department directors and their deputies were party members, and only 14 percent were not party members. Forty out of 49 voivods (chief regional administrators) belonged to the PUWP; 8 to the United Peasant Party; and only 1 was not a party member. Eighty-two percent of all city, town, and county heads were PUWP members; 13 percent were ZSL members; 2 percent were SD members; and a mere 3 percent did not belong to either the PUWP or one of the two government-controlled parties. Between 70 and 100 percent of the heads of officially recognized associations were party members, and all the presidents and deputy presidents of labor organizations were party members. Finally, 80 percent of all enterprise directors were party members. At the same time, the *nomenklatura* had aged considerably; on average, only 11 men and 8 women among the 444 central administrators were below 35 years of age. According to official figures released in 1988, out of 1.2 million managerial jobs (*stanowisko kierownicze*) in the country, 900,000 were occupied by party members.[24] At no time in the history of People's Poland had the PUWP enjoyed comparable control over administrative appointments in all sectors of public life. Addressing a PUWP plenum, Jaruzelski emphasized that "the party would not abandon its historical responsibility for the socialist direction of Poland's social and economic development."[25] Tight control over the government's personnel policy would remain a crucial elements of the party's "socialist renewal."

For all the discussion of economic reform, Jaruzelski's program prior to 1986 deserves only a brief mention. Jaruzelski's economic strategy in 1982 and 1983, all the talk of "enterprise self-financing" and "market socialism" notwithstanding, was limited to severe austerity measures in the face of the Western economic boycott, coupled with strenuous efforts to renegotiate Poland's foreign debt. The government's economic program, outlined in 1983, envisaged that the prices of food, energy, and consumer goods would rise about 40 percent on average by 1987, while Poland's capital investment would be cut by 50 percent over the same period.[26] At the same time, Jaruzelski displayed his government's determination not to give in to strikes and demonstrations; ZOMO troopers were routinely dispatched to crush street demonstrations, while newly enacted criminal legislation ensured that protesters would face swift punishment.

Reclaiming the Military Tradition

The image of the Polish soldier-patriot suffered terribly as a result of martial law. Hence, as part of the normalization campaign, the military moved to prop up the army's prestige. The most obvious manifestation of this policy was Jaruzelski's decision to dust off a number of national Polish symbols, such as the reintroduction of the four-cornered army cap (*czapka rogatywka*), a symbol of Poland's Insurrectionary Tradition and a part of the prewar Polish army uniform. At one point, there were even hints that the Polish eagle might regain its traditional crown, which for forty years of communist rule had been absent from the national insignia.[27]

The regime made renewed efforts to repatriate the remains of Gen. Władysław Sikorski, the wartime leader of Poland's government-in-exile and a great symbol to the Poles of national struggle for liberation. Jaruzelski also filed a formal request with the Sikorski Institute in London for the return of Poland's World War II national and military colors; in 1983, unconfirmed reports suggested that Warsaw was even considering bringing to Poland the remains of General Sosnkowski, another prominent leader of the London government-in-exile, a staunch anticommunist, and a fervent proponent of Poland's struggle for independence.[28] Official state media devoted an unprecedented amount of space to the discussion of the contribution of the Poles fighting in the West to the victory over Germany, implying that the Polish forces on all fronts of World War II shared in the same military tradition. Finally, attempts were made to come to terms with another communist taboo, namely the history of Polish-Jewish relations. While continuing to deny vehemently that anti-Semitism had ever been a part of Poland's past, the government nevertheless organized in 1983 an elaborate commemorative ceremony at the monument of the Warsaw Ghetto rising and for the first time invited members of the World Jewish Congress to attend.

Jaruzelski made repeated efforts to commemorate the history of Polish arms in order to claim Poland's military past as his army's legitimate heritage. Prominent among those attempts was the celebration in 1983 of the Rescue of Vienna, a Polish military expedition led by King Jan III Sobieski that lifted the Turkish siege of the Austrian capital in 1683. Sobieski's brilliant victory over the Ottoman Empire, which the majority of the Poles regard as exemplary of Poland's traditional role as the defender of European Christianity, was commemorated in a series of historical essays published in the governmental press, by television specials, and by parades of soldiers dressed in seventeenth-century uniforms.

The regime also tried some more practical steps to prop up the reputation of the Polish People's Army, especially among the country's youth, who had been badly shaken by the soldiers' role in the imposition of martial law. Considerable effort was made to indoctrinate the new recruits[29] and to attract more officer candidates. As reported by the army daily on September 1, 1985, the government opened new military high schools (*wojskowe licea ogólnokształcące*) in the cities of Lublin, Toruń, and Wrocław, with an entering first-year class of 300; plans were made to open three more such schools in Katowice, Olsztyn, and Gdynia by 1986. The new high schools were chartered as preparatory military academies, which would direct their graduates to various officers schools, where they would be turned into commissioned officers. The schools were placed under the supervision of the Ministry of Defense, which provided the buildings, audiovisual equipment, computers, and generous funding.[30] By 1988, in addition to the military academies, the air force had opened two specialized high schools for future pilots, in Dęblin and Zielona Góra.[31]

While the regime had little to offer to improve the lot of the increasingly destitute workers, it appealed to the Poles' patriotism to win popular support. Shortly after the Tenth Congress, the government celebrated the 576th anniversary (sic!) of the Polish-Lithuanian victory over the Teutonic Knights at Grunwald.[32] The celebration at the Grunwald fields was resplendent with military insignia, regimental banners, and parades in traditional Polish uniforms. As the army saw it, the victory by Poland-Lithuania in 1410 laid the foundations for the Polish-Soviet comradeship-in-arms of today. The most dramatic development in the military's campaign to reclaim Poland's heroic past came in November 1988. As part of the national celebration of the 70th anniversary of Poland's independence, government representatives laid a wreath at the crypt of Józef Piłsudski in the Wawel Castle in Cracow; an honor guard was posted at the marshal's grave. The inscription on the wreath's ribbons read: "For Józef Piłsudski on the 70th Anniversary of Poland's Independence—the Government of the Polish People's Republic."[33] The army's postwar patriotic pantomime had finally come full circle.

National Defense Committee: Poland's New Center of Power

The most significant change in the organizational structure of the Polish government, one which would ensure the military's dominant role in the country's politics, was the restructuring of the National Defense Committee (Komitet Obrony Kraju; KOK), the body that had coordinated the planning and implementation of martial law. At Jaruzelski's request, the 1967 Law on Universal Military Service was amended on November 21, 1983, to alter the KOK's function as the principal governmental agency in case of war or national emergency.

According to the provisions of the 1967 law, the KOK was headed by the prime minister, while the defense minister assumed the position of one of several KOK deputy chairmen designated by the Council of Ministers. Regular KOK members were chosen by the premier. The National Defense Committee was empowered to supervise all regional defense committees. These were set up in voivodships and chaired by regional administrators with the assistance of local military commanders and party secretaries. As stated in the 1967 law, the KOK's principal responsibility was to define policy guidelines in a national emergency, and to coordinate the work of regional and local defense committees.

Jaruzelski introduced fundamental changes into the KOK legislation. The revision of the law, enacted on November 21, 1983, stipulated that, in order to increase the KOK's effectiveness, its chairman would be appointed directly by the Sejm, while his deputies would be chosen by the Council of State. The newly appointed KOK chairman would enjoy the "institutional prerogatives of Commander in Chief," while in case of war a "Supreme Commander of the Armed Forces" would be appointed, presumably the same person as the KOK chairman.[34] On November 22, Jaruzelski resigned from his position as defense minister and, on the same day, was unanimously elected KOK chairman. As of this writing, he continues to occupy that position. Also in 1983, on Jaruzelski's recommendation, the general's closest associate since the 1968 invasion of Czechoslovakia, Gen. Florian Siwicki, was promoted to defense minister.

The crucial importance of the KOK's restructuring and Jaruzelski's appointment to the position of KOK chairman became clear two years later, in 1985, when, ostensibly as part of a routine government reshuffling, Jaruzelski resigned his post of prime minister and accepted the position of chairman of the Council of State. There can be little doubt that this change had been planned already in 1983, when the constitution was amended to give the chairman of the Council of State virtually presidential powers. Jaruzelski's election to the KOK chairmanship on November 22 was accompanied by the elevation of Politburo Member Zbigniew Messner to the position of deputy premier, a first step to Jaruzelski's eventual relinquishing of the premiership. As Messner was being gradually introduced to his new duties, Jaruzelski could rely on Gen. Michał Janiszewski, his trusted aide and the director of Jaruzelski's cabinet in the Council of Ministers to monitor Messner's work and report to Jaruzelski on the efficiency and loyalty of the central administration.

Although it passed almost unnoticed in the West, the modification of the 1967 Law on Universal Military Service was a watershed in the military's consolidation of its position in the government and a linchpin of Jaruzelski's "normalization" program. By creating in 1983 the preconditions for his resignation from the premiership in 1985, Jaruzelski made it clear that his goal was to claim the executive prerogatives of the president, relinquished in 1952 by Bolesław Bierut.[35]

The changes made in 1983 in the KOK's structure and its operational procedures weakened considerably the office of the prime minister. Not only did the premier lose the KOK chairmanship, he also no longer had direct control over appointments to the KOK. These were now the prerogative of the chairman of the Council of State, that is, General Jaruzelski. In effect, the functions of the office of prime minister were reduced solely to those of caretaker of the economy. Jaruzelski's resignation from the premiership and the promotion of Messner, an economist by training, was in keeping with the general's decision to limit the premier's executive authority. Finally, by relinquishing the position of prime minister, Jaruzelski was, at least formally, distancing himself from the country's economic policies and, should another economic disaster befall Poland, it would be easier for him to save face by pinning the blame on Messner. Since in 1983 the Polish standard of living declined on average by 20 percent relative to 1982, and a similar decline was expected in 1984, after new price increases announced in November 1983 had taken effect,[36] Jaruzelski probably considered it prudent to leave the economic mess to the apparatchiks. As the crisis of 1988 would demonstrate, the general displayed a remarkable foresight in doing so.

Even though Jaruzelski would no longer formally oversee the state administration, he by no means risked losing control over the bureaucracy. The army continued its practice of periodic inspections of local and regional administrative offices by small army detachments, first initiated as a reconnaissance in preparation for the imposition of martial law. Since the commander of each military unit reported to a plenipotentiary of the local defense committee, which in turn reported through established military channels to the KOK, Jaruzelski was guaranteed a constant flow of up-to-date intelligence on developments in all regions of the country and on the effectiveness of his local administrators. In fact, shortly after the crucial KOK reforms had taken effect, on December 7, 1983, Jaruzelski ordered his small army detachments into the countryside to check on the work of local administrators and "assess the country's defense readiness."[37] The exercise lasted two weeks, and (as in 1981) covered both towns and villages.

The KOK reform of 1983 also explains Jaruzelski's willingness to relinquish his post as defense minister. Since Jaruzelski became KOK chairman in 1983, and therefore exercised the powers of commander in chief, it was no longer necessary for him to hold on to the position of defense minister. Still, possibly as a bit of "extra insurance," Jaruzelski delegated his old job to General Siwicki, whose loyalty to him was beyond reproach. By promoting Siwicki to defense minister, Jaruzelski ensured that the armed forces remained tightly under his control.

Jaruzelski could feel confident that his officers would remain loyal to him because changes in the KOK structure and Siwicki's appointment came only after the general had purged his Defense Ministry staff. Two senior officers, Gen. Eugeniusz Molczyk and Gen. Włodzimierz Sawczuk, who had proved disloyal to Jaruzelski during the period of confrontation with Solidarity by pressuring him to move against Solidarity ahead of schedule, were pushed aside and eventually removed.[38] General Sawczuk, a one time MPA Chief who had been replaced on May 7, 1980, by Gen. Józef Baryła, was dismissed from the general staff in July 1982 and sent out of the country as Poland's ambassador to Libya.[39] General Molczyk, who at one time had ranked among the country's most influential political officers, was eased out of power, and finally retired in 1986. The official reason given in the military press for Molczyk's retirement was "poor health."[40]

The "normalization process" of 1982–1986 also included a maneuver aimed at tightening Jaruzelski's control over the security police (Służba Bezpieczeństwa; SB). Beyond the traditional competition between the army and the police, there had been several indications in the past that the relationship between the Polish army and the SB was strained. From 1980 to 1981, during the planning of the imposition of martial law, occasional clashes between Siwicki of the Defense Ministry and Poland's key policeman, General Milewski, delayed the planning process and demonstrated that the SB would not submit easily to Jaruzelski's control. The Bydgoszcz crisis of March 1981 and the near-disaster that followed demonstrated to Jaruzelski that direct supervision of the SB was necessary if similar surprises were to be prevented in the future.[41] Since Milewski was one of the key martial-law planners, in 1981 Jaruzelski simply could not afford to get rid of him right away; instead, Poland's police boss was co-opted into the Politburo, where Jaruzelski could keep an eye on him, while the day-to-day control over his ministry was transferred over to Gen. Czesław Kiszczak, Jaruzelski's trusted lieutenant.

In November 1983, as the crucial reforms of the KOK were taking shape, Jaruzelski moved to ensure his complete control over the SB. On his orders, a special interbranch Committee for the Protection of Law, Public Order, and Public Discipline was set up under the chairmanship of General Kiszczak, Poland's acting minister of the interior. On matters of security, Kiszczak's committee, staffed with his trusted appointees and reporting directly to the minister, was a supervisory body to all government agencies, including the SB; in effect, it became Jaruzelski's watchdog over the security forces. Since the committee's decisions were binding on the SB, Milewski's old police cadres found themselves overnight subordinated to Jaruzelski's military appointees. In 1984, the growing discontent within the SB, caused by the army's intrusion into security operations, would lead to a dramatic confrontation between Jaruzelski and Kiszczak and Milewski. The police murder in 1984 of a pro-Solidarity priest, Father Jerzy Popiełuszko, and the ensuing investigation and trial of the perpetrators ended with Jaruzelski finally bringing the security forces under his complete control.

The Popiełuszko Affair

As in 1981, there were indications in 1984 that a new challenge to Jaruzelski's authority had been gathering momentum inside the government. An argument over ideology and government policies in dealing with the opposition came again to the forefront. Throughout 1983 and 1984, the Central Committee periodically took up the discussion of the party's platform "What Are We Fighting For? Where Are We Heading?" first proposed in 1982. In the course of the discussion, the proposed revisions eventually abandoned all criticism of the party's mistakes and reverted to the traditional ideological orthodoxy of the past, emphasizing the "leadership role of the party." These scholastic debates over ideology were joined in early 1984 when several so-called Marxist discussion clubs in the countryside were reported to have brought up charges against Jaruzelski's regime for being too soft in dealing with the opposition.

The accusations were alarming enough for Jaruzelski to respond to them forcefully during the three-day National Party Conference (Krajowa Konferencja Delegatów) of March 1984, the first such mass party gathering in Poland since the Ninth PUWP Congress and an important stage in the preparations for the upcoming Tenth Congress. Evaluating the road the party had traveled since 1981, Jaruzelski demanded forcefully that regional activists focus on enforcing party discipline and work to strengthen the centralized structure of the PUWP.[42] The general emphasized in his address to some 1800 delegates that commitment to ideology and the party line *as defined by the leadership** was expected of every card-carrying member. To drive his point home, Jaruzelski reminded his audience that the recent Thirteenth Central Committee Plenum fully supported his demand for the removal of some 350 Central Committee staffers and 6000 apparatchiks from regional and local party organizations. The warning was clear: those who did not perform up to Jaruzelski's expectations, or who challenged his leadership, would be fired on the spot.

The speech had the desired effect. The National Party Conference adopted a resolution supporting the policies pursued by the Politburo since the Ninth Congress and expressing special thanks and recognition to Jaruzelski "for his service to the party"; it also fully confirmed the "correctness" of the general's policies. The document restated the party's commitment to Polish-Soviet friendship and cooperation, blamed the United States for interfering in Poland's internal affairs, and praised PRON for its efforts to bring about a new national accord. It adopted a revised version of the ideological declaration "What Are We Fighting For?" and expressed the party's commitment to combat "anarchy and counterrevolution," the two themes emphasized in Jaruzelski's speech.[43]

Even though criticism of Jaruzelski's policies was voiced chiefly by low-level party members, a direct challenge to his authority would ultimately come from within his own Politburo. It appears that Stefan Olszowski, the seasoned hard-line apparatchik who, together with Gen. Mirosław Milewski of the SB, had made his bid for party leadership during the Bydgoszcz crisis in 1981, was again scheming against Jaruzelski. Although Jaruzelski's position appeared strong at the moment, he could lose his grip on the PUWP if the Soviets threw their support behind another candidate. Olszowski, who at the time was both a member of the Politburo and Poland's foreign minister, was undoubtedly well aware of the turmoil and uncertainty within the CPSU, caused by Andropov's sudden death and the leadership transition thus necessitated in the Soviet Union. Although Gorbachev's name came up on several occasions in reports on the choice of the new general secretary, it was more likely at the time that the job would go either to Leningrad's hard-line party boss, Romanov, or to Brezhnev's former aide, Chernenko. In either case, with Soviet support Olszowski could gamble on displacing Jaruzelski on the grounds that the general was too soft on the opposition and would hence eventually drag the party into another crisis. The grumbling of regional apparatchiks could be just the pretext Olszowski was looking for.

* The author's emphasis.

In order to deflect hard-line criticism, Jaruzelski mounted a concerted effort to crack down on the remnants of Solidarity, thus confirming indirectly that the internal challenge to his leadership was indeed serious. In March 1984, the government conducted a series of operations against the underground, arresting in the process 35 opposition activists and confiscating underground printing equipment and publications. The crackdown, which came after ten successful major raids in January and February 1984, dealt a severe blow to the opposition's ability to publish and disseminate information.[44]

If Jaruzelski had been concerned about his standing with the new Soviet leadership, it soon became apparent that he had little to fear. Following Chernenko's selection as the new CPSU boss, Moscow announced in early April 1984 that Jaruzelski and his closest associate Gen. Florian Siwicki had been awarded the Order of Lenin. As after the 1968 Czechoslovak operation, the two trusted Poles were awarded the highest Soviet decorations for their service to the Socialist Commonwealth. Siwicki went to Moscow later that month to receive his decoration, confer with Soviet defense minister Marshal D. Ustinov, and make preparations for his boss's visit. On May 4, 1984, Jaruzelski flew in to meet with the new Soviet general secretary. After a warm reception, the medal-awarding ceremony, and an official dinner in honor of Jaruzelski, Chernenko expressed his full support for the general's policies; the joint communiqué released after the visit spoke of a "complete unity of views" between the PUWP leadership and the CPSU Politburo.[45] Jaruzelski's visit also had a sentimental touch to it; on May 5, he and Siwicki attended the unveiling of the Polish-Soviet Soldier Friendship Memorial in Ryazan, where the two had been trained as line officers in Berling's army. On their return to Moscow, Jaruzelski and Chernenko signed a new long-term Polish-Soviet agreement of cooperation, which covered the economy, science, and technology; the agreement would run through the year 2000.

After Jaruzelski's successful performance in Moscow and his government's success in rescheduling its debt, the conflict brewing within the Polish leadership became muted, probably owing in part to the June 17 elections to people's councils. The pre-election campaign of "consultations with the nation," conducted under the auspices of PRON, was intended to ensure the government's success in the election by encouraging a high voter turnout. Nevertheless, if the election was intended as a national referendum on Jaruzelski's regime, it proved to be only a partial success. By the government's own admission, only 74.95 percent of all citizens eligible to vote turned out at the polling stations, which was dismal by pre-Solidarity standards; in that period, voter turnout had been close to 100 percent.[46]

Still, the government claimed that the election was a success and proof that normalization was working. Jaruzelski drafted an amnesty proposal to be put before the Sejm; ostensibly, the amnesty was being considered in commemoration of the forty years of communist rule in Poland. Lest this gesture of reconciliation be misinterpreted, Jaruzelski made sure that the population knew who was in charge. While government propaganda heralded Jaruzelski's amnesty as a sign of normalization and national reconciliation, the courts dropped all charges against two policemen implicated in the murder of Grzegorz Przemyk, a Warsaw high-school student and son of an opposition activist, who had been beaten to death at a police station.[47] Apparently, police brutality directed against the opposition was not considered a punishable offense by the regime; a completely different message would be sent three months later, when police actions prefigured what by all indications was an aborted putsch inside the government.

The amnesty law was passed on July 21, 1984.[48] It led to the release of KOR and Solidarity activists who were either awaiting trial or had already been convicted of crimes against the state. Jaruzelski clearly expected that the clemency law would improve his international standing. The regime was moving vigorously to break out from the international isolation, caused in part by the American trade embargo imposed in retaliation for the imposition of martial law. In September 1984, Poland began to negotiate for readmission to the International Monetary Fund and made preparations for symbolically important state visits by several Western officials, including that of Austrian foreign minister Leopold Gratz planned for October 16. Other visits scheduled between October and December 1984 included those of Greek prime minister Andreas Papandreou; Finland's foreign minister, Paavo Vaerynen; Britain's minister of state at the Foreign and Commonwealth Office, Malcolm Rifkind; West Germany's foreign minister, Hans-Dietrich Genscher; and Italy's foreign minister, Giulio Andreotti. The planned display of Jaruzelski's international statesmanship was suddenly interrupted by dramatic internal developments. As the Austrian working visit had barely gotten underway, the news of the police murder of Father Jerzy Popiełuszko became public, throwing Poland into its most severe crisis since the declaration of martial law, and all but wrecking Jaruzelski's normalization campaign.

Jerzy Popiełuszko, an outspoken Warsaw priest and a supporter of Solidarity, was abducted on October 19, 1984, by three SB officers as he traveled by car from Warsaw to Toruń, in western Poland. His driver managed to escape by jumping out of the speeding car and immediately reported the incident. Popiełuszko's body was found the next day; he had been tied with a rope, tortured, strangled, and thrown into a water reservoir. The murderers, identified as two SB lieutenants and a captain, had been ordered to abduct Popiełuszko by their superior, a colonel in the security forces. They were told that the action had been sanctioned by a higher authority and were issued an official car with false license tags, three special passes in case they were stopped by a highway patrol, and service firearms.

The murder was a police operation from beginning to end. The news of the crime spread quickly and the nation's anger threatened to erupt in a wave of mass protest demonstrations. Aware of the gravity of the situation, the government responded by arresting the perpetrators, promising a full investigation, and announcing to the public that the guilty would be punished. On October 27, addressing the nation on the radio and television, Poland's minister of the interior Gen. Czesław Kiszczak labeled the murder a "political provocation" intended to damage Jaruzelski's government. Claiming that he himself was still confused as to the full motives for the action, he nevertheless identified the killers and announced that the investigation was under way. Kiszczak quoted from a Central Committee resolution that called for the swift punishment of those responsible and a complete inquiry into the operation of the security forces.[49]

It appears that for once the government spokesman was telling the truth. It is extremely unlikely that Jaruzelski himself would have planned or approved such an operation at the time when his efforts were directed toward legitimizing his regime in the international arena. Popiełuszko's murder threw the government into a deep internal crisis, wrecked Jaruzelski's international public-relations campaign, and brought his feud with Milewski to a head. Shortly after Kiszczak's speech, Jaruzelski announced that he was assuming direct personal supervision of all SB operations, which until then had been Milewski's prerogative in the Politburo and in the Central Committee Secretariat.[50] Next came Kiszczak's declaration reiterating that the crime was an "obvious political provocation" directed against the government. Although the interior minister stopped short of pointing his finger at the SB, he nevertheless said that the perpetrators were some "politicians and internal enemies of socialism."[51]

Popiełuszko's funeral on November 3 became a major political demonstration against the government. As preparations for the funeral were being made, Jaruzelski met individually with the heads of the party network within the Interior Ministry. Next on the general's agenda was a conference with the supervisory party commission responsible for monitoring the Interior Ministry's performance and for purging its compromised officials. The communiqué released afterwards tersely announced the suspension of one senior SB officer, Gen. Zenon Płatek, and the continuation of the investigation.[52] Col. Adam Pietruszka, Płatek's deputy, eventually became one of the four codefendants in the Popiełuszko murder trial. The trial itself, which opened in January 1985, and during which the four SB officers were charged with the crime, was skillfully stage-managed by government attorneys to demonstrate that the conspiracy did not reach into the higher echelons of the security agency. Once again, the Poles got only a glimpse of what had happened in the corridors of party power.

The Popiełuszko affair spelled out the end of General Milewski's political career and badly damaged the standing of Stefan Olszowski. Although the government never told the whole story, a connection between the three SB thugs who murdered Popiełuszko and Milewski was inadvertently established during the court proceedings when two of the defendants, Leszek Pękała and Waldemar Chmielewski, testified that they had been led to believe that Deputy Interior Minister Gen. Władysław Ciastoń was fully aware of the plan and, in fact, had authorized the whole operation. It appears that the "chain of command" ran from Colonel Pietruszka, who issued the orders to the murderers, through Brigadier General Płatek of the SB, who was subsequently called in to testify briefly during the trial and denied all charges of complicity on the higher level, to Deputy Minister of the Interior Gen. Władysław Ciastoń, a man promoted within the SB by Milewski prior to the latter's appointment to the Politburo in 1981, and finally up to the former interior minister himself.

Because Pękała and Chmielewski's testimony pointed at the interior minister's office, the government judge never pursued the matter. The day after their court revelations, Pękała and Chmielewski fully retracted their testimony linking Ciastoń to the affair, asserting that it had no relation to the truth.[53] The trial continued for several more weeks; in the end, the four codefendants were convicted and drew long prison terms, but the investigation never reached any higher than Colonel Pietruszka.

The high-level perpetrators of the crime were fired after some time had elapsed after the trial, in order not to make their removal appear directly related to the affair. The purge of the SB took place in 1985 and 1986 under Jaruzelski's personal supervision, and the list of those fired strongly suggests that the Popiełuszko affair reached into the very heart of the SB, the Ministry of the Interior, and the Politburo. In 1985, Stefan Olszowski and Mirosław Milewski were both removed from the Politburo. Subsequent reports described a fiery confrontation between Jaruzelski and Olszowski, during which, among a number of accusations, Olszowski was reproached for his personal life and his liaison with a married woman. Olszowski dropped out of Poland's political life and, relying on his diplomatic passport, divided his residence between Warsaw and an apartment of his mistress in Queens, New York.[54] Milewski simply disappeared from sight after 1985, when he was stripped of his Politburo membership, fired from his job as Central Committee secretary, and purged from the Central Committee altogether. Gen. Władysław Ciastoń was retired from the Interior Ministry to the diplomatic corps.[55] As reported by Radio Warsaw on December 23, 1986, Jaruzelski's new appointee as Kiszczak's deputy at the Ministry of the Interior was General Pożoga, the same SB officer who in 1980 and 1981 had called for swift retribution against Solidarity in the pages of *Wojsko Ludowe* and had worked closely with the army during the period of martial law. Before the convening of the PUWP's Tenth Congress in June of 1986, Jaruzelski had succeeded in destroying the last potential source of opposition to his authority inside the government. The supremacy of the general as the most powerful man in Poland's history since Gomułka's brief ascendancy in 1956 would become obvious during the congress.

Normalization Completed: The Tenth Party Congress

The formal lifting of martial law, on Poland's communist holiday of July 22, 1983, was preceded by the announcement of limited amnesty granted by an enactment passed by the Sejm.[56] The clemency law did not extend to some seventy political prisoners charged with plotting to overthrow the state; this group included the most active underground Solidarity leaders and the members of the nationalist Confederation of Independent Poland. In his address to the Sejm, Jaruzelski declared that, although the Military Council of National Salvation (WRON), would eventually be dissolved, military officers would continue to serve in the country's civilian administration.

The Tenth PUWP Congress was preceded by several important changes in the government that further solidified Jaruzelski's power. The KOK reform of 1983 was brought to its logical conclusion; on November 6, 1985, Jaruzelski resigned from his position as prime minister. At the same time, he replaced Henryk Jabłoński, Poland's veteran politician serving since the 1970s, as the country's chairman of the Council of State. Zbigniew Messner, selected by Jaruzelski in 1983 as his deputy premier, was promoted to prime minister.[57] Olszowski, who had been forced out from the Politburo, was also removed from the office of Foreign Minister; Milewski's SB was purged. As a result of those personnel changes, Jaruzelski could feel confident that he would arrive at the congress having eliminated all potential sources of opposition within the leadership and, through his new appointment as chairman of the Council of State, he would continue to exercise overall control of the government as the country's commander in chief (being chairman of the KOK), its communist party leader, and its de facto president.

The Tenth PUWP Congress, held in Warsaw from June 27 to July 4, 1986, was attended by Polish party delegates and 107 representatives of foreign communist parties. In a sign of the Soviets' trust in Jaruzelski and their appreciation for his "normalizing" of Poland's party politics, the CPSU delegation was headed by General Secretary Mikhail Gorbachev.[58] The cordial meeting between the Polish and the Soviet leaders was highlighted in the Polish and Soviet reporting of the proceedings. During his address to the delegates on June 30, Gorbachev expressed his unqualified support for Jaruzelski and the general's approach to solving the PUWP's problems.[59] The achievements of "normalization" thereby received official Soviet blessing. Gorbachev's personal approval of Jaruzelski's policies served to strengthen further the latter's position in the PUWP and sent a clear message to the general's potential opponents that he enjoyed Moscow's backing.

The congress marked the final reversal of the modest intraparty reforms undertaken in 1981. Jaruzelski's efforts during the meeting focused on strengthening the Central Committee's control over regional and local party organizations in order to prevent any future challenges to the center's authority similar to the "horizontal structures" movement of 1980–1981. On his recommendation, the congress decided to require that each basic party cell (Podstawowa Organizacja Partyjna; POP) be assigned a party activist from the central or regional administration who would be obliged to attend his POP's meeting at least once a month. To make this direct intrusion by Central Committee apparatchiks into plant-level party organizations more palatable to local leaders, Jaruzelski emphasized that the POPs would be given an effective veto power over administrative appointments. According to the new regulations, appointments to "positions of responsibility" would be contingent upon the recommendation of the candidate's POP, and the appointee would be forced to resign should his POP withdraw its support.[60] Both regulations gave Jaruzelski additional means to control regional party and governmental organizations. One the one hand, the monthly Central Committee visits ensured high-level supervision of the party's performance in the countryside; on the other hand, it made the POPs the watchdog over local government administration.

The proceedings of the Tenth Congress demonstrated that Jaruzelski had achieved a degree of personal power unprecedented in postwar Polish politics. The list of Central Committee secretaries submitted by the general to the congress was accepted unanimously and without question. Jaruzelski was the only candidate nominated for the post of first secretary and the announcement of his nomination was "greeted with enthusiastic applause"; of the 229 Central Committee members who were to elect the first secretary, 228 cast their votes for Jaruzelski (the general abstained). Finally, the newly elected Politburo was packed with Jaruzelski's cronies, including three military officers: Kiszczak, Siwicki, and Baryła, and two of Jaruzelski's most trusted apparatchiks: Czyrek and Messner. The composition of the Politburo and the list of key government appointments indicated that Jaruzelski's personnel policy of joint party and government appointments would be maintained. Thus, Politburo Member Messner retained his position as prime minister; Politburo Member Kiszczak continued as minister of the interior; and Politburo Member Siwicki remained Poland's defense minister.[61]

The election bylaws adopted by the Tenth Congress contained an interesting procedural detail. Formally, the secret ballot, first introduced during the Ninth Congress and touted as a breakthrough in party democracy, was retained but only for the final vote for the first secretary, the Politburo, and the Central Committee Secretariat. However, prior to the voting, candidates for these positions had to be "approved" by the Central Committee through an open show of hands. Jaruzelski also reinstituted one of the key rules of democratic centralism, namely that only Central Committee members have the authority to vote for the first secretary.[62] This in effect nullified the most important procedural change introduced in 1981, whereby all delegates had the right to elect their leader through direct vote. Jaruzelski could claim that the election in the Tenth Congress was done through secret ballot, while at the same time ensuring that every Central Committee member would have to declare openly what vote he or she intended to cast. The result of this petty trick was predictable: a "unanimous vote" of Central Committee members in support of Jaruzelski's policies.

Finally, the Tenth Congress witnessed a clear reaffirmation of Jaruzelski's suport for Gorbachev's policies of economic restructuring, first declared by the general during the Twentieth Central Committee Plenum of June 12–13, 1985.[63] During the Tenth Congress, the issue was taken up by Politburo Member Czyrek in his report to the congress, in which he outlined the new party program. Prominent among its goals was economic change that would lead to increased economic development and higher standards of living for the population.[64] But these goals lay beyond the scope of internal party politics. Hence, as far as Jaruzelski was concerned, in 1986 his "normalization program" was completed.

The Army Under Siege

Jaruzelski's success in controlling the party and the government was indeed impressive. Nevertheless, even while the general accepted congratulations during the Tenth Party Congress, the ultimate value of his success was coming increasingly into question. The PUWP had been consolidated, but its authority in society remained practically nil. The regime's inability or unwillingness to gauge realistically the degree to which it had become alienated from the citizenry was indeed astounding. Addressing a gathering of party apparatchiks in Zielona Góra, Jaruzelski asserted that the "Poland of today has become a different country than five years ago. Today, the strength of the government is measured not by the number of neutralized opponents, but by the number of new supporters. . . . A chapter in Polish history has ended."[65] Such self-congratulatory official optimism was again expressed by Jaruzelski at the end of November 1986 in his address to the second congress of the National Association of Trade Unions (Ogólnopolskie Porozumienie Związków Zawodowych; OPZZ), the new official trade unions that had replaced Solidarity. "We have endured," said the general, "we have reached the end of the deep crisis and have begun moving forward."[66]

Similar displays of official self-confidence notwithstanding, Jaruzelski faced an increasingly serious challenge to his traditional power base: the People's Army and the institution of the military as such. As early as 1983, the People's Army had seen the publication of its first underground paper, prepared for army personnel by a group of Polish reserve officers. The samizdat *Reduta* (The redoubt) appeared until April 1985, when the officers involved in its publication were arrested.[67] The suppression of *Reduta* proved only a temporary solution; in 1988 *Reduta* was replaced by *Honor i Ojczyzna* (Honor and fatherland) a new underground publication for the military, its name harking back to the traditional code of duty of the Polish officer.[68] Describing itself as a "paper for officers, cadets, and NCOs of the Polish People's Army," the first issue of *Honor i Ojczyzna* defined its task as "awakening the conscience" of the army and "fighting the propaganda lies spread in the army and security services."[69] Relying on the accounts of former army personnel, as well as the anonymous testimony of active duty officers, *Honor i Ojczyzna* described the People's Army's officer corps as increasingly polarized, full of self-doubt, and riven with guilt over its role in the country's postwar history.

Even when taken with a grain of salt, *Honor i Ojczyzna* presented a fascinating insight into the least-understood aspect of the Polish communist army: the morale and mind-set of its officers during and after the crisis of 1980–1981. According to Wincenty Heinrich, one of the paper's editors, the majority of the officer corps remained totally passive during the period of martial law. At best, one could point out sporadic cases of passive resistance, which never became an open challenge to Jaruzelski's orders. According to Heinrich, this behavior could be explained by the impact of the political indoctrination the officers had been subjected to since 1968, when Jaruzelski became defense minister.[70]

Apparently, some junior army officers attempted to resist. As recounted by Stanisław Dronicz, a 32-year army veteran and another member of the newspaper's editorial board, initially several young line officers entertained plans for at least token passive resistance in case of direct Soviet intervention, including plans for the intentionally slow execution of orders and interfering with Warsaw Pact communications. Reportedly, in one garrison in northwestern Poland, a clandestine soldiers' council was created to organize resistance in the event of a Warsaw Pact intervention. However, Jaruzelski's insistence that martial law was a "Polish solution to a Polish problem" apparently effectively neutralized the junior officers' resistance plans. According to Dronicz, the majority of the soldiers and NCOs were at first convinced that they were acting to prevent a national catastrophe and to remove corrupt local administrators.

The gradual recognition of the true purposes of Jaruzelski's action eventually led to bitter soul-searching in the army.[71] As one of the anonymous contributors to *Honor i Ojczyzna*, himself an active duty officer, put it "the Polish People's Army [officers] are frustrated by the inadequacy of their equipment, poor training, and most of all the [regime's] use of the army against society. The officer corps lives in apathy and is incapable of any resistance to the government. Everyone minds his own business. . . . The majority are incapable of action to improve the appalling conditions in our country. This leads not so much to the demoralization of the army, but to a sense of resignation and a belief that nothing is going to change."[72]

The picture that emerges from the description in the army's samizdat newspaper is one of an apathetic officer corps, full of self-doubt and moral ambivalence about its profession—a far cry from the official image of the professional military painted by Jaruzelski's propaganda machine. The diagnosis of the Polish army's low morale offered by *Honor i Ojczyzna* was indirectly corroborated by the pressure exerted by the military to increase the party's penetration of the armed forces. *Wojsko Ludowe* touted a statistically negligible increase in the number of party candidates recruited from the military (from 9364 in 1985 to 8300 in the first three quarters of 1986) as a "stable achievement."[73] Apathy in the army compelled the Main Political Administration to emphasize in 1987 that "the most important task was the constant strengthening of the army's morale (*stan moralno-polityczny*)," and that "strengthening discipline continued to be a fundamental task." As the military finally admitted, Polish youth "perceived a disparity between the ideals of socialism and reality."[74] The Polish army also had to grapple with a growing shortage of conscripts. According to Gen. Lesław Wojtasik of the MPA, in 1987 the army expected to have roughly 90,000 fewer men available for drafting than in 1978.[75] The shortage of conscripts aside, such low morale in a key non-Soviet WTO army could hardly be considered an asset by the Soviet Army's general staff when it drafted its contingency plans for war against NATO.

The price of the army's betrayal in 1981 of its traditional role as the nation's defender proved even higher in terms of the prestige of the military profession. Polish youth expressed its disillusionment with the army by rejecting the claim that military service was the most sacred duty of every patriotic Pole. Epitomized by the draft resistance movement Freedom and Peace (Wolność i Pokój), set up in April 1985, the antimilitary sentiment in the country had, by 1986, reached proportions alarming enough to move the regime to address the issue openly.

On the anniversary of the 1939 German invasion, *Trybuna Ludu* editorialized on the "patriotic duties of the citizen." According to the Central Committee's organ, "military service in the People's Army is one such [special duty], since the army has proved throughout Poland's postwar history that it prepares the citizens well for the defense of the fatherland."[76] Commenting on the army's role in the crackdown against Solidarity, *Żołnierz Wolności* felt compelled on the fifth anniversary of the imposition of martial law to justify once again the military's involvement in domestic politics. "On the 13th of December 1981," wrote the army daily, "the fatherland gave us an order. We executed it swiftly and with dedication. *By defending socialism [in Poland] we defended the country's independence. We fulfilled our patriotic duty to the nation, which armed us and vested its trust in us.*"[77]*

By 1986 the military had unabashedly used the threat of a Soviet invasion in 1981 as a justification for its actions. In a vein similar to Gomułka's *raison d'état* argument, Jaruzelski painted the country's democratic opposition as "a fervently antisocialist margin of society, fanatically dedicated to rejecting Poland's *raison d'état*."[78] Calls went out to combat pacifism among draft-eligible youth. The military admitted that university students—potential future officers of the People's Army—displayed the greatest hostility to the institution of the military. Sounding the alarm, Col. Bazyli Lewczuk, the army's authority on education, demanded a revision of military curricula at Poland's universities. Conceding that, for the most part, university students entering the mandatory one-year officer's curriculum, offered during the final year of their academic education, had their worldview already formed, Lewczuk called for the military instructors at universities to "infuse the students with a sense of patriotic duty, to combat pacifism, explain the need to defend People's Poland and resist the imperialist threat."[79] On November 13, 1986, during a special meeting of the KOK chaired by Jaruzelski, great emphasis was placed on the need to improve the effectiveness of the patriotic education of Polish youth.[80]

In January 1987, the army's Main Political Administration moved to increase its pressure on all paramilitary organizations to indoctrinate the youth about the importance of military service. Wrote *Wojsko Ludowe*:

> It is particularly important [to emphasize] the army's participation in the educational work with the youth.... The network of Officer Reserve Clubs must do more. We must pay special attention to university students in their last year, students in the university military curriculum, and the technical intelligentsia.[81]

Subsequently, the campaign to improve the image of the military among Polish youth became an ongoing feature of *Wojsko Ludowe* throughout 1987 and

---

* The author's emphasis.

1988. It found expression both in elaborate academic treatises, such as Col. Bazyli Lewczuk's convoluted essay on how to "shape patriotism among the university population,"[82] and in simple propaganda pieces hammering at "internationalist education [of the youth] according to the principles of friendship with Soviet nationalities and other nations of the socialist bloc, according to the principles of comradeship-in-arms with the Soviet Army and other armies of the Warsaw Pact."[83]

In 1987 and 1988, Poland's peace movement became a target of often vicious attacks by military propaganda. In an interview for *Żołnierz Wolności* the press spokesman for the Defense Ministry, Brig. Gen. Lesław Wojtasik charged that Freedom and Peace served foreign interests and undermined the nation's defense capability.[84] Subsequently, the peace movement was accused of acting "against socialist Poland" and of being little more than a "U.S.-sponsored propaganda war [waged against Poland] after December 1981," its goal being to "lower the social prestige [of the army] and its credibility with the allies."[85] According to the military, refusal to serve in the People's Army was part of an elaborate plan to "soften and break up the army and weaken the authorities' self-confidence."[86] Pacifism and draft resistance were allegedly a part of an elaborate Western propaganda campaign targeted against the People's Army.[87]

Traditional methods of political indoctrination were not likely to accomplish much with Poland's embittered youth. By the army's own admission, young people were becoming increasingly hostile to the very notion of military service. In an interview for *Żołnierz Polski*, the army's weekly, Col. Tadeusz Rzepecki of the KOK's staff, while contending that young Poles supported the institution of the military, nevertheless admitted that according to the army's latest polls only about 60 percent of Polish youth believed that military service was their duty, and only 20 percent believed it would benefit them professionally.[88] In order to attract candidates to officer schools, military academies, and the newly established military high schools, the Ministry of Defense resorted to advertising; *Żołnierz Polski* carried two-page ads informing potential candidates of the admission procedures and encouraging young people to apply.[89] In the spring of 1988, *Żołnierz Wolności* printed on its front page a series of testimonies from recently discharged servicemen and officers arguing that for them the army had been a valuable experience, and that only those who were not true Poles would try to avoid serving their country.[90]

In the end, the propaganda efforts to prop up the army's sagging image among Polish youth failed, and the military was compelled to concede defeat. A campaign organized by Freedom and Peace to change the contents of the military oath, in the aftermath of the jailing of a conscientious objector who had refused to swear loyalty to the Soviet Union, was crowned with success. On January 20, 1988, *Trybuna Ludu* reported that a draft bill for alternatives to military service would be submitted to the Sejm. Shortly after the first wave of strikes in 1988, the session of the Sejm on June 16 and 17 approved a revised version of the oath. In the new version, the clause about "brotherly alliance with the Soviet Union and other allied armies" was replaced by the pledge to "guard the peace in brotherhood-in-arms with the allied armies." The new version made no mention of defending Poland against "imperialist encroach-ment," dropped the pledge of loyalty to the communist government, and instead required the soldier to "serve faithfully his nation and the fa-therland."[91] In another concession to the pressure from the peace movement, the Council of Ministers announced on June 21, 1988, that men who did not wish to serve in the army because of religious or moral objections to such service could instead apply to do community service; the new law would require students to serve two years and ordinary draftees three years.[92] It was passed by the Sejm on July 13, 1988.[93]

The "Second Stage"

Jaruzelski's triumph during the Tenth PUWP Congress proved short-lived in part because his regime, preoccupied with internal party politics, failed to arrest Poland's economic decline. While the traditional party controls had been restored, and government propaganda continued to herald the "irrevers-ibility of socialist renewal in Poland," the country plummeted ever faster into economic chaos. By 1987, the Poles were once again approaching the limits of their endurance, while the regime was preparing for yet another round of "economic reform." Jaruzelski's "normalization" of the party and the govern-ment administration would be supplemented by a program of economic restructuring. Entitled the "Second Stage of Reform," the program was going to ensure a dramatic leap forward in Poland's economy, reduce foreign debt, impose austerity measures in the country by raising prices to account for real production costs, and encourage private business ventures in Poland. In February 1987, the Polish złoty was devalued for the ninth time in the past five years. In a telling display of regime priorities, the drafting of the program and the Sejm debate were left for the most part to Prime Minister Messner and his cabinet; Jaruzelski and his generals focused on winning the "hearts and minds" of the population.

The "Second Stage" economic-reform program, adopted by the Sejm after a prolonged debate, was built around a series of dramatic price increases. Effective as of February 1, 1988, food, tobacco, and alcohol prices would go up 40 percent; on March 1, day care costs, bus and streetcar fares, and rents would rise on average 50 percent; on April 1, energy costs would go up dramatically, including a 200 percent increase in the price of coal, and a 100 percent increase in the prices of gas, electricity, and heating. The workers were to be compensated 6000 zł. to offset partially the impact of the price increases.[94] To show that everyone in Poland would bear the hardships of the reform, Jaruzelski authorized a 20 percent cut in the Central Committee apparat, a 10 percent cut in the staff of regional and local party organizations, and a transfer of 10 percent of full-time apparatchiks from regional committees to basic party cells (POPs), effective January 1, 1988. The personnel reductions were advertised as a means to "cut costs of the party's day-to-day operation."[95]

The impact of the drastic price increases, introduced in 1988 without fundamental changes in the country's economic mechanism, could be only one: runaway inflation and a further dramatic decline in the living standards. The economic prospects of the younger generation had become truly hopeless. In Warsaw, for example, the average waiting period for a new apartment in 1987 was 56 years; opposition economists estimated that if the current trends continued, Poland would not reach the housing construction levels of 1978 for another 65 years.[96] Social unrest, which had simmered since the introduction of the first round of price increases in February, came to a boil in April.

In Bydgoszcz, municipal transport workers went on strike on April 25, demanding pay increases in compensation for the February price hikes and the reinstatement of Solidarity. Strikes quickly spread throughout Poland. There were work stoppages at the Stalowa Wola Heavy Machinery Plant, the Nowa Huta Steel Mill outside Cracow, and the Lenin Shipyard in Gdańsk; in Inowrocław bus drivers struck in support of Bydgoszcz workers. The government moved to resolve the strikes through a combination of concessions to individual plants and an occasional show of force. In Bydgoszcz and Stalowa Wola, the government quickly yielded to the workers' demands for higher pay. The decision to compromise at Stalowa Wola was probably due in part to the plant's vital importance to Poland's defense sector: the plant manufactures tank components. Then, on May 5 ZOMO thugs stormed Nowa Huta, breaking up a ten-day-old strike by some 14,000 workers; the regime also ordered the Gdańsk shipyard closed "until further notice."[97] Despite these actions, however, uncoordinated local strikes continued to spread almost as quickly as the government managed to put them down; after Nowa Huta, the Dolmel Electronics Plant in Wrocław stopped working. On May 7, Interior Minister Kiszczak opened negotiations with the Gdańsk strikers; on May 10, the Lenin Shipyard strike was broken off when the workers simply walked out of the plant, without having resolved any of the key political issues. Two years after the government had heralded its success in "normalizing" the political situation, the country was again in a deadlock.

Jaruzelski kept a low profile throughout the strikes, while the official mass media launched a propaganda campaign against the strike organizers to intimidate them. In a speech to the nation, transmitted by Polish Radio on

May 1, the communist workers' holiday, the general tersely announced that "there would be no return to chaos and anarchy." "Let no one pin their hopes," said Jaruzelski, "on our being deterred from the line of the [1981 and 1986] party congresses. . . . There will be no dismantling of the foundations of the [political] system."[98] Proving his determination, Jaruzelski's next step was to push through the Sejm a bill granting his government "extraordinary powers," including one-year mandatory imprisonment for anyone organizing strikes or any other form of protest. The bill would allow the government to freeze prices and wages, summarily dismiss managers, and declare financially troubled enterprises bankrupt. While the "second stage" touted market-oriented economic restructuring, in reality Jaruzelski asked the parliament to strengthen further the powers of central government. On May 11, the Sejm voted overwhelmingly in favor of the bill; the new law froze wages and prices, but also forbade even the official trade unions (OPZZ) to bargain collectively without first obtaining sanction from their leadership in Warsaw.[99]

The deadlock between the government and the Polish population did not mean, however, that Jaruzelski's position as Poland's leader was weakened. On the contrary, during Gorbachev's visit to Poland on July 11, 1988, the CPSU general secretary had nothing but praise for his Polish friend. Clearly pleased with Jaruzelski's handling of the unrest of April and May, Gorbachev spoke of similarities between *perestroika* and Jaruzelski's "socialist renewal." Addressing the Polish TV audience, Gorbachev was unequivocal in his support for the general. "You are lucky," said the Soviet leader, "to have a man of Jaruzelski's stature and importance at this stage of history."[100]

When a second wave of strikes paralyzed Poland's key export industry, coal mining, in August 1988, the government's façade of self-confidence finally began to crack. On August 15, the Manifest Lipcowy Mine in Jastrzębie Zdrój stopped working. The strikers' demands were identical to those made three months before: higher pay and the legalization of Solidarity. As in the spring, strikes quickly spread throughout Silesia; their sites included the Morcinek Mine in Kaczyce and the Andaluzja Mine in Piekary Śląskie. By August 21, the workers in at least 11 Silesian coal mines were on strike. As in the spring, the government's initial reaction was to stand firm. On August 16, Żołnierz Wolności declared the strikes "illegal"; three days later the army daily restated the government's position: "discussion–yes, blackmail–no." Jaruzelski apparently hoped that by simply refusing to negotiate he would win the war of nerves with the strikers. However, while the government stalled, unrest began to spread to other parts of the country; on August 17, dock workers in Szczecin went on strike.

Jaruzelski finally responded with a show of force. In a manner reminiscent of the early days of martial law, the army once again began patrolling the streets. Large army and police forces were moved to the vicinity of Jastrzębie and Szczecin—a clear warning that the regime was getting ready to attack.[101] Once again, threats and intimidation against the strikers filled the media. It appeared that an all-out confrontation was imminent when an unexpected dénouement was brought about by a special Eighth Central Committee Plenum, convened in Warsaw on August 27 and 28 to evaluate the situation and chart the government's course of action.

It is unclear what transpired during the Eighth Plenum. The official communiqué spoke of "continuing untiringly on the path of renewed and people-oriented socialism."[102] During the meeting, Jaruzelski spoke in general terms of the need for "broad dialogue with society"; his interior minister, Kiszczak, publicly invited the strikers to participate in a "broad roundtable discussion." Kiszczak's offer ostensibly set no preconditions for the talks; however, the minister expressly excluded from the discussion "those who reject the constitution."[103] Since Solidarity was an illegal organization, it appeared that Kiszczak's "roundtable" would not include Wałęsa or his advisors. However, in yet another surprising turn of events, three days later, on August 31, Kiszczak met with Lech Wałęsa in the presence of Deputy Politburo Member Stanisław Ciosek and Deputy Secretary of the Polish Episcopate Bishop Jerzy Dąbrowski.[104] After the meeting Wałęsa asked the workers to call off the strike.

It appears that the Interior Ministry, best aware of the mood in the country, was in favor of a resolution by means other than an all-out confrontation. The solution proposed by Kiszczak in fact promised nothing, and yet presented the government with an alternative to direct use of force as a means to end the strikes. The August meeting between Kiszczak and Wałęsa was followed by other such meetings, with little immediate progress to report. Typically, Kiszczak and Wałęsa would meet, "discuss problems concerning the procedures of the roundtable dialogue, and schedule another meeting."[105]

Kiszczak's promise of a dialogue ended the second wave of strikes in 1988. In the aftermath of the unrest, Premier Messner's cabinet came under increasingly open official criticism in the Polish media. It could very well be that Jaruzelski was genuinely angry with Messner's handling of the economy and felt that all his work to rebuild the party was being undone by Messner's clumsy economic management. The fact that Messner had become virtually invisible during the crisis was indicative of the premier's standing with the general; the management of the strikes was left completely to Kiszczak, Jaruzelski's trusted "point man." Two weeks after the first meeting between Wałęsa and Kiszczak, on September 19, in a development without precedent in the Soviet bloc, Messner's cabinet submitted its resignation to the Sejm.[106]

The government's resignation made clear the advantages of Jaruzelski's 1983 restructuring of the KOK and the government. In 1988, the fiasco of the regime's economic policies was blamed wholesale on Messner and his team, who were subjected to blistering criticism from Alfred Miodowicz, chairman of the official trade unions, and from the media. What made the 1988 crisis so different from all other postwar confrontations in Poland was that, unlike those of 1956, 1970, or 1980–1981, the blame for the "errors and deviations" was put not on the party, but on the government. Although politically expedient for Jaruzelski and his generals, this ostensible separation of responsibilities between the party and the government was largely fictitious. In his resignation speech to the Sejm, Messner bitterly complained that his government had never been given the necessary freedom to implement its economic program, and warned that if the same errors were to be avoided in the future, the "government should know the extent of its authority and freedom to act; so far such a clear delineation of duties has been missing."[107]

On September 27 Messner's post was assumed by Mieczysław Rakowski, a former editor in chief of the party weekly *Polityka*, a Politburo member, and a Central Committee secretary in charge of propaganda. During the time of martial law, Rakowski had become notorious as Jaruzelski's deputy premier and a bitter foe of Solidarity. Reportedly, in mid-1987 Rakowski submitted a "secret report" to the Politburo, entitled "Observations on Certain Aspects of Poland's Political and Economic Situation," which delivered a realistic critique of the situation in Poland. Among others, Rakowski argued that the population was ready to explode again as the effect of martial law was beginning to wear off, and that under the present circumstances the Soviet Union might not intervene even if the PUWP lost control in the country. He identified the Catholic Church and Solidarity as the main enemies of the party and called for a "strong charismatic leader" to take over the government. Shortly after his "secret report" had been delivered, the Sixth Central Committee Plenum in December 1987 made Rakowski a full Politburo member.[108]

As Jaruzelski put it in his speech, "Poland needed an effective, strong government."[109] The general hastened to stress that the foundations of Poland's political system were not negotiable. In 1988, Rakowski was brought in to re-establish the government's authority. He moved quickly, announcing the closing down of the Gdańsk shipyard, a blatantly political decision explained by the regime as an attempt to improve the industry's efficiency. A seasoned opportunist, Rakowski was out to become the "strongman" Jaruzelski needed; as the premier himself put it succinctly before a PRON gathering in October, "there was a clear longing in the country for an effective and consistent government."[110] This declaration seemed to encapsulate the real goal of Jaruzelski's "second stage" of reform.

As with Messner, Jaruzelski retreated into the background, leaving the spotlight to his new prime minister. The general made only a few public statements in October, insisting once again that the PUWP did not intend to give up control of the country. In an address to a gathering of local party officials in Warsaw on October 5, broadcast on Polish Radio, Jaruzelski asserted that "the party has always had a directing role, and we have never lost it because we have had the army, the security [police], [and] the *nomenklatura* [i.e., control of administrative appointments]; and when it was needed we have used other means." About two weeks later, in a radio broadcast on October 21, he vowed again that the leadership would not hesitate to use force, "should attempts emerge to destabilize or overthrow the socialist state."[111] As the general saw it, roundtable discussions would involve only those members of the opposition who "acted within the law."[112] The guidelines for Rakowski and Kiszczak's dialogue with the nation had thus been set.

The re-emergence of Rakowski on Poland's political scene was greeted with skepticism. After his first three months in office, Rakowski's approval ratings were dismal; according to official data, only 37 percent of the adult Polish population believed that the new premier cared at all about public opinion.[113] Still, what Rakowski lacked in public trust, he made up for in unabashed self-confidence. His new "economic consolidation plan," announced with great fanfare on November 3, was to guarantee "equality for all sectors of the economy" and independence of state enterprises, to decentralize banking and credit, to lift the limits on the number of workers privately owned plants could employ, to shift some resources from the defense sector to the production of consumer goods, and to attract foreign investment. Rakowski promised that in five to seven years, the Polish złoty would be convertible and by 1995 inflation would go down to 5–6 percent.[114] Once again, the government was promising the workers the moon in the hope that an economic upturn would silence the calls for political pluralism.

However, as 1988 drew to a close, it had become apparent to the regime that, unless it was prepared to face another major explosion of national discontent, it had to modify its belief that Poland's economics and politics could be kept separate. The wave of strikes in 1988 finally convinced Jaruzelski and his associates that they needed a modicum of social cooperation to implement economic reform. The government's invitation to "private citizen" Lech Wałęsa to discuss the country's economic and political situation was the ultimate vindication of the opposition's perseverance in resisting the regime's attempts to destroy the civil society that had emerged after the crisis of 1980 and 1981. By inviting Lech Wałęsa to enter into negotiations with General Kiszczak eight years after the military's assault on Solidarity, the government was forced to concede that the ideals of political pluralism symbolized by the independent trade union had proved stronger than Jaruzelski's policies of normalization.

Conclusion

— 10 —

A Pattern of Intervention

The history of civil-military relations in postwar Poland shows that the army and the party have for the most part worked together to defend the country's communist system. At the same time, the Polish People's Army has served Soviet imperial goals.

Because of Poland's national tradition, which bestowed upon the military the highest patriotic virtues, army officers have played a role in governing the country almost as a matter of course. First, as Polish communists fought to consolidate their political position after World War II, the military's help was instrumental in destroying the democratic opposition. Subsequently, in 1956, when it had become clear during Marshal Rokossovskii's tenure that direct Soviet control of the Polish army would in effect eradicate the last vestiges of the Polish communists' autonomy, an alliance between the apparatchiks and the officers was formed. The army gave its support to Gomułka's "national communism"; in return, the party gave the immediate control of the People's Army back to Polish officers. However, the balance in Polish civil-military relations achieved in 1956 did not last long. As the party's strength declined in the late 1960s and during the turbulent 1970s, the military became almost by default the senior partner in the alliance. The party's strength reached its nadir in 1981, when the executive powers in the Polish party and government shifted to Jaruzelski and his adjutants.

The politics of the People's Army after World War II have been marked by a pattern of intrusion into Poland's internal affairs unparalleled elsewhere in Eastern Europe. The apparatchiks repeatedly called upon the army to intervene in domestic politics, first to help them build their power base, then to defend their right to micromanage their own affairs, and in the 1970s and 1980s increasingly to prop up the faltering regime.

Poland's past was only one reason why the army's intervention in domestic politics seemed justifiable. The practice was also given the official sanction of Marxist-Leninist ideology. The Poles have repeatedly asserted that under communism, the army's involvement in politics is not only acceptable, but also "natural" and desirable. As one Polish sociologist put it, "under the dictatorship of the proletariat . . . the army is created as an arm of the revolution, and it is from the start linked to the revolutionary communist party."[1] Hence, the Polish army has had a clearly defined role in civilian affairs; it has been an instrument of government power and, presumably, has had no institutional goals of its own.

On the surface, the history of civil-military relations in Poland after 1944, taken together with the party's theoretical justification of the army's intervention in domestic politics, accords with William Odom's argument that the civil-military relationship in communist states is "by nature symbiotic," and that the "military is an administrative arm of the Party, not something separate from and competing with it."[2] However, at least in the Polish case, civil-military relations are more complex than that. The difference between the role of the army in the Soviet Union and in Poland lies ultimately in Poland's lack of state sovereignty. Furthermore, contrary to official Polish assertions, the People's Army does have a clearly defined set of institutional interests, which have not always coincided with those of the party.

Since Soviet interests in Poland are first and foremost strategic, the Polish People's Army, from its inception, has been regarded by Moscow as unqualifiedly a political actor as well as a military force. The Soviet decision during the war to renege on their commitments to develop the Anders army was dictated by purely political considerations. Stalin insisted that the Polish divisions that would return home alongside the Soviet Army had to be completely subordinated to Moscow, as they would be essential to a communist takeover in Poland. The new People's Army was staffed and trained by Soviet officers, and it was purged of all "unreliable elements," including prewar officers and Polish guerrillas from the anti-Nazi underground. Only a "proletarian officer corps" was considered by Stalin reliable in obeying Soviet orders without ever questioning them.

Between 1949 and 1956, the Polish army was fully subordinated to Soviet hegemonic interests in Eastern Europe and appeared powerless to resist Soviet demands. Yet, in 1956 this army won for Gomułka's apparatchiks a modicum of autonomy in their relationship with Moscow. A decade later, in still another political about-face, the Polish military moved closer to the Soviet Army's general staff, becoming another channel for Soviet intervention in Polish politics. In so doing, the military, beginning in the 1960s, went against the Polish party's institutional interest. In each instance of political reorientation, the army behaved not simply as a tool of the party or of Soviet power, but as a political actor in its own right. In effect, since the end of World War II, the Polish army has shifted its position between accepting and affirming complete Soviet hegemony, on the one hand, and the PUWP's "national communism" on the other.

Ever since Poland lost her national sovereignty after World War II, the country's domestic politics (including those of the armed forces) have depended ultimately on Moscow's sanction. While the Soviets have come to accept that the Poles have the prerogative to select their party leaders, the Kremlin's support will be automatically withdrawn from any Polish leadership that fails to protect Soviet strategic interests. In 1981, regardless of the extent and significance of political infighting within the Polish politburo, the Soviet decision to invade was in effect a wholesale condemnation of the PUWP leadership; Jaruzelski was a member of that leadership. Hence, by rescuing the party in 1981, the Polish generals were also protecting themselves.

In 1981, the Polish army intervened in domestic politics to support the party because its most vital institutional interests were identical with those of the party. Ironically, in the final analysis, in 1981 the interests of these two institutions coincided with the most vital Polish national interest. For reasons that have little to do with nationalism or the Polish patriotic ideal, it was imperative for the military to prevent direct Soviet military action and another occupation of Poland. Notwithstanding Jaruzelski's insistence that the "Polish solution" to the crisis was a sign of the army's patriotism, in reality the invasion would have consigned the senior Polish officer corps to political irrelevance and destroyed the army that Jaruzelski had built for more than a decade. Leaving Jaruzelski's motivation aside, it is also true that Soviet occupation would have become another great tragedy in the history of the Polish nation. Herein lies the bitter paradox of the Polish upheaval of 1980–1981.

It is true, as Jaruzelski hastened to point out after the declaration of martial law, that Soviet action would have most likely led to bloodshed. But these motives were secondary in his calculations, despite the military's self-image of a force of patriots coming to rescue the nation from anarchy and chaos. When the officers moved to prevent a Soviet invasion of Poland in 1981, they were defending their own vested political interests, and ultimately the Polish communist party.

Polish People's Army officers have built their entire careers around the party's monopoly of power. In 1956, they defended the party because it was being torn apart by Stalin's purges; had it lost the last vestiges of its autonomy, the military's own political future would have held no promise. In the 1970s, the officers helped the Soviets control Poland because Gierek's policies were destroying the party's ability to govern. In the 1980s, the army's institutional interest dictated that the Soviet Army not be permitted to force a resolution of the Polish August, and the same imperative required that the army come to the party's rescue.

The End of the Military's Mystique

In 1981, Polish society simply did not believe that the army could move against it. Poland's history of foreign occupations and costly insurrections made it easier, after martial law had been introduced, for Jaruzelski to claim that he had acted as a patriotic soldier. One cannot tell to what degree the WRON officers believed that they had saved their fellow Poles from bloodshed, and how many of them had been motivated purely by the army's institutional interest. It is plain, however, that in 1981, in the eyes of Polish society, the military forfeited all claims to the nation's military tradition. For the first time since the end of World War II, Poland saw the emergence of an organized and vigorous pacifist and draft-resistance movement. The young generation's rejection of the military ethos is today epitomized in the program of the Movement "Freedom and Peace" (Ruch "Wolność i Pokój"), which calls upon Polish youth to refuse to take the soldier's oath and questions the merit of military service.[3]

The army's success in taking over the government at the height of the crisis and suppressing Solidarity depended to a considerable degree on the country's military tradition and the widely held belief that the army could never act against Poland's national interest. Poland's long history of struggle against occupation by foreign powers and a vague, idealized historical memory of the "noble democracy" of the prepartition period made the Polish nation particularly prone to draw upon the military ethos as the embodiment of the country's glorious past. It matters a great deal to our understanding of Jaruzelski's success to know the degree to which Polish society was aware, before the imposition of martial law, of the fundamental differences between the Polish insurrectionary armies of the past and the Soviet-dominated People's Army. The images of continuity were powerful. The army of communist Poland claimed to have inherited the country's insurrectionary-patriotic tradition. From that army's inception, national symbols were used to make up for the lack of national sovereignty. The first division of the Soviet-sponsored Polish People's Army was named the Kościuszko Division; the traditional Polish military ranks were retained; the Polish military insignia, the white eagle, was only slightly modified; the hat worn by the military was still the traditional *czapka rogatywka*, which dated back to the garb worn by the insurrectionists in the eighteenth and nineteenth centuries. In deference to the Poles' ardent Catholicism, the People's Army has retained the institution of the army chaplain. The military salute is given with two fingers, which allegedly symbolize the Polish soldier's creed: Honor and Fatherland. Before 1981, even if the Poles had never regarded Jaruzelski as another Kościuszko or Piłsudski, the officers' ability to appeal to the images of Poland's former greatness helped the military to catch the opposition by surprise.

There is, however, nothing intrinsically Polish about relying on the National Defense Committee as the coordinating agency for all military and security operations, including repression of domestic dissent. Like similar agencies in other Soviet client states in Eastern Europe, Jaruzelski's KOK is modeled after the USSR Defense Council and performs similar functions. Communist control and the satellites' lack of national sovereignty have made Soviet influence a powerful determinant of policy. The role of Marshal Kulikov's Warsaw Pact headquarters in the planning of 1980–1981 for martial law in Poland, and as a transmission belt for orders from Moscow, was not significantly different from that played by Yakubovskiy's staff in the preparation of the "Danube" plan for the 1968 invasion of Czechoslovakia. By the same token, there is nothing specifically Polish in Soviet reliance on the senior officers of a satellite military as an alternative channel of communication and control. For example, during the months leading up to the declaration of martial law, there took place frequent contacts between Kulikov and the GDR's defense minister Heinz Hoffmann that paralleled official meetings between CPSU and SED officials.

Still, general systemic traits of Soviet domination in Eastern Europe should be balanced against the national traditions of individual client states. As this book has sought to demonstrate, in the Polish crisis of 1980–1981, national tradition played an especially important role. It is another paradox of the Polish crisis that Jaruzelski owed some of his popularity before 1981 to the Piłsudskiites and the strong anti-Russian sentiment of the Poles. Poland's past, which in 1981 allowed the Poles initially to forget Jaruzelski's connection to Moscow and consider him a Pole first, taught that service to a foreign power and patriotism were not mutually exclusive; in the 1920 Polish-Soviet war, Piłsudski's officer corps had proved just that.

This is not to imply by any means that Piłsudski's May Coup in 1926 was similar to Jaruzelski's assumption of power from a weak civilian government in 1981. Such analogies, which were frequently offered by Western journalists in 1981, would be, to say the least, misleading. The 1926 May Coup was a strictly Polish affair; Piłsudski, aided by a conspiracy inside the army, and only after a fair amount of fighting between his partisans and the troops loyal to the prime minister, overthrew a legitimate Polish government. While the Piłsudskiites acted on their own, Jaruzelski was backed by Moscow's power and acted as its agent. Jaruzelski worked inside the government and party apparat, and was accepted by the PUWP's Central Committee as the leader capable of suppressing the opposition and maintaining the communists in power. Jaruzelski's action was intended to preserve the existing political order in Poland, while Piłsudski's May Coup strove to overthrow it. Jaruzelski's target was a mass political movement that challenged the government; Piłsudski's target was the government itself. If prior to the crisis there could be doubt about where Jaruzelski's allegiance lay, that doubt was dispelled by the imposition of martial law. In 1981, the Polish military's mystique was shattered.

The Next Chapter

The Tenth PUWP Congress effectively ended the period of "normalization" in Poland. From the government's point of view, the June gathering in Warsaw symbolized the re-emergence of the communist party as the leading actor on Poland's political scene. That was the military's true vested interest, as only the party guaranteed its own institutional survival. On the surface Jaruzelski could claim an impressive record of achievement. Solidarity had been crushed and subsequently outlawed. The series of purges of the *nomenklatura* and of the party's rank and file had strengthened party discipline and re-established the centralized hierarchy of authority. The repressive measures at the government's disposal have been vastly strengthened through civil and criminal legislation introduced in the aftermath of martial law.

The Polish regime also succeeded in breaking out of the international isolation imposed upon it by U.S. economic sanctions and the trade boycott of the martial-law period. By 1986, Jaruzelski had been accepted by Western governments as Poland's leader. Shortly thereafter, the United States lifted its remaining sanctions against Poland, a step followed up in 1987 with an official visit to Poland by Vice President George Bush. In 1986, Poland reached another debt rescheduling agreement with the Paris Club and rejoined the International Monetary Fund; this opened to Jaruzelski an additional source of Western loans. Finally, Jaruzelski managed to establish a cordial personal relationship with Mikhail Gorbachev, and the new Soviet leader repeatedly expressed his full support for the Polish general.

Today Jaruzelski and his officers remain the custodians of the communist party. Jaruzelski's dilemma, and ultimately that of the Kremlin, is the enduring nature of the Polish crisis. The military's "normalization" program addressed only the issue of party politics; in terms of Poland's larger problems, it has been a failure. The rejection of the government's reform proposals by the majority of the Polish population in the 1987 referendum, and the subsequent wave of strikes in April and May and in August 1988, were signals that the fundamental economic and political problems have not been solved.

Where does this leave the never-ending Polish drama? The Polish economic crisis will only get worse. Considering the bankruptcy of the Polish economy, the pay increases granted to the striking workers in 1988 are nothing but a temporary solution. Premier Rakowski's "consolidation plan" promises too much too soon, and probably comes too late to generate much popular support. The Polish government, which has lied to its citizens so many times in the past, has no credibility. Workers in Gdańsk and Cracow know all too well that what the regime gives with one decree today, it may take away tomorrow with another. In 1970, the workers asked for pay increases and guarantees that food prices would not be raised; in 1980, they demanded that the government accept their independent trade union. In both cases government concessions proved only temporary, and similar solutions will therefore probably no longer suffice. The strikes of 1988 demonstrated quite clearly that Polish society would not give up its struggle for genuine political pluralism. In the final analysis, though, as was the case during the 1980–1981 crisis, it will be up to the Soviets to determine the course of Polish events in the 1990s.

At present, Gorbachev appears to be satisfied with Jaruzelski's performance. The military's rise to power destroyed Solidarity's national organization, thus removing the imminent threat to the party's monopoly of political power. In return, the apparatchiks had to submit themselves to the authority of the military in order to survive both the pressure from without and the tension within. For almost a decade now, the army has held the party together and preserved its dominant position in the country's politics, but it has paid for this achievement with its prestige. The army that kept its distance from internal party struggles and took no responsibility for the party's inefficiency and corruption, used to be, in the eyes of the Poles, a guardian of the country's past and its hope for the future. The generals who are now wearing the suits of party apparatchiks are no longer trusted by their countrymen. Nevertheless, this was considered by Jaruzelski a small price compared to the perceived direct threat that Solidarity constituted in 1980–1981 to the army's ultimate goal of institutional self-preservation. In 1981, the regime of the virtually incapacitated Brezhnev displayed a revealing flexibility by accepting the Polish military solution as a means to ensure continuing Soviet control over Poland. Jaruzelski's personal ambition should not be overlooked, however. The restructuring of the Polish government apparat, whereby the National Defense Committee has become the key agency, has made Jaruzelski (who is both the chairman of the Council of State and of the KOK) the most powerful man in the country.

Jaruzelski's "normalization" and his structural reform of the Polish government suggest that Soviet control in Eastern Europe has become increasingly based on personalities, rather than on institutions. So long as the East

European leader has demonstrated his loyalty and is deemed trustworthy, the Soviets appear increasingly indifferent to the manner in which he has arranged his domestic political environment. Jaruzelski's position as the strongman of Poland is a case in point; the organizational and personnel changes that he instituted have made him arguably the strongest leader in Warsaw party politics since the early years of Gomułka's stewardship in the 1950s. So far, Gorbachev does not seem to mind.

Today, the Polish army and the security forces, the latter since 1985 dominated by the Ministry of Defense, are the guarantors of Soviet interests in Poland. The military has strengthened the PUWP, although the apparatchiks remain junior partners in the alliance and Jaruzelski's "normalization program" brought about a lasting transformation inside the Polish regime. Structural changes, such as the KOK reform of 1983 that has vastly increased the executive powers of the chairman of the Council of State, have strengthened the central government and have made Jaruzelski Poland's undisputed leader. The officers who crushed Solidarity in 1981 are now Poland's regime. They command not only the allegiance of the army, but also of the party apparat and, after the Popiełuszko affair in 1985, of the security forces. For the first time since World War II, the institutional interests of the officers and the apparatchiks have become unequivocally one and the same. At the same time, the gap between the regime and the Polish people has become ever wider.

The military's primary concern in the late 1980s has been to ensure that the party should weather another storm of rising national discontent. In this respect, the military's institutional interests and the Polish nation's political aspirations have nothing in common. It is striking that the alleged identity of the army's and the party's political objectives, which Polish party ideologues have so long professed, and which some Western observers accepted as true, has finally come to pass. Since 1981, the Polish army has come ever closer to identifying its interests with those of the party apparat, without having the option any longer of using its influence to achieve a balance between Polish apparatchiks and the Soviets. This unity of institutional and political goals has not come about as a natural extension of civil-military relations under communism; on the contrary, it has happened in Poland because in 1981 the pattern of the relationship was permanently altered.

Notes

Chapter 1

1. See Jacques Rupnik, "The Military and 'Normalization' in Poland," in Paul G. Lewis, ed., *Eastern Europe: Political Crisis and Legitimation* (New York: St. Martin's Press, 1984), p. 164.

2. For example, George Sanford's *Military Rule in Poland: The Rebuilding of Communist Power, 1981–1983* (New York: St. Martin's Press, 1986); referred to hereafter as "Sanford."

3. Roman Kolkowicz, *The Soviet Military and the Communist Party* (Princeton, N.J.: Princeton University Press, 1967).

4. Timothy Colton, *Commissars, Commanders, and Civilian Authority* (Cambridge, Mass.: Harvard University Press, 1979).

5. William E. Odom, "The Party-Military Connection: A Critique," in Dale Herspring, ed., *Civil-Military Relations in Communist Systems* (Boulder, Colo.: Westview Press, 1978), pp. 13–42.

6. Condoleezza Rice, *The Soviet Union and the Czechoslovak Army, 1948–1983: Uncertain Alliance* (Princeton, N.J.: Princeton University Press, 1984). Hereafter referred to as "Rice."

7. Rice, p. 8.

8. Rice, p. 21.

9. For an extensive discussion of Soviet control in Eastern Europe, see Christopher D. Jones, *Soviet Influence in Eastern Europe: Political Autonomy and the Warsaw Pact* (New York: Praeger Publishers, 1981).

10. Zdzisław Rurarz, "Komuniści polscy czy polscy komuniści" (Polish communists or communist Poles), *Pomost*, July 1985: 3.

11. Andrzej Korbonski and Sarah M. Terry, "The Military as a Political Actor in Poland," in Roman Kolkowicz and Andrzej Korbonski, eds., *Soldiers, Peasants, and Bureaucrats: Civil-Military Relations in Communist and Modernizing Societies* (London: Allen & Unwin, 1982), p. 160.

12. Ibid., p. 174.

13. George C. Malcher, *Poland's Politicized Army: Communists in Uniform* (New York: Praeger Publishers, 1984); Sanford.

14. The term "mythology" is used here to mean the nation's heritage, codified through its literary tradition and constituting an essential element of national identity. In the Polish case, national mythology blends patriotism, soldierly duty, and Catholicism into national character.

15. "Przemówienie na promocji oficerów w Wyższej Szkole Oficerskiej Wojsk Obrony Przeciwlotniczej w Koszalinie, wygłoszone 30 sierpnia, 1981r.," in Wojciech Jaruzelski, *Przemówienia 1981–1982* (Speeches 1981–1982) (Warsaw: Ksiażka i Wiedza, 1983), p. 133.

16. Teresa Rakowska-Harmstone, "Patterns of Political Integration," in Teresa Rakowska-Harmstone, Christopher D. Jones, John Jaworsky, and Ivan Sylvain, *Warsaw Pact: The Question of Cohesion, Phase II*, vol. 1, *The Greater Socialist Army: Integration and Reliability* (Ottawa: ORAE Extra-Mural Paper No. 29, February 1984), p. 45.

17. Ibid., p. 133.

18. *Regulamin Dyscyplinarny Sił Zbrojnych Polskiej Rzeczpospolitej Ludowej* (Warsaw: Ministerstwo Obrony Narodowej, 1977), p. 8.

19. It is remarkable to what degree General Jaruzelski's official statements appear to reflect his private beliefs. According to Col. Ryszard Kukliński, one of the senior Polish officers who had frequent contact with the general, the issue of Poland's political system and her alliance with the Soviet Union was the foundation of the Polish officers' political views. Kukliński's testimony was published in the April 1987 issue of the Polish emigré quarterly *Kultura*; hereafter referred to as "Kukliński."

20. Zdzisław Kosyrz, Walerian Magoń, and Bogdan Nowakowski, *Wychowanie w Ludowym Wojsku Polskim* (Upbringing in the Polish People's Army) (Warsaw: Wydawnictwo Ministerstwa Obrony Narodowej, 1978), pp. 20–21.

21. Ibid., p. 38.

22. This premise and argument were put forward by Jaruzelski in his speech to graduating cadets of the Officer School of Armored Forces: "Przemówienie na promocji oficerów w Wyższej Szkole Oficerskiej Wojsk Pancernych im. Stefana Czarnieckiego w Poznaniu," in Wojciech Jaruzelski, *Przemówienia 1981–1982* (Warsaw: Ksiażka i Wiedza, 1983), p. 436.

23. *Wall Street Journal*, July 6, 1981.

24. See Albert L. Michaels, "Background to a Coup: Civil-Military Relations in Twentieth-Century Chile and the Overthrow of Salvador Allende," in Claude E. Welch, Jr., ed., *Civilian Control of the Military: Theory and Cases from Developing Countries* (Albany, N.Y.: State University of New York Press, 1976), pp. 283–306.

Chapter 2

1. The designation "Second Commonwealth" (Druga Rzeczpospolita) is traditionally applied to the Poland of the interwar years, to distinguish pre-World War II Poland from the old Commonwealth of Poland-Lithuania, which ceased to exist as a sovereign state following the third partition of Poland in 1795. Communist Poland is officially known as the Polish People's Republic.

2. *The Military Balance, 1986–1987* (London: The International Institute for Strategic Studies, 1986), pp. 52–53.

3. For more background information on Poland-Lithuania, see Norman Davies's *God's Playground: A History of Poland* (New York: Columbia University Press, 1984), vol. 1. Hereafter referred to as "Davies."

4. Tadeusz Nowak and Jan Wimmer, *Dzieje oręża polskiego* (History of Polish arms) (Warsaw: Ministerstwo Obrony Narodowej, 1968), vol. 1, p. 281.

5. Marian Kukiel, *Zarys historii wojskowości w Polsce* (Short history of the army in Poland) (Kraków: Krakowska Spółka Wydawnicza, 1929), pp. 168–70. Hereafter referred to as "Kukiel."

6. In fact, the Polish forces brought out against the Russians in 1792 never exceeded 50,000. See Kukiel, p. 172.

7. For a discussion of the Polish nobility's "golden freedoms" and their decline, see Maria Bogucka, *Dawna Polska: Narodziny, rozkwit, upadek* (Old Poland: Origins, acme, decline) (Warsaw: Wiedza Powszechna, 1985), pp. 262–79 and 369–80.

8. A remarkable first-hand account of the Polish nobility's mores during the twilight of the Commonwealth is given in Jan Chryzostom Pasek, *Memoirs of the Polish Baroque*, trans. and ed. by Catherine S. Leach (Berkeley, Calif.: University of California Press, 1976).

9. *Hetmans* were regional military commanders appointed by the king. Beginning in the sixteenth century, two "great hetmans" were appointed, one for the Crown (Poland proper) and one for Lithuania. These were assisted by several deputies, or field *hetmans*, who were de facto in control of the armies. See Kukiel, p. 44.

10. The Lubomirski mutiny against King Jan Casimir from 1661 to 1667 was among the most notorious. See Joanna Bąkowa, *Szlachta województwa krakowskiego wobec opozycji Jerzego Lubomirskiego w latach 1661–1667* (The nobility of the Kraków voivodship and the opposition camp of Jerzy Lubomirski, 1661–1667) (Warsaw: Państwowe Wydawnictwo Naukowe, 1974). The army played an important role in the mutiny; see pp. 45–79.

11. See *Poland's Constitution of May 3, 1791* (Monterey, Calif.: Defense Language Institute, 1985).

12. Davies, vol. 1, p. 535.

13. Immediately after the rising, Kościuszko left for Sweden; he died in exile in Switzerland. See Monica Gardner, *Kościuszko: A Biography* (London: Allen & Unwin, 1942), pp. 118–19.

14. Gabriel Zych, *Jan Henryk Dąbrowski, 1755–1818* (Warsaw: Wydawnictwo Ministerstwa Obrony Narodowej, 1964), p. 290. The People's Army has made the history of Dąbrowski's legions a part of its tradition; see the essay "Generał J. H. Dąbrowski w

tradycjach wychowania wojskowego" (General J. H. Dąbrowski in the tradition of military upbringing), by Lt. Col. Jerzy Cytowski, in the collection *Generał Jan Henryk Dąbrowski 1755–1818: Conference Papers* (Poznań: Uniwersytet im. Adama Mickiewicza, 1970), pp. 55–69. The conference was sponsored by the Dzierżynski Military Political Academy in Warsaw.

15. A first-hand account of the uprising can be found in Maurycy Mochnacki, *Powstanie narodu polskiego w roku 1830* (The uprising of the Polish nation in 1830) (Warsaw: Państwowy Instytut Wydawniczy, 1984). On the reaction of Polish senior officers, see vol. 2, p. 38.

16. The debate that followed the rising, and that continued in the Polish emigré community in France for several years after the 1831 defeat, blamed the failure on the Polish politicians who had led the rising. The heroism of the Polish soldier was beyond reproach. See Adam Mickiewicz, *Księgi pielgrzymstwa i narodu polskiego* (The books of pilgrimage and of the Polish nation) (Warsaw: Czytelnik, 1982).

17. To talk about national identity in Poland's case presents a number of problems. The partitions occurred when the process of modern nation-formation had barely begun, not only in Poland but in most other countries of Europe as well. Because of over two centuries in Prussian, Russian, and Austrian administration, the inhabitants of the territories that used to constitute the Commonwealth missed an opportunity to develop early a broadly based consensus about the allegiance and cultural heritage of Polish society. See Davies, vol. 2, pp. 3–81.

18. For an exhaustive and balanced biography of Piłsudski, see Wacław Jędrzejewicz, *Józef Piłsudski, 1867–1935* (London: Polska Fundacja Kulturalna, 1982). This study is also available in English. Hereafter referred to as "Jędrzejewicz."

19. Jędrzejewicz, p. 27.

20. Joseph Rothschild, *East Central Europe Between the Two World Wars* (Seattle, Wash.: University of Washington Press, 1974), pp. 31–34.

21. The legions consisted of three brigades. Piłsudski commanded the first; the second was led by Cols. Huttner and Haller, and the third by Col. Szeptycki. The legions crossed the border into the Russian partition on August 6, 1914, and, having proclaimed a nonexistent national government, marched into a provincial town. Following a brief skirmish with a Russian patrol, the legions withdrew into Galicja, and Piłsudski subordinated his troops to the Austrian high command. See Davies, p. 382.

22. Steven Zaloga and Victor Madej, *The Polish Campaign, 1939* (New York: Hippocrene Books, 1985), pp. 3–4. Hereafter referred to as "Zaloga."

23. The career of Gen. Władysław Anders is a case in point. A cavalry officer in the Russian army and a graduate of the St. Petersburg Military Academy, Anders joined the Polish army and proved himself an ardent patriot during the 1919 fighting in the Wielkopolska region, the Soviet-Polish war of 1919–1920, and the 1939 campaign. Released from Soviet prison after the Sikorski-Stalin agreement of 1941, Anders organized the first Polish units in the Soviet Union and became commander in chief of the Second Polish Corps that fought in the Middle East and Italy. See Władysław Anders, *Bez ostatniego rozdziału: Wspomnienia z lat 1939–1946* (Without the final chapter: Recollections from 1939–1946) (London: Gryf Publications, 1981). Hereafter referred to as "Anders."

24. For an extensive analysis of the Polish-Soviet war, see Norman Davies, *White Eagle, Red Star: The Polish-Soviet War, 1919–1920* (London: Orbis, 1983), and Jędrzejewicz, pp. 78–107.

25. Jędrzejewicz, p. 187.

26. Zaloga, pp. 127–28.

27. Zaloga, pp. 131–37.

28. A critical evaluation of the 1939 campaign can be found in Stefan Korboński, *W imieniu Rzeczypospolitej* (In the name of Poland) (Paris: Instytut Literacki, 1954). Korboński's memoirs show that, in the aftermath of the 1939 defeat, both the general public and prewar opposition politicians, in particular the leadership of the Polish Peasant Party, held the prewar government responsible for the tragedy of the September campaign.

29. A good discussion of the Home Army's objectives and its performance record can be found in lectures given by one of its commanders, Gen. Tadeusz Bór-Komorowski, at the Colditz POW camp immediately after the collapse of the Warsaw Rising of 1944. See Tadeusz Bór-Komorowski, *Trzy Wykłady o AK* (Three lectures on the Home Army) (Paris: Zeszyty Historyczne #49, 1979).

30. Mieczysław Młotek, *Krótki zarys historii Brygady Strzelców Karpackich, 1940–1942* (Short history of the Carpathian Brigade, 1940–1942) (London: Zarząd Główny Związku Tobrukczyków, 1985), pp. 3–5.

31. During the Battle of Britain, Polish pilots shot down 186 German planes (roughly 12 percent of the total German losses); by the end of the war, the Poles had shot down about 1000 planes of the Luftwaffe. These figures come from *XVII Rocznica Udziału Lotnictwa Polskiego w Bitwie o Anglię* (Seventeenth anniversary of the Polish air force's participation in the Battle of Britain) (Toronto: Związkowiec, 1977), p. 6. For an eyewitness account of the role of Polish fighter pilots during the Battle of Britain, see Arkady Fiedler, *Squadron 303* (New York: Roy, 1943).

32. Anders, pp. 196–221.

33. In fact, the insistence of the Polish government-in-exile on at least a semi-independent status in relation to the Soviets was not based on wishful thinking alone. The London government enjoyed complete authority in the occupied country; moreover, the Home Army, Poland's resistance force, numbered 380,000 soldiers by 1944. The communist-sponsored underground in Poland was insignificant compared to the magnitude of the Home Army's effort. Krystyna Kersten's authoritative study on the beginnings of communist government in Poland puts the number of resistance fighters in 1943 at 200,000 members of the Home Army (AK) and 10,000 People's Guards (GL). See Krystyna Kersten, *Narodziny systemu władzy: Polska 1943–1948* (The birth of the political system: Poland, 1943–1948) (Paris: Libella, 1986), p. 22. Hereafter referred to as "Kersten."

For more on Poland's contribution to the WWII effort, see Oscar Halecki, "The Armed Forces and National Security," in Oscar Halecki, ed., *Poland* (New York: Praeger Publishers, 1957), pp. 149–75.

34. On the Katyn Forest massacre, see Janusz K. Zawodny, *Death in the Forest: The Story of the Katyn Forest Massacre* (Notre Dame, Ind.: University of Notre Dame Press, 1962); *Zbrodnia Katyńska w świetle dokumentów* (Documents on the Katyn crime) (London: Gryf Publishers, 1948); or J. Abramski and R. Żywiecki, *Katyń* (Warsaw: Społeczny Instytut

Pamięci Narodowej im. J. Piłsudskiego, 1977). The Abramski/Żywiecki study is an underground *samizdat* publication.

35. An excellent discussion of Sikorski's policy reorientation is given in chapter 4: "Sikorski's Russian Gambit," of Sarah Meiklejohn Terry, *Poland's Place in Europe: General Sikorski and the Origin of the Oder-Neisse Line, 1939–1943* (Princeton, N.J.: Princeton University Press, 1983).

36. Anders, p. 76.

37. Gen. Anders's account reflects the brewing conflict between the new Polish army and the Soviets. The Poles were not issued the promised weapons and supplies; food rations were repeatedly cut; and the arriving recruits told of the NKVD's efforts to keep remaining Poles in the labor camps. See Anders, p. 130.

38. Because of the propaganda distortions of numerous official government publications on the origins of the People's Army, the story of the Kościuszko Division is one of the least known aspects of Poland's military history. A rare eyewitness account of the formation of the Kościuszko Division and its soldiers' odyssey, from their imprisonment in 1939, through the gulag, the Seltse recruiting station, and the Eastern Front campaign, was published in 1984 by Poland's underground press. See Wiktor Kulerski, ed., *Kościuszkowcy* (Kosciuszkovites) (Warsaw: Niezależne Wydawnictwo Harcerskie, 1984). Hereafter referred to as "*Kościuszkowcy.*"

39. It appears that the new Polish People's Army was to be used primarily for political and propaganda reasons inside Poland. In his memoirs, Gen. S. Shtemenko, who was chief of the Soviet general staff during the war, talks about the plan to use the First Polish Army to liberate Warsaw, which was foiled by the outbreak of the Warsaw Rising in 1944. See S. M. Shtemenko, *Generalnii shtab v gody voiny* (Moscow: Voyenizdat Publishers, 1968), vol. 1.

40. Anders, p. 111.

41. According to Anders, in August of 1942 Berling deserted to the Soviets, taking with him the military records of the Krasnovodsk base. See Anders, p. 111.

42. This mood among the Poles serving in the pro-Soviet armed forces was brilliantly captured by Nobel Prize–winner Czesław Miłosz in his novel *The Seizure of Power* (New York: Farrar, Straus, Giroux, 1982). The book shows that the soldiers of the new army regarded their service in the Soviet-controlled armed forces primarily as a way of getting out of the gulag and back to Poland. From this vantage point, the decision of young Jaruzelski to join the Polish People's Army in the Soviet Union does not necessarily mean his acceptance of Soviet-style communism; prior to his enlistment, Jaruzelski was deported in 1939 and worked as a forced laborer in the Karaganda mines. See Chap. 4 for a detailed account of Jaruzelski's early life and military career.

43. This section is based in part on M. Dowda, *Armia i Naród* (The army and the nation) (Warsaw: Książka i Wiedza, 1969); M. Checinski, *The Postwar Development of the Polish Armed Forces* (Rand Internal Note: September, 1979); S. Komornicki, ed., *Wojsko Polskie 1939–1945: Barwa i Broń* (The Polish army 1939–1945: Uniforms, insignia, and weapons) (Warsaw: Interpress, 1984); Henryk Kacała, *Kształt Ludowego Wojska* (The shape of the People's Army) (Warsaw: Ministerstwo Obrony Narodowej, 1972); and Davies, vol. 2.

44. An eyewitness described the battle as a slaughter of untrained and poorly led troops, the aftermath of which almost led to a mutiny against the officers (*Kościuszkowcy*, p. 12).

Official Polish sources give the casualty rates at about 2,500, including over 500 dead. See Marian Dowda, *Armia i Naród* (Warsaw: Książka i Wiedza, 1969), p. 27. Hereafter referred to as "Dowda."

45. Józef Buszko, *Historia Polski: 1864–1948* (History of Poland: 1864–1948) (Warsaw: Państwowe Wydawnictwo Naukowe, 1983), pp. 384–89.

46. Tadeusz Pióro, "Zaczęło się w Armii Berlinga" (It began in Berling's army), *Polityka*, October 15, 1988. Pióro's account is based on a book by Franciszek Kusiak, *Oficerowie 1 Armii Wojska Polskiego w latach 1944–1945* (The officers of the First Polish Army 1944–1945) (Warsaw: PAN, 1987). All data on the breakdown of the officer corps of "Berling's army" quoted in this section have been taken from Pióro's article.

47. Dowda, p. 28.

48. The plan for the creation of the Third Army, which together with the First and Second Armies would constitute a separate Polish front, was abandoned because of the approaching date of the Soviet winter offensive of 1944. The already formed units of the Third Army were incorporated into the First and the Second Armies.

49. Kersten, pp. 46–47 and p. 61.

50. For eyewitness testimony describing Soviet methods in dealing with the Home Army, see Leonard Mosiejko, "Protokół sporządzony w dniu 15 lutego, 1946" (Deposition taken on February 15, 1946), box 39, Stanisław Mikołajczyk Collection, Hoover Institution Archives.

51. Kersten, p. 80.

52. Interview with Jakub Berman quoted in Teresa Toranska, *Them: Stalin's Polish Puppets* (New York: Harper & Row, 1987), p. 229. Hereafter referred to as "Toranska."

53. Toranska, p. 230.

54. Toranska, p. 228.

55. Toranska, p. 229.

56. The biographical information about Żymierski given here has been taken from *Marszałek Polski Michał Żymierski* (Marshal of Poland Michał Żymierski) (Warsaw: Wydawnictwo Ministerstwa Obrony Narodowej, 1983). Hereafter referred to as "Żymierski."

Chapter 3

1. Kersten, p. 89. According to T. Rakowska-Harmstone, deserters from the People's Army during the civil war numbered in the thousands, as attested by the fact that over 7,000 deserters were included in the amnesties of 1945 and 1947; see T. Rakowska-Harmstone, Christopher Jones, and Ivan Sylvain, *Warsaw Pact: The Question of Cohesion, Phase II*, vol. 2, *Poland, German Democratic Republic, and Romania* (Ottawa: ORAE Extra-Mural Paper No. 33, November 1984). Hereafter referred to as "Rakowska-Harmstone."

2. Testimony of Poland's underground network signed "Zrąb." See *Konspiracja w Kraju Pod Okupacją Sowiecką* (The Polish underground under Soviet occupation), Hoover Institution Archives. Hereafter referred to as "Zrąb."

3. Zrąb, pp. 9–10.

4. Kersten, p. 116.

5. An intelligence report on the morale of the Polish army, submitted in February 1947 and signed "Zbyszek," emphasizes strong anti-Soviet and antigovernment feelings among the draftees. "Zbyszek" reports that despite government efforts to control the soldiers, during the 1947 election a substantial number of them voted for the opposition Polish Peasant Party (Polskie Stronnictwo Ludowe). See "Zbyszek—Wojsko Polskie (Zbyszek—The Polish army), box 39, Stanisław Mikołajczyk Collection, Hoover Institution Archives.

6. This data is given in the unpublished memoirs of Edward Osóbka-Morawski, then Poland's prime minister; see folder 3, Edward Osóbka-Morawski Collection, Hoover Institution Archives.

7. See Antoni B. Szczęśniak and Wiesław Z. Szota, *Droga do Nikąd: Działalność Organizacji Ukraińskich Nacjonalistów i Jej Likwidacja w Polsce* (Road to nowhere: The activities of the Organization of Ukrainian Nationalists and their suppression in Poland) (Warsaw: Wydawnictwo Ministerstwa Obrony Narodowej, 1973). Hereafter referred to as "Szczęśniak/Szota."

8. Kersten, pp. 260–61.

9. Adam Michalski, *Los się przychylił* (Good fortune) (Warsaw: Wydawnictwo Ministerstwa Obrony Narodowej, 1986), pp. 200–01. Hereafter referred to as "Michalski."

10. Michalski, pp. 212–13.

11. Michalski, p. 213.

12. Kersten, p. 295.

13. The extent to which military tribunals violated the law to serve the purposes of the regime was only revealed in 1981 in an extensive report on the most important trials before military tribunals, published in the last four issues of *Tygodnik Solidarność*. See "Procesy przed Najwyższym Sądem Wojskowym: Raport opracowany na zamówienie Komisji do Badania Odpowiedzialności za Łamanie Praworządności w Sądownictwie Wojskowym" (Trials before the Supreme Military Tribunal: A report prepared for the Commission on the Responsibility of Military Courts for Breaking the Law), *Tygodnik Solidarność*, Nov. 20 and 27, Dec. 4 and 11, 1981.

14. Tadeusz Pióro, "Zaczęło sie w Armii Berlinga" (It began in Berling's army), *Polityka*, Oct. 15, 1988. Pióro's account is based on Franciszek Kusiak's *Oficerowie 1 Armii Wojska Polskiego w latach 1944–45* (The officers of the First Polish Army 1944–45) (Warsaw: PAN, 1987).

15. Kersten, p. 297.

16. Kazimierz Łączyński and Stanisław Przyjemski, "Na marginesie artykułu Tadeusza Pióro: Jak Powstawała Sprawa 'Spisku w Wojsku'" (The origins of the "military conspiracy" affair: Marginal comments on the article by Tadeusz Pióro), *Polityka*, Nov. 26, 1988.

17. Kersten, p. 354.

18. Berling formally retired in 1963. See Toranska, p. 361.

19. Józef Światło's testimony. See Zbigniew Błażynski, *Mówi Józef Światło: Za Kulisami Bezpieki i Partii, 1940–1955* (Józef Światło reports: Behind the scenes of the secret police and

the party, 1940–1955) (London: Polska Fundacja Kulturalna, 1985), p. 56. Hereafter referred to as "Światło."

20. Toranska, p. 381.

21. Żymierski was arrested while in a government-owned villa in Szklarska Poręba. See Tadeusz Pióro, "Przed Najwyższym Sądem Wojskowym 1951–1953: Procesy Odpryskowe" (Before the Supreme Military Tribunal, 1951–1953: Ripple-effect trials), Sept. 17, 1988.

22. Światło, p. 56.

23. Żymierski, p. 260.

24. See Michael Checinski, "Poland's Military Burden," *Problems of Communism*, May–June 1983.

25. Stanisław Mikołajczyk, "Can Russia Depend Upon the Armies of its Satellites," box 122, Stanisław Mikołajczyk Collection, Hoover Institution Archives, p. 8.

26. Some authors give what appears to be an exaggerated estimate of the number of Soviet officers in the Polish army. For example, according to Halecki, at the end of World War II, the Polish armed forces, which totaled approximately 500,000 soldiers, included about 14,000 Soviet officers. See Oscar Halecki, "The Armed Forces and National Security," in O. Halecki, ed., *Poland* (New York: Praeger Publishers, 1957), p. 154. Mikołajczyk's estimate appears somewhat more accurate, although the numbers are still in dispute. According to Mikołajczyk, of the 11,000 Soviet officers assigned to the Polish army in 1944, roughly 6,000 were sent back home after the war, while the remainder was given Polish citizenship and retained (see "Can Russia Depend Upon the Armies of its Satellites?" box 122, Stanisław Mikołajczyk Collection, Hoover Institution Archives). This core of Soviet officers was supplemented by young Polish line officers of Jaruzelski's generation and Soviets from Rokossovskii's entourage.

27. See Paul C. Latawski "The Polish Military and Politics," in Jack Bielasiak and Maurice D. Simon, eds., *Polish Politics: Edge of the Abyss* (New York: Praeger Publishers, 1984), pp. 268–92.

28. Bordziłowski remained in the Polish army even after it had been purged, in 1956, of most of the Soviet generals. Following Rokossovskii's dismissal in 1956, Bordziłowski chose to remain in Poland, took Polish citizenship, and continued to serve in the Polish army until his retirement in 1968. See Rakowska-Harmstone, p. 63.

29. A. Ross Johnson, et al. *East European Military Establishments: The Warsaw Pact Northern Tier* (RAND, R-2417/1-AF/FF, 1980), p. 22. Referred to as hereafter as "Ross Johnson."

30. Tadeusz Pióro, "Generałowie Przed Sądem" (The generals on trial), *Polityka*, Sept. 10, 1988.

31. Ibid.

32. Gen. Józef Kuropieska, *Nieprzewidziane Przygody* (Unforeseen adventures) (Krakow: Wydawnictwo Literackie, 1988).

33. Tadeusz Pióro, "Generałowie Przed Sądem," *Polityka*, Sept. 10, 1988.

34. Światło, p. 140.

35. The date of Spychalski's arrest is based on the testimony given on March 6, 1958,

by Anatol Fejgin of the Ministry of Internal Affairs, quoted in Kazimierz Łączyński and Stanisław Przyjemski, "Na marginesie artykułu Tadeusza Pióro: Jak Powstawała Sprawa 'Spisku w Wojsku,'" *Polityka*, Nov. 26, 1988.

36. Tadeusz Pióro, "Przed Najwyższym Sądem Wojskowym 1951–1953: Procesy Odpryskowe," *Polityka*, Sept. 17, 1988.

37. Gen. S. Tatar died in 1980. See Toranska, p. 382.

38. Swiatło, p. 82.

39. Quoted from Utnik's unpublished manuscript, in Tadeusz Pióro, "Generałowie Przed Sądem," *Polityka*, Sept. 10, 1988.

40. Ibid.

41. This date of Komar's arrest is given in Tadeusz Pióro, "Przed Najwyższym Sądem Wojskowym, 1951–1953: Procesy Odpryskowe," *Polityka*, Sept. 17, 1988. Teresa Toranska gives 1953 as the date of Komar's arrest (Toranska, p. 371). Juliusz Hibner in a letter to the editor of *Polityka* gives the details of Komar's arrest; see *Polityka*, Nov. 19, 1988. It is ironic that Komar himself fell victim to the purge, because in 1947 he was the officer who, upon a denunciation by two army officers, ordered the investigation of Tatar. See Kazimierz Łączyński and Stanisław Przyjemski, "Na marginesie artykułu Tadeusza Pióro: Jak Powstawa-la Sprawa 'Spisku w Wojsku,'" *Polityka*, Nov. 26, 1988.

42. Światło, p. 84. Świerczewski was killed in a skirmish with Ukrainian nationalist forces of the UPA.

43. Juliusz Hibner's letter to the editor; *Polityka*, Nov. 19, 1988.

44. Tadeusz Pióro, "Przed Najwyższym Sądem Wojskowym, 1951–1953: Procesy Odpryskowe," *Polityka*, Sept. 17, 1988. According to Teresa Toranska, Komar was not released until 1956 (Toranska, p. 371).

45. Tadeusz Pióro, "Generałowie Przed Sądem," *Polityka*, Sept. 10, 1988.

46. Tadeusz Pióro, "Przed Najwyższym Sądem Wojskowym 1951–1953: Procesy Odpryskowe," *Polityka*, Sept. 17, 1988; and Kazimierz Łączyński and Stanisław Przyjemski, "Na marginesie artykułu Tadeusza Pióro: Jak Powstawała Sprawa 'Spisku w Wojsku,'" *Polityka*, Nov. 26, 1988. Łączyński and Przyjemski give 84 as the total number of officers tried in the course of the "ripple-effect trials"; the 84th officer, Naval Lt. Zdzisław Ficek, was sentenced to death on Aug. 9, 1954, and executed.

47. Kazimierz Łączyński and Stanisław Przyjemski, "Na marginesie artykułu Tadeusza Pióro: Jak Powstawała Sprawa 'Spisku w Wojsku,'" *Polityka*, Nov. 26, 1988.

48. Ibid.

49. Światło, p. 23.

50. Document no. 21: "Treść wystąpienia W. Gomułki w dniu 12 X 1956 na posiedzeniu Biura Politycznego KC PZPR, Section 'Sprawa doradców w wojsku'" (W. Gomułka's address to the Politburo of the PUWP Central Committee, Oct. 12, 1956; section "The question of military advisors"), in Jakub Andrzejewski, ed., *Gomułka i Inni: Dokumenty z Archiwum KC, 1948–1982* (Gomułka and others: Documents from the archives of the Central Committee, 1948–1982) (London: Aneks, 1987), p. 94. Hereafter referred to as "*Dokumenty KC*."

51. This information is taken from Edmund Makowski, ed., *Wydarzenia Czerwcowe w*

Poznaniu, 1956 (June events in Poznań, 1956) (Poznań: Uniwersytet im. Adama Mickie-wicza, 1981), pp. 58–59. The Makowski publication is a collection of papers presented at a conference on May 4, 1981, organized by the History Department of Poznań University to commemorate the Poznań revolt. The book was cleared for publication in Poland thanks to the relaxation of government censorship during Solidarity's first period of legal existence. Hereafter referred to as "Makowski."

52. Makowski, p. 70.

53. In fact, Khrushchev had known Gomułka for some time prior to 1956 and on one occasion had "recommended him very highly to Stalin." See *Khrushchev Remembers* (Boston: Little, Brown, 1970), p. 360.

54. Zbigniew Brzezinski, in his *Soviet Bloc: Unity and Conflict* (New York: Praeger Publishers, 1962), argues that in 1956 the threat of protracted Polish resistance to a Soviet invasion was not a key factor in forcing Khrushchev to accept Gomułka; yet he notes that during the October crisis the Polish army was restive, and it was likely that, "in a critical situation, [the army] would not obey Rokossovsky." (p. 258) On the other hand, both Rakowska-Harmstone and A. Ross Johnson emphasize the importance of Gen. Komar's military demonstration to the outcome of the crisis.

55. Rakowska-Harmstone, p. 66.

56. Ross Johnson, p. 24.

57. Spychalski was always regarded as a civilian. According to Osóbka-Morawski, Spychalski was promoted to colonel in a most unorthodox fashion. In late 1944, minutes before Spychalski was to be received by an American diplomat to whom he would plead for military aid to the AL, Osóbka-Morawski realized that his protégé was "only a major." Without a moment's hesitation, Osóbka-Morawski announced to Spychalski that he had decided to promote him to colonel, effective immediately. Minutes later, "Colonel Spychalski" was announced to the American envoy. See folder 3, Edward Osóbka-Morawski Collection, Hoover Institution Archives.

58. According to one source, Spychalski's intermittent fits of fury were frighteningly unexpected. See Romuald Spasowski, *The Liberation of One* (San Diego: Harcourt, Brace, Jovanovich, 1986), pp. 447–48. Hereafter referred to as "Spasowski."

59. Rakowska-Harmstone, p. 77.

60. A. Ross Johnson, Robert W. Dean, and Alexander Alexiev, *East European Military Establishments: The Warsaw Pact Northern Tier* (New York: Crane Russak, 1982), pp. 28–29. Hereafter referred to as "Johnson/Dean/Alexiev."

61. In addition to a book on this concept, Chocha has written extensively on strategy and tactics of modern warfare. His key theoretical works include *Rozważania o sztuce wojennej* (On military art) (Warsaw: Wydawnictwo Ministerstwa Obrony Narodowej, 1984) and *Wojna i doktryna wojenna* (War and military doctrine) (Warsaw: Wydawnictwo Minis-terstwa Obrony Narodowej, 1980); the latter study was written jointly with Julian Kaczmarek.

62. Johnson/Dean/Alexiev, p. 30.

63. George C. Malcher, in his study *Poland's Politicized Army: Communists in Uniform* (New York: Praeger Publishers, 1984) views the Main Political Administration as a "military communist party." He writes:

The military communist party is an integral part of the civilian Communist Party and is governed by the party statute. This means that party members serving in the army can play a full part in the life of the civilian party. At the same time the military party enjoys semi-autonomy because it has its own political apparatus of full-time functionaries (political officers) who are responsible for planning, direction, organization, and coordination of political work in the army. (p. 38)

The role of the MPA in the PUWP's internal politics is discussed later in the book, referred to hereafter as "Malcher."

64. Johnson/Dean/Alexiev, p. 46.

65. According to Zdzisław Rurarz, a onetime Polish ambassador to Japan and himself a counterintelligence officer, Soviet liaison officers have 24-hour-a-day access to all Polish military installations. This penetration assures that no important development inside the Polish army can take place without the Soviets knowing of it. See Z. Rurarz, "Komuniści polscy czy polscy komuniści" (Polish communists or communist Poles), *Pomost*, July 1985. Hereafter referred to as "Rurarz."

66. Duszyński reportedly had pressed for the eventual withdrawal of the Soviet troops stationed in Poland. T. Rakowska-Harmstone suggests that may be why he fell into disfavor with Moscow. See Rakowska-Harmstone, p. 71.

Chapter 4

1. Kukliński considers the story a sheer fabrication (Kukliński, p. 13); still, it survived in Poland until 1981. Timothy Garton Ash, in *The Polish Revolution: Solidarity* (New York: Charles Scribner's Sons, 1983), quotes Lech Wałęsa and other prominent Solidarity leaders who expressed, prior to the crackdown, their confidence in Jaruzelski as a professional, patriotic soldier; referred to hereafter as "Garton Ash."

2. The opinion that Jaruzelski was not involved in the 1970 riots was also accepted by Western students of Polish affairs. A. Ross Johnson suggests that Jaruzelski chose to oppose the use of the army against the strikers, and that, although several military units were deployed during the riots, their involvement was minimal. Johnson bases his assessment of Jaruzelski's position during the 1970 riots on several statements made by the general following the crisis, as well as on the "Letter from the Officers of the Gdańsk Garrison," published in February 1971 by *Żołnierz Wolności*, the army daily, which attempted to minimize the army's role in the suppression of the strike. Johnson writes:

The brunt of the repression in December 1970 was carried out by the militia (police), but it was backed up by the military. When the internal security forces of the coastal region proved insufficient for this task, regular units of the Gdańsk garrison were called in and they inflicted some casualties. But in a situation of leadership crisis in Warsaw and subjected to what Defense Minister Jaruzelski later called "uncoordinated orders," the military leadership refused to act on orders from Gomułka's chief lieutenant in the coastal area, Politburo member

Zenon Kliszko, to use immediate and overwhelming force to crush the worker demonstrations. (A. Ross Johnson, p. 60)

3. The biography of Jaruzelski contained in this section is based on *Mała Encyklopedia Wojskowa* (Short military encyclopedia) (Warsaw: MON, 1967–1971); *Rocznik Wojskowo-Historyczny, 1961* (Yearbook of military history, 1961) (Warsaw: Wydawnictwo Ministerstwa Obrony Narodowej, 1961), p. 446; Rurarz; *Current Biography Yearbook: 1982* (New York: The H. Wilson Co., 1982); *Who's Who in Poland* (Warsaw: Interpress Publishers, 1982); and *Sovyetskaya Voyennaya Entsiklopediya* (Moscow: Voyenizdat, 1980), vol. 8, p. 673.

4. Szczęśniak's and Szota's study of the Ukrainian nationalist movement contains a rare photograph of the young Jaruzelski, then a newly commissioned lieutenant of the Fifth Infantry Regiment, taken in 1947 during the "Vistula" operation. See Szczęśniak/Szota, p. 379.

5. For more about the national and ethnic background of the Polish officer corps immediately after World War II, see Ross Johnson, pp. 48–50.

6. Whether or not Jaruzelski attended Voroshilov is still debatable; Jaruzelski's official Polish biography makes no mention of this. It is possible that he attended only a short course at Voroshilov and never formally graduated. In the light of his subsequent career, it is highly unlikely that he would have been promoted to general without attending at least for a brief period of time the Moscow General Staff Academy. As a rule, training at the Voroshilov academy is a prerequisite for all high-level appointments in the Polish army.

7. Polish general-officer ranks are as follows: (1) one-star general (*generał brygady*); (2) two-star general (*generał dywizji*); (3) three-star general (*generał broni*); (4) four-star general (*generał armii*); and (5) marshal (*marszałek*).

8. It is interesting to note that Jaruzelski's 1960 appointment coincided with the elevation of Marshal Andrey Grechko to the position of commander in chief of the Warsaw Pact Forces. Grechko was instrumental in modernizing the WTO armies.

9. *Trybuna Ludu* Feb. 29, 1968.

10. Spychalski's promotion marked his downfall. In Poland at that time, the position of chairman of the Council of State—formally the head of state—was a purely honorific one. Two years later another prominent Polish government official, Gomułka's prime minister, J. Cyrankiewicz, was retired in a manner closely resembling Spychalski's dismissal. In 1970, after the Gomułka regime had been replaced by the Gierek group, Cyrankiewicz succeeded Spychalski as chairman of the Council of State, in part to assure continuity in foreign policy after Gomułka's accommodation with West Germany in 1970.

11. Franciszek Szlachcic, "Ze wspomnień Ministra Spraw Wewnętrznych" (Recollections of the interior minister), *Życie Literackie*, March 6, 1988.

12. Zdzisław Rykowski and Wiesław Władyka, "Marzec '68" (March 1968), *Polityka*, Feb. 20, 1988.

13. Zenobiusz Kozik, "O wydarzeniach marcowych 1968" (The events of March 1968), *Nowe Drogi*, Feb. 1988.

14. For more on the 1968 purge, see Michael Checinski, *Poland: Communism, Nationalism, Anti-Semitism* (New York: Karz-Cohl, 1982).

15. *Trybuna Ludu*, April 11, 1968.

16. Z. Rurarz has emphasized that throughout the 1970s Jaruzelski had direct access to the Soviet top brass, without having to clear his contacts with the Gierek party leadership. According to Rurarz, such contacts between the Polish senior officers and their Soviet counterparts are today routine. It is likely that in Jaruzelski's case such direct access had its roots in the late 1960s, around the time of his appointment as defense minister. See Rurarz, p. 3.

17. *Trybuna Ludu*, March 7, 1968.

18. *Trybuna Ludu*, March 8, 1968.

19. Such early planning would not be out of pattern. I argue in the subsequent chapters that contingency plans for a military solution to the 1980 Polish crisis were prepared immediately after the eruption of workers' discontent.

20. *Żołnierz Wolności*, April 13–15, 1968 (weekend edition).

21. It would be interesting to speculate whether, indeed, the appointment of Jaruzelski marked the Soviet decision to start preparing for military intervention in Czechoslovakia. By 1968, Spychalski's once-strong position in the Polish officer corps was completely eroded. Therefore, Gomułka, an ardent supporter of the invasion, must have realized that Spychalski was not the right man to lead the Polish troops into Czechoslovakia.

22. Testimony of Col. Ryszard Kukliński, who participated in the preparation of the invasion plans. See Kukliński, p. 10.

23. *Trybuna Ludu*, April 20, 1968.

24. *Trybuna Ludu*, April 29, 1968. The first announcement of joint WTO "staff maneuvers" to be held on Czechoslovak territory in June came on May 24, 1968.

25. *Trybuna Ludu*, Aug. 7, 1968. The inclusion in the Polish delegation of the principal invasion planners strongly suggests that the objective of Jaruzelski's meeting with Grechko and Shtemenko was to review the details of the Czechoslovak contingency plan.

26. *Trybuna Ludu*, April 29, 1968.

27. Jaruzelski's visit was reported in *Żołnierz Wolności*, Aug. 21, 1968.

28. *Trybuna Ludu*, May 10, 1968.

29. The text of Jaruzelski's speech was printed in *Żołnierz Wolności*, Sept. 2, 1968, p. 4.

30. These two high decorations are awarded both to Polish civilians and soldiers for exceptional service to the nation.

31. *Trybuna Ludu*, Sept. 1, 1968.

32. *Trybuna Ludu*, Sept. 30, 1968.

33. *Trybuna Ludu*, Oct. 11, 1968.

34. *Trybuna Ludu*, Oct. 13, 1968.

35. *Trybuna Ludu*, Oct. 13, 1968. Spychalski received his order of Lenin during a morning ceremony hosted by Gomułka in Belvedere. During the ceremony honoring the "Czechoslovak veterans," the only "civilian" present was Minister of the Interior Moczar, who had been a communist resistance fighter during World War II and had been promoted shortly thereafter to the rank of general.

36. *Trybuna Ludu*, Oct. 25, 1968.

37. Kukliński, p. 12.

38. Ross Johnson, p. 59.

39. The attempts of the military press to depict the Polish soldier in Czechoslovakia as a devout defender of the Socialist Commonwealth often reached heights of absurdity. On one occasion in 1968, immediately after the invasion, *Żołnierz Wolności* described the circumstances in which a Polish tank driver on duty in Bratislava had died. The army daily reported that the soldier had died while trying not to hit a Slovak pedestrian who was attempting to jaywalk in front of the Polish tank. The description of the event was accompanied by the writer's rendition of the tank driver's last thoughts as he struggled to regain control of his tank and ultimately chose to die rather than hurt the innocent Slovak civilian.

40. *Trybuna Ludu*, Nov. 17, 1968. As Gomułka's concession to the "partisans," the Fifth Congress also elected Moczar a candidate Politburo member. This, however, effectively limited Moczar's ability to act. See Franciszek Szlachcic, "Ze wspomnień Ministra Spraw Wewnętrznych," *Życie Literackie*, March 6, 1988.

41. Jeffrey Simon, *Warsaw Pact Forces: Problems of Command and Control* (Boulder, Colo.: Westview Press, 1985), pp. 62–67.

42. Dale R. Herspring, "The Warsaw Pact at 25," *Problems of Communism*, Sept.–Oct. 1980:5. Hereafter referred to as "Herspring."

43. According to one observer, the dramatic rise in WTO joint military exercises was an indication of the growing integration of the pact and the renewed emphasis by the Soviets on multilateral cooperation of the satellite armies within the framework of Soviet military strategy. During the first fourteen years of the pact's existence, only 18 joint exercises were held; the period 1969–1972 witnessed 21 of them. See Herspring, p. 5.

44. *Dokumenty K.C.*, p. 195.

45. Kukliński, p. 14.

46. Jaruzelski's own admission, contained in the transcript of a recording made during a discussion on January 24, 1971, between Gierek, Jaroszewicz, and Jaruzelski, on one side, and the strikers of Szczecin on the other. See *Od Października 1956 do Grudnia 1970: Materiały z Dziejów Polski* (Between October 1956 and December 1970: Sources on Polish history) (Warsaw: Wydawnictwo Społeczne KOS, 1985), zeszyt 2, p. 137. The book is an underground Polish publication, available from the Hoover Institution's Polish Underground Press Collection. Hereafter referred to as "*Materiały*."

47. *Dokumenty K.C.*, p. 195.

48. "List Władysława Gomułki z 6 II 1971 do I Sekretarza KC PZPR Edwarda Gierka" (A letter of Władysław Gomułka to First Secretary Edward Gierek, dated Feb. 6, 1971), in *Dokumenty K.C.*, p. 194. Gomułka doesn't mention Jaruzelski, but it is likely that as a Politburo member he was also present.

49. Kukliński, p. 14.

50. Poland's ex-ambassador to the U.S., R. Spasowski, who defected in 1981, claims in his memoirs that Gierek was a compromise choice accepted by Moscow only hours before the plenum that approved his appointment. This information is based on the account by Kazimierz Sidor, a high-ranking official in the Foreign Ministry and Poland's onetime ambassador to Egypt. See Spasowski, p. 477.

51. From a transcript of the tape recording of the meeting published by an underground press. See *Materiały*, pp. 136–38.

52. Kukliński, p. 13.

53. *Materiały*, p. 94.

54. In preparation for the commemorative celebrations of the 1970 Gdańsk riots, *Tygodnik Solidarność* published in the winter of 1980 a series of eyewitness accounts of the Polish December, among them memoirs of the Polish draftees involved in the bloody confrontation.

55. Tadeusz Podgórski, *Wojsko w PRL* (The army in the Polish People's Republic) (London: Centralny Komitet Polskiej Partii Socjalistycznej, 1976), p. 7.

56. Davies, vol. 2, p. 591.

57. *Materiały*, p. 137.

58. On Jaruzelski's elevation to the Politburo in 1970, see Zbigniew Pelczynski, "The Downfall of Gomułka," in Adam Bromke and John W. Strong, eds., *Gierek's Poland* (New York: Praeger Publishers, 1973), p. 16.

59. As Z. Rurarz observes, Jaruzelski had an additional line of communication to Moscow through his direct contacts with the commanding officers of the Warsaw Pact forces; he used this line repeatedly throughout the 1970s, thus bypassing the party's control. See Rurarz, p. 3.

60. On the impact of the WTO invasion on the morale of the Czechoslovak military, see A. Ross Johnson, "Soviet Military Policy in Eastern Europe," in Sarah Meiklejohn Terry, ed., *Soviet Policy in Eastern Europe* (New Haven, Conn.: Yale University Press, 1984), p. 267.

61. Adam Bromke, "Poland under Gierek: A New Political Style," *Problems of Communism*, Sept.–Oct. 1972:14.

62. See John P. Farrell, "Growth, Reform, and Inflation: Problems and Policies," and Zbigniew Fallenbuchl, "Policy Alternatives in Polish Foreign Economic Relations," in Maurice D. Simon and Roger E. Kanet, eds., *Background to Crisis: Policy and Politics in Gierek's Poland* (Boulder, Colo.: Westview Press, 1981).

63. Solidarity published a detailed account of the 1976 strikes. See *Tygodnik Solidarność*, June 26, 1981.

64. *Trybuna Ludu*, June 29, 1976.

65. *Tygodnik Solidarność*, June 26, 1981.

66. Quoted in A. Ross Johnson's RAND study from one of D. Herspring's 1978 interviews with former Polish officers. See Ross Johnson, p. 61.

67. Even if one disregards the arrest in 1981, ordered by Jaruzelski, of Gierek and his cronies on charges of economic mismanagement as merely a propaganda ploy, there are indications that Jaruzelski had much more respect for Gomułka than he ever did for Gierek. As late as 1986, during the Tenth Congress of the PUWP, First Secretary Jaruzelski paid tribute in his opening speech to Gomułka's leadership and asked the congress to honor Gomułka's memory with a minute's silence. See *Trybuna Ludu*, July 1, 1986.

68. Rurarz, p. 3. Rurarz's assessment is confirmed by Spasowski: "[In February 1980] Olszowski was not elected to the Politburo either, and many wondered why. I recalled him saying: 'All or nothing!'" See Spasowski, p. 611.

69. The 1977 change in the constitution, which described the country's alliance with the Soviet Union as one of the constitutive principles of Poland's statehood, infuriated Poland's intelligentsia and further contributed to the development of Poland's dissident movement.

70. On Gierek's détente policies, see Spasowski, pp. 527 and 585–87.

71. *Trybuna Ludu*, June 30, 1976.

72. *Trybuna Ludu*, July 8, 1976.

73. Dale R. Herspring, "Civil-Military Relations in Poland and East Germany: The External Factor," *Studies in Comparative Communism*, Autumn 1978:231. For comparison, party membership among the officers in the East German army was 99 percent of the total; in Bulgaria and Romania, 90 percent; and in Hungary, 80 percent.

74. Figures taken from Jack Bielasiak, "Recruitment Policy, Elite Integration, and Political Stability in People's Poland," in Maurice D. Simon and Roger E. Kanet, eds., *Background to Crisis: Policy and Politics in Gierek's Poland* (Boulder, Colo.: Westview Press, 1981), pp. 106–7.

75. The two figures are taken, respectively, from Eugeniusz Walczuk, "Oficerowie" (The officers), *Polityka*, April 29, 1972, and Michael Sadykiewicz, "Jaruzelski's War," *Survey* 3 (26), as cited in Rakowska-Harmstone, p. 78.

76. Data from *The Military Balance, 1983–1984* (London: The Institute for Strategic Studies, 1983).

77. Dale R. Herspring, "The Warsaw Pact at 25," *Problems of Communism*, Sept.–Oct. 1980:6.

78. According to Jan Zakrzewski, a Polish journalist, Olszowski probably challenged Gierek openly in 1978 and lost. Subsequently, Gierek removed him from Warsaw by sending him into "forced exile" as Poland's ambassador to East Germany, from which post he returned following the 1980 crisis. The information about the 1978 confrontation between Gierek and Olszowski is based on the author's conversation in the same year with Zakrzewski, at the time one of Poland's leading journalists. Zakrzewski indicated that Olszowski enjoyed considerable support in the PUWP's Central Committee.

79. As reported by Zdzisław Rurarz, neither Gierek nor Kania dared interfere with military appointments. See Rurarz, p. 3.

80. Biographical information for this section is taken from *Who's Who in Poland* (Warsaw: Interpress Publishers, 1982); Rurarz; and *Trybuna Ludu*, July 4, 1986.

81. Rakowska-Harmstone speculates that Kiszczak might have fought in one of the Soviet partisan groups. See Rakowska-Harmstone, p. 230.

82. The list of WRON members was published in *Żołnierz Wolności*, Dec. 14, 1981. Gen. Cz. Kiszczak was promoted in 1973; Gen. J. Baryła in 1970; Gen. Longin Łozowicki in 1970; Gen. M. Janiszewski in 1976; and Gen. J. Jarosz in 1978. See *Who's Who in Poland* (Warsaw: Interpress Publishers, 1982).

83. Rakowska-Harmstone, p. 149.

84. Kukliński, p. 43.

85. Kukliński, p. 48.

86. Kukliński, p. 23.

87. Gen. Florian Siwicki, "Centrum, jego struktura, zadania: Ministerstwo Obrony Narodowej" (The central government, its structure and its tasks: The Ministry of Defense), *Rzeczpospolita*, April 26, 1988.

88. See Timothy J. Colton, *Commissars, Commanders, and Civilian Authority: The Structure of Soviet Military Politics* (Cambridge, Mass.: Harvard University Press, 1979), pp. 58–84.

89. *Trybuna Ludu*, July 18–19, 1981.

90. The appointments of Czapla and Huszcza are listed in Appendix I of Malcher, pp. 273–80.

91. Malcher, p. 49.

92. Malcher, pp. 32–35.

93. Malcher, p. 93. Malcher suggests that the guidelines were the Central Committee's attempt to control the unauthorized incursions of political officers into party and governmental affairs on the regional level.

Chapter 5

1. In his introduction to J. S. Staniszkis, *Poland's Self-Limiting Revolution* (Princeton, N.J.: Princeton University Press, 1984), Jan T. Gross notes that the very existence of Solidarity constituted a challenge to the PUWP. Writing a year after the Gdańsk Agreements of 1980, Gross observes that

> it seems nearly impossible to stabilize a quasi-liberal, authoritarian-bureaucratic regime in Poland based on a "social contract" legitimacy on the one hand and on a conciliatory pattern of problem solving on the other hand. The totalitarian temptation of reverting to organized coercion is openly formulated. Some of these voices represent the *ultima ratio* of party-state power. Some are a rigid response caused by an ideological interpretation of Solidarity's claims. Others are linked to institutional-sectoral interests. Such temptations are reinforced by the desire of party members for a more active policy and for an end to the serious status problem linked with a tactic of permanent retreat. (p. 12)

2. Franciszek Szlachcic, "Ze wspomnień Ministra Spraw Wewnętrznych" (Recollections of the interior minister), *Życie Literackie*, March 6, 1988.

3. "List Edwarda Gierka z listopada 1982 do I sekretarza KC PZPR Wojciecha Jaruzelskiego" (Letter from Edward Gierek to First Secretary Wojciech Jaruzelski, dated November 1982), in *Dokumenty KC*, p. 252.

4. *Trybuna Ludu*, Aug. 25, 1980.

5. Malcher, p. 49.

6. *Trybuna Ludu*, Sept. 6–7, 1980.

7. Franciszek Szlachcic, "Ze wspomnień Ministra Spraw Wewnętrznych," *Życie Literackie*, March 6, 1988.

8. Moczar died in 1986.

9. *Trybuna Ludu*, Dec. 3, 1980.

10. Although Kania was a member of the Gierek team, he was associated with the internal party bureaucracy rather than with the managing of the economy or making important political decisions. Kania's party career was quite impressive. In 1971, he was elected to the Central Committee and in 1975 became full member of the PUWP's Politburo. Clearly, his concessions to Solidarity were never meant to go as far as power sharing. For more on Kania's position, see Jan B. de Weydenthal, Bruce D. Porter, and Kevin Devlin, eds., *The Polish Drama: 1980–1982* (Lexington, Mass.: Lexington Books, 1983). Hereafter referred to as "Weydenthal."

11. The evolution of Soviet policies toward Poland during the critical two years (1980–1982) is discussed in Chapter 8.

12. Kukliński describes Molczyk as the leader of the hard-line Stalinist faction within the army with frequent contacts with Moscow, some of which took place outside Jaruzelski's control and supervision. See Kukliński, pp. 23–24.

13. During 1980–1981, Baryła became a key figure in Jaruzelski's administration; he was eventually coopted into the Politburo. The author therefore considers his statements to be representative of Jaruzelski's own views.

14. *Trybuna Ludu*, Sept. 12, 1980.

15. Clearly, the army enjoyed considerable authority in Poland. For example, on July 6, 1981, *The Wall Street Journal* published the results of a public-opinion poll taken among the Poles to evaluate their level of confidence in particular institutions of their country. The military was placed third on the list of the most trustworthy institutions, following the Catholic Church and Solidarity. The PUWP had the lowest ranking, with only 32 percent of the sample mentioning it at all.

It is noteworthy that the Poles, who have been notorious for their skepticism about all agencies affiliated with their communist government, chose to trust the army more than Poland's postwar history might have warranted. A possible explanation of this could lie in the Poles' ardent nationalism and their conviction that communism is inherently alien to the Polish ethos. The desire to regard the People's Army as willing to support the Poles' national aspirations is a striking testimony to the strength of the military tradition in the country.

16. Kukliński, p. 21.

17. The Soviets did not know that the CIA had an agent in place within the Polish general staff, who participated in the drafting of the plans for imposing martial law, and until his removal in November of 1981 provided the U.S. intelligence service with up-to-date reports on the talks.

18. See Chapter 8.

19. Thus it should be emphasized that Jaruzelski's appeals to the Poles' patriotism and his protestations that the declaration of martial law was based on patriotic concern for the nation were not entirely a smoke screen. In a sense, they were determined by a mind-set

similar to the one that in 1956 allowed Gomułka both to defy the Soviets and then reimpose tight controls in the name of Poland's *raison d'état*.

20. Kukliński, p. 17. On Jaruzelski's instructions, Kukliński drafted a memorandum for the Soviets advising them that the preparation was proceeding according to plan.

21. Kukliński, pp. 17–18.

22. Kukliński, p. 18.

23. This law was eventually modified in 1983; see Chapter 9.

24. Mechanized Units of the Citizens' Militia (Zmotoryzowane Odwody Milicji Obywatelskiej; ZOMO) number approximately 30 thousand members and are stationed in Golędzinów, outside Warsaw. Cf. Lawrence Weschler, *The Passion of Poland* (New York: Pantheon Books, 1984), p. 225. Hereafter referred to as "Weschler."

25. Kukliński, p. 19.

26. There is no doubt that Baryła acted on Jaruzelski's instructions. Had Baryła overstepped his authority by initiating the campaign on his own, he would have been purged after 1981; far from it, in 1986 Baryła was promoted by the Tenth Party Congress to full membership in the Politburo.

27. Mieczysław Krajewski, "Silne państwo w interesie demokracji" (A strong state is in the interest of democracy), *Wojsko Ludowe*, Sept. 1980:16. Krajewski's "nonantagonistic contradictions" refer to the economic crisis in Poland.

28. Wojciech Jaruzelski, "Bezcenną zdobyczą socjalizmu w Polsce—polityka istnienia narodowego" (Policies ensuring national existence are the priceless achievement of socialism in Poland); speech given during the Sixth Plenary Session of the PUWP's Central Committee on Sept. 5, 1980. Printed in *Wojsko Ludowe*, Oct. 1980:26.

29. Ibid.

30. *Trybuna Ludu*, Sept. 8, 1980.

31. Col. Jerzy Muszyński, "Dysydenci polscy roku 1980" (Polish dissidents of 1980) *Wojsko Ludowe*, Dec. 1980. Interestingly, while describing the dissident movement as inspired by counterrevolution from abroad, Muszyński's article directly attacked the party for its inability to control opposition to it. "True socialism," wrote Muszyński,

> eliminates political pluralism, but in such socialism there is no place for contradictions between the working class and its communist vanguard anyway. The party must realize this first and foremost, precisely because it has taken upon itself the difficult task of creating a new socioeconomic formation with the help of the working people and in their interest. It is the party that is responsible for the realization of this historic mission of the working class, for making communist theory identical with social practice. (p. 19)

32. Józef Baryła, "Sprawie partii i narodu żołnierze oddani są całym sercem" (Soldiers are totally devoted to the cause of the party and the nation); speech given at the Seventh Plenary Session of the PUWP's Central Committee on Dec. 2, 1980. Printed in *Wojsko Ludowe*, Jan. 1981:13.

33. Ibid.

34. *Trybuna Ludu*, Dec. 2, 1980.

35. Ibid.

36. Kukliński, p. 22.

37. "Odezwa Komitetu Centralnego PZPR" (An appeal of the PUWP Central Committee), *Trybuna Ludu*, Dec. 4, 1980.

38. *Trybuna Ludu*, Dec. 6–7, 1980.

39. Kukliński, p. 24.

40. Kukliński, p. 25.

41. See Chapter 8.

42. Kukliński, pp. 22–23.

43. Kukliński, p. 26.

44. After the declaration of martial law, Jasiński was promoted and is currently deputy defense minister for general administration. See *Rzeczpospolita*, April 26, 1988.

45. Following the introduction of martial law, Puchała was promoted to general.

46. Kukliński, pp. 26–27.

47. Kukliński, p. 28.

48. Kukliński, p. 28.

49. In his article "Soviet Decision-Making in Poland," Richard D. Anderson argues that the Soviets were ready to invade in December 1980. Analyzing the Soviet troop movements in the Baltic area, Anderson concludes that an invasion of Poland was prepared at least twice prior to Jaruzelski's crackdown, and each time it was called off at the last minute. See *Problems of Communism*, March–April 1982:21–37. The setting of December 1980 as the time of the invasion has been confirmed by Kukliński's testimony; however, as this book contends, Soviet mobilization and troop movements in early spring of 1981 were a part of Kulikov's contingency planning for dealing with the failure of martial law (the declaration of which was originally planned for the spring) to destroy Solidarity. This argument is developed in greater detail in the last section of this chapter.

50. *Rozkaz Ministra Obrony Narodowej nr. 1 z dnia 11 lutego, 1981* (Order from the defense minister, no. 1, dated Feb. 11, 1981). The order was published on Feb. 12, 1981, in both *Żołnierz Wolności* and *Trybuna Ludu*, the PUWP's central daily, as well as in other newspapers.

51. As customary in the Soviet bloc on similar occasions, all official newspapers reprinted cables with greetings to Jaruzelski from the "fraternal governments."

52. Rurarz, p. 4.

53. *Wojsko Ludowe*, Feb. 1981.

54. Maj. Ryszard Maluta, "Miary ofensywnosci" (Taking the offensive), *Wojsko Ludowe*, Feb. 1981. Describing the meeting of the Silesian Military District's party organization, Maluta notes that the political administration of the district decided to focus on "demonstrating [to the soldiers] the level of threat to the nation's existence coming from the forces of counterrevolution, showing the real origins of the antisocialist forces, and unmasking the content, form, and methods of the enemies' actions." This, in Maluta's opinion, would lead

to the strengthening of the army's resistance to ideological subversion and to "the establishment of close collaboration with the MPs and the police." (p. 10)

55. The question of the party's place in society was raised by Col. Zdzisław Czerwiński in "Przewodnia Siła" (The vanguard), *Wojsko Ludowe*, Feb. 1981:21.

56. *Trybuna Ludu*, Feb. 13, 1981.

57. Kukliński, p. 28.

58. *Trybuna Ludu*, Feb. 23, 1981.

59. Kukliński, p. 31.

60. Kukliński, p. 29.

61. *Trybuna Ludu*, March 5, 1981.

62. Kukliński describes Jaruzelski as being at that time exhausted by constant arguments with the Russians. See Kukliński, pp. 30–31.

63. Kukliński, p. 31.

64. Kukliński, p. 32.

65. Stanisław Dymek, "Pomówmy i o tym" (Let's talk about it), *Żołnierz Polski*, Feb. 8, 1981, p. 5.

66. "Trzon wojska" (The core of the army), *Żołnierz Polski*, March 1, 1981, p. 14.

67. Background data based on *Radio Free Europe/Radio Liberty Research: Polish Situation Report/5*, March 20, 1981.

68. The chronology of Bydgoszcz events is based in part on "Wydarzenia Bydgoskie" (Bydgoszcz events), a reconstruction of the crisis printed in the first issue of *Tygodnik Solidarność*, April 3, 1981.

69. *Tygodnik Solidarność*, April 3, 1981.

70. Kukliński, p. 33.

71. Kukliński, pp. 33–34.

72. This is the interpretation proposed by Kukliński, who regards Bydgoszcz as a test of wills brought about by the government. George Sanford shares Kukliński's interpretation, but points his finger at Interior Minister Milewski as the principal culprit. See Kukliński, p. 32, and Sanford, pp. 102 and 246.

73. For Moscow's behavior during the crisis see Chapter 8.

74. Garton Ash, p. 153.

75. Col. Jan Ignaczak, "Pytania na które trzeba odpowiedzieć" (Questions that must be answered), *Żołnierz Polski*, March 29, 1981, p. 2.

76. *Radio Free Europe/Radio Liberty Research: Polish Situation Report/14*, Aug. 4, 1981.

Chapter 6

1. *Radio Free Europe/Radio Liberty Research: Polish Situation Report/8*, May 14, 1981, pp. 2–4. ("Radio Free Europe/Radio Liberty" abbreviated hereafter to "RFE/RL.")

2. *RFE/RL Polish Situation Report/8*, May 14, 1981, p. 2.

3. RFE/RL *Polish Situation Report/8*, May 14, 1981, pp. 19–20.

4. *Żołnierz Wolności*, May 6, 1981.

5. RFE/RL *Research: Poland Background Report/13*, May 11, 1981, p. 5.

6. *Trybuna Ludu*, May 1, 1981.

7. Jaruzelski repeatedly reminded the Soviets that the Polish military had to postpone the crackdown until the plans were ready, intelligence gathered, and forces deployed. See Kukliński, p. 31.

8. *Wokół Października* (Polish October) (Warsaw: Zeszyty Edukacji Narodowej, 1984), p. 12.

9. Kukliński, p. 37.

10. "Przyjaźń z Krajem Rad gwarancją naszego bezpieczeństwa," *Wojsko Ludowe*, April 1981.

11. Col. Ireneusz Ruszkiewicz, "Gwarant bezpieczeństwa Polski, wspólnoty, socjalizmu" (The guarantor of Poland's security, of the Socialist Commonwealth, of socialism), *Wojsko Ludowe*, May 1981:17.

12. Kukliński, p. 35.

13. Kukliński, p. 36.

14. Kukliński, p. 40.

15. Throughout the crisis, Jaruzelski's motives appear to have oscillated between patriotic sentiment and communist zeal. At one point in his account, while describing the general's behavior before one of his meetings with Kulikov, Col. Kukliński gives us a rare insight into Jaruzelski's personality. Appearing distressed at the prospect of the approaching deadline for the military's action, Jaruzelski exclaimed: "In the darkest depths of my mind I can't envision that we can do something like that"; and "I'd rather not be Prime Minister when the time comes to sign the orders." This patriotic outburst was immediately followed by a vicious attack on Solidarity activists, whom (in the best traditions of communist rhetoric) the general branded "social fascists." See Kukliński, p. 37.

16. No relationship to this author.

17. Norbert Michta, "Czego oczekuję od IX Zjazdu Partii?" (What do I expect of the Ninth Party Congress?), *Wojsko Ludowe*, June 1981:14.

18. Ibid., pp. 14–15.

19. *Wojsko Ludowe*, June 1981:17.

20. Stanisław Dymek, "Państwo nie jest sługą," *Żołnierz Polski*, June 7, 1981.

21. J. B. de Weydenthal, in his *Polish Drama: 1980–1982* (Lexington, Mass.: Lexington Books, 1983), views the June letter as an attempt on the part of the Soviets to test Kania's leadership. "A more likely explanation," writes Weydenthal, "is that the Soviet leadership sent the letter both to warn Kania and to precipitate a test of his leadership and influence in the Central Committee. Once Kania proved he could retain control of the committee, the Kremlin seems to have acquiesced in his new-found status in the PUWP. In any event, the personal snubs of Kania and criticism of the PUWP that had filled the Soviet media during April and May all but disappeared during June and July." (p. 129)

Weydenthal disputes the interpretation of the letter provided by ex-ambassador Rurarz, who suggested in a statement to the U.S. Commission on Security and Cooperation in Europe that, by accusing Kania and Jaruzelski of nationalism, the letter was aimed at strengthening their position in the country. For Rurarz, the letter was a precondition of the great popularity enjoyed by Jaruzelski during the congress.

22. Kukliński, p. 42.

23. See Chapter 5.

24. Olszowski, who towards the end of the Gierek years fell into disfavor and was sent out of Poland as ambassador to East Germany, staged a brilliant comeback at the very beginning of the crisis and reclaimed his prominent position with Poland's communist elite. After the Ninth Congress, Olszowski returned to relative obscurity.

25. *Trybuna Ludu*, July 18–19, 1981.

26. See Chapter 8.

27. Jaruzelski's speech published in *Wojsko Ludowe*, Aug. 1981:34–35.

28. *RFE/RL Research Department: Background Report/221*, Aug. 7, 1981, p. 25.

29. Gen. Józef Baryła, "Socializmu będziemy bronić tak jak niepodległości" (We will defend socialism like our independence), *Wojsko Ludowe*, Aug. 1981:36.

30. *RFE/RL Research Department: Background Report/240*, Aug. 25, 1981, pp. 1–12.

31. *Trybuna Ludu*, July 18–19, 1981.

32. *RFE/RL Research Department: Background Report/219*, Aug. 3, 1981, p. 13.

33. *RFE/RL Research Department: Background Report/221*, Aug. 7, 1981, p. 7.

34. *RFE/RL Research Department: Background Report/219*, Aug. 3, 1981, p. 19.

35. The relative eclipse of Olszowski is especially surprising in light of his previous ranking as "heir apparent" to Gierek. As this author was told in 1978 by Jan Zakrzewski, a prominent Polish radio journalist with very strong connections to the PUWP's Central Committee, Olszowski was then considered one of the few tough-minded party apparatchiks capable of leading the country out of the impending economic crisis.

36. *Życie Partii*, the party monthly, greeted the congress with a call for renewed activism and militancy within the rank and file as well as its leadership, a call which reflected the earlier assertions of the military press. See "Odbudować Siłę Partii" (To rebuild the party's power), *Życie Partii*, July 1981:3.

37. Gierek followed this tactic in defusing the tensions created by the 1970 Gdańsk riots. The workers' committees, created ostensibly to ensure the workers' participation in management, were, within a year, reduced to mere façades of the party's power. See *Nowe Wstrząsy: Grudzień, 1970* (New upheaval: December 1970) (Warsaw: Zeszyty Edukacji Narodowej, 1985).

38. See Chapter 8.

39. *RFE/RL Research Department: Background Report/240*, Aug. 25, 1981, p. 5.

40. *RFE/RL Research Department: Background Report/219*, Aug. 3, 1981, p. 7.

41. *Trybuna Ludu*, Aug. 12–13, 1981.

42. For the complete list of new voivodship first secretaries, see *Życie Partii*, Sept. 2, 1981.

43. Solidarity anticipated that a "state of emergency" was being readied. Two months before the crackdown, the Wrocław chapter of Solidarity issued a leaflet outlining with remarkable accuracy future government action and instructing its members on how to prepare for a general strike. See "Polish Collection: Trade Union Movement— Miscellaneous," Hoover Institution Archives.

44. In addition to Kania and Jaruzelski, the meeting on September 13 was attended by Gen. Cz. Kiszczak and Gen. B. Stachura, both of the Ministry of Internal Affairs; the Ministry of Defense was represented by Gen. F. Siwicki, Gen. T. Hupałowski, Gen. J. Skalski, Gen. A. Jasiński, and Gen. M. Dachowski. See Kukliński, p. 43.

45. Kukliński, p. 46.

46. For the full chronology of the official Polish-Soviet visits see *Wojskowy Przegląd Historyczny* (The military historical review) 98 (1981). Compared with the reports of previous meetings between high-level Soviet and Polish military officers, for example in 1978, the contacts in 1980–1981 were more frequent, with a significant increase in the number of such consultations immediately prior to and after clashes between Solidarity and the Polish government. Furthermore, unlike the contacts in 1980–1981, the 1978 meetings were distributed more evenly throughout the year and, as a rule, took place in connection with specific military matters, such as commemoration ceremonies of particular anniversaries or preparations for joint exercises.

47. Rurarz, p. 3.

48. This is confirmed by both Kukliński's testimony and Poland's ex-ambassador Z. Rurarz. See Rurarz, p. 19.

49. See "Uchwała I Krajowego Zjazdu Delegatów NSZZ 'Solidarność'" (A resolution by the First National Congress of Solidarity representatives), *Tygodnik Solidarność*, Sept. 11, 1981, p. 3.

50. *Serwis Informacyjny: I Krajowy Zjazd Delegatów NSZZ "Solidarność"* (News release: First National Congress of Solidarity representatives) (Gdańsk: Biuro Informacji Prasowej KKP NSZZ "Solidarność," 1981), p. 44.

51. *Życie Partii*, Sept. 23, 1981, p. 3.

52. "Przeciw Polskiej racji stanu," *Żołnierz Wolności*, Sept. 11–13, 1981.

53. *Życie Partii*, Sept. 23, 1981, p. 2.

54. Gen. Wojciech Jaruzelski, "Pozostawajcie niestrudzeni w służbie socjalistycznej Polski" (Remain indefatigable in your service to socialist Poland), *Żołnierz Polski*, Sept. 6, 1981, p. 4.

55. Stanisław Dymek, "Opozycyjny spektakl" (A spectacle by the opposition), *Żołnierz Polski*, Sept. 20, 1981.

56. Brig. Gen. Władysław Pożoga, "Chronić będziemy socjalistyczną Polskę" (We will protect socialist Poland), *Wojsko Ludowe*, Oct. 1981, p. 12.

57. Pożoga's loyalty to Jaruzelski was rewarded; after martial law was declared, Pożoga retained his job as deputy minister of the interior even after the purge of Milewski's supporters. See the CIA's *Directory of Polish Officials* (Washington, D.C.: Directorate of Intelligence, 1987).

58. Kukliński, p. 47.

59. Jerzy Holzer, *Solidarność 1980–1981: Geneza i Historia* (Solidarity 1980–1981: Origins and history) (Paris: Instytut Literacki, 1984), p. 278. Hereafter referred to as "Holzer."

60. The view that the October confrontation was a provocation engineered by Jaruzelski's government is supported by Kukliński's testimony. According to Kukliński, one of the new variants of the plan for imposing martial law, devised after the meeting of the KOK on September 13, called for the army and security forces to move in the face of a growing wave of strikes. See Kukliński, p. 46; Holzer, p. 278.

61. Brig. Gen. Władysław Honkisz, "Zrodzone z idei partii" (Born of the party's ideals), *Życie Partii*, Sept. 14, 1981, p. 3.

62. Kukliński recalls that on October 31, during a briefing by Gen. Molczyk, he learned that the "decision had already been made." See Kukliński, p. 47.

63. See Chapter 8. It is unclear to what extent Jaruzelski's decision to act quickly was influenced by the discovery, made by Poland's military counterintelligence, that the martial-law plans had been leaked to the Americans. Col. Kukliński, who throughout the crisis supplied the CIA with information on the planning of the imposition of martial law, learned of the ongoing investigation on November 2. See Kukliński, pp. 48–49.

64. From Gen. Wojciech Jaruzelski's speech to the Fourth Plenum of the PUWP, published in *Żołnierz Wolności*, Oct. 19, 1981.

65. Rurarz ranked Jaruzelski, Kiszczak, and Siwicki as the leading members of the new ruling elite. Hence the importance of Kiszczak's speech. See Rurarz, pp. 18–19. For more on Siwicki, Kiszczak, and other principal lieutenants of Jaruzelski, see Chapter 3.

66. From Gen. Cz. Kiszczak's speech, published in *Żołnierz Wolności*, Oct. 19, 1981.

67. See Weydenthal.

68. This information was reported in mid-October in a bulletin of the Solidarity news agency. Quoted in Garton Ash, p. 234. It is unclear why Solidarity disregarded the report.

69. Kukliński, p. 47.

70. "Pierwsze terenowe grupy operacyjne przystąpiły do działania" (First small detachments are in action), *Żołnierz Wolności*, Oct. 27, 1981.

71. There is a striking similarity between Jaruzelski's "small-detachment program" and the "defense-propaganda" campaign of 1947. For a comparison, see Chapter 3.

72. "Nadużywanie strajków—społecznym samobójstwem," *Żołnierz Wolności*, Oct. 28, 1981.

73. See "V Plenum KC" (Fifth Plenum of the Central Committee). *Żołnierz Wolności*, Oct. 29, 1981.

74. "Wezwanie pod adresem Solidarności" (An appeal to Solidarity), *Wojsko Ludowe*, Nov. 1981.

75. Stanisław Dymek, "Racja Stanu—Racje Polaków" (*Raison d'état*—Polish arguments), *Żołnierz Polski*, Nov. 1, 1981.

76. Jan Ignaczak, "Kilka refleksji o przeszłości i dniu współczesnym" (A few reflections on the past and the present), *Żołnierz Polski*, Nov. 8, 1981.

77. Jan Budziński, "Fundament, którego podważać nie wolno" (The foundation that must remain unchanged), *Żołnierz Polski*, Nov. 22, 1981.

78. For example, this argument was used by Deputy Prime Minister M. Rakowski during his 1984 meeting with Gdańsk shipyard workers.

Chapter 7

1. Gen. W. Jaruzelski, "Musimy dowieść, że Polski jesteśmy warci" (We must prove that we are worthy of Poland), *Trybuna Ludu*, Dec. 14, 1981.

2. The full membership of WRON consisted of the following: Gen. Wojciech Jaruzelski, chairman; members: Gen. Florian Siwicki, Gen. Eugeniusz Molczyk, Adm. Ludwik Janczyszyn, Gen. Czesław Kiszczak, Gen. Tadeusz Hupałowski, Gen. Czesław Piotrowski, Gen. Józef Baryła, Gen. Włodzimierz Oliwa, Gen. Henryk Rapacewicz, Gen. Józef Użycki, Gen. Tadeusz Krępski, Gen. Longin Łozowicki, Gen. Michał Janiszewski, Gen. Jerzy Jarosz, Col. Tadeusz Makarewicz, Col. Kazimierz Garbacik, Col. (reserves) Roman Leś, Col. Jerzy Włosiński, and Lt. Col. Mirosław Hermaszewski. The ruling directorate did not include Gen. Tadeusz Tuczapski, in charge of OTK (national territorial defense); the author could not ascertain why Tuczapski had been left out.

3. These claims were subsequently abandoned. In an interview with *The Washington Post* on June 4, 1986, the Polish government spokesman admitted that plans for the crackdown had been in preparation for months.

4. *RFE/RL Research Department: Background Report/3*, Jan. 8, 1982, p. 2.

5. "Duty to the motherland" was the major theme of Jaruzelski's speeches during the first critical months of martial law. See Wojciech Jaruzelski, *Przemówienia 1981–1982* (Speeches 1981–1982) (Warsaw: Książka i Wiedza, 1983), pp. 6, 42, 87–89. Hereafter referred to as "*Przemówienia*." For a detailed description of Solidarity's defiance of the general's orders, including strikes and street demonstrations, see Garton Ash, pp. 262–73; Weydenthal, pp. 237–63; and Sanford, pp. 116–82.

6. On the Soviet position, see Chapter 8.

7. The Law Against Parasitism was brought before the Sejm by Jaruzelski already in June of 1982. See "The Institutionalization of Martial Law," *Survey* 4(26):61.

8. See Chapter 5.

9. *Przemówienia*, pp. 287, 294–95, 297.

10. "Kraj-Kronika 1982" (Home affairs chronicle), *Wojsko Ludowe*, Dec. 1982:13.

11. *Życie Partii* provides a good insight into the modus operandi of the small army units. It describes the kinds of information collected by the officers dispatched into the field, while it inadvertently reveals how the army investigated local bureaucracies. See Włodzimierz Wodecki, "Wreszcie skutecznie" (Finally effective action), *Życie Partii*, Nov. 25, 1981, p. 17.

12. These and the following figures on the PUWP membership are as given by Ryszard Łukasiewicz in "Partia odradza się w działaniu" (The party is being reborn through action), *Życie Partii*, March 3, 1982, p. 3.

13. Brig. Gen. Tadeusz Dziekan, "Polityka kadrowa partii" (The party's personnel policy), *Życie Partii*, Dec. 8, 1982.

14. The figures are those given by Brig. Gen. Tadeusz Dziekan, chief of the PUWP

Central Committee's Department of Cadres, in his "Polityka kadrowa partii," *Życie Partii*, Dec. 8, 1982, p. 4.

15. *Wojsko Ludowe*, Jan. 1982.

16. *Przemówienia*, p. 257.

17. Col. Józef Borgosz, "Przeciw totalnej negacji" (Against total negation), *Wojsko Ludowe*, Jan. 1982:42.

18. *Przemówienia*, p. 327.

19. *Przemówienia*, p. 221.

20. *Życie Partii*, March 3, 1982.

21. Ibid.

22. *Życie Partii*, March 17, 1982, p. 5.

23. "O co walczymy, dokąd zmierzamy," *Nowe Drogi*, March 1982:48.

24. From Gen. Jaruzelski's speech before the Seventh Plenum of the PUWP's Central Committee as quoted in *Nowe Drogi*, March 1982:54.

25. The competition was announced in the March 17, 1982 edition of *Życie Partii*.

26. Teresa Rakowska-Harmstone has suggested that even after the events of 1981, the Poles have been unwilling to give up completely their traditional image of the country's military as defenders of the nation. On the basis of poll data, Rakowska-Harmstone concludes that at least junior officers (below the rank of colonel) have retained some remnants of social prestige. See Rakowska-Harmstone, p. 181.

Still, the mushrooming of draft resistance in Poland in the second half of the 1980s strongly suggests that, even if Polish society has not utterly condemned the institution of the military, the army has nevertheless experienced a lasting decline of its influence on the people.

27. Ryszard Łukasiewicz, "Partia odradza się w działaniu" (The party is being reborn through action), *Życie Partii*, March 3, 1982, p. 3.

28. Ibid.

29. The proceedings were published in a special issue of *Nowe Drogi*, July–August 1982. Another example of the ideological exegesis performed at the time is Stefan Olszowski's position paper "Konsolidacja partii—warunkiem odrodzenia" (The consolidation of the party as the condition of renewal), *Nowe Drogi*, Jan.–Feb. 1982:5.

30. See *RFE/RL Polish Situation Report/2*, Jan. 29, 1982; *RFE/RL Polish Situation Report/13*, July 27, 1982; *RFE/RL Polish Situation Report/19*, Nov. 9, 1982.

31. Anecdotes often reflect the mood of a society better than public opinion polls. Two of them, circulating immediately after the introduction of martial law, will serve to illustrate the change in the Poles' view of their military. Referring to Jaruzelski's brutal police methods, the Poles called him mockingly the "Polish ZOMOsa." In an even more telling expression of the social mood, Warsaw was covered with graffiti declaring that "The Eagle will not be defeated by the Crow" (Orła WRONa nie pokona), a slogan that pitted Poland's national symbol, the eagle, against the "crow," formed from the acronym of Jaruzelski's Military Council of National Salvation (WRON).

32. Wojciech Jaruzelski, "Przemówienie na posiedzeniu Komisji Inicjujacej utworzenie

Tymczasowej Rady Krajowej Patriotycznego Ruchu Odrodzenia Narodowego" (Speech during the meeting of the founding commission of the Provisional National Council of the Patriotic Movement of National Rebirth) (given on Sept. 15, 1982), in *Przemówienia*, p. 445.

33. See *Przemówienia*, pp. 390 and 488–90.

34. On the structure of the "military communist party" in Poland, especially the Main Political Administration of the Polish army, see Malcher, pp. 34–35.

35. "Postanowienia związane z wprowadzeniem stanu wojennego" (Decrees concerning the introduction of martial law), *Wojsko Ludowe*, Jan. 1982:13.

36. Ibid., p. 14.

37. *Przemówienia*, p. 490.

38. See Roman Stefanowski, comp., *Radio Free Europe Background Report/Chronology 5 (Poland)—Poland Under Martial Law: A Chronology of Events 13 December, 1981–30 December, 1982* (1983), p. 8.

39. *Raport: Polska 5 lat po Sierpniu* (A report: Poland five years after August 1980) (London: Aneks, 1986), p. 57. Hereafter referred to as "*Raport*."

40. These official figures, taken from the *Biuletyn Statystyczny* of Główny Urząd Statystyczny (Chief accounting office), are quoted in Weydenthal, p. 293.

41. *Raport*, p. 93.

Chapter 8

1. Zbigniew A. Pelczynski, "The Downfall of Gomułka," in Adam Bromke and John W. Strong, eds., *Gierek's Poland* (New York: Praeger Publishers, 1973), p. 21.

2. Sidney Ploss suggests that work stoppages in or around Gorky occurred approximately around the same time. See Sidney I. Ploss, *Moscow and the Polish Crisis: An Interpretation of Soviet Policies and Intentions* (Boulder, Colo.: Westview Press, 1986), p. 12. Hereafter referred to as "Ploss."

3. *Pravda*, Aug. 20, 1980.

4. Throughout the Polish crisis, *Izvestiya* maintained low-key coverage of Poland, limiting itself to reprinting TASS press releases. *Krasnaya Zvezda* ran its first item on Poland on Sept. 6, 1980.

5. Kukliński, p. 16.

6. The Soviet leadership frequently uses articles published under pseudonyms to express the Politburo's views on a particular subject. "Petrov" is one such pseudonym.

7. A. Petrov, "Proiski vragov sotsialisticheskoy Polshi," *Pravda*, Sept. 1, 1980.

8. *Dokumenty KC*, p. 252.

9. *Pravda*, Sept. 5, 1980.

10. Kukliński, p. 17.

11. *Pravda*, Sept. 7, 1980. The same issue brought a congratulatory telegram from A.

Kosygin to Poland's newly appointed prime minister, Józef Pińkowski. Pińkowski's name was the only one mentioned in TASS's report of the Sejm debate, released the day before the appearance of the *Pravda* article. See "V seyme PNR," *Krasnaya Zvezda*, Sept. 6, 1980.

12. Kukliński, p. 18.

13. *Pravda*, Sept. 13, 1980.

14. Kukliński, p. 18.

15. "Druzheskiy rabochiy visit," *Pravda*, Oct. 31, 1980. Identical releases were printed on the same day in *Izvestiya* and *Krasnaya Zvezda*.

16. "Ukreplyaya druzhbu i sotrudnichestvo," *Pravda*, Nov. 2, 1980.

17. Kukliński, p. 21.

18. As reported by Kukliński, from the start the Soviets regarded the Polish August as nothing but "counterrevolution." See Kukliński, p. 16.

19. Kukliński, p. 21.

20. Kukliński, p. 22.

21. *Rzeczpospolita* became an authoritative official newspaper under Jaruzelski's regime in the early 1980s.

22. TASS, Oct. 10, 1981.

23. "Reshayushchiy faktor," *Pravda*, Nov. 11, 1980.

24. Oliwa was subsequently promoted by Jaruzelski to quartermaster of the Polish army. See *Rzeczpospolita*, April 26, 1988.

25. Kukliński gives this date as the target for full operational readiness of the task force. See Kukliński, p. 22.

26. "K sobytiyam v Polshe," TASS, *Pravda*, Nov. 25, 1980.

27. Richard D. Anderson's "Soviet Decision-Making in Poland" (*Problems of Communism*, March–April 1982) supports the thesis that the Soviets did in fact prepare for an invasion, pointing to the troop movements and shifts in the command structure of the Soviet forces in the territories bordering on Poland.

28. Garton Ash, p. 94.

29. Kukliński, p. 22.

30. In his memoirs, Spasowski recalls an emergency meeting held in Warsaw on September 13, 1981, during which Emil Wojtaszek, the Central Committee secretary for foreign affairs, briefed the diplomatic staff on the situation in the country. During the meeting, Wojtaszek is said to have declared: "Our friends are most afraid of a general strike, just as we are. They think we should be evasive, yield, sign agreements, so long as there's no nationwide strike." See Romuald Spasowski, *The Liberation of One* (San Diego, Calif.: Harcourt, Brace, Jovanovich, 1986), p. 628.

31. "Priziv TsK PORP k narodu," TASS, *Pravda*, Dec. 5, 1980.

32. During his visit to Warsaw in December 1980, Spasowski asked Foreign Minister J. Czyrek whom he should consult before returning to Washington; he was reportedly told: "Only one person counts, Wojciech Jaruzelski." See Spasowski, p. 634.

33. "Priziv TsK PORP," *Krasnaya Zvezda*, Dec. 5, 1980.

34. Quoted in Garton Ash, p. 94.

35. This was suggested by Col. Kukliński. See Kukliński, p. 25.

36. *Pravda*, Jan. 14, 1981.

37. Reported in *Pravda* on Jan. 21, 1981.

38. "V prokurature PNR," *Pravda*, Feb. 10, 1981.

39. This theme would be subsequently used by Baryła's propagandists in their anti-Solidarity campaign. See Chapter 6.

40. "Plenum TsK PORP," *Pravda*, Feb. 11, 1981.

41. "Plenum TsK PORP," *Pravda*, Feb. 12, 1981.

42. *Pravda*, Feb. 24, 1981.

43. *Pravda*, Feb. 25, 1981.

44. "Vystupleniye tovarishcha Stanislava Kanii," *Pravda*, Feb. 25, 1981.

45. Ibid.

46. Kukliński, p. 29.

47. "Sovetsko-polskaya vstrecha," *Pravda*, March 5, 1981.

48. Kukliński, p. 31.

49. In his testimony, Kukliński emphasized that throughout the negotiations the Russians "heard what they wanted to hear." See Kukliński, pp. 33–35.

50. For example, on March 13, *Pravda* ran an article charging that Solidarity was financed by the CIA and the AFL-CIO.

51. "Vstrecha v Varshave," *Pravda*, March 19, 1981.

52. Kukliński, p. 31.

53. "Boyevoye Bratstvo: V Edinom Stroyu," *Krasnaya Zvezda*, March 22, 1981.

54. "Mosty druzhby i bratstva: Soyuz-81," *Krasnaya Zvezda*, March 25, 1981.

55. "K polozheniyu v Polshe," *Pravda*, March 27, 1981.

56. Kukliński, p. 33.

57. "K polozheniyu v Polshe," *Pravda*, March 28, 1981.

58. Weydenthal, pp. 69–72.

59. Ploss argues, based on Alexander Haig's recollections of the event, that the Soviets did not intend to invade directly, but rather to display force in case a confrontation in Poland would require a use of Poland's internal security forces or the army (Ploss, p. 77). Kukliński's account suggests that the threat of invasion was much greater, and that events could have easily escalated beyond anybody's control (Kukliński, pp. 35–37).

60. "Provokatsionniye zayavleniye," *Pravda*, March 31, 1981.

61. "Antisotsyalisticheskoye sborishche," *Pravda*, April 2, 1981.

62. Kukliński, p. 35.

63. Kukliński, p. 36.

64. Kukliński, p. 37.

65. "IX cherezvichayniy s'yezd PORP," *Pravda*, July 15, 1981.

66. Ibid.

67. "Na forumie pol'skikh kommunistov," *Pravda*, July 20 and 21, 1981.

68. Weschler, p. 222.

69. Garton Ash, p. 213.

70. *Pravda*, Oct. 13, 1981.

71. Another interesting development at the time, which supports the view that the implementation of Jaruzelski's plan commenced immediately upon his taking office, is Marshal V. Kulikov's sudden visit to East Berlin on Oct. 20, 1981. As reported by *Krasnaya Zvezda*, Kulikov met with East Germany's leader, E. Honecker; his defense minister, Gen. H. Hoffman; commander of the Soviet Group of Forces in the GDR, Gen. M. Zaytsev; and a number of senior Soviet and East German officers. It is probable that Kulikov went to East Berlin to discuss with the East Germans Jaruzelski's plans for imposing martial law and to devise a contingency plan for using the Soviet forces in East Germany in case the Poles required "fraternal assistance." See "Vstrecha v Berline," *Krasnaya Zvezda*, Oct. 21, 1981.

72. "K polozheniyu v Polshe," *Pravda*, Oct. 26, 1981.

73. *Pravda*, Oct. 30, 1981.

74. Ploss, p. 135.

75. Printed in *Pravda* on Nov. 8, 1981.

76. See Chapter 7.

77. According to *Pravda* (Nov. 26, 1981), Kulikov arrived on Nov. 25. Weschler and Weydenthal contend, on the basis of their Polish sources, that Kulikov had arrived in Warsaw at least a day earlier. In his testimony Kukliński stated that Kulikov had virtually resided in Poland since spring of 1981.

78. Ploss, p. 141.

79. Quoted in Weschler, p. 224.

80. "K plozheniyu v Polshe," *Pravda*, Dec. 12, 1981.

81. *Pravda*, Dec. 15, 1981.

82. "Dirizhery za kulisami," *Krasnaya Zvezda*, Dec. 18, 1981.

83. "O vmeshatelstve spetssluzhb SShA v dela PNR," *Pravda*, Dec. 25, 1981.

84. Weschler, p. 226.

85. For example, see "K vizitu partiyno-gosudarstvennoy delegatsii PNR vo glave s Pervym sekretarem tsentralnogo komiteta Polskoy obyedinyonnoy rabochey partii, Predsedatelem Soveta Ministrov PNR Voytsekhom Yaruzelskim," *Izvestiya*, March 1, 1981.

86. "S ofitsyalnym vizitom/Sovetsko-Polskiye peregovory," *Pravda*, March 2, 1982.

87. *Pravda*, March 2, 1982.

88. Ibid.

89. Ibid.

90. Ibid.

91. TASS, March 3, 1982.

92. "Druzheskaya vstrecha," TASS, Aug. 17, 1982.

93. Ibid.

94. Ibid.

Chapter 9

1. *RFE/RL Polish Situation Report/19*, Dec. 16, 1988. p. 9.

2. *Trybuna Ludu*, Oct. 9, 1982.

3. "The Institutionalization of Martial Law," *Survey* 4(26):61.

4. *Trybuna Ludu*, Oct. 27, 1982.

5. For an overview of the Sejm activities during the first year of martial law, see "Kraj-Kronika 1982" (Home-affairs chronicle), *Wojsko Ludowe*, Dec. 1982:12–31. For more on the Special Emergency Powers Act see also "The Institutionalization of Martial Law," *Survey*, 4(26):60–61.

6. *RFE/RL Research Department: Background Report/72*, March 5, 1983, p. 3.

7. Discussion of the new legislation is based on announcements by Polish Radio reported in *RFE/RL Polish Situation Report/11*, July 18, 1983, pp. 4–8.

8. Before 1983, the constitution had been last amended by Gierek in 1977.

9. *RFE/RL Polish Situation Report/12*, Aug. 4, 1983, p. 7.

10. *Trybuna Ludu*, Feb. 13, 1983.

11. *Trybuna Ludu*, Feb. 11, 1983.

12. *RFE/RL Polish Situation Report/3*, Feb. 23, 1983, p. 8.

13. *Trybuna Ludu*, Dec. 19, 1982.

14. Ibid.

15. *RFE/RL Polish Situation Report/3*, Feb. 21, 1983, p. 10.

16. *Życie Partii*, Dec. 22, 1982.

17. *Trybuna Ludu*, Feb. 16, 1983.

18. *Pravda*, June 15, 1983.

19. *Trybuna Ludu*, Jan. 10–11, 1983.

20. During the crisis, Oliwa spoke on Jaruzelski's behalf against a Soviet invasion of Poland; during the critical days of December 1980, he argued before the Sejm for an internal Polish solution of the problem. See Chapter 7.

21. *Trybuna Ludu*, March 23–24, 1983.

22. *Rzeczpospolita*, March 25, 1983.

23. *RFE/RL Polish Situation Report/9*, June 11, 1983, p. 5.

24. Marek Henzler, "Drabina" (The ladder), *Polityka*, May 14, 1988.

25. *RFE/RL Polish Situation Report/10*, June 30, 1988, p. 7.

26. *Trybuna Ludu*, March 7, 1983.

27. Col. Janusz Przymanowski, a popular Polish author of fiction set during World War

II, formally suggested to the Sejm that the crown be restored to the Polish eagle as a sign of Poland's sovereignty. See *Trybuna Ludu*, Jan. 27, 1982.

28. *RFE/RL Research Department: Background Report/232*, Sept. 29, 1983, pp. 2–3.

29. See "Wojsko Socjalistyczne i Wychowanie" (Socialist army and upbringing), *Żołnierz Wolności*, Nov. 24, 1983.

30. *Żołnierz Wolności*, Jan. 17, 1986.

31. *Żołnierz Polski*, Jan 17, 1988, p. 20.

32. "Patriotyczna Manifestacja na Polach Grunwaldu" (Patriotic demonstration on the Grunwald fields), *Żołnierz Wolności*, July 16, 1986.

33. *Żołnierz Wolności*, Nov. 11, 1988.

34. Announcement by Polish Radio, as reported by *RFE/RL Polish Situation Report/17*, Nov. 27, 1983, pp. 4–5.

35. It would be interesting to speculate about the extent to which Soviet leader Gorbachev's insistence on similar changes within his own government, outlined during the national conference of the CPSU in June 1988, draws upon Jaruzelski's effort in 1983 to centralize in his hands both party and executive authority. Since Jaruzelski is on the best of terms with the Soviet leader, Gorbachev is certainly thoroughly familiar with the organizational restructuring of the Polish government.

36. *RFE/RL Research Department: Background Report/295*, Dec. 31, 1983, p. 6.

37. *Trybuna Ludu*, Dec. 8, 1983.

38. Kukliński, p. 48.

39. *Trybuna Ludu*, July 26, 1982.

40. "Pożegnanie wiceministra ON, Głównego Inspektora Szkolenia, gen. broni Eugeniusza Molczyka" (Farewell to the deputy defense minister, chief inspector of training, Gen. Eugeniusz Molczyk), *Żołnierz Wolności*, Feb. 27, 1986.

41. See Chapter 6.

42. *Trybuna Ludu*, March 19, 1984.

43. "Rezolucja w sprawie realizacji uchwał IX Zjazdu PZPR" (Resolution on the implementation of the decisions of the Ninth PUWP Congress), *Żołnierz Wolności*, March 19, 1984. Also see *Trybuna Ludu*, March 19, 1984.

44. *RFE/RL Research Department: Background Report/57*, April 10, 1984.

45. *Trybuna Ludu*, May 6, 1984.

46. Voter-turnout data published in *Trybuna Ludu*, June 18, 1984.

47. *RFE/RL Polish Situation Report/14*, Aug. 3, 1984, p. 2.

48. *Trybuna Ludu*, July 22, 1984.

49. Kiszczak's address is quoted in *RFE/RL Polish Situation Report/18*, Oct. 19, 1984.

50. *RFE/RL Polish Situation Report/19*, Nov. 15, 1984. p. 5.

51. Ibid.

52. Ibid., p. 4.

53. *RFE/RL Polish Situation Report/1*, Jan 1, 1985, p. 6.

54. A story on Olszowski's living in New York City appeared in *The New York Times*, May 20, 1988, and Flora Lewis's account of his 1985 confrontation with Jaruzelski can be found in *The New York Times*, May 25, 1988.

55. *Poland's Leaders* (Washington, D.C.: CIA Reference Aid, 1987), p. 8.

56. *Trybuna Ludu*, July 22, 1983.

57. *Trybuna Ludu*, Nov. 7, 1985.

58. *Trybuna Ludu*, June 28–29, 1986.

59. *Trybuna Ludu*, July 1, 1986.

60. "Referat Komitetu Centralnego PZPR na X Zjazd PZPR" (Report of the PUWP Central Committee to the Tenth PUWP Congress), *Trybuna Ludu*, June 30, 1986.

61. *Żołnierz Wolności*, July 4, 1986.

62. *Trybuna Ludu*, July 4, 1986.

63. *Trybuna Ludu*, June 17, 1985.

64. *Trybuna Ludu*, July 4, 1986.

65. *Żołnierz Wolności*, Sept. 18, 1986.

66. *Żołnierz Wolności*, Nov. 1986.

67. This information comes from an RFE/RL broadcast "Underground Press No. 201: Sytuacja w polskim wojsku w latach powojennych" (Conditions in the Polish army since World War II), *Radio Free Europe/Polish Broadcasting Department*, air date: Nov. 9, 1988, p. 1. Hereafter referred to as "Underground Press No. 201."

68. "Underground Press No. 201," p. 1.

69. Replica edition of *Honor i Ojczyzna* published in RFE Research and Analysis Department's *Polish Independent Press Summary*, no. 42 (Nov. 4, 1988). Hereafter referred to as "*Independent Press Summary*, no. 42."

70. Wincenty Heinrich, "Opozycja w wojsku, 1944–1988" (Opposition in the army, 1944–1988), *Honor i Ojczyzna*, no. 1(1988), in *Independent Press Summary*, no. 42, p. 16.

71. Stanisław Dronicz, "Dlaczego w siłach zbrojnych PRL istnieje opozycja?" (Why is there an opposition in the armed forces of the Polish People's Republic?), ibid., pp. 17–18.

72. "Głos I" (Voice I), *Honor i Ojczyzna*, ibid., p. 21.

73. *Wojsko Ludowe*, Jan. 1987:3.

74. *Wojsko Ludowe*, Jan. 1987:4.

75. *Życie Warszawy*, Jan. 17–18, 1987.

76. *Trybuna Ludu*, Sept. 1, 1986.

77. *Żołnierz Wolności*, Dec. 12, 1986.

78. *Żołnierz Wolności*, Dec. 6, 1986.

79. Col. Bazyli Lewczuk, "Wychowanie nie tylko obronne" (Upbringing not only military), *Żołnierz Wolności*, Nov. 11, 1986.

80. *Żołnierz Wolności*, Nov. 14, 1986.

81. *Wojsko Ludowe*, Jan. 1987:4.

82. Col. Bazyli Lewczuk, "Kształtowanie patriotyzmy i obronne szkolenie studentów"

(Shaping the patriotism and military education of university students), *Wojsko Ludowe*, Feb. 1987:47.

83. *Wojsko Ludowe*, March 1987:3.

84. *Żołnierz Wolności*, June 26, 1987.

85. Lt. Col. Ireneusz Czyżewski, "Politykierstwo w osłonie frazesów: Grupa Wolność i Pokój" (Political machinations hiding behind slogans: The group Freedom and Peace), *Wojsko Ludowe*, Nov. 1987:46–49.

86. *Wojsko Ludowe*, Dec. 1987:42.

87. Jadwiga Prymek, "LWP jako obiekt zachodniej propagandy" (The Polish People's Army as a target of Western propaganda), *Wojsko Ludowe*, April 1988:62.

88. *Żołnierz Polski*, Jan. 24, 1988, p. 5.

89. See "Akademie i szkoły oficerskie czekają" (Academies and officer schools await), *Żołnierz Polski*, Jan. 24, 1988; and "MON ogłasza ochotniczą rekrutacje kandydatów do niżej wymienionych szkół" (Ministry of Defense announces recruitment for the following schools), *Żołnierz Polski*, Feb. 14, 1988.

90. See "Wojsko nie jest przerwą w życiorysie" (The army is not a blank page in your life), *Żołnierz Wolności*, April 19, 1988; "Pożyteczne lata" (Useful years), *Żołnierz Wolności*, April 20, 1988; and "Mamy się czym pochwalić" (We have a lot to be proud of), *Żołnierz Wolności*, April 21, 1988.

91. *RFE/RL Polish Situation Report/10*, July 1, 1988, p. 11.

92. *Żołnierz Wolności*, June 21, 1988.

93. *RFE/RL Polish Situation Report/11*, July 21, 1988, p. 27.

94. *RFE/RL Polish Situation Report/2*, Feb. 1, 1988, p. 3.

95. *Trybuna Ludu*, May 25, 1987.

96. *RFE/RL Polish Situation Report/8*, May 13, 1988, p. 3.

97. *RFE/RL Polish Situation Report/7*, May 6, 1988, pp. 17 and 27.

98. Reported in *RFE/RL Polish Situation Report/7*, May 6, 1988, p. 21.

99. *RFE/RL Polish Situation Report/8*, May 13, 1988, p. 25.

100. *RFE/RL Polish Situation Report/11*, July 21, 1988, p. 11.

101. *RFE/RL Polish Situation Report/13*, Aug. 26, 1988, p. 8.

102. *Żołnierz Wolności*, Aug. 29, 1988.

103. *Żołnierz Wolności*, Aug. 27–28, 1988.

104. *Trybuna Ludu*, Sept. 1, 1988.

105. *Trybuna Ludu*, Sept. 16, 1988.

106. *Trybuna Ludu*, Sept. 20, 1988.

107. *Trybuna Ludu*, Sept. 20, 1988.

108. *Trybuna Ludu*, Dec. 16, 1987, and *RFE/RL Polish Situation Report/16*, Oct. 7, 1988, p. 14. Rakowski's "secret report" was published reportedly in Poland by Myśl Publishing House, an independent underground publisher.

109. *Trybuna Ludu*, Sept. 28, 1988.

110. *Trybuna Ludu*, Oct. 7, 1988.

111. This and the preceding quotation taken from *RFE/RL Research Department: Background Report/213*, Oct. 25, 1988, p. 3.

112. Editorial, *Trybuna Ludu*, Oct. 15–16, 1988.

113. *Trybuna Ludu*, Nov. 29, 1988.

114. *RFE/RL Polish Situation Report/9*, Dec. 16, 1988, p. 9.

Chapter 10

1. Jerzy J. Wiatr, *Socjologia Wojska* (Sociology of the army) (Warsaw: Wydawnictwo Ministerstwa Obrony Narodowej, 1982), p. 354.

2. William E. Odom, "The Party-Military Connection: A Critique," in Dale R. Herspring and Ivan Volgyes, eds., *Civil-Military Relations in Communist Systems* (Boulder, Colo.: Westview Press, 1978), p. 41.

3. See *Kiążeczka cywilna* (The civilian's book) (Warsaw: Ruch Wolność i Pokój, 1988) and *Seminarium pokojowe w Warszawie, 7-9-V-87: Dokumenty* (Peace seminar in Warsaw: May 7–9, 1987: Proceedings) (Warsaw: Dezerter, 1987) in the collection of Polish underground publications held by the Hoover Institution Library.

Bibliography

Books and Articles

Abramski, J., and Żywiecki, R. *Katyń*. Warsaw: Społeczny Instytut Pamięci Narodowej im. J. Piłsudskiego, 1977.

"Akademie i szkoły oficerskie czekają" (Academies and officer schools await). *Żołnierz Polski*, Jan. 24, 1988.

Anders, Władysław. *Bez ostatniego rozdziału: Wspomnienia z lat 1939–1946* (Without the final chapter: Recollections from 1939–1946). London: Gryf Publications, 1981.

Anderson, Richard D. "Soviet Decision-Making in Poland." *Problems of Communism*, March–April 1982.

Andrzejewski, Jakub, ed. *Gomułka i Inni: Dokumenty z Archivum KC, 1948–1982* (Gomułka and others: Documents from the archives of the Central Committee, 1948–1982). London: Aneks, 1987.

"Antisotsyalisticheskoye sborishche." *Pravda*, April 2, 1981.

Bąkowa, Joanna. *Szlachta województwa krakowskiego wobec opozycji Jerzego Lubomirskiego w latach 1661–1667* (The nobility of the Kraków voivodship and the opposition camp of Jerzy Lubomirski, 1661–1667). Warsaw: Państwowe Wydawnictwo Naukowe, 1974.

Baryła, Gen. Józef. "Socjalizmu będziemy bronić tak jak niepodległości" (We will defend socialism like our independence). *Wojsko Ludowe*, Aug. 1981.

———. "Sprawie partii i narodu żołnierze oddani sa całym sercem" (Soldiers are totally devoted to the cause of the party and the nation). *Wojsko Ludowe*, Jan. 1981.

Bielasiak, Jack. "Recruitment Policy, Elite Integration, and Political Stability in People's

Poland." In Maurice D. Simon and Roger E. Kanet, eds., *Background to Crisis: Policy and Politics in Gierek's Poland*. Boulder, Colo.: Westview Press, 1981.

Błażyński, Zbigniew. *Mówi Józef Światło: Za Kulisami Bezpieki i Partii, 1940–1955* (Józef Światło reports: Behind the scenes of the secret police and the party, 1940–1955). London: Polska Fundacja Kulturalna, 1985.

Bogucka, Maria. *Dawna Polska: Narodziny, rozkwit, upadek* (Old Poland: Origins, acme, decline). Warsaw: Wiedza Powszechna, 1985.

Bór-Komorowski, Tadeusz. *Trzy Wykłady o AK* (Three lectures on the Home Army). Paris: Zeszyty Historyczne no. 49, 1979.

Borgosz, Józef. "Przeciw totalnej negacji" (Against total negation). *Wojsko Ludowe*, Jan. 1982.

"Boyevoye Bratstvo: V Edinom Stroyu." *Krasnaya Zvezda*, March 22, 1981.

Bromke, Adam. "Poland Under Gierek: A New Political Style." *Problems of Communism*, Sept.–Oct. 1972.

Brzezinski, Zbigniew. *Soviet Bloc: Unity and Conflict*. New York: Praeger Publishers, 1962.

Budziński, Jan. "Fundament, którego podważać nie wolno" (The foundation that must remain unchanged). *Żołnierz Polski*, Nov. 22, 1981.

Buszko, Józef. *Historia Polski: 1864–1948* (History of Poland: 1864–1948). Warsaw: Państwowe Wydawnictwo Naukowe, 1983.

Central Intelligence Agency. *Directory of Polish Officials*. Washington, D.C.: Directorate of Intelligence, 1987.

Checinski, Michael. *Poland: Communism, Nationalism, Anti-Semitism*. New York: Karz-Cohl, 1982.

———. *The Postwar Development of the Polish Armed Forces*. Rand Internal Note: Sept. 1979.

———. "Poland's Military Burden." *Problems of Communism*, May–June 1983.

Chocha, Bolesław. *Rozważania o sztuce wojennej* (On military art). Warsaw: Wydawnictwo Ministerstwa Obrony Narodowej, 1984.

Chocha, Bolesław, and Kaczmarek, Julian. *Wojna i doktryna wojenna* (War and military doctrine). Warsaw: Wydawnictwo Ministerstwa Obrony Narodowej, 1980.

Colton, Timothy. *Commissars, Commanders, and Civilian Authority*. Cambridge, Mass.: Harvard University Press, 1979.

Current Biography Yearbook: 1982. New York: The H. Wilson Co., 1982.

Cytowski, Jerzy. "Generał J. H. Dąbrowski w tradycjach wychowania wojskowego" (General J. H. Dąbrowski in the tradition of military upbringing). In *General Jan Henryk Dąbrowski 1755–1818: Conference Papers*. Poznan: Uniwersytet im. Adama Mickiewicza, 1970.

Czerwiński, Zdzisław. "Przewodnia Siła" (The vanguard). *Wojsko Ludowe*, Feb. 1981.

Czyżewski, Lt. Col. Ireneusz. "Politykierstwo w osłonie frazesów: Grupa Wolność i Pokój" (Political machinations hiding behind slogans: The group Freedom and Peace). *Wojsko Ludowe*, Nov. 1987.

Davies, Norman. *God's Playground: A History of Poland*. New York: Columbia University Press, 1984.

Davies, Norman. *White Eagle, Red Star: The Polish-Soviet War, 1919–1920*. London: Orbis, 1983.

"Dirizhery za kulisami." *Krasnaya Zvezda*, Dec. 18, 1981.

Dowda, Marian. *Armia i Naród* (The army and the nation). Warsaw: Książka i Wiedza, 1969.

"Druzheskaya vstrecha." TASS, Aug. 17, 1982.

"Druzheskiy rabochiy visit." *Pravda*, Oct. 31, 1980.

Dymek, Stanisław. "Opozycyjny spektakl" (A spectacle by the opposition). *Żołnierz Polski*, Sept. 20, 1981.

———. "Państwo nie jest sługą" (The state is not a servant). *Żołnierz Polski*, June 7, 1981.

———. "Pomówmy i o tym" (Let's talk about it). *Żołnierz Polski*, Feb. 8, 1981.

———. "Racja Stanu—Racje Polaków" (*Raison d'état*—Polish arguments). *Żołnierz Polski*, Nov. 1, 1981.

Dziekan, Brig. Gen. Tadeusz. "Polityka kadrowa partii" (The party's personnel policy). *Życie Partii*, Dec. 8, 1982.

Fallenbuchl, Zbigniew. "Policy Alternatives in Polish Foreign Economic Relations." In Maurice D. Simon and Roger E. Kanet, eds., *Background to Crisis: Policy and Politics in Gierek's Poland*. Boulder, Colo.: Westview Press, 1981.

Farrell, John P. "Growth, Reform, and Inflation: Problems and Policies." In Maurice D. Simon and Roger E. Kanet, eds., *Background to Crisis: Policy and Politics in Gierek's Poland*. Boulder, Colo.: Westview Press, 1981.

Fiedler, Arkady. *Squadron 303*. New York: Roy, 1943.

"V Plenum KC" (Fifth Plenum of the Central Committee). *Żołnierz Wolności*, Oct. 29, 1981.

Gardner, Monica. *Kościuszko: A Biography*. London: Allen & Unwin, 1942.

Garton Ash, Timothy. *The Polish Revolution: Solidarity*. New York: Charles Scribner's Sons, 1983.

Halecki, Oscar. "The Armed Forces and National Security." In Oscar Halecki, ed., *Poland*. New York: Praeger Publishers, 1957.

Henzler, Marek. "Drabina" (The ladder). *Polityka*, May 14, 1988.

Herspring, Dale R. *Civil-Military Relations in Poland and East Germany: The External Factor." Studies in Comparative Communism*, Autumn 1978.

———. "The Warsaw Pact at 25." *Problems of Communism*, Sept.–Oct. 1980.

Holzer, Jerzy. *Solidarność 1980–1981: Geneza i Historia* (Solidarity 1980–1981: Origins and history). Paris: Instytut Literacki, 1984.

Honkisz, Brig. Gen. Władysław. "Zrodzone z idei partii" (Born of the party's ideals). *Życie Partii*, Sept. 14, 1981.

Ignaczak, Col. Jan. "Pytania na które trzeba odpowiedzieć" (Questions that must be answered). *Żołnierz Polski*, March 29, 1981.

———. "Kilka refleksji o przeszłości i dniu współczesnym" (A few reflections on the past and the present). *Żołnierz Polski*, Nov. 8, 1981.

"The Institutionalization of Martial Law." *Survey* 4(26), Autumn 1982.

Jaruzelski, Wojciech. "Bezcenną zdobyczą socjalizmu w Polsce—polityka istnienia narodowego" (Policies ensuring national existence are the priceless achievement of socialism in Poland). *Wojsko Ludowe*, Oct. 1980.

——. "Musimy dowieść, że Polski jesteśmy warci" (We must prove that we are worthy of Poland). *Trybuna Ludu*, Dec. 13, 1981.

——. "Pozostawajcie niestrudzeni w służbie socjalistycznej Polski" (Remain indefatigable in your service to socialist Poland). *Żołnierz Polski*, Sept. 6, 1981.

——. *Przemówienia 1981–1982*. Warsaw: Książka i Wiedza, 1983.

——. *Rozkaz Ministra Obrony Narodowej nr. 1 z dnia 11 lutego, 1981* (Order from the defense minister, no. 1, dated Feb. 11, 1981). *Żołnierz Wolności*, Feb. 12, 1981; *Trybuna Ludu*, Feb. 12, 1981.

Jędrzejewicz, Wacław. *Józef Piłsudski, 1867–1935*. London: Polska Fundacja Kulturalna, 1982.

Jones, Christopher D. *Soviet Influence in Eastern Europe: Political Autonomy and the Warsaw Pact*. New York: Praeger Publishers, 1981.

"K polozheniyu v Polshe." *Pravda*, March 27, 1981.

"K sobytiyam v Polshe." TASS, *Pravda*, Nov. 25, 1980.

"K vizitu partiyno-gosudarstvennoy delegatsii PNR vo glave s Pervym sekretarem tsentralnogo komiteta Polskoy obydinyonnoy rabochey partii, Predsedatelem Soveta Ministrov PNR Voytsekhom Yaruzelskim." *Izvestiya*, March 1, 1981.

Kacała, Henryk. *Kształt Ludowego Wojska* (The shape of the People's Army). Warsaw: Ministerstwo Obrony Narodowej, 1972.

Kersten, Krystyna. *Narodziny systemu władzy: Polska 1943–1948* (The birth of the political system: Poland 1943–1948). Paris: Libella, 1986.

Khrushchev, Nikita. *Khrushchev Remembers*. Boston: Little, Brown, 1970.

Kiążeczka cywilna (The civilian's book). Warsaw: Ruch Wolność i Pokój, 1988.

Kolkowicz, Roman. *The Soviet Military and the Communist Party*. Princeton, N.J.: Princeton University Press, 1967.

Komornicki, S., ed. *Wojsko Polskie 1939–1945: Barwa i Broń* (The Polish army 1939–1945: Uniforms, insignia, and weapons). Warsaw: Interpress, 1984.

"Konspiracja w Kraju Pod Okupacją Sowiecką." In the Stanisław Mikłajczyk Collection. Hoover Institution Archives.

Korbonski, Andrzej, and Terry, Sarah M. "The Military as a Political Actor in Poland." In Roman Kolkowicz and Andrzej Korbonski, eds., *Soldiers, Peasants, and Bureaucrats: Civil-Military Relations in Communist and Modernizing Societies*. London: Allen & Unwin, 1982.

Korboński, Stefan. *W imieniu Rzeczypospolitej* (In the name of Poland). Paris: Instytut Literacki, 1954.

Kosyrz, Zdzisław; Magoń, Walerian; and Nowakowski, Bogdan. *Wychowanie w Ludowym Wojsku Polskim* (Upbringing in the Polish People's Army). Warsaw: Wydawnictwo Ministerstwa Obrony Narodowej, 1978.

Kozik, Zenobiusz. "O wydarzeniach marcowych 1968" (The events of March 1968). *Nowe Drogi*, Feb. 1988.

"Kraj-Kronika 1982" (Home-affairs chronicle). *Wojsko Ludowe*, Dec. 1982.

Krajewski, Mieczysław. "Silne państwo w interesie demokracji" (A strong state is in the interest of democracy). *Wojsko Ludowe*, Sept. 1980.

Kukiel, Marian. *Zarys historii wojskowości w Polsce* (Short history of the army in Poland). Cracow: Krakowska Spółka Wydawnicza, 1929.

Kukliński, Col. Ryszard J. "Wojna z narodem widziana od środka" (War against the nation seen from within). *Kultura* (Paris), April 1987.

Kulerski, Wiktor, ed. *Kościuszkowcy* (Kosciuszkovites). Warsaw: Niezależne Wydawnictwo Harcerskie, 1984.

Kuropieska, Gen. Józef. *Nieprzewidziane Przygody* (Unforeseen adventures). Cracow: Wydawnictwo Literackie, 1988.

Kusiak, Franciszek. *Oficerowie 1 Armii Wojska Polskiego w latach 1944–1945* (The officers of the First Polish Army 1944–1945). Warsaw: PAN, 1987.

Łączyński, Kazimierz, and Przyjemski, Stanisław. "Na marginesie artykułu Tadeusza Pióro: Jak Powstawała Sprawa 'Spisku w Wojsku'" (The origins of the "military conspiracy" affair: Marginal comments on the article by Tadeusz Pióro). *Polityka*, Nov. 26, 1988.

Latawski, Paul C. "The Polish Military and Politics." In Jack Bielasiak and Maurice D. Simon, eds., *Polish Politics: Edge of the Abyss.* New York: Praeger Publishers, 1984.

Lewczuk, Col. Bazyli. "Kształtownaie patriotyzmu i obronne szkolenie studentów" (Shaping the patriotism and military education of university students). *Wojsko Ludowe*, Feb. 1987.

———. "Wychowanie nie tylko obronne" (Upbringing not only military). *Żołnierz Wolności*, Nov. 11, 1986.

Łukasiewicz, Ryszard. "Partia odradza się w działaniu" (The party is being reborn through action). *Życie Partii*, March 3, 1982.

Makowski, Edmund, ed. *Wydarzenia Czerwcowe w Poznaniu, 1956* (June events in Poznań, 1956). Poznan: Uniwersytet im. Adama Mickiewicza, 1981.

Mała Encyklopedia Wojskowa (Short military encyclopedia). Warsaw: MON, 1967–1971.

Malcher, George C. *Poland's Politicized Army: Communists in Uniform.* New York: Praeger Publishers, 1984.

Maluta, Maj. Ryszard. "Miary ofensywnosci" (Taking the offensive). *Wojsko Ludowe*, Feb. 1981.

"Mamy się czym pochwalić" (We have a lot to be proud of). *Żołnierz Wolności*, April 21, 1988.

Marszałek Polski Michał Żymierski (Marshal of Poland Żymierski). Warsaw: Wydawnictwo Ministerstwa Obrony Narodowej, 1983.

Michaels, Albert L. "Background to a Coup: Civil-Military Relations in Twentieth-Century Chile and the Overthrow of Salvador Allende." In Claude E. Welch, Jr., ed., *Civilian Control of the Military: Theory and Cases from Developing Countries.* Albany, N.Y.: State University of New York Press, 1976.

Michalski, Adam. *Los się przychylił* (Good fortune). Warsaw: Wydawnictwo Ministerstwa Obrony Narodowej, 1986.

Michta, Norbert. "Czego oczekuję od IX Zjazdu Partii?" (What do I expect of the Ninth Party Congress?). *Wojsko Ludowe*, June 1981.

Mickiewicz, Adam. *Księgi pielgrzymstwa i narodu polskiego* (The books of pilgrimage and of the Polish nation). Warsaw: Czytelnik, 1982.

Mikołajczyk, Stanisław. "Can Russia Depend Upon the Armies of its Satellites." In the Stanisław Mikołajczyk Collection (box 122). Hoover Institution Archives.

The Military Balance, 1983–1984. London: The International Institute for Strategic Studies, 1986.

The Military Balance, 1986–1987. London: The International Institute for Strategic Studies, 1986.

Miłosz, Czesław. *The Seizure of Power.* New York: Farrar, Straus, Giroux, 1982.

Młotek, Mieczysław. *Krótki zarys historii Brygady Strzelców Karpackich, 1940–1942* (Short history of the Carpathian Brigade: 1940–1942). London: Zarząd Główny Związku Tobrukczyków, 1985.

Mochnacki, Maurycy. *Powstanie narodu polskiego w roku 1830* (The uprising of the Polish nation in 1830). Warsaw: Państwowy Instytut Wydawniczy, 1984.

"MON ogłasza ochotniczą rekrutację kandydatów do niżej wymienionych szkół" (Ministry of Defense announces recruitment for the following schools). *Żołnierz Polski*, Feb. 14, 1988.

Mosiejka, Leonard. "Protokół sporządzony w dniu 15 lutego, 1946" (Deposition taken on February 15, 1946). In the Stanisław Mikołajczyk Collection (box 39). Hoover Institution Archives.

"Mosty druzhby i bratstva: Soyuz-81." *Krasnaya Zvezda*, March 25, 1981.

Muszyński, Col. Jerzy. "Dysydenci polscy roku 1980" (Polish dissidents of 1980). *Wojsko Ludowe*, Dec. 1980.

"Na forumie pol'skikh kommunistov." *Pravda*, July 20 and 21, 1981.

"Nadużywanie strajków-społecznym samobójstwem" (The abuse of the right to strike equals social suicide). *Żołnierz Wolności*, Oct. 28, 1981.

"IX cherezvichayniy s'yezd PORP." *Pravda*, July 15, 1981.

Nowak, Tadeusz, and Wimmer, Jan. *Dzieje oręża polskiego* (History of Polish arms). Warsaw: Ministerstwo Obrony Narodowej, 1968.

Nowe Wstrząsy: Grudzień, 1970 (New upheaval: December 1970). Warsaw: Zeszyty Edukacji Narodowej, 1985.

"O co walczymy, dokąd zmierzamy" (What are we fighting for, where are we heading?). *Nowe Drogi*, March 1982.

"O vmeshatelstve spetssluzhb SShA v dela PNR." *Pravda*, Dec. 25, 1981.

Od Października 1956 do Grudnia 1970: Materiały z Dziejów Polski (Between October 1956 and December 1970: Sources on Polish history). Warsaw: Wydawnictwo Społeczne KOS, 1985. In Polish underground publication collection, Hoover Institution Library.

"Odbudować Siłę Partii" (To rebuild the party's power). *Życie Partii*, July 1981.

"Odezwa Komitetu Centralnego PZPR" (An appeal of the PUWP Central Committee). *Trybuna Ludu*, Dec. 4, 1980.

Odom, William E. "The Party-Military Connection: A Critique." In Dale R. Herspring and Ivan Volgyes, ed., *Civil-Military Relations in Communist Systems.* Boulder, Colo.: Westview Press, 1978.

Olszowski, Stefan. "Konsolidacja partii-warunkiem odrodzenia" (The consolidation of the party as the condition of renewal). *Nowe Drogi*, Jan.–Feb. 1982.

Osóbka-Morawski, Edward. Unpublished memoirs. In Edward Osóbka-Morawski Collection. Hoover Institution Archives.

Pasek, Jan Chryzostom. *Memoirs of the Polish Baroque*. Translated and edited by Catherine S. Leach, Berkeley, Calif.: University of California Press, 1976.

"Patriotyczna Manifestacja na Polach Grunwaldu" (Patriotic demonstration on the Grunwald fields). *Żołnierz Wolności*, July 16, 1986.

Pelczynski, Zbigniew A. "The Downfall of Gomułka." In Adam Bromke and John W. Strong, eds., *Gierek's Poland*. New York: Praeger Publishers, 1973.

Petrov, A. "Proiski vragov sotsialisticheskoy Polshi" (Intrigues of the enemies of socialist Poland). *Pravda*, Sept. 1, 1980.

"Pierwsze terenowe grupy operacyjne przystąpiły do działania" (First small detachments are in action). *Żołnierz Wolności*, Oct. 27, 1981.

Pióro, Tadeusz. "Generałowie Przed Sądem" (The generals on trial). *Polityka*, Sept. 10, 1988.

———. "Zaczęło się w Armii Berlinga" (It began in Berling's army). *Polityka*, October 15, 1988.

———. "Przed Najwyższym Sądem Wojskowym 1951–1953: Procesy Odpryskowe" (Before the Supreme Military Tribunal, 1951–1953: Ripple-effect trials). *Polityka*, Sept. 17, 1988.

"Plenum TsK PORP." *Pravda*, Feb. 11 and 12, 1981.

Ploss, Sidney I. *Moscow and the Polish Crisis: An Interpretation of Soviet Policies and Intentions*. Boulder, Colo.: Westview Press, 1986.

Podgórski, Tadeusz. *Wojsko w PRL* (The army in the Polish People's Republic). London: Centralny Komitet Polskiej Partii Socjalistycznej, 1976.

Poland's Constitution of May 3, 1791. Monterey, Calif.: Defense Language Institute, 1985.

Poland's Leaders. Washington, D.C.: CIA Reference Aid, 1987.

Polish Collection. Hoover Institution Archives.

"Postanowienia związane z wprowadzeniem stanu wojennego" (Decrees concerning the introduction of martial law). *Wojsko Ludowe*, Jan. 1982.

"Pożegnanie wiceministra ON, Głównego Inspektora Szkolenia, gen. broni Eugeniusza Molczyka" (Farewell to the deputy defense minister, chief inspector of training, Gen. Eugeniusz Molczyk). *Żołnierz Wolności*, Feb. 27, 1986.

Pożoga, Władysław, "Chronić będziemy socjalistyczną Polskę" (We will protect socialist Poland). *Wojsko Ludowe*, Oct. 1981.

"Pożyteczne lata" (Useful years). *Żołnierz Wolności*, April 20, 1988.

"Priziv TsK PORP k narodu." TASS, *Pravda*, Dec. 5, 1980.

"Priziv TsK PORP." *Krasnaya Zvezda*, Dec. 5, 1980.

"Procesy przed Najwyższym Sądem Wojskowym: Raport opracowany na zamówienie Komisji do Badania Odpowiedzialności za Łamanie Praworządnosci w Sądownictwie Wojskowym" (Trials before the Supreme Military Tribunal: A report prepared for the

Commission on the Responsibility of Military Courts for Breaking the Law). *Tygodnik Solidarność*, Nov. 20 and 27, Dec. 4 and 11, 1981.

"Provokatsionniye zayavleniye." *Pravda*, March 31, 1981.

Prymek, Jadwiga. "LWP jako obiekt zachodniej propagandy" (The Polish People's Army as a target of Western propaganda). *Wojsko Ludowe*, April 1988.

"Przeciw polskiej racji stanu" (Against Poland's *raison d'état*). *Żołnierz Wolności*, Sept. 11–13, 1981.

Rakowska-Harmstone, Teresa. "Patterns of Political Integration." In Teresa Rakowska-Harmstone, Christopher D. Jones, John Jaworsky, and Ivan Sylvain, *Warsaw Pact: The Question of Cohesion, Phase II.* Vol. 1, *The Greater Socialist Army: Integration and Reliability.* Ottawa: ORAE Extra-Mural Paper No. 29, February 1984.

Rakowska-Harmstone, Teresa; Jones, Christopher; and Sylvain, Ivan. *Warsaw Pact: The Question of Cohesion, Phase II.* Vol. 2, *Poland, German Democratic Republic, and Romania.* Ottawa: ORAE Extra-Mural Paper No. 33, November 1984.

Raport: Polska 5 lat po Sierpniu (A report: Poland five years after August 1980). London: Aneks, 1986.

"Referat Komitetu Centralnego PZPR na X Zjazd PZPR" (Report of the PUWP Central Committee to the Tenth PUWP Congress). *Trybuna Ludu*, June 30, 1986.

Regulamin Dyscyplinarny Sił Zbrojnych Polskiej Rzeczpospolitej Ludowej. (Disciplinary regulations of the armed forces of the Polish People's Republic). Warsaw: Ministerstwo Obrony Narodowej, 1977.

"Reshayushchiy faktor" (The decisive factor). *Pravda*, Nov. 11, 1980.

"Rezolucja w sprawie realizacji uchwał IX Zjazdu PZPR" (Resolution on the implementation of the decisions of the Ninth PUWP Congress). *Żołnierz Wolności*, March 19, 1984.

Rice, Condoleezza. *The Soviet Union and the Czechoslovak Army, 1948–1983: Uncertain Alliance.* Princeton, N.J.: Princeton University Press, 1984.

Rocznik Wojskowo-Historyczny, 1961 (Yearbook of military history, 1961). Warsaw: Wydawnictwo Ministerstwa Obrony Narodowej, 1961.

Ross Johnson, A. "Soviet Military Policy in Eastern Europe." In Sarah Meiklejohn Terry, ed., *Soviet Policy in Eastern Europe.* New Haven, Conn.: Yale University Press, 1984.

Ross Johnson, A., et al. *East European Military Establishments: The Warsaw Pact Northern Tier.* RAND, R-2417/1-AF/FF, 1980.

Ross Johnson, A.; Dean, Robert W.; and Alexiev, Alexander. *East European Military Establishments: The Warsaw Pact Northern Tier.* New York: Crane Russak, 1982.

Rothschild, Joseph. *East Central Europe Between the Two World Wars.* Seattle, Wash.: University of Washington Press, 1974.

Rupnik, Jacques. "The Military and 'Normalization' in Poland." In Paul G. Lewis, ed., *Eastern Europe: Political Crisis and Legitimation.* New York: St. Martin's Press, 1984.

Rurarz, Zdzisław. "Komuniści polscy czy polscy komuniści" (Polish communists or communists Poles). *Pomost*, July 1985.

Ruszkiewicz, Col. Ireneusz. "Gwarant bezpieczeństwa Polski, wspólnoty, socjalizmu" (The guarantor of Poland's security, of the Socialist Commonwealth, of socialism). *Wojsko Ludowe*, May 1981.

Rykowski, Zdzisław, and Władyka, Wiesław. "Marzec '68" (March 1968). *Polityka*, Feb. 20, 1988.

"S ofitsyalnym vizitom/Sovetsko-Polskiye peregovory." *Pravda*, March 2, 1982.

Sadykiewicz, Michael. "Jaruzelski's War." *Survey* 3(26), Summer 1982.

Sanford, George. *Military Rule in Poland: The Rebuilding of Communist Power, 1981–1983.* New York: St. Martin's Press, 1986.

Seminarium pokojowe w Warszawie, 7-9-V-87: Dokumenty (Peace seminar in Warsaw, May 7–9, 1987: Proceedings). Warsaw: Dezerter, 1987. In Polish underground publication collection, Hoover Institution Library.

Serwis Informacyjny: I Krajowy Zjazd Delegatów NSZZ "Solidarność" (News release: First National Congress of Solidarity representatives). Gdańsk: Biuro Informacji Prasowej KKP NSZZ "Solidariność," 1981.

XVII Rocznica Udziału Lotnictwa Polskiego w Bitwie o Anglie (Seventeenth anniversary of the Polish air force's participation in the Battle of Britain). Toronto: Zwiazkowiec, 1977.

Shtemenko, S. M. *Generalnii shtab v gody voiny.* Moscow: Voyenizdat Publishers, 1968.

Simon, Jeffrey. *Warsaw Pact Forces: Problems of Command and Control.* Boulder, Colo.: Westview Press, 1985.

Siwicki, Gen. Florian. "Centrum, jego struktura, zadania: Ministerstwo Obrony Narodowej" (The central government, its structure and its tasks: The Ministry of Defense). *Rzeczpospolita*, April 26, 1988.

Sovyetskaya Voyennaya Entsiklopediya. Moscow: Voyenizdat, 1980.

"Sovetsko-polskaya vstrecha." *Pravda*, March 5, 1981.

Spasowski, Romuald. *The Liberation of One.* San Diego, Calif.: Harcourt, Brace, Jovanovich, 1986.

Staniszkis, J. S. *Poland's Self-Limiting Revolution.* Princeton, N.J.: Princeton University Press, 1984.

Szczęśniak, Antoni B., and Szota, Wiesław Z. *Droga do Nikąd: Działalność Organizacji Ukraińskich Nacjonalistów i Jej Likwidacja w Polsce* (Road to nowhere: The activities of the Organization of Ukrainian Nationalists and their suppression in Poland). Warsaw: Wydawnictwo Ministerstwa Obrony Narodowej, 1973.

Szlachcic, Franciszek. "Ze wspomnień Ministra Spraw Wewnętrznych" (Recollections of the interior minister). *Życie Literackie*, March 6, 1988.

Terry, Sarah Meiklejohn. *Poland's Place in Europe: General Sikorski and the Origin of the Oder-Neisse Line, 1939–1943.* Princeton, N.J.: Princeton University Press, 1983.

Toranska, Teresa. *Them: Stalin's Polish Puppets.* New York: Harper & Row, 1987.

"Trzon wojska" (The core of the army). *Żołnierz Polski*, March 1, 1981.

"Uchwała I Krajowego Zjazdu Delegatów NSZZ 'Solidarność'" (A resolution by the First National Congress of Solidarity representatives). *Tygodnik Solidarność*, Sept. 11, 1981.

"Ukreplyaya druzhbu i sotrudnichestvo." *Pravda*, Nov. 2, 1980.

"V prokurature PNR." *Pravda*, Feb. 10, 1981.

"V seyme PNR." *Krasnaya Zvezda*, Sept. 6, 1980.

"Vstrecha v Berline." *Krasnaya Zvezda*, Oct. 21, 1981.

"Vstrecha v Varshave." *Pravda*, March 19, 1981.

"Vystupleniye tovarishcha Stanislava Kanii." *Pravda*, Feb. 25, 1981.

Walczuk, Eugeniusz. "Oficerowie" (The officers). *Polityka*, April 29, 1972.

Weschler, Lawrence. *The Passion of Poland*. New York: Pantheon Books, 1984.

Weydenthal, Jan B. de; Porter, Bruce D.; and Devlin, Kevin, eds. *The Polish Drama: 1980–1982*. Lexington, Mass.: Lexington Books, 1982.

"Wezwanie pod adresem Solidarności" (An appeal to Solidarity). *Wojsko Ludowe*, Nov. 1981.

Who's Who in Poland. Warsaw: Interpress Publishers, 1982.

Wiatr, Jerzy J. *Socjologia Wojska* (Sociology of the army). Warsaw: Wydawnictwo Ministerstwa Obrony Narodowej, 1982.

Wodecki, Włodzimierz. "Wreszcie skutecznie" (Finally effective action). *Życie Partii*, Nov. 25, 1981.

"Wojsko nie jest przerwą w życiorysie" (The army is not a blank page in your life). *Żołnierz Wolności*, April 19, 1988.

"Wojsko Socjalistyczne i Wychowanie" (Socialist army and upbringing). *Żołnierz Wolności*, Nov. 24, 1983.

Wojskowy Przeglad Historyczny (The military historical review), 98(1981).

Wokół Października (Polish October). Warsaw: Zeszyty Edukacji Narodowej, 1984.

"Wydarzenia Bydgoskie" (Bydgoszcz events). *Tygodnik Solidarność*, April 3, 1981.

Zaloga, Steven, and Madej, Victor. *The Polish Campaign, 1939*. New York: Hippocrene Books, 1985.

Zawodny, Janusz K. *Death in the Forest: The Story of the Katyn Forest Massacre*. Notre Dame, Ind.: University of Notre Dame Press, 1962.

Zbrodnia Katyńska w swietle dokumentów (Documents on the Katyń crime). London: Gryf Publishers, 1948.

"Zbyszek—Wojsko Polskie" (Zbyszek—The Polish army). In the Stanisław Mikołajczyk Collection (box 39). Hoover Institution Archives.

Zych, Gabriel. *Jan Henryk Dąbrowski, 1755–1818*. Warsaw: Wydawnictwo Ministerstwa Obrony Narodowej, 1964.

Periodicals

Izvestiya

Krasnaya Zvezda

Kultura (Paris)

New York Times

Nowe Drogi
Polityka
Pomost
Pravda
Radio Free Europe/Radio Liberty Research: Polish Situation Report; Background Report.
Rocznik Wojskowo-Historyczny
Trybuna Ludu
Tygodnik Solidarność
Wall Street Journal
Washington Post
Wojsko Ludowe
Wojskowy Przegląd Historyczny
Żołnierz Polski
Żołnierz Wolności
Życie Literackie
Życie Partii

Index

About the Author

Andrew A. Michta is Assistant Professor of International Studies at Rhodes College, Memphis, Tennessee, where he specializes in Soviet and East European politics. He was a Visiting Scholar at the Hoover Institution in 1988. He holds a Ph.D. in international relations from the Johns Hopkins University School of Advanced International Studies.

Reproduction and Sexuality in Marine Fishes

Patterns and Processes

Edited by

Kathleen S. Cole

UNIVERSITY OF CALIFORNIA PRESS

Berkeley   Los Angeles   London

University of California Press, one of the most distinguished university presses in the United States, enriches lives around the world by advancing scholarship in the humanities, social sciences, and natural sciences. Its activities are supported by the UC Press Foundation and by philanthropic contributions from individuals and institutions. For more information, visit www.ucpress.edu.

For a digital version of this book, see the press website.

University of California Press
Berkeley and Los Angeles, California

University of California Press, Ltd.
London, England

Library of Congress Cataloging-in-Publication Data

Reproduction and sexuality in marine fishes : patterns and processes / Kathleen S. Cole, editor.
       p. cm.
   Includes bibliographical references and index.
   ISBN 978-0-520-26433-5 (cloth : alk. paper)   1. Marine fishes—Reproduction.   2. Marine fishes—Sexual behavior.
I. Cole, Kathleen S. (Kathleen Sabina), 1950–
   QL620.R47 2010
   597.177—dc22

                                              2010027053

16   15   14   13   12   11   10
10   9   8   7   6   5   4   3   2   1

The paper used in this publication meets the minimum requirements of ANSI/NISO Z39.48-1992 (R 1997)(*Permanence of Paper*).

Cover illustration: Detail from "Sauvez la mer, sauvez les poissons" (Save the Sea, Save the Fish), a poster by David Lance Goines, 1998.

*This book is dedicated to the oceans and to the fishes
that live in them.*

CONTENTS

CONTRIBUTORS

KATHLEEN S. COLE
Department of Zoology
University of Hawaii at Mānoa
Honolulu, Hawaii, United States
colek@hawaii.edu

BRUCE B. COLLETTE
National Marine Fisheries Service
  Systematics Laboratory
Smithsonian Institution
Washington DC, United States
collettb@si.edu

JOHN GODWIN
Department of Biology and W. M. Keck
  Center for Behavioral Biology
North Carolina State University
Raleigh, North Carolina, United States
John_Godwin@ncsu.edu

PHILIP A. HASTINGS
Marine Biology Research Division
Scripps Institution of Oceanography
University of California, San Diego
La Jolla, California, United States
phastings@ucsd.edu

INGRID M. KAATZ
Department of Environmental and
  Forest Biology
State University of New York
College of Environmental Science and
  Forestry
Syracuse, New York, United States
ingridmkaatz1@yahoo.com

FREDERIEKE J. KROON
CSIRO Sustainable Ecosystems
Atherton, Queensland, Australia
frederieke.kroon@csiro.au

TETSUO KUWAMURA
School of International Liberal
  Studies
Chukyo University
Yagoto-honmachi, Nagoya, Japan
kuwamura@lets.chukyo-u.ac.jp

PHILLIP S. LOBEL
Department of Biology
Boston University
Boston, Massachusetts, United States
plobel@bu.edu

CARLOTTA MAZZOLDI
Department of Biology
University of Padova
Padova, Italy
carlotta.mazzoldi@unipd.it

PHILIP L. MUNDAY
ARC Centre of Excellence for Coral Reef
    Studies and School of Marine and Tropical
    Biology
James Cook University
Townsville, Queensland, Australia
philip.munday@jcu.edu.au

MARTA MUÑOZ
Àrea de Zoologia
Departament Ciències Ambientals
Universitat de Girona, Campus de Montilivi
Girona, Spain
marta.munyoz@udg.edu

JOHN A. MUSICK
Virginia Institute of Marine Science
Gloucester Point, Virginia, United
    States
jmusick@vims.edu

CHRISTOPHER W. PETERSEN
College of the Atlantic
Bar Harbor, Maine, United States
chrisp@coa.edu

AARON N. RICE
Bioacoustics Research Program
Cornell Laboratory of Ornithology
Cornell University
Ithaca, New York, United States
arice@cornell.edu

PREFACE

When Rachel Carson's *Silent Spring* was released in 1962, it raised an alarm regarding the disappearance of North American songbirds due to pesticide toxins. Everyone could identify with the loss of birds from our immediate environments and recognize the consequences of species extinction happening in their own back yards. Unfortunately, most of us are not so readily attuned to the sounds and rhythms of the oceans. Yet we are facing no less of a crisis in the current decline of marine fish populations worldwide. Ever-intensifying fishing practices, increasing climate and temperature oscillations, and significant losses of coastal habitats are all contributing to the decline, and possible disappearance, of marine fish species worldwide. But unlike Rachel Carson's songbirds, the fishes of the world's oceans have limited public appeal. While other warm-blooded animals are perceived as kindred spirits, a more muted response is generated when it comes to fish. This no doubt is due in part to the very different appearance of fishes, with their finned bodies and fixed facial expressions. In addition, most marine fish species live in an effectively hidden universe that the average individual rarely, if ever, visits or otherwise experiences. Unfortunately, for fishes occupying this invisible world, the adage "out of sight, out of mind" is particularly fitting.

This volume, however, is less about the challenges to survival that currently face marine fishes worldwide and more about the celebration of their continued existence. The chapters included here focus on biological patterns and processes that are most critical for species survival: those of reproduction and sexuality. The included authors have labored to reveal the amazing diversity and complexity that is to be found among many marine fish taxa. The chapter themes range from reproductive and sexual patterns in several major fish taxa, including pelagics, to processes associated with acoustic behavior, neuroendocrinology, fertilization, and reproductive ontogeny. Topic coverage includes the evolution of reproduction in cartilaginous fishes, the amazing reproductive diversity in scorpaeniforms, and mating systems and hermaphroditism in blennioids and gobiids, respectively. Both blennies and gobies represent some of the smallest-sized and least conspicuous of marine fishes, and these two taxa make up the majority of the cryptobenthic fish communities of coastal and reef habitats. They also constitute a critical link between bottom-end and higher trophic levels that is essential for energy cycling in these environments. Yet very little is known regarding the most basic aspects of their biology. At the other extreme, epipelagic fishes, many of which are large-sized or occur in schools, are primarily open water species and in many cases are targets for commercial exploitation. As a consequence of their offshore lifestyle, much of their biology, especially their reproductive biology, remains unknown. Nowhere is this information vacuum more critically felt than within the context of current efforts to develop effective management and conservation policies for the continued existence of these highly vulnerable fishes.

The following chapters outline what is known, and what remains to be discovered, with regard to patterns and processes of reproductive and sexual biology among a variety of marine fishes. As will become evident, our knowledge deficit is much greater than our existing understanding of the biology of coastal and oceanic fishes. This book highlights the remarkable biological diversity to be found just beyond our shores, if only we would look. Hopefully, it will encourage an increase in research efforts directed toward achieving a better understanding, both of the challenges to survival that face many marine fish species, and of our mutual dependency on meeting those challenges.

Kathleen S. Cole, editor

INTRODUCTION

Kathleen S. Cole

The study of evolutionary biology is like a detective story, complete with the classic three word mantra of "what, how, and why?" Shared biological patterns of new characters or modifications of existing characters suggest the possibility, if not probability, of a shared evolutionary history. Consequently, the "what" referred to above is an initial observation of an apparent shared character trait that leads to a hypothesis of homology-based evolutionary relatedness. The question of "how" leads naturally into investigations of formative biological processes underlying observed patterns. This frequently involves the study of molecules, patterns of gene expression and regulation, endocrine production and function, and/or ontogenetic events involved in trait or pattern expression. Lastly, new characters or modifications of existing characters do not persist in a vacuum. "Why" investigates hypotheses regarding historical biotic and abiotic conditions and consequent selection pressures that may have favored the retention of a particular trait. The combination of such what, how, and why investigations inevitably leads to increased insight into the evolutionary history of taxa and a deeper understanding of evolutionary processes. Therefore, identifying both patterns and underlying processes is central to an understanding of how taxa have evolved and why they may have evolved in diverse directions.

The contents of this volume represent a selection of studies of patterns and processes associated with reproductive biology and sexuality in marine fishes. For such a broad topic, the number of possible subjects is vast, and a comprehensive coverage would fill several encyclopedias. This book, however, represents a more modest undertaking. The collection of complementary themes related to the reproductive and sexual biology of marine fishes that is presented here is viewed by the authors as a first step, hopefully of many, toward developing a more inte-grated understanding of the reproductive and sexual diversity that exists among marine fishes. The selection of issues addressed herein was based on two criteria: What issues have eluded comprehensive reportage in the past? And what topics are of increasing concern in light of both documented and possible future changes to our ocean environments?

The first part of this volume is entitled Patterns. Identifying patterns is the first step in any biological investigation that seeks an increased understanding of taxon and trait evolution. Hence, the examination of reproductive and sexual pat-terns within and among taxa becomes increasingly informative when viewed in the context of a shared environmental or evolutionary history. The five chapters in this first section examine diverse aspects of reproductive biology, sexual biol-ogy, or both within a taxon-specific or habitat-specific context.

Reproduction in marine fishes exhibits an astonishing level of biological diver-sity and sophistication. Nowhere is this more evident than in the chondrichthyans, which share the character of an entirely cartilaginous skeleton and constitute one of the two major groups of extant fishes. Chondrichthyans diverged from bony fishes early in the evolutionary history of jawed vertebrates. Since this divergence, their reproductive biology has evolved along several highly specialized and di-verse pathways. Chapter 1, by John Musick, examines reproductive diversity in this group from a phylogenetic perspective. In doing so, he provides a wealth of detail regarding reproductive mode and morphology and offers strong support for hypothesized ancestral reproductive states and more recently derived repro-ductive traits within the taxon. Here, phylogenetic patterns both inform our un-derstanding of the origins of diverse reproductive modes in chondrichthyan fishes and provide insights into the evolutionary potential for reproductive pro-cesses among vertebrates as a whole.

Chapter 2, by Bruce Collette, switches from a taxon-centric to a habitat-centric viewpoint. Oceanic epipelagic fishes live most or all of their lives in blue water en-vironments, far from continental coasts. Many oceanic epipelagic species are of major commercial importance and provide a significant proportion of harvested fish biomass. However, the inaccessibility of their environment has made studies of their biology—and in particular their reproductive biology—extremely diffi-cult. Consequently, we know next to nothing regarding basic biological processes, the understanding of which is critical to successful management and conser-vation efforts. In this chapter, Collette has gathered together all of the available information on reproduction and development of oceanic epipelagic fishes. In do-ing so, he has been able to highlight the limits of our knowledge, which are con-siderable, and identify the necessary directions for research in the immediate future. As his chapter demonstrates, the gaps in our knowledge of the repro-ductive biology of oceanic epipelagic fishes are extensive. Should we wish to have a better understanding of how to proceed in our efforts to conserve both commercially important epipelagic species and, by association, the oceanic epipelagic ichthyofauna community (upon which the effects of commercially important species removal are unknown), this chapter provides essential reading.

Chapter 3, by Marta Muñoz, returns to a taxon-based perspective and offers a phylogenetic treatment for reproductive traits among the Scorpaeniformes. This taxon, as indicated in the chapter introduction, is one of the most morphologically diverse of all teleostean orders and, perhaps not surprisingly, is also one of the most reproductively diverse. Scorpaenids as a group exhibit both internal and external fertilization modes. Among internal fertilizers, offspring may be released from the maternal body at varying stages of development. Among externally spawning species in which ova are released directly into the environment prior to fertilization, the resulting embryos may be anchored, drift free, or raft with other embryos. As this chapter reveals, an impressive array of reproductive variations is exhibited within this taxon. With such a variety, the Scorpaeniformes offer a unique opportunity to investigate the evolution of diverse reproductive modes, an opportunity of which the author takes full advantage by applying a phylogenetic framework to her coverage and analysis.

Blennioid fishes comprise almost 900 described species, most of which are associated with coastal environments. Yet, as Philip Hastings and Christopher Petersen point out in chapter 4, essentially nothing has been published regarding the reproductive biology of more than 90% of blennioid species. The authors seek to redress this omission by presenting a review of spawning, mate choice, and parental care within an evolutionary context. The ecological importance of this taxon cannot be overstated. Blennioids, along with gobioids, constitute the dominant component of cryptic reef and coastal fishes and as such play a key role in coastal and reef community ecology, trophic cycling, and within-habitat energy flow. This chapter provides an informative review of their reproductive biology and in so doing focuses much-needed attention on this under-recognized group.

Gobiid fishes constitute the second largest family of vertebrates, and with more than 235 genera and over 1,400 species, they are by a considerable margin the largest marine family of fishes. As such, they comprise a dominant taxon of tropical coastal and coral reef fish communities. However, because of their small size and cryptic lifestyles, they are significantly underrepresented in both ichthyological surveys and in studies of coral reef community ecology. As a result, much remains unknown regarding their biodiversity and basic biology. Among gobiids the reproductive mode of external fertilization, oviposition of demersal eggs, and parental care until hatching is relatively simple. What makes this group unusual is the capability of some taxa to produce both ova and sperm during adult life. While this ability among marine fish taxa is not limited to gobiids, the diversity of patterns of sexual expression in this group reaches a level unmatched in other hermaphroditic fish taxa. Chapter 5, by Kathleen Cole, examines this aspect of reproductive biology among hermaphroditic goby taxa from a phylogenetic viewpoint. Patterns of gonad morphology are examined as possible clade traits in order to investigate whether hermaphroditism has multiple origins within the Gobiidae and to what extent shared patterns of gonad morphology may be predictive of phylogenetic relatedness. By investigating the origins of differing sexual patterns in this group, we can hopefully begin to understand why sexual lability, which is so rare in all other vertebrate groups, is so common among marine fishes.

The second part of this volume is entitled Processes. Reproductive processes reflect the drivers of adaptive innovations. How developmental processes may have become modified to generate variable sexual expression is the topic of Chapter 6, also by Kathleen Cole. Here, events associated with reproductive morphogenesis in teleosts are examined to determine whether diverse patterns of reproductive morphology among hermaphroditic gobiids can be explained in terms of ontogenetic modifications. This chapter reviews the chain of ontogenetic events, starting with the early formation of the germ cell line and carrying through to the formation of a sexually differentiated gonad, to evaluate various possibilities regarding the ontogenetic origins of labile sexual expression among hermaphroditic gobiid fishes. The hypotheses put forward in this chapter remain to be tested. However, they do offer a blueprint for the further exploration of regulatory mechanisms and morphogenic processes associated with sexual determination and sexual expression in gobiids and other hermaphroditic teleosts.

Living in an aquatic environment is not unique to marine fishes. However, the physical and chemical nature of marine systems differs substantially from freshwater environments, and many aspects of reproduction in marine fishes reflect this. Nowhere is this more evident than in the topic of Chapter 7. This chapter by Christopher Petersen and Carlotta Mazzoldi deals with fertilization success in marine fishes. As the authors query in their introduction, what could be more straightforward? But as their chapter reveals, processes associated with fertilization success are anything but. Whether or not sperm meets egg and becomes a zygote reflects the outcome of a delicate balance of numerous factors, including spawning mode, mating behavior, sperm quality, and environmental conditions. We live in a world where ocean environments are clearly changing in terms of temperature, acidity, CO_2, and calcium carbonate levels. At the same time, protein dependence on fishery resources is growing at an unprecedented rate, and the documentation of fishery depletions is ever increasing. Consequently, our understanding of fertilization processes in marine fishes is central to understanding the factors that influence reproductive success. Current efforts for the effective management of commercially important fish species and the conservation of noncommercial species make this a timely chapter in any discussion of reproduction in marine fishes.

Among marine fishes, the topic of reproduction would not be complete without the inclusion of a discussion of ecological and evolutionary patterns of sexuality. Fishes exhibit the greatest variety of sexual expression of all vertebrate taxa. Gonochorism, which refers to the expression of constant (i.e., fixed) sex among individuals, is nearly universal among most vertebrate taxa. Among marine fishes, however, reportage of labile sexual patterns is becoming increasingly common. Early research in this area focused on documentation of the phenomenon (e.g., Chapter 5) and the development of evolutionary models based on individual costs and benefits. Subsequently, attention turned to the internal and external regulators of sexual expression (see Chapter 6). The drivers of this research include not only scientific interest but, more recently, the documented effects of environmental factors on sexual development in fishes as well. In light of recent findings on the effects of warming waters on adult reproductive output and on the masculinization of genetic females among some fish species, a fresh look at processes associated with teleost sexuality is timely.

Chapter 8, by Philip Munday, Tetsuo Kuwamura, and Frederieke Kroon, explores the unusual phenomenon of bidirectional sex change, consisting of the alternating expression of male and female function. The initial discovery of this phenomenon in a fish species was instrumental in challenging our fundamental assumptions regarding the nature of vertebrate sexuality. The concept that behavior, brain function, endogenous endocrine levels, and reproductive system morphology could all shift not once, but numerous times, opened up new avenues of exploration for improving our understanding of vertebrate sexuality. In this chapter, taxon-specific features of reproductive biology, social systems, and environmental factors are all explored in an effort to answer the question as to why such a complex sexual pattern has evolved in some marine fish taxa.

The early findings of sequential sexual function (i.e., unidirectional sex change) among fishes, followed by the discovery of serial sexuality as described in Chapter 8, made it clear that the vertebrate model of sexual genotype determining sexual phenotype was in need of a reexamination as to how, precisely, sexuality is regulated and how external social conditions can influence that regulation. In Chapter 9, John Godwin investigates how physiological and neurobiological mechanisms in concert with social environmental cues can generate discrete sexual phenotypes within a common genotype. At the heart of this investigation is the question as to how external environments can generate differing physiological and neural responses that are responsible for altering biological processes as complex as sexual expression and function. Here, the sexual phenotype of an individual is not a singular condition. Rather, sexual phenotype is independent of any specific genotype and can have multiple expressions within a single individual. As stated in the author's introduction, identifying related regulatory mechanisms and how they respond to external cues is a hopeful approach to better our understanding of evolutionary patterns of sexual expression.

The three chapters examining various aspects of labile sexual expression that are included in Part Two collectively engage in the what, how, and why of teleost sexuality. Our increased understanding of this topic is a matter of growing urgency. Changing environmental conditions associated with direct anthropogenic disturbance and climate change are becoming increasingly associated with abnormalities in sex ratios among both freshwater and marine fishes. In a number of cases, genotypic females are masculinized by environmental conditions and irreversibly develop into phenotypic males. The possibility of increasingly unbalanced, male-biased sex ratios among numerous fish species, including commercially important ones, clearly has serious implications for both coastal ecology and human welfare.

The sensory environment of the world oceans is also changing. The anthropogenic addition of increased noise levels has as yet unknown impacts on fish reproduction. Sound travels farther and faster in water than in air. Therefore, the introduction of artificial noise can interfere substantially with reproductive behaviors that include the production and reception of auditory signals. As discussed in Chapter 10 by Phillip Lobel, Ingrid Kaatz, and Aaron Rice, sound production associated with reproductive behavior among marine fishes serves to synchronize the behavior of potential mates, thereby leading to successful fertilization. In oceanic environments, coastal waters receive the most exposure to introduced artificial noise. However, increases in shipping activities, commercial fishing, and off-shore drilling are also steadily increasing artificial noise levels in offshore waters. Acoustic interference in marine waters will only grow with time, and the effects on fish reproduction are virtually unknown. This final chapter demonstrates how sound production and acoustical communication are integral to the reproductive biology of many marine fish species, yet are frequently overlooked in reproductive studies.

The overall goal of this volume is to raise awareness of how little we know about the reproductive and sexual biology of most marine fishes, and how critical this lack of knowledge may be. We are facing a future that holds the promise of progressively declining resources within our oceans, decreasing biodiversity in marine floral and faunal communities, and the potentially irreversible depletion of much of the world's primary source of protein. For many third world countries with tropical coasts, fish collecting and fish rearing for the aquarium trade and local consumption provide important sources of sustenance and income. Yet the ways in which both commercial and noncommercial fishes constituting a major component of coastal and reef communities contribute to ecological stability in those environments are poorly understood. Our best hope for the protection, effective management, and ultimate conservation of the fishes of marine environments lies in having a comprehensive knowledge of their basic biology, and especially of their reproductive biology. The authors hope that this volume moves us closer toward that goal.

PART ONE

Patterns

Chondrichthyan Reproduction

John A. Musick

The chondrichthyan fishes have evolved separately from the Osteichthyes (Euteleostomi) since the dawn of gnathostomy more than 450 million years ago (Miller 2003; Kikugawa et al. 2004). Indeed, the chondrichthyans may be the oldest gnathostome group, perhaps having evolved from some thelodont agnathan ancestor in the Silurian (Marss et al. 2002). Whatever their origins, the Chondrichthyes and Osteichthyes underwent rapid divergent radiations during the Devonian (Miles 1967). This early divergence resulted in quite different reproductive trajectories in the two clades, probably initiated by high egg and larval predation from the newly evolved gnathostomes themselves (Musick & Ellis 2005). Osteichthyan reproductive evolution has been based on oviparity, with vulnerable ova lacking a maternally derived protective shell or case. Consequently, several adaptations have evolved multiple times to decrease egg predation (nest building, parental care, viviparity, etc.), or to maintain fitness despite predation (production of huge numbers of pelagic eggs). In contrast, chondrichthyan reproductive evolution has been based on lecithotrophic viviparity (i.e., yolk provides sole source of nutrients during development), matrotrophy (i.e., nutrients include maternally derived supplements), and in a small number of clades, oviparity with protective leathery egg cases. This chapter will review the evidence for this conclusion recently proposed by Musick & Ellis (2005).

THE CHONDRICHTHYAN REPRODUCTIVE SYSTEM

The elasmobranch reproductive system is predicated exclusively on internal fertilization. All male chondrichthyans have intromittent organs called claspers

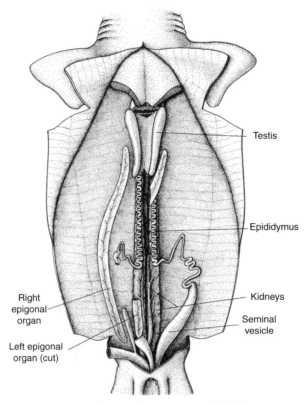

FIGURE 1.1. Male reproductive system (after Castro, 1973, Texas A&M Press by permission).

(myxopterygia), which are paired, grooved extensions of the posterior base of the pelvic fin, supported by cartilaginous endoskeletal elements (Compagno 1999).

Sperm is produced by the paired testes, then discharged into the ductus efferens and passed onto the convoluted epididymis, from which it passes on to the vas deferens and seminal vesicle (Conrath 2005)(Figure 1.1). The vas deferens and seminal vesicle function as storage areas for the semen, which may be packaged into spermatozeugmata or spermatophores (Wourms 1977). The paired seminal vesicles empty into a single urogenital sinus, which leads into a common cloaca. From there the semen enters the clasper grooves. Most male Chondrichthyes also posses siphon sacs, paired subcutaneous muscular bladders located just anterior to the base of the claspers. Each sac opens posteriorly through the apopyle and ends blindly anteriorly (Gilbert & Heath 1972). During copulation, the male usually inserts a single clasper into the female's urogenital opening and the siphon

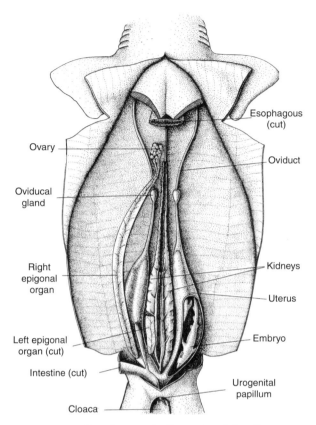

FIGURE 1.2. Female reproductive system (after Castro, 1973, Texas A&M Press by permission).

sac, which fills with seawater, functions under pressure to squirt semen into the female oviduct (Conrath 2005). The evolution of claspers has involved not only the coordinated development of the muscular siphon sac but also the muscles required to maneuver the clasper during copulation (Musick & Ellis 2005). The presence of claspers and prismatic skeletal calcification (i.e., a mineralized form of cartilage) are the two principal synapomorphies that define the Chondrichthyes (Grogan & Lund 2004). Thus, claspers and internal fertilization probably have been defining features of the group since its origin (Musick & Ellis 2005).

Prominent in both Figures 1.1 and 1.2 are the epigonal organs—long, white, strap-like bodies closely associated with the reproductive system in both sexes—however, epigonal organs are composed of myeloid tissue and are part of the immune system (Luer et al. 2004).

The female reproductive system (Figure 1.2) in Chondrichthyes is comprised of one or two ovaries, and paired oviducts into which the eggs enter through funnel-shaped ostia (Hamlett & Koob 1999). The oviducts pass into paired oviducal (= shell, = nidmental) glands. These are complex structures and histologically differentiated into four zones (Hamlett et al. 1998). Fertilization takes place in the anterior part of the oviducal glands, or just forward of them, in the oviduct. After an egg is fertilized, the oviducal gland surrounds the egg with a jelly coat and other egg investments and a tertiary egg envelope to form an egg capsule (Hamlett et al. 2005b). In many species, the oviducal gland may also store sperm in the posterior section from a few weeks to more than a year, leading to delayed fertilization after mating (Conrath 2005). The largest and most complex oviducal glands occur in oviparous species (Hamlett et al. 1998; Musick & Ellis 2005). Egg capsules pass out of the oviducal gland through the isthmus to the paired uteri. Function of the uteri varies depending on the reproductive mode of the species at hand. In yolk-sac viviparous and oophagous species, the uterus regulates the uterine environment; supplies oxygen, water, and minerals; and regulates wastes (Hamlett & Koob 1999). In other matrotrophic viviparous species, the uterus provides the above services, but it also produces nutritious mucous in limited histotrophs, and copious uterine "milk" in lipid histotrophs, and is the site of embryonic placentation in placental species (Hamlett & Hysell 1998). The uterus in oviparous species contributes to polymerization and scleratization of the egg capsule, which may be retained for several days before oviposition (Hamlett & Hysell 1998).

The uteri unite posteriorly to form a cervical and urogenital sinus (Hamlett & Koob 1999), which empties into the cloaca. In many species of viviparous sharks, only the right ovary develops, but the rest of the reproductive system is paired (Conrath 2005). Conversely, in many myliobatid rays, the entire reproductive system on the right side may be reduced.

CHONDRICHTHYAN MODES OF REPRODUCTION

Although the extant chondrichthyans are a relatively small class of vertebrates, including about 1100 species of elasmobranchs (sharks and rays) and 30+ species of holocephalans (chimaeras), they exhibit a surprising diversity of reproductive modes (Hamlett et al. 2005b).

These modes may be classified into lecithotrophic and matrotrophic based on whether fetal nutrition is supported solely by the yolk in the egg or augmented by additional maternal input of nutrients during development (Wourms 1981)(Table 1.1). Lecithotrophy includes two forms of oviparity (single and multiple) and one form of viviparity (yolk sack viviparity). Matrotrophy includes five different forms of viviparity (Wourms 1981; Hamlett et al. 2005b; Musick & Ellis 2005)(Table 1.1).

TABLE 1.1 Chondrichthyan reproductive modes

Reproductive strategies	Lecithotrophic	Matrotrophic
Oviparity		
Single	+	
Multiple	+	
Viviparity		
Yolk-sac	+	
Limited histotrophy		+
Lipid histotrophy		+
Carcharhinid oophagy		+
Lamnid oophagy		+
Placental		+

Oviparity

Oviparous chondrichthyans all deposit benthic eggs with leathery, structurally complex shells (Hamlett & Koob 1999). Chondrichthyan oviparity is limited to clades that are benthic in habit. Single oviparity, in which eggs are usually deposited on the sea floor in pairs, one from each uterus, is the only form of reproduction in the extant holocephalans. However, this group is but a small relic of a once diverse group of Mississippian chondrichthyans within which viviparity has been well documented in different taxa (Lund 1980, 1990; Grogan 1993, 2000, 2009, unpublished data). Evidence of oviparity is sparse in the Bear Gulch, the most intensively studied Mississippian fossil deposit, despite the high quality of preservation there (Grogan & Lund 2004). Within the elasmobranchs, oviparity occurs in only a small number of clades (some speciose).

Single oviparity is the sole form of reproduction in the horn sharks (Heterodontiformes), the batoid family Rajidae (skates), and in most cat sharks (Scyliorhinidae) and occurs along with various forms of viviparity in the carpet sharks (Orectolobiformes). In single oviparity, eggs are usually deposited every few days over a period of months. This results in an annual fecundity of 20 to 100 or more eggs per year in most species (Musick & Ellis 2005), an order of magnitude higher than that of viviparous elasmobranchs of similar size. Oviparity in elasmobranchs has evolved as an adaptation to increase fecundity in groups in which most members have small body size (<100cm TL) and thus limited uterine capacity (Musick & Ellis 2005). In addition, oviparity in small elasmobranchs may represent a form of "bet hedging" (Stearns 1992). Small individuals suffer a proportionally higher predation rate than do large individuals (Cortés 2004). If a pregnant viviparous shark is eaten, her immediate fitness is zero, whereas if an oviparous species is predated, her most recently produced offspring may still survive (Frisk et al. 2002; Musick & Ellis 2005). Multiple oviparity (Table 1.1) occurs in a small number of Scyliorhinidae and represents an evolutionary reversal. In this reproductive mode, females retain developing eggs in the uterus for most of the developmental period, then deposit them before they hatch (Nakaya 1975). This obviously limits the fecundity and probably has evolved in response to very high egg predation rates (Musick & Ellis 2005). The same may be said about a small number of scyliorhinids in the terminal sub-tribe Galeini, which have reverted to yolk-sac viviparity (Musick & Ellis 2005).

Lecithotrophic Viviparity

Yolk-sac viviparity is the simplest form of viviparity, wherein the developing eggs are retained within the uterus until parturition and fetal nutrition is supplied solely by the yolk and thus is lecithotrophic (Hamlett et al. 2005b). This form of reproduction is basal and most widespread in elasmobranchs and is present in all extant orders except the Heterodontiformes, which are oviparous, and the Lamniformes, which have a more advanced form of viviparity (oophagy)(Musick & Ellis 2005)(Figure 1.3). Yolk-sac viviparity occurs in many species formally classified as "ovoviviparous." The term ovoviviparous was abandoned because some of the species so classified actually exhibited a limited form of matrotrophy (Ranzi 1934; Budker 1958; Hoar 1969). Subsequently, "ovoviviparity" was replaced by the term "aplacental viviparity," which included three major modes of elasmobranch reproduction (yolk-sac viviparity, histotrophy, and oophagy), thus obscuring the true reproductive diversity in the group. In addition to being based on a negative attribute (lack of a placenta), by inference, the term elevated the relative importance of placental viviparity, a mode of reproduction restricted to a small number of terminal nodes within the Carcharhiniformes (Musick & Ellis 2005). The term "aplacental viviparity" should be abandoned and replaced with "yolk-sac viviparity," "histotrophy," or "oophagy" as appropriate.

Matrotrophic Viviparity

Mucoid (Limited) Histotrophy.   Mucoid histotrophy is the simplest form of matrotrophic viviparity wherein developing embryos receive additional nutrients above those supplied in the yolk (Hamlett et al. 2005b; Musick & Ellis 2005) by ingesting mucus produced by the uterus. This form of matrotrophy may be insidious and difficult to detect without obtaining ash-free dry weights from newly fertilized ova to compare with those of full -term embryos (Ranzi 1934; Needham 1942, Hamlett et al. 2005b). During embryogenesis, nutrients are expended to support the metabolic requirements for embryonic maintenance, growth, and development. Thus, in truly lecithotrophic species, more than a 20 percent reduction of ash-free dry weight should occur during development from egg to term embryo (Hamlett et al. 2005b). Ranzi (1932, 1934) noted early on that although some lecithotrophic species of Torpediniformes and Squaliformes lost 23 to 46 percent organic content during development, other squaliforms and some Triakidae supposed to be lecithotrophic actually gained 1 to 369 percent in organic content. Evidence for mucoid histotrophy may also be provided by histological examination of the uterine walls, which should exhibit high mucus secretory activity at least during early and midterm development (Hamlett et al. 2005b). Mucoid histotrophy appears to be widespread among viviparous groups, and further research is needed to determine the frequency of this reproductive mode (Hamlett et al. 2005b).

Lipid Histotrophy.   Lipid histrophy is restricted to the myliobatiform stingrays. This reproductive mode involves the secretion of a lipid-rich histotroph from highly developed secretory structures called trophonemata located in the uterine lining. Embryos supported by lipid histotrophy may undergo an increase in organic content of 1680 to 4900 percent (Needham 1942).

Oophagy.   Oophagy is a form of matrotrophic viviparity where embryonic development is supplemented by the mother's production of unfertilized eggs, which are ingested by the embryo. (Musick & Ellis 2005). This nominal mode of reproduction has evolved twice among elasmobranchs: in the lamniforms, and in the small carcharhiniform family, Pseudotriakidae. The mechanics of oophagy in these two groups differ and are not homologous (Musick & Ellis 2005). Oophagy is the only mode of reproduction known in the lamniforms, where large numbers of unfertilized eggs are produced by the mother and ingested by the embryos during most of the pregnancy (Gilmore et al. 2005). Adelphophagy (intrauterine cannibalism), where the first embryo that develops in each uterus attacks and eats its developing siblings, is an extension of oophagy and is known to occur in only one species, the sand tiger (*Carcharias taurus*). After the embryos have eaten their siblings, subsequent development in this species is supported through oophagy, as in all other Lamniformes (Gilmore et al. 2005). Adelphophagy results in the birth of only two large (>1m TL) neonates, one from each uterus.

In the carcharhiniform Pseudotriakidae, a number of unfertilized eggs are included within the egg envelope with the embryo, which then ingests the eggs during development. No further unfertilized eggs are produced to support the developing embryos above those included in the egg envelope, but the Pseudotriakidae may also be limited histotrophs (Yano 1992, 1993).

Placental Viviparity.   Placental viviparity is present in five higher families within the Carcharhiniformes. The "placenta" in elasmobranchs is analogous, but not homologous, to that in mammals and has been termed a yolk-sac placenta (Hamlett et al. 2005b). In elasmobranchs, the yolk sac forms the attachment with the uterine epithelium and the yolk stalk elongates to form an umbilical cord. The developing embryos are maintained in separate uterine compartments. All placental sharks utilize yolk stores from the egg for initial development, and then mucoid histotrophy before, and for some species, even during placentation (Hamlett 1989; Hamlett et al. 2005b).

ELASMOBRANCH PHYLOGENY

The Neoselachii are a monophyletic sub-class that includes all living elasmobranchs as well as some extinct Mesozoic forms and possibly, a small number of Paleozoic fossils (Maisey et al. 2007). Historical classifications of modern elasmobranchs have recognized two major clades: the Batoidei and the Selachii (Bigelow & Schroder 1948, 1953). This classification was radically changed in the 1990s following morphological cladistic analyses that placed the Batoidei as a terminal group within the squalomorph sharks in a new clade, the Hypnosqualea (Shirai 1992, 1996; de Carvalho 1996), an arrangement that was in conflict with the paleontological data. The earliest known batoids had separated from and were concurrent with the earliest heterodontiform, hexanchiform, and orectolobiform sharks by the Jurassic if not earlier (Thies 1983; Capetta 1987; Maisey et al. 2007), contradicting the batoid terminal position in the cladistic analysis. This contradiction was resolved by more recent molecular and paleontological analyses (Douady et al. 2003; Naylor et al. 2005; Maisey et al. 2007), which clearly showed the Batoidei to be the sister group to the Selachii. Cladistic misclassification of the Batoidei based on morphology may have been mitigated by homoplasies shared by the benthic, dorsoventrally flattened batoids and the squalean Squantiniformes (Nelson, 2006).

PHYLOGENETIC REPRODUCTIVE PATTERNS

Six major modes of elasmobranch reproduction have been mapped on the most recently accepted cladogram for neoselachians (Figure 1.3)(Musick & Ellis 2005; Naylor et al. 2005; Nelson 2006). This figure provides considerable insight into the evolutionary polarity of the various modes of reproduction. Among the 10 major clades within the Batoidei, oviparity has evolved in only one family, Rajidae, which is clearly terminal and derived from yolk-sac viviparous ancestors (McEachran & Aschliman 2004). Lipid histotrophy has evolved in the myliobatid stingrays. The mode of reproduction found in all the batoid basal clades is yolk-sac viviparity (Musick & Ellis 2005).

Within the Selachii two superorders, the Squalomorphii and the Galeomorphii, have been recognized. Oviparity is absent in the Squalomorphii and yolk-sac viviparity is the plesiomorphic mode of reproduction in all five orders (Figure 1.3).

Limited histotrophy is a derived state present in some squalomorphs, and more research is required to determine the extent of this cryptic, derived mode of fetal nutrition (Hamlett et al 2005b; Musick & Ellis 2005).

Reproductive patterns among the Galeomorphii are more diverse and complex (Musick & Ellis 2005). This superorder has been divided into two major, distantly-related clades, the Heterodontoidea and Galeoidea (Musick & Ellis 2005; Naylor et al. 2005; Maisey et al. 2007)(Figure 1.3). The Heterodontoidea includes only one relict order (Heterodontiformes) limited to one family with a handful of species each restricted to a specific coastal region of the world. The extant heterodontoids are all oviparous with complex, unique corkscrew-shaped egg capsules and specialized oviducal glands (Hamlett et al. 1998).

Among the Galeoidea, the Orectolobiformes are basal and have been divided into two suborders: the Parascylloidei, and Orectoloboidei (Goto 2001; Maisey et al. 2007). Whereas the Parascylloidei is comprised of one family of small, benthic, oviparous sharks (Compagno 2001), Orectoloboidei includes two superfamilies which contain six families, four of which are yolk-sac viviparous, and two of which are oviparous (the small benthic speciose Hemiscyliidae and the larger monotypic Stegostomatidae). The two oldest families, Brachaeluridae (lower Jurassic, 180mya) and Orectolobidae (middle Jurassic, 160mya)(Capetta et al. 1993) are both in the superfamily Orectoloboideia, and both have yolk-sac viviparity (Musick & Ellis 2005).

The order Lamniformes, as far as known, is uniformly oophagous (including adelphophagy in *C. taurus*)(Figure 1.3). The earliest stages of development in lamniformes are supported by the yolk sac, and yolk-sac viviparity appears to have been a necessary ancestral precursor to oophagy.

The Carcharhiniformes have usually been subdivided into two suborders: the Scyliorhinoidei and the Carcharhinoidei (Compagno 1988, 1999) (Figure 1.4). The Scyliorhinoidei, as presently recognized (Musick & Ellis 2005; Maisey et al. 2007), includes two families: the Scyliorhinidae and the Proscylliidae. The Scyliorhinidae, a speciose, benthic group of small, bathyal sharks, was considered to be the most primitive group of Carcharhiniformes (White 1937). This conclusion was based on their attenuate body and caudal fin, the posteriorly placed dorsals and poor vertebral calcifications. However, an attenuate body and tail, with posteriorly placed dorsals is typical of many benthic sharks (including the Orectolobiformes)(Compagno 1988, 1999), and reduced vertebral calcification is found in most bathyal sharks including many of the squalomorphs. Further, Compagno (1988) suggested that given that lamnoids and carcharhinoids are sister groups, the proscylliid body form with a high, forward-placed first dorsal, may be primitive for the Carcharhiniformes, with the scyliorhinids derived.

The proscylliids are currently comprised of three genera: *Ctenacis* and *Eridacnis*, which have yolk-sac viviparity, and *Proscyllium*, which is oviparous. *Ctenacis*

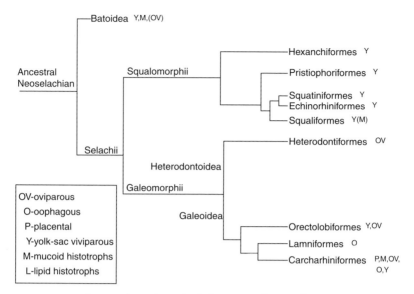

FIGURE 1.3. Recent elasmobranch phylogeny, with reproductive modes mapped for major clades.

and *Eridacnis* are more closely related to each other than either is to *Proscyllium*, and the latter is closest to the Scyliorhinidae, sharing characteristics with *Schroederichthys* (Compagno 1988). Thus, the position of *Proscyllium* is equivocal as it may be the primitive sister group to the Scyliorhinidae (Figure 1.4). Regardless, *Ctenacis* and *Eridacnis* comprise a yolk-sac viviparous clade that is most likely the primitive sister group to the rest of the Carcharhiniformes (Musick & Ellis 2005). In addition, the sister group relationship between Lamniformes (which has no oviparous clades) and Carcharhiniformes would dictate a viviparous group to be basal in the latter. Other than the scyliorhinids, which are mostly oviparous, with a reversal to yolk-sac viviparity in a small number of species in the subtribe Galeini, all the other families of Carcharhiniformes are viviparous: the Pseudotriakidae are oophagous and probably have mucoid histotrophy (Yano 1992, 1993); the monotypic Leptochariidae has a form of placental viviparity; the Triakidae have placental viviparity and/or mucoid histotrophy, the Hemigaleidae are placental, and all of the Carcharhinidae save one, the tiger shark (*Galeocerdo cuvier*), are placental. *Galeocerdo*, considered to be the most primitive member of the family, is yolk-sac viviparous.

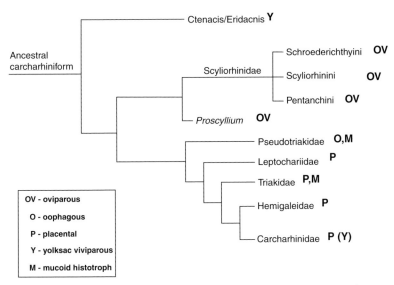

FIGURE 1.4. Recent carcharhiniform phylogeny with reproductive modes mapped. Note equivocal position of *Proscylium*.

YOLK-SAC VIVIPARITY: THE PLESIOMORPHIC STATE

The hypothesis that yolk-sac viviparity is unequivocally the plesiomorphic reproductive state in neoselachians, and plausibly in the Chondrichthyes, is supported by multiple sources of evidence:

Female reproductive system. The simplest, least specialized oviducal glands and uteri are found in species with yolk-sac viviparity (Hamlett et al. 2005a; Musick & Ellis 2005).

Male reproductive system. All male Chondrichthyes, both recent and fossil (so far as known) possess claspers (Grogan & Lund 2004; Musick & Ellis 2005). These have no other use than internal fertilization during copulation. Internal fertilization along with the presence of well-developed uteri in females provides the potential, if not the probability, for viviparity.

Urea retention. Chondrichthyans retain urea in marine environments as the principal mechanism to maintain osmotic equilibrium (Smith 1953). Urea is produced through the ornothine-urea cycle, which is found in all gnathostome classes except the Aves, in which it has been lost (Griffith 1991). The ornothine-urea cycle probably evolved in early gnathostomes as a means of detoxifying ammonia produced by catabolism in internally developing embryos (Griffith 1991). Thus, viviparity must have evolved quite early in the evolution of chondrichthyans or their ancestors. Conversion of ammonia to urea would not be necessary in oviparous marine forms because ammonia is rapidly diluted and carried away in seawater. (In recent oviparous chondrichthyans with horny egg capsules, pores in the leathery shell and embryonic movements produce seawater flushing through the egg case.) In early chondrichthyans, post-embryonic urea retention probably evolved through paedomorphosis, and allowed more efficient osmoregulation and greater euryhalinity than in their isosmotic, stenohaline ancestors (Musick & Ellis 2005).

Parsimony. Earlier studies that have been based on oviparity as the plesiomorphic reproductive state in modern elasmobranchs are less parsimonious than one based on plesiomorphous yolk-sac viviparity. In the oviparity "camp," Wourms & Lombardi (1992) estimated that viviparity evolved from oviparity 18 to 20 times. Dulvy & Reynolds (1997) estimated there were 9 to 10 transitions from oviparity to viviparity. Blackburn (2005) invoked 15 transitions from oviparity to viviparity among recent elasmobranchs. These three and related studies were based in part on older elasmobranch classifications and either assumed that oviparity was plesiomorphous, or used an oviparous out-group, the holocephalans, in their cladistic analyses. (Recent paleontological evidence suggests that the Paleozoic basal group from which both the Holocephalii and Elasmobranchii evolved was viviparous [Grogan & Lund unpublished data]). Thus the possibility that viviparity might be plesiomorphous was never considered or adequately tested. In contrast, hypothesizing yolk-sac viviparity as the plesiomorphic state, and analyzing the most recently accepted elasmobranch phylogeny (Naylor et al. 2005; Nelson 2006; Maisey et al. 2007), Musick & Ellis (2005) found six transitions from viviparity to oviparity (Table 1.2). Thus, with yolk-sac viviparity as ancestral there are 3 to14 fewer transitions.

Phylogeny. Yolk sac viviparity is unequivocally the plesiomorphous reproductive state in the Batoidea, and in the selachien Squalomorphii. The latter is

TABLE 1.2 Parsimony and the plesiomorphic reproductive state

State			
Plesiomorphic →	*Apomorphic*	Transitions	Source
Oviparity	Viviparity	18–20	Wourms 1992
Oviparity	Viviparity	9–10	Dulvy & Reynolds 1997
Oviparity	Viviparity	15	Blackburn 2005
Viviparity	Oviparity	6	Musick & Ellis 2005

the sister group to the Galeomorphii, in which reproductive patterns in the most primitive clades are not so well defined; Heterodontiformes are oviparous, and Orectolobiformes includes both oviparous and viviparous clades. However, in the latter order the oldest families (Brachaeluridae, Orectolobidae) are yolk sac viviparous. Thus the preponderance of evidence supports the hypothesis that yolk sac viviparity is plesiomorphous in neoselachians.

Paleontology. Viviparity has been well documented in Paleozoic chondrichthyans, whereas evidence of oviparity is sparse (Lund 1980, 1990; Grogan 1993; Grogan & Lund 2000, 2009, submitted). In addition, viviparity has recently been documented among the Devonian Placodermi, the Paleozoic sister group to the Chondrichthyes, and perhaps all the other gnathostome groups (Long et al. 2008, 2009).

Plesiomorphic yolk-sac viviparity simplifies the pattern of reproductive evolution in living elasmobranchs and forms the unspecialized basis for all other modes of elasmobranch reproduction. Early chondrichthyans possessed intromittent organs, internal fertilization, viviparity, and precocial young. Thus, their eggs and developing embryos had a large measure of protection from newly evolving gnathostome egg predators. In contrast, the Actinopterygii with vulnerable unprotected eggs and small larvae, evolved adaptations to decrease egg and larval predation (egg hiding, nest building, parental protection), or to increase fitness by producing huge numbers of small pelagic eggs (Balon 1975). Such adaptations have been superfluous for the chondrichthyans.

ACKNOWLEDGMENTS

This is VIMS Contribution 3014. Thanks are due to José Castro and the Texas A&M Press for use of Figures 1.1 and 1.2 (modified). Eileen Grogan, Dick Lund, and Nick Dulvy contributed to stimulating conversations leading to the ideas presented in this paper. "Ain't science fun?" (S. P. Applegate pers. comm.)

REFERENCES

Balon EK (1975). Reproductive guilds of fishes: A proposal and definition. Journal of Fisheries Research Board of Canada 32: 821–864.

Bigelow HB, Schroeder WC (1948). Sharks. In: Tee-Van J, Breder CM, Parr AE, Schroeder WC, and Schultz LP (eds.), *Fishes of the Western North Atlantic.* Memoirs of the Sears Foundation for Marine Research, Yale University, New Haven, Connecticut, pp. 59–546.

Bigelow HB, Schroeder WC (1953). *Fishes of the Western North Atlantic, Part II, Sawfishes, Guitarfishes, Skates and Rays; Chimaeroids.* Memoirs of the Sears Foundation for Marine Research, Yale University, New Haven, Connecticut.

Blackburn DG (2005). Evolutionary origins of viviparity in fishes. In: Grier HJ, Uribe MC (eds.), *Viviparous Fishes*. New Life Publications, Homestead, Florida, pp. 287–301.

Budker P (1958). La viviparité chez les sélaciens. In: Grasse P (ed.), *Traité de Zoologie*. Masson, Paris, pp. 1755–1790,

Capetta H (1987). Chondrichthyes II: Mesozoic and Cenozoic Elasmobranchii, vol. 3, In: Schultze HP (ed.), *Handbook of Paleoichthyology*. Verlag Friedrich Pfeil, Munich, Germany.

Capetta H, Duffin CJ, Zidek J (1993). Chondrichthyes. In: Benton MJ (ed.), *The Fossil Record*. Chapman and Hall, London, pp. 539–609.

Castro J (1973). *Sharks of North American Waters*. Texas A&M Press, College Station, Texas.

Compagno LJV (1988). *Sharks of the Order Carcharhiniformes*. Princeton University Press, Princeton, New Jersey.

Compagno LJV (1999). Systematics and body form. In: Hamlett WC (ed.), *Sharks, Skates, and Rays: The Biology of Elasmobranch Fishes*. Johns Hopkins University Press, Baltimore and London, pp. 1–42.

Compagno LJV (2001). Sharks of the World: An Annotated and Illustrated Catalogue of Shark Species Known to Date, Vol. 2. Bullhead, Mackerel and Carpet Sharks (Heterodontiformes, Lamniformes and Orectolobiformes). FAO Species Catalogue for Fishery Purposes 1(2), FAO, Rome.

Conrath CL (2005). Reproductive biology. In: Musick JA and Bonfil R (eds.), Management Techniques for Elasmobranch Fisheries. FAO Fisheries Technical Paper 474, pp. 103–127.

Cortés E (2004). Life-history patterns, demography, and population dynamics. In: Carrier J, Musick J and Heithaus M (eds.), *The Biology of Sharks and Their Relatives*. CRC Press, Boca Raton, Florida, pp. 449–470.

de Carvalho MR (1996). Higher level elasmobranch phylogeny, basal squaleans, and paraphyly. In: Stassny MLJ, Parenti LR, Johnson DG (eds.), *Interrelationships in Fishes*. Academic Press, London, pp. 35–62.

Douady CJ, Dosay M., Shivji MS, Stanhope MJ (2003). Molecular phylogenetic evidence refuting the hypothesis of Batoidea (rays and skates) as derived sharks. Molecular Phylogenetics and Evolution 26: 215–221.

Dulvy NK, Reynolds JD (1997). Evolutionary transitions among egg-laying, live-bearing, and maternal inputs in sharks and rays. Proceedings of the Royal Society B. 264(1386): 1309–1315.

Frisk MG, Miller TJ, Fogarty MJ (2002). The population dynamics of little skate *Leucoraja erinacea*, winter skate *Leucoraja ocellata*, and barndoor skate *Dipturus laevis*: predicting exploitation limits using matrix analyses. ICES Journal of Marine Science 59: 576–586.

Gilbert PW, Heath GW (1972). The clasper-siphon sac mechanism in *Squalus acanthias* and *Mustelus canis*. Comparative Biochemistry and Physiology 42a: 97–119.

Gilmore RG, Putz O, Dodrill JW (2005). Oophagy, intrauterine cannibalism and reproductive strategy in Lamnoid sharks. In: Hamlett WC (ed.), *Reproductive Biology and Phylogeny of Chondrichthyes*. Science Publishers, Inc., Enfield, New Hampshire, pp. 435–462.

Goto T (2001). Comparative anatomy, phylogeny and cladistic classification of the order Orectolobiformes (Chondrichthyes, Elasmobranchii). Memoirs of the Graduate School of Fisheries Sciences, Hokkaido University 48(1): 1–100.

Griffith RW (1991). Guppies, toadfish, lungfish, coelacanths and frogs: A scenario for the evolution of urea retention in fishes. In: Musick JA, Bruton MN, Balon EK (eds.), The biology of *Latimeria chalumnae* and the evolution of Coelacanths. Environmental Biology of Fishes 32: 1–4, The Hague, pp. 199–218.

Grogan ED (1993). The structure of the holocephalan head and the relationships of the Chondrichthyes. Ph.D. dissertation, School of Marine Science, College of William and Mary, Williamsburg, Virginia.

Grogan ED, Lund R (2000). *Debeerius ellefseni* (Fam. Nov., Gen. Nov., Spec. Nov.), an autodiastylic chondrichthyan from the Mississippian Bear Gulch Limestone of Montana (USA), the relationships of the Chondrichthyes, and comments on gnathostome evolution. Journal of Morphology 243(3): 219–245.

Grogan ED, Lund R (2004). Origin and relationships of early Chondrichthyes. In: Carrier JC, Musick JA, Heithaus MR (eds.), *Biology of Sharks and Their Relatives*. CRC Press, Boca Raton, Florida, pp. 3–31.

Grogan ED, Lund R (2009). Live birth and superfetation in a 318 million year old Carboniferous chondrichthyan. Joint Meeting of Ichthyologists and Herpetologists, Portland, Oregon, 22–27 July 2009 (Abst.)

Hamlett WC (1989). Evolution and morphogenesis of the placenta in sharks. In: Hamlett WC, Tota B (eds.), Eighth International Symposium on Morphological Sciences, Rome, Italy. Journal of Experimental Zoology, Suppl. 2: 35–52.

Hamlett WC, Hysell MK (1998). Uterine specializations in elasmobranchs. Journal of Experimental Zoology 282(4–5): 438–459.

Hamlett WC, Koob T (1999). Female reproductive system. In: Hamlett WC (ed.), *Sharks, Skates, and Rays: The Biology of Elasmobranch Fishes*. Johns Hopkins University Press, Baltimore and London, pp. 398–443.

Hamlett WC, Knight DP, Koob TJ, Jezior M, Loung T, Rozycki T, Brunette N, Hysell MK (1998). Survey of oviducal gland structure and function in elasmobranchs. Journal of Experimental Zoology 282: 399–420.

Hamlett WC, Knight DP, Pereira FTV, Steele J, Sever DM (2005a). Oviducal glands in Chondrichthyans. In: Hamlett WC (ed.), *Reproductive Biology and Phylogeny of Chondrichthyes*. Science Publishers, Inc., Enfield, New Hampshire, pp. 301–336.

Hamlett WC, Kormarik CG, Storrie M, Serevy B, Walker TI (2005b). Chondrichthyan parity, lecithotrophy and matrotrophy. In: Hamlett WC (ed.), *Reproductive Biology and Phylogeny of Chondrichthyes*. Science Publishers Inc., Enfield, New Hampshire, pp. 395–434.

Hoar WS (1969). Reproduction. In: Hoar WS, Randall DJ (eds.), *Fish Physiology, Volume III, Reproduction and Growth; Bioluminescence, Pigments and Poisons*. Academic Press, New York and London, pp. 1–72.

Kikugawa K, Katoh K, Kuraku S, Sakurai H, Ishida O, Iwabe N, Miyata T (2004). Basal jawed vertebrate phylogeny inferred from multiple nuclear SNA-coded genes. BioMed Central Biology 2: 3.

Long JA, Trinajstic K, Young GC, Senden T (2008). Live birth in the Devonian period. Nature 453: 650–652.

Long JA, Trinajstic K, Johanson Z (2009). Devonian arthrodire embryos and the origin of internal fertilization in the vertebrates. Nature 457: 1124–1127

Luer C, Walsh CJ, Bodine AB (2004). The immune system in sharks and rays. In: Carrier JC, Musick JA, Heithaus MR (eds.), *Biology of Sharks and Their Relatives*. CRC Press, Boca Raton, Florida, pp. 369–398.

Lund R (1980). Viviparity and intrauterine feeding in a new holocephalan fish from the Lower Carboniferous of Montana. Science 209: 697–699.

Lund R (1990). Chondrichthyan life history styles as revealed by the 320 million year old Mississippian of Montana. Environmental Biology of Fishes 27(1): 1–19.

Maisey JG, Naylor GJP, Ward D (2007). Mesozoic elasmobranchs, neoselachian phylogeny, and the rise of modern neoselachian diversity, In: Arratria G, Tintori A (eds.), *Mesozoic Fishes III. Systematics, Paleoenvironments and Biodiversity*. Verlag Pfeil, Munich, Germany, pp. 17–56.

Marss T, Wilson MVH, Thorsteinsson R (2002). New thelodont (Agnatha) and possible chondrichthyan (Gnathostomata) taxa established in the Silurian and lower Devonian of the Canadian Arctic Archipelago. Proceedings of the Estonian Academy of Science Geology 51(2): 88–120.

McEachran JD, Aschliman N (2004). Phylogeny of Batoidea. In: Carrier JC, Musick JA, Heithaus MR (eds.), *Biology of Sharks and Their Relatives*. CRC Press, Boca Raton, Florida, pp. 79–114.

Miles RS (1967). Observations on the ptyctodont fish, *Rhamphodopsis* Watson. Journal of the Linnean Society of London, Zoology 47: 99–120.

Miller RF (2003). The oldest articulated chondrichthyan from the Early Devonian period. Nature 425: 501–504.

Musick JA, Ellis J (2005). Reproductive evolution of chondrichthyans. In: Hamlett WC (ed.), *Reproductive Biology and Phylogeny of Chondrichthyans*. Science Publishers Inc., Enfield, New Hampshire, pp. 45–79.

Nakaya K (1975). Taxonomy, comparative anatomy and phylogeny of Japanese catsharks, Scyliorhinidae. Memoirs of the Faculty of Fisheries, Hokkaido University 23(1): 1–94.

Naylor GJP, Ryburn JA, Fedrigo O, Lopez JA (2005). Phylogenetic relationships among the major lineages of modern elasmobranchs. In: Hamlett WC (ed.), *Reproductive Biology and Phylogeny of Chondrichthyans*. Science Publishers Inc., Enfield, New Hampshire, pp. 1–44.

Needham J (1942). *Biochemistry and Morphogenesis*. Cambridge University Press, Cambridge.

Nelson J (2006). *Fishes of the World*. 4th ed. John Wiley & Sons, Hoboken, New Jersey.

Ranzi S (1932). Le basi fisio-morfologische dello sviluppo embrionale dei Selaci—Parti I. Pubblicazioni Della Stazione Zoologica di Napoli 13: 209–240.

Ranzi S (1934). Le basi fisio-morfologische dello sviluppo embrionale dei Selaci—Parti II and III. Pubblicazioni Della Stazione Zoologica di Napoli 13: 331–437.

Shirai S (1992). *Squalean Phylogeny. A New Framework of "Squaloid" Sharks and Related Taxa*. Hokkaido University Press, Sapporo.

Shirai S (1996). Phylogenetic interrelationships of neoselachians (Chondrichthyes, Euselachii). In: Stiassny MLG, Parenti LR, Johnson GD (eds.), *Interrelationships of Fishes*. Academic Press, San Diego, London, pp. 9–34.

Smith HW (1953). *From Fish to Philosopher*. Little, Brown and Co., Boston.

Stearns SC (1992). *The Evolution of Life Histories*. Oxford University Press, Oxford.

Thies, D (1983). Jurazeitlicher Neoselachier aus Deutschland und S. England. Courier For-
shungsinstitut Senckenberg 58: 1–116.

White EG (1937). Interrelationships of the elasmobranchs with a key to the order Galea.
Bulletin of the American Museum of Natural History 74: 25–138.

Wourms JP (1977). Reproduction and development in chondrichthyan fishes. American
Zoologist 17: 379–410.

Wourms JP (1981). Viviparity: The maternal-fetal relationship in fishes. American Zoologist 21(2): 473–515

Wourms JP, Lombardi J (1992). Reflections on the evolution of piscine viviparity. American Zoologist 32: 276–293.

Wourms JP, Grove BD, Lombardi J (1988). The maternal-embryonic relationship in viviparous fishes. In: Hoar WS, Randall DJ (eds.), *Fish Physiology*, vol. 2. Academic Press,
San Diego, pp. 1–134.

Yano K (1992). Comments on the reproductive mode of the false cat shark *Pseudotriakis
microdon*. Copeia 1992(2): 460–468.

Yano K (1993). Reproductive biology of the slender smoothhound, *Gollum attenuata*, collected from New Zealand waters. Environmental Biology of Fishes 38: 59–71.

Reproduction and Development in Epipelagic Fishes

Bruce B. Collette

The marine pelagic environment is the largest realm on Planet Ocean, constituting 99% of the biosphere volume and supplying about 80% of the fish consumed by humans (Angel 1993; Game et al. 2009). The epipelagic or holoepipelagic region of Parin (1970) is a thin upper fraction of the pelagic realm. Epipelagic fishes spend all or almost all of their lives in the open ocean, mostly above the thermocline, usually in the upper 20 to 30 meters, although many species move deeper to feed. This treatment of the reproductive biology and development of epipelagic fishes excludes sharks and deeper-dwelling mesopelagic fishes. It also excludes Sargassum-associated species such as *Histrio histrio* (Antennariidae), *Syngnathus pelagicus* (Syngnathidae), and *Xanthichthys ringens* (Balistidae), which are representatives of benthic or inshore families that secondarily become members of the Sargassum complex. I have selected representatives of true oceanic epipelagic fishes from groups of fishes with which I am most familiar. Those treated in this chapter belong to four orders: (1) Lampriformes (Lampridae, opahs); (2) Beloniformes (Scomberesocidae, sauries; Belonidae, needlefishes; Hemiramphidae, halfbeaks; and Exocoetidae, flyingfishes); (3) three suborders of the Perciformes: Xiphioidei (Xiphiidae, swordfish; and Istiophoridae, billfishes), Percoidei (Echeneidae, remoras), and Scombroidei (Scombridae, tunas and mackerels); and (4) Tetraodontiformes (Molidae, ocean sunfishes). Other groups of epipelagic fishes, such as the Rainbow Runner (*Elagatis bipinnulata*) of the Carangidae and many species of the suborder Stromateoidei, are omitted due to lack of time and space.

Relatively little is known about the reproduction of most oceanic epipelagic fishes, particularly on aspects of reproduction that rely on direct field observations of courtship and mating (Iversen et al. 1970), although there are observations on captive Pacific Bonito and Yellowfin Tuna (Magnuson & Prescott 1966; Margulies et al. 2007). Selected species accounts will summarize available information on (see Table 2.1): distribution; maximum size; all-tackle game fish record (International Game Fish Association [IGFA] 2009); longevity; sexual dimorphism; size at first maturity; size at 50% maturity (when available); spawning location, season, and temperature; migrations; breeding habits; fecundity; egg characteristics; and sources of larval illustrations followed by comments on fishery importance and threat status of the species using the Red List categories of the International Union for the Conservation of Nature (IUCN 2009). Problems facing epipelagic fishes include finding a mate in the right place and at the right time of year for successful reproduction and having mechanisms for keeping eggs near the surface where young fish can find adequate food supplies.

Several species of tunas and billfishes are highly migratory, tolerating a wide thermal range while feeding but returning to warmer waters for spawning (Boyce et al. 2008). This is particularly true of the three species of bluefin tunas. Most epipelagic fishes show little external differentiation between the sexes, although female billfishes are usually larger than males, and male dolphinfishes and tunas are larger than females. Epipelagic fishes practice external fertilization, and functional hermaphroditism is typically absent (Sadovy & Liu 2008). This chapter will concentrate on a sample of oceanic epipelagic fishes and will not treat coastal pelagic species such as most jacks (Carangidae), bonitos (*Sarda*), mackerels (*Scomber* and *Rastrelliger*), Spanish mackerels (*Scomberomorus*), or inshore needlefishes (*Strongylura*) and halfbeaks (*Hyporhamphus*).

ORDER LAMPRIFORMES

The Lampriformes contains seven families and about 21 species of highly modified epipelagic fishes characterized by a unique type of protrusible upper jaw (Olney 1984).

Family Lampridae

Lampris guttatus (Brünnich 1788), Opah.   Found worldwide in tropical and temperate waters and replaced in the Southern Hemisphere by *L. immaculata* Gilchrist 1904. Maximum size at least 185 cm TL and 220 to 275 kg, commonly to 120 cm. IGFA all-tackle record 73.9 kg. Spawning behavior unknown. Fecundity of a 963-mm FL female from Puerto Rico estimated as 7.2 to 9.7 million eggs. A 119-cm FL running ripe female caught in February in the South Pacific contained large eggs, 2.3 mm in diameter with no oil globules. Larvae illustrated by Olney (1984, 2005). Opah are taken incidentally by tuna longliners and are an excellent food fish. See Bane 1965; Klawe 1966; Olney 1984, 2005.

ORDER BELONIFORMES

The Beloniformes (or Synentognathi) is an order of atherinomorph fishes containing two suborders, six families, 37 genera, and at least 230 species (Rosen & Parenti 1981; Collette et al. 1984a; Collette 2004). Species of one suborder, Adrianichthyoidei, inhabit Asian fresh and/or brackish waters. Most species of the five families of Exocoetoidei are tropical epipelagic marine fishes, but the internally fertilizing Zenarchopteridae and most genera of Belonidae and Hemiramphidae are restricted to coastal marine waters or freshwater.

Development has long been of interest in beloniform fishes (Schlesinger 1909; Nichols & Breder 1928; Collette et al. 1984a; Lovejoy 2000; Collette 2003; Lovejoy et al. 2004). Most beloniform fishes produce large spherical eggs with attaching filaments, characters they share with other atherinomorph fishes (Rosen & Parenti 1981). Freshwater and estuarine genera of halfbeaks in the Asian family Zenarchopteridae practice internal fertilization and three genera are viviparous (Meisner & Collette 1999). Adrianichthyid eggs are the smallest (1.0 to 1.5 mm in diameter), followed by exocoetids (generally 1.5 to 2.0 mm), Hemiramphidae (typically 1.5 to 2.5 mm), Scomberesocidae (slightly elliptical, 1.5 to 2.5 mm), and belonid eggs, which are generally the largest (most 3.4 mm). The eggs typically have a homogeneous yolk and a relatively small perivitelline space. The incubation period is relatively long in exocoetoids (Kovalevskaya 1982). Belonids hatch at the largest sizes (6.8 to 14.4 mm), followed by halfbeaks (4.8 to 11 mm), sauries (at least as small as 6.0 to 8.5 mm), flyingfishes (3.5 to 6.1 mm), and adrianichthyids (3.5 to 4.5 mm)(Collette et al. 1984a). Fin formation generally begins during the embryonic stage or soon after hatching. Caudal, dorsal, and anal fins generally form first, followed by the pectorals, and lastly, the pelvics (except in exocoetids, where the pectorals form last). During post-embryonic development, exocoetoids undergo complex changes in barbel development, beak length, melanistic dorsal fin lobe, body bars, and pelvic fin pigmentation, and these features are important both in phylogeny and identification of species.

Family Scomberesocidae (Sauries)

The Scomberesocidae is the sister group of the Belonidae (discussed next) and is defined by the series of 4 to 7 finlets behind the dorsal and anal fins. This family and the Belonidae form the superfamily Scomberesocoidea based on two derived characters: presence of a premaxillary canal and upper jaw at least slightly elongate (Collette et al. 1984a). Maximum size of the two large species, *Cololabis saira* and *Scomberesox saurus*, 400 to 762 mm SL respectively; maximum size of the two dwarf species, *C. adocoetus*, 126 mm and *S. simulans*, 68 mm.

The four species of sauries are either placed in four monotypic genera (Hubbs & Wisner 1980): *Scomberesox* and its dwarf derivative *Nanichthys*, and *Cololabis*

TABLE 2.1 Summary of some reproductive information for selected epipelagic fishes

Family/Species	Max. size[a]	Longevity (years)	Sex. dimorph.[b]	Size at first maturity	Size at 50% maturity	Spawning time/ season	Spawning temp. (°C)
Lampridae							
Lampris guttatus	105 cm FL	?	?	?	?	?	?
Scomberesocidae							
Cololabis saira	400 mm SL	2	no	?	?	all	?
C. adocoetus	126 mm SL	<2?	no	?	?	?	?
Scomberesox saurus	762 mm SL	2?	?	?	?	?	?
Belonidae							
Ablennes hians	70 cm SL	?	no	?	?	?	?
Platybelone argalus	38 cm SL	?	no	?	?	May– June	?
Tylosurus acus	129 cm SL	?	no	?	?	?	?
T. crocodilus	105 cm SL	?	no	?	?	May– June	?
Hemiramphidae							
Euleptorhamphus velox	310 mm SL	?	no	?	?	March	?
Hemiramphus balao	280 mm SL	?	no	?	?	spring– summer	?
H. brasiliensis	350 mm SL	?	no	?	?	spring– summer	?
Oxyporhamphus micropterus	185 mm SL	?	no	120 mm SL	?	?	?
Exocoetidae							
Exocoetus obtusirostris	196 mm SL	1	no	140–150 mm SL	?	?	?
E. volitans	189 mm SL	1+	no	140 mm SL	?	all	?
Coryphaenidae							
Coryphaena hippurus	200 cm FL	4	male> female		458 mm FL	all	?
C. equiselis	75 cm FL	?	male> female		?	?	>21

Spawning migration	Fecundity[c]	Batch spawning	Egg diameter (mm)	Oil globule	Filaments	Fishery importance[d]	Threat status[e]
?	7.2–4.7M	?	23	no	no	*	LC
?	?	?	1.5–1.8	no	yes	**	LC
?	?	?	2	no	no	no	LC
?	?	?	2.3–2.5	no	no	*	LC
?	660	?	3.0–3.5	no	yes	+	LC
?	2100	?	>1.5–1.8	?	yes	+	LC
?	?	?	3.2–4.0	?	yes	+	LC
?	25–31T	?	4.0–4.6	?	yes	+	LC
?	?	?	?	?	yes?	no	LC
?	3700	yes	1.6	?	yes	+	LC
?	1200	yes	2.4	?	yes	+	LC
?	?	?	1.8–2.1	no	short	no	LC
?	10,300	yes	?	no	no		LC
?	?	yes	1.7–3.0	no?	no	no	LC
?	58T–1.5M	yes	1.3	one	no	***	LC
?	?	yes?	1.35	?	no	+	LC

(*continued*)

TABLE 2.1 (*continued*)

Family/Species	Max. size[a]	Longevity (years)	Sex. dimorph.[b]	Size at first maturity	Size at 50% maturity	Spawning time/ season	Spawning temp. (°C)
Xiphiidae							
Xiphias gladius	445 cm TL	9+	female > male	70–100 cm	?	?	?
Istiophoridae							
Istiophorus platypterus	340 cm TL	11+	female > male	162 cm	?	all	
Istiompax indica	448 cm TL	?	female > male	140–160 LJFL	?	all	27–28
Kajikia albida	280 cm TL	12+	female > male	130–140 LJFL	?	spring	20–29
K. audax	350 cm TL	12+	female > male	140–160 LJFL	?	spring– summer	27.5– 31.9
Makaira nigricans	440 cm TL	17	female > male	130–140 LJFL	?	Mar– Nov	20–29
Tetrapturus angustirostris	200 cm TL	?	female > male	?	?	winter	25
T. belone	240 cm BL	?	?	?	?	winter– spring	?
T. georgii	160 cm BL	?	?	?	?	?	?
T. pfluegeri	200 cm BL	4	no	?	?	?	?
Scombridae							
Acanthocybium solandri	210 cm FL	9	female > male	?	93–102 cm FL	May– Oct	?
Allothunnus fallai	96 cm FL	?	?	71.5 cm FL	?	summer	?
Auxis rochei	53 cm FL	5	no	35–37 cm FL	24 cm	all	24+
A. thazard	58 cm FL	4	no?	29–35 cm FL	30– 34 cm	all	24+
Gasterochisma melampus	195 cm FL	?	?	?	?	?	?
Katsuwonus pelamis	108 cm FL	8	?	40–45 cm FL	?	Apr– Nov	24+
Thunnus alalunga	127 cm FL	13	no	85– 97 cm	?	all	24+
T. albacares	>200 cm FL	6+	no	50–60 cm FL	62–92 cm FL	all	24+

Spawning migration	Fecundity[c]	Batch spawning	Egg diameter (mm)	Oil globule	Filaments	Fishery importance[d]	Threat status[e]
yes	2–5M	?	1.6–1.8	one	no	***	NT
	1–19.5M	yes	1.3	one	no	**	VU
yes	~40M	?	?	?	no?	**	NT
yes	?	no?	?	?	no?	**	VU
?	11–29M	?	~1.0	?	no?	**	VU
yes	?	?	~1.0	?	no?	**	VU
?	?	?	1.3–1.6	?	no?	*	
?	?	?	1.48	?	no?	*	LC
?	?	?	?	?	no?	*	LC
?	?	?	?	?	no?	*	LC
?	6M	yes	0.8	?	no?	**	LC
?	?	?	?	?	no?	*	LC
?	31–148T	yes	0.82–0.88	one	no?	*	LC
?	1.37M	?	0.84–0.92	one	no?	*	LC
?	?	?	?	?	no?	*	LC
no	80T–2M	yes	0.80–1.17	one	no?	***	LC
yes	2–3M	yes	0.84–0.94	one	no	***	VU
little	163T–8M	yes	0.90–1.04	one	no	***	LC

(continued)

TABLE 2.1 *(continued)*

Family/Species	Max. size[a]	Longevity (years)	Sex. dimorph.[b]	Size at first maturity	Size at 50% maturity	Spawning time/ season	Spawning temp. (°C)
Scombridae (continued)							
T. atlanticus	110 cm FL	8	male > female	48–52 cm FL	50–52 cm FL	Apr– Nov	24+?
T. maccoyii	225 cm FL	20+	no	120 cm FL	152 cm	summer	24+
T. obesus	>200 cm FL	16+	no	80–102 cm FL	102–135 cm	all	24–30
T. orientalis	300 cm FL	16	no	150 cm FL	?	Apr– July	24+
T. thynnus	>300 cm FL	35+	?	115–200 cm FL	?	?	?
T. tonggol	130 cm FL	5+	?	?	39.6 mm	Jan–Apr Aug–Sept	?
Luvaridae							
Luvarus imperialis	200 cm	?	?	?	?	spring– summer	?
Molidae							
Masturus lanceolatus	259 cm TL	?	?	?	?	?	?
Mola mola	368 cm TL	?	?	?	?	Aug–Oct	?
Ranzania laevis	200 cm TL	?	?	?	?	?	?

NOTE: A solitary question mark indicates unknown; information followed by a question mark indicates that the information is a good inference based on data for closely related species but there is no direct support for it.

[a] Size: FL = fork length; SL = standard length; LJFL = lower jaw fork length (for billfishes); BL = body length, end of opercle to base of tail.

[b] Sex. dimorphism: "No?" and "yes?" indicate the author's opinions based on phylogeny.

[c] Fecundity: T = thousand; M = million.

[d] Fishery importance: + indicates slight, artisanal fishing; increasing numbers of * indicates increasing importance of the fishery.

[e] Threat status: Red List categories LC = least concern; NT = near threatened; VU = vulnerable; EN = endangered; CR = critically endangered.

Spawning migration	Fecundity[c]	Batch spawning	Egg diameter (mm)	Oil globule	Filaments	Fishery importance[d]	Threat status[e]
?	?	?	?	?	no?	*	LC
yes	14–15M	yes	0.66–1.05	?	no	***	EN
yes	2.9–6.3M	yes	1.03–1.08	one	no?	***	NT
yes	5–25M	?	?	?	?	***	NT
?	?	?	1.00–1.12	one	no	***	EN
?	1.2–1.9M	?	?	one	no?	*	LC
?	47.5M	?	?	?	no?	*	LC
?	?	?	1.8	40	no	?	LC
?	300M	yes	?	multiple?	?	?	LC
?	?	?	1.42–1.65	20–30	no	?	LC

and its dwarf derivative *Elassichthys*; or in two genera, considering *Nanichthys* a synonym of *Scomberesox* and *Elassichthys* a synonym of *Cololabis* (Collette et al. 1984a). Both species of *Scomberesox* develop an elongate beak; the snout increases in length in *S. simulans* throughout its life span and in *S. saurus* until a length of about 200 mm SL. The two dwarf species, *Cololabis adocoetus* and *Scomberesox simulans*, differ convergently from the two larger species, *C. saira* and *S. saurus*, in being much smaller, losing one ovary and the swimbladder, and in having fewer vertebrae, branchiostegal rays, pectoral fin rays, and gill rakers. *Scomberesox* inhabits all three oceans; *Cololabis* is restricted to the Pacific Ocean. As a group, sauries spawn large oval eggs that contain an unpigmented yolk.

Cololabis adocoetus (Böhlke 1951).   Eastern Pacific. Maximum size 126 mm SL. Spawning period unknown. Only one ovary. Eggs within ovary 2 mm in diameter lack filaments and sculpturing. See Orton 1964; Hubbs & Wisner 1980.

Cololabis saira (Brevoort 1856), Pacific Saury.   Restricted to the North Pacific Ocean north of about 20°N. Maximum size about 400 mm SL. Longevity not more than two years. Both ovaries present. Spawn year-round with a spring peak in California Current Region. Egg slightly ovoid, 1.5 to 1.8 mm in diameter, no oil globule. Cluster of 12 to 20 filaments at one end of the egg, plus one thicker filament at the other end. Hatching at about 5 to 7 mm, flexion before hatching. Illustrations of eggs and larvae provided by Mukhacheva (1960) and Watson (1996). Of great commercial importance, particularly in Japan. See Mukhacheva 1960; Orton 1964; Hubbs & Wisner 1980; Watson 1996.

Scomberesox saurus, Atlantic Saury.   Antitropical in temperate parts of the Atlantic, Pacific, and Indian oceans. Hubbs & Wisner (1980) recognized two subspecies with the nominal subspecies, *scomberesox saurus saurus*, in the Northern Hemisphere and *S. saurus scombroides* (Richardson 1843) in the Southern Hemisphere. This saury spends most of its life in warm homogeneous surface layers of the open sea, far from shallow continental shelf waters. Sauries are one of the most abundant epipelagic planktivores inhabiting the open part of the Atlantic Ocean, feeding mainly on siphonophores, copepods, euphausiids, amphipods, fish eggs and larvae, protozoans, algae, and larvae of polychaetes, decapods, isopods, ostracods, cirripeds, and siphonophores. Sauries serve as food for many inhabitants of the sea, such as squids, Swordfish, marlins, sharks, tunas, dolphins, whales, and birds. The great abundance of sauries and their wide distribution make them an important link in the epipelagic food chain of the ocean by transferring energy from lower to higher trophic levels. Maximum size 762 mm SL. They spawn offshore between the 26.5°C isotherm in the north and the 23.5° isotherm in the south. Both ovaries developed. Greatest diameter of eggs, 2.32 to 2.52 mm, oil globules absent. Yolk clear and without any vesicles. The long filaments characteristic of *Cololabis saira* and most other beloniform eggs are absent with only numerous, uniformly spaced, short rigid bristles remaining. Incubation 14 to 16 days depending on water temperature. Hatching at 6.8 to 8.5 mm, flexion at about 6.4 mm. Complete development of fins and finlets at about 25 mm. Sauries are valuable food fishes in some parts of the world such as the Mediterranean. See Orton 1964; Nesterov & Shiganova 1976; Hubbs & Wisner 1980; Boehlert 1984; Hardy & Collette 2005.

Family Belonidae (Needlefishes)

Belonidae, the needlefishes, is the sister group of the Scomberesocidae (sauries). The family contains 10 genera and 34 species (Collette 2003), of which two genera, the monotypic *Ablennes*, and *Tylosurus* with six species, contain oceanic epipelagic species. The other genera contain either freshwater or coastal epipelagic species.

Needlefishes are oviparous and the eggs are released to the external environment prior to fertilization. There is a tendency for the right gonad to be reduced in length or even lost in some species, particularly in females. Needlefishes deposit large eggs with well-developed chorionic filaments that attach to vegetation. The filaments are typically long, numerous, and uniformly spaced over the chorion. Needlefish eggs are generally larger (2.3 to 4.3 mm in diameter) than other beloniform eggs (Collette et al. 1984a: table 90). Correlated with large egg size, belonids hatch at the largest sizes (6.8 to 14.4 mm) among beloniforms.

During post-embryonic development, needlefishes, like other beloniform fishes, undergo a number of complex changes in beak length, melanistic dorsal fin lobe, and body bars. Most species of Belonidae pass through a "halfbeak" stage in which the lower jaw, but not the upper jaw, is greatly elongated. Juveniles of *Belone belone* remain in the halfbeak stage for a longer time than other needlefishes. *Petalichthys* and *Platybelone* also remain in the halfbeak stage for a long time. Comparative development of *Platybelone* (as *Strongylura longleyi*), *Strongylura marina*, *S. notata*, and two species of *Tylosurus* (*T. acus* and *T. crocodilus*) has been illustrated by Breder (1932: figs. 7 and 10, plates 1 and 2). *Tylosurus crocodilus* lacks a halfbeak stage, with upper and lower jaws growing at the same rate from larval to adult stages of development (Breder 1932: plate 2, fig. 2, as *T. raphidoma*).

Ablennes and *Tylosurus* share a prominent, enlarged, melanistic lobe in the posterior part of the dorsal fin. Other genera of needlefishes lack any trace of this posterior dorsal lobe. Breder (1932: plates 3–5) illustrated the development of this posterior lobe in *T. acus* and *T. crocodilus* and its absence in *Strongylura* and *Platybelone*. Juveniles of two species of *Tylosurus*, *T. gavialoides* and *T. acus* (see Collette & Parin 1970: fig. 12), and *Ablennes hians* have bars. These bars are retained in adult *Ablennes* as is the melanistic posterior dorsal fin lobe.

Ablennes hians (Valenciennes 1846), Flat Needlefish.   Worldwide in tropical and subtropical waters. Maximum size 70 cm SL, 63 cm body length. IGFA all-tackle record 4.8 kg. Spawning season unknown. Oviparous; only the right gonad developed. A 278 mm female had 660 eggs, 3.0 to 3.5 mm in diameter, oil globules absent. Uniformly spaced tufts of filaments on chorion, 1 to 6 per tuft, 37 to 59 total, filaments longer than diameter of egg. The enlarged black dorsal fin lobe characteristic of juveniles is retained in adult *Ablennes*. Illustrations of juveniles 12.3 to 187 mm are in Collette (2005a). Harvested by artisanal fisheries in some countries such as India and considered a game fish by IGFA. See Chen 1988; Watson 1996; Collette 2005a.

Platybelone argalus (LeSueur 1821), Keeltail Needlefish.   Worldwide in tropical and subtropical waters with seven subspecies recognized (Collette 2003). Particularly abundant around islands. Maximum size 38.2 cm SL, 25.6 cm body length. Ripe females taken in June in the Caribbean Sea. Oviparous, right ovary longer than left. A 266 mm BL female had 944 eggs in the left ovary, 1,136 in the right. Juveniles remain in the halfbeak stage longer than most other species of needlefishes, at least to 100 mm BL. Of minor importance in artisanal fisheries. See Erdman 1977; Chen 1988; Collette 2005a.

Tylosurus acus (Lacepède 1803), Agujon Needlefish.   Worldwide in tropical and subtropical seas within the 23.9°C isotherm, except replaced in the eastern Pacific by *T. pacificus* (Steindachner 1876). Maximum size 128.5 cm SL, 95 cm body length. Oviparous, left gonad absent or greatly reduced in size, ratio of left gonad length to right 2.3 to 15.5+. Ovarian egg counts in two females, 485 and 500 mm BL (body length), 116 (2.3 to 3.0 mm in diameter) and 196 (1.0 to 1.2) in the left ovary, 1,676 (2.5 to 2.9) and 12,017 (0.9 to 1.3) in the right for totals of 1,792 and 12,313 eggs. Diameter of fertilized eggs 3.2 to 4.0 mm. Egg with uniformly spaced tufts of 2 to 3 filaments that are longer than egg diameter. Incubation about 10 to 12 days at 25.0 to 30.4°C. Hatching at 10.2 mm, flexed at hatching. Dorsal and anal fins develop prior to hatching at 168 hours post-fertilization, pectoral fin rays by hatching, and pelvic fin rays at 14 mm TL. The enlarged melanistic posterior dorsal fin lobe forms at about 23 mm BL, reaches maximum development from 169 to 244 mm, is still evident up to 605 mm, and is then resorbed. Flesh is of good quality so harvested in many tropical countries and also considered a game fish by IGFA. See Breder & Rasquin 1954; Mito 1958; Collette 2005a.

Tylosurus crocodilus (Peron & LeSueur 1821), Hound Needlefish.   Worldwide in tropical and subtropical waters, the nominal subspecies, *Tylosurus crocodilus crocodilus,* in the Atlantic and Indo-West Pacific, *T. c. fodiator* Jordan and Gilbert in the eastern Pacific. Maximum size 101.3 cm SL, 71.5 cm body length. IGFA all-tackle record 3.74 kg. Spawning in May through June in Brazil, but ripe females found in the Caribbean in October through November. Both ovaries developed but the right is longer than the left, ratio of right to left 1.1 to 1.5. An 860 mm BL (body length) female had 7,535 eggs in left ovary (3.6 to 4.4 mm in diameter), 23,721 in the right (3.9 to 4.8 mm), for a total of 31,256. Diameter of eggs 4.0 to 4.6 mm. Egg with numerous long, fine, transparent thread-like filaments. Incubation 8 to 10 days. Hatching at 10.7 to 12.0 mm, flexed at hatching. The enlarged melanistic posterior dorsal fin lobe forms at 25 to 30 mm, reaches maximum development at 100 to 200 mm, and begins to disintegrate at 200 to 250 mm. Flesh is of good quality so harvested in many tropical countries and also considered a game fish by IGFA. See Breder & Rasquin 1952; Randall 1960; Masurekar 1968; Erdman 1977; Collette 2005a.

Family Hemiramphidae (Halfbeaks)

Hemiramphidae, the halfbeaks, is the sister group of the Exocoetidae, the flying-fishes, which together form the superfamily Exocoetoidae (Collette et al. 1984a). Most halfbeaks have an elongate lower jaw that distinguishes them from the fly-ingfishes, which lack an elongate lower jaw, and from the needlefishes (Belonidae) and sauries (Scomberesocidae), which have both jaws elongate.

The Hemiramphidae contains nine genera and subgenera and at least 63 species and subspecies (Collette 2004). Three genera contain epipelagic oceanic species: *Oxyporhamphus* (two species), *Euleptorhamphus* (two species), and *Hemiramphus* (10 species). The family Zenarchopteridae contains five genera and 54 sexually dimorphic Indo-West Pacific estuarine or freshwater species that were previously included in the Hemiramphidae.

Halfbeak eggs are typically 1.5 to 2.5 mm in diameter and have attaching filaments, although these are greatly reduced in length in the pelagic eggs of *Oxyporhamphus*. Halfbeaks hatch at a size (4.8 to 11 mm) smaller than needlefishes but larger than flyingfishes and sauries (Collette et al. 1984a). Larvae are well developed at hatching with partially to fully pigmented eyes, an open mouth, fully flexed notochord, developing rays in the dorsal, anal, and caudal fins, and a small to moderate sized yolk sac (Watson 1996). A preanal fin fold is typically present throughout much of the larval stage. Like other beloniform fishes, post-embryonic development of halfbeaks includes complex changes in beak length, melanistic dorsal fin lobe, body bars, and pelvic fin pigmentation. Adults of four genera lack the elongate lower jaw that characterizes most members of this family, but juveniles of all four genera have a distinct beak. Juveniles of *Hemiramphus* and *Oxyporhamphus* develop a darkened posterior lobe on the dorsal fin similar to that present in two genera of needlefishes, *Ablennes* and *Tylosurus*. The ten species of *Hemiramphus* have a series of broad vertical bars on the body during some stages of their development. Body bars are retained for different periods of time during development: all body bars are lost before 120 mm SL in *He. bermudensis* and *He.*

brasiliensis but are retained past 175 mm in *He. balao*, and all are retained throughout life in the Indo-Pacific *He. far*. Species of *Hemiramphus* also have pigmented pelvic and caudal fins as juveniles. Patterns of pelvic fin pigmentation divide the genus into two species groups, one with pigment concentrated proximally on the fin (*He. balao* group), and the other with pigment absent basally and concentrated distally (*He. brasiliensis* group, including *He. bermudensis*). As indicated below, much less information is available on reproduction compared to post-fertilization stages, among open ocean halfbeaks.

Halfbeaks are valued food fishes in many parts of the world such as Australia and New Zealand (Collette 1974). They are utilized for food in the West Indies and South America but are not presently considered an important resource in the United States. Their value to man in the western Atlantic is largely as forage and bait for a wide variety of important food and game species such as tunas, Spanish mackerels, billfishes, dolphinfishes, Bluefish, and also sea birds. The most direct use of halfbeaks in the western North Atlantic is as bait for some of the game species mentioned above (Berkeley et al. 1975; McBride et al. 1996).

Euleptorhamphus velox, Flying Halfbeak.   *Euleptorhamphus velox* Poey 1868 in the Atlantic and *E. viridis* (van Hasselt 1823) in the Pacific. Maximum size 310 mm SL. Ripe females found in the Caribbean in March. Reproductive biology of both species is poorly known. Illustrations of larvae from 8.6 to 135 mm SL are in Collette (2005b). Neither species is of any fisheries interest. See Erdman 1977; Chen 1988; Watson 1996; Collette 2005b.

Oxyporhamphus micropterus (Valenciennes 1847), Smallwing Flyingfish.   The nominal subspecies, *Oxyporhamphus micropterus micropterus,* is widespread in tropical and subtropical waters of the Indo-Pacific and is replaced in the Atlantic by *O. micropterus similis* Bruun 1935. Maximum size 185 mm SL. A second species, *O. convexus* (Weber & de Beaufort 1922) is found in the Indo-Pacific. Females are ripe at about 120 mm SL. Ripe females have been found in March, August, and November in the Caribbean Sea, suggesting year round spawning. Egg diameter 1.8 to 2.1 mm, no oil globules. The chorion is decorated with 74 to 120, very short (0.08 to 0.12 mm), filaments, unlike the condition in most other beloniforms. Hatching at 4.0 mm SL, flexion before hatching. A lower jaw beak occupies more than 20% SL at lengths of 20 to 40 mm SL, decreases rapidly to less than 5% of SL until about 50 mm SL, and disappears by about 100 mm SL. Juveniles develop a melanistic lobe in the posterior part of the dorsal fin at about 38 mm SL which remains until at least 70 mm SL. Larvae of *O. micropterus micropterus* from 3.4 to 66.0 mm SL have been illustrated by Watson (1996), of *O. micropterus similis* 4.2 to 146.0 mm by Collette (2005b). Neither species is of any fisheries interest. See Bruun 1935; Breder 1938; Khrapkova-Kovalevskaya 1963; Erdman 1977; Watson 1996; Collette 2005b.

Hemiramphus. The most complete reproductive information for any of the 10 species of *Hemiramphus* is for two Atlantic species, *He. balao* (LeSueur 1823) Balao Halfbeak and *He. brasiliensis* Linnaeus 1758, Ballyhoo Halfbeak. Both species are widespread in tropical and subtropical waters of the Atlantic and are replaced by other species of the genus in the Indo-Pacific. Maximum size 280 to 350 mm SL and 400 mm TL, respectively. Cyclic patterns of gonadosomatic indices indicate that both species spawn during spring and summer months in south Florida. Hydration of oocytes begins in the morning and spawning occurs at dusk the same day. All mature females spawn daily, in June for *He. balao,* in April for *He. brasiliensis.* Batch fecundity in *He. balao* averages 3,734 hydrated oocytes in a 100 g female compared to 1,164 in *He. brasiliensis.* Spawning in *He. brasiliensis* occurs inshore, all along the coral reef tract of the Atlantic Ocean; spawning in *He. balao* is over deeper, more offshore waters. Illustrations of larvae of *He. balao* from 5.2 to 117 mm SL and of eggs and juveniles of *He. brasiliensis* 13.5 to 119 mm SL are in Collette (2005b). Illustrations of larvae of the eastern Pacific *He. saltator* (Gilbert & Starks 1904) from 5.2 to 14.1 mm are in Watson (1996). Valued food fishes in the West Indies and South America but more important as baitfish in Florida. Indo-West Pacific species of *Hemiramphus* are also valued food fishes. See Berkeley & Houde 1978; Watson 1996; McBride et al. 2003; McBride & Thurman 2003; Collette 2005b.

Family Exocoetidae (Flyingfishes)

Exocoetidae contains seven genera and about 50 species divided into four subfamilies (Collette et al. 1984a). Flyingfishes are a significant component of the epipelagic food chain. They feed on small zooplankton, predominantly copepods and chaetognaths. They are eaten by a large variety of predatory fishes, such as dolphinfishes, tunas, snake mackerels, and also by omastrephid squids, seabirds, and dolphins. Flyingfishes are an important fishery resource in many parts of the world (Oxenford et al. 1995). In the southeastern Caribbean, the catch of the gill-net flyingfish fishery is almost entirely the Four-wing Flyingfish *Hirundichthys affinis* (Khokiattiwong et al. 2000), so more information is available about the biology of this species than of the more oceanic *Exocoetus.*

The Exocoetinae contains the single genus *Exocoetus,* the two-wing flyingfishes, which have only the pectoral fins enlarged compared to the more advanced four-wing flyingfishes, which have both pectoral and pelvic fins enlarged. *Exocoetus* is the most oceanic genus of flyingfishes and is the only genus treated here. Five species of *Exocoetus* are recognized (Parin & Shakhovskoy 2000): circumtropical *E. volitans,* Indo-West Pacific *E. monocirrhus* Richardson, Atlantic *E. obtusirostris, E. gibbosus* Parin & Shakhovskoy from the southern subtropical Pacific, and *E. peruvianus* Parin & Shakhovskoy from off Peru and Ecuador in the eastern Pacific. The eggs of all five species are pelagic, without the filaments characteristic of other flyingfishes and most beloniform fishes. Juveniles either lack barbels or have a single chin barbel (*E. monocirrhus*).

Exocoetus obtusirostris (Günther 1866), Oceanic Two-Wing Flyingfish.   Widely distributed on both sides of the Atlantic, between 40°N and 40°S, including the Gulf of Mexico and Caribbean Sea in the western Atlantic and between 30°N and 30°S in the eastern Atlantic at water temperatures varying from 17.6–29.2°C. Maximum known size 196 mm SL. Females and males attain sexual maturity at about 140–150 mm SL and all females larger than 170 mm SL are in spawning condition during the year. Otoliths of mature fishes, including the largest specimens, constantly show one opaque and one hyaline zone, indicating that longevity may be about one year and all individuals die after the first reproductive season. Spawning is intermittent with up to 20 batches laid in five or more days; each batch consisting of 420 to 890 (mean 630) eggs. Estimated total fecundity averages 10,300 eggs. See Breder 1938; Cotten & Comyns 2005.

Exocoetus volitans (Linnaeus 1758), Tropical Two-wing Flyingfish.   The most abundant flying fish in offshore tropical waters of all oceans at 20.0 to 29.0°C. In the Atlantic Ocean common between 30 to 35°N and 25 to 30°S in the west and between 20 to 28°N and 20 to 25°S in the east. Maximum known size 189 mm SL. As with *E. obtusirostris*, all specimens of *E. volitans* below 140 mm SL are immature and all above 170 mm SL are ripe. The maximum age is 1+ year. Spawning is year round in the Caribbean Sea. Spawning intermittent, each batch numbering 327 to 418 (mean 370) eggs. Egg diameter 1.7 to 3.0 mm, no oil globule. Hatch at 3.5 to 4 mm, flexion before hatching. Illustrations of larvae 3.7 to 26.4 mm are in Watson (1996). See Erdman 1977; Watson 1996; Cotten & Comyns 2005.

ORDER PERCIFORMES

This is the largest order of fishes, containing 20 suborders, 160 families and more than 10,000 species (Nelson 2006). Epipelagic species from three suborders and five families are treated here.

Family Coryphaenidae (Dolphinfishes)

There are two cosmopolitan species of *Coryphaena* (Gibbs & Collette 1959): the Common Dolphinfish, *C. hippurus*; and the Pompano Dolphinfish, *C. equiselis*. Adult males develop a bony crest on front of head in both species but more dramatically in *C. hippurus*. Dolphinfishes are epipelagic, inhabiting open waters, but also approach the coast and follow ships. They show a high affinity for floating objects. Both feed mainly on fishes, but also on crustaceans and squids. Both species spawn in the open sea, probably approaching the coast as water temperatures rise.

Caught by trolling and on tuna longlines; also occasionally with purse seines. Highly appreciated food fishes.

Coryphaena equiselis (Linnaeus 1758), Pompano Dolphinfish.   Maximum size 75 cm FL, commonly to 50 cm FL. IGFA all-tackle record 3.86 kg. Much smaller and less important to fisheries than *C. hippurus*. Age at first maturity 3 to 4 months. Spawning is probably year-round at water temperatures greater than 21° C. Egg diameter 1.35 mm. Length at flexion 7.5 to 9.0 mm SL. Length at transformation 25 to 30 mm SL. Juveniles illustrated by Gibbs & Collette (1959), Ditty et al. (1994), and Ditty (2005). See Gibbs & Collette 1959; Palko et al. 1982; Ditty et al. 1994; Ditty 2005.

Coryphaena hippurus (Linnaeus 1758), Common Dolphinfish.   Maximum size 200 cm FL, commonly to 100 cm FL. IGFA all-tackle record 39.46 kg. Longevity up to four years but usually less than two years. Growth is extremely rapid, first year growth ranging from 1.43 to 4.71 mm/d. Age at first maturity three to four months in the Gulf of Mexico, six to seven months in the northeastern North Atlantic. Off North Carolina, males reach 50% maturity at 476 mm, 100% at 645 mm; females reach 50% maturity at 458 mm, 100% at 560 mm. Spawning is probably year-round in tropical regions with water temperatures greater than 21° C. In temperate areas such as North Carolina, peak spawning occurs from April through July. Batch spawner spawning at least two or three times per spawning period. Batch fecundity estimates in the west central Atlantic range from 58,000 to 1.5 million eggs and are strongly influenced by female size. Diameter of ripe eggs off Taiwan 1.0 to 1.6 mm, one oil globule present. Hatch at 3 mm TL, flexion at 7.5 to 9.0 mm SL. Juveniles illustrated by Gibbs & Collette (1959), Ditty et al. (1994), and Ditty (2005). A very highly appreciated sports fish and food fish, frequently marketed under the Hawaiian name "mahi-mahi." Caught by trolling and on tuna longlines. See Gibbs & Collette 1959; Beardsley 1967; Palko et al. 1982; Oxenford & Hunte 1986; Ditty et al. 1994; Oxenford 1999; Wu et al. 2001; Ditty 2005; Schwenke & Buckel 2008.

Family Echeneidae (Remoras)

The Echeneidae is divided into two subfamilies, four genera, and eight species (Gray et al. 2009). Six species are oceanic epipelagic; the two species of *Echeneis* are more coastal. They are perciform fishes with a transversely laminated, oval-shaped, cephalic disc on their head. This structure is derived from the spinous dorsal fin. Juveniles of some species have an elongate median caudal filament.

Remoras attach themselves to many different marine vertebrates including sharks, rays, larger teleost fishes, sea turtles, whales, and dolphins (O'Toole 1999). They may also attach to ships and various floating objects. Some species have a preference or specificity for certain hosts. *Remora australis* (Bennett 1839), the

Whalesucker, is only known from marine mammals. *Remora osteochir* (Cuvier 1829), the Marlinsucker, is usually found in the gill cavities of billfishes, particularly Sailfish and White Marlin. Frequently they occur in pairs, a male under one opercle, a female under the other (Strasburg 1964 and pers. obs.), perhaps increasing the probability of finding a mate. The preferred host of *Remora albescens* (Temminck & Schlegel 1850), the White Suckerfish, is the Manta Ray. Species of *Remora* are almost always captured on their host, where they may be found attached to the body, in the mouth, or in the gill cavity. Many species feed on parasitic copepods on their hosts (Cressey & Lachner 1970).

Breeding behavior of *Echeneis naucrates* has been described in an aquarium (Nakajima et al. 1987) but almost nothing else is known about their reproductive biology. Echeneid eggs have not been described. Young are free-swimming until about 40 to 80 mm SL. Development of the sucking disc occurs at early stages. Postflexion stage, larvae, and juveniles of some echeneids have been illustrated by Richards (2005a). See Strasburg 1964; Cressey & Lachner 1970; Nakajima et al. 1987; O'Toole 1999; Richards 2005a; Gray et al. 2009.

Family Xiphiidae (Swordfish)

Xiphias gladius (Linnaeus 1758), Swordfish. A single cosmopolitan epi-mesopelagic, oceanic species usually found from 45°N to 45°S in surface waters warmer than 13°C. It is primarily a warm-water species that migrates toward temperate or cold waters for feeding in the summer and back to warm waters in winter for spawning and overwintering. Maximum size 445 cm TL and about 540 kg. IGFA all-tackle record 536.15 kg. Longevity 9+ years. Females are usually larger than males and most Swordfish over 140 kg or 210 cm LJFL (lower jaw fork length) are females. First spawn at five to six years of age in the Pacific. Males reach sexual maturity at about 100 cm and females at about 70 cm in the Atlantic. Ovaries contain 2 to 5 million eggs. Egg diameter 1.6 to 1.8 mm. One oil globule, about 0.4 mm in diameter. Incubation 2.5 days. Hatching size 4.2 mm NL (notochord length). Length at flexion 12 mm. Young Swordfish lack the strong pterotic and preopercular spines characteristic of juvenile Istiophoridae. Jaws start to elongate and distinct highly modified prickle-like scales form in juveniles by 7 mm TL. Although previously thought to be naked, scales persist in adults but become embedded deep in the dermis as the stratum spongiosum increases in thickness above the scale. Illustrations of juveniles are in Arata (1954), Sun (1960), Palko et al. (1981), Potthoff & Kelley (1982), Collette et al. (1984b), and Richards (2005c). A highly important food and game species. The North Atlantic stock was rated as "Endangered" in the IUCN Red List based on a 1996 assessment (IUCN 2009), but seems to be recovering. See Arata 1954; Sun 1960; Palko et al. 1981; Potthoff & Kelley 1982; Collette et al. 1984b; Nakamura 1985; Govoni et al. 2004; Richards 2005c; Wang et al. 2006.

Family Istiophoridae (Billfishes)

Billfishes include nine species of epipelagic oceanic fishes: *Istiophorus* (monotypic), *Istiompax* (monotypic), *Makaira* (monotypic), *Kajikia* (two species), and *Tetrapturus* (four species) following Collette et al. (2006). Billfishes are at or near the apex of pelagic food webs, have broad diets, grow very rapidly, have high fecundity and, in some cases show long-distance migrations (Kitchell et al. 2006). More information is available on the reproductive biology of billfishes than for most of the fishes previously discussed in this chapter. Synopses on the biology of billfish species are included in Shomura and Williams (1975). Females are usually larger than males. Oviparous, buoyant eggs, pelagic larvae. Spawning: warm months. Fecundity: 0.75 to 19 million eggs, increasing with size. Age: 9 to 12+ years. All but the smallest young billfishes are quite easily identified to family because the snout starts to elongate by 3 mm notochord length although it does not take on the adult spear shape until a length of 50 mm or longer. However, identification of larvae and juveniles to species is extremely difficult (Richards & Luthy 2005).

All are important sport fishes and many are also taken in long-lining operations and used for food. Several species are under intense fishing pressure and since the early 1980s, stock assessments have indicated that Atlantic stocks of some billfishes are overfished (Restrepo et al. 2003; Die 2006). Size limitations, encouragement of catch-and-release sport fishing, and recommendations for using circle hooks instead of J-hooks are measures designed to increase survival in catch-and-release sport fishing and may be instrumental in their successful management.

Istiophorus platypterus (Shaw & Nodder 1792), Sailfish.   Widely distributed in tropical and temperate waters. Maximum size more than 340 cm TL and 100 kg. IGFA all-tackle record 100.24 kg (Pacific), 64 kg (Atlantic). Longevity 11+ years, but the sport fishery in Florida is largely dependent on fish between 6 and 18 months old. No external sexual dimorphism but females grow larger than males. Proportion of females in the catch off Taiwan increased with size as LJFL (lower jaw to fork length) increased beyond 145 cm and reached nearly 100% at sizes greater than 227 LJFL. Estimated mean LJFL at sexual maturity of females is 166 cm off Taiwan; smallest mature female, 162 cm LJFL. Spawning occurs with males and females swimming in pairs or with two or three males chasing a single female. Spawning takes place throughout the year in tropical waters. Off southeast Florida, presence of three distinct groups of maturing ovocytes in the ovaries of ripe females shows that ovocyte development is asynchronous, resulting in fractional or multiple spawning. Fecundity 1 to 19.5 million eggs, sharply increasing with female size. Egg diameter 1.3 mm, one oil globule. Length at flexion about 6 mm. Juveniles are illustrated by Gehringer (1956, 1970), Sun (1960), Ueyanagi (1964), Beardsley et al. (1975), Fritzsche (1978), Collette et al. (1984b), and Richards & Luthy (2005).

Taken as bycatch by tuna longliners and also with surface driftnets and by trolling and harpooning but more important as a valued sports fish. See Gehringer 1956, 1970; Sun 1960; Ueyanagi 1964; Beardsley et al. 1975; Fritzsche 1978; Collette et al. 1984b; Nakamura 1985; de Sylva & Breder 1997; Richards & Luthy 2005; Chiang et al. 2006; Wang et al. 2006.

Istiompax indica (Cuvier 1832), Black Marlin.   Found throughout the tropical and subtropical waters of the Indo-Pacific and extending a short distance into the South Atlantic. Maximum size more than 448 cm TL and 700 kg. IGFA all-tackle record 707.61 kg. Longevity unknown. Males and females indistinguishable externally but females attain a much larger size. Sex ratio varies with area and season. In Taiwan waters, all Black Marlin greater than 270 cm LJFL were females. Length of males at first maturity about 140 cm, 230 cm for females. Age at first maturity not known. Intensive spawning occurs in the Coral Sea, especially during October and November. Water temperatures about 27 to 28°C during spawning. A large fish (presumably a female) seen followed by several smaller fish (presumably males) off Cairns. Egg counts of ripe females totaled about 40 million. Juveniles illustrated by Ueyanagi (1960, 1964) and Nakamura (1975). Caught by tuna longliners and also a very important sports fish off Peru, Ecuador, and northeastern Australia. See Ueyanagi 1960, 1964; Nakamura 1975, 1985; Wang et al. 2006; Matsumoto & Bayliff 2008.

Kajikia albida (Poey 1860), White Marlin.   Found throughout warm waters of the Atlantic from 45°N to 45°S including the Gulf of Mexico, Caribbean Sea, and the Mediterranean. Maximum size over 280 cm TL and over 82 kg. IGFA all-tackle record 82.5 kg. Longevity 12+ years. No apparent sexual dimorphism but females attain larger sizes than males. Length at first maturity 130 cm orbit to fork length or about 20 kg in the female. Spawning areas are in deep-blue oceanic waters, generally at high surface temperatures (20 to 29°C). Migrates into subtropical waters to spawn with peak spawning in spring and early summer, March through June. Apparently spawn once a year. Eggs undescribed. Length at flexion about 6 mm. Juveniles illustrated by Gehringer (1956), Fritzsche (1978), and Richards & Luthy (2005). Over 90% of the reported landings are attributed to longline fisheries and there are also important directed recreational fisheries (Restrepo et al. 2003). Despite voluntary conservation measures, mandated minimum size limits and wide acceptance of catch-and-release, White Marlin are currently considered to be severely overfished (Restrepo et al. 2003; Jesien et al. 2006). A recent petition to declare White Marlin an endangered species in the United States was not accepted (White Marlin Review Team 2002). See Gehringer 1956; Mather et al. 1975; Fritzsche 1978; Nakamura 1985; de Sylva & Breder 1997; Restrepo et al. 2003; Richards & Luthy 2005; Jesien et al. 2006.

Kajikia audax (Philippi 1887), Striped Marlin.   Latitudinally the most widely distributed billfish occurring throughout tropical, subtropical, and temperate waters of the Pacific and Indian oceans. Maximum size exceeds 350 cm TL and 200 kg. IGFA all-tackle record 224.1 kg. Longevity 12+ years. Little size difference between males and females but proportion of females increases with size in Taiwan waters. Size at first maturity estimated to be between 140 and 160 cm eye-fork length around Taiwan and off east Africa. Ripe Striped Marlin found from May through December in the southern Gulf of California, larvae at temperatures of 27.5 to 31.5°C. Fecundity 11 to 29 million eggs. Ovarian eggs from New Zealand averaged 0.85 mm in diameter shortly before spawning so ovulated eggs should exceed 1 mm in diameter. Larvae primarily found during late spring and early summer in both hemispheres of the Pacific. Larvae in four spatially discrete regions: eastern North Pacific, eastern South Pacific, western North Pacific, and central South Pacific, suggesting spawning site fidelity. Larvae illustrated by Ueyanagi (1964), Ueyanagi & Wares (1975), and Hyde et al. (2006). An important commercial and recreational resource throughout its range, with the largest catches taken as bycatch by the pelagic longline fisheries targeting tunas. See Ueyanagi 1964; Ueyanagi & Wares 1975; Nakamura 1985; González-Armas et al. 2006; Hyde et al. 2006; Wang et al. 2006; McDowell & Graves 2008.

Makaira nigricans (Lacepède 1802), Blue Marlin.   Cosmopolitan in tropical and temperate waters. Latitudinal range varies seasonally and extends from 45°N to 35°S in the Atlantic, 48°N to 48°S in the Pacific. Maximum size over 906 kg and 420 cm TL in the Pacific, smaller in the Atlantic. IGFA all-tackle record 636 kg. Longevity 17 years. Females grow larger than males; around the Bonin Islands, all fish over 200 cm eye-fork length were females; in Taiwan waters all over 180 cm eye-fork length or 280 cm LJFL were females. Estimated size at first maturity 130 cm eye-fork length for males, 180 cm for females. Make seasonal north-south migrations. Ripe or subripe individuals found from March to October in the Caribbean, May to September in the western Pacific. Spawn between April and September in the northeast Atlantic at temperatures between 26 and 29°C. Multiple spawners, spawning every two to three days on average. Batch fecundity 2.11 to 13.5 million eggs. Eggs within ovary or intra-ovarian 1 mm in diameter. Flexion at about 6 mm. Juveniles illustrated by Gehringer (1956), Ueyanagi (1964), Fritzsche (1978), and Richards & Luthy (2005). More than 73% of reported landings are incidental to large offshore longline fisheries; other major fisheries are the directed recreational fisheries of the United States and other countries (Restrepo et al. 2003). See Gehringer 1956; Ueyanagi 1964; Rivas 1975; Erdman 1977; Fritzsche 1978; Collette et al. 1984b; Nakamura 1985; de Sylva & Breder 1997; Restrepo et al. 2003; Richards & Luthy 2005; Wang et al. 2006; Sun et al. 2009.

Tetrapturus angustirostris (Tanaka 1915), Shortbill Spearfish. Distributed throughout the tropical and temperate waters of the Pacific and Indian Oceans. Maximum size about 2 m and 52 kg in weight. IGFA all-tackle record 36.8 kg. Females may average slightly larger than males. Spawning is believed to occur mainly during winter months, especially in warm offshore currents with surface temperatures of about 25°C. Diameters of shed eggs range from 1.3 to 1.6 mm, mean 1.442 mm, in the equatorial western Indian Ocean. Illustration of larvae provided by Sun (1960), Ueyanagi (1964), and Kikawa (1975). No special fisheries but caught incidentally by tuna longliners and rarely by trolling or sport fishing. See Sun 1960; Ueyanagi 1964; Kikawa 1975; Nakamura 1985.

Tetrapturus belone (Rafinesque 1810), Mediterranean Spearfish. Distribution limited to the Mediterranean Sea. Maximum size exceeds 240 cm in body length and 70 kg in weight. IGFA all-tackle record 41.2 kg. Nothing is known about the biology of this species. Probably spawns in winter or spring. Pelagic eggs from the Straits of Messina averaged 1.48 mm in diameter with a single oil globule. Taken at the surface by harpoons, longlines, driftnets and set nets incidental to fishing for swordfish, bluefin tuna, and albacore. See de Sylva 1975; Nakamura 1985.

Tetrapturus georgii (Lowe 1841), Roundscale Spearfish. Originally described from Madeira and reported from several other eastern Atlantic localities but only recently known with certainty from the western Atlantic as well (Shivji et al. 2006). Maximum size at least 160 cm body length and 21.5 kg weight. IGFA all-tackle record 31.2 kg. Little is known of the reproductive biology of this species. Taken by sports fishermen along with White Marlin. See Nakamura 1985; Shivji et al. 2006.

Tetrapturus pfluegeri (Robins & de Sylva 1963), Longbill Spearfish. Widely distributed in Atlantic offshore waters from approximately 40°N to 35°S. Maximum size exceeds 200 cm in body length and 58 kg in weight. IGFA all-tackle record 58 kg. Longevity probably four years. No sexual dimorphism reported. First spawning probably occurs at the end of the first year and few females apparently survive beyond a second spawning. Females probably spawn once a year. Spawning takes place throughout wide areas of the tropical and subtropical Atlantic from late November to early May. Eggs undescribed. Drawing of a 368-mm juvenile included in Robins (1975). Taken as bycatch by tuna longliners and also by sports fishermen. See Robins 1975; Nakamura 1985; de Sylva & Breder 1997; Richards & Luthy 2005.

Family Scombridae (Mackerels, Tunas, and Bonitos)

The Scombridae contains 15 genera and 51 species (Collette et al. 2001) and is divided into two subfamilies: Gasterochismatinae, which contains only the peculiar southern ocean *Gasterochisma melampus*; and Scombrinae. On the basis of internal osteological characters, Collette and Chao (1975) and Collette & Russo (1985) divided the Scombrinae into two groups of tribes. The more primitive mackerels (Scombrini) and Spanish mackerels (Scomberomorini) are characterized by (i) a distinct notch in the hypural plate that supports the caudal fin rays, (ii) absence of a bony support for the median fleshy keel (when present), and (iii) preural vertebrae centra not greatly shortened as compared to those of the other vertebrae. Bonitos (tribe Sardini) are a group of four genera and seven species that are intermediate between Spanish mackerels (tribe Scomberomorini) and higher tunas (tribe Thunnini). They lack any trace of a specialized subcutaneous vascular system or dorsally projecting cartilaginous ridges on the tongue, and the bony structure underlying their median fleshy caudal peduncle keel is incompletely developed; they also lack the prominent paired frontoparietal fenestra on the dorsal surface of the skull characteristic of most Thunnini. The Thunnini contains five genera, four of which (all except *Allothunnus*) are unique among bony fishes in having countercurrent heat exchanger systems that allow them to retain metabolic heat so that the fish is warmer than the surrounding water. Three genera of this tribe (*Auxis, Euthynnus,* and *Katsuwonus*) and the yellowfin group of *Thunnus* have central and lateral heat exchangers, while the specialized bluefin group of *Thunnus* have lost the central heat exchanger and evolved very well-developed lateral heat exchangers (Graham & Dickson 2000).

Scombrids are swift, epipelagic or epi-mesopelagic predators; some species occur in coastal waters, others far from shore. Spanish mackerels, bonitos, and tunas feed on larger prey, including small fishes, crustaceans, and squids. The main predators of smaller scombrids are other predacious fishes, particularly large tunas and billfishes. Scombrids are dioecious (separate sexes) and most display little or no sexual dimorphism in structure or color pattern. Reports of courting behavior in scombrids are rare (Magnuson & Prescott 1966; Iversen et al. 1970). Males of many species attain larger sizes than females. Batch spawning of most species takes place in tropical and subtropical waters. The eggs are pelagic and hatch into planktonic larvae. Mackerels and tunas support very important commercial and recreational fisheries as well as substantial artisanal fisheries throughout the tropical and temperate waters of the world. Catches in cold and warm temperate waters predominate over tropical catches, with more than half of the world catch being taken in the northwestern Pacific, the northeastern Atlantic, and the southeastern Pacific. Many species of tunas and mackerels are the target of long-distance fisheries. The principal fishing methods used for fish schooling near the surface include purse seining, driftnetting, hook and line/bait boat fishing, and trolling; standard and deep longlining are used for (usually bigger) fish occurring at least temporarily in deeper water. Recreational fishing methods involve mostly surface trolling and pole-and-line fishing, while numerous artisanal fisheries deploy a great variety of gear including bag nets, cast nets, lift nets, gill (drift) nets, beach seines, hook-and-line, handlines, harpoons, specialized traps, and fish corrals.

Early life-history pattern: dioecious; usually no sexual dimorphism in external characters (except size); sex ratio does not deviate significantly from the expected 1:1 ratio; oviparous; asynchronous oocyte development; multiple or batch spawners; epipelagic or mesopelagic; spawning dependent on warm water temperature, usually at least 24°C (Schaefer 2001). Larvae are characterized by large heads, triangular gut, and large jaws but are very difficult to identify to species (Richards 2005b).

Acanthocybium solandri (Cuvier 1832), Wahoo.   Tropical and subtropical waters of all oceans including the Caribbean and Mediterranean seas. Nuclear and mitochondrial DNA show extensive sharing of haplotypes across the Wahoo's entire global range and analyses are unable to detect significant structure (Theisen et al. 2008). Maximum size 210 cm FL and more than 83 kg. IGFA all-tackle record 83.46 kg. Females grow larger than males. A fast growing species with a high mortality. Longevity nine years. Spawning seems to extend over a long period of time, in the western Atlantic from at least May to October. In the northern Gulf of Mexico, 50% sexual maturity in males is reached before 935 mm FL, probably at an age of one year; in females, size at 50% maturity is approximately 1,020 mm FL, at an estimated age of two years. Females are multiple batch spawners and fecundity is quite high, a mean batch fecundity of 1,146,395 ±291,210 eggs/female. An individual female might spawn every two to six days, a total of 20 to 62 times during a spawning season, resulting in a total fecundity for a five-year-old female of 30–92.8 million eggs. Mature eggs 0.8 mm in diameter. Hatching at 2.5 mm NL, flexion at about 6 mm. Drawings of larvae in Wollam (1969), Fritzsche (1978), Collette et al. (1984b) and Richards (2005b). There do not appear to be organized fisheries for Wahoo in most areas but they are targeted in the western Atlantic by both commercial and recreational fisheries and are highly appreciated as a food fish. See Wollam 1969; Erdman 1977; Fritzsche 1978; Collette & Nauen 1983; Collette et al. 1984b; Brown-Peterson et al. 2000; Oxenford et al. 2003; Richards 2005b; McBride et al. 2008; Theisen et al. 2008.

Allothunnus fallai (Serventy 1948), Slender Tuna.   Circumglobal in the Southern Ocean from 20°S to 50°S. Maximum size 96 cm FL and 12 kg. IGFA all-tackle record 11.85 kg. Size at first maturity 71.5 cm FL. Active spawning is presumed to take place during the summer months over a wide range of the temperate Indian and South Pacific oceans. Fecundity unknown. Five larvae probably referable to *Allothunnus fallai* were described and illustrated by Watanabe et al. (1966). Slender tuna are taken incidentally by tuna longliners fishing for Southern Bluefin Tuna and by purse seiners. See Watanabe et al. 1966; Collette & Nauen 1983; Graham & Dickson 2000.

Auxis rochei (Risso 1810), Bullet Tuna.   Cosmopolitan in warm waters. Maximum size 50 cm FL, common to 35 cm FL. IGFA all-tackle record 1.84 kg. Longevity five years. Males and females of equal length. Length at first maturity in the Philippines 17 cm. Length at 50% maturity of both sexes off India 24 cm, 18.8 cm in the Philippines. The spawning season varies from region to region at sea surface temperatures of 24°C or higher. In the Gulf of Mexico, peaks of batch spawning are reported from March to April; from June to August in coastal waters from Cape Hatteras to Cuba; and in the Straits of Florida, spawning begins in February. Fecundity estimates range between 31,000 and 162,800 eggs per spawning event correlated with the size of the female. Hydration occurs between 1100 and 1300 hrs, ovulation at about 1500 hrs, followed by spawning. Egg diameter 0.82 to 0.88 mm, one oil globule. Hatch at 2.14 mm NL, flexion at approximately 6 mm SL. Illustrations of larvae in Fritzsche (1978) and Richards (2005b). Caught by pole and line and as bycatch in a variety of gear including gill nets. Particularly important in the Philippines, Japan, and the Mediterranean Sea. See Yoshida & Nakamura 1965; Rodríguez-Roda 1966; Fritzsche 1978; Uchida 1981; Collette & Nauen 1983; Grudtsev 1992; Yesaki & Arce 1994; Collette & Aadland 1996; Niiya 2001a, b; Schaefer 2001; Richards 2005b.

Auxis thazard (Lacepède 1800), Frigate Tuna.   Probably cosmopolitan in warm waters but relatively few documented occurrences in the Atlantic Ocean. Maximum size 58 cm FL. IGFA all-tackle record 1.72 kg. Longevity four years. Smallest maturing female off the west coast of Thailand 31 to 33 cm FL. Length at 50% maturity in the Gulf of Thailand 34 to 37 cm FL. In the southern Indian Ocean, spawning extends from August to April, north of the equator from January to April at sea surface temperatures of 24°C or higher. Fecundity estimates range from 78,000 to 1.37 million eggs in 31.5- to 44.2-cm females. Egg diameter 0.84 to 0.92 mm, one oil globule. Hatch at 2.32 mm NL, flexion at approximately 6 mm SL. Illustrations of larvae 4.5 mm NL to 25.0 mm SL in Richards (2005b). Caught by pole and line and as by catch in a variety of gear including gill nets. Particularly important in the Philippines and Japan. See Yoshida & Nakamura 1965; Uchida 1981; Collette & Nauen 1983; Grudtsev & Korolevich 1986; Yesaki & Arce 1994; Collette & Aadland 1996; Schaefer 2001; Richards 2005b.

Gasterochisma melampus (Richardson 1845), Butterfly Kingfish.   Circumglobal in southern temperate waters, mostly between 35°S and 50°S. Maximum size 195 cm FL. Originally described in three different genera: as *Gasterochisma melampus* based on a 181-mm juvenile from New Zealand; as *Chenogaster holmbergi* based on a 132-cm adult from Uruguay; and as *Lepidothynnus huttoni* based on a 167-cm adult from New Zealand. One reason for this is that earlier workers were not aware of the dramatic allometric growth changes, particularly in the length of the pelvic fin (Ito et al. 1994). Reproductive biology, eggs, and larvae unknown. Taken as bycatch by tuna longliners fishing for Southern Bluefin Tuna. See Collette & Nauen 1983; Kohno 1984; Ito et al. 1994.

Katsuwonus pelamis (Linnaeus 1758), Skipjack Tuna.   Cosmopolitan in tropical and warm temperate waters within the 15° isotherms. Maximum size 108 cm FL and 34.5 kg. IGFA all-tackle record 20.54 kg. Longevity at least eight years. Sex ratio about 1:1, but fisheries that rely on young, immature fish are dominated by females; older captured fish are mostly male. Size at first maturity 40 to 55 cm FL, depending on area. Spawn several times per season. Spawn in batches at sea surface temperatures of 24°C to 29°C throughout the year in the Caribbean and other equatorial waters, in the Atlantic, Pacific and Indian oceans, and from spring to early fall in subtropical waters, with the spawning season becoming shorter as distance from the equator increases. Models of migration have been proposed, especially from the central Pacific into the eastern Pacific. Apparent courtship involved one fish following another with its snout close to the caudal fin of the lead fish, the following fish displaying dark vertical bars, and the lead fish wobbling from side to side; similar to observations made in large tanks of Pacific Bonito, *Sarda chiliensis,* and Yellowfin Tuna (Magnuson & Prescott 1966; Margulies et al. 2007). Fecundity increases with size but is highly variable, the number of eggs per season in females 41 to 87 cm FL ranges from 80,000 to 2,000,000. Diameter of eggs still within the ovary 0.80 to 1.17 mm, with a single oil globule, 0.22 to 0.45 mm. Hatching at 2.3 to 3.0 mm NL, flexion at 5.0 to 7.0 mm SL. Illustrations of larvae in Sun (1960), Fritzsche (1978); Ambrose (1996), and Richards (2005b). Skipjack make up 59% of the commercial tuna catch and are mostly canned as light meat tuna. They are taken at the surface mostly with purse seines and pole-and-line gear. Majkowski (2007) categorized most stocks as "Moderately Exploited"; Joseph (2009b) concluded that overfishing of Skipjack stocks was not occurring and that the stocks were not overfished. See Sun 1960; Iversen et al. 1970; Erdman 1977; Fritzsche 1978; Collette & Nauen 1983; Matsumoto et al. 1984; Wild & Hampton 1994; Pagavino & Gaertner 1995; Ambrose 1996; Schaefer 2001; Richards 2005b; Majkowski 2007; Joseph 2009a, b.

Thunnus alalunga (Bonnaterre 1788), Albacore.   Cosmopolitan in tropical and temperate waters of all oceans including the Mediterranean Sea but not at the surface between 10°N and 10°S. Maximum size 127 cm FL. IGFA all-tackle record 40.0 kg. Longevity 13 years. Immature Albacore (<80 cm) generally have a sex ratio of 1:1 but males predominate in catches of mature fish. Maturity attained at about 90 to 94 cm FL for females, 94 to 97 cm FL for males. Spawning occurs at sea surface temperatures of 24°C or higher. Use of combined Japanese and U.S. tagging data confirm the frequent westward movement of young Albacore and infrequent eastward movements, in the North Pacific. This corresponds to Alba-core life history in which immature fish recruit into fisheries in the western and eastern Pacific and then gradually move nearer to their spawning grounds in the central and western Pacific before maturing. Fecundity increases with size but there is no clear correlation between fork length, ovary weight, and number of eggs. A 20 kg female may produce between 2 and 3 million eggs per season, re-leased in at least two batches. Egg diameter 0.84 to 0.94 mm, one oil globule, 0.24 mm in diameter. Hatching at 2.60 mm NL, flexion at about 6.0 mm SL. Lar-vae illustrated by Fritzsche (1978) and Richards (2005b). An important fishery exists for this species, which is mainly marketed as canned white meat tuna, the most expensive canned tuna. They are caught by longlining, live-bait fishing, purse seining, and trolling. The North Atlantic stock was considered "Vulnera-ble" and the South Atlantic stock "Critically Endangered" based on 1996 assess-ments (IUCN 2009). Majkowski (2007) considered the North Atlantic stock to be "Overexploited"; Joseph (2009b) feels that this stock is in an overfished state and that overfishing is currently taking place. Majkowski (2007) considered the In-dian Ocean and North Pacific stocks to be "Fully Exploited." See Fritzsche 1978; Collette & Nauen 1983; Chang et al. 1993; Labelle et al. 1993; Richards 2005b; Majkowski 2007; Ichinokawa et al. 2008; IUCN 2009; Joseph 2009b.

Thunnus albacares (Bonnaterre 1788), Yellowfin Tuna.   Widespread throughout tropical and temperate waters of the world. Maximum size over 200 cm FL. IGFA all-tackle record 176.35 kg. Longevity at least six years. Smallest mature individuals in the Pacific off the Philippines and Central America in the 50 to 60 cm size group at an age of 12 to 15 months. Length at 50% maturity in the eastern Pacific 69 cm for males, 92 cm for females. Spawning occurs throughout the year in the core areas of distribution at sea surface temperatures of 24°C or higher, but peaks are observed in the northern and southern summer months respectively. Spawning occurs almost entirely at night between 2200 and 0600 hrs. Reproductively active Yellowfin spawn almost daily. Courtship behavior in aquaria consisted of one to three males follow-ing a female and often flashing vertical bars on the body. Estimated average batch fecundity 2.5 million ova or 67.3 ova/g of body weight. Batch fecundity estimates in the eastern Pacific ranged from 162,918 ova for a 1180-mm female to 8,026,026 ova for a 1460-mm female. Egg diameter 0.90 to 1.04 mm, one oil globule. Incubation 24 to 38 hours at 26°C. Hatching at 2.6 to 2.7 mm TL, flexion at 4.5 to 6.1 mm. Il-lustrations of larvae and juveniles in Sun (1960), Fritzsche (1978), Ambrose (1996), and Richards (2005b). Yellowfin is the second most important species of tuna for canning, constituting 24.0% of the tuna catch, and is the primary target of the purse-seine fishery in the eastern Pacific. They are also taken primarily by pole-and-line fishing. Considered of "Least Concern" based on a 1996 assessment (IUCN 2009) and "Fully Exploited" by Majkowski (2007), but Joseph (2009b) considered the Indian Ocean stock as being overfished with overfishing currently taking place. See Sun 1960; Fritzsche 1978; Collette & Nauen 1983; Ambrose 1996; Schaefer 1998, 2001; Richards 2005b; Majkowski 2007; Margulies et al. 2007; IUCN 2009; Joseph 2009a, b.

Thunnus atlanticus (Lesson 1830), Blackfin Tuna.   Confined to the western North Atlantic from Cape Cod to southern Brazil in waters of at least 20°C. Maximum size 110 cm FL. IGFA all-tackle record 22.39 kg. Longevity eight years. Males grow larger than females. Length of females at 50% maturity 49.8 cm FL and for males 52.1 cm FL off northeastern Brazil; both sexes mature at age two years. Around Florida, the spawning season extends from April to November with a peak in May, while in the Gulf of Mexico, spawning apparently lasts from June to September. Eggs unknown. Length at flexion about 6 mm SL. Illustrations of larvae and juveniles in Fritzsche (1978) and Richards (2005b). The largest fisheries for Blackfin Tuna are a live-bait and pole fishery off the southeastern coast of Cuba and a handline artisanal fishery off northeastern Brazil but there are also important sports fisheries in Florida and the Bahamas. See Erdman 1977; Fritzsche 1978; Collette & Nauen 1983; Neilson et al. 1994; Freire et al. 2005; Richards 2005b.

Thunnus maccoyii (Castelnau 1872), Southern Bluefin Tuna.   Found throughout the Southern Ocean between 30 and 50°S but migrating to warm waters between northwest Australia and Indonesia for spawning. Maximum size 225 cm FL and 200 kg. IGFA all-tackle record 158 kg. Longevity 20+ years. Sex ratio in catches shows that as juveniles, females outnumber males; the situation is reversed in adults. Maturity can occur at 120 cm FL but more commonly at 130 cm (about eight years old). Age at first maturity five to seven years at 110 to 125 cm FL. Size at 50% maturity 152 cm FL. The spawning season extends throughout the southern summer from about September/October to March at water surface temperatures in excess of 24°C. Once females start spawning, they appear to spawn daily. Migration pattern shown in Caton (1994). An asynchronous indeterminate spawner with annual batch fecundity of 57 ova/g body weight. Fecundity of a 158-cm female with gonads weighing about 1.7 kg each was estimated at about 14 to 15 million eggs. Intraovarian eggs 0.66 to 1.10 mm in diameter with one or two large oil globules. A very important commercial species especially off Australia. The meat is highly prized for the sashimi markets of Japan. Considered "Critically Endangered" by a 1996 assessment (IUCN 2009), "Depleted" by Majkowski (2007), and seriously overfished by Joseph (2009a). See Collette & Nauen 1983; Thorogood 1986; Caton 1994; Farley & Davis 1998; Schaefer 2001; Majkowski 2007; IUCN 2009; Joseph 2009a.

Thunnus obesus (Lowe 1839), Bigeye Tuna.   Worldwide in tropical waters of the Atlantic, Indian, and Pacific oceans but absent from the Mediterranean Sea. Maximum size over 200 cm FL. IGFA all-tackle record 197.31 kg. Maximum age 16 years, although 80% of fish caught in Australia were less than five years. Males tend to predominate in catches over the entire size range but particularly at larger sizes. Minimum length at maturity for females 80 to 102 cm FL and predicted length at 50% maturity 102 to 135 cm in different regions. In the eastern and central Pacific, spawning has been recorded between 15°N and 15°S and between 105° and 175°W during most months when sea surface temperatures exceeded 24°C, with a peak from April through September in the northern hemisphere and between January and March in the southern hemisphere. Spawning is primarily at night between 1900 and 0400 hr. The average mature female spawns every 2.6 days. The estimated mean batch fecundity is 24 ova/g body weight. The number of eggs per spawning has been estimated at 2.9 to 6.3 million. Eggs 1.03 to 1.08 mm in diameter with one oil droplet 0.23 to 0.24 mm in diameter. Length at flexion about 6 mm SL. Illustrations of larvae in Fritzsche (1978) and Richards (2005b). An extremely valuable fishery resource especially for the sashimi market. In the Pacific, Bigeye are exploited by longliners from 40°N to 40°S and by purse seiners from 10°N to 20°S. Bigeye were considered "Vulnerable" but the Pacific stock was considered "Endangered" by a 1996 assessment (IUCN 2009). Majkowski (2007) considered the Atlantic and Indian Ocean stocks to be "Fully Exploited" and both Pacific stocks to be "Overexploited." Joseph (2009b) considered the eastern Pacific stock to be overfished and the Atlantic stock slightly overfished. See Fritzsche 1978; Collette & Nauen 1983; Miyabe 1994; Schaefer 2001; Richards 2005b; Schaefer et al. 2005; Farley et al. 2006; Majkowski 2007; IUCN 2009; Joseph 2009b.

Thunnus orientalis (Temminck & Schlegel 1844), Pacific Bluefin Tuna.   Known from the Gulf of Alaska to southern California and Baja California in the eastern Pacific; from Sakhalin Island in the southern Sea of Okhotsk south to the southeastern Australia and New Zealand in the western Pacific; most abundant near Japan. Maximum length 300 cm FL and maximum weight 555 kg. IGFA all-tackle record 325 kg. Longevity 16 years. Spawning occurs between Japan and the Philippines in April, May, and June, off southern Honshu in July, and in the Sea of Japan in August. A model of migration is presented by Bayliff (1994). The sex ratio is about 1:1. Size at first maturity is 150 cm FL and 60 kg at an age of five years. Batch fecundity increases with length, from about 5 million eggs at 190 cm FL to about 25 million eggs at 240 cm FL. The linear relationship between batch fecundity F and fork length L (cm) is

$$F = 3.2393 \times 10^5 \times L - 5.2057 \times 10^7$$

Broodstock of Pacific Bluefin that were artificially hatched and reared, spawned in captivity. The resulting eggs hatched and the young were reared to the juvenile stage (Sawada et al. 2005). A highly valuable species. See Collette & Nauen 1983; Bayliff 1994; Schaefer 2001; Sawada et al. 2005; Chen et al. 2006.

Thunnus thynnus (Linnaeus 1758), Atlantic Bluefin Tuna.   Genetic differentiation and homing to breeding sites indicates that there are two reproductively isolated stocks although there is considerable transatlantic migration of individuals from both stocks. The western Atlantic stock is found from Labrador and Newfoundland south into the Gulf of Mexico and Caribbean Sea; the eastern Atlantic stock occurs from off Norway south to the Canary Islands and the Mediterranean Sea. Maximum size over 300 cm FL, common to 200 cm. IGFA all-tackle record 678.58 kg. Longevity at least 35 years. Maturity is reached at about four or five years and 115 to 121 cm FL in the Mediterranean Sea. Maturity is delayed in the Gulf of Mexico to age eight to ten years and 200 cm FL. The western Atlantic stock spawns in the Gulf of Mexico from mid-April to early July at temperatures of 22.6 to 27.5°C starting at age eight although most fish first spawn closer to age 12. The eastern Atlantic stock spawns in the Mediterranean Sea from May to August at temperatures of 22.5 to 25.5°C starting at age three and full recruitment is reached by age five. There are distinct behaviors during the spawning period, most noticeably changes in diving times and depths. Estimated relative batch fecundity is greater (more than 90 ova/g of body weight) than estimated for other tunas in the genus *Thunnus*. Egg diameter 1.00 to 1.12 mm, one oil globule, 0.25 to 0.28 mm. Hatching size 2.0 to 3.0 mm TL, flexion at about 6 mm SL. Illustrations of larvae in Fritzsche (1978) and Richards (2005b). A highly valued species for the Japanese sashimi markets that has led to severe overfishing in both the eastern and western Atlantic. Also an important gamefish, particularly in the United States and Canada. The eastern Atlantic stock was considered "Endangered" and the western Atlantic stock "Critically Endangered" by 1996 assessments (IUCN 2009). The two stocks were considered "Overexploited" and "Depleted," respectively by Majkowski (2007), seriously overfished by Joseph (2009a), and "Critically Endangered" by MacKenzie et al. (2009). High priority needs to be given to protecting spawning adults in the Gulf of Mexico and Mediterranean Sea. Large adults in the northern foraging region in the Gulf of Maine and Gulf of St. Lawrence also need protection because this region represents a critical refugium for the largest fishes, so-called western "giants." See Fritzsche 1978; Collette & Nauen 1983; Sissenwine et al. 1998; Corriero et al. 2003; Richards 2005b; Majkowski 2007; Rooker et al. 2007, 2008; Boustany et al. 2008; IUCN 2009; Joseph 2009a; MacKenzie et al. 2009.

Thunnus tonggol (Bleeker 1851), Longtail Tuna.   An epipelagic species that is widely distributed along the tropical shores of the Indo-West Pacific. Maximum size about 130 cm FL. IGFA all-tackle record 35.9 kg. Longevity at least five years. Sex ratio 1:1. Probably spawn more than once a year, perhaps in two spawning seasons in the Gulf of Thailand. Smallest mature female in Thailand was 43 cm FL. Fifty percent of females in the Gulf of Thailand were mature at 39.6 cm. Long-tail Tuna from Southeast Asia mature at a smaller size than fish from Australia-Papua New Guinea. Fecundity of fish ranging in size from 43.8 to 49.1 cm varied from 1.2 to 1.9 million eggs. No information available on fertilized eggs but intra-ovarian eggs had a diameter of 1.09 mm and an oil globule of 0.31 to 0.33 mm. There are two major fishing grounds for Longtail Tuna, one off the South China Sea coast of Thailand and Malaysia and the other off countries bordering the North Arabian Sea. Catch of this species is increasing in many areas but landings are frequently confused with Yellowfin Tuna in some regions. Caught mostly with purse seines and gillnets, not with longlines. See Collette & Nauen 1983; Yesaki 1994.

Family Luvaridae (Louvar)

A monotypic cosmopolitan family found in tropical and temperate waters and containing only *Luvarus imperialis* (Rafinesque 1810), Louvar. This is a large, heavily built, blunt-snouted species reaching 2 m TL, commonly 1 m TL. It feeds on jellyfish, ctenophores, and salps and has an extremely long gut, 5 to 11 times standard length. Apparently solitary. Spawns in late spring and summer in the Mediterranean. Estimated total number of eggs from a 173.5-cm FL female from the Gulf of Mexico is 47.5 million. Eggs undescribed. Hatching at 3.5 mm or smaller. Flexion at 6 to 7 mm, length at transformation 9 to 10 mm, larvae pelagic. Pelagic juveniles infrequently collected in coastal waters between 40°N and 90°S. Juveniles go through a dramatic metamorphosis in the shape and size of the head and fins leading to the names hystricinella, astrodermella, and luvarella for three growth stages of juveniles. Occasionally captured with purse seines. See Gottschall & Fitch 1968; Topp & Giradin 1971; Tyler et al. 1989; Farooqui et al. 2005.

ORDER TETRAODONTIFORMES

This order contains the most highly evolved fishes with nine families with about 350 species (Nelson 2006).

Family Molidae (Ocean Sunfishes)

Three cosmopolitan species in three monotypic genera: *Mola mola* (Linnaeus 1758), *Ranzania laevis* (Pénnant 1776), and *Masturus lanceolatus* (Liénard 1840). These highly specialized epipelagic fishes reach enormous sizes of more than 2 m TL and 1000 kg). Ocean sunfishes are considered to be among the most fecund of bony fishes, spawning large, spherical pelagic eggs that measure 1.42 to 1.8 mm in diameter and contain 20 to 40 oil globules. Time to hatching takes at least seven to eight days. Newly hatched larvae are extremely rotund and measure 1.8 mm NL. Flexion does not occur, the tip of the notochord atrophies. Ocean sunfishes have lost the caudal fin; dorsal and anal fin rays grow around the posterior part of the fish and meet in the middle to form what has been termed a clavus (Johnson & Britz 2005).

Masturus lanceolatus (Liénard 1840), Sharptail Mola.   Spawning season and fecundity unknown. Egg diameter 1.8 mm. About 40 oil globules. Hatching size unknown. Transformation takes place at about 5 mm TL. Illustrations of larvae from 2.8 mm TL to 22.5 mm preclaval length in by Lyczkowski-Shultz (2005).

Mola mola (Linnaeus 1758), Ocean Sunfish.   Based on seasonal changes in gonad index and gonad maturation phases, the spawning period off Japan is estimated to be from August to October. Asynchronous oocyte development suggests that Ocean Sunfish are multiple spawners. The ovary of a 150-cm female contained about 300 million eggs. Eggs undescribed but probably similar to other molids and containing multiple oil globules. Larval transformation takes place at about 4 mm TL. Illustrations of larvae from 1.8 mm TL to 11.0 mm TL in Lyczkowski-Shultz (2005). See Schmidt 1921; Lyczkowski-Shultz 2005; Nakatsubo et al. 2007.

Ranzania laevis (Pénant 1776), Slender Mola.   Reproductive biology unknown. Egg diameter 1.42 to 1.65 mm, 20 to 30 oil globules, 0.05 to 0.16 mm in diameter. Hatching size 1.8 mm NL. Length at transformation about 15 mm. Illustrations of eggs and larvae from 1.8 mm TL to 11.0 mm preclaval length were presented by Lyczkowski-Shultz (2005).

CONCLUSIONS

Even the basic knowledge of reproductive biology of most epipelagic fishes is limited (see summary in Table 2.1). Most epipelagic fishes show little evidence of sexual dimorphism except in body size. They are highly fecund and spawn in warm waters, usually 24°C or warmer. Fertilization appears to be external in all oceanic epipelagic fishes. Most eggs have one or more oil globules, enabling them to float at the surface, or filaments that facilitate attachment to floating vegetation. Most species of the Beloniformes have filaments on the eggs, but the most oceanic species have lost these filaments. Important, fast-growing food fishes with widespread spawning sites such as both species of dolphinfishes, Skipjack, and Yellowfin Tuna, seem to still be in relatively stable condition and are probably not in danger of extinction, in spite of high fishing pressures. Long-lived species with restricted spawning sites such as the three species of bluefin tunas are threatened and in need of protection from over-fishing. Efforts to successfully manage pelagic fish stocks are likely to fail until adequate information regarding their reproductive biology becomes available. It may be necessary to implement marine protected areas (MPAs) for pelagic conservation (Game et al. 2009).

These have had some successes with inshore fishes and fishes that live associated with benthic habitats and may be useful in conserving some marine epipelagic species.

ACKNOWLEDGMENTS

Kurt M. Schaefer and William J. Richards read early drafts of the manuscript and provided useful comments, and Maria Jose Juan Jorda read the section on Scombridae and provided many additional references.

REFERENCES

Ambrose DA (1996). Scombroidei. In: Moser HG (ed.), The early stages of fishes in the California Current region. California Cooperative Oceanic Fishery Investigations Atlas 33: 1257–1293.

Angel, MV (1993). Biodiversity of the pelagic ocean. Conservation Biology 7: 760–772.

Arata GF Jr (1954). A contribution to the life history of the swordfish, *Xiphias gladius* Linnaeus, from the south Atlantic coast of the United States and the Gulf of Mexico. Bulletin of Marine Science of the Gulf and Caribbean 4: 183–243.

Bane, GW Jr (1965). The opah (*Lampris regius*), from Puerto Rico. Caribbean Journal of Science 5: 63–66.

Bayliff WH (1994). A review of the biology and fisheries for northern bluefin tuna, *Thunnus thynnus*, in the Pacific Ocean. FAO Fisheries Technical Paper 336(2): 244–295.

Beardsley GL Jr (1967). Age, growth, and reproduction of the dolphin *Coryphaena hippurus*, in the straits of Florida. Copeia 1967: 441–451.

Beardsley GL Jr, Merrett NR, Richards WJ (1975). Synopsis of the biology of the sailfish, *Istiophorus platypterus* (Shaw and Nodder, 1791). NOAA Technical Report NMFS SSRF-675(3): 95–120.

Berkeley SA, Houde ED (1978). Biology of two exploited species of halfbeaks, *Hemiramphus brasiliensis* and *H. balao* from southeast Florida. Bulletin of Marine Science 28: 624–644.

Berkeley SA, Houde ED, Williams F (1975). Fishery and biology of ballyhoo on the southeast Florida coast. University of Miami Sea Grant Special Report 4: 1–15.

Boehlert GW (1984). Scanning electron microscopy. In: Moser HG et al. (eds.), Ontogeny and systematics of fishes. American Society of Ichthyologists and Herpetologists Special Publication 1: 43–48.

Boustany AM, Reeb CA, Block BA (2008). Mitochondrial DNA and electronic tracking reveal population structure of Atlantic bluefin tuna (*Thunnus thynnus*). Marine Biology 156: 13–24.

Boyce DG, Tittensor DP, Worm B (2008). Effects of temperature on global patterns of tuna and billfish richness. Marine Ecology Progress Series 355: 267–276.

Breder CM Jr (1932). On the habits and development of certain Atlantic Synentognathi. Carnegie Institution of Washington Publication 435, Papers from the Tortugas Laboratory 28(1): 1–25.

Breder CM Jr (1938). A contribution to the life histories of Atlantic Ocean flying fishes. Bulletin of the Bingham Oceanographic Collection 6(5): 1–126.

Breder CM Jr, Rasquin P (1952). The sloughing of the melanic area of the dorsal fin, an ontogenetic process in *Tylosurus raphidoma*. Bulletin of the American Museum of Natural History 99: 1–24.

Breder CM Jr, Rasquin P (1954). The nature of post-larval transformation in *Tylosurus acus* (Lacepède). Zoologica, New York 39: 17–30.

Brown-Peterson NJ, Franks JS, Burke AM (2000). Preliminary observations on the reproductive biology of wahoo, *Acanthocybium solandri*, from the northern Gulf of Mexico and Bimini, Bahamas. Proceedings of the Gulf and Caribbean Fisheries Institute 51: 414–427.

Bruun AF (1935). Flying-fishes (Exocoetidae) of the Atlantic. Dana Report 6: 1–106.

Caton AE (1994). Review of aspects of southern bluefin tuna biology, population, and fisheries. FAO Fisheries Technical Paper 336(2): 96–343.

Chang S-K, Liu H-C, Hsu C-C (1993). Estimation of vital parameters for Indian albacore through length-frequency data. Journal of the Fisheries Society of Taiwan 20: 1–13.

Chen C-H (1988). Beloniformes. In: Okiyama M (ed.), *An Atlas of the Early Stage Fishes in Japan*. Tokai University Press, Tokyo, pp. 259–301.

Chen K-S, Crone P, Hsu C-C (2006). Reproductive biology of female Pacific bluefin tuna *Thunnus orientalis* from south-western North Pacific Ocean. Fisheries Science 72: 985–994.

Chiang W-C, Sun C-L, Yeh S-Z, Su W-C, Liu D-C, Chen W-Y (2006). Sex ratios, size at sexual maturity, and spawning season seasonality of sailfish *Istiophorus platypterus* from eastern Taiwan. Bulletin of Marine Science 79: 727–737.

Collette BB (1974). The garfishes (Hemiramphidae). of Australia and New Zealand. Records of the Australian Museum 29: 11–105.

Collette BB (2003). Family Belonidae Bonaparte 1832: needlefishes. California Academy of Sciences Annotated Checklists of Fishes No. 16.

Collette BB (2004). Family Hemiramphidae Gill 1859: halfbeaks. California Academy of Sciences Annotated Checklists, Fishes No. 22.

Collette BB (2005a). Belonidae: needlefishes. In: Richards WJ (ed.), *Early Stages of Atlantic Fishes: An Identification Guide for the Western Central North Atlantic*. CRC Press, Boca Raton, Florida, pp. 909–931.

Collette BB (2005b). Hemiramphidae: halfbeaks. In: Richards WJ (ed.), *Early Stages of Atlantic Fishes: An Identification Guide for the Western Central North Atlantic*. CRC Press, Boca Raton, Florida, pp. 933–953.

Collette BB, Aadland CR (1996). Revision of the frigate tunas (Scombridae, *Auxis*), with descriptions of two new subspecies from the eastern Pacific. Fishery Bulletin 94: 423–441.

Collette BB, Chao LN (1975). Systematics and morphology of the bonitos (*Sarda*) and their relatives (Scombridae, Sardini). Fishery Bulletin 73: 516–625.

Collette BB, Nauen CE (1983). FAO species catalogue. Vol. 2. Scombrids of the world. An annotated and illustrated catalogue of tunas, mackerels, bonitos and related species known to date. FAO Fisheries Synopsis 125(2): 1–37.

Collette BB, Parin NV (1970). Needlefishes (Belonidae) of the eastern Atlantic Ocean. Atlantide Report 11: 7–60.

Collette BB, Russo JL (1985). Morphology, systematics, and biology of the Spanish mackerels (*Scomberomorus*, Scombridae). Fishery Bulletin 82: 545–692.

Collette BB, McGowen GE, Parin NV, Mito S (1984a). Beloniformes: development and relationships. In: Moser HG et al. (eds.), *Ontogeny and Systematics of Fishes*. American Society of Ichthyologists and Herpetologists Special Publication 1, Allen Press, Lawrence, Kansas, pp. 335–354.

Collette BB, Potthoff T, Richards WJ, Ueyanagi S, Russo JL, Nishikawa Y (1984b). Scombroidei: development and relationships. In: Moser HG et al. (eds.), *Ontogeny and Systematics of Fishes*. American Society of Ichthyologists and Herpetologists Special Publication 1, Allen Press, Lawrence, Kansas, pp. 591–620.

Collette BB, Reeb C, Block BA (2001). Systematics of the tunas and mackerels (Scombridae). In: Block BA, Stevens ED (eds.), *Tuna: Physiology, Ecology, and Evolution*. Academic Press, San Diego, pp. 1–33.

Collette BB, McDowell JR, Graves JE (2006). Phylogeny of recent billfishes (Xiphioidei). Bulletin of Marine Science 79: 455–468.

Corriero A, Desantis S, Deflorio M, Acone F, Bridges CR, de la Serna JR, Megalofonou P, De Metrio G (2003). Histological investigation on the ovarian cycle of the bluefin tuna in the western and central Mediterranean. Journal of Fish Biology 63: 108–119.

Cotten N, Comyns BH (2005). Exocoetidae: flyingfishes. In: Richards WJ (ed.), *Early Stages of Atlantic Fishes: An Identification Guide for the Western Central North Atlantic*. CRC Press, Boca Raton, Florida, pp. 955–989.

Cressey RF, Lachner EA (1970). The parasitic copepod diet and life history of diskfishes (Echeneidae). Copeia 1970: 310–318.

de Sylva DP (1975). Synopsis of biological data on the Mediterranean spearfish, *Tetrapturus belone* Rafinesque. NOAA Technical Report NMFS SSRF-675(3): 121–131.

de Sylva DP, Breder PR (1997). Reproduction, gonad histology, and spawning cycles of North Atlantic billfishes (Istiophoridae). Bulletin of Marine Science 60: 668–697.

Die DJ (2006). Are Atlantic marlins overfished or endangered? Some reasons why we may not be able to tell. Bulletin of Marine Science 70: 529–543.

Ditty JG (2005). Coryphaenidae: dolphinfishes. In: Richards WJ (ed.), *Early Stages of Atlantic Fishes: An Identification Guide for the Western Central North Atlantic*. CRC Press, Boca Raton, Florida, pp. 1511–1515.

Ditty JG, Shaw RF, Grimes CB, Cope JS (1994). Larval development, distribution, and abundance of common dolphin *Coryphaena hippurus*, and pompano dolphin, *C. equiselis*. Fishery Bulletin 92: 275–291.

Erdman DS (1977). Spawning patterns of fish from the northeastern Caribbean. In: Stewart HB (ed.), Cooperative investigations of the Caribbean and adjacent regions II. FAO Fisheries Report No. 200: 145–169.

Farley JH, Davis TLO (1998). Reproductive dynamics of southern bluefin tuna, *Thunnus maccoyii*. Fishery Bulletin 96: 223–236.

Farley JH, Clear NP, Leroy B, Davis TLO, McPherson G (2006). Age, growth and preliminary estimates of maturity of bigeye tuna, *Thunnus obesus*, in the Australian region. Australian Journal of Marine and Freshwater Research 57: 713–724.

Farooqui TW, Shaw RF, Lindquist DC. (2005). Luvaridae: louvar. In: Richards WJ (ed.), *Early Stages of Atlantic Fishes: An Identification Guide for the Western Central North Atlantic*. CRC Press, Boca Raton, Florida, pp. 2111–2117.

Freire KMF, Lessa R, Lins-Oliveria JE (2005). Fishery and biology of blackfin tuna *Thunnus atlanticus* off northeastern Brazil. Gulf and Caribbean Research 17: 15–24.

Fritzsche RA (1978). Chaetodontidae through Ophidiidae. Vol. 5, Development of fishes of the mid-Atlantic Bight. U.S. Fish and Wildlife Service FWS/OBS-78/12.

Game ET, Grantham HS, Hobday AJ, Pressey RL, Lombard, AT, Beckley LE, Gjerde K, Bustamente R, Possingham HP, Richardson AJ (2009). Pelagic protected areas: the missing dimension in ocean conservation. Trends in Ecology and Evolution 24: 360–369.

Gehringer JW (1956). Observations on the development of the Atlantic sailfish *Istiophorus americanus* (Cuvier), with notes on an unidentified species of istiophorid. Fishery Bulletin 57: 139–171.

Gehringer JW (1970). Young of the Atlantic sailfish *Istiophorus platypterus*. Fishery Bulletin 68: 177–189.

Gibbs RH Jr, Collette BB (1959). On the identification, distribution, and biology of the dolphins, *Coryphaena hippurus* and *C. equiselis*. Bulletin of Marine Science of the Gulf and Caribbean 9: 117–152.

González-Armas R, Klett-Traulsen A, Hernández-Herrera A (2006). Evidence of billfish reproduction in the southern Gulf of California, Mexico. Bulletin of Marine Science 70: 705–717.

Gottschall DW, Fitch JE (1968). The louvar, *Luvarus imperialis* in the eastern Pacific, with notes on its life history. Copeia 1968: 181–183.

Govoni JJ, West MA, Zivotofsky D, Zivotofsky AZ, Bowser PR, Collette BB (2004). Ontogeny of squamation in Swordfish, *Xiphias gladius*. Copeia 2004: 301–306.

Graham JB, Dickson KA (2000). The evolution of thunniform locomotion and heat conservation in scombrid fishes: new insights based on the morphology of *Allothunnus fallai*. Zoological Journal of the Linnean Society 129: 419–466.

Gray KN, McDowell JR, Collette BB, Graves JE (2009). A molecular phylogeny of the Echeneoidea (Perciformes: Carangoidei). Bulletin of Marine Science 84: 183–198.

Grudtsev ME (1992) Particularites de repartition et caracteristiques biologiques de la melva *Auxis rochei* (Risso) dans les eaux du Sahara. International Commission for the Conservation of Atlantic Tunas Collective Volume of Scientific Papers 39(1): 284–288.

Grudtsev ME, Korolevich LI (1986). Studies of frigate tuna *Auxis thazard* (Lacepede) age and growth in the eastern part of the equatorial Atlantic. International Commission for the Conservation of Atlantic Tunas Collective Volume of Scientific Papers 25: 269–274.

Hardy JD Jr, Collette BB (2005). Scomberesocidae: sauries. In: Richards WJ (ed.), *Early Stages of Atlantic Fishes: An Identification Guide for the Western Central North Atlantic*. CRC Press, Boca Raton, Florida, pp. 905–907.

Hubbs CL, Wisner RL (1980). Revision of the sauries (Pisces, Scomberesocidae), with descriptions of two new genera and one new species. Fishery Bulletin 77: 521–566.

Hyde JR, Humphreys R Jr, Musyl M, Lynn E, Vetter, R (2006). A central North Pacific spawning ground for striped marlin, *Tetrapturus audax*. Bulletin of Marine Science 70: 683–690.

Ichinokawa M, Coan AL Jr, Y. Takeuchi Y (2008). Transoceanic migration rates of young North Pacific albacore, *Thunnus alalunga*, from conventional tagging data. Canadian Journal of Fisheries and Aquatic Science 65: 1681–1691.

IGFA (2009). International Game Fish Association World Record Game Fishes. International Game Fish Association, Dania Beach, FL.

Ito RY, Hawn DR, Collette BB (1994). First record of the butterfly kingfish *Gasterochisma melampus* (Scombridae) from the North Pacific Ocean. Japanese Journal of Ichthyology 40: 482–486.

IUCN (2009). IUCN Red List of threatened species. Version 2009. www.iucnredlist.org (accessed 13 November 2009).

Iversen RTB, Nakamura EL, Gooding RM (1970). Courting behavior in skipjack tuna, *Katsuwonus pelamis*. Transactions of the American Fisheries Society 99: 93.

Jesien RV, Barse AM, Smyth S, Prince ED, Serafy JE (2006). Characterization of the white marlin (*Tetrapturus albidus*) recreational fishery off Maryland and New Jersey. Bulletin of Marine Science 79: 647–657.

Johnson GD, Britz R (2005). Leis' Conundrum: homology of the clavus of ocean sunfishes. 2. Ontogeny of the median fins and axial skeleton of *Ranzania laevis* (Teleostei, Tetraodontiformes, Molidae). Journal of Morphology 266: 11–21.

Joseph J (2009a). Plenty more tuna in the sea? New Scientist 203(2719): 22–23.

Joseph J (2009b). Status of the world fisheries for tuna. International Seafood Sustainability Foundation. www.iss-foundation.org (accessed 15 April 2009).

Khokiattiwong S, Mahon R, Hunte W (2000). Seasonal abundance and reproduction of the fourwing flyingfish, *Hirundichthys affinis*, off Barbados. Environmental Biology of Fishes 59: 43–60.

Khrapkova-Kovalevskaya, NV (1963). Data on reproduction, development and distribution of larvae and young fish of *Oxyporhamphus micropterus* Val. (Pisces, Oxyporhamphidae). Trudy Instituta Okeanologii Akademiya Nauk SSSR 62: 49–61 (in Russian).

Kikawa S (1975). Synopsis of biological data on the shortbill spearfish, *Tetrapturus angustirostris* Tanaka, 1914 in the Indo-Pacific areas. NOAA Technical Report NMFS SSRF-675(3): 39–54.

Kitchell JF, Martell SJD, Walters CJ, Jensen OP, Kaplan IC, Watters J, Essington TE, Boggs CH (2006). Billfishes in an ecosystem context. Bulletin of Marine Science 79: 669–682.

Klawe WL (1966). Observations on the opah, *Lampris regius* (Bonnaterre). Nature 210: 965–966.

Kohno, H (1984). Osteology and systematic position of the butterfly mackerel, *Gasterochisma melampus*. Japanese Journal of Ichthyology 31: 268–286.

Kovalevskaya NV (1982). Reproduction and development of flying fishes of the family Exocoetidae. Voprosy Ikhtiologii 22: 582–587 (in Russian, translated in Journal of Ichthyology 22: 48–54).

Labelle M, Hampton J, Bailey K, Murray T, Fournier DA, Sibert JR (1993). Determination of age and growth of South Pacific albacore (*Thunnus alalunga*) using three methodologies. Fishery Bulletin 91: 649–663.

Lovejoy NR (2000). Reinterpreting recapitulation: systematics of needlefishes and their allies (Teleostei: Beloniformes). Evolution 54: 1349–1362.

Lovejoy NR, Iranpour M, Collette BB (2004). Phylogeny and jaw ontogeny of beloniform fishes. Integrative and Comparative Biology 44: 366–377.

Lyczkowski-Shultz L (2005). Molidae: ocean sunfishes. In: Richards WJ (ed.), *Early Stages of Atlantic Fishes: An Identification Guide for the Western Central North Atlantic*. CRC Press, Boca Raton, Florida, pp. 2457–2465.

MacKenzie BR, Mosegaard H, Rosenberg AA (2009). Impending collapse of bluefin tuna in the northeast Atlantic and Mediterranean. Conservation Letters 2: 25–34.

Magnuson JL, Prescott JH (1966). Courtship, locomotion, feeding, and miscellaneous behaviour of Pacific bonito (*Sarda chiliensis*). Animal Behaviour 14: 54–67.

Majkowski J (2007). Global fishery resources of tuna and tuna-like species. FAO Fisheries Technical Paper 483.

Margulies D, Suter JM, Hunt SL, Olson RJ, Scholey VP, Wexler JB, Nakazawa A (2007). Spawning and early development of captive yellowfin tunas (*Thunnus albacares*). Fishery Bulletin 105: 249–265.

Masurekar VB (1968). Eggs and development stages of *Tylosurus crocodilus* (Lesueur). Journal of the Marine Biological Association of India 9: 70–76.

Mather FJ III, Clark HL, Mason JM Jr (1975). Synopsis of the biology of the white marlin, *Tetrapturus albidus* Poey, (1861). NOAA Technical Report NMFS SSRF-675(3): 55–94.

Matsumoto T, Bayliff WH (2008). A review of the Japanese longline fishery for tunas and billfishes in the eastern Pacific Ocean, 1998–2003. Bulletin of the Inter-American Tropical Tuna Commission 24: 1–187.

Matsumoto WM, Skillman RA, Dizon AE (1984). Synopsis of biological data on skipjack tuna, *Katsuwonus pelamis*. NOAA Technical Report NMFS Circular 451.

McBride RS, Thurman PE (2003). Reproductive biology of *Hemiramphus brasiliensis* and *H. balao* (Hemiramphidae): maturation, spawning frequency, and fecundity. Biological Bulletin, Woods Hole 204: 57–67.

McBride RS, Foushee L, Mahmoudi B (1996). Florida's halfbeak, *Hemiramphus* spp., bait fishery. Marine Fisheries Review 58(1–2): 29–38.

McBride RS, Styer JR, Hudson R (2003). Spawning cycles and habitats for ballyhoo (*Hemiramphus brasiliensis*) and balao (*Hemiramphus balao*) in south Florida. Fishery Bulletin 101: 583–589.

McBride RS, Richardson AK, Maki KL (2008). Age, growth, and mortality of wahoo, *Acanthocybium solandri*, from the Atlantic coast of Florida and the Bahamas. Marine and Freshwater Research 59: 799–807.

McDowell JR, Graves JE (2008). Population structure of striped marlin (*Kajikia audax*) in the Pacific Ocean based on analysis of microsatellite and mitochondrial DNA. Canadian Journal of Fisheries and Aquatic Science 65: 1307–1320.

Meisner AD, Collette BB (1999). Generic relationships of the internally-fertilized southeast Asian halfbeaks (Hemiramphidae: Zenarchopterinae). In: Proceedings of the Fifth Indo-Pacific Fish Conference, Nouméa, 1997. Societe Francaise d'Ichthyologie, pp. 69–76.

Mito S (1958). Eggs and larvae of *Tylosurus melanotus* (Bleeker) (Belonidae). In: Uchida K et al. (eds.), Studies on the eggs, larvae and juveniles of the Japanese fishes. Series 1. Second Laboratory of Fisheries Biology, Fisheries Department, Faculty of Agriculture, Kyushu University, Fukuoka, Japan, p. 22.

Miyabe N (1994). A review of the biology and fisheries for bigeye tuna, *Thunnus obesus*, in the Pacific Ocean. FAO Fisheries Technical Paper 336(2): 207–243.

Mukhacheva VA (1960). Some data on the breeding, development and distribution of saury: *Cololabis saira* (Brevoort). Trudy Instituta Okeanologii 41: 163–174 (in Russian).

Nakajima H, Kawahara H, Takamatsu S (1987). The breeding behavior and the behavior of larvae and juveniles of the sharksucker, *Echeneis naucrates*. Japanese Journal of Ichthyology 34: 66–70.

Nakamura I (1975). Synopsis of the biology of the black marlin, *Makaira indica* (Cuvier), 1831. NOAA Technical Report NMFS SSRF-675(3): 17–27.

Nakamura I (1985). FAO species catalogue. Vol. 5. Billfishes of the world. An annotated and illustrated catalogue of marlins, spearfishes, and swordfishes known to date. FAO Fisheries Synopsis 125(5).

Nakatsubo T, Kawachi M, Mano N, Hirose H (2007). Spawning period of ocean sunfish *Mola mola* in waters of the eastern Kanto Region, Japan. Aquaculture Science 55: 613–618 (in Japanese with English abstract).

Neilson JD, Manickhand-Heileman S, Singh-Renton, S (1994). Assessment of hard parts of blackfin tuna (*Thunnus atlanticus*) for determining age and growth. International Commission for the Conservation of Atlantic Tunas Collective Volume of Scientific Papers 42(2): 369–376.

Nelson JS (2006). *Fishes of the World*, 4th ed. John Wiley & Sons, Hoboken, NJ.

Nesterov AA, Shiganova TA (1976). The eggs and larvae of the Atlantic saury, *Scomberesox saurus* of the North Atlantic. Voprosy Ikhtiologii 16: 315–322 (in Russian, translated in Journal of Ichthyology 16: 277–283).

Nichols JT, Breder CM Jr (1928). An annotated list of the Synentognathi with remarks on their development and relationships. Collected by the Arcturus. Zoologica, New York 8: 423–448.

Niiya Y (2001a). Age, growth, maturation and life of bullet tuna *Auxis rochei* in the Pacific waters off Koch Prefecture. Nippon Suisan Gakkaishi 67(3): 429–437 (in Japanese with English abstract).

Niiya Y (2001b). Maturation cycle and batch fecundity of the bullet tuna *Auxis rochei* off Cape Ashizuri, southwestern Japan. Nippon Suisan Gakkaishi 67: 10–16 (in Japanese with English abstract).

Olney JE (1984). Lampriformes: development and relationships. In: Moser HG et al. (eds.), Ontogeny and systematics of fishes. American Society of Ichthyologists and Herpetologists Special Publication 1, Lawrence, Kansas, pp. 368–379.

Olney JE (2005). Chapter 81. Family Lamprididae. In: Richards WJ (ed.), *Early Stages of Atlantic Fishes: An Identification Guide for the Western Central North Atlantic*. CRC Press, Boca Raton, Florida, pp. 995–997.

Orton GL (1964). The eggs of scomberesocid fishes. Copeia 1964: 144–150.

O'Toole B (1999). Phylogeny of the species of the superfamily Echeneoidea (Perciformes: Carangoidei: Echeneidae, Rachycentridae, and Coryphaenidae) with an interpretation on echeneid hitchhiking behaviour. Canadian Journal of Zoology 80: 596–623.

Oxenford, HA (1999). Biology of the dolphinfish (*Coryphaena hippurus*) in the western central Atlantic: a review. Scientia Marina 63: 277–301.

Oxenford HA, Hunte W (1986). A preliminary investigation of the stock structure of the dolphinfish (*Coryphaena hippurus*) in the eastern Caribbean. Fishery Bulletin 84: 451–460.

Oxenford HA, Mahon R, Hunte W (1995). Distribution and relative abundance of flying fish (Exocoetidae) in the eastern Caribbean. I. Adults. Marine Ecology Progress Series 117: 11–23.

Oxenford HA, Murray PA, Luckhurst BE (2003). The biology of wahoo (*Acanthocybium solandri*) in the western central Atlantic. Gulf and Caribbean Research 15: 33–49.

Pagavino M, Gaertner D (1995). Ajuste de una curva de crecimiento a frecuencias de tallas de atún listado (*Katsuwonus pelamis*) pescado en el mar Caribe suroriental. International Commission for the Conservation of Atlantic Tunas Collective Volume of Scientific Papers 44(2): 303–309.

Palko BJ, Beardsley GL, Richards WJ (1981). Synopsis of the biology of the swordfish, *Xiphias gladius* Linnaeus. NOAA Technical Report NMFS Circular 441.

Palko BJ, Beardsley GL, Richards WJ (1982). Synopsis of the biological data on dolphin-fishes, *Coryphaena hippurus* Linnaeus and *Coryphaena equiselis* Linnaeus. NOAA Technical Report NMFS Circular 443.

Parin NV (1970). Ichthyofauna of the epipelagic zone (translated from Russian by M. Ravah). Israel Program for Scientific Translations, Jerusalem.

Parin NV, Shakhovskoy IB (2000). A review of the flying fish genus *Exocoetus* (Exocoetidae) with descriptions of two new species from the Southern Pacific Ocean. Journal of Ichthyology 40, Supplement 1: S31–S63.

Potthoff T, Kelley S (1982). Development of the vertebral column, fins and fin supports, branchiostegal rays, and squamation in the swordfish, *Xiphias gladius*. Fishery Bulletin 80: 161–186.

Randall JE (1960). The living javelin. Sea Frontiers 6: 228–233.

Restrepo V, Prince ED, Scott GB, Uozumi Y (2003). ICCAT stock assessments of Atlantic billfish. Australian Journal of Marine and Freshwater Research 54: 361–367.

Richards WJ (2005a). Echeneidae: remoras. In: Richards WJ (ed.), *Early Stages of Atlantic Fishes: An Identification Guide for the Western Central North Atlantic*. CRC Press, Boca Raton, Florida, pp. 1433–1438.

Richards WJ (2005b). Scombridae: mackerels and tunas. In: Richards WJ (ed.), *Early Stages of Atlantic Fishes: An Identification Guide for the Western Central North Atlantic*. CRC Press, Boca Raton, Florida, pp. 2187–2227.

Richards WJ (2005c). Xiphiidae: swordfish. In: Richards WJ (ed.), *Early Stages of Atlantic Fishes: An Identification Guide for the Western Central North Atlantic*. CRC Press, Boca Raton, Florida, pp. 2241–2243.

Richards WJ, Luthy SA (2005). Istiophoridae: billfishes. In: Richards WJ (ed.), *Early Stages of Atlantic Fishes: An Identification Guide for the Western Central North Atlantic*. CRC Press, Boca Raton, Florida, pp. 2231–2240.

Rivas LR (1975). Synopsis of biological data on blue marlin, *Makaira nigricans* Lacepède, 1802. NOAA Technical Report NMFS SSRF-675(3): 1–16.

Robins CR (1975). Synopsis of biological data on the longbill spearfish, *Tetrapturus pfluegeri* Robins and de Sylva. NOAA Technical Report NMFS SSRF-675(3): 28–38.

Rodríguez-Roda J (1966). Estudio de la bacoreta, *Euthynnus alleteratus* (Raf.), bonito, *Sarda sarda* (Bloch), y melva, *Auxis thazard* (Lac.), capturados por las almadrabas españolas. Investigacion Pesquera, Barcelona 30: 247–292.

Rooker JR, Alvarado Bremer JR, Block BA, Dewar H, de Metrio G, Corriero A, Kraus RT, Prince ED, Rodríguez-Marín E, Secor DH (2007). Life history and stock structure of Atlantic bluefin tuna (*Thunnus thynnus*). Reviews in Fishery Science 15: 265–310.

Rooker JR, Secor DH, de Metrio G, Schloesser R, Block BA, Neilson JD (2008). Natal homing and connectivity in Atlantic bluefin tuna populations. Science 322: 742–744.

Rosen DE, Parenti LR (1981). Relationships of *Oryzias*, and the groups of atherinomorph fishes. American Museum Novitates 2719: 1–25.

Sadovy Y, Liu M (2008). Functional hermaphroditism in teleosts. Fish and Fisheries 9: 1–43.

Sawada Y, Okada T, Miyashita S, Murata O, Kumai H (2005). Completion of the Pacific bluefin tuna *Thunnus orientalis* (Temminck et Schlegel) life cycle. Aquaculture Research 36: 413–421.

Schaefer KM (1998). Reproductive biology of yellowfin tuna (*Thunnus albacares*) in the eastern Pacific Ocean. Bulletin of the Inter-American Tropical Tuna Commission 21: 201–272.

Schaefer KM (2001). Reproductive biology of tunas. In: Block BA, Stevens ED (eds.), *Tuna: Physiology, Ecology, and Evolution*. Fish Physiology 19. Academic Press, San Diego, pp. 25–270.

Schaefer KM, Fuller DW, Miyabe N (2005). Reproductive biology of bigeye tuna (*Thunnus obesus*) in the eastern and central Pacific Ocean. Bulletin of the Inter-American Tropical Tuna Commission 23: 1–31.

Schlesinger G (1909). Zur Phylogenie und Ethologie der Scombresociden. Verhandlungen der Zoologisch-Botanischen Gesellschaft in Wien 59: 302–339.

Schmidt J (1921). New studies of sun-fishes made during the "Dana" expeditions 1920. Nature 107: 76–79.

Schwenke KL, Buckel JA (2008). Age, growth, and reproduction of dolphinfish (*Coryphaena hippurus*) caught off the coast of North Carolina. Fishery Bulletin 106: 82–92.

Shivji MS, Magnussen JE, Beerkircher LR, Hinteregger G, Lee DW, Serafy JE, Prince ED (2006). Validity, identification, and distribution of the roundscale spearfish, *Tetrapturus georgii* (Teleostei: Istiophoridae): morphological and molecular evidence. Bulletin of Marine Science 79: 483–491.

Shomura RS, Williams F, eds. (1975). Proceedings of the International Billfish Symposium Kailua-Kona, Hawaii, 9–12 August 1972. Part 3. Species synopses. NOAA Technical Report NMFS SSRF-675(3): 1–159.

Sissenwine, MP, Mace PM, Powers JE, Scott, GP (1998). A commentary on western Atlantic bluefin tuna assessments. Transactions of the American Fisheries Society 127: 838–855.

Strasburg, DW (1964). Further notes on the identification and biology of echeneid fishes. Pacific Science 18: 51–57.

Sun C-L, Chang Y-J, Tszeng C-C, Su N-J (2009). Reproductive biology of blue marlin (*Makaira nigricans*) in the western Pacific Ocean. Fishery Bulletin 107: 420–432.

Sun Z-G (1960). Larvae and juveniles of tunas, sailfish and swordfish (Thunnidae, Istiophoridae, Xiphiidae) from the central and western parts of the Pacific Ocean. Trudy Instituta Okeanologii 41: 175–191 (in Russian).

Theisen TC, Bowen BW, Lanier W, Baldwin JD (2008). High connectivity on a global scale in the pelagic wahoo, *Acanthocybium solandri* (tuna family Scombridae). Molecular Ecology 17: 4233–4247.

Thorogood J (1986). Aspects of the reproductive biology of the southern bluefin tuna (*Thunnus maccoyii*). Fisheries Science 4: 297–315.

Topp RW, Giradin DL (1971). An adult louvar, *Luvarus imperialis* (Pisces, Luvaridae), from the Gulf of Mexico. Copeia 1971: 181–182.

Tyler JC, Johnson GD, Nakamura I, Collette BB (1989). Morphology of *Luvarus imperialis* (Luvaridae) with a phylogenetic analysis of the Acanthuroidei (Pisces). Smithsonian Contributions to Zoology 485.

Uchida RN (1981). Synopsis of biological data on frigate tuna *Auxis thazard*, and bullet tuna, *A. rochei*. NOAA Technical Report NMFS Circular 436.

Ueyanagi S (1960). On the larvae and the spawning areas of the shirokajiki, *Marlina marlina* (Jordan & Hill). Report of the Nankai Regional Fisheries Research Laboratory 12: 85–96 (in Japanese with English abstract).

Ueyanagi S (1964). Description and distribution of larvae of five istiophorid species in the Indo-Pacific. Proceedings of the Symposium on Scombroid Fishes, Marine Biological Association of India Symposium Series 1: 499–528.

Ueyanagi S, Wares PG (1975). Synopsis of biological data on striped marlin, *Tetrapturus audax* (Philippi), 1887. NOAA Technical Report NMFS SSRF-675(3): 132–159.

Wang S-P, Sun C-L, Yeh S-Z, Chiang W-C, Su N-J, Chang Y-J, Liu C-H (2006). Length distributions, weight-length relationships, and sex ratios at lengths for the billfishes in Taiwan waters. Bulletin of Marine Science 79: 865–869.

Watanabe H, Yukinawa M, Nakazawa S, Ueyanagi S (1966). On the larva probably referable to slender tuna, *Allothunnus fallai* Serventy. Report of the Nankai Regional Fisheries Research Lab. No. 23: 85–94 (in Japanese with English summary).

Watson W (1996). Beloniformes. In: Moser HG (ed.), The early stages of fishes in the California Current region. California Cooperative Oceanic Fisheries Investigation Atlas No. 33, pp. 625–657.

White Marlin Status Review Team (2002). Atlantic white marlin status review document. Report to the National Marine Fisheries Service, Southeast Regional Office, St. Petersberg, Florida.

Wild A, Hampton J (1994). A review of the biology and fisheries for skipjack tuna, *Katsuwonus pelamis*, in the Pacific Ocean. FAO Fisheries Technical Paper 336(2): 1–51.

Wollam MB (1969). Larval wahoo, *Acanthocybium solandri* (Cuvier), (Scombridae) from the Straits of Yucatan and Florida. Florida Department of Natural Resources Leaflet Series 4(12): 1–7.

Wu C-C, Su W-C, Kawasaki T (2001). Reproductive biology of the dolphin fish *Corphaena* [sic] *hippurus* on the east coast of Taiwan. Fisheries Science 67: 784–793.

Yesaki M (1994). A review of the biology and fisheries for longtail tuna (*Thunnus tonggol*) in the Indo-Pacific region. FAO Fisheries Technical Paper 336(2): 370–387.

Yesaki M, Arce F (1994). A review of the *Auxis* fisheries of the Philippines and some aspects of the biology of frigate (*A. thazard*) and bullet (*A. rochei*) tunas in the Indo-Pacific region. FAO Fisheries Technical Paper 336(2): 409–439.

Yoshida HO, Nakamura EL (1965). Notes on schooling behavior, spawning, and morphology of Hawaiian frigate mackerels, *Auxis thazard* and *Auxis rochei*. Copeia 1965: 111–114.

3

Reproduction in Scorpaeniformes

Marta Muñoz

The Scorpaeniformes, or mail-cheeked fishes, are one of the largest and most morphologically diverse teleostean orders with more than 1400 species classified in 24 to 36 families, depending on the taxonomy (e.g., Washington et al. 1984b; Eschmeyer 1998; Nelson 2006). After Cuvier's (1829) initial characterization, phylogenetic relationships of this group have been considered by many authors (e.g., Matsubara 1943, 1955; Yabe 1985; Gill 1988; Shinohara 1994; Imamura 1996). Although it has been traditionally retained as a taxonomic unit, recent studies indicate that the mail-cheeked fish group is polyphyletic (see Shinohara & Imamura 2007 for a review comparing findings of Imamura & Yabe 2002; Miya et al. 2003; Smith & Wheeler 2004). As a result, this chapter is structured according to the two recognized major scorpaeniform lineages: the Cottoidei and the Scorpaenoidei (Washington et al. 1984b; Kendall 1991; Imamura & Shinohara 1998).

As Washington et al. (1984a) has pointed out, the Scorpaeniformes show a wide range of reproductive strategies. Some families spawn individual pelagic eggs (Anoplopomatidae, Congiopodidae, and Triglidae) while others spawn demersal clusters of adhesive eggs (Cyclopteridae, Cottidae, and Agonidae). However, most of them spawn pelagic egg masses embedded in a gelatinous matrix. There are strong trends toward internal fertilization, and the genera *Sebastes* and *Sebasticus* give birth to live young.

Following the excellent discussion about the evolution of piscine viviparity in rockfishes made by Wourms (1991) and summarized in Table 3.1, it seems that the ancestral stock of scorpaeniforms was probably unspecialized. It is reasonable to assume that their reproduction involved a simple form of oviparity, such as broadcast spawning of pelagic, or oviposition of demersal, eggs. This ancestral

TABLE 3.1 Scenario for evolution of viviparity in scorpaeniform fishes, from Wourms (1991)

Cottoids (mostly demersal)
Recent cottoids. Oviparous.
Internal fertilization in some taxa. Demersal eggs spawned in masses. Parental care. Exception
  Comephorus, pelagic and viviparous.

Scorpaenoids (primarily demersal, secondarily pelagic)
Oviparous ovuliparous. Broadcast spawning of individual pelagic eggs. External fertilization.
Oviparous, ovuliparous. Pelagic spawning, groups of eggs enclosed in gelatinous mass. External
  or internal fertilization.
Oviparous, zygoparous or embryoparous. Pelagic spawning, groups of developing eggs or
  embryos enclosed in gelatinous mass. Internal fertilization.
Viviparous. Internal fertilization. Developing embryos enclosed in gelatinous mass that is
  extruded at parturition. Embryonic nutrition, lecithotrophic.
Viviparous. Internal fertilization. Developing embryos not enclosed in gelatinous mass.
  Embryonic nutrition ranges from lecithotrophic to matrotrophic.

stock diverged into two groups: the lineages Cottoidei and Scorpaenoidei. This is in concordance with the reproductive dichotomy found between demersal spawning cottoids and pelagic spawning scorpaenoids, which according to Washington et al. (1984b) led to a reproductive partitioning of shared habitats. The wide distribution and extensive speciation of the two lineages indicate that they are both successful groups, and as Wourms (1991) states, it is reasonable to assume that reproductive modes account, at least in part, for their success.

In this chapter, the diversity and evolutionary trends of reproduction in scorpaeniform fishes will be presented and discussed.

COTTOID LINEAGE

In most species of cottoids, the general aspects of the mode of reproduction are similar. Oviparity is retained, clusters of adhesive demersal eggs are generally laid, and parental care is common. This reproductive style has proved to be highly successful and is retained in modern cottoids (Washington et al. 1984a). However, there are a few exceptions: species of Anoplopomatidae secondarily adopted a pelagic lifestyle and produce pelagic eggs, and some freshwater species are viviparous.

At least one of the two existing species of pelagic anoplopomids, the sablefish, *Anoplopoma fimbria*, is long-lived (up to 113 years; McFarlane & Beamish 1983, 1995), with pelagic spawning at depths of 300 to 500 m, near the edges of the continental slopes (McFarlane & Nagata 1988). Eggs develop at these depths; following hatching, larvae develop near the surface as far offshore as 180 miles (Wing 1997). Females of *A. fimbria* are extremely fecund, producing up to one million eggs (Alderdice et al. 1988; McFarlane & Nagata 1988). This reproductive style of non-guarding, egg-scattering pelagic spawners and nutrient-poor ova produced in high numbers coincides with that of most fishes and seems to be the ancestral condition (Balon 1984).

Nowadays most cottoids are guarders, including Hexagrammidae, Cottidae, Cyclopteridae, Hemitripteridae, and others. However, they display a wide range of different types of fertilization and parental behavior modes. Among cottids, the reproductive mode can be either copulatory or non-copulatory (Breder & Rosen 1966; Munehara et al. 1989).

Non-copulatory refers to the release of both ova and sperm to the external environment. This mode appears to be widespread among the hexagrammids. Where recorded, hexagrammids also exhibit either a promiscuous or polygamic mating system, or both. This has been demonstrated for species of several genera: *Pleurogrammus monopterygius* (Dermott et al. 2007), *Hexagrammos* spp. (Crow et al. 1997), *Oxylebius pictus* (DeMartini 1987), and the polyandric *Ophidion elongatus* (King & Withler 2005). Most of them exhibit clear courtship behavior involving—at least in different species of *Hexagrammos*—rushing, butting, and undulation of the trunk (Munehara et al. 2000). These actions have also been observed for *Pleurogrammus azonus* (Gomelyuk 1988). When a female enters the nest, the male leans his head on the spawning surface in the nest and spasmodically undulates his trunk. After the female has released her eggs within the seaweed bed, the male passes over them, touching his genital pore to the egg mass and releasing sperm. Sneaking by other males was frequently observed by Gomelyuk (1988) following the release of sperm.

With regard to the diversity of cottid fishes, their phylogenic relationships together with their reproductive modes are shown in Figure 3.1 (Abe & Munehara 2009). Among cottids, there are also some non-copulating marine species. In *Hemilepidotus gilberti*, females spawn adhesive demersal eggs on the spawning substratum. Under these conditions sperm release should take place close to the eggs to ensure that many spermatozoa will encounter eggs. However, males typically cannot get close to the egg mass, which is deposited between the spawning substratum and the female's belly (Hayakawa & Munehara 1996). Consequently, they position themselves behind the spawning female and emit semen at a distance from the eggs, raising hypotheses regarding the pattern of sperm motility in this species. Hayakawa & Munehara (1998) noted high motility and longevity of spermatozoa of this species when placed in experimentally provided ovarian fluid, a feature of spermatozoa that is similar to that of copulatory cottids. Subsequently, Hayakawa & Munehara (2001) demonstrated that internal fertilization occurs frequently in natural conditions in *H. gilberti*, although all of the internally fertilized eggs developed abnormally. Together with the fact that this species is regarded, based on morphology, as one of the most primitive species among Cottidae (Yabe 1985), this suggests that copulation of marine cottids may have evolved

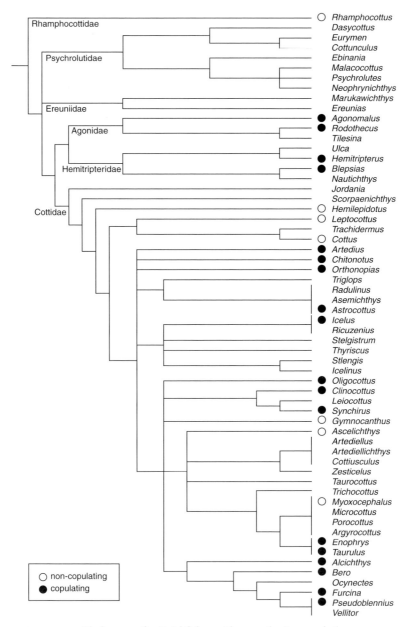

FIGURE 3.1. Phylogeny of cottoid fishes with reproductive mode (non-copulating or copulating). From Abe & Munehara (2009), modified after Yabe (1985). Reprinted with permission from Science Publishers, Enfield, NH.

from the facultative insemination of non-copulatory species, in which the physiological characteristics of spermatozoa are adapted for ovarian fluid conditions.

In copulating species of cottids, spermatozoa are introduced into the female reproductive tract during copulation and associate with ova in the ovarian cavity. However, the entry of spermatozoa into ova and subsequent fertilization occur externally, when the ova come into contact with seawater. This differs from the more typical internal fertilization in fishes because, although sperm enter the ovary and may even enter the micropyle, it does not penetrate the ooplasmic membrane and initiate fertilization and development until eggs are released. This unique reproductive mode is called internal gametic association (IGA) and has been described for several cottid species, including *Alcichthys alcicornis* (Munehara et al. 1989), *Hemitripterus villosus* (Munehara 1992, 1996), *Blepsias cirrhosus* (Munehara et al. 1991), *Radulinopsis taranetzi* (Abe & Munehara 2005), *Bero elegans*, and *Pseudoblennius cottoides* (Koya et al. 1993). Moreover, it is thought to occur in *Artedius harringtoni* (Ragland & Fischer 1987) and the other copulating cottids that have previously been reported to be internal fertilizing species (Munehara et al. 1989), but for which true internal fertilization has not been documented. Hayakawa & Munehara (2001) suggest that the deficiency of calcium ions in the ovarian fluid, which inhibits internal fertilization in copulatory marine sculpins, might have evolved after the establishment of copulatory behavior. It could have developed to preserve eggs until their release to the environment as an alternative to viviparity, since the ovary of these IGA-mode species appears to be unable to supply developing embryos with a suitable environment and enough of essential elements such as oxygen. An excellent review about the reproductive mode in copulating cottoid species has been recently published (Abe & Munehara 2009).

Most of these copulating sculpins transfer sperm by using a large, flexible genital papilla (Ragland & Fischer 1987; Munehara 1988), and copulation can be aided by various morphological features (Munehara 1996). In *Oligocottus snyderi*, the male's first anal ray is enlarged so that it can clasp the female while copulating (Morris 1956). In *Synchirus gilli*, the opposing grip of the male's lower jaw and its pelvic fins are modified to embrace the female body (Krejsa 1964). However, *Blepsias cirrhosus* and *Hemitripterus villosus*, which do not possess such a functional genital organ, have also been inferred to copulate (Munehara et al. 1991). Male *H. villosus* have no intromittent organ and sperm transfer is external, but insemination occurs internally (Munehara 1996). The female first everts the genital papilla and emits gelatinous ovarian fluid from its tip. The male then releases semen in the direction of the gelatinous ovarian fluid, after which the female retracts the gelatinous mass and associated spermatozoa into the ovary, where it is stored. During sperm emission, semen is released at a distance from the gelatinous ovarian fluid, resembling the spawning and ejaculation of *Hemilepidotus gilberti* described above (Hayakawa & Munehara 1996).

In relation with these fertilization tactics, it should be pointed out that spermio-genesis in many cottoids is known to involve atypical paraspermatozoa (i.e., di-morphic spermatozoa) as well as normal euspermatozoa (Hann 1927, 1930; Quinitio et al. 1988; Quinitio 1989; Quinitio & Takahashi 1992; Hayakawa et al. 2002c, 2007; Hayakawa 2007). Parasperm are the nonfertile sperm that are regularly produced along with normal fertile sperm in reproductive males, unlike aberrant sperm, which are irregularly crippled by some errors during spermatogenesis (Healy & Jamieson 1981; Swallow & Wilkinson 2002). It is not always easy to find a biological explanation for the existence of considerable amounts of paraspermato-zoa, but Hayakawa & Munehara (2004) state that in these cottoids, the lump forma-tion of paraspermatozoa can help euspermatozoa move directly toward the eggs by preventing the lateral dispersion of semen. Without paraspermatozoa, semen would have difficulty reaching the egg mass due to lateral dispersion caused by drag before reaching the egg mass (Hayakawa et al. 2002a). Consequently, males with parasper-matozoa can increase the number of euspermatozoa which will reach the egg mass (Hayakawa et al. 2002c, 2004). In addition, parasperm can help eusperm fertilize the egg mass by blocking sperm from other males, when sperm competition arises as a result of several males releasing sperm at the same time (Hayakawa et al. 2002b).

Intraovarian sperm storage has been described in only a few cottids, and no specialized structures within the female reproductive tract have been found asso-ciated with this reproductive feature. However, Koya et al. (2002) have been able to relate some differences in the characteristics of the location of the stored sperm with differences in the storage period. For example, in *Alcichthys alcicornis*, in which sperm only spends a short time in the female ovary, the intraovarian sperm remain freely floating in the ovarian fluid. In contrast, in the marine cottids *Pseudoblennius cottoides*, *P. percoides,* and *Furcina ishikawae*, in which the sperm is maintained in the ovary for a longer period of time, spermatozoa are located in the posterior end of the ovary and are arranged perpendicular to the ovarian wall epithelium (Shinomiya 1985).

Cottoids are one of the most reproductively diverse groups of marine fishes in terms of providing parental care. Most of them produce demersal eggs, which is considered a fundamental step in the evolution of parental care in fish (Potts 1984), since if the embryos are not protected in some way, they are more vulner-able to predation and other environmental hazards. Hexagrammid males guard benthic nests containing several clutches of eggs deposited from multiple females, as has been described for *Ophidion elongatus* (King & Withler 2005), *Hexagram-mos decagrammus* (Crow et al. 1997), or *Pleurogrammus monopterygius* (Dermott et al. 2007). In the cottoid family Psychrolutidae, the blob sculpin *Psychrolutes phrictus* represents the first direct evidence of parental care in an oviparous deep-sea fish. Drazen et al. (2003) observed, with a remote operating vehicle, aggregations of egg-brooding blob sculpins attending nests of large pinkish eggs. Parents often sat directly on, or were otherwise in contact with, the eggs that were free of sediment, suggesting that the adults cleaned or fanned their nest sites. Finally, although freshwater cottids typically exhibit male parental care of demersal eggs, within the marine cottids a greater variety of care patterns has been documented. Strictly paternal care has been found in *Alcichthys alcicornis* (Koya et al. 1994) and *Artedius harringtoni* (Ragland & Fischer 1987). In contrast, Abe & Munehara (2005) showed that *Radulinopsis taranetzi* females practice exclusive maternal egg care. Biparental care with limited maternal care has been observed in *Hemilepidotus gilberti* (Hayakawa & Munehara 1996) and *H. hemilepidotus* (DeMartini & Patten 1979). In these two species, females remain near the eggs for a few days after spawning, while the males continue to care for them until they hatch several weeks later.

As Petersen et al. (2005) have pointed out, the pattern of male parental care and internal fertilization (or at least internal gamete association) is very unusual in fishes (Clutton-Brock 1991). Yet it appears to have evolved multiple times within the cottids. It appears, for example, in the two genera, *Alcichthys* and *Artedius*, which are located in very different lineages within the phylogeny (Yabe 1985). It seems that eggs serve as courtship devices, with males defending eggs and oviposition sites to obtain additional copulations with females (Rohwer 1978; Ragland & Fischer 1987). Munehara et al. (1994) found support for this hypothesis in *Alcichthys alcicornis*, with males commonly providing care to clutches they had not fathered. In this respect, Petersen et al. (op. cit.) point out that the ability of males to continue to obtain matings at a spawning site, and the role of eggs in attracting additional mates, have been suggested as important components of selection pressure for the evolution of paternal care in fishes (Barlow 1964; Jamieson 1995; Petersen 1995; among others).

Among cottoids, egg hiding, as opposed to parental care, is also common. Some cottids, such as *Pseudoblennius cottoides*, *P. percoides*, and *Furcina ishikawae*, deposit eggs in the peribranchial cavity of sea squirts (Uchida 1932), and *Blepsias cirrhosus* injects eggs into the tissue near the gastral cavity of a sponge (Munehara 1991). All of these fishes deposit eggs only on specific invertebrates. Among the family Hemitripteridae, *Hemitripterus americanus* also attaches its eggs near the base of a sponge (Warfel & Merriman 1944), and *H. villosus* deposits them on polychaete tubes (Munehara 1992, 1996). These last two species probably use invertebrates both as spawning substrates and as protection for the eggs from predators. *Pseudoblennius cottoides*, *P. percoides*, *F. ishikawae*, and *B. cirrhosus* eggs may also take additional advantage of available oxygen, as the eggs obtain oxygen for respiration from the seawater passing through the cavities of the invertebrates (Munehara 1992).

Another cottoid family that is a close relative of sculpins is Liparidae. Snailfish, or liparids, are known to lay eggs attached to hydroids (Able & Musick 1976), algae (Detwyler 1963), in empty bivalve shells (DeMartini 1978), and among polychaete tubes or barnacle colonies (Marliave & Peden 1989). In the case of the liparid genus *Careproctus*, the eggs form compact masses within the branchial chambers of lithodid crabs (Somerton & Donaldson 1998). According to these authors and to Yau et al. (2000), such an association may provide snailfish with protection from potential predators, an optimum aerated environment, and even a means of transport toward food falls, at no apparent cost to the crabs.

SCORPAENOID LINEAGE

The reproductive modes of the cottoid sister taxon, Scorpaenoidei, are also extremely varied, consistent with their broad polyphyly as determined by Smith & Wheeler (2004). Most of scorpaenoid species have separate sexes, although some platycephalids (Shinomiya et al. 2003) and caracanthids are hermaphroditic (Cole 2003). Nearly all the families are oviparous and spawn pelagic eggs, but within the subfamily Sebastinae, most species are viviparous. In this respect, there are many examples of intermediate stages between the two basic modes of reproduction, oviparity, and viviparity. These include ovuliparity, zygoparity, and embryoparity as defined by Blackburn et al. (1985) and Wourms et al. (1988). Ovuliparity refers to the release of ova from the female reproductive tract followed by their fertilization within the external environment (i.e., classical oviparity). Zygoparity refers to the oviparous reproductive mode in which fertilized ova are retained within the female reproductive tract for a short period of time before their release. Embryoparity is the pattern of oviparous reproduction in which the embryo is formed and may develop to an advanced state prior to its release from the female reproductive tract. Consequently, the extreme limits of embryoparity can overlap with those of viviparity.

The least specialized mode of reproduction occurs in non-guarding families like Triglidae, Platycephalidae, and Synanceiidae. Most representatives of these three families are ovuliparous broadcast spawners of individual pelagic eggs, and fertilization is external. Members of the family Triglidae are found on sandy and muddy substrates or rubble, using the free pectoral rays for support and to search for food. According to Potts (1984), fish that live on, or in association with, such relatively mobile substrates normally have pelagic eggs, thereby preventing the risk of abrasion or smothering by moving particles. In fact, the eggs of triglids are pelagic and spherical, with a single oil droplet and a diameter over 1 mm (Dulcic et al. 2001; Muñoz et al. 2001, 2002a, 2003). Triglids can emit growling or grunting sounds, related to reproduction, with their swim bladder (Moulton 1963). Aspects of the biology of the triglids suggest that they have a generalist and opportunistic

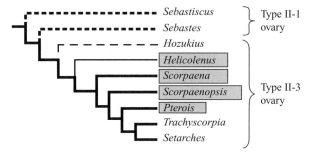

FIGURE 3.2. Phylogenetic tree of scorpaenoids showing their reproductive modes (after Imamura 2005, modified from Koya & Muñoz 2007). Bold dotted line = viviparous. Thin dashed line =, unknown. Thin solid line = zygoparous or embryoparous. Bold line = oviparous. Boxes label those taxa that release the egg mass within a gelatinous matrix.

life style. Triglid growth patterns reveal an extended longevity in most species—16 years for *Chelidonichthys capensis* (McPhail et al. 2001) and 21 years for *Aspitrigla cuculus* Baron (1985)—and many of them exhibit extremely rapid growth before sexual maturity. As Booth (1997) has pointed out, early maturity in long-lived species, with reproduction initiated at a large size, ensures high individual reproductive output.

Another ovuliparous family is Platycephalidae, which seems to contain several species with protandrous sex change, as *Cociella crocodila, Inegocia japonica, Kumococcius rodericensis,* and *Onigocia macrolepis* (Aoyama et al. 1963; Fujii 1970, 1971). In fact, Shinomiya et al. (2003) demonstrated both the existence of this kind of hermaphroditism and of a courtship behavior, at least in *I. japonica.*

According to Wourms (1991), the next phase in the evolutionary scenario of this lineage occurs in Sebastolobine, Scorpaenine, and Pteroine species, and involves a shift from the primitive, unspecialized pattern of spawning individual pelagic eggs to a more specialized pattern of oviparity. Fertilization is still external and the mode of reproduction is ovuliparous, but the small (0.7 to 1.2 mm), spherical to slightly ovoid eggs are now embedded in a large, pelagic, gelatinous matrix (Washington et al. 1984a). Phylogenetic relationships of the scorpaenoids together with their reproductive modes are shown in Figure 3.2 (Koya & Muñoz 2007), where the ovuliparous mode of reproduction of the genera *Setarches, Trachyscorpia, Pterois, Scorpaenopsis* and *Scorpaena* is marked.

Several characteristics of this specialized mode of oviparity distinguish many scorpaenids from the simpler ovuliparous species widely described in the literature. Wourms & Lombardi (1992) have suggested that this specialized mode of

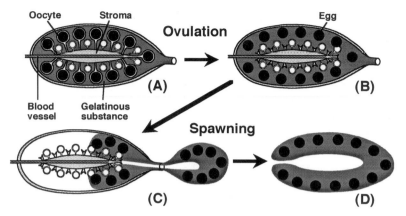

FIGURE 3.3. Schematic illustration of the formation of gelatinous egg masses in the kichiji rockfish. (A) Ovary at the pre-ovulatory period, (B) ovary at post-ovulatory period, (C) spawning, and (D) gelatinous egg mass spawned. From Koya et al. (1995).

oviparity first appeared in the genus *Scorpaena*, so the following discussion focuses on *Scorpaena notata*, and compares the results obtained in our work (Muñoz et al. 2002b, c) with those for other scorpaenids that share this reproductive strategy.

The ovarian stroma of *S. notata* is located in the center of the gonad, and the developing oocytes are connected to it by peduncles extending out into the surrounding lumen. Though the ovarian structure of *S. notata* differs from that of most Teleostei, it is similar to that described for some other scorpaenid species, such as *Dendrochirus brachypterus* (Fishelson 1977, 1978), *Sebastolobus alascanus* (Erickson & Pikitch 1993), *Sebastolobus macrochir* (Koya & Matsubara 1995), *Scorpaenodes littoralis* (Yoneda et al. 2000), *Helicolenus hilgendorfi* (Takano 1989), and *H. dactylopterus dactylopterus* (Muñoz et al. 1999). This type of organization corresponds to the cystovarian type II-3 ovary defined by Takano (1989), and seems to be related to the production of a gelatinous matrix that surrounds the expelled eggs, as shown in Figure 3.3 (Koya et al. 1995).

The peduncles connecting the ovarian follicles to the stroma, the detected paucity and small size of the cortical alveoli, and the thinness of the zona radiata of the oocytes are all characteristics typical of viviparous species (Wourms 1976; Fleger 1977; Takemura et al. 1987). The peduncles are usually considered to be protuberances of placentary or pseudo-placentary connections (Erickson & Pikitch 1993). In oviparous species, their presence may act to prevent oocytes from being too tightly packed (Fishelson 1975) or facilitate the ovulation of mature oocytes directly into the gelatinous mass. The role of the cortical alveoli in the strengthening of the chorion immediately after the fertilization of the egg is well known (Selman & Wallace 1989; West 1990; Iwamatsu et al. 1995; Shibata & Iwamatsu 1996). Their paucity and small size here suggest that less physical protection is needed by the eggs. This is further supported by the presence of a thin zona radiata, which normally provides mechanic protection. In the case of the scorpionfishes, mechanical protection is provided instead by the gelatinous matrix that encloses the eggs.

The testes of *Scorpaena* spp. also show some unusual features not typical in the most basic form of oviparity. In fish, the male germinal epithelium is normally composed of spermatocysts formed when a single clone of primary spermatogonia is enclosed by Sertoli cells. The germ cells develop inside these cysts. At the end of the process, the cysts open and spermatozoa are released into the lobular lumen. However, spermatogenesis among analyzed species of *Scorpaena* does not follow this pattern. Instead, cysts open before spermatogenesis is complete, and therefore sperm maturation finishes in the lobule lumen, without any physical connection with Sertoli cells (Muñoz et al. 2002b; Sàbat et al. 2009). This is semicystic spermatogenesis first described by Mattei et al. (1993) in the *Ophidion* genus, and has rarely been reported in fish.

The spermatozoa of these *Scorpaena* species are classified as primitive, despite exhibiting some modifications related to the specialization of semicystic spermatogenesis that occurs in the genus. As defined by Jamieson & Leung (1991), these are Type I anachrosomal aquasperm, which are characteristic of species using external fertilization. However, while the midpiece is usually shorter than 1 μm in this type of spermatozoon, in *Scorpaena angolensis* (Mattei 1970), *S. notata*, *S. porcus,* and *S. scrofa* it is longer (for example 1.35 μm in *S. notata*, as described by Muñoz et al. 2002b). As the midpiece is made up of mitochondria used to power movement of the flagellum, this extra length provides more energy for the sperm to move (Baccetti & Afzelius 1976) and is generally considered to be an adaptation to internal fertilization (Jamieson 1991; Mattei 1991), since the viscosity of the medium in which fertilization occurs demands more energy supply (Idelman 1967).

As we have seen, there are several reproductive features that place the *Scorpaena* genus, together with other oviparous scorpenids, in a position of having an intermediate reproductive strategy between the simplest ovuliparity and the development of internal fertilization. Among all of the functions attributed to ovarian fluid in fishes, perhaps the most important in the case of scorpenids is keeping the spawn together. If sperm are released onto the grouped mass of eggs within the gelatinous matrix, fertilization is assured and thereby reduces the need for the female to produce large number of eggs, which could explain their relative low fecundity (Muñoz et al. 2005). Observations on scorpionfishes forming pairs during certain times of the year seem to support this hypothesis.

Complex courtship and mating behaviors in oviparous scorpaenids have been described for *Pterois volitans* (Ruiz-Carus et al. 2006), in which males have an elaborate courting display and use their spines in agonistic displays with competing males (Fishelson 1975). Subsequently, females release two mucus-filled egg clusters that dissolve and release the eggs into the water column

At some time in the evolution of this lineage, internal fertilization appeared. According to Wourms (1991), once evolved, its presence was a strong, positive developmental feature that would facilitate the evolution of viviparity.

It is believed that viviparity evolved from oviparity in teleosts, as well as in Scorpaenidae. But despite the repeated suggestion of a scenario in which viviparous genera such as *Sebastes* and *Sebasticus* evolved from oviparous ancestral scorpaenids (such as *Scorpaena*) via embryoparity similar to that of *Helicolenus* (i.e., through the described specialization and a progressively longer retention of embryos), the comparative study of ovarian structures by Koya & Muñoz (2007) does not support this hypothesis. Their analysis suggests that the evolution of the reproductive mode in scorpaenid fishes is based on the primitive dorsal lamella-type ovary (i.e. in which the lamella-like stroma develops from the ovarian hilus located on the dorsal side of the ovary) of *Sebastes* and *Sebasticus*. In these genera, viviparity evolved later, from this ancestral type of ovary. Nevertheless, in the genera that spawn a floating egg mass, such as *Scorpaena* and *Sebastolobus*, the ovarian structure evolved from the primitive one to the previously described central stroma type. Subsequent internal fertilization and embryoparity, such as that of *Helicolenus*, evolved from them.

Ovaries of the dorsal lamella type are the general structure in other families of Scorpaeniformes, although within the family Scorpaenidae, they are only found in viviparous genera. In addition, the ovary of the central stroma type described for many scorpaenid oviparous genera and for the embryoparous *Helicolenus*, has only been observed in scorpaenids and caracanthids (Cole 2003), so it seems to be a structure that originally evolved in this lineage.

The scenario of the evolution of the reproductive mode of scorpaenids, which could be based on the evolution of the above-mentioned ovarian structures, is described as follows (Koya & Muñoz 2007). Current scorpaenids may have evolved from an ancestral clade that had the typical dorsal lamella-type ovary and in which ova were released and fertilized in the external environment. At some time during evolution, copulation behavior developed from this ancestral mode, leading to the development of viviparous species such as *Sebastiscus* and *Sebastes*. However, along a different evolutionary pathway from the ancestral species, other species that spawn floating eggs masses developed, accompanied by a shift in ovarian structure to the central stroma type, which facilitates the formation of the gelatinous matrix (e.g., *Scorpaena*, *Scorpaenopsis*, *Scorpaenodes*, *Pterois*, *Dendrochirus*, and *Sebastolobus*). The ancestral scorpaenid species possessing an ovary of the dorsal lamella-type and releasing eggs that are fertilized externally may have disappeared following such a bipolarization of reproductive mode. Later, copulation behavior appeared within the group having the central stroma-type ovary. They had not yet evolved to viviparity but stayed in the reproductive mode where they spawn developing embryos embedded in the floating egg mass, as presently seen in *Helicolenus* (Krefft 1961; Sequeira et al. 2003).

Features that suggest a separate evolutionary line for *Sebastes* with viviparity and *Helicolenus* with zygoparity are not limited to their ovarian structures. It is known that the gonadal cycles of males and females in several species of *Sebastes* are not synchronized, and there is a long period of time between spermatogenesis and oogenesis within a copulating pair. This occurs in *Sebastes marinus* and *S. mentella* (Sorokin 1961), *S. pachycephalus pachycephalus* (Shiokawa 1962), *S. serranoides* (Love & Westphal 1981), *S. taczanowskii* (Takemura et al. 1987), and *S. elongatus* (Shaw & Gunderson 2006). The same phenomenon has also been described for *Helicolenus dactylopterus* (Muñoz & Casadevall 2002). In these species, plus others of the same genus like *Sebastes atrovirens* (Sogard et al. 2008) or *Helicolenus lengerichi* (Lisovenko 1979), after copulation—described in depth together with the courtship for *Sebastes inermis* (Shinomiya & Ezaki 1991) and *S. mystinus* (Helvey 1982)—the spermatozoa are retained in the ovaries until the oocytes are mature and fertilization can take place.

However, if the viviparity in scorpaenids evolved from the embryoparity of *Helicolenus*, we would expect that sperm storage structures would also reveal this evolutionary pattern, being simpler in *Helicolenus* and more complex in *Sebastes*. In spite of this, we found that storage of spermatozoa in *Helicolenus* takes place in structures much more complex than those found in viviparous species. In *Sebastiscus* and *Sebastes*, sperm is stored but there are neither specialized ovarian structures nor any unique structural modifications of sperm that can be linked to its storage (Tateishi et al. 1958; Takemura et al. 1987; Eldridge et al. 1991; Takahashi et al. 1991), excepting the invasion by sperm of the follicular epithelia, as described for *Sebastes schlegeli* (Mori et al. 2003). In contrast, in *Helicolenus* there is a crypt (Figure 3.4), probably formed by an epithelial inclusion at the base of the lamellae, which takes up and encloses the sperm (Muñoz et al. 1999, 2000). The stored spermatozoa subsequently seem to be nourished in two ways: through their own energy reserves contained in a large cytoplasm mass that surrounds the sperm head during storage (Vila et al. 2007), and by means of a nutritive contribution from the cryptal epithelium that surrounds the spermatozoa (Muñoz et al. 2002d). Sperm remain protected against the female's immune system by a large number of intercellular junctions among cells of the cryptal epithelium (Vila et al. 2007). This fact has been documented in other scorpaeniform species having intraovarian sperm storage, such as *Alcichthys alcicornis*, in which traces of peroxidase confirm a breakdown of junctional complexes after the spawning period ends (Koya et al. 1997).

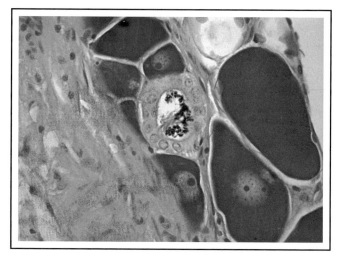

FIGURE 3.4. Intraovarian sperm storage crypt of *Helicolenus dactyopterus*. Epithelial cells surrounding stored sperm are clearly distinguishable.

The differences in ovarian morphology associated with the storage of sperm suggest that viviparous *Sebastiscus* and *Sebastes*, and embryoparous *Helicolenus*, evolved copulation and internal fertilization independantly. This hypothesis is supported by phylogenetic analyses (i.e., Imamura 2004), in which *Sebastiscus* is contained in the most basal clade, *Sebastes* is in the second most basal clade, with the ovary of dorsal lamella type present in both genera, and all genera with ovaries of the central stroma-type are in more recently derived clades. However, it should be pointed out that other recent phylogenetic studies (Smith & Wheeler 2004; Frehlick et al. 2006) consider or suggest that sebastids represent a more derived lineage.

Among viviparous teleosts, members of the genus *Sebastes* are considered relatively primitive with respect to the development of maternal-fetal relationships (Nagahama et al. 1991; Wourms 1991). Gestation is lumenal (i.e., within the ovarian lumen) and the embryos usually develop to term within the egg envelope during a gestation period which is generally longer, compared to the developmental period of oviparous embryos of similar sizes (Yamada & Kusakari 1991). Dygert & Gunderson (1991) suggest that although matrotrophy viviparity (i.e., involving the provision of maternal nutrition for the developing embryo) may be the common mode of reproduction, having been already demonstrated in different species of the genus (Boehlert & Yoklavich 1984; Boehlert et al. 1986; Shimizu et al. 1991; Yoklavich & Boehlert 1991; among others), energy contribution to the development of the embryo varies greatly between species.

Finally, it should be pointed out that most scorpaenids show high fecundities and long reproductive life spans. *Helicolenus dactylopterus* has a fecundity on par with, or even higher than, oviparous scorpaenids, despite the internal fertilization and temporal incubation of the eggs that occurs in this species (Muñoz & Casadevall 2002). In addition, members of the genus *Sebastes* are considered the most fecund of all the teleost viviparous species (Wourms & Lombardi 1992), and that those of the genus *Sebastodes* are also exceptionally fecund (MacGregor 1970). Moreover, their extreme longevity (Pearson & Gunderson 2003; Tsang et al. 2007)—with many species of *Sebastes* reaching maximum ages of 50 to 150 years (Archibald et al. 1981; Love et al. 1990) and a recorded maximum age of 205 years (Cailliet et al. 2001; Munk 2001)—in combination with the evidence that oogenesis continues at advanced ages (de Bruin et al. 2004) reveals a long reproductive life span among members of this group. These traits support the suggestion of Wourms (1991) that scorpaenids have evolved an effective reproductive style that incorporates the best of both possible worlds, namely the fecundity of oviparity combined with the enhanced survival of embryos and larvae conferred by viviparity.

ACKNOWLEDGMENTS

The research was supported in part by contract CTM2006-13964-C03-01 from the "Ministerio de Educación y Cultura" of Spain. I would like to thank reviewers Y. Koya and H. Munehara; their suggestions greatly improved the manuscript.

REFERENCES

Abe T, Munehara H (2005). Spawning and maternal-care behaviors of a copulating sculpin *Radulinopsis taranetzi*. Journal of Fish Biology 67(1): 201–212.

Abe T, Munehara H (2009). Adaptation and evolution of reproductive mode in copulating cottoid species. In: Jamieson B (ed.), *Reproductive Biology and Phylogeny of Fishes (Agnathans and Bony Fishes)*, vol. 8B. Science Publishers, Enfield, New Hampshire, pp. 221–247.

Able KW, Musick JA (1976). Life history ecology and behavior of *Liparis inquilinus* (Pisces Cyclopteridae) associated with the sea scallop *Placopecten magellanicus*. Fishery Bulletin 74(2): 409–421.

Alderdice DF, Jensen JOT, Velsen F (1988). Preliminary trials on incubation of sablefish eggs (*Anoplopoma fimbria*). Aquaculture 69: 271–290.

Aoyama T, Kitajima C, Mizue K (1963). Study of the sex reserval of inegochi, *Cociella crocodila* (Tilesius). Bulletin of Seikai Region Fishery Research Laboratory 29: 11–23.

Archibald CP, Shaw W, Leaman BM (1981). Growth mortality estimates of rockfish (Scorpaenidae) from BC coastal waters 1977–1979. Canadian Technical Reports of Fisheries and Aquatic Sciences 1048.

Baccetti B, Afzelius BA (1976). The biology of the sperm cell. Monographs in Developmental Biology 10: 1–254.

Balon EK (1984). Patterns in the evolution of reproductive styles in fishes. In: Potts GW, Wootton RJ (eds.), *Fish Reproduction: Strategies and Tactics.* Academic Press, London and Orlando, Florida, pp. 36–53.

Barlow GW (1964). Ethology of the Asian teleost *Badis badis.* V. Dynamics of fanning and other parental activities with comments on the behavior of larvae and postlarvae. Zeitschrift für Tierpsychogie 21: 99–123.

Baron J (1985). Les Triglidés (Teleostéens Scorpaeniformes) de la Baie de Douarnenez. 2. La reproduction de: *Eutrigla gurnardus, Trigla lucerna, Trigloporus lastoviza* et *Aspitrigla cuculus.* Cybium 9: 255–281.

Blackburn DG, Evans HE, Vitt LJ (1985). The evolution of fetal nutritional adaptations. Fortschritte der Zoologie 30: 437–439.

Boehlert GW, Yoklavich MM (1984). Reproduction, embryonic energetics and the maternal-fetal relationship in the viviparous genus *Sebastes* (Pisces: Scorpaenidae). The Biological Bulletin 167: 354–370.

Boehlert GW, Kusakari M, Shimizu M, Yamada J (1986). Energetics during embryonic development in kurosoi, *Sebastes schlegeli* Hilgendorf. Journal of Experimental Marine Biology and Ecology 101: 239–256.

Booth AJ (1997). On the life history of the lesser gurnard (Scorpaeniformes: Triglidae) inhabiting the Agulhas Bank, South Africa. Journal of Fish Biology 51: 1155–1173.

Breder CM, Rosen DE (1966). *Modes of Reproduction in Fishes.* TFH Publications, Neptune City, New Jersey.

Cailliet GM, Andrews AH, Burton EJ, Watters DL, Kline DE, Ferry-Graham LA (2001). Age determination and validation studies of marine fishes: do deep-dwellers live longer? Experimental Gerontology 36: 739–764.

Clutton-Brock TH (1991). *The Evolution of Parental Care.* Princeton University Press, Princeton, New Jersey.

Cole KS (2003). Hermaphroditic characteristics of gonad morphology and inferences regarding reproductive biology in *Caracanthus* (Teleostei, Scorpaeniformes). Copeia 2003 (1): 68–80.

Crow KD, Powers DA, Bernardi G (1997). Evidence for multiple maternal contributors in nests of kelp greenling (*Hexagrammus decagrammus*, Hexagrammidae). Copeia 1997: 9–15.

Cuvier G (1829). Le règne animal distribué d'àpres son organisation pour servir de base à l'historie naturelle des animaux et d'introduction à l'anatomie comparée. 2. Nouvelle Édition. Chez Déterville, Paris.

de Bruin JP, Gosden RG, Finch CE, Leaman BM (2004). Ovarian aging in two species of long-lived rockfish, *Sebastes aleutianus* and *S. alutus*. Biology of Reproduction 71: 036–1042.

DeMartini E (1978). Apparent paternal care in *Liparis fucensis* (Pisces: Cyclopteriade). Copeia 1978: 537–539.

DeMartini EE (1987). Paternal defense cannibalism and polygamy: factors influencing the reproductive success of painted greenling (Pisces, Hexagrammidae). Animal Behaviour 35: 1145–1158.

DeMartini EE, Patten BG (1979). Egg guarding and reproductive biology of the red Irish lord, *Hemilepidotus hemilepidotus* (Tilesius). Syesis 12: 41–55.

Dermott SF, Maslenikov KP, Gunderson DR (2007). Annual fecundity, batch fecundity and oocyte atresia of atka mackerel (*Pleurogrammus monopterygius*) in Alaskan waters. Fishery Bulletin 105: 19–29.

Detwyler R (1963). Some aspects of the biology of the seasnail, *Liparis atlanticus* (Jordan and Evermann). Ph.D. thesis, University of New Hampshire, Durham New Hampshire.

Drazen JC, Goffredi SK, Schlining B, Stakes DS (2003). Aggregations of egg-brooding deep-sea fish and cephalopods on the Gorda Escarpment: a reproductive hot spot. The Biological Bulletin 205: 1–7.

Dulcic J, Grubisic L, Katavic I, Skakelja N (2001). Embryonic and larval development of the tub gurnard *Trigla lucerna* (Pisces: Triglidae). Journal of the Marine Biological Association of the United Kingdom 8: 313–316.

Dygert P, Gunderson DR (1991). Energy utilization by embryos during gestation in viviparous copper rockfish, *Sebastes caurinus*. Environmental Biology of Fishes 30: 165–171.

Eldridge MB, Whipple JA, Bowers MJ, Jarvis BM, Gold J (1991). Reproductive performance of yellowtail rockfish *Sebastes flavidus*. Environmental Biology of Fishes 30: 91–102.

Erickson DL, Pikitch EK (1993). A histological description of shortspine thornyhead, *Sebastolobus alascanus,* ovaries: structures associated with the production of gelatinous egg masses. Environmental Biology of Fishes 36: 273–282.

Eschmeyer WN (1998). *Catalog of Fishes.* Vol. 3, *Genera of Fishes, Species and Genera in a Classification.* California Academy of Sciences, San Francisco.

Fishelson L (1975). Ethology and reproduction of pteroid fishes found in the Gulf of Aqaba (Red Sea), especially *Dendrochirus brachypterus* (Cuvier) (Pteroidae: Teleostei). Pubblicazioni della Stazione Zoologica di Napoli 39: 635–656.

Fishelson L (1977). Ultrastructure of the epithelium from the ovary wall of *Dendrochirus brachypterus* (Pteroidae: Teleostei). Cell and Tissue Research 177: 375–381.

Fishelson L (1978). Oogenesis and spawn-formation in the pigmy lion fish *Dendrochirus brachypterus* (Pteroidae). Marine Biology 46: 341–348.

Fleger C (1977). Electron microscopic studies on the development of the chorion of the viviparous teleost *Dermogenys pusillus* (Hemirhamphidae). Cell and Tissue Research 179: 255–270.

Frehlick LJ, Eirín-López J M, Prado A, Su HW (Harvey), Kasinsky HE, Ausió J (2006). Sperm nuclear basic proteins of two closely related species of Scorpaeniform fish (*Sebastes maliger, Sebastolobus* sp.) with different sexual reproduction and the evolution of fish protamines. Journal of Experimental Zoology 305: 277–287.

Fujii T (1970). Hermaphroditism and sex reversal in the fishes of the Platycephalidae. I. Sex reversal of *Onigocia macrolepis* (Bleeker). Japanese Journal of Ichthyology 17: 14–21.

Fujii T (1971). Hermaphroditism and sex reversal in the fishes of the Platycephalidae. II. *Kumococius detrusus* and *Inegocia japonica.* Journal of Ichthyology 18: 109–117.

Gill T (1988). On the classification of the mail-cheeked fishes. Proceedings of the United States National Museum 11: 567–592.

Gomelyuk VE (1988). Spawning behavior of Asian greenling, *Pleurogrammus azonua*, in Peter the Great Gulf. Journal of Ichthyology 28: 82–90.

Hann HM (1927). The history of the germ cell of *Cottus bairdii* Girard. Journal of Morphology and Physiology 43: 427–498.

Hann HM (1930). Variation in spermiogenesis in the teleost family Cottidae. Journal of Morphology and Physiology 50: 393–411.

Hayakawa Y (2007). Parasperm: morphological and functional studies on nonfertile sperm. Ichthyological Research 54: 111–130.

Hayakawa Y, Munehara H (1996). Non-copulatory spawning and female participation during early egg care in a marine sculpin, *Hemilepidotus gilberti*. Ichthyological Research 43: 73–78

Hayakawa Y, Munehara H (1998). The environment for fertilization of the non-copulating marine sculpin, *Hemilepidotus gilberti*. Environmental Biology of Fishes 52: 181–186.

Hayakawa Y, Munehara H (2001). Facultatively internal fertilization and anomalous embryonic development of a non-copulatory sculpin, *Hemilepidotus gilberti* Jordan and Starks (Scorpaeniformes: Cottidae). Journal of Experimental Marine Biology and Ecology 256: 51–58.

Hayakawa Y, Munehara H (2004). Ultrastructural observations of euspermatozoa and paraspermatozoa in a copulatory cottoid fish, *Blepsias cirrhosus*. Journal of Fish Biology 64: 1530–1539.

Hayakawa Y, Akiyama H, Munehara H, Komaru A (2002a). Dimorphic sperm influence semen distribution in a non-copulatory sculpin, *Hemilepidotus gilberti*. Environmental Biology of Fishes 65: 311–317.

Hayakawa Y, Komaru A, Munehara H (2002b). Obstructive role of the dimorphic sperm in a non-copulatory marine sculpin, *Hemilepidotus gilbertii*, to prevent other males' eusperm from fertilization. Environmental Biology of Fishes 64: 419–427.

Hayakawa Y, Komaru A, Munehara H (2002c). Ultrastructural observations of eu- and paraspermiogenesis in the cottid fish, *Hemilepidous gilbertii* (Teleostei: Scorpaeniformes: Cottidae). Journal of Morphology 253: 243–254.

Hayakawa Y, Akiyama R, Munehara H (2004). Antidispersive effect induced by parasperm contained in semen of a cottid fish, *Helmilepidotus giberti*: estimation by models and experiments. Japanese Journal of Ichthyology 51: 31–42.

Hayakawa Y, Kobayashi M, Munehara H (2007). Spermatogenesis involving parasperm production in the marine cottoid fish, *Hemilepidotus gilberti*. Raffles Bulletin of Zoological Sciences 14: 29–35.

Healy JM, Jamieson BGM (1981). An ultrastructural examination of developing and mature paraspermatozoa in *Pyrazus ebeninus* (Mollusca, Gastropoda, Potamididae). Zoomorphology 98: 101–119.

Helvey M (1982). First observations of courtship behaviour in the rockfish genus *Sebastes*. Copeia 1982: 763–770.

Idelman S (1967). Données récentes sur l'infrastructure du spermatozoïde. Annales Biologiques 6: 113–190.

Imamura H (1996). Phylogeny of the family Platycephalidae and related taxa. Species Divers 1: 123–233.

Imamura H (2004). Phylogenetic relationships and new classification of the superfamily Scorpaenoidea (Actinopterygii: Perciformes). Species Divers 9: 1–36.

Imamura H, Shinohara G (1998). Scorpaeniform fish phylogeny: an overview. Bulletin of the Natural Science Museum, Series A 24: 185–212.

Imamura H, Yabe M (2002). Demise of the Scorpaeniformes (Actinopterygii: Percomorpha): an alternative phylogenetic hypothesis. Bulletin of Fisheries Sciences, Hokkaido University 53: 107–128.

Iwamatsu Y, Shibata Y, Kanie T (1995). Changes in chorion proteins induced by the exudate released from the egg cortex at the time of fertilization in the teleost *Oryzias latipes*. Development, Growth, Differentiation 37: 747–759.

Jamieson BGM (1991). *Fish Evolution and Systematics: Evidence from Spermatozoa.* Cambridge University Press, Cambridge.

Jamieson BGM, Leung LKP (1991). Introduction to fish spermatozoa and the micropyle. In: Jamieson BGM (ed.), *Fish Evolution and Systematics: Evidence from Spermatozoa.* Cambridge University Press, Cambridge, pp. 6–72.

Jamieson I (1995). Do female fish prefer to spawn in nests with eggs for reasons of mate choice copying or egg survival? American Naturalist 145: 824–832.

Kendall AW Jr (1991). Systematics and identification of larvae and juveniles of the genus *Sebastes*. Environmental Biology of Fishes 30: 173–190.

King JR, Withler RE (2005). Male nest site fidelity and female serial polyandry in lingcod (*Ophidion elongates*, Hexagrammidae). Molecular Ecology 14: 653–660

Koya Y, Matsubara T (1995). Ultrastructural observations on the inner ovarian epithelia of kichiji rockfish, *Sebastolobus macrochir*, with special reference to the production of gelatinous material surrounding the eggs. Bulletin of the Hokkaido Natural Fisheries Research Institute 59: 1–17.

Koya Y, Muñoz M (2007). Comparative study on ovarian structures in scorpaenids: possible evolutional process of reproductive mode. Ichthyological Research 54: 221–230

Koya Y, Munehara H, Takano K, Takahashi H (1993). Effects of extracellular environments on the motility of spermatozoa in several marine sculpins with internal gametic association. Comparative Biochemistry and Physiology 106: 25–29.

Koya Y, Munehara H, Takano K (1994). Reproductive cycle and spawning ecology in elkhorn sculpin, *Alcicthys alcicornis*. Japanese Journal of Ichthyology 41: 39–45.

Koya Y, Hamatsu T, Matsubara T (1995). Annual reproductive cycle and spawning characteristics of the female kichiji rockfish, *Sebastolobus macrochir*. Fisheries Science 61: 203–208.

Koya Y, Munehara H, Takano K (1997). Sperm storage and degradation in the ovary of a marine copulating sculpin, *Alcichthys alcicornis* (Teleostei: Scorpaeniformes): role of intercellular junctions between inner ovarian epithelial cells. Journal of Morphology 233: 153–163.

Koya Y, Munehara H, Takano K (2002). Sperm storage and motility in the ovary of the marine sculpin, *Alcichthys alcicornis* (Teleostei: Scorpaeniformes) with internal gametic association. Journal of Experimental Zoology 292: 145–155.

Krefft G (1961). A contribution to the reproductive biology of *Helicolenus dactylopterus* (De la Roche 1809) with remarks on the evolution of the Sebastinae. Rapports et Procès

Verbaux des Réunions du Conseil International pour l'Exploration de la Mer 150: 243–244.

Krejsa RJ (1964). Reproductive behavior and sexual dimorphism in the manacled sculpin, *Synchirus gilli* Bean. Copeia 1964: 448–450.

Lisovenko LA (1979). Reproduction of rockfishes (family Scorpaenidae) off the Pacific coast of South America. Journal of Ichthyology 18: 262–268.

Love MS, Westphal WV (1981). Growth, reproduction, and food habits of olive rockfish, *Sebastes serranoides*, off central California. Fishery Bulletin 79: 533–545.

Love MS, Morris P, McCrae M, Collins R (1990). Life history aspects of 19 rockfish species (Scorpaenidae: *Sebastes*) from the southern California Bight. Technical Report of the National Marine Fisheries Service 87. La Jolla, California.

MacGregor JS (1970). Fecundity, multiple spawning, and description of the gonads in *Sebastodes*. Special Scientific Reports US Fish Wildlife Service Fisheries 596, pp. 1–12.

Marliave JB, Peden AE (1989). Larvae of *Liparis fucensis* and *Liparis callyodon*: is the "cottoid bubblemorp" phylogenetically significant? Fishery Bulletin US 87: 735–743.

Matsubara K (1943). Studies on the scorpaenoid fishes from Japan: anatomy, phylogeny and taxonomy. I. Transactions of the Sigenkagaku Kenkyusho 1: 1–170.

Matsubara K (1955). Fish morphology and hierarchy. Ishizaki-shoten, Tokyo.

Mattei X (1970). Spermiogenèse comparée des poissons. In: Baccetti B (ed.), *Comparative Spermatology*. Academic Press, New York, pp. 57–69.

Mattei X (1991). Spermatozoa ultrastructure and taxonomy in fishes. In: Baccetti B (ed.), *Spermatology 20 Years After*. Raven Press, New York, pp. 985–990.

Mattei X, Siau Y, Thiaw OT, Thiam D (1993). Peculiarities in the organization of testis of *Ophidion* sp. (Pisces: Teleostei). Evidence for two types of spermatogenesis in teleost fish. Journal of Fish Biology 43: 931–937.

McFarlane GA, Beamish RJ (1983). Biology of adult sablefish (*Anoplopoma fimbria*) in waters of western Canada. Proceedings of the International Sablefish Symposium, Anchorage, Alaska. Alaska Sea Grant Report 83—08, pp. 59–80.

McFarlane GA, Beamish RJ (1995). Validation of the otolith cross-section method of age determination for sablefish (*Anoplopoma fimbria*) using oxytetracycline. In: Secor DH Dean JM, Campana SE (eds.), *Recent Developments in Fish Otolith Research*. The Belle W. Baruch Library in Marine Science 19, University of South California Press, Columbia, South California, pp. 319–329.

McFarlane GA, Nagata WD (1988). Overview of sablefish mariculture and its potential for industry. Proceedings of the Fourth Alaska Aquaculture Conference. Alaska Sea Grant Report 88–4, pp. 105–120.

McPhail AS, Shipton TA, Sauer WHH, Leslie RW (2001). Aspects of the biology of the Cape Gurnard, *Chelidonichthys capensis* (Scorpaeniformes: Trigilidae) on the Agulhas Bank, South Africa. Vie et Milieu-Life and Environment 51: 217–227.

Miya M, Takeshima H, Endo H, Ishiguro NB, Inoue JG, Mukai T, Satoh TP, Yamaguchi M, Akira K (2003). Major patterns of higher teleostean phylogenies: a new perspective based on 100 complete mitochondrial sequences. Molecular Phylogenetics and Evolution 26: 121–138.

Mori H, Nakagawa M, Soyano K, Koya Y (2003). Annual reproductive cycle of black rock-fish, *Sebastes schlegeli*, in captivity. Fisheries Science 69: 910–923.

Morris RW (1956). Clasping mechanism of the cottid fish *Oligocottus snydery* (Greely). Pacific Science 10: 314–317.

Moulton JM (1963). Acoutic behaviour of fishes. In: Busnel RG (ed.), *Acoustic Behaviour of Animals*. Elsevier, Amsterdam, pp. 655–693.

Munehara H (1988). Spawning and subsequent copulating behavior of elkhorn sculpin, *Alcichthys alcicornis*, in an aquarium. Japanese Journal of Ichthyology 35: 358–364.

Munehara H (1991). Utilization and ecological benefits of a sponge as spawning bed by the little dragon sculpin, *Blepsias cirrhosus*. Japanese Journal of Ichthyology 38: 179–184.

Munehara H (1992). Utilization of polychaete tubes as spawning substrate by the sea raven, *Hemitripterus villosus* (Scorpaeniformes). Environmental Biology of Fishes 33: 395–398.

Munehara H (1996). Sperm transfer during copulation in the marine sculpin *Hemitripterus villosus* (Pisces: Scorpaeniformes) by means of a retractable genital duct and ovarian secretion in females. Copeia 1996: 452–454.

Munehara H, Takano K, Koya Y (1989). Internal gametic association and external fertilization in the elkhorn sculpin, *Alcichthys alcicornis*. Copeia 1989 3: 673–678.

Munehara H, Takano K, Koya Y (1991). The little dragon sculpin, *Blepsias cirrhosus*: another case of internal gametic association and external fertilization. Japanese Journal of Ichthyology 37: 391–394.

Munehara H, Takenaka A, Takenaka O (1994). Alloparental care in the marine sculpin *Alcichtys alcicornis* (Pisces: Cottidae): copulating in conjunction with parental care. Journal of Ethology 12: 115–120.

Munehara H, Kanamoto Z, Miura T (2000). Spawning behaviour and interspecific breeding in three Japanese greenlings (Hexagrammidae). Ichthyological Research 47: 287–292.

Munk KM (2001). Maximum ages of groundfishes in waters off Alaska and British Columbia and considerations of age determination. Alaska Fisheries Research Bulletin 8: 12–21.

Muñoz M, Casadevall M (2002). Reproductive indices and fecundity of *Helicolenus dactylopterus dactylopterus* (Teleostei: Scorpaenidae) in the Catalan Sea (Western Mediterranean). Journal of the Marine Biological Association of the UK 82: 995–1000.

Muñoz M, Cadasevall M, Bonet S (1999). Annual reproductive cycle of *Helicolenus dactylopterus dactylopterus* (Teleostei: Scorpaeniformes) with special reference to the ovaries sperm storage. Journal of the Marine Biological Association of the UK 79: 521–529.

Muñoz M, Casadevall M, Bonet S, Quagio-Grassiotto I (2000). Sperm storage structures in the ovary of *Helicolenus dactylopterus dactylopterus* (Teleostei: Scorpaenidae): an ultrastructural study. Environmental Biology of Fishes 58: 53–59.

Muñoz M, Casadevall M, Bonet S (2001). Gonadal structure and gametogenesis of *Aspitrigla obscura* (Pisces: Triglidae). Italian Journal of Zoology 68: 39–46.

Muñoz M, Casadevall M, Bonet S (2002a). Testicular structure and semicystic spermatogenesis in a specialized ovuliparous species: *Scorpaena notata* (Pisces Scorpaenidae). Acta Zoologica (Stockholm) 83: 213–219.

Muñoz M, Casadevall M, Bonet S (2002b). The ovarian morphology of *Scorpaena notata* shows a specialized mode of oviparity. Journal of Fish Biology 61: 877–887.

Muñoz M, Koya Y, Casadevall M (2002c). Histochemical analysis of sperm storage in *Helicolenus dactylopterus dactylopterus* (Teleostei: Scorpaenidae). Journal of Experimental Zoology 292: 156–164.

Muñoz M, Sàbat M, Malloll S, Casadevall M (2002d). Gonadal structure and gametogenesis of *Trigla lyra* (Pisces: Triglidae). Zoological Studies 41: 412–420.

Muñoz M, Hernández MR, Sàbat M, Casadevall M (2003). Annual reproductive cycle and fecundity of *Aspitrigla obscura* (Teleostei, Triglidae). Vie et Milieu 53(2–3): 123–129.

Muñoz M, Sàbat M, Vila S, Casadevall M (2005). Annual reproductive cycle and fecundity of *Scorpaena notata* (Teleostei: Scorpaenidae). Scientia Marina 69: 555–562.

Nagahama Y, Takemura A, Takano K, Adachi S, Kusakari M (1991). Serum steroid hormone levels in relation to the reproductive cycle of *Sebastes tackzanowskii* and *S. schlegeli*. Environmental Biology of Fishes 30: 31–38.

Nelson JS (2006). *Fishes of the World*. 4th ed. John Wiley & Sons, New York.

Pearson KE, Gunderson DR (2003). Reproductive biology and ecology of shortspine thornyhead rockfish, *Sebastolobus alascanus*, and longspine thornyhead rockfish, *S. altivelis*, from the northeastern Pacific Ocean. Environmental Biology of Fishes 67: 117–136.

Petersen CW (1995). Male mating success and female choice in permanently territorial damselfishes. Bulletin of Marine Science 57: 690–704.

Petersen CW, Mazzoldi C, Zarrella KA, Hale RE (2005). Fertilization mode, sperm characteristics, mate choice and parental care patterns in *Artedius* spp. (Cottidae). Journal of Fish Biology 67: 239–254.

Potts GW (1984). Parental behaviour in temperate marine teleosts with special reference to the development of nest structures. In: Potts GW, Wootton RJ (eds.), *Fish Reproduction: Strategies and Tactics*. Academic Press, London and Orlando, Florida, pp. 223–242.

Quinitio GF (1989). Studies on the functional morphology of the testis in two species of freshwater sculpins. Ph.D. thesis, Hokkaido University, Sapporo, Japan.

Quinitio GF, Takahashi H (1992). An ultrastructural study on the aberrant spermatids in the testis of the river sculpin, *Cottus hangiongensis*. Japanese Journal of Ichthyology 39: 235–241.

Quinitio GF, Takahashi H, Goto A (1988). Annual changes in the testicular activity of the river sculpin, *Cottus hangiongensis* Mori, with emphasis on the occurrence of aberrant spermatids during spermatogenesis. Journal of Fish Biology 33: 871–878.

Ragland HC, Fischer EA (1987). Internal fertilization and male parental care in the scalyhead sculpin, *Artedius harringtoni*. Copeia 1987: 1059–1062.

Rohwer S (1978). Parent cannibalism of offspring and egg raiding as a courtship strategy. American Naturalist 112: 429–440.

Ruiz-Carus R, Matheson Jr RE, Roberts Jr DE, Whitfield PE (2006). The western Pacific red lionfish, *Pterois volitans* (Scorpaenidae), in Florida: evidence for reproduction and parasitism in the first exotic marine fish established in state waters. Biology and Conservation 128: 384–390.

Sàbat M, Lo Nostro F, Casadevall M, Muñoz M (2009). A light and electron microscopic study on the organization of the testis and the semicystic spermatogenesis of the genus *Scorpaena* (Teleostei, Scorpaenidae). Journal of Morphology 270: 662–672.

Selman K, Wallace RA (1989). Cellular aspects of oocyte growth in teleosts. Zoological Science 6: 211–231.

Sequeira V, Figueredo I, Muñoz M, Gordo LS (2003). New approach to the reproductive biology of *Helicolenus dactylopterus*. Journal of Fish Biology 62: 1206–1210.

Shaw FR, Gunderson DR (2006). Life history traits of the greenstriped rockfish, *Sebastes elongates*. California Department of Fish and Game 92: 1–23.

Shibata Y, Iwamatsu T (1996). Evidence for involvement of the exudate released from the egg cortex in the change in chorion proteins at the time of egg activation in *Oryzias latipes*. Zoological Science 13: 271–275.

Shimizu M, Kusakari M, Yoklavich MM, Boehlert GW, Yamada J (1991). Ultrastructure of the epidermis and digestive tract in *Sebastes* embryos with special reference to the uptake of exogenous nutrients. Environmental Biology of Fishes 30: 155–163.

Shinohara G (1994). Comparative morphology and phylogeny of the suborder Hexagrammoidei and related taxa. Memoirs of the Faculty of Fisheries Hokkaido University 41: 1–97.

Shinohara G, Imamura H (2007). Revisiting recent phylogenetic studies of "Scorpaeniformes." Ichthyological Research 54: 92–99.

Shinomiya A (1985). Studies on the reproductive physiology and ecology in three marine cottid fish. Ph.D. thesis, Hokkaido University, Sapporo, Japan.

Shinomiya A, Ezaki O (1991). Mating habits of the rockfish *Sebastes inermis*. Environmental Biology of Fishes 30: 15–22.

Shinomiya A, Yamada M, Sunobe T (2003). Mating system and protandrous sex change in the lizard flathead, *Inegocia japonica* (Platycephalidae). Ichthyological Research 50: 383–386.

Shiokawa T (1962). Studies on habits of coastal fishes in the Amakusa Islands. Part II. Growth and maturity of the purple rockfish, *Sebastes pachycephalus pachycephalus* Temminck et Schlegel. Recent Oceanographic Works, Japan 6: 103–111.

Smith WL, Wheeler WC (2004). Polyphyly of the mail-cheeked fishes (Teleostei: Scorpaeniformes): evidence from mitochondrial and nuclear sequence data. Molecular Phylogenetics and Evolution 32: 627–646.

Sogard SM, Gilbert-Horvath E, Anderson EC, Fishee R, Berkeley SA, Garza JC (2008). Multiple paternity in viviparous kelp rockfish, *Sebastes atrovirens*. Environmental Biology of Fishes 81: 7–13.

Somerton DA, Donaldson W (1998). Parasitism of the golden king crab, *Lithodes aequispinus*, by two species of snailfish genus *Careproctus*. Fishery Bulletin US 96: 871–884.

Sorokin VP (1961). The redfish: gametogenesis and migrations of the *Sebastes marinus* (L) and *Sebastes mentella* Travin. Rapports et Proces-Verbaux des Reunions du Conseil International pour l'Exploration de la Mer 150: 245–250.

Swallow JG, Wilkinson GS (2002). The long and short sperm polymorphism in insects. Biological Reviews 77: 153–182.

Takahashi H, Takano K, Takemura A (1991). Reproductive cycles of *Sebastes*. Environmental Biology of Fishes 30: 23–29.

Takano K (1989). Ovarian structure and gametogenesis. In: Takashima F, Hanyu I (eds.), *Reproductive Biology of Fish and Shellfish*. Midori-shobo, Tokyo, pp. 3–34.

Takemura A, Takano K, Takahashi H (1987). Reproductive cycle of a viviparous fish, the white-edged rockfish, *Sebastes taczanowski*. Bulletin of the Faculty of Fisheries of Hokkaido University 38: 111–125.

Tateishi S, Mizue K, Inao T (1958). Histological study about the ovaries of several kinds of oviviviparous teleost. Bulletion of the Faculty of Fisheries of Nagasaki University 7: 47–50

Tsang WN, Chaillé PM, Collins PM (2007). Growth and reproductive performance in cultured nearshore rockfish (*Sebastes* spp.). Aquaculture 266: 236–245.

Uchida K (1932). On the fish spawning in sea squirt. Kagaku 2: 56–57.

Vila S, Muñoz M, Sabat M, Casadevall M (2007). Annual cycle of stored spermatozoa within the ovaries of *Helicolenus dactylopterus dactylopterus* (Teleostei Scorpaenidae). Journal of Fish Biology 71: 596–609.

Warfel HE, Merriman D (1944). The spawning habits, eggs and larvae of the sea raven *Hemipterus americanus*, in southern New England. Copeia 1944: 197–205.

Washington BB, Eschmeyer WN, Howe KM (1984a). Scorpaeniformes: relationships. In: Moser HG, Richards WJ, Cohen DM, Fahay MP, Kendall Jr AW, Richardson SL (eds.), *Ontogeny and Systematics of Fishes*. American Society of Ichthyologists and Herpetologists, Special Publication 1. Allen Press, Lawrence, Kansas, pp. 438–447.

Washington BB, Moser HG, Laroche WA, Richards WJ (1984b). Scorpaeniformes: development. In: Moser HG, Richards WJ, Cohen DM, Fahay MP, Kendall Jr AW, Richardson SL (eds.), *Ontogeny and Systematics of Fishes*. American Society of Ichthyologists and Herpetologists, Special Publication 1. Allen Press, Lawrence, Kansas, pp. 405–428.

West G (1990). Methods of assessing ovarian development in fishes: a review. Australian Journal of Marine and Freshwater Research 41: 199–222

Wing BL (1997). Distribution of sablefish, *Anoplopoma fimbria*, larvae in the eastern Gulf of Alaska. In: Wilkins M, Saunders M (eds.), Proceedings of the International Symposium on the Biology and Management of Sablefish, *Anoplopoma fimbria*. Seattle, Washington. NOAA National Marine Fisheries Service Technical Report 130, pp. 13–26.

Wourms JP (1976). Annual fish oogenesis. I. Differentiation of the mature oocyte and formation of the primary envelope. Developmental Biology 50: 338–354.

Wourms JP (1991). Reproduction and development of *Sebastes* in the context of the evolution of piscine viviparity. Environmental Biology of Fishes 30: 111–126.

Wourms JP, Lombardi J (1992). Reflections on the evolution of piscine viviparity. American Zoologist 32: 276–293.

Wourms JP, Grove BD, Lombardi J (1988). The maternal embryonic relationship in viviparous fishes. In: Hoar WS, Randall DJ (eds.), *Fish Physiology 11B*. Academic Press, San Diego, pp. 1–134.

Yabe M (1985). Comparative osteology and myology of the superfamily Cottoidea (Pisces: Scorpaeniformes) and its phylogenetic classification. Memoirs of the Faculty of Fisheries of Hokkaido University 32: 1–130.

Yamada J, Kusakari M (1991). Staging and the time course of embryonic development in kurosoi, *Sebastes schlegeli*. Environmental Biology of Fishes 30: 103–110.

Yau C, Collins MA, Everson I (2000). Commensalism between a liparid fish (*Careproctus* sp.) and stone crabs (Lithodidae) photographed *in situ* using a baited camera. Journal of the Marine Biological Association of the UK 80: 379–380.

Yoklavich MM, Boehlert GW (1991). Uptake and utilization of ^{14}C-glycine by embryos of *Sebastes melanops*. Environmental Biology of Fishes 30: 147–153.

Yoneda M, Miura H, Mitsuhashi M, Matsuyama M, Matsuyama S (2000). Sexual maturation, annual reproductive cycle, and spawning periodicity of the shore scorpionfish, *Scorpanenodes littoralis*. Environmental Biology of Fishes 58: 307–319.

4

Parental Care, Oviposition Sites, and Mating Systems of Blennioid Fishes

Philip A. Hastings and Christopher W. Petersen

Mating systems of species result from a complex interaction of phylogenetic constraints and a host of environmental factors (Emlen & Oring 1977; Shuster & Wade 2003). Well-documented, fundamental features of the reproductive biology of fishes affecting their mating systems include mode of fertilization, egg type, and parental care pattern (Gross & Shine 1981). These features evolve relatively slowly in most fishes as they vary little within lineages (Mank et al. 2005). Environmental factors in general are more variable within lineages and consequently are more often responsible for variation in the mating systems within particular lineages. These include the ability of males to sequester females or resources critical to females, as well factors that influence the timing of mating and the distribution of mating sites. In this chapter, we review the fundamental reproductive features of blennioid fishes, as well as the role of various environmental factors on the form of the mating system. We focus on aspects of oviposition sites as the major environmental factor in externally fertilizing species, which includes the majority of blennioids.

Blennioid fishes are common in many coastal regions of the world and prominent members of most reef communities in both tropical and temperate areas. Blennies and other small, benthic fishes have received considerable research attention in recent years as their important roles in coastal communities are becoming more widely evident (Munday & Jones 1998; Depczynski & Bellwood 2003; Smith-Vaniz et al. 2006) and their value as study organisms more widely appreciated (Patzner et al. 2009).

The Blennioidei is a monophyletic lineage of perciform fishes and includes at least 883 species allocated among six families (Springer 1993; Hastings &

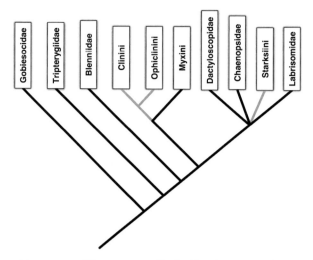

FIGURE 4.1. Character map for fertilization pattern in lineages of blennioid fishes and their sister group the cling-fishes (Gobiesocidae). Solid black = external fertilization of demersal eggs. Solid gray = internal fertilization.

Springer 2009a). The bulk of this diversity is found in the combtooth blennies (Blenniidae) with 387 species (Hastings & Springer 2009a) and the triplefin blennies (Tripterygiidae) with 163 species (Fricke 2009). Both of these lineages are global in distribution. The remaining families are smaller and have more restricted distributions with the Clinidae (85 species) found primarily in temperate oceans and the Chaenopsidae (91), Labrisomidae (109) and Dactyloscopidae (48) found primarily in the Neotropics (Hastings 2009). Five of the six families have evidence of monophyly, while the Labrisomidae lack known morphological synapomorphies (Hastings & Springer 2009b). The phylogenetic relationships of blennioids are largely unresolved. Preliminary phylogenetic analyses based on nuclear and mitochondrial markers (Lin 2009) are largely consistent with the phylogenetic hypothesis proposed by Springer & Orrell (2004) based on selected morphological features (Hastings & Springer 2009b). In that hypothesis, tripterygiids, blenniids, and clinids are sequential sister groups to an unresolved lineage that includes chaenopsids, labrisomids, and, tentatively, dactyloscopids (Figure 4.1).

The biology of blennies, including several aspects of their reproductive biology, has received increased study in recent years (Patzner et al. 2009). In a brief survey of the primary literature, we found 113 journal articles covering some aspect of blenny reproductive biology or reproductive behavior. These papers re-

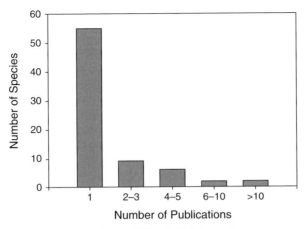

FIGURE 4.2. Numbers of blennioid fish species per quantity of publications covering some aspect of their reproductive biology.

ported on one or more of 74 blennioid species. This represents only 8 percent of the 883 known species; thus, nothing is published concerning the reproductive biology of over 90 percent of blenny species. In addition, the published studies on blennies are heavily biased towards a surprisingly few well-studied species (Figure 4.2). Twenty-seven papers involve some aspect of the reproductive biology of the peacock blenny, *Salaria pavo* (Blenniidae), while 12 concern the reproductive biology of the Azoran rock-pool blenny, *Parablennius parvicornis* (Blenniidae). The vast majority of blennies that have been studied, 55 of 74 species, are treated in a single published study. The distribution of published studies is also biased towards certain families. In particular, it might appear that the reproductive biology of the Clinidae is relatively well known with 27 percent of its species covered in one or more publications. However, most of these are from surveys of specific aspect of their reproductive biology, such as the morphology of male copulatory organs and sperm transmission mechanisms (Fishelson et al. 2006, 2007), details of maternal investment in offspring (Gunn & Thresher, 1993) or general ecology (Prochazka & Griffiths 1992), and do not provide detailed insight into the mating system of most of these species.

In spite of this uneven coverage, several general patterns regarding the reproductive biology and mating systems of blennies emerge. In the present study, we explore the role of selected constraints on the mating systems of blennioids with an emphasis on parental care pattern and oviposition sites. We view these as key features influencing multiple aspects of their mating systems.

FERTILIZATION MODE AND PARENTAL CARE

A fundamental determinant of mating systems in animals is the mode of fertilization (Gross & Shine 1981; Mank et al. 2005). The majority of blennioids are assumed to have external fertilization of demersal eggs deposited on the substrate (Breder & Rosen 1966) or carried on the body of the male (see below). Although unconfirmed for most species, assuming that this feature follows phylogenetic lines, this includes all species of the Tripterygiidae (163 species), Blenniidae (387), Chaenopsidae (91), and Dactyloscopidae (48), most members of the Labrisomidae (78 of 109 species) and a few of the Clinidae (including 9 of the 85 clinid species). Thus, 88 percent (776 of 883) of the species of blennioids probably exhibit external fertilization. In addition to being by far the predominant condition, all available evidence, including the similar condition in the Gobiesocoidei (clingfishes and relatives; Breder & Rosen 1966), the apparent sister group of the Blennioidei, (Hastings & Springer 2009b), indicates that external fertilization of demersal eggs is the plesiomorphic condition in the Blennioidei (Figuvre 4.1).

Internal fertilization (IF) evolved independently at least twice and probably only twice within the Blennioidei (Figure 4.1). IF is seen in two tribes of the Clinidae: the Clinini, with 64 species, and the Ophiclinini, with 12 species. George & Springer (1980) hypothesized that these tribes were sister groups based primarily on the presence of "ovoviviparity" and intromittent organs in males. This relationship was corroborated by earlier (Stepien et al. 1997) and more recent (S. von der Heiden pers. comm.) molecular analyses, implying that internal fertilization evolved once in their common ancestor. Males of both lineages have prominent intromittent organs that represent modifications of the genital papilla, and females retain fertilized eggs within the follicles until hatching (Gunn & Thresher 1993; Fishelson, et al. 2006; Moser 2007). Among blennioids, IF evolved a second time in the unrelated labrisomid tribe Starksiini, a monophyletic lineage that includes two genera, *Starksia* with 30 species, and *Xenomedea* with only one (Rosenblatt & Taylor 1971). All starksiines have putative intromittent organs (Hubbs 1952), and although unconfirmed for most species, *Xenomedea* and at least four species of *Starksia* are confirmed to have internal fertilization (Rosenblatt & Taylor 1971).

Mode of fertilization appears to dictate the pattern of parental care in fishes in general (Ridley 1978; Gross & Shine 1981; Gross & Sargent 1985; Mank et al. 2005), as well as in blennioids. So far as is known, all species of blennioids with external fertilization exhibit male guarding of eggs that are deposited either in the male's territory, in a shelter, or on a modified (cleared) patch of substrate, or are carried on their body (Figure 4.3). Eggs may be deposited on the substrate in a monolayer (e.g., Clarke & Tyler 2003) or in a mass held together with filaments (e.g., Breder 1941). In most cases, parental care takes on the form of egg defense by chasing conspecific and heterospecific egg predators. Predators on the eggs of blennies include a variety of other fish species and invertebrates (e.g., Sunobe 1998; Hirayama et al. 2005), and conspecifics including paternal males themselves (e.g., Ohta & Nakazono 1988; Hamada & Nakazono 1989; Kraak & van der Berghe 1992; Vinyoles et al. 1999).

Parental care in blennies also includes behaviors that appear to increase the survivorship of developing embryos. The most commonly reported behavior of this type is fanning of eggs (e.g., Gibran et al. 2004; Lengkeek & Didderen 2006). In *Aidablennius sphinx,* the frequency of egg fanning is positively correlated with brood size (Kraak & Videler 1991; Oliveira et al. 2000) and with female mate preference (e.g., Neat & Locatello 2002). However, not all paternal blennioids fan eggs (e.g., Petersen 1988). Other parental behaviors of blennies include nest cleaning (e.g., Oliveira et al. 2000), mouthing of eggs to increase circulation and/or remove debris and dead eggs (e.g., Breder 1941; Kraak 1996), and application of antibiotics via the prominent anal-fin glands of male blenniids (Giacomello et al. 2006). Secretions from these glands are attractive to receptive females (Barata et al. 2008). While similar fin glands are present in other lineages of blennioids such as the triplefins (Northcott & James 1996), their function in these latter groups has not been documented.

Importantly, these forms of parental care in blennioids are shareable care in that the per-egg cost of parental care is not additive (Wittenberger 1979, 1981); that is, once a male is caring for eggs, it costs very little more to care for additional eggs as long as they can be accommodated within the spawning site. As a consequence, parental males often continue courting females and may obtain additional clutches of eggs. Thus parental males often guard clutches of eggs that are in different stages of development (see Neat & Lengkeek 2009). However, defense of eggs is costly to males in reduced feeding opportunities because their movements may be restricted to nest sites (e.g., Gonçalves & Almada 1997).

The importance of male egg guarding is reflected in female mate preferences in some blenny species. Females have been demonstrated to prefer mating with males that are already mating with other females (e.g., Petersen 1989) and those males already guarding other clutches of eggs (e.g., Kraak & Videler 1991; Kraak & Groothuis 1994; Kraak & Weissing 1996). In the redlip blenny, females appear to monitor survivorship of eggs in the nests of males and adjust their mating preferences accordingly (Côté & Hunte 1989b). The commonly observed correlations between male body size and female preference (e.g., Hastings 1988a, b, 1992) and male body size and male reproductive success (reviewed in Neat & Lengkeek 2009) have been hypothesized to be a consequence of increased parental abilities (i.e., defense of eggs) by larger males (e.g., Côté & Hunte 1989a, 1993).

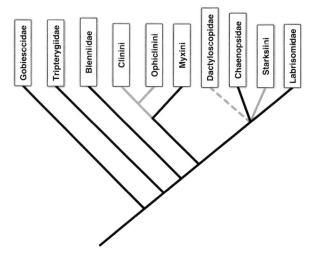

FIGURE 4.3. Character map for parental care pattern in lineages of blennioid fishes and their sister group, the cling-fishes (Gobiesocidae). Solid black = male defense of eggs deposited on the substrate. Dashed gray = male egg carrying. Solid gray = female internal gestation.

The sand stargazers (Dactyloscopidae) exhibit a unique form of parental care that may be related to their unusual habitat. These fishes occur on sand and rubble substrates adjacent to or sometimes far from reefs (Hastings & Springer 2009b). They typically burrow in the substrate and exhibit a number of extraordinary features associated with this behavior. These behaviors include upwardly directed mouth and eyes, the lateral line placed high on the body, lip fimbriae preventing sand from entering the buccal cavity, and a modified branchial pump (Todd 1973). One of the most striking features of sand stargazers is their method of parental care. Sand and rubble habitats often lack suitable substrate for egg deposition and egg guarding, and, unique among blennioids (Figure 4.3), dactyloscopid males carry clutches of eggs in one or two balls behind each pectoral fin. The eggs, about 1 mm in diameter, are attached to one another by fine adhesive filaments and a thicker adhesive thread is located in the central portion of each egg mass. Eggs are held in place between the large pectoral fins and the recurved spines in the anterior anal fin of males of species in the genera *Dactyloscopus*, *Dactylagnus*, and *Myxodagnus* (Böhlke & Chaplin 1968; Petti 1969). Males of some species reportedly carry two distinct egg balls, one behind each pectoral fin (Robins et al. 1999). A single egg mass in *M. opercularis* reportedly included 404 eggs, while one in *Dactyloscopus mundus* contained 3,342 eggs (Petti 1969). Little else is known of this behavior including how eggs are transferred from the female to the male, the number of eggs and number of clutches that are carried by males and consequently how many females mate with single males. It seems likely that this does not represent sharable care, and a male may be constrained to carry the eggs of a single female until they hatch, much like the situation in pipefishes and seahorses (e.g., Berglund et al. 1989) and oral brooders such as cardinalfishes (e.g., Okuda et al. 2003).

Blennies with internal fertilization exhibit a shift from male care of eggs to internal female care and, often, provisioning of embryos (Figure 4.3). This transition from external to internal fertilization in the Starksiini was accompanied by a shift from male parental care, typical of other labrisomid blennies (e.g., Petersen 1988), to female care of internally developing embryos (Rosenblatt & Taylor 1971). In the more well-studied internally fertilizing clinids, care also shifted from male guarding of eggs in the Myxiodini (Stepien 1986) to internal retention of developing eggs by females. Female clinids also contribute significant resources to embryos in addition to those present in the eggs (Veith 1979, 1980). This is clearly not shareable care, although several features of females appear to maximize their fecundity. Chief among these is superfoetation in which clutches of eggs in as many as eight different stages are maintained within the ovary of single females (Gunn & Thresher 1993; Moser 2007).

OVIPOSITION SITES IN EXTERNALLY FERTILIZING BLENNIOIDS

Diversity of Sites

Among blennioids with paternal care of demersal eggs, the variety of spawning sites is immense. These range from temporary territories in the intertidal (Almada et al. 1992; Almada & Santos 1995; Gonçalves & Almada 1998), to holes or crevices (Almada et al. 1994), to species-specific dependence on empty tests of invertebrates (Hastings 1988a, b, 1992). These spawning sites are defended by resident males, and courtship activities are centered around these sites. Courtship may include a variety of visual, chemical, and auditory displays (e.g., Almada et al. 1990; de Jong et al. 2007; Barata et al. 2008). Receptive females approach and enter the nest site and deposit eggs directly on the substrate where they are fertilized by the resident male (and sometimes by nonresident males; see below). Following egg deposition, females leave the spawning site. In some cases entire clutches of eggs are deposited with a single male (e.g., *Ophioblennius macclurei*, Côté & Hunte 1989a), while in others, females may immediately spawn with nearby males (e.g., *Acanthemblemaria macrospilus*, Stephens et al. 1966). After spawning, males continue guarding the oviposition site and consequently the eggs (Petersen 1988) and may also perform one or more egg maintenance behaviors (see above). Parental males often continue courtship, and in many species, successful males may attract multiple mates to oviposition sites (see Neat & Lengkeek 2009). Thus, the typical pattern in blennioids is the combination of paternal care and male courtship, because the main factor limiting male reproductive success is access to females.

In species where males and females differ in habitat utilization, males are often found in either more protected microhabitats such as vacant invertebrate tests as opposed to open surfaces (e.g., Hastings 2002), shallower sites within a rock reef (e.g., Petersen 1988; Almada et al. 1992) or more frequently on living versus dead corals (e.g., Clarke & Tyler 2003).

Because male reproductive success is typically dependent upon defense of an oviposition site, male-male competition for these limited resources (Buchheim & Hixon 1992; Hastings & Galland 2009) may be intense (e.g., Shibata & Kohda 2006), especially where shelters vary in quality as reproductive sites (Hastings 1988a, b). A number of features of blennioids appear to maximize their fighting capabilities, including large body size (Faria & Almada 2001), and large jaws and robust associated muscles (Kotrschal 1988; Hastings 2002).

In a well-studied population of the peacock blenny, S. pavo, that occurs in an area of sandy substrate, suitable oviposition sites are limited, being found only in artificial tiles that are defended by large males (Almada et al. 1994, 1995). This shortage of suitable oviposition sites excludes small males from shelter defense and leads to sex role reversal where females actively court males. While this situation is unusual in blennioids, similar sex role shifts have been observed in the blenniid *Petroscirtes breviceps* during the middle of an extended breeding season when free space for egg deposition becomes limiting (Shibata & Kohda 2006).

Sites and Male Reproductive Success

Reproductive success of male blennioids results from a complex interaction of male-male competition for oviposition sites and female preference for various aspects of males and the oviposition sites they defend. Mate choice parameters in blennies were recently reviewed by Neat & Lenkeek (2009). Here we expand their analysis to discuss aspects of oviposition sites in greater detail.

Females typically show preferences for larger males in mating, and this has been demonstrated for several blennies (e.g., *Coralliozetus angelicus*, Hastings 1988b; *Acanthemblemaria crockeri*, Hastings 1988a; *Ophioblennius macclurei,* Côté & Hunte 1989a; *Emblemaria hypacanthus*, Hastings 1991; *Salarias pavo*, Fagundes et al. 2007). This preference may also be reflected in the field, where the reproductive success of male blennies is often correlated with their size for these and many other species (e.g., the above species plus *Fosterygion varium*, Thompson 1986; *Malacoctenus macropus*, Petersen 1988; *Ophioblennius macclurei*, Côté &

Hunte 1989; *Salaria pavo*, Oliveira et al. 1999; *Parablennius parvicornis*, Oliveira et al. 2000; *Aidablennius sphinx*, Neat & Locatello 2002; and Fagundes et al. 2007; but no effect found by Kraak & Videler 1991). In *Aidablennius sphinx*, females lay more eggs, and do so more quickly, with larger males, reflecting either or both a preference for large males and perhaps sperm limitation in small males (Locatello & Neat 2005). In *Ophioblennius macclurei*, females pay a cost of increased aggression from territorial damselfish in order to mate with larger (preferred) males far from their home territory (Reynolds & Côté 1995)

The degree that this pattern of greater reproductive success by larger males is found in field populations may vary over a spawning season (e.g., Oliveira et al. 1999) and depends on the ability of larger males to sequester more successful sites. For example, within populations of *Emblemaria hypacanthus*, Hastings (1992) found that although females preferred larger males in mate choice experiments where other factors were controlled, in the field larger males only obtained higher reproductive success (RS) in a population where nest sites were larger and allowed for high levels of simultaneous egg development. Additionally, preferences for larger males can be masked in populations when larger males are not associated with preferred oviposition sites. Petersen (1988) found that larger males did not have higher RS in *Malacoctenus hubbsi*, but when the effects of oviposition site were statistically removed, larger males were preferred as mates. Females of the angel blenny (*Coralliozetus angelicus*), a barnacle specialist, prefer large males, but at some sites, larger barnacles are lower quality, tending to be more heavily fouled internally where eggs are deposited. Because large, preferred males are forced to occupy especially large shelters (barnacles) and the quality of the largest shelters is below a threshold required by females, the reproductive success of large males is reduced (Hastings 1988b).

In species where the sexes differ in habitat utilization, females often show preferences for males in the direction of the habitat differences (e.g., Petersen 1988). For example, in the carmine triplefin, *Axoclinus storyae*, male territories are at greater depth than female territories, and males defending deeper sites have higher mating success (Petersen 1989). In the chaenopsid *Acanthemblemaria spinosa*, males occupying shallower shelters have increased reproductive success although the sexes do not differ in the depth of shelters occupied; in both sexes larger individuals were found in more shallow shelters (Clarke & Tyler 2003) where their feeding rate is greater because of increased availability of planktonic prey (Clarke 1992). The greater reproductive success of males defending more shallow shelters may be a result of the preference of females for larger males (Clarke & Tyler 2003).

In some blennies, females prefer to mate with males defending protected sites. For example, in the labrisomid *Malacoctenus macropus*, males with the most protected oviposition sites had the highest mating success (Petersen 1988). This suggests that sexual selection through female choice is one of the selective factors favoring males to live in more protected sites.

In species that lay eggs in the open, more vertical (as opposed to more horizontal) surfaces probably have two advantages as oviposition sites, both related to egg development. First, vertical surfaces probably receive more current flow than horizontal surfaces, which should increase oxygenation rates of eggs. Secondly, eggs should be less likely to receive excess amounts of sediments that might reduce egg development rates or increase egg mortality through infection or hypoxia. Species that spawn in open sites often do not fan eggs (e.g., *Tripterygion*, Wirtz 1978; *Malacoctenus*, Petersen 1988), but may provide other forms of parental care, such as guarding eggs and removing dead eggs (Wirtz 1978).

Although some aspects of oviposition sites are preferred by females, these sites can have limited areas for oviposition and thereby constrain male mating success. This appears to limit male reproductive success in several species (e.g., *Emblemaria hypacanthus*, Hastings 1992; *Aidablennius sphynx*, Neat & Locatello 2002). In these species, females lay eggs in a monolayer and, although clutches can be contiguous, they do not overlap. Other species that deposit eggs on exposed surfaces have cryptically colored eggs that are deposited more loosely with algae (Petersen pers. obs.); it is less clear in these species if oviposition substrate ever becomes limiting.

The long-term predictability of the quality of oviposition sites appears to vary substantially among species. For some, such as *M. hubbsi*, sites in the intertidal have decreased success during spring tides when the sites are exposed to air, and this appears to change preferred oviposition sites at those times (Petersen 1988). In response to this temporal variability in oviposition site attractiveness, males in some species appear to assess territory quality indirectly by their mating success. In *M. hubbsi,* males abandon territories within three days when females are kept from mating in those territories (Petersen 1988), and in *Ophioblennius macclurei,* males are more likely to abandon sites after periods of low male reproductive success (Côté & Hunte 1989b). In this second case, males move oviposition sites but stay within the same feeding territories.

In many species of fishes with paternal care, females prefer to mate with males guarding eggs, especially when those eggs or clutches are at early stages of development (Kraak & Videler 1991). In *Ophioblennius atlanticus*, males taking over sites with surviving eggs present realize an increase in mating success over males occupying sites with no eggs (Santos 1995). This has several potential benefits for females, the most obvious one being increased survivorship of eggs due to either dilution of egg predation by the paternal male, increased parental care by the male, or a lower likelihood of abandonment of an oviposition site. In blennioids, this pattern has been suggested by female preferences for mating with males guarding eggs (Kraak & Videler 1991; Kraak & Groothuis 1994; Kraak & Weissing 1996, Fagundes et al. 2007) or mating males (Petersen 1989; Geertjes & Videler 2002). The most intriguing study of this kind is the work of Kraak & van der Berge (1992) on *Aidablennius sphynx*. These authors showed that if a male is given eggs, his future reproductive success increases, and if eggs are removed, his future reproductive success decreases. When nests are empty, females appear to lay a few eggs (1 to 10) in a nest, and if these "test" eggs survive, females will subsequently lay larger clutches with that male.

In some hole nesting combtooth blennies, a positive association between male size and size of the shelter opening has been reported (e.g., Crabtree & Middaugh 1982; Takegaki et al. 2008). Relative fit of males within their shelter entrance in the chaenopsids *Coralliozetus angelicus* and *Acanthemblemaria crockeri* shows considerable variation, ranging from 20 to 98 percent of the shelter opening filled by the resident's head; however, relative fit of males within their shelter entrance was unrelated to their body size or to the number of eggs they defended in either species (Hastings 1988a, b).

Size assortative pairing has been reported in at least two blenniids, *Ophioblennius macclurei* (Côté & Hunte 1989a) and *Istiblennius enosimae* (Sunobe et al. 1995). The preference of large females for large males is not surprising, given that a preference for large males occurs in many blennioids (see above). The important point here is that small females appear to be restricted from mating with large males. In species with relatively open oviposition sites, multiple females spawning simultaneously or consecutively with a male is common (Petersen 1988; Hamada & Nakazono 1989; Petersen 1989; Neat 2001; Geertjes & Videler 2002), and size assortative spawning is not reported in these species. In these species, males maximize mating success by mating with as many females as possible; small females are not excluded from oviposition sites and may mate at the same time that large females are spawning. However, if the number of females a male can mate with is restricted, then preferences for large females can evolve either because these females have qualitatively or quantitatively better offspring, or because their rates of oviposition during individual spawning events are higher. Restrictions on female mates would most likely occur in species where oviposition sites are limited to single females spawning at a time, and spawning is limited either to specific diel or lunar cycles. All of these conditions occur in *Ophioblennius macclurei*; spawning occurs during a limited period at dawn, is concentrated within a lunar cycle (Robertson et al. 1990) and the oviposition sites appear to restrict spawning to one female at a time. With limited opportunities to spawn, we would expect males to differentially select large females. An interesting prediction from this hypothesis is that we would expect male choice and size assortative pairing to be most intense during the peak of spawning in the lunar month. Thus, we would expect sexual selection for male choice to be less intense during other times in the lunar month when fewer females are spawning. Shibata & Kohda (2006) reported a shift in sex roles in *Petroscirtes breviceps* at the middles of an eight-month breeding season when spawning sites were restricted in availability, but they did not report the size of mating pairs.

A second possible reason for size assortative pairing would be if individuals assort in the habitat according to size, and females travel limited distances to find mates, thereby reducing their mating options. Size assortative habitat use has been reported in *Acanthemblemaria spinosa* (Clarke & Tyler 2003), but it is unclear whether this pattern ever leads to size assortative mating.

There is no evidence in any blennioid species that sperm limits fertilization success in the field, and sperm limitation is unlikely to be a constraint on fertilization success in these and similar fishes (Giacomello et al. 2007). Spawning in enclosed areas such as cracks or invertebrates probably leads to very effective fertilization at very low sperm concentrations. Spawning in open areas with greater current flow is more likely to result in sperm dilution and reduced fertilization rates, but no data exist to address this prediction for marine blennioids. However, in the freshwater blenniid *Salaria fluviatilis,* males in riverine populations were currents may disperse sperm have larger testes and release more sperm compared to males from lake populations (Vinyoles et al. 2002; Neat et al. 2003a).

OVIPOSITION SITES AND ALTERNATIVE
REPRODUCTIVE TACTICS

Alternative male reproductive tactics (ARTs), including both sneak spawning and female mimicry, are known for several species of blennioids. This topic has been recently reviewed (Taborsky 2001 for fishes, and Oliveira et al. 2001a and Almada & Robalo 2008 for blennioids). Within blennioids, alternative reproductive tactics appear to take three forms: small males sneaking into nests and releasing sperm (e.g., *Axoclinus* spp. and *Tripterygion spp.*, Wirtz 1978; Neat 2001); satellite males that associate with specific nests and their territorial males, do some nest defense, but also sneak spawn (e.g., *Parablennius parvicornis* and *Salaria pavo*; Oliveira et al. 2002; Gonçalves et al. 2003a, b); and males that mimic female behavior and morphology to gain access to oviposition sites in what has been described for fishes as pseudofemale behavior (e.g., *Salaria pavo*, Gonçalves et al. 1996, 2005). Males practicing ARTs often forego investment in accessory gonadal structures associated with mate attraction in territorial males (de Jonge et al. 1989; Oliveira et al. 2001b; Neat et al. 2003b) and often have larger testes (Ruchon et al. 1995; but see Geertjes & Videler 2002 for an exception).

Oliveira et al. (2008) reviewed the nine species of blennioids where ARTs have been documented, which includes only the Tripterygiidae and Blenniidae. However, the absence of reports from the less well-studied Labrisomidae is probably a result of less published work on these species. For example, in the labrisomid *Malacoctenus hubbsi*, one of us has observed individuals adopting pseudofemale behavior, either for multiple days or as a potential season-long tactic. In addition, territorial males that do not attract females early during the breeding period lose their courtship coloration and attempt to enter nearby nests with active spawning (Petersen, unpublished observations). Although these sightings were rare events (only one individual of each type was observed), it suggests that ARTs are more widely distributed across the blennioids than currently reported.

With the recent proliferation of microsatellite primers for a variety of fish species, the genetic confirmation of multiple paternity, and thus the success of ARTs is now possible. Multiple paternity was recently demonstrated within clutches of eggs defended by single males in the blenniid *Scartella cristata* (Mackiewicz et al. 2005). Because male replacement at oviposition sites is well known in blennioids (e.g., Santos 1995; Tyler & Tyler 1999), some cases of males guarding unrelated eggs may represent nest turnover rather than successful sneak fertilizations. Nest turnover should be distinguishable from lost fertilizations to competing males because in the former, eggs fathered by a different male should be the oldest eggs at the oviposition site.

Reports on ARTs in blennioids conform to a pattern of smaller males "making the best of a bad situation," suggesting that they have lower current reproductive success than territorial males, and that the mating tactic is conditional and not an equally successful mating strategy (Ruchon et al. 1995; Gonçalves & Almada 1997). Generally, we expect alternative mating tactics in blennioids to exist when there is a class of males, typically significantly smaller males, that have substantially lower expected mating success than larger territorial males.

Blennioids vary substantially in how physically isolated oviposition sites are within the environment. These range from small holes in virtually all chaenopsids and some blenniids, to the often relatively open oviposition sites in the labrisomids and many of the tripterygiids. Oviposition sites located in holes or crevices, especially when they are relatively small compared to individual adults (i.e., in chaenopsids), often lead to single females spawning with males at any one time, and make it relatively easy for males to defend these sites from conspecific male intruders (Hastings 1986). ARTs have never been reported within the Chaenopsidae, and instead, neighboring males exhibit vigorous courtship from their own shelter when in sight of a spawning pair (Hastings pers. obs.) and females may spawn consecutively with multiple males (Stephens et al. 1966). This is in contrast to open substrate spawners, like tripterygiids, where as many as five females of *Axoclinus storyae* may spawn with a male at once. ARTs have been reported for several of these triplefin species (Wirtz 1978; Neat 2001). Generally, we expect ARTs to be more likely in open substrate spawning species than in hole nesting species, simply because of increased access to nests by small males, either as a sneaker male making quick intrusions into relatively open oviposition site, or as one of many conspecifics in a nest at once (Neat & Locatello 2002). ARTs are known in some non-blennioid species that are hole nesters, but in these species the hole or crevice is either large enough for multiple spawning partners to be in a nest at once, or males appear to release sperm at a distance from the female and fan the sperm toward the nest with their pectoral fins (Mazzoldi & Rasotto 2002).

The second characteristic that we predict will exist in species with ARTs is that of having a class of males that have a low expectation of mating success for a given time in the reproductive season. In species that live for several years, this will most often consist of younger year classes of males or, in short-lived species with prolonged spawning seasons, those males that have recently recruited to the re-productive population. For example, in the Gulf of California triplefin, *Axoclinus nigricaudus*, during the summer months there are two size classes of males. The smaller size class does not take on male secondary sexual characteristics, does not have a well-developed accessory gland, and can be observed sneak spawning with larger territorial males (Neat 2001; Petersen pers. obs.). In contrast, *Axoclinus storyae* (= *A. carminalis*) appears to be largely an annual species, with breeding restricted to the summer months. All males are mature, have well-developed secondary sexual characteristics including red coloration and developed acces-sory glands, and attempt to court females to oviposition sites (Petersen 1989, pers. obs.). However, late in the breeding season, small individual males do ap-pear, presumably young of the year from spawnings earlier in the season, and at-tempt to sneak spawn (Petersen, pers. obs.). Thus, in Gulf of California *Axoclinus* species, variation in body size within a species appears to have a direct relation-ship with the existence of ARTs, as predicted generally by Taborsky (2001). In species such as hole nesters where there is a large variation in male size and large males can become associated with successful (and limited) oviposition sites, we expect the more likely life-history tactic will be for males to delay maturation, and only the largest males to have well-developed secondary sexual characteristics. However, where size assortative mating provides mating opportunities for young, small males such as in the angel blenny (*Coralliozetus angelicus*), males of all sizes defend shelters from which they court and spawn with similarly sized females (Hastings 1986, 1988b).

Alternative mating tactics have evolved in at least three families of blennies and several times within the blenniids (Oliveira et al. 2001a; Almada & Robalo 2008), so this characteristic appears to have high evolvability in this group, especially where oviposition sites are more exposed and more accessible. ARTs have not been reported in species with readily defensible oviposition sites (i.e., within small shelters), and they may also be absent in internally fertilizing blennioids, but the mating behaviors of these species are largely unknown.

SIZE DIMORPHISM AND PATTERNS
OF MALE REPRODUCTIVE SUCCESS

Blennioid species differ in their pattern of sexual size dimorphism, ranging from males being larger, to sexes similar in size, to females being larger. Because small changes in body size of males and/or females can affect the presence or absence of size dimorphism, it appears that body size dimorphism is a phylogenetically labile feature in blennioids. This is not surprising given the varied nature of growth and mortality in fishes such as blennies and the fact that sexual size dimorphism results from separate but related selection on male and female body size (Blankenhorn 2005). For example, angel blennies are highly dimorphic in body size, with the frequency of males increasing disproportionately in the larger size classes (Hastings 1991); however, this may result from differential mortality of females because they experience greater exposure to predators (Hastings 2002); faster growth of males (not tested); or both (Hastings 1991).

Similar to externally fertilizing clinids (e.g., *Heterostichus rostratus*, Stepien 1986), males of internally fertilizing clinids are the larger sex in several species (Gunn & Thresher 1993). The larger size of males in internally fertilizing species is surprising given persistent selection on gestating females to maximize fecundity. This observation predicts a large male advantage in mating in these fishes, but this has yet to be demonstrated.

Externally fertilizing blennies exhibit a range of dimorphism patterns. Large male size dimorphism is predicted in species where larger males are able to obtain higher reproductive success (RS), which often will be related to their ability to sequester preferred oviposition sites. Stable patterns of female preference with respect to oviposition site should select for larger males that can defend these sites. The intensity of this selection will be proportional to the variance in male reproductive success due to variation in oviposition site. However, several factors may restrict the ability of males to maintain sites that allow them to continue to mate with females and obtain high levels of RS. First, as mentioned earlier, size of oviposition sites in some species may place upper limits on male RS due to limited oviposition site area (e.g., *Emblemaria hypacanthus*, Hastings 1992). Additionally, preferred sites must be predictable and not change in quality over the reproductive season, and must continue to be preferred after males begin defending them. In *Malacoctenus hubbsi*, high spring tides may expose otherwise preferred oviposition sites during the spawning period, reducing the RS of males defending them (Petersen 1988). Similarly, over time, barnacle tests used for oviposition sites may became fouled and thus less preferred as oviposition sites in *Corallioze-tus angelicus* (Hastings 1988b). While most studies of male RS have treated oviposition sites as fixed-quality entities, these studies, and those where males change oviposition sites in response to changes in RS (e.g., Côté & Hunte 1989b), suggest that such temporal instability of oviposition-site quality may be common in blennioids.

Under what circumstances will females prefer larger males? We expect that females should select males defending oviposition sites that maximize the fitness of their young. This could occur if their offspring have better survivorship at specific sites or if spawning with particular males has genetic benefits. Although there is some suggestion that females in some species do prefer larger males because of increased survivorship of young guarded by large males (e.g., Giacomello & Rasotto 2005), we cannot discern any a priori predictions of where this association might exist. We cannot, for example, find any reason to predict that variance in egg survivorship should be greater for species that nest in holes versus species that nest in more open oviposition sites.

ANALYSIS OF FIFTEEN SPECIES OF BLENNIOIDS

We examined patterns of sexual size dimorphism (SSD) and the correlation between male size and male mating success in several species of blennioids where we have recorded field data on male mating success and male size. These 15 study species are distributed across four of the six families of blennioids, with most data coming from species from the Gulf of California (13 of 15; Table 4.1).

Data on sexual size dimorphism were either collected from individuals at the same time that mating success data were being collected, or were obtained from museum collections. In all species, immature individuals were excluded from analysis. In chaenopsids, only those individuals whose sex could be accurately identified based on sex-specific genital papillae (Hastings 1991) were included. For several genera (e.g., *Malacoctenus, Ophioblennius*), only individuals with gonadal evidence of active reproduction, as assessed by visual inspection of gonads, were included. In *Axoclinus nigricaudus*, SSD was estimated using only year 2+ males and females (i.e., as estimated from size frequency distributions), effectively excluding males employing ARTs.

Data on male mating success in the field was determined in one of two general ways. For species that had readily visible eggs, eggs were censused either once (several chaenopsids) or multiple times up to one month (e.g., *Acanthemblemaria crockeri* and *Ophioblennius* spp.). RS was inferred based on either total area of

TABLE 4.1 Sexual size dimorphism and male reproductive success
in 15 species of blennioid fishes

Family/species	M/F SL	Correlation coefficient (r) for SL vs. RS (N)	p	Source
Labrisomidae				
Malacoctenus tetranemus	1.11*	0.076 (26)	0.714	CP
M. macropus	1.07*	0.554 (19)	0.014	Petersen 1988
M. hubbsi	0.96*	0.205 (36)	0.792	Petersen 1988
M. margaritae	0.94*	0.015 (21)	0.948	CP
Tripterygiidae				
Axoclinus nigricaudus	1.04*	0.26 (29)	0.173	CP
A. storyae	1.00	−0.362 (21)	0.107	Petersen 1989
Blenniidae				
Ophioblennius macclurei	0.98*	0.699 (19)	0.001	CP
O. steindachneri	1.00	−0.04 (8)	0.920	CP
Chaenopsidae				
Acanthemblemaria balanorum	1.06	0.4003 (17)	0.110	PH
A. crockeri	1.10*	0.3469 (56)	0.009	Hastings 1988a
A. macrospilus	1.10*	0.1852 (38)	0.266	PH
Coralliozetus angelicus	1.08*	0.3442 (133)	0.001	Hastings 1988b
C. micropes	1.04*	0.1987 (38)	0.232	PH
C. rosenblatti	1.33*	0.6839 (11)	0.020	PH
Emblemaria hypacanthus	1.10*	0.5232 (34)	0.001	Hastings 1992

M/F SL = male to female ratio of mean standard length (SL).

*indicates male and female sizes are significantly different based on a t-test.

r = correlation coefficient of SL vs. RS (N = number of males sampled; RS = reproductive success).

p = significance level for coefficient r.

CP = Petersen unpublished data.

PH = Hastings unpublished data.

eggs oviposited (*Ophioblennius*) or exact counts of eggs (chaenopsids). This number was then run in a correlation against standard length of males guarding the eggs. For more detail on these methods, see Hastings (1988a, b). This technique was used for all chaenopsids and blenniids.

For species with open oviposition sites and more cryptic eggs, we used the techniques reported in Petersen (1988, 1989) for estimating reproductive success. Individuals were censused during the morning spawning period, and the relative mating success of a male was estimating by integrating the amount of time a male spawned with females over a period of weeks. This technique was used for all labrisomids and tripterygiids.

There were substantial differences in SSD among the 15 species, with nine species having larger males, three species having larger females, and two species showing no pattern of SSD (Table 4.1). Although chaenopsids tended to be more likely to show male SSD (six of seven species), generally there was little clear phylogenetic signal with four of the six genera showing interspecific variation in the pattern of SSD.

The general prediction that species where males are larger would have a stronger correlation between male size and mating success was only weakly supported in our data set. Ignoring the phylogenetic signal, five of nine species where there was a significant male SSD showed a positive correlation between male size and male RS. Only one (*Ophioblennius macclueri*) of five species where males were not larger showed a positive correlation between male size and male RS (Fisher exact test $p = 0.168$). Similarly, there was a non-significant trend for SSD to be correlated with the correlation between male size and male RS ($r = 0.453$, $p = 0.104$, 2-tailed).

Although there are slight trends toward a positive correlation between male SSD and a size advantage in male mating success for territorial males in these blennioid species, the pattern is not striking, and clearly other factors are affecting the observed patterns. Within some genera like *Malacoctenus*, the species with the most striking pattern of male SSD showed a notable lack of correlation between RS and male size. While there are many possible explanations for these patterns, here we mention three types of reasons why sexual selection on increased male size is not strictly mirrored in our data set.

First, male and female blennies may have different energy budgets or different survivorship due to differences in their ecology or reproductive behavior. There may be selection for increased male size. But in some species, defense of oviposition sites may change feeding rates, or may change male mortality rates relative to females. Second, our estimates of male RS with size are based on our best censusing of reproductive males. It is possible that males with no mating success are underrepresented in some species, and if they are smaller, these uncounted males would limit our ability to determine positive correlations between reproductive success and male size. Finally, our estimate of short-term reproductive success may not represent the selective differential on male size versus female size. This might be because short-term male RS is not a good predictor of lifetime RS for males, or that species differ in selection on female RS and female size.

With the relatively simple analysis presented here, we cannot distinguish between the possibilities listed above and other potential reasons accounting for lack of a strong correlation between male RS and male SSD. We consider this analysis an initial step in understanding how patterns of SSD and male reproductive success interact with oviposition site and other elements of the reproductive biology of these fishes to produce the rich patterns of mating systems we see in blennioids.

SUMMARY

This brief overview of the factors impinging on the mating systems of blennioid fishes reveals the importance of fertilization mode and parental care pattern in setting the selective arena in which environmental factors act to determine a species' mating system. A key component in the majority of blennioids with external fertilization of demersal eggs is the predictability and defensibility of oviposition sites. These determine to a large extent the options for resource defense by dominant males, the patterns of female mate choice, and the reproductive options of non-territorial males.

REFERENCES

Almada VC, Robalo JI (2008). Phylogenetic analysis of alternative reproductive tactics: problems and possibilities. In: Oliveira RF, Taborsky M, Brockmann HJ (eds.), *Alternative Reproductive Tactics: An Integrative Approach*. Cambridge University Press, Cambridge, pp. 52–62.

Almada VC, Santos RS (1995). Parental care in the rocky intertidal: a case study of adaptation and exaptation in Mediterranean and Atlantic blennies. Reviews of Fish Biology and Fisheries 5:23–37.

Almada VC, Oliveira RF, Barata EN, Gonçalves EJ, Rito AP (1990). Field observations on the behaviour of the breeding males of *Lipophrys pholis* (Pisces: Blenniidae). Portugaliae Zoologica 1: 27–36.

Almada VC, Gonçalves EJ, Oliveira RF, Barata EN (1992). Some features of the territories in the breeding males of the intertidal blenny *Lipophrys pholis* (Pisces: Blenniidae). Journal of the Marine Biological Association, UK 72: 187–197.

Almada VC, Gonçalves EJ, Santos AJ, Baptista C (1994). Breeding ecology and nest aggregations in a population of *Salaria pavo* (Pisces: Blenniidae) in an area where nest sites are very scarce. Journal of Fish Biology 45: 819–830.

Almada VC, Gonçalves E, Oliveira RF, Santos AJ (1995). Courting females: ecological constraints affect sex roles in a natural population of the blenniid fish, *Salaria pavo*. Animal Behaviour 49: 1125–1127.

Barata EN, Serrano RM, Miranda A, Nogueira R, Hubbard PC, Canário AVM (2008). Putative pheromones from the anal glands of male blennies attract females and enhance male reproductive success. Animal Behaviour, 75: 379–389.

Berglund A, Rosenqvist G, Svensson I (1989). Reproductive success of females limited by males in two pipefish species. American Naturalist 133: 506–516.

Blanckenhorn WU (2005). Behavorial causes and consequences of sexual size dimorphism. Ethology 111: 977–1016.

Böhlke JE, Chaplin CG (1968). *Fishes of the Bahamas and Adjacent Tropical Waters*. Livingston Press, Wynnewood, Pennsylvania.

Breder CM (1941). On the reproductive behavior of the sponge blenny, *Paraclinus marmoratus* (Steindachner). Zoologica 26: 233–236.

Breder CM, Rosen DE (1966). *Modes of Reproduction in Fishes*. Natural History Press, Garden City, New York.

Buchheim JR, Hixon MA (1992). Competition for shelter holes in the coral-reef fish, *Acanthemblemaria spinosa* Metzelaar. Journal of Experimental Marine Biology and Ecology 164: 45–54.

Clarke R, Tyler JC (2003). Differential space utilization by male and female spinyhead blennies, *Acanthemblemaria spinosa* (Teleostei: Chaenopsidae). Copeia 2003: 241–247.

Clarke RD (1992). Effects of microhabitat and metabolic rate on food intake, growth and fecundity of two competing coral reef fishes. Coral Reefs 11: 199–205.

Côté IM, Hunte W (1989a). Male and female mate choice in the redlip blenny: why bigger is better. Animal Behaviour 38: 78–88.

Côté IM, Hunte W (1989b). Self-monitoring of reproductive success: nest switching in the redlip blenny (Pisces: Blenniidae). Behavioral Ecology and Sociobiology 24: 403–408.

Côté IM, Hunte W (1993). Female blennies prefer older males. Animal Behaviour 46: 203–205.

Crabtree RE, Middaugh DP (1982). Oyster shell size and the selection of spawning sites by *Chasmodes bosquianus*, *Hypleurochilus geminatus*, *Hypsoblennius ionthas* (Pisces, Blenniidae) and *Gobiosoma bosci* (Pisces, Gobiidae) in two South Carolina estuaries. Estuaries 5: 150–155.

de Jonge J, de Ruiter AJH, van den Hurk R (1989). Testis-testicular gland complex of two *Tripterygion* species (Blennioidei, Teleostei): differences between territorial and non-territorial males. Journal of Fish Biology 35: 497–508.

de Jong K, Bouton N, Slabbekoorn H (2007). Azorean rock-pool blennies produce size-dependent calls in a courtship context. Animal Behaviour 74(5): 1285–1292.

Depczynski M, Bellwood DR (2003). The role of crytobenthic reef fishes in coral reef trophodynamics. Marine Ecology Progress Series 256: 183–191.

Emlen ST, Oring LW (1977). Ecology, sexual selection and the evolution of mating systems. Science 197: 215–223.

Fagundes T, Gonçalves DM, Oliveira RF (2007). Female mate choice and mate search tactics in a sex role reversed population of the peacock blenny *Salaria pavo* (Risso, 1810). Journal of Fish Biology 71: 77–89.

Faria C, Almada V (2001). Agonistic behaviour and control of access to hiding places in two intertidal blennies, *Lipophrys pholis* and *Coryphoblennius galerita* (Pisces: Blenniidae). Acta Ethologica 4: 51–58.

Fishelson L, Gon O, Holdengreber V, Delarea Y (2006). Comparative morphology and cytology of the male sperm-transmission organs in viviparous species of clinid fishes (Clinidae: Teleostei, Perciformes). Journal of Morphology 267: 1406–1414.

Fishelson L, Gon O, Holdengreber V, Delarea Y (2007). Comparative spermatogenesis, spermatocytogenesis, and spermatozeugmata formation in males of viviparous species of clinid fishes (Teleostei: Clinidae, Blennioidei). The Anatomical Record 290: 311–323.

Fricke, R (2009). Systematics of the Tripterygiidae. In: Patzner R, Gonçalves E, Hastings P, Kapoor B (eds.), *The Biology of Blennies*. Science Publishing, Enfield, New Hampshire, pp. 37–67.

Geertjes GJ, Videler JJ (2002). A quantitative assessment of the reproductive system of the Mediterranean cave-dwelling triplefin blenny *Tripterygion melanurus*. PSZN: Marine Ecology 23: 327–340.

George A, Springer VG (1980). Revision of the clinid fish tribe Ophiclinini, including five new species, and definition of the family Clinidae. Smithsonian Contributions to Zoology 307: 1–31.

Giacomello E, Rasotto MB (2005). Sexual dimorphism and male mating success in the tentacle blenny *Parablennius tentacularis* (Teleostei: Blenniidae). Marine Biology 147: 1221–1228.

Giacomello E, Marchini D, Rasotto MB (2006). A male sexually dimorphic trait provides antimicrobials to eggs in blenny fish. Biology Letters 2: 330–333.

Giacomello E, Neat F, Rasotto MB (2007). Mechanisms enabling sperm economy in blenniid fishes. Behavioral Ecology and Sociobiology 62: 671–680.

Gibran FG, Santos FB, dos Santos HF, Sabino J (2004). Courtship behavior and spawning in the hairy blenny *Labrisomus nuchipinnis* (Labrisomidae) in southeastern Brazil. Neotropical Ichthyology 2: 163–166.

Gonçalves EJ, Almada VC (1997). Sex differences in resource utilization by the peacock blenny. Journal of Fish Biology 51: 624–633.

Gonçalves EJ, Almada VC (1998). A comparative study of territoriality in intertidal and subtidal blennioids (Teleostei: Blennioidei). Environmental Biology of Fishes 51: 257–264.

Gonçalves EJ, Almada VC, Oliveira RF, Santos AJ (1996). Female mimicry as a mating tactic in males of the blenniid fish *Salaria pavo*. Journal of the Marine Biological Association, UK 76: 529–538.

Gonçalves D, Fagundes T, Oliveira R (2003a). Reproductive behaviour of sneaker males of the peacock blenny. Journal of Fish Biology 63: 528–532.

Gonçalves D, Oliveira RF, Körner K, Schlupp I (2003b). Intersexual copying by sneaker males of the peacock blenny. Animal Behaviour 65: 355–361.

Gonçalves, DM, Matos R, Fagundes T, Oliveira R (2005). Bourgeois males of the peacock blenny, *Salaria pavo*, discriminate female mimics from females? Ethology 111: 559–572.

Gross MR, Sargent RC (1985). The evolution of male and female parental care in fishes. American Zoologist 25: 807–822.

Gross MR, Shine R (1981). Parental care and mode of fertilization in ectothermic vertebrates. Evolution 35: 775–793.

Gunn JS, Thresher RE (1993). Viviparity and the reproductive ecology of clinid fishes (Clinidae) from temperate Australian waters. Environmental Biology of Fishes 31: 323–344.

Hamada H, Nakazono A (1989). Reproductive ecology of the triplefin, *Enneapterygius etheostomus*, with special reference to the occurrence of fish eggs in the digestive tract of the male. Science Bulletin of the Faculty of Agriculture, Kyusu University 43: 127–134.

Hastings PA (1986). Habitat selection, sex ratio and sexual selection in *Coralliozetus angelica* (Blennioidea: Chaenopsidae). In: Uyeno T, Arai R, Taniuchi T, Matsuura K. (eds.),

Indo-Pacific Fish Biology: Proceedings of the Second International Conference on Indo-Pacific Fishes. Ichthyological Society of Japan, pp. 785–793.

Hastings PA (1988a). Correlates of male reproductive success in the brown cheeked blenny, *Acanthemblemaria crockeri* (Blennioidei: Chaenopsidae). Behavioral Ecology and Sociobiology 22: 95–102.

Hastings PA (1988b). Female choice and male reproductive success in the angel blenny, *Coralliozetus angelica* (Teleostei: Chaenopsidae). Animal Behaviour 38: 115–124.

Hastings PA (1991). Ontogeny of sexual dimorphism in the angel blenny, *Coralliozetus angelica* (Blennioidei: Chaenopsidae). Copeia 1991: 969–978.

Hastings PA (1992). Nest-site size as a short-term constraint on the reproductive success of paternal fishes. Environmental Biology of Fishes 34: 213–218.

Hastings PA (2002). Evolution of morphological and behavioral ontogenies in females of a highly dimorphic clade of blennioid fishes. Evolution 58: 1644–1654.

Hastings PA (2009). Biogeography of Neotropical blennies. In: Patzner R, Gonçalves E, Hastings P, Kapoor B (eds.), *The Biology of Blennies*. Science Publishing, Enfield, New Hampshire, pp. 95–118.

Hastings PA, Galland GR (2010). Ontogeny of microhabitat use and two-step recruitment in a specialist reef fish, the Browncheek Blenny (Chaenopsidae). Coral Reefs in 29: 155–164.

Hastings PA, Springer VG (2009a). Systematics of the Blenniidae (Blennioidei). In: Patzner R, Gonçalves E, Hastings P, Kapoor B (eds.), *The Biology of Blennies*. Science Publishing, Enfield, New Hampshire, pp. 69–99.

Hastings PA, Springer VG (2009b). Systematics of the Blennioidei and the included families Chaenopsidae, Clinidae, Labrisomidae and Dactyloscopidae. In: Patzner R, Gonçalves E, Hastings P, Kapoor B (eds.), *The Biology of Blennies*. Science Publishing, Enfield, New Hampshire, pp. 3–30.

Hirayama ST, Shiiba Y, Sakai H, Hashimota, Gushima K (2005). Fish-egg predation by the small clingfish *Pherallodischthys meshimaensis* (Gobiesocide) on the shallow reefs of Kuchierabu-Jima Island, southern Japan. Environmental Biology of Fishes 73: 237–242.

Hubbs CL (1952). A contribution to the classification of blennioid fishes of the family Clinidae, with a partial revision of the eastern Pacific forms. Stanford Ichthyological Bulletin 4: 41–165.

Kotrschal K (1988). A catalogue of skulls and jaws of eastern tropical Pacific blennioid fishes (Blennioidei: Teleostei): A proposed evolutionary sequence of morphological change. Zeitschrift für Zoologisches Systematik und Evolutionsforschung 26: 442–466.

Kraak SBM (1996). A quantitative description of the reproductive biology of the Mediterranean blenny *Aidablennius sphynx* (Teleostei, Blenniidae) in its natural habitat. Environmental Biology of Fishes 46: 329–342.

Kraak SBM, Groothuis TGG (1994). Female preference for nests with eggs is based on the presence of the eggs themselves. Behaviour 131: 189–206.

Kraak SBM, van der Berghe EP (1992). Do female fish assess paternal quality by means of test eggs? Animal Behaviour 43: 865–867.

Kraak SBM, Videler JJ (1991). Mate choice in *Aidablennius sphynx* (Teleostei, Blenniidae): females prefer nests containing more eggs. Behaviour 119: 243–266.

Kraak SBM, Weissing FJ (1996). Female preference for nests with many eggs: a cost-benefit analysis of female choice in fish with paternal care. Behavioral Ecology 7: 353–361.

Lengkeek W, Didderen K (2006). Breeding cycles and reproductive behaviour in the river blenny (*Salaria fluviatilis*). Journal of Fish Biology 69: 1837–1844.

Linn HC (2009). Evolution of the suborder Blennioidei: Phylogeny and phylogeography of a shallow water fish clade. Unpublished Dissertation, University of California, San Diego.

Locatello L, Neat FC (2005). Reproductive allocation in *Aidablennius sphynx* (Teleostei: Blenniidae): females lay more eggs faster when paired with larger males. Journal of Experimental Zoology 303A: 992–926.

Mackiewicz M, Porter BA, Dakin EE, Avise JC (2005). Cuckoldry rates in the molly miller (*Scartella cristata*, Blenniidae) a hole nesting marine fish with alternative reproductive tactics. Marine Biology 148: 213–221.

Mank JE, Promislow DEL, Avise JC (2005). Phylogenetic perspective on the evolution of parental care in ray-finned fishes. Evolution 59: 1570–1578.

Mazzoldi C, Rasotto MB (2002). Alternative male mating tactics in *Gobius niger*. Journal of Fish Biology 61: 157–172.

Moser HG (2007). Reproduction in the viviparous South African clinid fish *Fucomimus mus*. African Journal of Marine Science 29: 423–436.

Munday PL, Jones GP (1998). The ecological implications of small body size among coral-reef fishes. Annual Review of Oceanography and Marine Biology 36: 373–411.

Neat FC (2001). Parasitic spawning in two species of triplefin blenny: contrasts in demography, behaviour and gonadal characteristics. Environmental Biology of Fishes 55: 57–64.

Neat FC, Lengkeek W (2009). Sexual selection in blennies. In: Patzner R, Gonçalves E, Hastings P, Kapoor B (eds.), *The Biology of Blennies*. Science Publishing, Enfield, New Hampshire, pp. 249–278.

Neat FC, Locatello L (2002). No reason to sneak: why males of all sizes can breed in the hole-dwelling blenny, *Aidablennius sphynx* (Teleostei: Blenniidae). Behavioral Ecology and Sociobiology 52: 66–73.

Neat FC, Lengkeek W, Westerbeek P, Laarhoven B, Videler JJ (2003a). Behavioural and morphological differences between lake and river populations of *Salaria fluviatilis*. Journal of Fish Biology 63: 374–387.

Neat FC, Locatello L, Rasotto MB (2003b). Reproductive morphology in relation to alternative reproductive tactics in *Scartella cristata*. Journal of Fish Biology 62: 1381–1391.

Northcott SJ, James MA (1996). Ultrastructure of the glandular epidermis on the fins of male estuarine triplefins *Fosterygion nigripenne*. Journal of Fish Biology 49: 95–107.

Ohta T, Nakazono A (1988). Mating habits, mating system and possible filial cannibalism in the triplefin, *Enneapterygius etheostomus*. In: Choat JH, Barnes D, Borowitzka MA, Coll JC, Davies PJ, Flood P, Hatcher BG, Hopley D, Hutchings PA, Kinsey D, Orme GR, Pichon M, Sale PF, Sammarco P, Wallace CC, Wilkinson C, Wolanski E, Bellwood O (eds.), Proceedings of the Sixth International Coral Reef Symposium. Vol. 2, Contributed Papers. Townsville, Australia, pp. 797–801.

Okuda N, Fukumori K, Yanagisawa Y (2003). Male ornamentation and its condition-dependence in a paternal mouthbrooding cardinalfish with extraordinary sex roles. Journal of Ethology 21: 153–159.

Oliveira RF, Almada VC, Forsgren E, Gonçalves EJ (1999). Temporal variation in male traits, nesting aggregations and mating success in the peacock blenny. Journal of Fish Biology 53: 499–512.

Oliveira RF, Miranda JA, Carvalho N, Gonçalves EJ, Grober MS, Santos RS (2000). Male mating success in the Azorean rock-pool blenny: the effects of body size, male behaviour and nest characteristics. Journal of Fish Biology 57: 1416–1428.

Oliveira RF, Canario AVM, Grober MS (2001a). Male sexual polymorphism, alternative reproductive tactics, and androgens in combtooth blennies (Pisces: Blenniidae). Hormones and Behavior 40: 266–275.

Oliveira RF, Gonçalves EJ, Santos RS (2001b). Gonadal investment of young males in two blenniid fishes with alternative mating tactics. Journal of Fish Biology 59: 459–462.

Oliveira RF, Carvalho N, Miranda J, Gonçalves EJ, Grober M, Santos RS (2002). The relationship between the presence of satellite males and nest-holders' mating success in the Azorean rock-pool blenny *Parablennius sanguinolentus parvicornis*. Ethology 108: 223–235.

Oliveira RF, Gonçalves DM, Ros A (2008). Alternative reproductive tactics in blennies. In: Patzner R. Gonçalves E, Hastings P, Kapoor B (eds.), *The Biology of Blennies*. Science Publishing, Enfield, New Hampshire, pp. 279–308.

Patzner R, Gonçalves E, Hastings P, Kapoor B (2009). *The Biology of Blennies*. Science Publishing, Enfield, New Hampshire.

Petersen CW (1988). Male mating success, sexual size dimorphism, and site fidelity in two species of *Malacoctenus* (Labrisomidae). Environmental Biology of Fishes 21: 173–183.

Petersen CW (1989). Females prefer mating males in the carmine triplefin, *Axoclinus carminalis*, a paternal brood-guarder. Environmental Biology of Fishes 26: 213–221.

Petti JC (1969). Behavioral and morphological adaptations to burrowing of two species of dactyloscopid fishes from the northern Gulf of California. Master's thesis, University of Arizona, Tucson.

Prochazka K, Griffiths CL (1992). Observations on the distribution patterns, behaviour, diets and reproductive cycles of sand-dwelling clinids (Perciformes: Clinidae) from South Africa. Environmental Biology of Fishes 35: 371–379.

Reynolds JD, Côté IM (1995). Direct selection on mate choice: female redlip blennies pay more for better mates. Behavioral Ecology 6: 175–181.

Ridley M (1978). Parental care. Animal Behaviour 26: 904–932.

Robertson DR, Petersen CW, Brawn JD (1990). Lunar reproductive cycles of benthic-brooding reef fishes: reflections of larval-biology or adult-biology? Ecological Monographs 60: 311–329.

Robins CR, Ray C, Douglas J (1999). *A Field Guide to Atlantic Coast Fishes: North America*. Houghton Mifflin and Harcourt, Boston.

Rosenblatt RH, Taylor Jr LR (1971). The Pacific species of the clinid fish tribe Starksiini. Pacific Science 25: 436–463.

Ruchon F, Laugier T, Quignard JP (1995). Alternative male reproductive strategies in the peacock blenny. Journal of Fish Biology 47: 826–840

Santos RS (1995). Allopaternal care in the redlip blenny. Journal of Fish Biology 47: 350–353.

Shibata J, Kohda M (2006). Seasonal sex role changes in the blenniid *Petroscirtes breviceps*, a nest brooder with paternal care. Journal of Fish Biology 69: 203–214.

Shuster SM, Wade MJ (2003). *Mating Systems and Strategies*. Princeton University Press, Princeton, New Jersey.

Smith-Vaniz WF, Jelks HL, Rocha LA (2006). Relevance of cryptic fishes in biodiversity assessments: a case study at Buck Island Reef National Monument, St. Croix. Bulletin of Marine Science 79: 17–48.

Springer VG (1993). Definition of the suborder Blennioidei and its included families (Pisces: Perciformes). Bulletin of Marine Science 52: 472–495.

Springer VG, Orrell TM (2004). A phylogenetic analysis of 147 families of acanthomorph fishes based primarily on dorsal gill-arch muscles and skeleton. Bulletin of the Biological Society of Washington 11: 237–260.

Stephens JS Jr, Hobson ES, Johnson RK (1966). Notes on distribution, behavior and morphological variation in some chaenopsid fishes from the tropical eastern Pacific, with descriptions of two new species, *Acanthemblemaria castroi* and *Coralliozetus springeri*. Copeia 1966: 424–438.

Stepien CA (1986). Life history and larval development of the giant kelpfish, *Heterostichus rostratus* Girard, 1854. Fisheries Bulletin 84: 809–826.

Stepien CA, Dillon AK, Brooks MJ, Chase KL, Hubers AN (1997). The evolution of blennioid fishes based on an analysis of mitochondrial 12S rDNA. In: Kocher TT, Stepien CA (eds.), *Molecular Systematics of Fishes*. Academic Press, San Diego, pp. 245–270.

Sunobe T (1998). Notes on the mating system of *Omobranchus elegans* and *O. fasciolatoceps* (Blenniidae) at Maizuru, Japan. Ichthyological Research 45: 319–321.

Sunobe T, Ohta T, Nakazono A (1995). Mating system and spawning cycle in the blenny *Istiblennius enosimae*, at Kagoshima, Japan. Environmental Biology of Fishes 43: 195–199.

Taborsky M (2001). The evolution of bourgeois, parasitic and cooperative reproductive behaviors in fishes. Journal of Heredity 92: 100–110.

Takegaki T, Matsumoto Y, Tawa A, Miyano T, Natsukari Y (2008). Size-assortative nest preference in a paternal brooding blenny *Rhabdoblennius ellipes* (Jordan & Starks). Journal of Fish Biology 72: 93–102.

Thompson S (1986). Male spawning success and female choice in the mottled triplefin, *Forsterygion varium* (Pisces: Tripterygiidae). Animal Behaviour 34: 580–589.

Todd ES (1973). A preliminary report on the respiratory pump in the Dactyloscopidae. Copeia 1973: 115–119.

Tyler JC, Tyler DM (1999). Natural history of the sea fan blenny, *Emblemariopsis pricei* (Teleostei: Chaenopsidae), in the western Caribbean. Smithsonian Contribution to Zoology 601: 1–24.

Veith WJ (1979). The chemical composition of the follicular fluid of the viviparous teleost *Clinus superciliosus*. Comparative Biochemistry and Physiology 63A: 37–40.

Veith WJ (1980). Viviparity and embryonic adaptations in the teleost *Clinus superciliosus*. Canadian Journal of Zoology 58: 1–12.

Vinyoles D, Côté IM, De Sostoa A (1999). Egg cannibalism in river blennies: the role of natural prey availability. Journal of Fish Biology 55: 1223–1230.

Vinyoles D, Côté IM, de Sostoa A (2002). Nest orientation patterns in *Salaria fluviatilis*. Journal of Fish Biology 61: 405–416.

Wirtz P (1978). The behaviour of the Mediterranean *Tripterygion* species (Pisces, Blennioidei). Zeitschrift für Tierpsychologie 48: 142–174.

Wittenberger JF (1979). The evolution of mating systems in birds and mammals. In: Marler P, Vanderberg J (eds.), *Handbook of Behavioral Neurobiology: Social Behavior and Communication*. Plenum Press, New York, pp. 271–349.

Wittenberger JF (1981). *Animal Social Behavior*. Duxbury Press, Boston.

5

Gonad Morphology in Hermaphroditic Gobies

Kathleen S. Cole

Gobiid fishes (Family Gobiidae, Order Perciformes), consisting of at least 214 genera and 1,400 species (E. Murdy pers. comm.), constitute the second largest vertebrate family (second only to the Cyprinidae) and the largest family of vertebrates occupying marine environments (Nelson 2006). Among species for which there is information on reproductive biology, all are oviparous, having external fertilization in which gametes are released and fertilization occurs in the external environment. Typically, the female oviposits demersal eggs on a spawning surface prepared by the male, and the male guards the embryos until they hatch.

The reproductive anatomy of gobiids, particularly among males, exhibits considerable morphological diversity. In many species, extensive modifications of the sperm duct form specialized, secretion-producing structures referred to as seminal vesicles (Eggert 1931; Young & Fox 1937; Egami 1960; Arai 1964) or more commonly as sperm duct glands (Miller 1984). These structures show considerable taxon-specific variation in morphology (Miller 1984; Fishelson 1989). Testis morphology is also variable across gobiid taxa. Among some gonochoric (i.e., fixed-sex) species, a portion of the testis is made up of an aggregation of Leydig-like cells, which is referred to as the mesorchial gland (Colombo & Burighel 1974). These cells synthesize and secrete steroids, some of which act to attract gravid female conspecifics (Colombo et al. 1980; Belanger et al. 2004). The size of this gland has been shown to relate to mating tactics, with small sneaker males having a much smaller mesorchial gland than larger, conventionally spawning males (Locatello et al. 2002; Rasotto & Mazzoldi 2002). In other species, such as *Pomatoschistus microps*, organized mesorchial glands are absent and steroid production depends on interstitial cells that are embedded in the sperm duct glands.

In two hermaphroditic genera, *Paragobiodon* and *Gobiodon*, Fishelson (1989) has reported that the mesorchial gland is absent during the female phase but develops at the time of sex change.

Among functionally hermaphroditic goby taxa, the reproductive morphology of the gonad proper has become even further modified, substantially in some cases. These modifications vary considerably across hermaphroditic goby taxa. However, both morphological features and their patterns of development and transition throughout life have been shown to be highly conserved within some hermaphroditic clades (i.e., Cole 1990; Cole & Shapiro 1990). This clade-based distribution of reproductive morphological diversity raises the question as to whether hermaphroditism within the Gobiidae has singular or multiple origins.

As one of the two largest vertebrate families, gobiids have undergone considerable adaptive radiation and speciation, particularly in marine environments. Their success seems likely to be based at least in part on a capacity for developing morphological and physiological innovations. This, in turn, would have increased their ability to become morphologically and functionally specialized, leading to increased micropartitioning of complex habitats and the invasion of new niches. A finding of numerous independent origins of hermaphroditism within the taxon would provide additional support for the hypothesis that character innovation has been a major driver of evolutionary diversity within the Gobiidae.

In this chapter, information has been compiled from a variety of sources to examine the biological implications of diverse reproductive morphologies found among hermaphroditic goby taxa. In the first section, the generalized model of the teleost reproductive complex is compared with those of gonochoric (i.e., fixed-sex, or non-hermaphroditic) and functionally hermaphroditic gobiids to characterize differences and identify patterns of reproductive morphology among hermaphroditic goby taxa. In the second section, the distribution patterns of different forms of reproductive morphology among hermaphroditic goby taxa are examined from a phylogenetic perspective to answer two questions: First, are developmental patterns consistent with known phylogenetic relationships within the Gobiidae (i.e., does reproductive morphology accurately predict clade relationships among hermaphroditic gobies)? And second, to what extent may the evolution of different reproductive morphologies across clades represent independent evolutionary events within the Gobiidae?

A GENERALIZED MODEL OF THE REPRODUCTIVE COMPLEX OF EXTERNALLY FERTILIZING TELEOSTS

The following is a brief overview of teleost gonad morphology. For more detailed information, the reader is referred to Hoar (1955), Grier (1981), Nagahama (1983), Maack & Segner (2003), and Parenti & Grier (2004).

The basic morphology of the ovary among externally fertilizing teleosts is one of a bilobed, caudally united structure that is continuous with the oviduct, the latter extending through the body of the genital papilla and terminating at the genital pore. The ovary consists of peripheral tissue layers forming an ovarian wall that encloses and protects ovigerous (i.e., ova-producing) tissue making up the body of the gonad. The ovigerous tissue is typically anchored to the entire inner layer of the ovarian wall and takes the form of lamellar folds projecting into a central lumen.

The ovigerous tissue contains a variety of developmental stages of female sex cells, including oogonia and more mature stages of oocytes. At ovulation, mature oocytes—now termed ova—are released from their surrounding follicle cells into the ovarian lumen. Among externally fertilizing, non-inseminating teleosts, ova move from the ovarian lumen into the common genital sinus, an open region formed by the union of the two ovarian lobes and which has no ovigerous tissue directly associated with the genital sinus wall. From here, ova pass through a relatively short oviduct and are delivered to the outside of the body via the genital pore.

The typical testis of externally fertilizing teleosts consists of a bilobed, caudally united structure that is continuous with a sperm duct, which in turn leads to the genital papilla and terminates at the genital pore. In its simplest form, the testis consists of an external testis wall and, internally, spermatogenic tissue organized into blind-ended, seminiferous lobules (i.e., seminiferous tubules) *sensu* Grier et al. (1980). The terminal apices of these lobules are usually located at the testis lobe periphery. The proximal, open end of each lobule is oriented toward either a medially located sperm sinus; an internal sperm-collecting duct; or a caudally located common collecting region, frequently referred to as the common genital sinus. In mature males, free spermatozoa can be found in the lobule lumina and in the common collecting region(s) into which lobule lumina empty. The common genital sinus of the male reproductive complex is formed by the posterior union of the testis lobes; it contains no directly affixed spermatogenic tissue, and is continuous with the sperm duct.

Individual seminiferous lobules of the testis consist of a lobule wall made up of support cells and of male germ cells in various stages of development. Among teleosts, the seminiferous lobules may be of the restricted or the unrestricted type (Grier et al. 1980). In the unrestricted type testis, the lobule lumen extends the full length of the lobule and is surrounded along its length by developing germ and support cells. In the restricted type testis, the germ and support cells are confined to the distal end of the blind-ended lobule.

THE REPRODUCTIVE COMPLEX
OF GONOCHORIC GOBY TAXA

In general, the female reproductive complex of gonochoric (i.e., non-hermaphroditic, or constant-sex) goby taxa reiterates the basic teleost model of two ovarian lobes united posteriorly to form a common genital sinus. This non-gametogenic region is confluent with the oviduct and provides the pathway by which ova pass from the gonad to the outside environment. Lamellae of ovigerous tissue extend into a central cavity—the ovarian lumen—and within these lamellae various stages of female sex cells are present. Among immature individuals, these include oogonia and primary oocytes. The primary oocytes may consist of a number of developmental stages identified on the basis of cytological features, including chromatin nucleolar, perinucleolar, and cortical alveolar stages. Among reproductively active females, various stages of vitellogenic oocytes will dominate the ovigerous tissue. In most gonochoric gobiid taxa, a bilobed ovary, common genital sinus, and oviduct constitute the reproductive complex. *Schindleria praematura*, a planktonic paedomorphic goby, is an exception to this pattern. Ovigerous tissue forms a ventrally anchored ridge that projects dorsally into a surrounding lumen within the gonad and is surrounded on three sides by the lumen (Thacker & Grier 2005). Within the ovigerous ridge, stromal tissue is limited, and much of the tissue is made up of oogonia and oocytes. This unusual morphology is likely an adaptation to the extremely small size that characterizes this species.

Among males of gonochoric gobiid taxa, the reproductive complex typically exhibits considerable structural modification. Across taxa there is an impressive diversity of morphology, of both the gonad and the accessory gonadal structures (Miller 1984; Fishelson 1991). The bilobed testis may have an associated testicular gland (Stanley et al. 1965; Columbo & Burighel 1974), also referred to as a mesorchial gland (Miller 1984). This glandular structure is embedded within the testis proper, but it is isolated from the spermatogenic tissue and does not contribute to seminal fluid (Seiwald & Patzner 1989); rather, it is exocrine in function, consists primarily of Leydig cells, and provides a source of steroid hormones (Columbo & Burighel 1974; Seiwald & Patzner 1989). It has also been shown in the black goby, *Gobius niger*, to produce sexual pheromones (Columbo et al. 1980; Locatello et al. 2002). In this species, the relative size of the mesorchial gland is large in conventionally spawning males and small in males that parasitize spawning events by adopting a sneaker strategy (Rasotto & Mazzoldi 2002; Immler et al. 2004). The reduction in the latter is hypothesized to prevent conventionally spawning males from recognizing sneakers on the basis of mesorchial-gland-produced, male-specific pheromones. The mesorchial gland is absent in a number of goby species including the common goby, *Pomatoschistus microps*, *Lebetus* sp. (Miller 1984); two-spotted goby, *Gobiusculus flavescens* (Fishelson 1991); pelagic crystal goby,

Crystallogobius linearis; transparent goby, *Aphia minuta* (Caputo et al. 2003); and *Coryphopterus* spp. (Cole unpublished data). When more information is collected, the mseorchial gland may be found to be more commonly absent than present in some gobiid clades.

The most prominent accessory structures associated with the male reproductive complex among gobiid fishes are paired secretory structures that are associated with the sperm duct. These structures have been referred to as seminal vesicles (Eggert 1931; Young & Fox 1937; Weisel 1949) or sperm duct glands (Miller 1984) and exhibit considerable morphological variation in size and architecture among goby taxa (Miller 1984; Fishelson 1991). In most cases they consist of enlarged lobules lined with a simple columnar epithelium that has a complex ultrastructure (Cinquetti 1997) responsible for producing a sialoglycoprotein-rich fluid (Fishelson 1991; Lahnsteiner et al. 1992). In some species the resulting secretions combine with sperm and seminal fluid to produce sperm trails (Marconato et al. 1996; Scaggiante et al. 1999) from which spermatozoa slowly dissolve out of the mucin-based matrix after their release and deposition on a spawning surface. The size of the secretory structures has been shown to vary among males exhibiting different mating strategies. In some species, parental males have large structures associated with conventional spawning and sperm trail production. In contrast, sneaker males have much smaller secretory structures that are used for sperm storage rather than mucin production and a relatively large testis suitable for releasing large bursts of sperm during sneaking events (Immler et al. 2004; Scaggiante et al. 2004; Mazzoldi et al. 2005). Secretory accessory gonadal structures associated with the male reproductive complex are widespread among goby taxa; however, they are reported to be extremely reduced or absent in several species, including *Amblygobius nocturnus*, *Cryptocentrus lutheri*, *Valenciennea strigata*, *V. sexguttata*, *V. muralis* (Mazzoldi et al. 2005), and *Schindleria praematura*. In the latter species, the secretory accessory structure is reduced, the secretory epithelium is restricted to the ventral region, and instead of consisting of secretory lobules, the structure forms as a single chamber (Thacker & Grier 2005).

THE REPRODUCTIVE COMPLEX
OF HERMAPHRODITIC GOBIIDS

In hermaphroditic gobies, gonadal function varies over an individual's lifetime. Consequently, the terms "female," "male," "ovary," and "testis" that are used to describe the reproductive anatomy and sexual state of gonochores have limited application to the hermaphroditic condition. Accordingly, gonadal state in a hermaphroditic individual is better characterized by a combination of morphology and function. In morphological terms, the gonad may be ovariform, ovotestiform, or testiform. In functional terms, the gonad is either ova producing, sperm producing, both ova and sperm producing, or in the absence of any mature gametes, inactive. Note that the term "inactive" as used here equally describes the gonad of immatures and of adults during a non-reproductive phase. Therefore, on its own, describing a gonad as inactive does not distinguish between these two developmental and functional states. The designation of "immature" or "inactive adult" can only be made in the context of other species-specific information such as size or age at first maturity. By applying the same convention, the functional state of an individual can be characterized as male-active (i.e., sperm producing), female-active (i.e., ova producing), bisexually active (i.e., both sperm and ova producing), or inactive (i.e., no mature gamete production).

The manner in which reproductive anatomy has become modified in hermaphroditic goby species appears to vary according to taxon. Among some taxa, morphological modifications are only associated with the ovariform gonad, while in others, elaborate anatomical modifications of various regions of the reproductive complex are associated with either the female-active or male-active phase. Reproductive modifications among hermaphroditic gobiids are exhibited in their least morphologically elaborated form in the goby genus *Coryphopterus*. In *Coryphopterus glaucofraenum*, the first hermaphroditic *Coryphopterus* species to be studied in detail (Cole & Shapiro 1992), most individuals initially develop an ovariform gonad in which no testis tissues or features are visible. (See Figure 5.1A. First maturation is characterized by the onset of a female-active phase and ova production (Figure 5.1B). Subsequent to the female-active phase, the gonad undergoes a transformation to form a secondary testis (Figure 5.1C). To accomplish this, all elements of prior ovarian structure are lost, including the ovigerous tissue and its lamellar configuration around a central lumen, and the gonad is rebuilt internally by the formation of longitudinally oriented and cell-lined channels. These develop into seminiferous lobules which come to entirely replace the preceding ovigerous tissue (Figure 5.1D). Thus, the gonadal tissue of the initial immature and subsequent female-active phases appears strictly ovariform (Figure 5.1A, B), while that of the secondary male is strictly testiform.

Based on the description above, the pattern of reproductive morphology exhibited by *C. glaucofraenum* involves the absence of testis-associated tissues or recognizable male sex cells within the gonad prior to sex change; the *de nouveau* development of seminiferous lobules within previously active ovigerous tissue at the time of transformation; and the complete disappearance of ovarian tissue and architecture in the secondary testis. In this ontogenetic sequence, female-specific and male-specific gonadal tissues only co-occur for a brief period of time during the transition from female to male function. During this period, the gonad takes the form of a nonfunctional ovotestis by virtue of its temporarily coexisting ovariform and testiform features. In comparison with gonochore gobies in which the

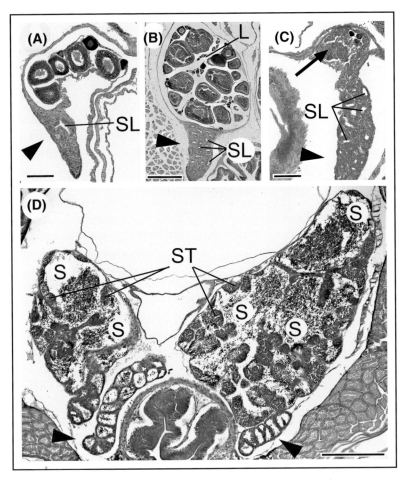

FIGURE 5.1. Histological features shown in transverse section of interim ovotestis gonad morphologies associated with immature and adult *Coryphopterus glaucofraenum*. In all images, dorsal is uppermost.

A. Ovariform gonad of immature, consisting solely of oocyte-bearing tissue, with pAGS (arrowhead) showing cell-bound lumen of future secretory lobule (SL). Scale bar is 100 μ.

B. Female-active gonad with lamellae of ovigerous tissue separated by branches of the central lumen (L) and showing prominent pAGS (arrowhead) with numerous lumina of future secretory lobules (SL). Scale bar is 500 μ.

C. Developing ovotestis (arrow) of transitional fish, with expanding seminiferous lobule lumina (SL) within developing AGS (arrowhead). Scale bar is 100 μ.

D. Reproductive complex of secondary male, including left and right lobes of the secondary testis (ST) made up solely of spermatogenic tissue, including seminiferous lobule lumina filled with sperm (S) and fully developed, actively secreting AGS (arrowhead). Scale bar is 200 μ.

reproductive complex is canalized early into either a male or female pathway, *C. glaucofraenum* expresses an ontogenetic sequence of gonadal morphologies comprising inactive ovariform, functional ovariform, transitional nonfunctional ovotestiform, and functional testiform, respectively.

During the immature and female-active phases, *C. glaucofraenum* does not exhibit any morphological indications of future spermatogenic capacity within the ovigerous tissue. However, there is a novel anatomical feature associated with the gonad proper that is necessary for the development of the reproductive anatomy of the male-active phase. In many gobiid taxa, and in all known hermaphroditic representatives, the male reproductive complex includes accessory structures that are lobular in architecture and secretory in function (i.e., sperm duct glands *sensu* Miller 1984). In hermaphroditic species, these structures usually develop at the time of sex change from female to male function. Among immature and ova-producing *C. glaucofraenum*, a small, ventro-lateral tissue mass located just anterior to the common genital sinus is associated with each gonadal lobe. These accessory masses, which are in close proximity to, but unassociated with, the ovigerous tissue (see arrowhead in Figure 5.1A), are made up of clusters of cells, some of which form a contiguous, single-celled layer around developing channels (Figure 5.1A, B).

In five additional *Coryphopterus* species for which morphological changes associated with a shift from female to male function have been tracked, these tissue masses are universally present among immature and female-active individuals and remain in a stable, undifferentiated state during the ovariform phase of the gonad (Cole & Robertson 1988; Cole & Shapiro 1990, 1992). During seminiferous lobule formation within the transforming gametogenic tissue, the accessory tissue masses undergo cell proliferation, rapid growth, and the development of numerous, epithelial-lined lobules (Figure 5.1C). With continued growth, the developing lobulated structures expand into the body cavity, the lining epithelium becomes columnar, and secretions produced by this epithelium start to be discharged into the lobule lumina (Figure 5.1D)(Cole & Robertson 1988; Cole & Shapiro 1992).

In terms of overall appearance, internal architecture, and secretory activities, the fully developed secretory structures of male-active fish among hermaphroditic *Coryphopterus* spp. appear identical to sperm duct glands associated with the male reproductive complex of gonochore goby taxa (Miller 1984, 1992). Among gonochore taxa, however, lobular secretory structures arise from the wall of the sperm duct, form early in development well before the initiation of sperm production, and are present only in males. The lobular secretory structures of hermaphroditic *Coryphopterus* spp., in contrast, arise from the lateral wall of the gonadal lobes and their precursors are present in all immatures and female-active adults. Because the lobular secretory structures of secondary male *Coryphopterus* spp. have no direct association with the gonoduct, they have been termed accessory gonadal structures, or AGS (Cole & Robertson 1988). The use of this term allows for a distinction to be made between the sperm duct glands *sensu* Miller (1984) that are associated only with the gonoduct of the male reproductive complex among gonochore goby taxa, and the gonadal wall derived structures of hermaphroditic *Coryphopterus* spp. which have the same differentiated appearance and apparent function as sperm duct glands. As AGS arise from the initially undifferentiated tissue masses associated with the ovariform gonad, the latter have been termed *precursive* accessory gonadal structures, or pAGS. The combination of pAGS and AGS that is characteristic of the *Coryphopterus* spp. reproductive complex of different functional states has not been described for any gonochore goby taxa and therefore represents a novel feature of reproductive morphology associated with some hermaphroditic gobies.

The ontogenetic pattern of gonad morphology expressed by *C. glaucofraenum*, in which pAGS associated with the ovariform gonadal phase develop into AGS and male and female gametogenic tissues only co-occur during a brief transitional phase associated with sex change, is also characteristic for all other *Coryphopterus* species that have been examined, including *C. personatus*, *C. dicrus*, *C. hyalinus*, and *C. lipernes* (Cole & Robertson 1988; Cole & Shapiro 1990). In four additional species, *C. alloides*, *C. eidolon*, *C. thrix*, and *C. urospilus*, morphogenic transformations of the gonad have not been tracked, but pAGS have been present in all examined immatures and female-active adults (Cole & Shapiro 1990).

The ovariform–nonfunctional transitional ovotestis–testiform pattern of gonad development exhibited by *Coryphopterus* spp. is also found among species of three other hermaphroditic gobiid genera, including *Rhinogobiops* (previously *Coryphopterus*) *nicholsii* (Cole 1983), *Lophogobius cyprinoides*, and *L. cristulatus* (Cole 1990; Cole unpublished data), and in two *Fusigobius* species, *F. neophytus*, and *F. signipinnis* (Cole 1990; Cole herein). A similar ovariform and testiform morphology has been found in both *L. cyprinoides* and *L. cristulatus* (Figure 5.2A–C and D–F, respectively), including the presence of pAGS associated with the immature and adult ovariform gonad (Figure 5.2A and D, respectively), and in *F. neophytus* (Figure 5.3A, B) and *F. signipinnis* (Figure 5.3C, D). In all four species, the gonad among immatures and ova-producing adults is entirely ovariform, and among sperm-producing adults is entirely testiform. Collectively, these four genera sharing a similar pattern of gonad morphology are referred to here as the Coryphopterus group. The form of gonad development characterized by the expression of a transient, nonfunctional ovotestis between ovariform and testiform phases as described above is termed here an *interim ovotestis* developmental pattern. This pattern involves a relatively straightforward process of tissue replacement and restructuring with no functional overlap in gamete production,

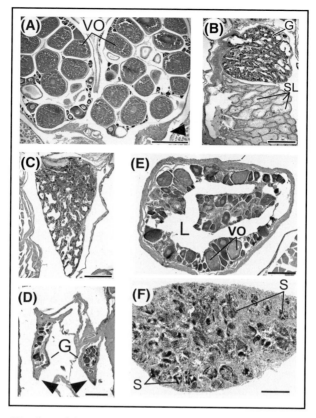

FIGURE 5.2. Histological features shown in transverse section of interim ovotestis gonad morphologies associated with differing reproductive states in *Lophogobius cyprinoides* and *L. crystulatus*. In all images, dorsal is uppermost.

A. *L. cyprinoides* female-active gonad made up entirely of ovigerous tissue containing
   vitellogenic oocytes (VO), with pAGS (arrowhead) of right lobe visible in this plane
   of cut. Scale bar is 500 μ.

B. *L. cyprinoides* reproductive complex of secondary male consisting of a gonad (G)
   made up solely of spermatogenic tissue and an enlarged, actively-secreting AGS consisting of enlarged secretory lobules (SL) filled with secretory material. Scale bar is
   500 μ.

C. Detail of gonad shown in (B) illustrating absence of oocyte-bearing tissue. Scale bar
   is 500 μ.

D. *L. cristulatus* ovariform gonad (G) of immature, consisting solely of oocyte-bearing
   tissue, with pAGS (arrowheads). Scale bar is 200 μ.

E. *L. cristulatus* female-active gonad made up entirely of ovigerous tissue containing
   vitellogenic oocytes (VO) surrounding a central lumen (L). Scale bar is 200 μ.

F. *L. cristulatus* secondary testis lobe made up solely of spermatogenic tissue, including
   seminiferous lobule lumina filled with sperm (S). Scale bar is 100 μ.

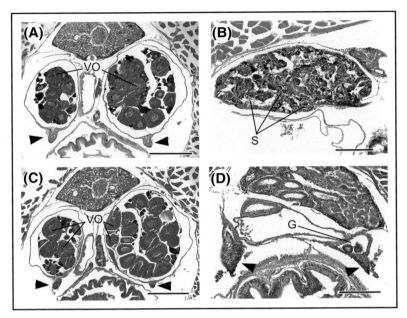

FIGURE 5.3. Histological features shown in transverse section of interim ovotestis gonad morphologies associated with differing reproductive states in *Fusigobius neophytus*, *F. signipinnis*, and *F.* sp.5 (DFH).

A. *F. neophytus* female-active gonad made up entirely of ovigerous tissue containing vitellogenic oocytes (VO), with pAGS (arrowheads). Dorsal is uppermost; scale bar is 500 μ.

B. *F. neophytus* secondary testis lobe made up solely of spermatogenic tissue including seminiferous lobule lumina filled with sperm (S). Dorsal is to the right; scale bar is 200 μ.

C. *F. signipinnis* female-active gonad made up entirely of ovigerous tissue containing vitellogenic oocytes (VO), with pAGS (arrowhead). Dorsal is uppermost. Scale bar is 200 μ.

D. *F.* sp.5 (DFH) (probably *F. melacron*) ovariform gonad (G) of immature, consisting solely of oocyte-bearing tissue, and with associated pAGS (arrowhead). Dorsal is uppermost. Scale bar is 200 μ.

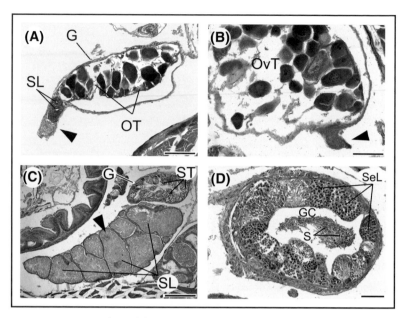

FIGURE 5.4. Histological features shown in transverse section of modified interim ovotestis gonad morphologies associated with differing reproductive states in *Elacatinus multifasciatus*.

A. Ovariform gonad (G) of immature, consisting solely of oocyte-bearing tissue (OT), and with associated pAGS (arrowhead) with cell-bound lumen of future secretory lobule (SL). Dorsal is to the right; scale bar is 500 μ.

B. Female-active gonad made up entirely of ovigerous tissue (OvT) containing vitellogenic oocytes, with associated pAGS (arrowhead). Dorsal is uppermost; scale bar is 500 μ.

C. Reproductive complex of secondary male consisting of a gonad (G) made up entirely of spermatogenic tissue (ST) and an enlarged, actively secreting AGS (arrowhead) consisting of greatly enlarged secretory lobules (SL) filled with secretory material. Dorsal is uppermost; scale bar is 200 μ.

D. Detail of spermatogenic gonad of fish shown in (C), illustrating a peripheral organization of seminiferous lobules (SeL), the absence of oocyte-bearing tissue, and the retention of a central gonadal lumen (GC) for the collection and egress of sperm (S). Dorsal is uppermost; scale bar is 50 μ.

thereby representing a minimally modified example of anatomical transformation among functional hermaphroditic goby taxa.

In the western Atlantic genus *Elacatinus* (recently removed from *Gobiosoma*)(Hoese & Reader 2001), a single species, *Gobiosoma multifasciatus* (Steindachner, 1876), now classified as *Elacatinus multifasciatus* (Steindachner 1876), is confirmed as a protogynous hermaphrodite (Robertson & Justines 1982). As with the Coryphopterus group, the only indication of future sperm-producing potential among immature and ova-producing individuals is the presence of pAGS (see Figure 5.4A, B)(Cole 2008). In the process of sex change, pAGS develop into AGS, and the ovigerous tissue is completely replaced by seminiferous lobules (Figure 5.4C); however, the former ovarian lumen persists (Figure 5.4C, D). Free spermatozoa pass from seminiferous lobules into the gonadal lumen, which now functions as a common collection region that is continuous with the common genital sinus. The Elacatinus pattern of gonad development is essentially the same as that of the Coryphopterus group, except for the retention of the gonadal lumen. Because of this difference, and to distinguish the *E. multifasciatus* pattern from that of the Coryphopterus group, *E. multifasciatus* is described as having a *modified interim ovotestis* developmental pattern, which constitutes a second pattern of hermaphroditic gonad morphology.

Eviota is a speciose gobiid genus found throughout the tropical Indo-West Pacific (Lachner & Karnella 1980; Karnella & Lachner 1981; Jewett & Lachner 1983; Gill & Jewett 2004). *Eviota epiphanes* is hermaphroditic (Cole 1990) and along with three other species, *E. afelei*, *E. disrupta*, and *E. fasciola*, exhibits a somewhat different pattern of gonad morphology than that described for the Coryphopterus group or for *Elacatinus multifasciatus*. The Eviota pattern is characterized by the presence of an ovotestis among all individuals, regardless of sexual function (see Figure 5.5). Immatures and female-active adults all have a predominantly ovariform gonad with oocytes and support cells organized into lamellae surrounding a central lumen (Figure 5.5A, B, C), pAGS or partially or fully developed AGS (Figure 5.5B, C), and clusters of small, haematoxylin-staining cells constituting spermatocysts scattered throughout the gonadal tissue (Figure 5.5A, B, C). A shift to male function involves a number of changes, including the proliferation of spermatocysts and surrounding somatic cells to become organized into seminiferous lobules, an overall reduction of oogenic tissue consisting of oocytes and support cells, the differentiation of pAGS into AGS, and the subsequent increase in AGS size accompanied by the initiation of secretory activity (Figure 5.5D). However, following a transition to male function, the Eviota gonad retains both a central lumen and numerous healthy, early-stage oocytes scattered among the interstices of the seminiferous lobules (Figure 5.5D).

Therefore, the Eviota pattern is one of a universally present ovotestis such that hermaphroditic capabilities are clearly evident within the gonad morphology of

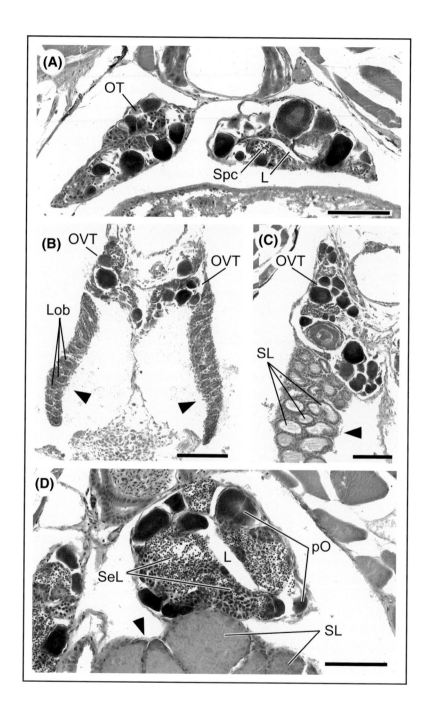

FIGURE 5.5. Histological features shown in transverse section of persistent integrated ovotestis morphologies associated with differing reproductive states in *Eviota epiphanes*. In all images, dorsal is uppermost and scale bar is 100 μ.

A. Integrated ovotestis of immature consisting of oocyte-bearing tissue (OT) and clusters of spermatocytes (SpC), surrounding a central lumen (L).

B. More posterior section of the reproductive complex shown in (A) showing the integrated ovotestis (OVT) and large, fully developed AGS (arrowhead) made up of numerous compressed lobules (Lob).

C. Reproductive complex of female-active adult (no vitellogenic oocytes present in this section) showing integrated ovotestis (OVT) and AGS (arrowhead) with secretory lobules (SL), expanded lobule lumina relative to (B), and containing small amounts of secretions.

D. Integrated ovotestis of male-active adult with sperm-filled seminiferous lobules (SeL) interspersed with pre-vitellogenic oocytes (pO) and retained central gonadal lumen (L). The dorsal-most portion of the AGS (arrowhead), with secretory lobules (SL) filled with secretions, is visible in the lower part of the image.

all individuals. This differs from the Coryphopterus group and *E. multifasciatus* patterns, in which the ovotestis is a transient feature and only the presence of pAGS among immatures and female-active adults indicates hermaphroditic capabilities. An ovotestis in which male and female components are intermixed, as is the case with *Eviota*, is frequently referred to as an undelimited ovotestis (Sadovy & Shapiro 1987). The intermingled distribution of male and female gametocytes observed in all phases of sexual function in *Eviota* produces a third reproductive morphology pattern, the *persistent integrated ovotestis* pattern, which is distinct from the Coryphopterus group and *E. multifasciatus* patterns characterized by a transient interim ovotestis pattern.

The genus *Lythrypnus* has a distribution that includes the eastern central Pacific, eastern Pacific, southeast Pacific, and the western Atlantic (Böhlke & Robins 1960; Greenfield 1988; Bussing 1990). The generalized pattern of gonad morphology in *Lythrypnus* is similar among examined species (Cole 1988; St. Mary 1998). Among immatures and female-active adults, the gonad is usually an ovotestis that is primarily ovarian in both architecture and sex cell type. In at least one species, *L. nesiotes*, rather than having pAGS, nonsecreting but differentiated AGS are associated with the immature ovotestis (see Figure 5.6A). The extent of AGS development among differing gonadal phases has not been reported for the remaining species (St. Mary 1993, 1998, 2000). Among several species, a small number of either pure females (i.e., completely ovarian gonad) or pure males (i.e., completely testicular gonad) may be present (St. Mary 1993, 2000). During the inactive ovariform and female-active phases, male components of the ovotestis consist of small clusters of spermatocytes confined to two regions, one dorsal-most and one ventral-most, in the gonad (Figure 5.6B). With reallocation of function from ova to sperm

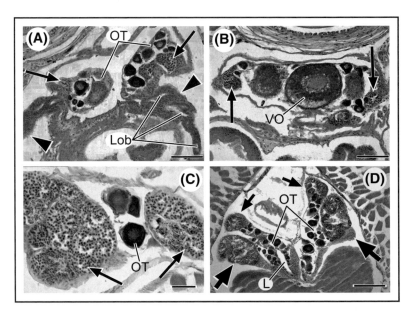

FIGURE 5.6. Histological features shown in transverse section of persistent re-gionalized ovotestis morphologies associated with differing reproductive states in *Lythrypnus nesiotes*.

A. Ovotestis of immature, consisting of oocyte-bearing tissue (OT) and region-alized spermatocyte-bearing tissue (arrows) with partially developed AGS (arrowhead) showing early lobule formation (Lob). Dorsal is uppermost; scale bar is 100 μ.

B. Female-active ovotestis with late-stage vitellogenic oocyte (VO) in the cen-tral ovigerous region, flanked dorsally and ventrally by spermatocyte-bearing tissue regions (arrows). Dorsal is to the right; scale bar is 100 μ.

C. Male-active ovotestis showing enlarged dorsal and ventral sperm-producing regions (arrows) and centrally located, regressed oocyte-bearing tissue (OT). Dorsal is to the right; scale bar is 50 μ.

D. Male-active ovotestis showing resulting lobe formation from expansion of the dorsal (small arrows) and ventral (large arrows) sperm-producing re-gions linked proximally by the regressed oocyte-bearing tissue region (OT) surrounding a central gonadal lumen (L). Dorsal is uppermost; scale bar is 200 μ.

production, the spermatocyte-occupied regions expand with newly formed semi-niferous lobules coming to constitute the majority of the gonad, and the oviger-ous portion becomes reduced to a relatively small and central region of the ovotestis (Figure 5.6C). In *L. nesiotes*, the independent growth pattern of the two antipodal regions of testis-function tissue results in a bifurcation of each of the gonadal lobes, with the central oogenic region anchoring dorsal and ventral pro-jections of spermatogenic tissue (Figure 5.6D).

The pattern of *Lythrypnus* gonad morphology is novel, having a localized con-centration of male gametocytes and spermatogenic tissues rather than an intermin-gled pattern like that of the persistent integrated ovotestis of *Eviota*. Among imma-tures and ova-producing individuals, the precursive sperm-producing tissues are situated in two separate regions. Moreover, in the male-functioning ovotestis, each of the two regions of precursive spermatogenic tissue develops independently to form two sublobes of spermatogenic tissues connected by a reduced region of tissue consisting of early-stage oocytes. The initial location and subsequent proliferation pattern of spermatocyte-bearing tissues consequently result in a *regionalized* (rather than integrated) *ovotestis* pattern. As a consequence, the gonad morphology of *Lythrypnus* exhibits a fourth pattern: that of a *regionalized persistent ovotestis* rather than an integrated persistent ovotestis pattern like that of *Eviota*.

A fifth pattern of hermaphroditic gonad morphology is shared by three other hermaphroditic genera: *Trimma*, *Priolepis*, and *Bryaninops*. *Trimma* is a speciose Indo-Pacific gobiine genus, while *Priolepis* and *Bryaninops* are less speciose. *Bryaninops* is widespread throughout the Indo-Pacific (Larson 1985), while *Pri-olepis* is found in the Indo-Pacific, the eastern Pacific, and the western Atlantic (Winterbottom & Burridge 1992; Nogawa & Endo 2007). Hermaphroditism is widespread among examined species of these three genera, and all share a num-ber of features of gonad morphology. As illustrated by *Bryaninops loki*, the go-nad develops at the outset as a partitioned structure (see Figure 5.7). Among im-matures and female-active adults, a larger region of oocyte-bearing tissue is organized into a lamellar configuration surrounding a central lumen, and the gonads of both of these functional states have undifferentiated pAGS (Figure 5.7A). Slightly more anteriorly, a smaller region extending along the ventral go-nad periphery from a medial to a ventro-lateral position appears as a thickened portion of the gonad wall. This region exhibits increased cell complexity and is separated from the ovigerous region by a thin boundary layer of connective tis-sue (Figures 5.7B, 5.8B), making this a delimited ovotestis (Sadovy & Shapiro 1987). In transitional individuals, the ova-producing region becomes reduced in size, the ventral region expands and becomes organized into seminiferous lob-ules, and secretory lobules develop within the pAGS in association with their transformation into AGS. In male-functioning adults, the spermatogenic tissue is expanded to occupy much of the gonadal body, and the lobule epithelium of

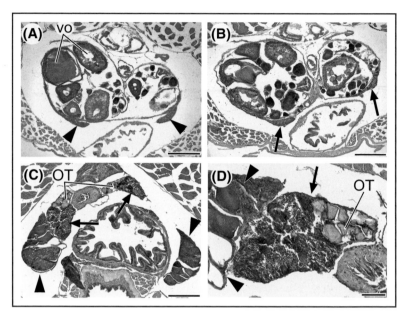

FIGURE 5.7. Histological features shown in transverse section of persistent partitioned ovotestis morphologies associated with differing reproductive states in *Bryaninops loki*.

A. Female-active ovotestis with late-stage vitellogenic oocytes (VO) and prominent, undifferentiated pAGS (arrowhead) posterior to spermatogenic tissue region. Dorsal is uppermost; scale bar is 200 μ.

B. Slightly more anterior section of female-active ovotestis shown in (A), showing future spermatogenic tissue region (arrows). Dorsal is uppermost; scale bar is 200 μ.

C. Reproductive complex with male-active ovotestis showing enlarged sperm-producing tissue regions (arrows for left and right lobes), regressed oocyte-bearing tissue region (OT), and AGS (arrowheads) filled with colloidal material. Dorsal is uppermost; scale bar is 200 μ.

D. Detail of dorsal portion of reproductive complex shown in (C), with oocyte-bearing tissue (OT) dorsal-most (to the right in the image), sperm-producing tissue (arrow) consisting of seminiferous lobules filled with sperm, and the dorsal-most portion of the enlarged AGS (arrowheads) to the left in the image. Dorsal is to the right; scale bar is 50 μ.

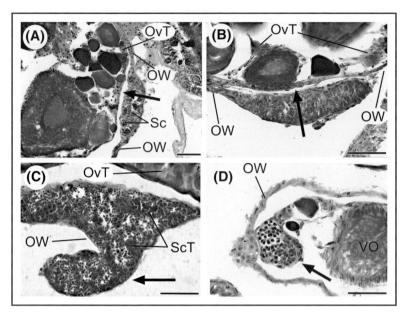

FIGURE 5.8. Persistent partitioned ovotestis morphology (A, B, C) illustrating the separation of oocyte-bearing and spermatocyte-bearing tissues within a partitioned ovotestis of three hermaphroditic goby genera as compared to regionalized persistent ovotestis morphology (D). Scale bar is 50 μ.

A. *Trimma taylori* female-active ovotestis with one region made up of ovigerous tissue (OvT), here containing vitellogenic oocytes, and a small, clearly separated region (see arrow at point of separation) located medially in the ovotestis made up of clusters of spermatocysts (Sc) containing spermatocytes, both enclosed by the ovotestis wall (OW). Dorsal is uppermost.

B. *Bryaninops loki* female-active ovotestis consisting ovigerous tissue (OvT) separated (see arrow at point of separation) from a spermatocyte-bearing region located medially in the ovotestis (arrow). OW is ovotestis wall; dorsal is to the right.

C. *Priolepis hipoliti* early developmental stage spermatocyte-bearing tissue (ScT) organized into a cohesive mass (arrow) within the female-active ovotestis, showing a broad separation from the ovigerous tissue (OvT). OW is ovotestis wall; dorsal is to the right.

D. *Lythrypnus nesiotes* female-active ovotestis with late-stage vitellogenic oocytes (VO) in the ovigerous region and showing a clear demarcation from the ventral spermatocyte-bearing tissue region (arrow). OW is ovotestis wall; dorsal is to the right.

the AGS is actively secreting (Figure 5.7C, D)(Cole 1990). In *Trimma* (Figure 5.8A), *Bryaninops* (Figure 5.8B), and *Priolepis* (Figure 5.8C), all examined individuals exhibit a partitioned ovotestis (Cole 1990, herein), a pattern of gonad morphology that is referred to here as a *persistent partitioned ovotestis* pattern. This pattern is most similar to that of the regionalized ovotestis pattern of *Lythrypnus* spp. (Figure 5.8D).

In one *Priolepis* species, *P. hipoliti*, a histological survey of gonad morphology by Cole (1990) revealed an unusual size-based sequence of ovotestis morphology. Small-sized adults exhibited a predominance of ovigerous tissue and a partially developed AGS showing early secretory lobule development. Large-sized adults had a reduced ovigerous region, a greatly expanded and active spermatogenic region, and fully developed and secreting AGS. Among intermediate-sized adults, both portions of the gonad contained healthy, mature gametes and the AGS were fully developed. The appearance of simultaneous mature gamete production among mid-sized adults indicates that this species appears likely to have an intervening functionally bisexual phase between female- and male-active phases. Pending experimental verification, *P. hipoloti* is tentatively identified as an *interim* (functional) *bisexual hermaphrodite*. A similar bisexual gonad containing mature gametes of both sexes has also been found in its congener, *P. eugenius*, which shows a pattern similar to that of *P. hipoliti* (see Figure 5.9). Among the smallest immatures, the gonad is already partitioned into a dorsal oocyte-bearing region and a ventral spermatocyte-bearing region (Figure 5.9A) and has large and fully differentiated AGS associated with the gonoduct (Figure 5.9B). Among some female-active adults, the ova-producing region makes up the majority of the ovotestis, while the inactive spermatocyte-bearing region consisting of fully differentiated, small-sized seminiferous lobules is relatively contracted (Figure 5.9C). Among other adults, the oocyte and spermatocyte-bearing regions are fully developed, and both regions include mature gametes (Figure 5.9D, E). Among female-active and putatively bisexually active adults, the AGS remain relatively small and shows no signs of secretory activity (Figure 5.9C, D). Among a third group of adults, the male-active ovotestis consists of an enlarged sperm-producing region, a relatively regressed oocyte-bearing tissue region, and extremely enlarged and actively secreting AGS (Figure 5.9F). The persistent partitioned ovotestis pattern exhibited by *P. eugenius* coupled with morphological evidence of an interim functional simultaneous hermaphroditic phase is unique among hermaphroditic gobies, excepting its congener, *P. hipoliti*. The possibility of such a combination of sexual functions has not been investigated among other *Priolepis* species and may be common or even synapomorphic for the genus.

The greatest complexity of reproductive anatomy among hermaphroditic gobiid taxa reported to date is in the Indo-Pacific genus *Gobiodon*. Among immatures and female-active adult *G. oculolineatus*, the gonad is ovariform and has no visible spermatogenic tissue (Cole 2009), a feature that has also been found in *G. okinawae* (Cole & Hoese 2001). Histological features of the tripartite secondary ovotestis are illustrated in Figure 5.10. Among male-active adults, the gonad proper is an ovotestis (Figure 5.10A, B, C) that exhibits three contiguous, intergraded regions: a dorsal gametogenic region, a ventro-lateral lobular region, and a medial stromal region (Figure 5.10B). The gametogenic region is made up of seminiferous lobules and healthy perinucleolar oocytes situated in lobule interstices, which resembles the persistent integrated ovotestis condition of *Eviota* (Figure 5.10C). However, the ventro-lateral region of the gonad consists of enlarged lobules filled with eosinophilic colloidal secretions and is separated from the gametogenic region by medially located stromal tissue that gradually merges with each (Figure 5.10B, D). The tripartite ovotestis configuration formed by regionalization of gametogenic tissue, stromal tissue, and secretion-storing lobules observed within *G. oculolineatus* and *G. okinawae* represents a novel gonad organization that has also been found in several other *Gobiodon* species (Cole unpublished data). It also represents a new pattern in which the adult ovotestis develops secondarily from an ovariform gonad, making it a secondary ovotestis. Because of these features, *Gobiodon* exhibits a sixth gonad morphology pattern, the *tripartite secondary ovotestis* pattern.

In addition to the lobular region of the ovotestis in which colloid secretions accumulate, the *Gobiodon* reproductive complex also includes a pair of lobular structures that are directly associated with the gonoduct. These accessory gonoduct-associated structures, or AGdS, are the production sites for colloidal secretions and are presumably the source for similar appearing material that occupies the secretion-accumulating lobule region of the ovotestis. In all previously described hermaphroditic goby taxa, the accessory structures responsible for secretion production arise from precursive tissues associated with the gonadal wall and develop with the onset of the male-active phase. In contrast, the AGdS of *Gobiodon* are clearly associated with the gonoduct and are fully differentiated in all individuals regardless of their functional phase. The presence of AGdS in *Gobiodon* represents a substantial departure from the secretory AGS found in all other hermaphroditic gobies.

Based on ontogenetic origin, morphology, and connectivity, the AGdS found in all examined *Gobiodon* species appear homologous with the sperm duct glands *sensu* Miller (1984) that are associated with the male reproductive complex of most gonochore goby species. AGdS have been found in *G. okinawae* (Cole & Hoese 2001), *G. oculolineatus* (Cole 2009), and four other *Gobiodon* species (Cole unpublished data), and they represent a novel feature among hermaphroditic gobies. The universal presence of AGdS among all *G. okinawae* and *G. oculolineatus* individuals, regardless of sexual state, constitutes an additional novel feature of the reproductive complex not reported for either gonochoric or other hermaphroditic

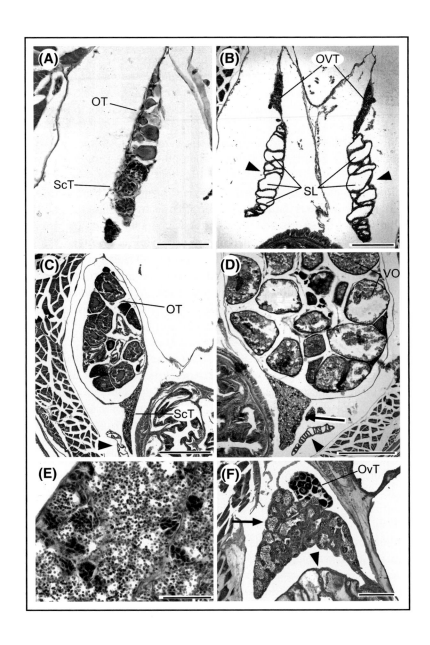

FIGURE 5.9. Histological features shown in transverse section of persistent partitioned ovotestis morphologies associated with differing reproductive states in *Priolepis eugenia*, including functional bisexual phase. In all images, dorsal is uppermost.

A. Ovotestis of immature consisting of oocyte-bearing tissue (OT) dorsally and spermatocyte-bearing tissue (ScT) ventrally. Scale bar is 200 μ.

B. More posterior section of reproductive complex shown in (A), showing ovotestis (OvT) and large, fully developed AGS (arrowhead) made up of broad-lumina, secretory lobules (SL). Scale bar is 100 μ.

C. Reproductive complex of female-active adult showing enlargement of the active oocyte-bearing tissue region (OT) dorsally, inactive spermatocyte-bearing tissue (ScT) ventrally, and fully differentiated but small-sized AGS (arrowhead). Scale bar is 500 μ.

D. Reproductive complex with simultaneous ova and sperm-producing ovotestis, with late-stage vitellogenic oocytes (VO), seminiferous lobules filled with sperm (arrow), and fully differentiated but small-sized AGS (arrowhead). Scale bar is 500 μ.

E. Detail of the sperm-producing region of the ovotestis shown in (D), with sperm-filled seminiferous lobules. Scale bar is 50 μ.

F. Male-active ovotestis showing enlarged sperm-producing region (arrow) and regressed ova-producing region (OvT). The dorsal-most portion of the enlarged, fully developed and secreting AGS (arrowhead) is visible at the bottom of the image. Scale bar is 200 μ.

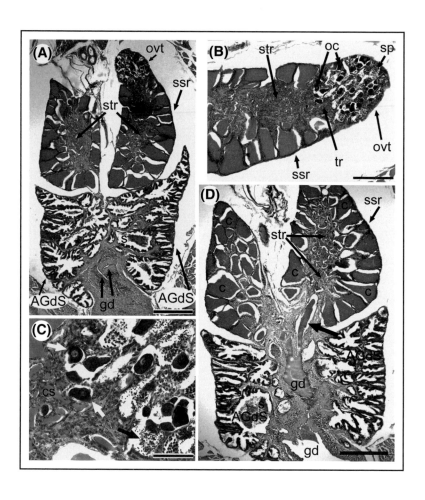

FIGURE 5.10. Histological features shown in transverse section of tripartite secondary ovotestis of *Gobiodon oculolineatus.*

A. Section through posterior region of the reproductive complex showing compressed lumen of gonoduct (gd), AGdS with secretions (s) within secretory lobules, secretion storing lobule region (ssr) of the ovotestis with lobules filled with colloidal material, stromal region (str) of the ovotestis, and posterior-most gametogenic region of the right ovotestis lobe (ovt). Dorsal is uppermost; scale bar is 500 μ.

B. Enlarged view of ovotestis lobe shown in image (A), showing peripherally arranged storage lobules, central stromal core (str) with smaller colloid-filled lumina and loosely packed stromal cells, transitional region (tr) consisting of stromal tissue and early-stage oocytes, and spermiated ovotestis (ovt)-containing oocytes (oc), developing male germ cells and spermatozoa (sp). Dorsal is to the right; scale bar is 250 μ.

C. Enlarged view of the transitional and gametogenic regions of ovotestis lobe detailed in image (B), showing colloid-filled lumina (cs), perinucleolar stage oocytes each surrounded by a ring of follicular cells (white arrows), and cell-delimited lumina containing spermatids (black arrow). Dorsal is to the right; scale bar is 100 μ.

D. More caudal transverse section of the reproductive complex shown in image (A), showing storage lobules (ssr) filled with colloidal material (c) and central stromal region (str) making up entirety of ovotestis (i.e., no gametogenic tissue present); AGdS with secretions (s) in some secretory lobule lumina; portions of the central channel of the gonoduct (gd) moving in and out of the plane of cut; and region of colloid-filled central channel of gonoduct that is continuous with the secretion-storing region (black arrow). Dorsal is uppermost; scale bar is 500. (From Cole 2009; reproduced with permission from Springer Science and Business Media.)

goby taxa. Lastly, the development of a specialized storage region within the gonad proper among all male-active *Gobiodon* (Cole & Hoese 2001; Cole 2008, unpublished data) constitutes a third novel reproductive feature that sets *Gobiodon* apart from other hermaphroditic goby genera so far discussed.

The presence of AGdS and a specialized lobular secretion-storing region within the gonad proper has been reported for only one other genus, *Paragobiodon*, which is also the proposed sister group of *Gobiodon* (Harold et al. 2008). There are few details available regarding the morphology of the reproductive complex in this group. However, in two species, *P. rivulatus* and *P. echinocephalus*, male-active fish also exhibit an enlarged pair of AGdS associated with the gonoduct where secretions are produced, and an enlarged lobular region of the ventral portion of the gonad where secretions are stored (Cole 1990, unpublished data).

The developmental pattern of gonad morphology characterized by *Gobiodon* does not resemble any other pattern among hermaphroditic gobies (except *Paragobiodon*) described here, and both the storage lobule and stromal regions of the gonad, and the derivation of the AGdS from the gonoduct, are so far unique among known hermaphroditic goby taxa.

SUMMARY OF REPRODUCTIVE MORPHOLOGY PATTERNS

Hermaphroditic gobies exhibit a range of reproductive morphologies that are organized into distinctive patterns which show a high degree of taxon-specificity (see Table 5.1 and Figures 5.11 and 5.12). These include (i) the interim ovotestis pattern of the Coryphopterus group (Figure 5. 11A, B, C); (ii) the modified interim ovotestis pattern of *Elacatinus multifasciatus* (Figure 5.11A, B, D); (iii) the persistent integrated ovotestis pattern of *Eviota* (Figure 5.11E, F, G); (iv) the regionalized persistent ovotestis of *Lythrypnus*; (v) the persistent partitioned ovotestis of *Trimma* and *Bryaninops* (Figure 5.11H, I, J) and the specialized pattern of *Priolepis hipoliti* and *P. eugenia*, with an interim functionally bisexual ovotestis (Figure 5.11K, L, M); and (vi) the tripartite secondary ovotestis of *Gobiodon* (Figure 5.12). In four of the first five reproductive morphology patterns listed above (i.e., excepting *Lythrypnus*), the AGS arise from tissues associated with the gonadal wall and only become fully differentiated and active at the onset of male function. In the sixth pattern, shown by *Gobiodon*, secretory structures (AGdS) are associated with the gonoduct rather than the gonadal wall and may be homologous with sperm duct glands *sensu* Miller (1984). However, the AGdS of *Gobiodon* differ from the male-specific sperm duct glands of gonochore goby taxa in that they occur as fully differentiated structures of the reproductive complex irrespective of reproductive state. How these different patterns of reproductive morphology and development may reflect evolutionary patterns associated

TABLE 5.1 Taxon-specific features of ovotestis and male-active gonad morphology in hermaphroditic gobies

Taxon	Ovotestis duration	Ovotestis gametogenic tissue distribution	Male-active gonad features
Coryphopterus *Lophogobius* *Rhinogobiops* *Fusigobius*	Interim	Integrated	Tissue completely spermatogenic; no retained ovariform features
Elacatinus *multifasciatus*	Interim	Integrated	Tissue completely spermatogenic; retained gonadal lumen
Eviota	Persistent	Integrated	Male-dominant ovotestis
Lythrypnus	Persistent	Regionalized	Spermatogenic tissue dorsally and ventrally, forming dorsal and ventral lobes
Trimma *Priolepis* *Bryaninops*	Persistent	Partitioned	Male-dominant ovotestis
Gobiodon	Secondary	Integrated	Tripartite gonad with gametogenic, stromal, and storage lobule regions

with the development of functional hermaphroditism within the Gobiidae is the topic of the next section.

DISTRIBUTION PATTERNS OF HERMAPHRODITISM AND PHYLOGENETIC RELATIONSHIPS WITHIN THE GOBIIDAE

The frequent appearance of hermaphroditic sexual patterns, coupled with taxon-linked diversity in reproductive morphology among gobiid fishes, suggests that hermaphroditism may have multiple independent origins within the family. To address this possibility requires an examination of the distribution of hermaphroditic sexual patterns among gobiid taxa within a phylogenetic context. Morphology and molecular-based analyses, either separately or in combination, have consistently identified a number of monophyletic gobiid clades, including the gobiines, sycidiines, oxudercines, amblyopines, and gobionellines (Hoese 1984; Hoese & Gill 1993; Pezold 1993). More recently, the Gobiidae has been expanded to include its former sister taxa, the microdesmids (Wang et al. 2001), the ptereleotrids and schindleriids (Thacker 2003), and the kraemeriids (Thacker 2009), as well as being contracted to exclude the sycidiines, oxydurcines, amblyopines, and gobionellines (Thacker 2009)(refer to Figure 5.13). Clearly, the determination of

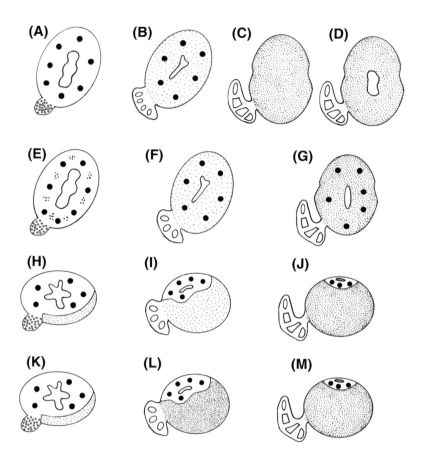

FIGURE 5.11. Progression of gonadal morphologies from female-active (left), to transitional (center), to male-active (right) for four taxon-specific patterns. White background represents oocyte-bearing tissue; large black dots are oocytes; medium-size gray dots represent pAGS tissue; light stipple is early-stage, non-active spermatogenic tissue; dark stipple is male-active spermatogenic tissue.

A. *Coryphopterus* ovariform female-active gonad with oocytes surrounding a central lumen and small channels visible in pAGS.

B. *Coryphopterus* interim ovotestis with regressing lumen, developing spermatocyte-bearing tissue, and developing AGS.

C. *Coryphopterus* secondary testis made up entirely of spermatogenic tissue, no retained gonadal lumen, and fully developed AGS.

D. *Elacatinus multifasciatus* secondary testis made up entirely of spermatogenic tissue, with retained gonadal lumen and fully developed AGS.

E. *Eviota* persistent integrated ovotestis of female-active individual, with oocytes surrounding a central lumen, small clusters of spermatocytes distributed throughout the ovotestis, and pAGS.

F. *Eviota* ovotestis of transforming fish, with developing but not yet mature spermatocyte-bearing tissue, a partially regressed lumen, oocytes (pre-vitellogenic), and developing AGS.

G. *Eviota* ovotestis of a male-active adult, consisting primarily of spermatogenic tissue along, with a small number of non-vitellogenic oocytes, reduced persistent gonadal lumen, and fully developed AGS.

H. *Trimma* persistent partitioned ovotestis of female-active individual, with a dorsal region consisting of oocytes surrounding a central lumen, a ventral region of partially developed but not yet mature spermatocyte-bearing tissue, and pAGS.

I. *Trimma* ovotestis of transforming fish, with a reduced oocyte-bearing region, an expanding region of spermatocyte-bearing tissue, and developing AGS.

J. *Trimma* persistent partitioned ovotestis of a male-active adult, consisting primarily of the expanded region of spermatogenic tissue, a much-reduced region of oocyte-bearing tissue, and fully developed AGS.

K. *Priolepis* persistent partitioned ovotestis of female-active individual identical to that of *Trimma*, with a dorsal oogenic region, a ventral spermatocyte-bearing tissue region, and pAGS.

L. *Priolepis* bisexual ovotestis, with a dorsal oogenic region, a ventral spermatogenic region, and small, fully developed AGS.

M. *Priolepis* persistent partitioned ovotestis of a male-active adult, consisting primarily of the expanded region of spermatogenic tissue, a much-reduced region of oocyte-bearing tissue, and fully developed AGS.

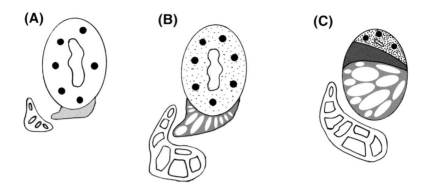

FIGURE 5.12. Progression of gonadal morphologies for *Gobiodon*, from female-active (left), to transitional (center), to male-active (right). White background represents oocyte-bearing tissue; large black dots are oocytes; light stipple is early stage, non-active spermatocyte-bearing tissue; dark stipple is male-active spermatogenic tissue; light gray background represents region of future storage lobules; medium gray is tissue surrounding developing storage lobules (white ovals); dark gray is stromal tissue region.

A. *Gobiodon* ovariform female-active gonad with oocytes surrounding a central lumen; a ventrally located, densely cellular region where storage lobules will later develop; and small-sized, fully developed AGdS associated with the gonoduct.

B. *Gobiodon* integrated ovotestis of transforming fish, with developing but not yet mature spermatocyte-bearing tissue interspersed with pre-vitellogenic oocytes; a developing, ventrally located storage lobular region; and enlarged AGdS.

C. *Gobiodon* tripartite secondary ovotestis of male-active adult, consisting dorsally of an integrated ovotestis region, centrally of a stromal region, and ventrally of a fully developed storage lobular region; and AGdS fully developed.

relationships within the gobiid and gobioid fishes remains challenging, with proposed phylogenies no doubt continuing to undergo revision for the foreseeable future. To date, all reported hermaphroditic gobiid taxa are found within the Gobiidae subfamily, Gobiinae, *sensu* Pezold (1993).

In Thacker's (2003) phylogenetic analysis, all of the hermaphroditic goby genera that were sampled, including *Coryphopterus, Lophogobius, Fusigobius, Priolepis, Elacatinus* (formerly *Gobiosoma*), *Eviota, and Gobiodon*, were placed within a monophyletic clade. In a redefined Gobiidae, which includes the Gobiinae *sensu* Pezold (1993), a number of clades were recovered (Thacker 2009). In this latest phylogeny (Figure 5.13), the deepest split separates the combined Trimma-Priolepis and Coryphopterus-Lophogobius (plus *Fusigobius signipinnis*) groups from all of the remaining examined gobiid taxa. The latter are further subdivided by a split that places one known hermaphroditic genus, *Elacatinus* (formerly *Gobiosoma*), in a monophyletic taxon well separated from the remaining three hermaphroditic goby genera included in that study. These three hermaphroditic genera further resolved into two constituent clades including *Eviota* plus *Gobiodon*, and *Fusigobius neophytus*, respectively.

If hermaphroditism has a singular point of origin within the Gobiidae, the dispersed distribution of hermaphroditic taxa across the family as illustrated in Figure 5.13 indicates that sexual lability has been lost in many more descendent lineages that it has been retained. Alternatively, hermaphroditism has arisen independently at least twice and possibly up to five times within the family (see vertical black arrows in Figure 5.13). In the latter instance, hermaphroditism may have arisen independently in each of five groups: the Coryphopterus-Lophobogius-*F. signipinnis* group; the Trimma-Priolepis-Bryaninops group; the Eviota-Gobiodon group; the Gobiosoma group *sensu* Rüber et al. (2003), which includes *Elacatinus*; and the group containing *F. neophytus sensu* Thacker (2009).

The widespread occurrence of hermaphroditism and shared interim ovotestis pattern of reproductive morphology within the Coryphopterus group, including *Coryphopterus, Lophogobius, Rhinogobiops nicholsii*, and *Fusigobius signipinnis*, supports the hypothesis of a recent common hermaphroditic ancestor proposed for these genera (Thacker & Cole 2002).

Trimma, Priolepis, and *Bryaninops* exhibit a different reproductive morphology pattern, characterized by a persistent partitioned ovotestis. On the basis of a number of morphological autapomorphies, Winterbottom & Emery (1981) have proposed that *Trimma* and *Priolepis* along with *Paratrimma* and *Trimmatom* form a monophyletic clade. In Thacker (2009), *Priolepis, Trimmatom*, and *Trimma* form a monophyletic clade that is sister to a group including *Coryphopterus, Lophogobius, Kraemeria*, and *Fusigobius signipinnis*. Reproductive morphology as described here supports both a close relationship between *Trimma, Priolepis*, and *Bryaninops* (reproductive morphology for *Paratrimma, Trimmatom*, and *Kraemeria* have not

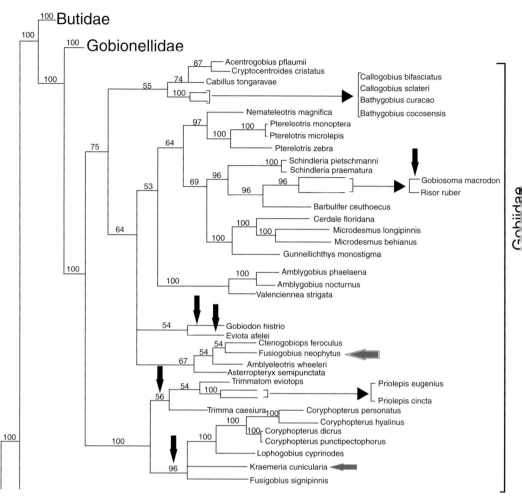

FIGURE 5.13. Phylogeny of Gobiidae based on Thacker (2009) showing distribution of gobiid clades having one or more hermaphroditic members. Black vertical arrows indicate basal region of clades proposed to have an independently evolved hermaphroditic sexual pattern, based on reproductive morphology. Horizontal, white-outlined gray arrow indicates questioned placement of *Fusiogobius neophytus*. Horizontal gray arrow indicates questioned placement of the genus *Kraemeria*, for which available information on gonad morphology indicates an absence of hermaphroditic features (Langston unpublished data, Cole unpublished data) and for which hermaphroditism has not been reported.

yet been reported on), and some phylogenetic separation from *Coryphopterus*, *Lophogobius*, *Rhinogobiops*, and *Fusigobius signipinnis*. There are currently no published phylogenies for the placement of *Bryaninops* within the Gobiidae. Larson (1985, 1990) proposed a close relationship between *Bryaninops* and another soft-coral associated goby genus, *Pleurosicya*. Herler (2007) commented on unpublished data that indicates that *Bryaninops* and *Pleurosicya* are somewhat distant from *Gobiodon* and *Paragobiodon*. Based on shared reproductive morphological traits described here, there is strong support for a close relationship between *Bryaninops* and the *Trimma-Priolepis* clade.

Compared with the persistent partitioned and transient unpartitioned ovotestis patterns described above, *Lythrypnus* exhibits a somewhat specialized condition. During the female-active phase, spermatocytes are present and concentrated in two small, localized regions at the dorsal and ventral apices of the gonad (St. Mary 1998, Drilling & Grober 2005). During the male-active phase, the testicular tissue expands from these two locations to take over most of the gonad, relegating the oogenic tissue to a small peripheral region in which early-stage oocytes are retained. The localized ovotestis pattern of *Lythrypnus* has not yet been described for any other hermaphroditic gobies. *Lythrypnus* was not included in either of the two phylogenies of Thacker (2003, 2009), nor has any sister group been proposed, although Böhlke & Robins (1960) noted that superficially, small specimens of *Lythrypnus elasson* sometimes resemble *Priolepis* (*Quisquilius*) *hipoliti*. Based on its persistent regionalized ovotestis morphology, *Lythrypnus* may be most closely related to the Trimma-Priolepis-Bryaninops group, which exhibits a persistent partitioned ovotestis.

The persistent integrated pattern of reproductive morphology of *Eviota* is distinct from that of the previously discussed Coryphopterus and Trimma-Priolepis-Bryaninops groups and of *Lythrypnus*. A comparative analysis by Winterbottom & Emery (1981) showed that *Eviota* shares none of the morphological autapomorphies that unite *Priolepis* and *Trimma*, thereby disassociating *Eviota* from the latter. Several recent molecular analyses indicate that *Eviota* and *Gobiodon* (and by implication, *Paragobiodon*, based on Harold et al. 2008) are closely related but do not share a recent common ancestor with either of the Coryphopterus-Lophogobius or Trimma-Priolepis-Bryaninops groups (Thacker 2003, 2009). A proposed close relationship between *Eviota* and *Gobiodon* is not well supported by reproductive morphology. *Eviota* exhibits a persistent integrated ovotestis pattern in which the ovotestis is present regardless of sexual state. In *Gobiodon*, the gonad is initially ovariform, with an ovotestis only evident among male-active individuals. Moreover, the gonad of male-active adults is highly modified into three functional regions resulting in a tripartite secondary ovotestis pattern. Lastly, secretory functions of the *Gobiodon* reproductive complex are provided by AGdS rather than secretory AGS, which are so far unique to *Gobiodon* and *Paragobiodon* among hermaphroditic gobies. If *Eviota* and *Gobiodon* are in fact sister taxa and hermaphroditism is a shared ancestral condition, the reproductive morphology has subsequently become highly modified in the *Gobiodon/Paragobiodon* lineage. Alternatively, and more likely, the novel features of reproductive morphology found in the latter reflect developmental processes different from that of all other hermaphroditic goby taxa, including *Eviota*, indicating that hermaphroditism in *Gobiodon* spp. (and putatively *Paragobiodon*) evolved independently from the other clades discussed here.

The Gobiosoma group underwent a period of rapid speciation and adaptive radiation early in its evolutionary history (Rüber et al. 2003). In a departure from other hermaphroditic goby clades in which hermaphroditism is widespread, functional hermaphroditism within the speciose Gobiosoma group has been reported for only a single species, *Elacatinus multifasciatus* (Robertson & Justines 1982). However, a number of species within the closely related genera, *Elacatinus*, *Gobiosoma* and *Elacatinus sensu* Rüber et al. (2003) show evidence of a possible ancestral hermaphroditic condition. In several species, immature females exhibit the transient development of pAGS that disappear by first maturity (Cole 2008). If hermaphroditism is an ancestral state within the Gobiosoma group, sexual lability may have played an important role in its adaptive radiation. Rüber et al. (2003) have suggested that behavioral diversification and microhabitat specialization have been instrumental in the rapid evolution and high rate of speciation within some of the more speciose Gobiosoma group clades. As suggested in Cole (2008), the successful exploitation of patchily distributed microniches in this group may have been successful, in part, due to labile sexual patterns that could counter potential constraints on reproductive opportunities. If, as the transient expression of pAGS suggests, hermaphroditism was a basal trait of the Gobiosoma group, it has been secondarily lost among most of the descendent lineages.

From a phylogenetic perspective, *Fusigobius* presents a challenge. Molecular analyses by Thacker (2003, 2009) indicate that *Fusigobius*, for which the species *F. neophytus* and *F. signipinnis* were sequenced, is polyphyletic. In both studies, *F. neophytus* falls into a clade with *Asterropteryx*, *Amblyeleotris*, and *Ctenogobiops* (see white-outlined, horizontal gray arrow in Figure 5.13). The second species, *F. signipinnis*, appears to be distant from *F. neophytus*, although its position changes between the two studies. In one study (Thacker 2003), *F. signipinnis* is placed in a clade along with *Ptereleotris*, *Gunnellichthys*, and *Schindleria*, while in the second (Thacker 2009) it comes out as part of the Coryphopterus-Lophogobius group. Gonad morphology in *F. neophytus* supports this move, as it shares all of the distinctive features of the female-active and male-active gonad of *Coryphopterus*, *Rhinogobiops nicholsii*, and *Lophogobius*. These features include pAGS associated with the gonad of immatures and ova-producing adults; the absence of testicular tissues or male sex cells associated with the ovariform gonad; and the reciprocal absence of ovarian features or female sex cells associated with the gonad of sperm-producing adults (Cole 1990). It is of interest to note that *F. signipinnis*, currently placed distant to *F. neophytus*, shows the same gonad morphology pattern as *F. neophytus*. This argues for a much closer association, and probable monophyly, for these two species and a shared ancestry with the Coryphopterus-Lophogobius-*Rhinogobiops nicholsii* group.

IMPLICATIONS OF FUNCTIONAL HERMAPHRODITISM IN GOBIID EVOLUTION

Within the gobiids, hermaphroditism appears to have arisen independently on several occasions. In one clade consisting of *Coryphopterus, Lophogobius, Rhinogobiops*, and *Fusigobius signipinnis*, all exhibit a unidirectional pattern of hermaphroditism involving a single shift from female to male. None of the above taxa are particularly speciose. *Fusigobius* is an Indo-Pacific genus with 11 described species (Randall 2001). *Coryphopterus* is a western Atlantic and eastern Pacific genus having 16 species including two newly described (Victor 2008). *Lophogobius* has three described species (Hoese 1995), although the validity of the current placement of *L. bleekeri* within this genus is in doubt (Hoese pers. comm.). All are relative habitat generalists and are primarily associated with coral reef habitats, except for *Rhinogobiops nicholsii*, which occupies rock and sand habitats of the northeastern Pacific (Eschmeyer et al. 1983), and *Lophogobius cyprinoides*, which is generally found in grass beds, mangroves, tidal creeks, brackish coastal waters, and inland bays of the western Atlantic (Böhlke & Chaplin 1993).

Compared with serial hermaphroditism, in which sexual function can shift back and forth to suit the existing social conditions, a unidirectional form of hermaphroditism appears at first glance to provide more limited adaptive advantages. However, unidirectional hermaphroditism is well suited for these species having broad habitat tolerances and an associated ubiquitous distribution of conspecifics. Under these conditions, the probability of finding a mate is likely high. Consequently, the evolution of unidirectional hermaphroditism in the Coryphopterus group most likely reflects an adaptation associated with the reproductive biology and social organization characteristics of this clade. For one species within the Coryphopterus group, *Rhinogobiops nicholsii*, high-quality nest sites for demersal eggs have been shown to be limited (Breitburg 1987; Kroon et al. 2000). Consequently, reproductive success corresponds to successful nest-site defense, for which large males have a competitive advantage. In having limited access to nest sites, small males are likely to have lower reproductive success than both large males and small adult females, leading to strong selection for size-based protogyny (Ghiselin 1969; Berglund 1990).

A second clade *sensu* Thacker (2009) includes the hermaphroditic genera *Trimma* and *Priolepis*, both of which are relatively speciose genera. *Priolepis* consists of 35 described species (Nogawa & Endo 2007) and an unknown number of undescribed species (Winterbottom pers. comm.), while *Trimma* consists of 58 described species and an estimated 30 to 40 as-of-yet undescribed species (Winterbottom & Southcott 2008). *Trimma* species either occur in hovering aggregations in caves and around overhangs or live more solitarily in reef crevices, while *Priolepis* species form small social groups or live solitarily in small reef holes and crevices (Winterbottom pers. comm.). Species of both genera exhibit serial hermaphroditism, and among some *Priolepis* species, a combination of serial hermaphroditism and simultaneous bisexuality may exist (Cole 1990, herein). The degree to which species of these two genera exhibit habitat segregation among congeners is unclear due to their small size, cryptic lifestyle, and the limited number of studies focusing on this topic. However, serial hermaphroditism is clearly adaptive in instances where mating opportunities may be diminished due to limited mobility relative to encounter rates with conspecifics. This circumstance seems more likely to apply to crevice-dwelling and more solitary species of *Trimma* and *Priolepis* than to the aggregating species of *Trimma*, some of which are also serially hermaphroditic (Sunobe & Nakazono 1993). However, serial hermaphroditism may be adaptive for some *Trimma* species for other reasons. *Trimma* is generally at the small end of the goby size spectrum and therefore faces considerable fecundity constraints on the part of females. In addition, many members of this genus may be very short-lived, as has been reported for *Trimma naso* (Winterbottom & Southcott 2008). These factors introduce considerable unpredictability into potential lifetime reproductive success for both sexes, regardless of the degree of mate access. Consequently, serial hermaphroditism may have developed in response to unpredictable conditions or, alternatively, the development of serial hermaphroditism was an ancestral condition and supported the subsequent evolution of small size, abbreviated life history patterns, or both.

Among the more cryptic and solitary-living *Priolepis* species, life span information is not available, but their larger size suggests a longer life span than that of *Trimma*. In terms of collection numbers, *Priolepis* is not encountered as frequently in rotenone collections as *Trimma* (Winterbottom pers. comm.; Cole pers. obs.) or other common benthic gobies of the western Atlantic (Cole unpublished data). Serial hermaphroditism in *Priolepis* may have evolved as a successful counterbalance to locally low population densities and unpredictability in lifetime reproductive success due to a strong potential for low encounter rates among adults. One recently discovered *Priolepis* species was collected from relatively deep (400m) waters of the Red Sea (Goren & Baranes 1995). If there are further discoveries of deepwater *Priolepis* species and these species prove also to be serially hermaphroditic, this form of flexible sexual pattern may have been instrumental in a bathydemersal radiation within this genus.

Bryaninops is an Indo-Pacific genus of nine described species, all of which are very small sized and form obligate associations with gorgonian and antipatharian corals (Okiyama & Tsukamoto 1989). Most species are microhabitat specialists, often with highly species-specific coral associations (Herler 2007). Due to their small size, associated limited mobility, and highly specific habitat needs, species of *Bryaninops* likely experience the greatest within-population spatial isolation found among hermaphroditic gobies, in which mating opportunities are limited to conspecifics occupying the same sea whip. In addition, their extremely small size imposes significant limitations on female fecundity and they may experience an abbreviated lifespan, which seems to be a common condition among small-sized fishes (Depczynski & Bellwood 2005). *Bryaninops* also expresses serial hermaphroditism and has a reproductive morphology that places it close to *Trimma* and *Priolepis*. To date, this genus has not been included in any phylogenetic analyses of gobiid fishes, so the nature of its relationship to *Trimma* and *Priolepis* remains to be tested. The expression of serial hermaphroditism within *Bryaninops* seems almost obligatory to sustain such a constrained lifestyle. The question as to whether serial hermaphroditism arose prior to, concomitant with, or subsequent to the development of this extreme lifestyle remains unanswered in the absence of any hypotheses of phylogenetic relationships for this genus relative to other gobiid taxa.

Eviota is a tropical Indo-Pacific genus consisting of 50 described species (Gill pers. comm.) and probably at least a similar number of undescribed species (Jewett & Lachner 1983). *Eviota* constitutes a genus of small-sized fishes, many of which have extensive distributions and are abundant within their range (Lachner & Karnella 1980; Gill & Jewett 2004). A number of species occur intertidally (Cole 1990; Gill & Jewett 2004) or subtidally in coral or rock reef crevices, and often in pairs (Sunobe 1988). In a recent Red Sea study, Herler (2007) found that *Eviota* species exhibited a much higher degree of niche segregation among congeners relative to heterogeneric species, indicating strong niche partitioning among coexisting *Eviota* species. The specific nature of the hermaphroditic pattern in *Eviota* remains unclear, but the persistent integrated ovotestis pattern of reproductive morphology suggests a capacity for serial hermaphroditism like that of *Trimma, Priolepis*, and *Bryaninops*. As pointed out earlier, the evolution of serial hermaphroditism in microhabitat specialists may offer the advantage of increased mating opportunities among adult conspecifics that are otherwise constrained by small size, limited mobility, highly specific microhabitat requirements, and/or a possibly short life span.

Gobiodon and *Paragobiodon* are proposed sister taxa (Harold et al. 2008) which share a similar pattern of reproductive morphology. *Gobiodon* consists of more than 30 described species, of which 19 are currently recognized as valid (Harold et al. 2008), while *Paragobiodon* has 6 described species (Akihito et al. 2002). Both *Gobiodon* and *Paragobiodon* are obligate coral-dwelling taxa, often with highly species-specific coral associations (Munday et al. 1997, 1999; Herler 2007). In a recent Red Sea study, *Gobiodon* and *Paragobiodon* were found to constitute some of the most habitat-specialized reef fishes examined (Herler 2007). As proposed for *Eviota*, the evolution of serial hermaphroditism in *Gobiodon* and *Paragobiodon* appears highly adaptive under the constraints of small size, limited mobility, and highly specific microhabitat requirements. However, in the absence of a known sister group for the Gobiodon/Paragobiodon clade, it cannot be determined whether a labile sexual pattern preceded, occurred concomitantly with, or followed the development of such an extreme form of obligate coral-dwelling lifestyle.

The Gobiosoma group of American seven-spined gobies (Gobiidae, Gobiosomatini *sensu* Rüber et al. [2003]) is a western Atlantic clade. Within this relatively speciose taxon, *E. multifasciatus* is the sole known hermaphroditic representative and exhibits a unidirectional protogynous pattern. *Elacatinus multifasciatus* is fairly abundant in intertidal and shallow subtidal habitats, occupying coral rubble and sponges and frequently associating with rock-boring sea urchins (Böhlke & Chaplin 1993; Toller 2005). The sexual pattern of the Gobiosoma group is of interest due to the occurrence of functional hermaphroditism in only a single species within the genus, which is unique among hermaphroditic goby taxa. However, it has been proposed (Cole 2008) that hermaphroditism may be an ancestral condition within the Gobiosoma group that has subsequently been lost in most of the descendent species, excepting *E. multifasciatus*. This hypothesis developed from the observation that there is a transient expression of pAGS prior to first maturity during the immature phase among females of several species closely related to *E. multifasciatus*. Many species within the monophyletic Gobiosoma group are microniche specialists, which has been proposed as an important factor in the adaptive radiation and rapid speciation of this group early in its evolutionary history (Rüber et al. 2003). Functional hermaphroditism may have been instrumental in supporting the success of microniche specialization and subsequent adaptive radiation within this group. By correlation, functional hermaphroditism may have also played a similar role in other speciose genera such as *Trimma*, *Eviota*, and *Priolepis*.

The goby genus *Lythrypnus* contains approximately 20 small-sized species and has a distribution that includes the eastern central Pacific, eastern Pacific, southeast Pacific, and the western Atlantic (Böhlke & Robins 1960; Greenfield 1988; Bussing 1990). All examined species appear to have a serial hermaphroditic sexual pattern (St. Mary 2000). The regionalized ovotestis of *Lythrypnus* exhibits both similarities and differences with that of the partitioned ovotestis of *Trimma*, *Priolepis*, and *Bryaninops*. If *Lythrypnus* is closely related to the Trimma-Priolepis clade (the placement of *Bryaninops* being currently unresolved), differences in the configuration of tissues associated with reproductive function between these two groups may represent a divergence from the ancestral reproductive morphology pattern on the part of either or both. Alternatively, as hypothesized by St. Mary (1998), differences between these two groups could reflect independent origins for hermaphroditism.

In summary, within the Gobiidae, functional hermaphroditism has likely arisen several times within different clades, under differing sets of selective pressures, and with different forms of expression. The development of labile sexuality among numerous goby taxa has also likely played a significant interactive role in the coevolution, and possible convergence, of widely varying social and mating systems and life histories among goby species. In addition, hermaphroditic sexual patterns may have played a central role in the evolution of species-rich genera among gobiids, and therefore contributed to the remarkable diversity of this group. Currently, the phylogenetic resolution of constituent taxa of the Gobiidae suffers from many sampling gaps that remain to be filled. Given the size of this taxon, the likelihood is that many more species—and even genera—remain to be discovered. With the information provided here, gobiid fishes offer an exciting and promising model taxon for the study of evolution processes and adaptive radiation among speciose vertebrate taxa, and of the inter-related evolutionary patterns of speciation, life history, reproductive biology, and sexual expression among marine fishes.

SUMMARY

Reproductive morphology among hermaphroditic goby taxa can be characterized by a number of differing anatomical and ontogenetic patterns that show a high degree of taxon specificity. In some instances, the gonad is either completely ovariform or completely testiform, according to sexual function. An ovotestis, defined here by the co-occurrence of sex-specific reproductive tissues with no ascribed functional connotation, may be present only briefly as an interim form. This transient ovotestis presence results from the brief temporal overlap of sex-specific reproductive tissues during the transition phase between sexual functions (e.g., Coryphopterus group). Among other hermaphroditic taxa, the ovotestis is a more durable feature that persists throughout life (e.g., *Eviota*) or may form secondarily from an ovariform state (e.g., *Gobiodon*). In the persistent ovotestis pattern, gametogenesis is typically limited to only ova or sperm production at any one time although an interim, possibly functional, bisexual ovotestis has been documented for *Priolepis hipoliti* and *P. eugenia*. Within the ovotestis, the organization of sex-specific reproductive tissues also demonstrates several different patterns. The distribution of oocyte-bearing and spermatocyte-bearing tissues may be integrated (e.g., *Eviota*, *Gobiodon*), regionalized (e.g., *Lythrypnus*), or partitioned (e.g., *Trimma*, *Priolepis*, *Bryaninops*).

Another morphological feature associated with the reproductive complex of hermaphroditic gobies is the elaboration of accessory structures. In most instances, the function of differentiated accessory structures is secretory and appears to be analogous to sperm duct glands of gonochore goby taxa. These secretory accessory structures may arise from the sperm duct (as with AGdS of *Gobiodon*) but more typically develop from precursive or partially developed tissues associated with the gonadal wall (pAGS and AGS, respectively). In *Gobiodon*, an additional elaborated region, which is located directly within the gonad, develops into storage lobules for secretions produced by the AGdS.

The diversity of reproductive morphologies exhibited by hermaphroditic goby taxa is due to a number of novel morphological traits not found in gonochoric goby taxa. Some of these traits may be shared among many, or all, hermaphroditic goby taxa. For example, the functional equivalent of sperm duct glands, the secretory AGS, arise from precursive gonad-associated tissues. These precursive tissues and their subsequent differentiation into gonad-associated AGS represent a novel anatomical feature found among most hermaphroditic goby species. In this review, *Gobiodon* is the only taxon that does not have pAGS that develop into gonad-associated AGS. Instead, their secretory accessory structures (AGdS) arise directly from the gonoduct and therefore may be homologous with gonochore sperm duct glands. However, the AGdS of *Gobiodon* are not entirely consistent with sperm duct glands of gonochore species. In the former, the AGdS are present and fully developed in immatures and in both female-active and male-active adults, while sperm duct glands of gonochoric goby taxa are found only in the male reproductive complex. Consequently, the AGdS of *Gobiodon* may represent a novel reproductive character that is unique to a limited number of gobiine species.

A number of other Gobiodon pattern novelties include the development of a secondary ovotestis during the male-active phase and the partitioning of the secondary ovotestis into gametogenic, stromal, and storage lobule regions. This tripartite form of ovotestis, as well as the presence of storage lobules which dominate the posterior region of the gonad, represent novel features that are currently unique to *Gobiodon*.

A comparison of distribution patterns for different hermaphroditic reproductive morphologies and phylogenetic relationships among hermaphroditic goby taxa indicates a strong concordance. Hermaphroditic reproductive morphology accurately predicts the majority of currently hypothesized clade relationships within the Gobiidae. And where phylogenetic relationships are still unresolved, shared patterns of reproductive morphology (i.e., *Eviota* and *Gobiodon*; *Bryaninops* and Trimma-Priolepis) may be phylogenetically informative. The combination of shared reproductive morphologies found among closely related goby taxa and differing reproductive morphologies among distantly related taxa supports a hypothesis of multiple independent origins for hermaphroditism within the

Gobiidae. This finding also argues for a significant capacity for morphological and physiological innovation within the Gobiidae, traits that have likely been instrumental in the frequent and extensive adaptive radiation that is characteristic of this speciose family.

ACKNOWLEDGMENTS

Portions of this chapter benefitted greatly from enlightening conversations with A.C. Gill, D.W. Greenfield, A.S. Harold, D.F. Hoese, H.K. Larson, P.L. Munday, L.R. Parenti, F. Pezold, C.E. Thacker, J.L. Van Tassel, and R. Winterbottom. Specimens were generously provided by D.W. Greenfield, D.F. Hoese, R.C. Langston, H.K. Larson, D.R. Robertson, and R. Winterbottom. Additional assistance and support in the field were kindly provided by L. Orsak and J. Masey (Christensen Research Institute, Papua, New Guinea); A. Hoggett, J. Leis, S. Reader, and L.Vail (Lizard Island Research Station, Australia); and L. Bell, P. Colin (Coral Reef Research Foundation, Palau), and Y. Sadovy (University of Hong Kong). Microphotography imaging assistance was provided by S. Raredon and B. Vine, and artwork by S. Mondon. Cladogram imaging assistance was kindly and patiently provided by S. Raredon. Portions of the research reported on in this chapter were supported by grants from the Smithsonian Institution through the National Museum of Natural History's Caribbean Coral Reef Ecosystems Program (CCRE Contribution no. 830), a Curatorial Fellowship from the Australian Museum, and from funds provided by the University of Hawaii at Mānoa.

REFERENCES

Akihito SK, Ikeda Y, Sugiyama K (2002). Suborder Gobioidei. In: Nakabo, T (ed.), *Fishes of Japan with Pictorial Keys to the Species*, 2nd edition. Tokai University Press, Tokyo, pp. 12139–12168.

Arai R (1964). Sex characters of Japanese gobioid fishes (I). Bulletin of National Science Museum, Tokyo 7: 295–306.

Belanger AJ, Arbuckle WJ, Corkum LD, Gammom DB, Li W, Scott AP, Zielinski S (2004). Behavioural and electrophysiological responses by reproductive female *Neogobius melanostomus* to odours released by conspecific males. Journal of Fish Biology 65: 933–946.

Berglund A (1990). Sequential hermaphroditism and the size-advantage hypothesis: an experimental test. Animal Behaviour 39: 426–433.

Böhlke JE, Chaplin CCG (1993). *Fishes of the Bahamas and Adjacent Tropical Waters*. University of Texas Press, Austin.

Böhlke JE, Robins CR (1960). Western Atlantic gobioid fishes of the genus *Lythrypnus*, with notes on *Quisquilius hipoliti* and *Germannia pallens*. Proceedings of the National Academy of Sciences, Philadephia 112: 73–101.

Breitburg DL (1987). Interspecific competition and the abundance of nest sites: factors affecting sexual selection. Ecology 68: 1844–1855.

Bussing WA (1990). New species of gobiid fishes of the genera *Lythrypnus, Elacatinus* and *Chriolepis* from the eastern tropical Pacific. Revista de Biologia Tropical 38: 99–118.

Caputo V, Mesa ML, Candi G, Cerioni PN (2003). The reproductive biology of the crystal goby with a comparison to that of the transparent goby. Journal of Fish Biology 62: 375–385.

Cinquette R (1997). Histochemical, enzyme histochemical and ultrastructural investigation on the sperm duct glands of *Padogobius martensi* (Pisces, Gobiidae). Journal of Fish Biology 50: 978–991.

Cole KS (1983). Protogynous hermaphroditism in a temperate zone territorial marine goby, *Coryphopterus nicholsii*. Copeia 1983: 809–812.

Cole KS (1988). Predicting the potential for sex change on the basis of ovarian structure in gobiid fishes. Copeia 1988: 1082–1086.

Cole KS (1990). Patterns of gonad structure in hermaphroditic gobies (Teleostei: Gobiidae). Environmental Biology of Fishes 28: 125–142.

Cole KS (2008). Transient ontogenetic expression of hermaphroditic gonad morphology within the Gobiosoma group of the Neotropical seven-spined gobies (Teleostei: Gobiidae). Marine Biology 154: 943–951.

Cole KS (2009). Modifications of the reproductive complex and implications for the reproductive biology of *Gobiodon oculolineatus* (Teleostei: Gobiidae). Environmental Biology of Fishes 84: 261–273.

Cole KS, Hoese DF (2001). Gonad morphology, colony demography and evidence for hermaphroditism in *Gobiodon okinawae* (Teleostei: Gobiidae). Environmental Biology of Fishes 61: 161–173.

Cole KS, Robertson DR (1988). Protogyny in a Caribbean reef goby, *Coryphopterus personatus*: gonad ontogeny and social influences on sex change. Bulletin of Marine Sciences 42: 317–333.

Cole KS, Shapiro DY (1990). Gonad structure and hermaphroditism in the gobiid genus *Coryphopterus* (Teleostei: Gobiidae). Copeia 1990: 996–1003.

Cole KS, Shapiro DY (1992). Gonadal structure and population characteristics of the protogynous goby *Coryphopterus glaucofraenum*. Marine Biology 113: 1–9.

Colombo L, Burighel P (1974). Fine structure of the testicular gland of the black goby, *Gobius jozo* L. Cell and Tissue Research 154: 39–49.

Colombo L, Marconato A, Belvedere PC, Frisco C (1980). Endocrinology of teleost reproduction: a testicular steroid pheromone in the black goby, *Gobius jozo* L. Bollettino di Zoologia 47: 355–364.

Depczynski M, Bellwood DR (2005). Shortest recorded vertebrate lifespan found in a coral reef fish. Current Biology 15: R288.

Drilling CC, Grober MS (2005). An initial description of alternative male reproductive phenotypes in the bluebanded goby, *Lythrypnus dalli* (Teleostei: Gobiidae). Environmental Biology of Fishes 72: 361–372.

Egami N (1960). Comparative morphology of the sex characters in several species of Japanese gobies, with reference to the effects of sex steroids on the characters. Journal of the Faculty of Science, University of Tokyo, Section IV 9: 67–100.

Eggert B (1931). Die Geschlechtsorgane der Gobiiformes und Blenniiformes. Zeitschrift Wissenschaftliche Zoologie 139: 249–517.

Eschmeyer WN, Herald ES, Hammann H (1983). *A Field Guide to the Pacific Coast Fishes of North America.* Houghton Mifflin Company, Boston.

Fishelson L (1989). Bisexuality and pedogenesis in gobies (Gobiidae: Teleostei) and other fish, or: why so many little fish in tropical seas? Senckenbergiana Maritima 20: 147–160.

Fishelson L (1991). Comparative cytology and morphology of seminal vesicles in male gobiid fishes. Japanese Journal of Ichthyology 38: 17–30.

Ghiselin MT (1969). The evolution of hermaphroditism among animals. The Quarterly Review of Biology 44: 189–208.

Gill AC, Jewett SL (2004). *Eviota hoesei* and *E. readerae,* new species of fish from the Southwest Pacific, with comments on the identity of *E. corneliae* Fricke (Perciformes: Gobiidae). Records of the Australian Museum 56: 2235–2240.

Goren M, Baranes A (1995). *Priolepis goldshmidtae* (Gobiidae), a new species from the deep water of the northern Gulf of Aqaba, Red Sea. Cybium 19: 343–347.

Greenfield DW (1988). A review of the *Lythrypnus mowbrayi* complex (Pisces: Gobiidae), with the description of a new species. Copeia 1988: 460–470.

Grier H, Linton JR, Leatherland JF, de Vlaming VL (1980). Structural evidence for two different testicular types in teleost fishes. American Journal of Anatomy 159: 331–345.

Grier HJ (1981). Cellular organization of the testis and spermatogenesis in fishes. American Zoologist 21: 345–357.

Harold AS, Winterbottom R, Munday PL, Chapman RW (2008). Phylogenetic relationships of Indo-Pacific coral gobies of the genus *Gobiodon* (Teleostei: Gobiidae), based on morphological and molecular data. Bulletin of Marine Science 82: 119–136.

Herler J (2007). Microhabitats and ecomorphology of coral- and coral rock-associated gobiid fish (Teleostei: Gobiidae) in the northern Red Sea. Marine Ecology 28, Supplement 1: 82–94.

Hoar WS (1955). Reproduction in teleost fish. Memoirs of the Society for Endocrinology 4: 5–24.

Hoese DF (1984). Gobioidei: relationships. In: Moser HG, Richards WJ, Cohen DM, Fahay MP, Kendall AW, Richardson SL (eds.), *Ontogeny and Systematics of Fishes.* American Society of Ichthyologists and Herpetologists Special Publication 1, Gainesville, Florida, pp. 588–591.

Hoese DF (1995). Gobiidae. Gobios, chanquetes y guasetas. In: Fischer W, Krupp F, Schneider W, Sommer C, Carpenter KE, Niem V (eds.), *Guia FAO para Identificación de Especies para lo Fines de la Pesca.* Pacifico Centro-Oriental, 3 Vols. FAO, Rome, pp. 1129–1135.

Hoese DF, Gill AC (1993). Phylogenetic relationships of eleotridid fishes (Perciformes: Gobioidei). Bulletin of Marine Science 52: 415–440.

Hoese DF, Reader S (2001). A preliminary review of the Eastern Pacific species of *Elacatinus* (Perciformes: Gobiidae). Revista De Biologia Tropical 49, Supplement 1: 157–167.

Immler S, Mazzoldi C, Rassoto MB (2004). From sneaker to parental male: change of reproductive traits in the black goby, *Gobius niger* (Teleostei: Gobiidae). Journal of Experimental Zoology 301A: 177–185.

Jewett SL, Lachner EA (1983). Seven new species of the Indo-Pacific genus *Eviota* (Pisces: Gobiidae). Proceedings of the Biological Society of Washington 96: 780–806.

Karnella SJ, Lachner EA (1981). Three new species of the *Eviota epiphanies* group having vertical trunk bars (Pisces: Gobiidae). Proceedings of the Biological Society of Washington 94: 264–275.

Kroon FJ, de Graaf M, Liley NR (2000). Social organisation and competition for refuges and nest sites in *Coryphopterus nicholsii* (Gobiidae), a temperate protogynous reef fish. Environmental Biology of Fishes 57: 401–411.

Lachner EA, Karnella SJ (1980). Fishes of the Indo-Pacific genus *Eviota* with descriptions of eight new species (Teleostei: Gobiidae). Smithsonian Contributions to Zoology 315: 1–136.

Lahnsteiner F, Seiwald M, Patzner RA, Ferrero EA (1992). The seminal vesicles of the male grass goby, *Zosterisessor ophiocephalus* (Teleostei: Gobiidae): Fine structure and histochemistry. Zoomorphology 111: 239–248.

Larson HK (1985). A revision of the gobiid genus *Bryaninops* (Pisces), with a description of six new species. The Beagle: Occasional Papers of the Northern Territory Museum of Arts and Sciences 2: 57–93.

Larson HK (1990). A revision of the gobiid genera *Pleurosicya* and *Luposicya*, with descriptions of eight new species of *Pleurosicya*. The Beagle: Records of the Northern Territory Museum of Arts and Sciences 7: 1–53.

Locatello L Mazzoldi C Rasotto MB (2002) Ejaculate of sneaker males is pheromonally inconspicuous in the black goby, *Gobius niger* (Teleostei: Gobiidae). Journal of Experimental Zoology 293: 601–605.

Maack G, Segner H (2003). Morphological development of the gonads in zebrafish. Journal of Fish Biology 62: 895–906.

Marconato A, Rasotto MB, Mazzoldi C (1996). On the mechanism of sperm release in three gobiid fishes (Teleostei: Gobiidae). Environmental Biology of Fishes 46: 321–327.

Mazzoldi C Petersen CW Rasotto MB (2005). The influence of mating system on seminal vesicle variability among gobies (Teleostei: Gobiidae). Journal of Zoological Systematics and Evolutionary Research 43: 307–314.

Miller PJ (1984). The tokology of gobioid fishes. In: Potts GW, Wootton RJ (eds.), *Fish Reproduction: Strategies and Tactics*. Academic Press, London, pp 119–153.

Miller PJ (1992). The sperm duct gland: a visceral synapomorphy for gobioid fishes. Copeia 1992: 253–256.

Munday PL, Harold AS, Winterbottom R (1999). Guide to the coral-dwelling gobies, genus *Gobiodon* (Gobiidae) from Papua New Guinea and the Great Barrier Reef. Revue Française d'Aquariologie 26: 49–54.

Munday PL, Jones GP, Caley MJ (1997). Habitat specialisation and the distribution and abundance of coral-dwelling gobies. Marine Ecology Progress Series 152: 227–239.

Nagahama Y (1983). The functional morphology of teleost gonads. In: Hoar WS, Randall DJ, Donaldson EM (eds.), *Fish Physiology*, vol. IXA. Academic Press, New York, pp. 223–275.

Nelson JS (2006). *Fishes of the World*. John Wiley & Sons, Inc., Hoboken, New Jersey.

Nogawa Y, Endo H (2007). A new species of the genus *Priolepis* (Perciformes: Gobiidae) from Tosa Bay, Japan. Bulletin of the National Museum of Nature and Science, Series A, Supplement 1: 153–161.

Okiyama M, Tsukamoto Y (1989). Sea whip goby, *Bryaninops yongei*, collected from outer shelf off Miyakojima, East China Sea. Ichthyological Research 36: 1341–8998.

Parenti LR, Grier HJ (2004). Evolution and phylogeny of gonad morphology in bony fishes. Integrative and Comparative Biology 44: 333–348.

Pezold F (1993). Evidence for monophyletic Gobiinae. Copeia 1993: 634–643.

Randall JE (2001). Five new Indo-Pacific gobiid fishes of the genus *Coryphopterus*. Zoological Studies 40: 206–225.

Rasotto MB, Mazzoldi C (2002). Male traits associated with alternative reproductive tactics in *Gobius niger*. Journal of Fish Biology 61: 173–184.

Robertson DR, Justines G (1982). Protogynous hermaphroditism and gonochorism in four Caribbean reef gobies. Environmental Biology of Fishes 7: 137–142.

Rüber L, Van Tassell JL, Zardoya R (2003). Rapid speciation and ecological divergence in the American seven-spined gobies (Gobiidae: Gobiosomatini) inferred from a molecular phylogeny. Evolution 57: 1584–1598.

Sadovy Y, Shapiro DY (1987). Criteria for the diagnosis of hermaphroditism in fishes. Copeia 1987: 136–156.

Scaggiante M, Grober MS, Lorenzi V, Rasotto MB (2004). Changes along the male reproductive axis in response to social context in a gonochoristic gobiid, *Zosterisessor ophiocephalus* (Teleostei: Gobiidae), with alternative mating tactics. Hormones and Behavior 46: 607–617.

Scaggiante M, Mazzoldi C, Petersen C W, Rasotto MB (1999). Sperm competition and mode of fertilization in the grass goby *Zosterisessor ophiocephalus* (Teleostei: Gobiidae). Journal of Experimental Zoology 283: 81–90.

Seiwald M, Patzner RA (1989). Histological, fine-structural and histochemical differences in the testicular glands of gobiid and blenniid fishes. Journal of Fish Biology 35: 631–640.

Stanley H, Chieffi G, Boote V (1965). Histological and histochemical observations on the testis of *Gobius paganellus*. Zeitschrift fiir Zellforschung 65: 350–362.

St. Mary CM (1993). Novel sexual patterns in two simultaneous hermaphroditic gobies, *Lythrypnus dalli* and *Lythrypnus zebra*. Copeia 1993: 1062–1072.

St. Mary CM (1998). Characteristic gonad structure in the gobiid genus *Lythrypnus dalli* with comparison to other hermaphroditic gobies. Copeia 1998: 720–724.

St. Mary CM (2000). Sex allocation in *Lythrypnus* (Gobiidae): variations on a hermaphroditic theme. Environmental Biology of Fishes 58: 321–333.

Sunobe T (1988). A new gobiid fish of the genus *Eviota* from Cape Santa, Japan. Japanese Journal of Ichthyology 35: 278–281.

Sunobe T, Nakazono A (1993). Sex change in both directions by alternation of social dominance in *Trimma okinawae* (Pisces: Gobiidae). Ethology 94: 339–345.

Thacker CE (2003). Molecular phylogeny of the gobioid fishes (Teleostei: Perciformes: Gobioidei). Molecular Phylogenetics and Evolution 26: 354–368.

Thacker CE (2009). Phylogeny of Gobioidei and placement within Acanthomorpha, with a new classification and investigation of diversification and character evolution. Copeia 2009: 93–104.

Thacker CE, Cole KS (2002). Phylogeny and evolution of the gobiid genus *Corypohopterus*. Bulletin of Marine Science 70: 837–850.

Thacker CE, Grier H (2005) Unusual gonad structure in the paedomorphic teleost *Schindleria praematura* (Teleostei: Gobioidei): A comparison with other gobioid fishes. Journal of Fish Biology 66: 378–391.

Toller W (2005). F7 Final Report—October 1, 2003 to September 30 2005, Recreational Fisheries Habitat Assessment Project Study 3. Patterns of habitat utilization by reef fish on St. Croix. Division of Fish and Wildlife, Department of Planning and Natural Resources, Government of the U.S. Virgin Islands.

Victor BC (2008). Redescription of *Coryphopterus tortugae* (Jordan) and a new allied species *Coryphopterus bal* (Perciformes: Gobiidae: Gobiinae) from the tropical eastern Atlantic Ocean. Journal of the Ocean Science Foundation 1: 1–19.

Wang H-Y, Tsai M-P, Dean J, Lee S-C (2001). Molecular phylogeny of gobioid fishes (Perciformes: Gobioidei) based on mitochondrial 12S rRNA sequences. Molecular Phylogenetics and Evolution 20: 390–408.

Weisel GF (1949). The seminal vesicles and testes of *Gillichthys*, a marine teleost. Copeia 1949: 101–110.

Winterbottom R, Burridge M (1992). Revision of *Egglestonichthys* and of *Priolepis* species possessing a transverse pattern of cheek papillae (Teleostei: Gobiidae), with a discussion of relationships. Canadian Journal of Zoology 70: 1934–1946.

Winterbottom R, Emery AR (1981). A new genus and two new species of gobiid fishes (Perciformes) from the Chagos Archipelago, Central Indian Ocean. Environmental Biology of Fishes 6: 139–149.

Winterbottom R, Southcott L (2008). Short lifespan and high mortality in the western Pacific coral reef goby *Trimma nasa*. Marine Ecology Progress Series 366: 203–208.

Young RT, Fox DL (1937). The seminal vesicles of the goby, with preliminary chemical and physiological studies of the vesicular fluid. Proceedings of the National Academy of Sciences 23: 461–467.

PART TWO

Processes

6

Gonad Development in Hermaphroditic Gobies

Kathleen S. Cole

Among hermaphroditic goby taxa (Perciformes, Gobiidae), considerable variability in the composition and configuration of gametogenic tissue within the gonad proper is coupled with a diversity of accessory structures of the reproductive complex (Cole 1990, 2009, this volume). Such diversity prompts the question as to how gonad ontogeny and morphogenesis may have become modified to produce such an impressive array of anatomical complexity. In the past decade, major advances in gene expression research have substantially improved our understanding of how cells and tissues first differentiate and then become organized to form the teleost reproductive complex. Genes and gene products such as *vasa, olvas, nanos, DMY/Dmrt1, SOX/STY, FOXl2,* and the enzyme aromatase figure prominently in these studies. While the number of fish species examined has been relatively limited, and mostly freshwater (i.e., zebrafish, *Danio rerio* and medaka, *Oryzias latipes*), collectively they have provided a working model and testable framework upon which to investigate early reproductive ontogeny in other teleosts. Studies of early ontogeny of the reproductive system in gobiids, although few in number, show numerous similarities with existing teleost model species. Therefore, what is known about the development of the reproductive complex in other teleosts may provide insights into the origins of reproductive morphological diversity found among hermaphroditic goby taxa. This chapter, consisting of three sections, addresses that possibility. The first section provides a brief overview of hermaphroditic gonad morphology among gobiid fishes. For a more detailed coverage, the reader is referred to Chapter 5 (Cole) of this volume. The second section reviews various aspects of early cell differentiation and tissue formation associated with the ontogeny of the teleost reproductive complex. The third section

165

concludes with a discussion as to how ontogenetic processes may inform our understanding of the evolution of gonad morphological diversity among hermaphroditic gobiid fishes. It is hoped that this approach may offer new avenues of investigation into ontogenetic processes that are instrumental in the development of labile sexual patterns among vertebrates.

DEVELOPMENTAL PATTERNS OF GAMETOGENIC TISSUES IN HERMAPHRODITIC GOBIES

Among gonochore goby species, in which all individuals produce only one gamete type, either ova or sperm, the reproductive complex follows the basic teleost pattern. Paired gonadal lobes are united posteriorly and are continuous with an oviduct in females, and a sperm duct in males. The gobiid oviduct is typically a short, simple, tubular structure that conveys ova to the outside of the body. The gobiid sperm duct, however, is rarely simple. In the majority of goby taxa, expanded regions of the sperm duct form lobular secretory structures that vary extensively in their morphology across the family (Miller 1984; Fishelson 1991). Because of their association with the sperm duct, these structures have been termed sperm duct glands (Miller 1984).

In hermaphroditic goby species, either most or all individuals pass through an immature ovariform phase followed by an adult, ova-producing (i.e., female-functioning) phase (Cole & Robertson 1988; Cole & Shapiro 1992; Munday et al. 1998). If there is no preformed spermatogenic tissue present and the gonad is strictly ovariform, the oogenic tissue has one of two fates following sex change. It may completely disappear, resulting in the formation of a *secondary testis* (i.e., develops secondarily from an ovary); or, alternatively, healthy oocytes may persist during and following the development of spermatogenic tissue, and the gonad becomes a *secondary ovotestis* (i.e., develops secondarily from an initial single-sex gonad).

If the ovariform gonad of both the juvenile and initial ova-producing phases includes early-stage spermatogenic tissue, the gonad develops directly as an ovotestis. In hermaphroditic gobies, a shift to male function following an initial ova-producing phase is typically accompanied by a concomitant regression, but not disappearance, of ova-producing tissue. Therefore, in this ontogenetic pattern the direct development of an ovotestis that is subsequently retained throughout life results in a *persistent ovotestis*.

In addition to gonadal transformation, sex change in hermaphroditic gobies includes the development of secretory structures that appear to fulfill the function of sperm duct glands of gonochore species. Accessory secretory structures associated with male function in hermaphroditic gobiids may arise from one of two locations. In most species, precursive tissue masses (pAGS) which are associated with the wall of the ovariform gonad differentiate to form gonad-derived secre-tory structures (i.e., accessory gonadal structures, or AGS) (Cole 1988, 1990). How-ever, in a small number of hermaphroditic species, secretory structures arise di-rectly from the gonoduct as gonoduct-derived structures (i.e., accessory gonoduct structures, or AGdS), much like the sperm duct glands of gonochore gobies (Cole & Hoese 2001; Cole 2009)

From the anatomical diversity described above, the sequence of morphologies exhibited during immature, ova-producing and sperm-producing phases among hermaphroditic goby species has the potential to vary considerably. These differ-ences can be expressed in terms of both the distribution of gamete-producing tissue(s) and the extent to which they co-occur. Applying these two criteria, her-maphroditic gobies exhibit a variety of developmental patterns of sequential mor-phological expression, which show a high degree of taxon specificity, as described by Cole earlier in this volume. Reproductive morphology patterns for hermaph-roditic gobies fall into a number of different patterns, which include: (i) the interim ovotestis pattern of the Coryphopterus group, including the genera *Coryphopterus*, *Rhinogobiops*, *Lophogobius*, and *Fusigobius*; (ii) the modified interim ovotestis pattern of *Elacatinus multifasciatus*; (iii) the persistent integrated ovotestis pat-tern of *Eviota*; (iv) the regionalized ovotestis of *Lythrypnus*; (v) the persistent par-titioned ovotestis of *Trimma* and *Bryaninops*, including the specialized persistent partitioned ovotestis pattern of *Priolepis hipoliti* and *P. eugenia,* which includes an interim functionally bisexual ovotestis; and (vi) the tripartite secondary ovotestis of *Gobiodon*. Most of these patterns are illustrated in detail in Chapter 5 of this volume (Figures 5.11, 5.12). Figure 6.1 illustrates ova-producing and sperm-producing gonad morphology for five of the six currently recognized go-nad developmental patterns.

In the majority of reproductive morphology patterns listed above, the AGS arise from tissues associated with the gonadal wall and become fully differentiated and active at the onset of male function. In the sixth pattern shown by *Gobiodon*, however, accessory secretory structures are associated with the gonoduct rather than the gonadal wall. Although similar in position with the sperm duct glands male gonochore gobies *sensu* Miller (1984), the gonoduct-derived AGdS of *Gobiodon* differ in their expression. Unlike sperm duct glands, AGdS occur as fully differentiated structures in all individuals, including immatures and ova-producing adults and therefore are a persistent feature of the reproductive com-plex throughout all phases of sexual expression.

The diversity of morphology patterns associated with the reproductive com-plex of hermaphroditic gobies reflects the intersection of ontogeny, morphogene-sis, and evolution. The question is, can variable patterns of morphology and de-velopment provide informative models for how reproductive structures and gene expression can be modified to generate complex functional morphologies?

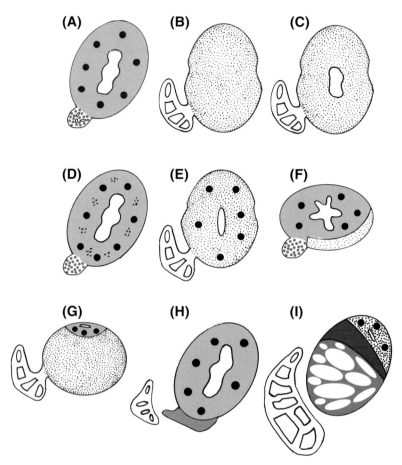

FIGURE 6.1. Illustration of ova-producing and sperm-producing gonad morphologies for four gonad developmental patterns exhibited by hermaphroditic gobies. (A) Coryphopterus group ovary and (B) secondary testis of interim ovotestis pattern. (C) *Elacatinus multifasciatus* secondary testis of modified interim ovotestis pattern. (D) *Eviota* ova-producing ovotestis and (E) sperm-producing ovotestis of persistent integrated ovotestis pattern. (F) *Trimma* and *Bryaninops* ova-producing ovotestis and (G) sperm-producing ovotestis of persistent partitioned ovotestis pattern. (H) *Gobiodon* ovary and (I) secondary ovotestis of tripartite secondary ovotestis pattern. Light gray background represents oocyte-bearing tissue. Large black dots are oocytes. Open circle clusters represent pAGS tissue. Light stipple (F) is early-stage, non-active spermatogenic tissue. Darker stipple is male-active spermatogenic tissue. Medium gray background (H) represents undifferentiated region of future storage lobules. White ovals (I) are storage lobules surrounded by supporting tissue (medium gray); dark gray (I) is stromal tissue.

EARLY REPRODUCTIVE DEVELOPMENT IN TELEOSTS
Primordial Germ Cell Origins

The teleost reproductive complex initially develops as a composite of two cell sources: primordial germ cells (PGCs) arising from the germ cell line, and somatic cells. The germ cell line appears early in teleost development and the arrival of PGCs at the site of the future gonad is closely timed to that of the earliest stage of gonadal development, the gonadal anlagen. In the zebrafish, it has been shown that the origin of the germ cell line is predetermined by an aggregation of substances within the developing ovum, which are present long before ovum maturation and fertilization (Yoon et al. 1997; Braat et al. 1999; Pelegri & Schulte-Merker 1999; Howley and Ho 2000; Knaut et al. 2000; Pelegri 2003). These substances consist in part of an electron-dense material called "nuage" (Andre & Rouiller 1957) and the aggregate is referred to as "germ plasm" (e.g., Eddy 1975; Selman et al. 1993; Rongo et al. 1997). The presence of mRNA for the gene *vasa* (an RNA-binding protein), which is associated with germ plasm, is detectable in the early stages of oocyte development (stages I and II) in the maternal gonad and therefore predates fertilization (Yoon et al. 1997; Howley and Ho 2000; Pelegri 2003). Following fertilization, daughter cells that acquire germ plasm during cleavage events go on to form the germ cell line.

Vasa and *vasa*-like proteins associated with the germ cell line have been described for a number of teleosts including the Nile tilapia, *Oreochromis niloticus* (Kobayashi et al. 2000), rainbow trout, *Oncorhynchus mykiss* (Yoshizaki et al. 2000); Gibel carp, *Carassius auratus gibelio* (Xu et al. 2005); and most recently, bluefin tuna, *Thunnus orientalis* (Nagasawa et al. 2009). Early ontogeny studies of *vasa* expression associated with germ plasm have not yet been carried out for any goby species as of yet. However, a similar "nuage-like" aggregation of subcellular, electron-dense structures has been described for cells tentatively identified as PGCs in the goby *Leucopsarion petersii*, also known as shiro-uo, or the ice-goby (Miyake et al. 2006). Removal of this nuage-like substance during early ontogeny results in a significant decline in PGC numbers later in development (Miyake et al. 2006) suggesting that the origin of the germ cell line in gobiid taxa is similar to that of other examined teleosts.

In zebrafish, transcripts of the gene *vas* (zebrafish *vasa* homologue) provide a specific marker for germ line cells. Following fertilization, *vasa*-specific mRNA signal exhibits a predictable localization pattern (Yoon et al. 1997; Braat et al. 1999; Knaut et al. 2000). The signal is first expressed along the first and second cleavage furrows, and then becomes localized into four aggregates at each end of the two cleavage furrows. At the 32-cell stage, the aggregates ingress into four cells. During subsequent cleavage events, the four *vasa*-expressing cells undergo asymmetric segregation such that only one of the two daughter cells retains the *vasa*-positive germ plasm. In this way, the germ plasm remains restricted to four cells up until the 1-k cell (i.e., late blastula) stage (Knaut et al. 2000). At this point, *vasa*-positive cells undergo symmetric segregation such that both daughter cells now acquire a *vasa* signal, an event that marks the start of proliferation of germ plasm-containing cells and the consequent formation of a germ cell line. Thus, in the developing zebrafish embryo, two cell lines are formed as early as the blastula stage. One cell line consists of cells having no germ plasm, from which the somatic cell line arises. The other line includes cells that retain and often enrich the germ plasm and subsequently gives rise to the germ cell line and future PGCs.

In other teleosts, *vasa*-positive expression associated with the development of the germ cell line shows similar patterns across several teleost families and orders. In the loach, *Misgurnus anguillicaudatus* (F. Cobitidae, Cypriniformes) anywhere from four to eight *vasa* mRNA aggregates develop prior to the 32-cell stage. Here, symmetrical segregation within the *vasa*-positive cell line that marks the beginning of cell proliferation within the germ cell line also occurs at the 1 k-cell (i.e., late blastula) stage (Fujimoto et al. 2006). In goldfish, *Carassius auratus* (F. Cyprinidae, Cypriniformes) a total of eight *vasa*-specific mRNA signals develop initially and the development of the germ cell line, signaled by the onset of symmetric segregation, is initiated at the 256-cell (i.e., early blastula) stage (Otani et al. 2002). In medaka (F. Adrianichthyidae, Beloniformes), PGCs identified through cell-specific expression of the *vasa*-like gene, *olvas*, initiate symmetric segregation slightly later, in the late gastrula (stage 16)(Shinomiya et al. 2000).

The few studies of *vasa* expression in gobiid fishes show a similar pattern. In the ice-goby, *L. petersii*, the pattern of appearance and localization of *vasa* mRNA is similar to that of the goldfish in that eight *vasa* mRNA aggregates form in early cleavage by the 16-cell stage (Miyake et al. 2006). In another goby, *Gymnogobius urotaenia*, also known as ukigori, anywhere from 4 to 8 *vasa* aggregates develop by the 16-cell stage (Saito et al. 2004). In both the ice-goby and ukigori, the initiation of symmetric segregation signaled by an increase in the number of *vasa*-positive cells also occurs after the late blastula, 512-cell stage.

In summary, there are broad similarities in PGC formation across numerous examined teleost taxa, including two goby species, ice-goby, and ukigori. These similarities include: the location and timing of appearance of *vasa* signal early in cleavage; the number of cells that express *vasa* mRNA prior to the initiation of cell division and establishment of the germ cell line; and the timing of symmetric segregation during the blastula stage that initiates the development and proliferation of the germ cell line.

Primordial Germ Cell Migration

Studies of a number of teleost taxa, including killifish, *Fundulus heteroclitus* (Richards & Thompson 1921); medaka (Hamaguchi 1982; Shinomiya et al. 2000;

Kurokawa et al. 2006); Celebes medaka, *Oryzias celebensis* (Hamaguchi 1983); and zebrafish (Weidinger et al. 1999) have demonstrated that *vasa*-positive cells, initially located outside the embryo proper, move to the interior of the developing embryo and migrate to the target site of the future gonad. The pathway followed by PGCs within the embryo starts along the ventral coelomic wall and ends at a dorsally located position, just below the developing mesonephric ducts. During their migration, PGCs become encircled by a small number of cells derived from the lateral plate mesoderm, or LPM (Hamaguchi 1982; Kobayashi et al. 2004).

PGC tracking in a number of teleost species has revealed a combination of shared and differing behaviors of germ cell movement and subsequent development of the gonadal anlagen. In medaka, PGCs become incorporated into the outer somatic layer of the LPM and then move dorsolaterally to arrive at the location of the presumptive gonad (Gamo 1961; Kurokawa et al. 2006). Here, the proliferation of dorsal coelomic peritoneal cells adjacent to PGCs rapidly increases their numbers, resulting in the formation of the gonadal anlagen (Hamaguchi 1982; Kobayashi et al. 2004). In zebrafish, PGCs migrate into the embryo interior during early gastrulation and become clustered bilaterally in the dorsoanterior trunk region (Weidinger et al. 1999; Weidinger et al. 2002; Reichman-Fried et al. 2004). This is followed by directed movement until they reach the site of the future gonad (Doitsidou et al. 2002). In rainbow trout (F. Salmonidae, Salmoniformes) PGCs have been tracked moving from the ventral mesentery first along the inner splanchnic layer of the LPM on either side of the gut mesentery, then along the dorsal mesentery and laterally to the left, or right, along the roof of the coelom (Moore 1937).

In two gobies, ukigori and ice-goby, PGCs are reported to move dorsally along the inner splanchnic layer of the LPM to the dorsal region of the gut, then to the site of the future gonadal anlage (Saito et al. 2002, 2004). In the round goby, *Neogobius melanostomus*, PGC migration along the LPM has been described as occurring along both the inner splanchnic and outer somatic layers (Moiseyeva 1983). Thus, gobies exhibit PGC migration patterns seen in other teleosts.

Early Gonad Development

PGC migration stops upon reaching a dorsal position adjacent to the mesonephric ducts. Here, PGCs, their surrounding LPM-derived somatic cells and adjacent, proliferating peritoneal cells of the dorsal coelom form the gonadal anlagen. The first conspicuous morphological indication of the formation of the gonadal anlagen is the development of a longitudinal ridge of cells, referred to as the peritoneal gonadal, or genital ridge, which extends along the length of the dorsal coelom on either side of the midline. The timing of formation of the peritoneal ridge varies among teleosts such that in some species, the peritoneal ridge forms prior to the arrival of PGCs, while in others it appears to develop in response to the arrival of PGCs.

In rainbow trout, after PGCs reach a position below the mesonephric ducts, they become surrounded by adjacent peritoneal epithelial cells, which proliferate to form the gonad anlagen (Moore 1937; Takashima et al. 1980). Subsequently, PGCs migrate anteriorly such that the developing gonadal anlagen extends nearly the length of the abdominal cavity (Moore 1937). A similar pattern of PGC migration and arrival at the site of the future gonad prior to peritoneal cell proliferation has been reported for a number of species, including: brown bullhead, *Ameiurus nebulosus* (Bachmann 1914); killifish, *Fundulus heteroclitus* (Richards & Thompson 1921); goldfish (Stromsten 1931); medaka (Hamaguchi 1982); rosy barb, *Puntius conchonius* (Timmermans & Taverne 1983); and carp, *Cyprinus carpio* (Parmentier & Timmermans 1985).

Information is less precise for gobies. In ukigori, brief descriptions provided by Saito et al. (2002, 2004) imply that the formation of a peritoneal ridge predates the arrival of the PGCs. In the round goby, however, a brief description of the site of the future gonad implies that the arrival of the PGCs may precede the proliferation of adjacent peritoneal cells to form a ridge (Moiseyeva 1983).

Gonadogenesis among teleosts starts with the initial formation of anlagen, which characterizes the *gonadal anlagen* stage. The term "gonadal anlage" refers to the structure that includes PGCs already surrounded by enveloping LPM cells plus additional surrounding, but non-enveloping, somatic (i.e., peritoneal) cells (Parmentier & Timmermans 1985). With subsequent cell proliferation the (usually two) gonadal anlagen expand into the coelomic cavity, being separated from the body cavity only by the portion of the peritoneum which envelops each anlage. This peritoneal layer also usually forms the suspensory mesentery—the mesorchium of the testis or the mesovarium of the ovary—which suspends each anlage from the dorsal coelomic wall. In the subsequent *indifferent gonad* stage, the gonad is still insufficiently differentiated morphologically to be identified as either an ovary or a testis. This stage is characterized by the mitotic increase of PGCs, the transformation of PGCs to gonial cells that cannot yet be distinguished as either oogonia or spermatogonia, and the proliferation of somatic cells of the former gonadal anlagen. The next stage—that of a *sexually differentiated* gonad—applies to gonads exhibiting identifiable male or female sex cells, distinctive ovarian or testiform morphology, or both. The final gonadal stage is that of a *mature* gonad and is identified by the presence of mature gametes (i.e., ova, sperm, or both). These stages of gonadal development can be applied to all teleosts, including hermaphroditic gobies.

Evidence of Predetermined Sex in Some Gonochore Teleosts

In some teleosts, gonial cells are insufficiently distinctive to identify as either oogonia or spermatogonia until later in development. However, predetermined sex may still be evident by differences in mitotic division rates of germ cells within the indifferent gonad. Medaka, for example, exhibit no obvious ultrastructural differences between male and female gonial cells (Satoh 1974). However, gonia among genetic female medaka mitotically increase to four times their original number between the time they become incorporated into the gonad anlagen and hatching, while only doubling in number among genetic males (Hamaguchi 1982; Kobayashi et al. 2004). As a result, medaka having relatively fewer gonial cells prior to hatching are male, while similar-aged embryos having relatively more gonial cells are female (Satoh & Egami 1972). Similar findings of an initial female-specific increase in PGCs have also been reported in the threespine stickleback, *Gasterosteus aculeatus* (Lewis et al. 2008), rainbow trout, *Oncorhynchus mykiss* (Lebrun et al. 1982) and Mozambique tilapia, *Oreochromis mossambicus* (Nakamura et al. 1998). These examples reflect the establishment of sexual determination, albeit morphologically cryptic, well before sex-specific characteristics of gonia or the gonad become evident. In such instances, it should be noted, the term "indifferent gonad" serves primarily as a point of reference for the absence of visible characteristics of gonad ontogeny, rather than an actual absence of sex determination.

In addition to differences in rates of germ cell division, females and males frequently exhibit different time lines in sex cell differentiation. Among female medaka, gonial cells differentiate into primary oocytes at about five days post-hatch, thereby transforming the indifferent gonad into a recognizable ovary. Among males, however, mitotic proliferation of gonial cells does not occur until around 45 days post-hatch. The differentiation of spermatogonia into primary spermatocytes occurs even later, well after the differentiation of interstitial (i.e., Leydig) cells and their subsequent sex steroid production (Satoh 1974; Yoshikawa & Oguri 1979). In female pejerrey, *Odontesthes bonariensis*, the proliferation of both gonial cells and gonadal somatic cells among females begins 49 to 63 days post-hatch compared to 98 days among males (Strüssmann et al. 1996). Exhibiting a similar pattern, the number of sex cells in Celebes medaka is greater in females at hatching, and primary oocytes differentiate in females before primary spermatocytes do so in males (Hamaguchi 1983). In the goldfish, mitotic division of germ cells starts around 6 to 7 weeks post-fertilization regardless of genetic sex. However, subsequent meiosis of primary oocytes begins at approximately 16 weeks post-fertilization while secondary spermatocyte formation following meiosis does not begin until 20 weeks post-fertilization (Parmentier & Timmermans 1985; van Winkoop et al. 1992).

Gonad differentiation characterized by sex-specific gonad morphology frequently shows a similar sex-specific gap in timing. In female channel catfish, *Ictalurus punctatus*, the initiation of ovarian cavity formation occurs at around 14 days post-hatch, prior to PGC differentiation into gonia, while testis-typical lobule formation among males does not take place until about 96 days post-hatch (Patiño et al. 1996). In the cichlid, *Cichlasoma dimerus*, ovarian differentiation marked by the development of the ovarian cavity and the concomitant differentiation of gonia into primary oocytes occurs at about 40 days post-hatch (Meijide et al. 2005). In contrast, the earliest sign of testis differentiation among males occurs at 65 days post-hatch, as signaled by the appearance of presumptive Sertoli cells surrounding individual gonial cells. Primary spermatocyte differentiation occurs even later, 70 days post-hatch, followed by the differentiation of seminiferous lobules at about 100 days post-hatch (Meijide et al. 2005). In the closely related Nile tilapia, histological sex differentiation is characterized in females by the onset of oocyte meiosis, which is simultaneous with the development of the ovarian cavity at around day 28 post-fertilization. Among males, the onset of first meiotic prophase in future spermatocytes occurs at about 55 days post-fertilization, resulting in a time lag of about three weeks between female and male time lines (Kanamori et al. 1985; Nakamura & Nagahama 1989; Nakamura et al. 1998; D'Cotta et al. 2001a). In a slight deviation from the general trend, early ovarian lamellar architecture and testis lobular structure in rainbow trout are both evident at 100 days. However, primary oocytes in females are first recognizable at 67 days post-fertilization while primary spermatocytes among males are not distinguishable until 168 days post-fertilization (Takashima et al. 1980).

In zebrafish, testis morphogenesis follows a sequential pathway. In all individuals, an ovariform gonad develops first, in tandem with the initial differentiation of primary oocytes, at around 16 to 24 days post-fertilization. Among genetic females, the ovarian components persist throughout life. Among genetic males, oocyte development is followed by degeneration, which occurs anywhere from 30 to 40 days post-fertilization and is then followed by the development of testis features (Takahashi 1977; Maack & Segner 2003; XG Wang et al. 2007). This ovariform to testiform pattern of early gonad ontogeny in otherwise gonochoric species has also been reported for carp, *Cyprinus carpio* (Davies & Takashima 1980); Sumatra barb, *Barbus tetrazona* (Takahashi & Shimizu 1983); red sea bream, *Pagrus major* (Matsuyama et al. 1988); mosquitofish, *Gambusia affinis* (Koya et al. 2003);Mekong ricefish, *Oryzias mekongensis*; and up to 50 percent of genetic males in the Luzon ricefish, *O. luzonensis* (Otake et al. 2008).

Thus, the overall trend among examined teleosts is one of differentiation of sex-specific features of the female reproductive complex prior to that of the male. Among gobiids, there is little information available on sex-specific rates of gonial development, timing of gonial differentiation according to sex, or for sex differentiation processes in general. In the round goby (*Neogobius melanostomus*), Moiseyeva (1984) reported that the first indication of sex differentiation among females was oocyte differentiation at 20 days post-hatch, followed by ovarian morphogenesis by 30 days post-hatch. Among males, features of testis morphology were first evident at 40 to 45 days post-hatch but spermatocytes did not appear until close to a year after hatching, thereby repeating the generalized teleost pattern of a time lag in male sex differentiation.

Formation of the Gonadal Ducts

The other component of the teleost reproductive complex in addition to the gonad is the gonoduct, for which developmental details among teleosts are scant. In fish taxa that have paired gonadal lobes, the lobes either unite posteriorly and empty into a common gonoduct, or each empties into a gonoduct that then unites to form a single duct that terminates at the distal orifice at the tip of a genital papilla. In some species, gonoducts of one or both sexes may be reduced or absent. Male yellow perch, *Perca flavescens*, have a short sperm duct which links with the posteriorly united testis lobes. In females, however, there is no oviduct. An ovarial sac enclosing the single ovary is fused posteriorly with the body wall. Shortly before ovulation, a protrusion develops at the junction of the ovarian sac and abdominal wall. As ovulation approaches, the overlying tissue of the protrusion thins, then ruptures, thereby providing an exit point for the ova from the ovarian lumen to the external environment (Parker 1942). In the Japanese sea bass, *Lateolabrax japonicus*, the gonoducts of both sexes are very short and in the female, the oviduct opens to the outside only at the time of ovulation (Hayashi 1969). In a somewhat different ontogenetic pattern, the gonadal ducts of the silver-stripe round herring, *Spratelloides gracilis*, form early in development but are incomplete, being unconnected to the gonad until maturity (Hatakeyama et al. 2005).

The origin(s) of gonoducts have been variously ascribed to the dorsal peritoneum, the suspensory mesentery of the gonad, a posterior continuation of the surrounding peritoneum of the gonad which becomes narrowed down to form a trough or tube, an extension of a somatic cell mass that develops in the posterior gonad, or some combination thereof. In coho salmon, *Oncorhynchus kisutch*, the oviduct forms anteriorly from both a continuation of the portion of the peritoneum forming an ovarian covering and from the suspensory mesovarium. A left and a right anterior oviduct leading from the ovarian lobes each extend posteriorly for a short distance, and then merge to form a single channel. More posteriorly, folding of the dorsal mesentery forms the posterior oviduct. However, unlike the female reproductive complex of most teleosts, the oviduct remains open dorsally due to incomplete folding and fusion and forms a trough rather than a true duct (Kendall 1921).

In the swordtail, *Xiphophorus helleri* (F. Poeciliidae, Cyprinodontiformes), elements of anterior oviduct development are reminiscent of that found in coho

(Essenberg 1923). Early in development, the left and right gonadal anlagen fuse, first along the ventral margin, then subsequently along the dorsal margins, to form a single ovary and ovarian cavity. The associated oviduct develops from two points of origin. While the gonad is still incompletely fused dorsally, cell proliferation takes place at the caudal end of the ovary to form a cell mass. This cell mass then widens and develops a ventral groove, mimicking the cross-sectional V shape of the still dorsally open ovary. Therefore, for a brief period, the developing swordtail oviduct is open dorsally, like that of coho. Subsequently, the groove becomes covered by a portion of the suspensory mesovarium lying directly above to become completely enclosed, thereby forming a lumen at the anterior end of the developing oviduct. In the posterior region of the abdominal cavity, a concomitant proliferation of peritoneal cells develops along the dorsal midline, which results in the formation of a solid cord of cells. The cell cord develops forward along the dorsal wall of the abdominal cavity and fuses with the anterior portion of the oviduct arising from the posterior gonad. Subsequently, first a slit, then a lumen forms within the proliferating peritoneal cell cord that becomes continuous with the lumen of the anterior oviduct.

The extra-gonadal portion of the swordtail sperm duct develops in much the same manner as that of the oviduct, with the initial formation of anterior and posterior gonoduct primordia. Anteriorly, the proliferation of peritoneal cells at the caudal end of the testis effectively becomes an extension of the internal (i.e., efferent) sperm duct system such that the efferent sperm duct lumen within the testis becomes continuous with that of the extra-gonadal sperm duct. Thus, in the development of both the female and male swordtail reproductive complex, the gonoduct forms from the proliferative activity of cells both from the caudal portion of the gonad and from the peritoneum of the posterior region of the abdominal cavity.

In female medaka, the oviduct also develops from two different sources (Suzuki & Shibata 2004) but the process differs from that of the swordtail. The anterior portion of the oviduct arises from somatic cell proliferation from the posterior end of the ovary. This cell mass grows caudally to the posterior extent of the bladder. Subsequent cavitation results in the formation of a lumen, transforming the cell mass into a duct that is continuous with the lumen of the ovary. However, at this stage the caudal portion of the anterior oviduct is blind-ended. In contrast, the posterior portion of the oviduct arises from mesenchymal cells surrounding the urethra. The portion of the mesenchymal cell layer lying ventral to the urethra becomes thickened and forms a cortical tissue layer (so termed in Suzuki & Shibata [2004]). A proliferation of anterior cells of the cortical layer extends forward until it almost reaches the posterior end of the anterior oviduct. Subsequently, two bilateral cavities develop along the length of the cortical layer.

At this point, the anterior and posterior portions of the oviduct are still separate from one another. With the approach of first maturity, the anterior oviduct and cortical layer extension meet and fuse. The partition separating the right and left cavities of the cortical layer disappears, leaving behind a common lumen, which becomes continuous with the anterior oviduct lumen. At the terminus of the urogenital papilla, the distal end of the posterior oviduct becomes open to the outside of the body, thereby providing an exit for ova to the outside environment. Thus, the final medaka oviduct arises from an anterior portion that is derived from gonadal somatic cells and from a posterior portion that arises from urethra-associated mesenchymal tissue in the form of a cortical layer.

In male medaka, the sperm duct also develops from two sources (Suzuki & Shibata 2004). Information provided on its development is not as detailed as that of the oviduct, but appears to share a number of similarities with the latter. The anterior portion of the sperm duct arises from a cell mass forming from the proliferation of somatic cells in the posterior end of the testis, then subsequently develops a lumen by cavitation, and extends caudally towards the ventral region of the bladder. The posterior portion arises in the ventral area of urethra-associated mesenchyme and extends caudally almost until it reaches the urinary pore. Here, the posterior sperm duct and urethra merge and the inner lumen epithelia of the two structures become confluent. The subsequent fusion of the anterior and posterior portions results in the formation of a single, continuous sperm duct that transmits sperm from the efferent duct system within the testis to a urogenital sinus before exiting the body.

The development of the oviduct in the guppy, *Poecilia reticulata*, follows a somewhat different ontogeny than that of medaka. In the guppy, oviduct development involves both the dorsal mesentery and dorsal peritoneum located just posterior to the fused ovarian lobe (Anteunis 1959). Two lateral folds of the dorsal mesentery develop, extend in opposite directions away from the midline, then each deflect upward towards the dorsal peritoneum. The fusion of the two recurved folds, either with each other or with the dorsal peritoneum, and the subsequent disappearance of the internal partition formed by the enclosed portion of the dorsal mesentery, results in the formation of an undivided duct that is continuous with the posterior portion of the ovary.

The two sperm ducts in male guppies have a slightly different developmental pattern. The sperm ducts originate as somatic cell masses arising from the posterior end of the two testis lobes (Takahashi & Iwasaki 1973). These become extended as solid, bilateral ridges that form the sperm duct anlagen. As they approach the urogenital sinus, the two ridges become fused to form a single ridge. Subsequently, an internal slit develops along the length of the fused and separate portions of the ridge, and becomes lined with epithelial cells to form a proper sperm duct. The lumen of the anterior paired sperm ducts becomes continuous with the main lumen of the efferent duct system within the testis while the posterior, unified portion remains closed at its terminus until later in development.

Finally, in female three-spined stickleback, *Gasterosteus aculeatus*, bilateral, sterile genital ridges form along the dorsal coelomic wall posterior to the ovary. Medial and lateral cellular extensions grow outward from the ridge, become extended towards each other, and then fuse to form a tubular structure. The tubular structure subsequently becomes continuous with the ovarian lobe and its lumen and becomes the oviduct (Shimizu & Takahashi 1980).

In summary, the origins of the gonoducts show considerable variation across fish taxa. They may develop from peritoneal epithelium that variously surrounds the gonad, forms the gonad suspensory mesentery and dorsal mesentery, or lines the dorsal region of the abdominal cavity. Their formation may result from somatic cell proliferation from the posterior gonad, posterior tubular extensions of gonadal serosa, peritoneal folds, dorsal mesentery folds, cavitation of a solid cord of cells, or by some combination of these. As a result, there is considerable scope for the development of new features and anatomical structures, a possibility that may have been instrumental in the development of the considerable diversity of gonoduct-associated accessory structures documented across fish taxa in general, and gobies in particular.

Ontogeny Summary

The earliest stage of teleost gonad development, the gonadal anlagen, is composed of PGCs or PGC-derived gonial cells, enveloping LPM cells and dorsal coelom peritoneal cells. The anlagen develop following the formation of germ line cells, the subsequent migration of PGCs to a location below the mesonephric ducts and their integration into genital (i.e., peritoneal) ridges extending along the dorsal coelom. Subsequently, the anlagen increase in size through somatic (peritoneal) cell proliferation to form an indifferent gonad. The indifferent gonad is characterized by germ cells and associated support cells and tissues, and an absence of morphological features indicative of future sex. With the differentiation of germ cells, or sex-specific gonadal features, or both, the gonad enters the sexually differentiated stage that persists until gamete production, at which time it becomes a mature gonad. In contrast, the gonoduct is characterized by the absence of identifiable germ cells or any directly associated gametogenic tissue. It may form from peritoneally derived cells, mesenchymal cells, somatic cells of the gonad, or some combination thereof. Typically, the junction of the gonoduct and gonad comprises an expanded region with no associated gametogenic tissue, which in hermaphroditic gobies is termed the common genital sinus (Cole & Robertson 1988; Cole 1990).

Based on the above information, the ontogeny of the teleost reproductive complex can be viewed in one of two ways. The entire complex may form as a construct of separate, independently arising components consisting of the gonad proper (germ line cells and peritoneal derivatives) and the gonoduct (only peritoneal or other derivatives) that are linked by a non-germinal, transition region (i.e., the common genital sinus of gobies). Alternatively, the reproductive complex represents a continuous peritoneally derived structure that is characterized by: the localized presence of germ cells, support cells, and tissues forming the initial anlagen and subsequent gonad proper; and the remaining non-gametogenic sections making up the common genital sinus and gonoduct.

Ontogenetic information related to the development of the reproductive complex is still extremely limited for gobiid species, especially for early anlage and indifferent developmental stages and for gonocyte differentiation. However, the broad similarity of developmental patterns across teleosts, coupled with similar features of early germ cell-line formation and PGC migration exhibited by shiro-uo, ukigori and round goby, suggest that general features of the development of the teleost reproductive complex may be predictive of gobies. A comparative examination of diverse morphologies of the reproductive complex among hermaphroditic gobies may therefore suggest possible modifications of ontogenetic processes that result in labile sexual expression and reveal the underlying morphogenic nature of the hermaphroditic reproductive complex as a whole

REPRODUCTIVE COMPLEXITY IN HERMAPHRODITIC GOBY TAXA FROM AN ONTOGENETIC PERSPECTIVE

Origins of Morphology Patterns of the Hermaphroditic Gonad

To date, all reported hermaphroditic gobiid taxa are found within the Gobiidae subfamily, Gobiinae, *sensu* Pezold (1993). Functional hermaphroditism has been demonstrated or inferred from gonad morphology in fourteen genera. These include the following:

Bryaninops (Fishelson 1989)

Coryphopterus (Robertson & Justines 1982; Cole 1983; Cole & Shapiro 1990)

Eviota (Cole 1990)

Fusigobius (Cole 1990)

Gobiodon (Cole 1990; Nakashima et al. 1995, 1996; Munday et al. 1998; Cole & Hoese 2001)

Elacatinus (formerly *Gobiosoma*)(Robertson & Justines 1982)

Lophogobius (Cole 1990)

Luposicya (Fishelson 1989)

Lythrypnus (St. Mary 1993, 1994)

Paragobiodon (Lassig 1977; Cole 1990; Kuwamura et al. 1994; Nakashima et al. 1995)

Pleurosicya (Fishelson 1989)

Priolepis (Cole 1990; Sunobe & Nakazono 1999)

Rhinogobiops (previously *Coryphopterus*)(Cole 1983)

Trimma (Fishelson 1989; Cole 1990; Sunobe & Nakazono 1990, 1993)

Four hermaphroditic genera making up the Coryphopterus group *sensu* Cole (see Chapter 5 of this volume) include *Coryphopterus, Rhinogobiops, Lophogobius,* and *Fusigobius,* all of which exhibit an interim ovotestis development pattern. In this pattern, the production of sex-specific gametes occurs during temporally disassociated phases of ova and sperm production, and the ovotestis phase is both transient and afunctional (see Cole, this volume, for more detailed description). *Elacatinus multifasciatus,* another hermaphroditic goby species, exhibits a "modified" interim ovotestis pattern which is identical to that of the Coryphopterus group excepting the retention of a gonadal lumen. The interim and modified interim ovotestis developmental patterns appear to represent the simplest gonad ontogeny pattern among hermaphroditic gobiids. Based on what we now know of sex determination and differentiation in other teleosts, a shift from gonochorism to simple sequential hermaphroditism in gobiids may have been achieved by the modification of two ontogenetic processes. The first involves temporal shifts in gene expression associated with sexual differentiation, which change the timing of upregulation and downregulation of various aspects of gonadogenesis. The second is the development and retention of gonial stem cells, or bipotential gonia, that are capable of differentiating along either an oogenic or a spermatogenic pathway.

Among examined gonochore teleosts, gametocytes and gonad morphology typically differentiate earlier in females than in conspecific males. As described in the previous section, in a number of species genetic males first develop an ovariform gonad, and sometimes oocytes, before spermatocyte differentiation and testis development (Takahashi 1977; Davies & Takashima 1980; Takahashi & Shimizu 1983; Matsuyama et al. 1988; Koya et al. 2003; Maack & Segner 2003; XG Wang et al. 2007; Otake et al. 2008). From here, it would only take a short, additional developmental step for the initial feminized phase of gonad development that occurs in all individuals to become extended past first maturity such that all individuals function first as an ova-producing female. Secondary male function associated with sperm production would follow with the delayed development of male sex cells and a testiform gonad. By means of such a heterochronic shift, a gonochore sexual pattern might be transformed into a protogynous sequence of sexual function.

In unidirectional hermaphroditism as expressed in the Coryphopterus group and *Elacatinus multifasciatus,* the first appearance of male sex cells is delayed until after a period of ova-production and is accompanied by the disappearance of all ovarian tissues. A mechanism for delayed masculinization of the reproductive complex in the interim ovotestis pattern can be found in events associated with the regulation of normal sexual differentiation in teleosts. Cytochrome P450 aromatase (referred to here as aromatase) is a steroidogenic enzyme that acts to catalyze androgens (mostly testosterone) to oestrogens (mostly oestradiol-17, or E_2) and plays a feminizing role in sexual ontogeny. In a number of gonochore teleosts, normal ovarian development among females has been shown to be accompanied by elevated levels of aromatase and E_2 while normal testis development is associated with a decrease in both E_2 and aromatase (Guiguen et al. 1999; Kitano et al. 1999; D'Cotta et al. 2001a, b; Uchida et al. 2004), demonstrating a direct relationship for aromatase production, E_2 levels and feminization of the gonad. Moreover, aromatase and E_2 appear to be essential for ovarian development. Treatment during early gonad differentiation with the non-steroidal aromatase inhibitor, fadrozole, has been shown to result in the masculinization of genetic females in a number of fish species including zebrafish (Fenske & Segner 2004), golden rabbitfish, *Siganus guttatus* (Komatsu et al. 2006) and European sea bass, *Dicentrarchus labrax* (Navarro-Martín et al. 2009).

Inhibition of aromatase production can also be induced by maintenance at higher than normal water temperatures. Among genetically female Nile tilapia, *Oreochromis niloticus*, elevated levels of aromatase enzyme activity and E_2 are normally associated with a shift from an indifferent gonad to a differentiated ovariform gonad. However, when maintained under high temperature regimes, reduced aromatase expression is followed by masculinization (D'Cotta et al. 2001a, b). In female Atlantic salmon, *Salmo salar*, warmer maintenance temperatures are associated with an inhibition of aromatase activity, a decrease in plasma E_2 levels and an increase in testosterone levels (Watts et al. 2004). And in Japanese flounder, *Paralichthys olivaceus*, rearing genetically female larvae at high water temperatures causes a suppression of aromatase gene expression and the conversion of genetic females into phenotypic males (Yoshinaga et al. 2004). Thus, in gonochore teleost development, the presence of aromatase has a feminizing influence through its mediation of E_2 production, and its absence has a masculinizing influence.

A similar feminizing role for E_2 has been demonstrated in a number of hermaphroditic teleosts in which elevated E_2 levels are characteristic of the ovarian phase while decreased levels are associated with the testiform phase (see Piferrer & Guiguen 2008 for a review). In two hermaphroditic goby species, *Rhinogobius* (previously *Coryphopterus*) *nicholsii* and *Gobiodon erythrospilus,* the inhibition of aromatase activity by fadrozole triggers adult female-to-male sex change (Kroon & Liley 2000; Kroon et al. 2005), implicating a role for declining E_2 in normal sex change events. The subsequent application of E_2 to male-phase adult *Gobiodon erythrospilus*, a serially hermaphroditic species that can shift between female and male adult function, results in a shift back to female function (Kroon et al. 2005). In another serial hermaphrodite, *Gobiodon histrio*, whole-body concentrations of testosterone, 11-ketotestosterone, and E_2 suggest that the upregulation or down-regulation of the aromatase/testosterone-to-E_2 conversion pathway is a probable candidate for mediating serial sex change in this species (Kroon et al. 2003). Based on the above findings, the delayed masculinization characteristic of the interim ovotestis pattern of the Coryphopterus group may be mediated by a prolonged period of aromatase upregulation. The brief appearance of an afunctional ovotestis presumably reflects an overlap between declining levels of aromatase and E_2 associated with oogenic regression, and the concomitant upregulation of testis development.

Genes involved in the morphogenesis of ovariform and testiform features of the teleost gonad are becoming better known and patterns of gene expression are starting to emerge. *FOXl2* expression is increasingly associated with ovarian morphogenesis in teleosts through the initiation and regulation of aromatase transcription. In female medaka, somatic cells directly surrounding germ cells exhibit *FOXl2* expression at the time of ovarian differentiation (Nakamoto et al. 2006). Similar findings have been made for the Japanese flounder (Yamaguchi et al. 2007) and Nile tilapia (D-S Wang et al. 2004, 2007; Ijiri et al. 2008). In the Luzon medaka, *O. luzonensis*, the expression of *FOXl2* in the somatic cells of the indifferent gonad is found in all genetic females and in almost half of all genetic males. In the latter, the downregulation of *FOXl2* directly precedes testis development and is thought to reflect the upregulation of one or more testis-determining genes that act to inhibit further ovarian differentiation (Nakamoto et al. 2009). A close association between *FOXl2* and teleost ovarian development is also indicated by the findings of over-expression of *FOXl2* in the developing ovary, but not the testis, in the Southern catfish, *Silurus meridionalis* (Liu et al. 2007), Nile tilapia (D-S Wang et al. 2007) and rainbow trout (Baron et al. 2004). Among hermaphroditic species, the downregulation of *FOXl2* is associated with ovarian degeneration during female-to-male sex change in the protogynous honeycomb grouper, *Epinephelus merra* (Wu et al. 2008), while *FOXl2* upregulation is associated with testicular regression during male-to-female sex change in the protandrous black porgy, *Acanthopagrus schlegeli* (Alam et al. 2008). And in genetic female rainbow trout that were artificially masculinized by the application of either an aromatase inhibitor or active androgens, ovarian regression was accompanied by reduced *FOXl2* expression (Vizziano et al. 2007). Therefore, *FOXl2* and the cells that express it are likely key to ovarian development in both gonochoric and hermaphroditic fish species, and a decline in *FOXl2* expression is likely necessary for the development of either a secondary testis or secondary ovotestis.

The gene *SOX9* has also been implicated in early sexual development in a number of teleosts. In medaka of both sexes, *SOX9b* is expressed in enveloping cells that surround PGCs. These enveloping cells differentiate into granulosa cells in females and Sertoli cells in males. As such, *SOX9b*-expressing cells are intimately associated with germ cells and are precursors of both male and female gonocyte support cells (Nakamura et al. 2008). *SOX9a2* is another gene within the *SOX9* group, which in medaka is expressed in germ-cell enveloping cells in both males and females prior to differentiation. However, its expression persists only in genetic males and appears to play a role in testis morphogenesis, specifically in seminiferous lobule formation (Nakamoto et al. 2005).

If the first step towards functional, female-first hermaphroditism in gobies involved a heterochronic shift in gonial and gonad differentiation, then this shift was likely mediated at least in part by the delayed expression of testis-determining gene(s). In medaka, *DMY* (also known as *Dmrt1bY*) has been identified as a testis-determining gene for this species (Matsuda et al. 2002; Nanda et al. 2002) In genetic males, its expression is found in somatic cells directly surrounding germ cells (i.e., presumptive Sertoli cells), is initiated at the end of the indifferent gonad phase, just prior to testis differentiation, and is involved in testis-specific PGC proliferation and testis differentiation (i.e., gonad morphogenesis)(Kobayashi et al. 2004). Spermatogonial differentiation in this species, however, is regulated by another gene, *Dmrt1* (Kobayashi et al. 2004). Similarly, in the protogynous orange-spotted grouper, *Epinephelus coioides*, the expression of an intronless version of *Dmrt1* is associated with male-phase germ cells and appears to play a central role in stimulating spermatogenesis (Xia et al. 2007). The role of *Dmrt1* in testis differentiation has been either implicated or demonstrated in a number of other teleosts including southern catfish (Liu et al. 2007), Nile tilapia (Injiri et al. 2008; Kobayashi & Nagahama 2009), and pejerrey, *Odontesthes bonariensis* (Fernandino et al. 2008). Further evidence of its importance in the development of male function is evident in several examples of ovary-testis transitioning events. *Dmrt1* upregulation occurs in genetically female, experimentally masculinized, rainbow trout at the time of testis development (Vizziano et al. 2008). Conversely, reduced *Dmrt1* expression characterizes male-to-female sex change in two protandrous fish species, gilthead bream, *Sparus auratus* (Liarte et al. 2007) and black porgy (Shin et al. 2009).

Thus, *DMY/Dmrt1bY* and *Dmrt1* play important roles in testis development across a wide range of teleost taxa. However, similarities of expression and proposed function across several taxa do not necessarily indicate automatic conservation within taxa. *DMY/Dmrt1bY* expression, which is present in both medaka and a congener, *O. curvinotus* (Matsuda et al. 2003), is absent in two other congeners, *O. mekongensis* (Otake et al. 2008) and *O. celebensis* (Kondo et al. 2003). Therefore, even closely related taxa may have different testis-determining regulatory genes. So far, little is known regarding gene(s) involved in the regulation of testis development and spermatogenesis in gobiids. In one study of the hermaphroditic blue-banded goby, *Lythrypnus dalli*, *Dmrt1* was found to undergo rapid upregulation and exhibit a two-fold increase shortly after the initiation of a transition from ova to sperm production (Rogers 2007). Whether *Dmrt1* is widely expressed across gobiid taxa, and what precise role it plays in testis development, remain to be discovered. Certainly, the identification of testis-determining gene(s) and their regulation properties will be central to the reconstruction of the evolutionary steps that have led to the development of functional hermaphroditism among the Gobiidae.

A second ontogenetic modification likely associated with a shift from gonochorism to functional hermaphroditism, particularly when involving the secondary development of spermatogenic tissue, entails the successful maintenance of a reservoir of gonial cells capable of developing into either oocytes or spermatocytes. There are a variety of potential sources for new oogonia and spermatogonia. In the mouse, embryonic stem cells have been shown to produce both male and female gametes under experimental conditions (Geijsen et al. 2003; Nayernia et al. 2006; Kerkis et al. 2007). In the rainbow trout, spermatogonia have been shown to be both developmentally plastic and sexually bipotent. Green fluorescent protein (GFP)-labeled spermatogonia taken from adult rainbow trout testes and transplanted into the undifferentiated genital ridges of conspecific fry subsequently differentiated into spermatocytes in the recipient gonad of genetic males and into oocytes in genetic females (Okutsu et al. 2006). Recent findings have demonstrated that there are different types of spermatogonia in several fish species. Genetic male zebrafish have several types of spermatogonia including: undifferentiated type A (two types), differentiated type A, type B (early), and type B (late). When undifferentiated type A spermatogonia divide, one daughter cell remains an undifferentiated type A spermatogonium, while the other becomes a differentiated type A spermatogonium. The latter gives rise to type B spermatogonia, which in turn give rise to spermatocytes (Leal et al. 2009). Based on the findings of Okutsu et al. (2006) regarding the lability of rainbow trout spermatogonia, it appears that spermatogonia with stem cell properties may also have the ability to dedifferentiate and give rise to oogonia. In hermaphroditic teleosts in which male sex cells are not evident prior to the development of male function (i.e., interim ovotestis and secondarily derived ovotestis patterns in gobiids), the source of newly-developed spermatogonia may be either embryonic stem cells or undifferentiated type A spermatogonia which are present in the gonad during the initial ovariform phase. Among serial hermaphrodites with alternating ova and sperm production, oocytes may arise from retained oogonia, embryonic stem cells, or type A spermatogonia.

The combination of extended feminization (likely mediated by prolonged aromatase upregulation and E_2 production) and the maintenance of a source of bipotential gonia or embryonic stem cells that are capable of differentiating into either oogonia or spermatogonia is sufficient to generate all known gobiid hermaphroditic sexual patterns. Hermaphroditic members of the Coryphopterus group (i.e., *Coryphopterus, Rhinogobiops, Lophogobius,* and *Fusigobius*) all express an interim ovotestis pattern in which initial ovariform development is either widespread or universal, and future male potential is not evident within the gametogenic tissue prior to sex change. The subsequent, unidirectional shift to a male phase is accompanied by the loss of ovarian features and female gametocytes such that healthy, late-stage male and female sex cells never co-occur. A similar developmental pattern is found during early gonad ontogeny in zebrafish in which an ovariform gonad develops in all individuals regardless of genetic sex. The initial development of oocytes within the zebrafish indifferent gonad which transforms it into an ovariform gonad is associated with an enhanced expression of *vasa*-dependent green fluorescent protein (EGFP)(XG Wang et al. 2007). Subsequently, among genetic males there is a drop in *vasa*-dependent EGFP signal concurrent with the first appearance of spermatocytes, which transforms the ovariform gonad into a testiform gonad (XG Wang et al. 2007). Thus, zebrafish exhibit the same ontogenetic pattern of interim ovotestis development seen in the Coryphopterus group, with the exception that the latter extend the ovariform phase in most or all individuals beyond first maturity, thereby generating a functional hermaphroditic sexual pattern. In both zebrafish and hermaphroditic members of the Coryphopterus group, a shift from ova to sperm production likely involves the downregulation of aromatase pathways such as *FOXl2* that maintain ovariform expression while upregulating pathways that initiate testiform development and expression (i.e., testis-determining genes such as *DMY, Dmrt1* and *SOX9* variants)(Kobayashi et al. 2004; Yoshinaga et al. 2004; Guiguen et al. 2009).

In the interim ovotestis pattern, all ovarian tissues disappear following testis development. Whether female expression among secondary male protogynous hermaphrodites is completely lost, or only suppressed following the development of male expression, is unknown. In two protogynous wrasses including the three-spot, *Halichoeres trimaculatus*, and the Chinese wrasse, *H. tenuispinis*, direct-developing males can be induced with estrogen treatment to secondarily become female, indicating a female potential among males that normally never function as females (Kojima et al. 2008; Miyake et al. 2008). In rainbow trout, testicular germ cells removed from an adult male and transplanted into the indifferent gonad of genetic males and females differentiate into viable spermatogonia and oogonia, respectively (Okutsu et al. 2006). Taken together, these findings suggest that some form of stem cell or bipotential sex cell may be retained in the gonad of both gonochoric and hermaphroditic species.

In the interim and modified interim ovotestis developmental pattern that is expressed by the Coryphopterus group and *Elacatinus multifasciatus*, the initial gonadal phase appears entirely ovarian. This is followed by the transient presence of an ovotestis until ovarian tissue is completely replaced by testis tissue. The tissue of the secondary testis here arises apparently *de novo* within the field of regressing ovarian tissue (Cole 1983; Cole & Robertson 1988; Cole & Shapiro 1990, 1992). Following the degeneration of oocytes, their supporting cells, and ovarian-specific tissues that marks the end of the transient ovotestis phase, the gonadal tissue of the secondary phase appears entirely spermatogenic. If gonadogenesis regulation in gobiids is similar to that of other teleosts, this likely reflects an end to *FOXl2*, or *FOXl2*-like, upregulation and the initiation of *DMY*, *Dmrt*, or similar testis-determining gene upregulation. There have been no reports of secondary males naturally reversing sex and returning to a female-active phase within the Coryphopterus group or *E. multifasciatus*, and efforts to reverse the sex-change process by manipulation of the social environment among some *Coryphopterus* species have been unsuccessful (Cole & Robertson 1988; Cole unpublished data). This failure suggests that either oogonial or bipotential gonial cells do not persist past sex change, alternative sources of oogonia are not available; upregulation of aromatase production is blocked, testis-determining genes cannot be downregulated, or that some combination of these is the case.

Members of the hermaphroditic genus *Eviota* exhibit a different developmental pattern in which all individuals develop an ovotestis early in ontogeny and retain it throughout life. Within the ovotestis, early-stage oogenic and spermatogenic tissues and their associated gonocytes are intermingled in close proximity to one another, resulting in a persistent integrated ovotestis pattern. In this type of gonad, aromatase/E_2 and testis-determining genes have to be jointly upregulated, at least to some extent, to simultaneously sustain gametocytes and support cells of both ova and sperm-generating tissues. Consequently, in *Eviota*, these two regulatory pathways are unlikely to have inhibitory effects on one another, as suggested by Nakamoto et al. (2009) for the Luzon rice fish, unless the inhibition is incomplete. The close proximity of intermingled ova-fated and sperm-fated gonocytes suggests that sex-specific regulatory cues for gametocyte differentiation and support tissue proliferation are highly localized and in close proximity to target cells. Germ cell enveloping cells meet the proximity requirement, and as future granulosa and Sertoli cells, their expression of *FOXl2* and *DMY/Dmrt1*, respectively argues for their central regulatory role in functional shifts of sexual expression in hermaphroditic fishes, including gobies.

Among the hermaphroditic genera *Trimma*, *Bryaninops*, and *Priolepis*, the gonad also develops initially as an ovotestis. However, early-stage oogenic and spermatogenic cells and tissues are physically separated from one another by a connective tissue boundary, resulting in a persistent partitioned ovotestis. In most instances, when one gonadal tissue is active it occupies much of the gonad while the other is reduced to a small area consisting of early-stage gonocytes and their support cells. The shared persistent ovotestis features of *Trimma, Bryaninops*, and *Priolepis* suggest shared patterns of regulatory gene expression.

Given the close proximity of healthy oocytes and spermatocytes in the *Eviota* pattern, it seems unlikely that partitioning is requisite for ovotestis development in *Trimma, Bryaninops*, and *Priolepis*. Consequently, the function of partitioning is unclear. Its presence, however, may have facilitated the apparent addition of an interim functional bisexual stage to the gonad developmental sequence in *Priolepis hipoliti* and *P. eugenius*. In these two species, mature, healthy oocytes and free spermatozoa co-occur for an undetermined period of time (Cole 1990, this volume). Consequently, a putative functional bisexual phase exists in addition to the strictly ova-producing and sperm-producing phases in *Priolepis hipoliti* and *P. eugenius*, which is novel among currently known sexual patterns of hermaphroditic gobiid taxa.

Gobiodon, which has a secondary ovotestis, initially mimics the interim ovotestis pattern of the Coryphopterus group. However, ovigerous tissue is retained during the sperm-producing phase, resulting in the formation of a secondary ovotestis. In this case, the testis-determining gene(s) may act to downregulate aromatase activity and E_2 production, leading to the development of a secondary ovotestis. Consequently, the Gobiodon developmental pattern of secondary ovotestis formation may reflect a combination of sequential and serial gene expression patterns associated with several other hermaphroditic goby developmental patterns. For example, the initial, strictly ovariform gonad development that persists through the juvenile and early maturation phases is similar to the interim ovotestis pattern of the sequentially protogynous Coryphopterus group. In *Gobiodon*, however, when testicular tissue develops after a period of ova production, oogenic tissue does not disappear. Instead, early-stage oocytes and supporting cells persist scattered throughout the testicular tissue, much like the integrated ovotestis of *Eviota*, which in *Gobiodon* results in a secondary ovotestis. Subsequently, the alternation of ova-producing and sperm-producing phases reflects shifts between the upregulation and downregulation of gene expression associated with these two gonadal phases. The serial expression of male and female function that is characteristic of *Gobiodon* likely involves maintaining a balance between the activities of testis-determining and aromatase-upregulating genes, which results in the generation of two functional gonad states in an alternating fashion. Such possibilities as those described above remains to be tested.

Origins of Accessory Structures

The most conspicuous and consistent synapomorphy of the reproductive complex of gobiid fishes is the presence among males of accessory secretory structures (i.e., sperm duct glands). These structures, described as "expanded leaflike hyaline appendages" are formed in most gobiids by the elaboration of the sperm duct wall (Miller 1984, 1992). In the majority of known hermaphroditic goby taxa however, the reproductive complex of male-active fishes does not have associated sperm duct glands *sensu* Miller (1984). Instead, lobulated secretory structures having a similar appearance and apparent function as sperm duct glands arise from small tissue masses associated with the ovariform gonadal wall during a transition to male function (Cole 1988; Cole & Robertson 1988; Cole & Shapiro 1992). In these instances, the resulting secretory lobules are referred to as accessory gonadal structures or AGS, and the tissue masses they arise from are referred to as precursive accessory gonadal structures, or pAGS. The pAGS are typically present throughout both the immature and female-active phases prior to sex change.

Neither the sperm duct glands of gonochore gobies nor the AGS of hermaphroditic gobies normally exhibit male gametogenic tissue or gametocytes. In spite of this, there are several sources of evidence that suggest a close ontogenetic affinity between the gametogenic regions of the gonad and the non-gametogenic regions consisting of specialized tissues and structures of the male gobiid reproductive complex. Testicular tissue, sperm duct glands, secretory and storage AGS, and AGdS are anatomically similar in that all are lobulated structures. Testicular tissues are organized into seminiferous lobules that extend along the longitudinal axis of the gonad. As discussed in Cole (this volume), both sperm duct glands of gonochore goby taxa and the AGdS found in *Gobiodon* are made up of longitudinally oriented secretory lobules that are associated with the gonoduct. The secretory AGS of hermaphroditic gobiids, which arise from gonad-associated pAGS, appear similar to both sperm duct glands and AGdS in their lobular structure and cytology. And the storage AGS of *Gobiodon,* which arise from the posterior region of the gonad proper, consist of longitudinally oriented lobules that are lined with a thin squamous epithelium.

In addition to shared lobular architecture, testicular tissue and the AGS of hermaphroditic gobiids also have a positional affinity. pAGS, which are an ovariform feature of all gonad developmental patterns of hermaphroditic gobies excepting that of *Gobiodon*, develop from the ventro-caudal region of each gonadal lobe just anterior to the common genital sinus. In the partitioned ovotestis of *Trimma, Priolepis,* and *Bryaninops,* the narrow region occupied by spermatogenic tissue during the juvenile and ova-producing phases also comprises the ventro-lateral margin of the ovotestis lobe (Cole 1990, this volume). And in the regionalized ovotestis of *Lythrypnus,* one of two centers of spermatogenic tissue originates in the same ventrolateral location (Cole, this volume). Collectively, these findings suggest that the ventro-lateral portion of the gonadal lobe in hermaphroditic gobies is a reactive site for the future development of testis-associated tissues and structures.

Lastly, there may be a close affinity between gametogenic and AGS regions of the male reproductive complex of hermaphroditic gobies based on ontogenetic origins and ontogenetic potential. In the gonochore goby, *Bathygobius soporator*, the surgical removal of the testis lobes from adult males resulted in the ectopic development of spermatogenic seminiferous lobules originating from the sperm duct glands (Tavolga 1955). These newly formed testis lobes arising from the body of the sperm duct gland contained all stages of male sex cells, including mature sperm. They were also functionally associated with the sperm duct gland, as evidenced by the presence of mature sperm within sperm duct gland lobule lumina. Thus, under certain conditions, sperm duct gland tissue of *B. soporator* appears competent to differentiate into functional spermatogenic tissue.

The source of spermatogonia found in the regenerated testis tissues of *B. soporator* is unknown. Tavolga (1955) thought that the removal of testis tissue may have been incomplete and that residual spermatogonial cells subsequently migrated into the AGS to induce the formation of spermatogenic support tissues. However, subsequent findings on the lability of germ cells associated with the teleost gonad suggest a possible alternative explanation. When 85 juvenile kokanee salmon (*Onchorhynchus nerka*) were gonadectomized and followed over a period of nine years, 95% of 59 males and 38% of 26 females had regenerated fully functional gametogenic tissue including mature ova among females and spermatozoa among males (Robertson 1961). Similarly, in an experimental group of grass carp, *Ctenopharyngodon idella*, ten months after the removal of the gonads and surrounding mesenteries in their entirety, all but one male and one female of the 30 surviving fish showed complete gonad regeneration. Most were producing either mature ova or releasing seminal fluid, the latter presumed to be laden with sperm (Underwood et al. 1986).

In the case of experimental male *B. soporator* described by Tavolga (1955), bipotential gonial cells or embryonic stem cells capable of differentiating into spermatogonia may reside within the AGS, the posterior region of the gonoduct, or both. Under appropriate conditions, these cells can be upregulated and provide the source of cells and tissues required for gonad regeneration. In the reproductive complex of hermaphroditic gobies, the ventrolateral portion of the gonadal lobes may have similar developmental capabilities. The retention of bipotential or embryonic stem cells in this region following initial gonad differentiation provides numerous options for differing gonad ontogeny patterns. Depending on clade-specific patterns of gene expression associated with gonad development, either pAGS, spermatogenic tissues, or in the case of the persistent regionalized and partitioned ovotestis, both can be formed in this region. A test of this possibility would be to remove all gonadal tissues, excepting undifferentiated pAGS, from the reproductive complex of pAGS-expressing hermaphroditic gobies. If the pAGS region contains bipotential or gonial stem cells, any regeneration of gonadal tissue would arise from the pAGS tissue. Depending on whether the regeneration occurred in an aromatase/E_2, or a $DMY/Dmrt1$, dominated environment, the newly formed gonad would presumably be either ovariform, or testiform, respectively.

In the past, it has been presumed that sperm duct glands of gonochore gobies and secretory AGS of hermaphroditic gobiids are not homologous (Cole & Robertson 1988). However, the findings of Tavolga (1955), Robertson (1961) and Underwood et al. (1986), in combination with the morphological similarities of spermatogenic tissue, sperm duct glands, AGS (both secretory and storage) and AGdS of hermaphroditic gobies suggest a much closer relationship. This has two interesting implications. The first is that the morphogenesis of lobulated structures of the reproductive complex may all be regulated by the same gene (or genes) being expressed in different regions of the reproductive complex. These include testis lobules, secretory AGS and AGdS lobules, and storage AGS lobules. The second is that most, if not all, regions of the reproductive complex are competent to form lobulated structures. If so, differences in the location of, or ontogenetic timing for, the development of the various lobulated structures that distinguish different gonad ontogeny patterns may simply reflect differences in temporal and regional patterns of gene expression.

In gonochore goby taxa, the upregulation of sperm duct gland development is localized to a region of the gonoduct and only occurs in males. In *Gobiodon*, the upregulation of AGdS formation is also localized to a region of the gonoduct but takes place early in ontogeny in all individuals, presumably in the presence of elevated aromatase/E_2 levels associated with ovariform gonad development. In other hermaphroditic goby taxa, the localization of pAGS and subsequent AGS development to the region of the posterior, ventrolateral portion of the gonadal lobes suggests a similar localization of either the presence of, or competence to respond to, associated developmental induction cues.

SUMMARY

Although little is known regarding the early development of germ cells and the gonadal anlagen among gobiids, what is known conforms to that of other teleosts. Consequently, general features of teleost gonadogenesis and development of the reproductive complex may be representative of similar processes occurring among gobiids. A number of morphological modifications have likely been instrumental in the evolution of various hermaphroditic patterns among gobies. Simple unidirectional hermaphroditism as expressed by the Coryphopterus group and *E. multifasciatus* may have involved the least number of ontogenetic alterations and been accomplished by a simple heterochronic shift in gonochore gonadogenesis events. As a consequence, instead of regulatory pathways becoming canalized along one of two mutually exclusive pathways, ovariform gonad development and gonia differentiation associated with higher levels of aromatase and E_2 occurs either in most, or all, individuals and persists into adulthood. Subsequently, the disappearance of oocytes, ova-producing tissues and ovariform features occurs in tandem with testiform gonad development and spermatocyte differentiation. In this manner, a pre-existing male pattern of early ovariform ontogeny followed by a shift to testiform development, as found in zebrafish and some other fish species, becomes universalized to all individuals, and produces a protogynous, unidirectional hermaphroditic sexual pattern.

Among goby taxa having a persistent ovotestis, the upregulation of both oocyte and spermatocyte development early in gonad differentiation is maintained throughout life. In the subsequent serial expression of male and female function, alternation of oogenic and spermatogenic function may be mediated through respective regulatory oscillations (i.e., possible alternation of *FOXl2*/gonadal aromatase and *DMRT1*/*SOX9* expression [Kobayashi et al. 2004]). In the case of the persistent ovotestis pattern, partial downregulation resulting in the regression of somatic tissue of one gonad morphology co-occurs with the upregulation of morphogenesis of the other gonadal tissue, and both sex-specific germ cell lines are retained.

FOXl2 has been implicated in ovarian differentiation of *Oryzias luzonensis* (Nakamoto et al. 2009) while the upregulation of *DMY* in medaka (*Oryzias latipes*) leads to testis differentiation (Kobayashi et al. 2004). In the protogynous hermaphrodite, *Epinephelus coioides*, *SOX3* protein is found within differentiating PGCs, oogonia and multiple developmental stages of oocytes of ovarian tissue, suggesting that *SOX3* is responsible, at least in part, for oogenesis (Yao et al. 2007). However, among males, *SOX3* expression is found only in the Sertoli cells of testicular tissue, suggesting a different role in testis differentiation (Yao et al. 2007). In medaka, *Dmrt1* may also be an important regulator of spermatogenesis (Kobayashi et al. 2004). Consequently, in hermaphroditic gobiids, sex cell and gonadal differentiation respectively are likely controlled by differing regulatory pathways. Whether these regulators act in concert or in opposition in hermaphroditic gobies ultimately determines the taxon-specific pattern of reproductive morphogenesis.

The pattern of secondary ovotestis development in *Gobiodon* appears intermediate to that of the Coryphopterus group and of *Eviota*. It differs from the persistent ovotestis pattern in its sole expression of ovariform development throughout the juvenile and early adult stages (i.e., a Coryphopterus group trait). During this period, the pattern of upregulation is likely similar to, or identical with, that of the Coryphopterus group. However, at the point where upregulation of male reproductive tissues coincides with the downregulation and extinction of female reproductive tissues in the Coryphopterus group pattern, female reproductive somatic tissues of the Gobiodon pattern simply regress to small groups of oocytes and support cells distributed throughout the ovotestis, much like the integrated ovotestis of *Eviota*. The oocytes, which are early-stage and relatively few in number during the sperm-producing phase, can subsequently be prompted to resume differentiation. Thus, the underlying regulatory processes governing gonad expression and function in *Gobiodon* shifts to that of the persistent integrated ovotestis pattern in which male and female adult function may be serially expressed.

In a number of *Gobiodon* species, it has been shown that the oocytes and surrounding cells within an ovotestis can be upregulated for a return to ova production (Nakashima et al. 1996; Munday et al. 1998; Cole & Hoese 2001). This form of serial or bidirectional hermaphroditism has been demonstrated in a number of other gobiid genera maintaining an ovotestis, including *Lythrypnus* (St. Mary 1994, 1996, 2000), *Trimma* (Sunobe & Nakazono 1993; Shiobara 2000; Manabe et al. 2007, 2008) and *Paragobiodon echinocephalus* (Kuwamura et al. 1994). Serial hermaphroditism has also been suggested, based on the presence of a persistent ovotestis, for *Priolepis cincta* (Sunobe & Nakazono 1999) and *Bryaninops yongei* (Munday et al. 2002).

The diversity of gonad and gonad-associated morphology described herein suggests that there is considerable ontogenetic lability in the reproductive complex of hermaphroditic gobies. A repeated structural pattern found in the male-active reproductive complex is one of lobulation. The teleost testis is lobule-based with seminiferous lobules (i.e., seminiferous tubules consisting of developing gametes and support tissues) typically making up the majority of the gonad. In hermaphroditic goby taxa, the close anatomical association between the seminiferous lobules and pAGS-derived secretory lobules, as well as their shared architecture, invites speculation of shared ontogenetic origins. Such speculation is strengthened by the findings following gonadectomy in one goby species, *B. soporator*. In gonadectomized males, the sperm duct gland was the site of testis regeneration and the subsequent production of mature, viable sperm. In *Gobiodon*, a portion of the gonad develops into a highly lobulated, non-gametogenic, secretion storage region following a shift to male function. These examples suggest that there is both considerable ontogenetic lability, and broadly distributed competency, of the reproductive complex of hermaphroditic gobies to develop into a diversity of tissues and structures serving diverse reproductive functions.

Among hermaphroditic gobies, the diversity and distinctiveness of different patterns of reproductive ontogeny described here suggest that modifications in ontogenetic processes have taken several different directions across hermaphroditic goby clades. For example, secretory structures secondarily arise from the gonad in some hermaphroditic taxa and from the gonoduct in others. The presence of an ovotestis can be transitory, persistent, or secondary. And the distribution of gametogenic tissues within the ovotestis may be intermingled, regionalized, or completely separated. All of these variations tend to be distributed along clade-specific lines. Based on known developmental processes associated with teleost gonad and germ cell differentiation, small changes in germ cell behavior and ontogenetic processes appear to be sufficient to explain the variety of developmental patterns of gonad ontogeny, despite the extensive morphological diversity among hermaphroditic gobies. In addition, the number of ontogenetic alterations required for the evolution of both hermaphroditic function, and for the considerable morphological diversity of the reproductive complex found among hermaphroditic gobiids, may be relatively small.

ACKNOWLEDGMENTS

Portions of this chapter benefitted greatly from conversations with A.C. Gill, D.W. Greenfield, A.S. Harold, D.F. Hoese, H.K. Larson, P.L. Munday, L.R. Parenti, F. Pezold, C.E. Thacker, J.L. Van Tassel and R. Winterbottom and from insightful review comments from J. Burns and J. Godwin. Specimens were generously provided by D.W. Greenfield, D.F. Hoese, R.C. Langston, H.K. Larson, D.R. Robertson and R. Winterbottom. Additional assistance and support in the field were kindly provided by: L. Orsak, J. Masey (at Christensen Research Institute, Papua New Guinea); A. Hoggett, J. Leis, S. Reader, L.Vail (at Lizard Island Research Station, Australia); and L. Bell, P. Colin, Y. Sadovy (at Coral Reef Research Foundation, Palau). Portions of the research reported on in this chapter were supported by grants from the Smithsonian Institution through the National Museum of Natural History's Caribbean Coral Reef Ecosystems Program (CCRE Contribution no. 889), a Curatorial Fellowship from the Australian Museum and from funds provided by the University of Hawaii at Mānoa.

REFERENCES

Alam MA, Kobayashi Y, Horiguchi R, Hirai T, Nakamura M (2008). Molecular cloning and quantitative expression of sexually dimorphic markers *Dmrt1* and *Foxl2* during female-to-male sex change in *Epinephelus merra*. General and Comparative Endocrinology 157: 75–85.

Andre J, Rouiller C (1957). L'ultrastructure de la membrane nucleaire des ovocytes de l'araignee (*Tegeneraria domestica* Clark). In: Sjostrand F, Rhodin J (eds.), *Proceedings of the European Conference on Electron Microscopy, Stockholm, 1956*. Academic Press, New York, pp. 162–164.

Anteunis A (1959). Recherches sur la structure et le développement de l'ovaire et l'oviducte chez *Lebistes reticulatus* (Téléostéen). Archives de Biologie (Liege) 70: 783–809.

Bachman FM (1914). The migration of the germ cells in *Amiurus nubulosus*. Biological Bulletin 26: 351–366.

Baron D, Cocquet J, Xia X, Fellous M, Guiguen Y, Veitia R (2004). An evolutionary and functional analysis of *FoxL2* in rainbow trout gonad differentiation. Journal of Molecular Endocrinology 33: 705–715.

Braat AK, Speksnijder JE, Zivkovic D (1999). Germ line development in fishes. International Journal of Developmental Biology 43: 745–760.

Cole KS (1983). Protogynous hermaphroditism in a temperate zone territorial marine goby, *Coryphopterus nicholsii*. Copeia 1983: 809–812.

Cole KS (1988). Predicting the potential for sex change on the basis of ovarian structure in gobiid fishes. Copeia 1988: 1082–1086.

Cole KS (1990). Patterns of gonad structure in hermaphroditic gobies (Teleostei: Gobiidae). Environmental Biology of Fishes 28: 125–142.

Cole KS (2009). Modifications of the reproductive complex and implications for the reproductive biology of *Gobiodon oculolineatus* (Teleostei: Gobiidae). Environmental Biology of Fishes 84: 261–273.

Cole KS, Hoese DF (2001). Gonad morphology, colony demography and evidence for hermaphroditism in *Gobiodon okinawae* (Teleostei, Gobiidae). Environmental Biology of Fishes 61: 161–173.

Cole KS, Robertson DR (1988). Protogyny in a Caribbean reef goby, *Coryphopterus personatus*: gonad ontogeny and social influences on sex change. Bulletin of Marine Sciences 42: 317–333.

Cole KS, Shapiro DY (1990). Gonad structure and hermaphroditism in the gobiid genus *Coryphopterus* (Teleostei: Gobiidae). Copeia 1990: 996–1003.

Cole KS, Shapiro DY (1992). Gonadal structure and population characteristics of the protogynous goby *Coryphopterus glaucofraenum*. Marine Biology 113: 1–9.

Davies PR, Takashima F (1980). Sex differentiation in common carp, *Cyprinus carpio*. Journal of the Tokyo University of Fisheries 66: 191–199.

D'Cotta H, Fostier A, Guiguen Y, Govoroun M, Baroiller J-F (2001a). Aromatase plays a key role during normal and temperature-induced sex differentiation of tilapia *Oreochromis niloticus*. Molecular Reproduction and Development 59: 265–276.

D'Cotta H, Fostier A, Guiguen Y, Govoroun M, Baroiller J-F (2001b). Search for genes involved in the temperature-induced gonadal sex differentiation in the tilapia, *Oreochromis niloticus*. Journal of Experimental Zoology 290: 574–585.

Doitsidou M, Reichman-Fried M, Stebler J, Köprunner M, Dörries J, Meyer D, Esguerra CV, Leung T, Raz E (2002). Guidance of PGC migration by the chemokine SDF-1. Cell 111: 647–659.

Eddy E (1975). Germ plasm and the differentiation of the germ cell line. International Review of Cytology 43: 229–280.

Essenberg JM (1923). Sex-differentiation in the viviparous teleost *Xiphophorus helleri* Heckel. Biological Bulletin 45: 46–97.

Fenske M, Segner H (2004). Aromatase modulation alters gonadal differentiation in developing zebrafish (*Danio rerio*). Aquatic Toxicology 67: 105–126.

Fernandino JI, Hattori RS, Shinoda T, Kimura H, Strobl-Mazzulla PH, Strüssmann CA, Somoza GM (2008). Dimorphoic expression of *dmrt1* and *cyp19a1* (ovarian aromatase) during early gonadal development in pejerrey, *Odontesthes bonariensis*. Sexual Development 2: 316–324.

Fishelson L (1989). Bisexuality and pedogenesis in gobies (Gobiidae: Teleostei) and other fish, or: why so many little fish in tropical seas? Senckenbergiana Maritima 20: 147–160.

Fishelson L (1991). Comparative cytology and morphology of seminal vesicles in male gobiid fishes. Japanese Journal of Ichthyology 38: 17–30.

Fujimoto T, Kataoka T, Sakao S, Saito T, Yamaha E, Arai K (2006). Developmental stages and germ cell lineage of the loach (Misgurnus anguillicaudatus). Zoological Science 23: 977–989.

Gamo H (1961). On the origin of germ cells and the formation of gonad primordia in the medaka, Oryzias latipes. Japanese Journal of Zoology 13: 101–115.

Geijsen N, Horoschak M, Kim K, Gribnau J, Eggan K, Daley GQ (2003). Derivation of embryonic germ cells and male gametes from embryonic stem cells. Nature 427: 148–154.

Guiguen Y, Baroiller J-F, Ricordel M-J, Iseki K, McMeel OM, Martin SAM, Fostier A (1999). Involvement of estrogens in the process of sex differentiation in two fish species: the rainbow trout (Oncorhynchus mykiss) and a tilapia (Oreochromis niloticus). Molecular Reproduction and Development 54: 154–162.

Guiguen Y, Fostier A, Piferrer F, Chang C-F (2009). Ovarian aromatase and estrogens: a pivotal role for gonadal sex differentiation and sex change in fish. General and Comparative Endocrinology 165: 351–558.

Hamaguchi S (1982). A light- and electron-microscopic study on the migration of primordial germ cells in the teleost, Oryzias latipes. Cell and Tissue Research 227: 139–151.

Hamaguchi S (1983). Asymmetrical development of the gonads in the embryos and fry of the fish, Oryzias celebensis. Development, Growth and Differentiation 25: 553–561.

Hatakeyama R, Shirafuji N, Nishimura D, Kawamura T, Watanabe Y (2005). Gonadal development in early life stages of Spratelloides gracilis. Fisheries Science 71: 1201–1208.

Hayashi I (1969). Some observations on the reproductive duct of the Japanese sea bass, Lateolabrax japonicus (Cuvier and Valenciennes). Japanese Journal of Ichthyology 16: 68–73.

Howley C, Ho RK (2000). mRNA localization patterns in zebrafish oocytes. Mechanisms of Development 92: 305–309.

Ijiri S, Keneko H, Kobayashi T, Wang D-S, Sakai F, Paul-Prasanth B, Nakamura M, Nagahama Y (2008). Sexual dimorphic expression of genes in gonads during early differentiation of a teleost fish, the Nile tilapia Oreochromis niloticus. Biology of Reproduction 78: 333–341.

Kanamori A, Nagahama Y, Egami N (1985). Development of the tissue architecture in the gonads of the medaka, Oryzias latipes. Zoological Science 2: 695–706.

Kendall WC (1921). Peritoneal membranes, ovaries, and oviducts of salmonoid fishes and their significance in fish-cultural practices. Bulletin of the United States Bureau of Fisheries 37: 183–208.

Kerkis A, Fonseca SAS, Serafim RC, Lavagnolli TMC, Abdelmassih S, Abdelmassih R, Kerkis I (2007). In vitro differentiation of male mouse embryonic stem cells into both presumptive sperm cells and oocytes. Cloning and Stem Cells 9: 535–548.

Kitano T, Takamune K, Kobayashi T, Nagahama Y, Abe S-I (1999). Suppression of P450 aromatase gene expression in sex-reversed males produced by rearing genetically female larvae at a high water temperature during a period of sex differentiation in the Japanese flounder (Paralichthys olivaceus). Journal of Molecular Endocrinology 23: 167–176.

Knaut H, Pelegri F, Bohmann K, Schwarz H, Nusslein-Volhard C (2000). Zebrafish *vasa* RNA but not its protein is a component of the germ plasm and segregates asymmetrically before germline specification. Journal of Cell Biology 149: 875–888.

Kobayashi T, Nagahama Y (2009). Molecular aspects of gonadal differentiation in the teleost fish, the Nile tilapia. Sexual Development 3: 109–117.

Kobayashi T, Kajiura-Kobayashi H, Nagahama Y (2000). Differential expression of *vasa* homologue gene in the germ cells during oogenesis and spermatogenesis in a teleost fish, tilapia, *Oreochromis niloticus*. Mechanisms of Development 99: 139–142.

Kobayashi T, Matsuda M, Kajiura-Kobayashi H, Suzuki A, Saito N, Nakamoto M, Shibata N, Nagahama Y (2004). Two DM domain genes, DMY and DMRT1, involved in testicular differentiation and development in the medaka, *Oryzias latipes*. Developmental Dynamics 231: 518–526.

Kojima Y, Bhandari RK, Kobayashi Y, Nakamura M (2008). Sex change of adult initial-phase male wrasse, *Halichoeres trimaculatus* by estradiol-17beta treatment. General and Comparative Endocrinology 156: 628–632.

Komatsu T, Nakamura S, Nakamura M (2006). Masculinization of female golden rabbitfish *Siganus guttatus* using an aromatase inhibitor treatment during sex differentiation. Comparative Biochemistry and Physiology Part C 143: 402–409.

Kondo M, Nanda I, Hornung U, Asakawa S, Shimizu N, Mitani H, Schmid M, Shima A, Schart M (2003). Absence of the candidate male sex-determining gene dmrt1b(Y) of medaka from other fish species. Current Biology 13: 416–420.

Koya Y, Fujita A, Niki F, Ishihara E, Miyama H (2003). Sex differentiation and pubertal development of gonads in the viviparous mosquitofish, *Gambusia affinis*. Zoological Science 20: 1231–1242.

Kroon FJ, Liley NR (2000). The role of steroid hormones in protogynous sex change in the blackeye goby, *Coryphopterus nicholsii*. General and Comparative Endocrinology 118: 273–283.

Kroon FJ, Munday PL, Pankhurst NW (2003). Steroid hormone levels and bi-directional sex change in the coral dwelling goby *Gobiodon histrio* (Teleostei: Gobiidae). Journal of Fish Biology 62: 153–167.

Kroon FJ, Munday PL, Westcott DA, Hobbs J-P, Liley NR (2005). Aromatase pathway mediates sex change in each direction. Proceedings of the Royal Society of London Series B 272: 1399–1405.

Kurokawa H, Aoki Y, Nakamura S, Ebe Y, Kobayashi D, Tanaka M (2006). Time-lapse analysis reveals different modes of primordial germ cell migration in the medaka *Oryzias latipes*. Development, Growth and Differentiation 48: 209–221.

Kuwamura T, Nakashima Y, Yogo Y (1994). Sex change in either direction by growth-rate advantage in the monogamous coral goby, *Paragobiodon echinocephalus*. Behavioral Ecology 5: 434–438.

Lassig BR (1977). Socioecological strategies adopted by obligate coral-dwelling fishes. In: Taylor DL (ed.), Proceedings of the Third International Coral Reef Symposium. Vol. 1, Biology. Rosenstiel School of Marine and Atmospheric Science, Miami, Florida, pp. 565–570.

Leal MC, Cardoso ER, Nóbrega RH, Batlouni SR, Bogerd J, França LR, Schulz RW (2009). Histological and stereological evaluation of zebrafish (*Danio rerio*) spermatogenesis with an emphasis on spermatogonial generations. Biology of Reproduction 81: 177–187.

Lebrun C, Billard R, Jalabert B (1982). Changes in the number of germ cells in the gonads of the rainbow trout (*Salmo gairdneri*) during the first 10 post-hatching weeks. Reproduction Nutrition Développement 22: 405–412.

Lewis ZR, McClellan MC, Postlethwait JH, Cresko WA, Kaplan RH (2008). Female-specific increase in primordial germ cells marks sex differentiation in threespine stickleback (*Gasterosteus aculeatus*). Journal of Morphology 269: 909–921.

Liarte S, Chaves-Pozo E, García-Alcazar A, Mulero V, Meseguer J, García-Ayala A (2007). Testicular involution prior to sex change in gilthead seabream is characterized by a decrease in DMRT1 gene expression and by massive leukocyte infiltration. Reproductive Biology and Endocrinology 5: 20.

Liu Z, Wu F, Jiao B, Zhang X, Hu C, Huang B, Zhou L, Huang X, Wang Z, Zhang Y, Nagamaha Y, Cheng CHK, Wang D (2007). Molecular cloning of doublesex and mab-3-related transcription factor 1, forkhead transcription factor gene 2, and two types of cytochrome P450 aromatase in Southern catfish and their possible roles in sex differentiation. Journal of Endocrinology 194: 223–241.

Maack G, Segner H (2003). Morphological development of the gonads in zebrafish. Journal of Fish Biology 62: 895–906.

Manabe H, Ishimura M, Shinomiya A, Sunobe T (2007). Field evidence for bi-directional sex change in the polygynous gobiid fish *Trimma okinawae*. Journal of Fish Biology 70: 600–609.

Manabe H, Matsuoka M, Goto K, Dewa S, Shinomiya A, Sakurai M, Sunobe T (2008). Bi-directional sex change in the gobiid fish *Trimma* sp.: does size-advantage exist? Behaviour 145: 99–113.

Matsuda M, Nagahama Y, Shinomiya A, Sato T, Matsuda C, Kobayashi T, Morrey CE, Shibata N, Asakawa S, Shimizu N, Hori H, Hamaguchi S, Sakaizumi M (2002). DMY is a Y-specific DM-domain gene required for male development in the medaka fish. Nature 417: 559–563.

Matsuda M, Sato T, Toyazaki Y, Nagahama Y, Hamaguchi S, Sakaizumi M (2003). *Oryzias curvinotus* has DMY, a gene that is required for male development in the medaka, *O. latipes*. Zoological Science 20: 159–161.

Matsuyama M, Torres Lara R, Matsuura S (1988). Juvenile bisexuality in the red sea bream, *Pagrus major*. Environmental Biology of Fishes 21: 27–36.

Meijide FJ, Lo Nostro FL, Guerrero GA (2005). Gonadal development and sex differentiation in the cichlid fish *Cichlasoma dimerus* (Teleostei, perciformes): a light- and electron-microscopic study. Journal of Morphology 264: 191–210.

Miller PJ (1984). The tokology of gobioid fishes. In: Potts GW, Wootton RJ (eds.), *Fish Reproduction: Strategies and Tactics*. Academic Press, London, pp. 119–153.

Miller PJ (1992). The sperm duct gland: a visceral synapomorphy for gobioid fishes. Copeia 1992: 253–256.

Miyake A, Saito T, Kashiwagi T, Ando D, Yamamoto A, Suzuki T, Nakatsuji N, Nakatsuji T (2006). Cloning and pattern of expression of the shiro-au *vasa* gene during embryogenesis and its roles in PGC development. International Journal of Developmental Biology 50: 619–625.

Miyake Y, Fukui Y, Kuniyoshi H, Sakai Y, Hashimoto H (2008). Examination of the ability of gonadal sex change in primary males of the diandric wrasses *Halichoeres poecilopterus* and *Halichoeres tenuispinis*: estrogen implantation experiments. Zoological Science 25: 220–224.

Moiseyeva YB (1983). The development of the gonads of the round goby, *Neogobius melanostomus* (Gobidae) during the embryonic period. Journal of Ichthyology 23: 64–74.

Moore GA (1937). The germ cells of the trout (*Salmo irideus* Gibbons). Transactions of the American Microscopical Society 56: 105–112.

Munday PL, Caley MJ, Jones GP (1998). Bi-direction sex change in a coral-dwelling goby. Behavioral Ecology and Sociobiology 43: 371–377.

Munday PL, Pierce SJ, Jones GP, Larson HK (2002). Habitat use, social organization and reproductive biology of seawhip goby *Bryaninops yongei*. Marine and Freshwater Research 53: 769–775.

Nagasawa K, Takeuchi Y, Miwa M, Higuchi K, Morita T, Mitsuboshi T, Miyaki K, Kadomura K, Yoshizaki G (2009). cDNA cloning and expression analysis of a vasa-like gene in Pacific bluefin tuna *Thunnus orientalis*. Fisheries Science 75: 71–79.

Nakamoto M, Suzuki A, Matsuda M, Nagahama Y, Shibata N (2005). Testicular type *Sox9* is not involved in sex determination but might be in the development of testicular structures in the medaka, *Oryzias latipes*. Biochemical and Biophysical Research Communications 333: 729–736.

Nakamoto M, Matsuda M, Wang DS, Nagahama Y, Shibata N. (2006). Molecular cloning and analysis of gonadal expression of *Foxl2* in the medaka, *Oryzias latipes*. Biochemical and Biophysical Research Communications 344: 353–361.

Nakamoto M, Muramatsu S, Yoshida S, Matsuda M, Nagahama Y, Shibata N (2009). Gonadal sex differentiation and expression of *Sox9a2*, *Dmrt1*, and *Foxl2* in *Oryzias luzonensis*. Genesis 47: 289–299.

Nakamura M, Nagahama Y (1989). Differentiation and development of Leydig cells, and changes of testosterone levels during testicular differentiation in tilapia *Oreochromis niloticus*. Fish Physiology and Biochemistry 7: 211–219.

Nakamura M, Kobayashi T, Chang X, Nagahama Y (1998). Gonadal sex differentiation in teleost fish. Journal of Experimental Zoology 281: 362–372.

Nakamura S, Aoki Y, Saito D, Kuroki Y, Fujiyama A, Naruse K, Tanaka M (2008). *Sox9b/sox9a2*-EGFP transgenic medaka reveals the morphological reorganization of the gonads and a common precursor of both the female and male supporting cells. Molecular Reproduction and Development 75: 472–476.

Nakashima Y, Kuwamura T, Yogo Y (1995). Why be a both-ways sex changer? Ethology 101: 301–307.

Nakashima Y, Kuwamura T, Yogo Y (1996). Both-ways sex change in monogamous gobies, *Gobiodon* spp. Environmental Biology of Fishes 46: 281–288.

Nanda I, Kondo M, Hornung U, Asakawa S, Winkler C, Shimizu A, Shan Z, Haaf T, Shimizu N, Shima A, Schmid M, Schartl M (2002). A duplicated copy of DMRT1 in the sex-determining region of the Y chromosome of the medaka, *Oryzias latipes*. Proceedings of the National Academy of Sciences 99: 11778–11783.

Navarro-Martín L, Blázquez M, Piferrer F (2009). Masculinization of the European sea bass (*Dicentrarchus labrax*) by treatment with an androgen or aromatase inhibitor involves different gene expression and has distinct lasting effects on maturation. General and Comparative Endocrinology 160: 3–11.

Nayernia K, Nolte J, Michelmann HW, Lee JH, Rathsack K, Drusenheimer N, Dev A, Wulf G, Ehrmann IE, Elliott DJ, Okpanyi V, Zechner U, Haaf T, Meinhardt A, Engel W (2006). In vitro-differentiated embryonic stem cells give rise to male gametes that can generate offspring mice. Developmental Cell 11: 125–132.

Okutsu T, Suzuki K, Takeuchi Y, Takeuchi T, Yoshizaki G (2006). Testicular germ cells can colonize sexually undifferentiated embryonic gonad and produce functional eggs in fish. Proceedings of the National Academy of Sciences 103: 2725–2729.

Otake H, Shinomiya A, Kawaguchi A, Hamaguchi S, Sakaizumi M (2008). The medaka sex-determining gene DMY acquired a novel temporal expression pattern after duplication of DMRT1. Genesis 46: 719–723.

Otani S, Maegawa S, Inoue K, Arai K, Yamaha E (2002). The germ cell lineage identified by vas-mRNA during the embryogenesis in goldfish. Zoological Science 19: 519–526.

Parker JB (1942). Some observations on the reproductive system of the yellow perch (Perca flavescens). Copeia 1942: 223–226.

Parmentier HK, Timmermans LPM (1985). The differentiation of germ cells and gonads during development of carp (Cyprinus carpio L.). A study with anti-carp sperm monoclonal antibodies. Journal of Embryology and Experimental Morphology 90: 13–32.

Patiño R, Davis KB, Schoore JE, Uguz C, Strüssmann CA, Parker NC, Simco BA, Goudie CA (1996). Sex differentiation of channel catfish gonads: normal development and effects of temperature. Journal of Experimental Zoology 276: 209–218.

Pelegri F (2003). Maternal factors in zebrafish development. Developmental Dynamics 228: 535–554.

Pelegri F, Schulte-Merker S (1999). A gynogenesis-based screen for maternal-effect genes in the zebrafish, Danio rerio. In: Detrich W, Zon LI, Westerfield M (eds.), The Zebrafish: Genetics and Genomics, vol. 60. Academic Press, San Diego, pp. 1–20.

Pezold F (1993). Evidence for monophyletic Gobiinae. Copeia 1993: 634–643.

Piferrer F, Guiguen Y (2008). Fish gonadogenesis. Part II. Molecular biology and genomics of sex differentiation. Reviews in Fisheries Science 16(S1): 33–53.

Reichman-Fried M, Minina S, Raz E (2004). Autonomous modes of behavior in primordial germ cell migration. Developmental Cell 6: 589–596.

Richards A, Thompson JT (1921). The migration of the primary sex-cells of Fundulus heteroclitus. The Biological Bulletin 40: 325–348.

Robertson DR, Justines G (1982). Protogynous hermaphroditism and gonochorism in four Caribbean reef gobies. Environmental Biology of Fishes 7: 137–142.

Robertson OH (1961). Prolongation of the life span of Kokanee salmon (Oncorhynchus nerka Kennerlyi) by castration before beginning of gonad development. Proceedings of the National Academy of Sciences 47: 609–621.

Rogers EW (2007). Sexual plasticity in a marine goby (Lythrypnus dalli): social, endocrine, and genetic influences on functional sex. Ph.D. dissertation, Georgia State University, Atlanta.

Rongo C, Broihier HT, Moore L, Van Doren M, Forbes A, Lehmann R (1997). Germ plasm assembly and germ cell migration in Drosophila. Cold Spring Harbor Symposia on Quantitative Biology 62: 1–11.

Saito T, Otani S, Nagai T, Nakatsuji T, Arai K, Yamaha E (2002). Germ cell lineage from a single blastomere at 8-cell stage in shiro-uo (ice goby). Zoological Science 19: 1027–1032.

Saito T, Otani S, Fujimoto T, Suzuki T, Nakatsuji T, Arai K, Yamaha E (2004). The germ line lineage in ukigori, *Gymnogobius* species (Teleostei: Gobiidae) during embryonic development. The International Journal of Developmental Biology 48: 1079.

Satoh N (1974). An ultrastructural study of sex differentiation in the teleost, *Oryzias latipes*. Journal of Embryology and Experimental Morphology 32: 195–215.

Satoh N, Egami N (1972). Sex differentiation of germ cells in the teleost, *Oryzias latipes*, during normal embryonic development. Journal of Embryology and Experimental Morphology 28: 385–395.

Selman S, Wallace RA, Sarka A, Qi X (1993). Stages of oocyte development in the zebrafish, *Brachydanio rerio*. Journal of Morphology 218: 203–224.

Shimizu M, Takahashi H (1980). Process of sex differentiation of the gonad and gonoduct of the three-spined stickleback, *Gasterosteus aculeatus* L. Bulletin of the Faculty of Fisheries, Hokkaido University 31: 137–148.

Shin HS, An KW, Park MS, Jeong MH, Choi CY (2009). Quantitative mRNA expression of *sox3* and DMRT1 during sex reversal, and expression profiles after GnRHa administration in black porgy, *Acanthopagrus schlegeli*. Comparative Biochemistry and Physiology B 154: 150–156.

Shinomiya A, Tanaka M, Kobayashi T, Nagahama Y, Hamaguchi S (2000). The *vasa*-like gene, *olvas*, identifies the migration path of primordial germ cells during embryonic body formation stage in the medaka, *Oryzias latipes*. Development, Growth and Differentiation 42: 317–326.

Shiobara Y (2000). Reproduction and hermaphroditism of the gobiid fish, from Suruga Bay, central Japan. Science Reports of the Museum, Tokai University 2: 19–30.

St. Mary CM (1993). Novel sexual patterns in two simultaneous hermaphroditic gobies, *Lythrypnus dalli* and *Lythrypnus zebra*. Copeia 1993: 1062–1072.

St. Mary CM (1994). Sex allocation in the simultaneous hermaphrodite, the bluebanded goby (*Lythrypnus dalli*): the effects of body size and behavioral gender and the consequences for reproduction. Behavioral Ecology 5: 304–313.

St. Mary CM (1996). Sex allocation in a simultaneous hermaphrodite, the zebra goby *Lythrypnus zebra*: insights gained through a comparison with its sympatric congener, *Lythrypnus dalli*. Environmental Biology of Fishes 45: 177–190.

St. Mary CM (2000). Sex allocation in *Lythrypnus* (Gobiidae): variations on a hermaphroditic theme. Environmental Biology of Fishes 58: 321–333.

Sunobe T, Nakazono A (1990). Polygynous mating system of *Trimma okinawae* (Pisces: Gobiidae) at Kagoshima, Japan with a note on sex change. Ethology 84: 133–143.

Sunobe T, Nakazono A (1993). Sex change in both directions by alteration of social dominance in *Trimma okinawae* (Pisces: Gobiidae). Ethology 94: 339–345.

Sunobe T, Nakazono A (1999). Mating system and hermaphroditism in the gobiid fish, *Priolepis cincta*, at Kagoshima, Japan. Ichthyological Research 46: 103–105.

Suzuki A, Shibata N (2004). Developmental process of genital ducts in the medaka, *Oryzias latipes*. Zoological Science 21: 397–406.

Stromsten FA (1931). The development of the gonads in the goldfish *Carassius auratus* L. Iowa Studies in Natural History 13: 3–45.

Strüssmann CA, Takashima F, Toda K (1996). Sex differentiation and hormonal feminization in pejerrey *Odontesthes bonariensis*. Aquaculture 139: 31–45.

Takahashi H (1977). Juvenile hermaphroditism in the zebrafish, *Brachydanio rerio*. Bulletin of the Faculty of Fisheries, Hokkaido University 28: 57–65.

Takahashi H, Iwasaki Y (1973). The occurrence of histochemical activity of 3-beta-hydroxysteroid dehydrogenase in the developing testes of *Poecilia reticulata*. Development, Growth and Differentiation 15: 241–253.

Takahashi H, Shimizu M (1983). Juvenile intersexuality in a cyprinid fish, the Sumatra barb, *Barbus tetrazona tetrazona*. Bulletin of the Faculty of Fisheries, Hokkaido University 34: 69–78.

Takashima F, Patiño R, Nomura M (1980). Histological studies on the sex differentiation in rainbow trout. Bulletin of the Japanese Society of Scientific Fisheries 46: 1317–1322.

Tavolga W N (1955). Effects of gonadectomy and hypophysectomy on prespawning behavior in males of the gobiid fish, *Bathygobius soporator*. Physiological Zoology 28: 218–233.

Timmermans LPM, Taverne N (1983). Origin and differentiation of primordial germ cells (PGCs) in the rosy barbs, *Barbus conchonius*, (Cyprinidae, Teleostei). Acta Morphologica Neerlando-Scandinavica 21: 182.

Uchida D, Yamashita M, Kitano T, Iguchi T (2004). An aromatase inhibitor or high water temperature induce oocyte apoptosis and depletion of P450 aromatase activity in the gonads of genetic female zebrafish during sex reversal. Comparative Biochemistry and Physiology A 137: 11–20.

Underwood JL, Hestand II RS, Thompson BZ (1986). Gonad regeneration in grass carp following bilateral gonadectomy. The Progressive Fish-Culturist 48: 54–56.

van Winkoop A, Booms GHR, Dulos GJ, Timmermans LPM (1992). Ultrastructural changes in primordial germ cells during early gonadal development of the common carp (*Cyprinus carpio* L., teleostei). Cell and Tissue Research 267: 337–346.

Vizziano D, Randuineau G, Baron D, Cauty C, Guiguen Y (2007). Characterization of early molecular sex differentiation in rainbow trout, *Oncorhynchus mykiss*. Developmental Dynamics 236: 2198–2206.

Vizziano D, Baron D, Randuineau G, Mahè S, Cauty C (2008). Rainbow trout gonadal masculinization induced by inhibition of estrogen synthesis is more physiological than masculinization induced by androgen supplementation. Biology of Reproduction 78: 939–946.

Wang D, Kobayashi T, Zhou L, Nagahama Y (2004). Molecular cloning and gene expression of *FOXl2* in the Nile tilapia, *Oreochromis niloticus*. Biochemical and Biophysical Research Communications 320: 83–89.

Wang D-S, Kobayashi T, Zhou L-Y, Paul-Prasanth B, Ijiri S, Sakai F, Okubo K, Morohashi K-i, Nagahama Y (2007). *Foxl2* up-regulates aromatase gene transcription in a female-specific manner by binding to the promoter as well as interacting with Ad4 binding protein/steroidogenic factor 1. Molecular Endocrinology 21: 712–725.

Wang XG, Bartfait R, Sleptsova-Freidrich I, Orban L (2007). The timing and extent of "juvenile ovary" phase are highly variable during zebrafish testis differentiation. Journal of Fish Biology 70 (SA): 33–44.

Watts M, Pankhurst NW, King HR (2004). Maintenance of Atlantic salmon (*Salmo salar*) at elevated temperature inhibits cytochrome P450 aromatase activity in isolated ovarian follicles. General and Comparative Endocrinology 135: 381–3990.

Weidinger G, Wolke U, Köprunner M, Raz E (1999). Identification of tissues and patterning events required for distinct steps in early migration of zebrafish primordial germ cells. Development 126: 5295–5307.

Weidinger G, Wolke U, Köprunner, M, Thisse C, Thisse C, Raz E (2002). Regulation of zebrafish primordial germ cell migration by attraction towards an intermediate target. Development 129: 25–36.

Wu G-C, Tomy S, Nakamura M, Chang C-F (2008). Dual roles of *cyp19a1a* in gonadal sex differentiation and development in the protandrous black porgy, *Acanthopagrus schlegeli*. Biology of Reproduction 79: 1111–1120.

Xia W, Zhou L, Yao B, Li C-J, Gui J-F (2007). Differential and spermatogenic cell-specific expression of DMRT1 during sex reversal in protogynous hermaphroditic groupers. Molecular and Cellular Endocrinology 263: 156–172.

Xu H, Gui J, Hong Y (2005). Differential expression of vasa RNA and protein during spermatogenesis and oogenesis in the Gibel carp (*Carassius auratus gibelio*), a bisexually and gynogenetically reproducing vertebrate. Developmental Dynamics 233: 872–882.

Yamaguchi T, Yamaguchi S, Hirai T, Kitano T (2007). Follicle-stimulating hormone signaling and Foxl2 are involved in transcriptional regulation of aromatase gene during gonadal sex differentiation in Japanese flounder, *Paralichthys olivaceus*. Biochemical and Biophysical Research Communications 359: 935–940.

Yao B, Zhou L, Wang Y, Xia W, Gui J-F (2007). Differential expression and dynamic changes of SOX3 during gametogenesis and sex reversal in protogynous hermaphroditic fish. Journal of Experimental Zoology 307A: 207–219.

Yoon C, Kawakami K, Hopkins N (1997). Zebrafish *vasa* homologue RNA is localized to the cleavage planes of 2- and 4-cell-stage embryos and is expressed in the primordial germ cells. Development 124: 3157–3166.

Yoshikawa H, Oguri M (1979). Gonadal sex differentiation in the medaka, *Oryzias latipes*, with special regard to the gradient of the differentiation of the testes. Bulletin of the Japanese Society of Scientific Fisheries 45: 1115–1121.

Yoshinaga N, Shiraishi E, Yamamoto T, Iguchi T, Abe S, Kitano T (2004). Sexually dimorphic expression of a teleost homologue of Müllerian inhibiting substance during gonadal sex differentiation in Japanese flounder, *Paralichthys olivaceus*. Biochemical and Biophysical Research Communications 322: 508–513.

Yoshizaki G, Sakatani S, Tominaga H, Takeuchi T (2000). Cloning and characterization of a *vasa*-like gene in rainbow trout and its expression in the germ cell lineage. Molecular Reproduction and Development 55: 364–371.

Fertilization in Marine Fishes

A Review of the Data and Its Application to Conservation Biology

Christopher W. Petersen and Carlotta Mazzoldi

Fertilization in fishes appears to be a relatively simple phenomenon to discuss. Individuals live in an aquatic medium, so sperm and eggs can be broadcast into the environment with spawning partners releasing gametes synchronously in close proximity. This suggests that fertilization success (the proportion of eggs fertilized) will be high in marine fishes, that ejaculates do not need special modifications, and that male ejaculates with sperm and seminal fluid similar to blood plasma would be adequate to allow for successful fertilization. In the early seminal papers on social and mating system evolution, sperm production costs were seen as trivial, and it was hypothesized that enough sperm would be produced by a single male to fertilize all of a female's clutch (e.g., Trivers 1972, p. 138).

This simplified scenario ignores a significant arena in which tradeoffs in reproductive allocation may play out. By viewing sperm production, morphology, and behavior as elements of allocation to reproduction in males to maximize lifetime reproductive success, with explicit tradeoffs among the ways males can partition their resources, a much clearer picture of fertilization and the evolution of reproductive traits in fishes emerges.

There are several places where tradeoffs may occur in fish fertilization strategies. Although maximizing the number of spawns a male takes part in might be seen as maximizing reproductive success, individuals also maximize reproductive success by reducing the number of spawns they take part in but increasing their proportional fertilization in those spawns by excluding other males. This appears to have led to a range of allocation patterns to testicular tissue and sperm production, both interspecifically and intraspecifically, with some males defending females or spawning sites while maintaining low levels of sperm production, and some males having high sperm production associated with chronic sperm competition (Stockley et al. 1997; Petersen & Warner 1998; Taborsky 1998). Another area for potential tradeoffs is the composition of the ejaculate of each spawn; males release not just sperm but other substances, some of which affect sperm performance. Additionally, individual sperm may vary in either the quantity of provisioned energy or their morphology and behavior, where characteristics like sperm swimming speed or longevity might be expected to trade off against one another (Snook 2005).

Given the diversity of fish reproductive biology, we expect that these patterns might play out differently for species with different types of fertilization (internal vs. external) and different types of eggs (demersal vs. pelagic). In addition, the degree of sperm competition should also affect tradeoffs in reproductive allocation.

In this chapter, we examine fertilization mode and fertilization success from the perspective of behavioral and evolutionary ecology. We start with an overview of the dynamics of fertilization in fishes, and then discuss how fertilization success has been measured in the field. We then summarize data on marine fishes with external fertilization (pelagic and demersal egg species) and internal fertilization. Following that overview, we examine the evolution of male ejaculates and examine how different ecological circumstances may select for different allocation strategies. Finally, we ask how this information interacts with and informs applied areas such as conservation biology and exploited species, such as Atlantic cod and large sex-changing tropical species such as groupers. This chapter will not include several very interesting and important areas of the field of fertilization; in particular, we do not discuss the cellular mechanisms of fertilization (e.g., Amanze & Iyengar 1990; Yanagimachi et al. 1992; Munehara et al. 1997; and for review on external fertilizers Cosson et al. 2008a, b). We also restrict our analysis to bony fishes.

FERTILIZATION DYNAMICS IN MARINE FISHES

In the behavioral ecology and evolutionary biology literature, the first authors to suggest that fertilization might be less than 100% in fishes were Nakatsuru & Kramer (1982). In this study, they showed that when male lemon tetras (*Hyphessobrycon pulchripinnis*, Characinidae) were serially exposed to receptive females, fertilization success fell off rather quickly so that after 40 spawning acts fertilization was near zero. Females discriminated against males that had recently spawned suggesting that females did encounter this situation in the field, and had developed behaviors that would increase their fertilization success.

The result poses a question: If sperm are cheap to produce, why do males not always produce enough sperm to fertilize all of a female's clutch? To understand how this quandary is resolved, an informative starting point is a fertilization curve for an externally fertilizing fish (Figure 7.1A). As the number of sperm released in a spawn increases, fertilization increases, but with diminishing returns as number of sperm released increases (Levitan & Petersen 1995; Warner et al. 1995). The marginal return in fitness to the male, the amount of fertilization gained for each incremental increase in sperm production, decreases to near zero as most of the eggs are fertilized (Figure 7.1B). Importantly, as long as the marginal return is above zero, not all of the eggs have been fertilized. Even though sperm are cheap, at some point the returns on increased male gametic investment may be less than fitness returns for alternative allocations of this energy.

Unlike males, female fitness from a spawning event may always be maximized when all of their eggs are fertilized. But even here, potential exceptions exist since females may do better by mating with males that produce higher quality offspring even if there is a fertilization cost, or mating events that give higher fertilization may have higher mortality risks for females. Thus, in many cases fertilization is probably best seen as a form of sexual conflict, in which the male's interests and the female's interests may not completely coincide.

Some work in the past has suggested that there is a threshold number of sperm needed to effect fertilization. We believe that this misconception has probably arisen due to the use of plotting log fertilization curves (Figure 7.2). This type of plot is a common way to graphically illustrate the effect of sperm number on fertilization success (e.g., Ginzburg 1968; marine invertebrate literature). This sharp increase after a range of x-values with very little increase gives the impression of a critical sperm concentration. This idea is embedded in the models of Shapiro & Giraldeau (1996). If we replot Figure 7.2, but instead plot number of sperm released on a linear scale we get Figure 7.1A. There is no threshold of sperm needed to begin fertilization, just as there is no guaranteed upper level of sperm release that will always fertilize all of the eggs in a spawning event.

These figures assume that the main factor affecting fertilization success of a batch of eggs is the concentration of sperm around the eggs at the time of spawning. In aquaculture, when determining how to maximize fertilization, researchers often refer to the ratio of sperm to eggs (e.g., Suquet et al. 1995; Rurangwa et al. 1998), thus explicitly including egg concentration into fertilization dynamics. In the previous examples, however, we have been assuming that fertilization success depended exclusively on the number of sperm, and was independent of egg concentration (or number). What is the cause of this difference? For egg number to affect the fertilization success of a spawn, eggs have to be at such a high concentration relative to sperm that by having an egg nearby being fertilized by one sperm (or attracting multiple sperm), it must be reducing the probability of fertilization for nearby eggs. The inclusion of egg number in models of fertilization rate implies that eggs are strongly competing for sperm, and that increasing egg concentration without increasing sperm number would decrease fertilization success.

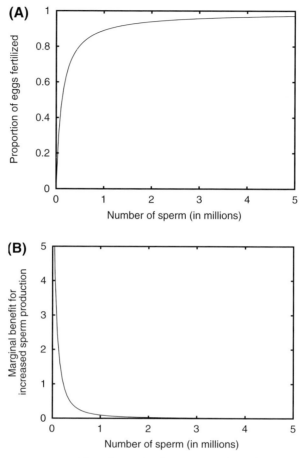

FIGURE 7.1. The relationship between number of sperm released and (A) the proportion of eggs fertilized and (B) the marginal benefit for producing more sperm at different sperm release levels. The fertilization curve used in this calculation is proportion of eggs fertilized = (0.994 × number of sperm released in millions) / (0.117 + number of sperm released in millions). It is the curve used to fit data for bluehead wrasse (*Thalassoma bifasciatum*) field data. Equation first used in Warner et al. 1995.

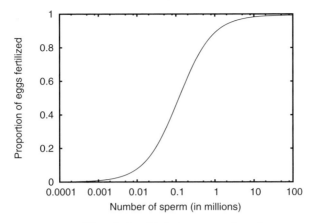

FIGURE 7.2. The relationship between number of sperm released and the proportion of eggs fertilized, plotted with a log-scale x-axis. The equation used is the same as in Figure 7.1.

The inclusion of egg concentrations in fertilization equations is probably warranted when egg concentrations are very high, as will occur in a bowl of eggs being fertilized by sperm, but is probably not important at the concentrations of sperm and eggs seen in natural environments. The exclusion of egg concentration from field estimates of fertilization success is supported by statistical analysis of field data in the best-studied example (Table 1 in Warner et al. 1995). In addition, Kiflawi (2000) modeled both types of scenarios in his detailed theoretical treatment of fertilization curves, and found that the data did not strongly support the results predicted from fertilization dynamics dependent on egg concentration. All of this suggests that sperm concentration will be the most important causal factor affecting fertilization success in nature.

METHODS FOR MEASURING FERTILIZATION SUCCESS IN THE FIELD

Measuring fertilization success in a marine fish species that spawns pelagic eggs is conceptually an easy task. Imagine that all eggs float post spawning, that spawning is predictable in time and in space, that fertilized and unfertilized eggs exhibit similar behavior in the water column, and that collecting does not damage eggs or interfere with fertilization. It would also be convenient if all eggs could easily be identified to species when multiple species synchronize spawning spatially and temporally. Then, by putting a plankton net downcurrent of a spawning aggregation, you could estimate fertilization for a species without too much difficulty. In fact, many of these conditions are probably met for some species, and some investigators have used similar techniques to estimate fertilization success (Colin 1983; Howell et al. 1991). The fact that sperm in at least the one tropical reef fish where it has been measured have a very short span of time that they are capable of fertilizing eggs (<1 minute) reduces many of the potential biases of taking eggs from the environment soon after spawning (*T. bifasciatum*, Petersen et al. 1992).

Unfortunately, nets, especially more durable nitex netting used in plankton nets, damage eggs collected immediately after spawning in a wide range of species (Markle & Waiwood 1985; Petersen et al. 1992; Marconato et al. 1997; Petersen pers. obs.). One alternative to nitex nets that has been used is softer hand held nylon aquarium nets (Petersen et al. 1992) although these nets have also been shown to create damage to eggs, biasing estimates of fertilization success (Marconato et al. 1997).

The methodology that appears to produce the least amount of bias in estimating fertilization success in spawns is collecting the eggs and the water around the spawn in a large plastic bag that is then taken to an above-water platform where samples can be taken for egg and sperm counts and for estimating fertilization. This technique was first developed by Andrea Marconato and has been used successfully in different species of small reef fishes (Shapiro et al. 1994; Marconato et al. 1995, 1997; Warner et al. 1995; Marconato & Shapiro 1996; Petersen et al. 2001). Collecting eggs in a bag after the spawn creates two logistical challenges. First, the diver needs to be relatively close to the spawning event to successfully sample eggs before they disperse in the water column, so only species that allow relatively close approach by divers can be collected with good reliability. Second, the bag needs to be taken to a boat, where a sample of eggs (and potentially sperm) can be taken. This requires more labor than the net technique. The potential for bags to produce biases in measurements of fertilization success was studied extensively by Marconato et al. (1997). They concluded that the bag used immediately after spawning caused a slight decrease in estimates of fertilization success (0.2% to 3.8% reported in Marconato et al. 1997).

In species with demersal eggs, eggs do not disperse and fertilization can be measured hours after fertilization when eggs have hardened and are less vulnerable to handling. Although few studies report fertilization success for marine fishes with demersal eggs, fertilization success appears to be very close to 100% (Petersen & Warner 2002). One possible bias in the estimation of fertilization rate hours after egg deposition comes from parental cannibalism. Cannibalism by the parental male has been recorded in several demersal spawners with male egg care, and part of this cannibalism is performed on unfertilized eggs (Manica 2002). If such cannibalism occurs in a short time after fertilization, fertilization rate would be overestimated.

MODES OF FERTILIZATION

Among marine fishes, patterns and modes of spawning and fertilization are characterized by an amazing degree of diversity; however, we have found it convenient to divide our summary and discussion of fertilization into three categories, fertilization of pelagic eggs, fertilization of demersal eggs, and internal fertilization. Much of the work is focused on a few well-studied species, including the Caribbean bluehead wrasse, *Thalassoma bifasciatum*, the gobies of the Mediterranean and the sculpins (Cottidae) of the Pacific.

Fertilization Success in Species with Pelagic Eggs

For tropical fishes with pelagic eggs, there have been no published accounts of fertilization success in the field since the data were last reviewed by Petersen & Warner (2002). Several of these papers have concluded that sperm limitation exists because there is a strong relationship between either direct measurements of sperm released in a spawn and fertilization success (measured as successful development of embryos), or a relationship between fertilization success and a feature of the mating system believed to correlate with sperm release patterns, such as number of males releasing sperm or the spawning rate of a male. Here we focus on data from bluehead wrasse, *Thalassoma bifasciatum*, and then briefly compare those results with other small tropical species.

Bluehead Wrasse *(Thalassoma bifasciatum).*   The bluehead wrasse is one of the most common shallow coral reef fishes in the Caribbean. Fertilization success of this fish in the wild has been studied more than any other marine fish. Bluehead wrasse spawn daily on coral reefs at predictable times, allowing collections of gametes and embryos from individual spawns. In a series of papers, Marconato, Shapiro, Warner, and Petersen have reported on a variety of details of fertilization in populations from Puerto Rico and St. Croix (Petersen et al. 1992; Shapiro et al. 1994; Warner et al. 1995; Marconato et al. 1997; Petersen et al. 2001).

Fertilization success of individual spawning events in bluehead wrasse is high, with most spawns well over 90% and an average of 95.3% (Petersen et al. 2001). The early reports of fertilization averaging 75% by Petersen et al. (1992) appear to be due to damage caused by nets causing reduced fertilization success. However, even with these high average levels of fertilization success, these studies consistently show that sperm limitation does cause a small reduction in fertilization success in some spawns.

These papers have shown that several factors predictably affect fertilization success in bluehead wrasse, and virtually all of them can be related to the concentration of sperm around eggs at fertilization. Fertilization success is positively related to the number of sperm released in a spawn, either when comparing pair spawns (single male spawning with a single female) to group spawns (single female and multiple males spawning in a single spawning rush)(Marconato et al. 1997) or when just examining the patterns within pair spawns (Warner et al. 1995; Petersen et al. 2001). The difference in average fertilization success for pair-spawning males can be considerable, with average male fertilization success ranging from 86 to 99% in St. Croix (Warner et al. 1995; Marconato et al. 1997; Petersen et al. 2001).

The lowest fertilization rates occur for pair spawns involving males with a high daily mating frequency who release less sperm per spawn than males with lower rates of spawning (Warner et al. 1995). Group spawns, which have much higher levels of sperm released per spawn (approximately 50x)(Shapiro et al. 1994), and much lower variation in fertilization success than pair spawns (Marconato et al. 1997), have as high or higher fertilization success than pair spawns on the same reef, and typically average 98% to 99% (Marconato et al. 1997). Within a reef, spawns involving pair-spawning males with the highest mating success (number of matings per day) have an average fertilization success as much as 12% below the average for group spawns on the same reef (Marconato et al. 1997).

At least one physical factor, water flow at a site, also appears to affect fertilization success in a spawn. Sites with higher level of water flow have lower fertilization success for the same amount of sperm released by a male, which would be expected if flow caused gametes to disperse faster (Petersen et al. 1992, 2001).

In addition to these very intuitive results, Petersen et al. (2001) also found that fertilization effectiveness, the fertilization success for a given number of sperm released per spawn, was negatively correlated with female size, and also negatively correlated with the mating success of the male after the number of sperm released per spawn was statistically removed. Since larger females tend to release more eggs per spawn, this might suggest that egg numbers affect fertilization success, but Warner et al. (1995) found that fertilization success was independent of number of eggs released in a spawn. If larger females create more turbulence in their spawns, gametes could be dispersed over a wider area, reducing the sperm concentration and subsequent fertilization success of the spawn, but this interpretation is speculative. The negative correlation between male mating success and fertilization success, controlling for the number of sperm released, could result from males with higher mating success either not being as well positioned with the female during spawning or having sperm of lower quality, but neither of these hypotheses has been tested.

In addition to the descriptive studies, this research group conducted two field experiments to determine how sperm release responded to changes in energy budget and mating success. In the first experiment, Warner et al. (1995) experimentally enhanced the energy budgets of territorial, terminal-phase male bluehead wrasse by feeding them daily for two weeks. They found that individuals increased mating success, but did not increase sperm output per spawn. In a second experiment, Petersen et al. (2001) experimentally changed mating success of individual males by either removing females from a patch reef or removing competing males. When a male's mating success was changed, his fertilization success decreased with increasing mating success, mirroring the natural population data.

Although fertilization success varies in predictable ways, and is less than 100% due to sperm limitation, there is no evidence in *T. bifasciatum* that females preferentially spawn in situations that provide higher fertilization success. None of the patterns that could be used to predict higher fertilization success for specific types of spawns, individual males, or individual sites, appear to be used by females to secure higher fertilization success (Warner et al. 1995; Petersen et al. 2001). The evolution of female choice in this species may be influenced by several selective forces, including not just fertilization success but many factors that influence lifetime reproductive success including mortality rate associated with spawning, male quality, and the energetic or time constraints of getting to a spawning site.

Other Species of Pelagic Spawners.   Although fertilization success has only been measured in the field for a few other species with pelagic eggs, the results from these studies suggest that the picture that emerges from bluehead wrasse may be a common one. In comparisons among spawns in another wrasse, the slippery dick, *Halichoeres bivattatus*, increased fertilization success was found in spawns with streakers (additional males that quickly join pair spawners, releasing sperm in competition with the male-role pair-spawning individual)(Petersen 1991). The addition of streakers presumably increases the total sperm released in a spawn compared to pair spawns. Fertilization success decreased with rougher sea conditions and increased water velocity (Petersen 1991). In the razorfish *Xyrichthys novacula*, Marconato et al. (1995) found high fertilization success (96% to 98%) and higher sperm release per spawn in two males with lower mating success, while a third male that had recently enlarged his harem had much lower sperm released per spawn and lower (87%) fertilization success. In the bucktooth parrotfish, *Sparisoma radians*, Marconato & Shapiro (1996) found fertilization success positively correlated with the amount of sperm released in a pair spawn, and more sperm released in spawns with larger females. The median fertilization success reported in this study was 93%.

One study that did not find differences in fertilization success with changes in the number of sperm presumably released in a spawn is the study by Kiflawi et al. (1998) for the group-spawning surgeonfish *Acanthurus nigrofuscus*. These investigators obtained very high fertilization success measurements, averaging 98% to 99%, for both group spawns (single spawns with multiple males) and mass spawning (multiple group spawns in an areas over a very short period, leaving large and visually persistent gamete clouds). In contrast to previous studies, they also found no effect of ambient current speed on fertilization success. Because all of the spawns in this species involved high levels of sperm competition, the total amounts of sperm released were probably quite high, and at high levels of sperm release, we expect consistently high levels of fertilization success, with little difference over large differences in sperm release (Figure 7.1A)(Petersen & Warner 2002).

Fertilization Success in Species with Demersal Eggs

In pelagic spawners, fertilization is affected by the rapid dispersal and dilution of sperm and eggs in the environment, and consequently, highly synchronous gamete release appears to be a prerequisite in order to achieve high fertilization rates. However, in demersal spawners eggs are attached to a substrate and not dispersed, providing the possibility of asynchronous or extended gamete release. Demersal spawners may scatter their eggs on the open substrate or release a defined clutch, often inside a nest. While in the first case sperm may be rapidly dispersed as in pelagic spawners, reproduction within a nest makes the oviposition site highly predictable and sperm may be retained for a long period inside the nest. This mode of reproduction is exhibited by dozens of different families, often with male parental care (Breder & Rosen 1966; Blumer 1979; Baylis 1981; Gross & Shine 1981; Thresher 1984), and with males occupying and/or building the nest and attracting females.

In one such family, the Gobiidae, asynchronous gamete release has been demonstrated, with males starting sperm release before females begin egg deposition. Such asynchronous gamete release is achieved by releasing sperm embedded in a mucous-enriched seminal fluid on the ceiling of the nest. During the spawning act, males turn upside down, intermittently rubbing the urogenital papilla and releasing sperm on the roof of the nest site (Marconato et al. 1996; Ota et al. 1996). The mucous component of these trails keeps sperm inactive, and sperm activate only when in direct contact with seawater. The mucins of the trails slowly dissolve, liberating active sperm into the seawater for hours (Scaggiante et al. 1999; Rasotto & Mazzoldi 2002). A single trail may release sperm for up to about 30 hours, while sperm in the water may be active for an average of 80 minutes, as observed in the grass goby *Zosterisessor ophiocephalus* (Scaggiante et al. 1999). Sperm reach eggs via the surrounding water, and eggs do not need to be released directly on sperm trails (Scaggiante et al. 1999; Giulianini et al. 2001). In these species females take a very long time (up to several hours) to lay an entire clutch one egg at a time (Mazzoldi et al. 2000). The intermittent gamete release that characterizes the laying of sperm trails frees males from spending all the spawning time releasing sperm and possibly reduces sperm production costs, allowing males to save energy (Mazzoldi et al. 2005).

There are many other families that deposit eggs cared for by males in a nest (Breder & Rosen 1966; Blumer 1979, 1982; Thresher 1984). In families such as the Blenniidae, it has been observed that males rub the urogenital region on the nest ceiling releasing sperm before (Giacomello pers. comm.) and during egg deposition (Giacomello et al. 2006). In some species, males actually spend part of the time outside the entrance while females are laying eggs (Kraak 1996). This fertilization style might be quite common among demersal spawners using enclosed nests.

Eggs of other demersal spawners, such as the cottid *Hemilepidotus gilberti,* are laid in a mass enclosed in the viscous ovarian fluid. In this species, egg deposition takes around one hour, and males start emitting sperm a few minutes after the beginning of oviposition, intermittently quivering the posterior trunk (Hayakawa & Munehara 1996). Fertilization occurs while the eggs are still embedded in the ovarian fluid. After several hours, the ovarian fluid dissolves and the demersal egg mass develops on the bottom (Hayakawa & Munehara 1998).

In mouthbrooding fish, such as cardinalfish, females release eggs, bound in a mass by threads, which are immediately taken in the mouth by males. The partners maintain a close proximity during courtship, turning in a circle side by side. Although Garnaud (1950) hypothesized internal fertilization for *Apogon imberbis,* external fertilization appears more likely for this species (Mazzoldi et al. 2008) as reported for all the other Apogonidae. Fertilization has been hypothesized to occur before the male turns to grab the eggs (Kuwamura 1983; Vagelli 1999). Males often wrap their anal fin around the female's abdomen (Thresher 1984) but given that the entire mating process takes two seconds (Vagelli 1999), males could also gulp sperm together with eggs, and actual fertilization might occur or continue within the male buccal cavity. If this is the case, fertilization would take place in a restricted volume without sperm competition, and consequently few sperm would be needed. An indication of low sperm production is suggested by the low values of the gonadosomatic index (GSI, the proportion of body weight devoted to gonads) reported for cardinalfish males (Okuda 2001). Jawfish, another group of marine mouthbrooders, also appears to have a low male GSI in both monogamous and polygynous species (Hess 1993; Marconato & Rasotto 1993; Hess pers. comm.).

Fertilization within a restricted volume also occurs in some pipefish and seahorses in which males have a brood pouch. In those species, eggs are released inside the male pouch where fertilization takes place (Watanabe et al. 2000; Foster & Vincent 2004). The confined volume where fertilization occurs allows the production of extremely small amounts of sperm, enabling the male to allocate more energy to embryo development (Watanabe et al. 2000; Van Look et al. 2007). In the seahorse *Hippocampus kuda* and the pipefish *Nerophis ophidion,* which does not have a brood pouch, sperm may be activated by ovarian fluid (Ah-King et al. 2006; Van Look et al. 2007).

Although a smaller amount of sperm is required for fertilization in demersal versus pelagic spawners, nonetheless, sperm limitation may occur in these species. The first fish species in which sperm limitation was reported is the freshwater demersal spawner, lemon tetra (Nakatsuru & Kramer 1982). Many species with demersal eggs exhibit high degrees of polygyny, which are correlated with sperm limitation in pelagic species. However, we expect that lower water flow around demersal oviposition sites will increase the probability of contact between sperm and eggs and enhance fertilization success for similar initial sperm concentrations, reducing sperm limitation for most demersal species. Sperm limitation is least likely in species in which males care for just one egg clutch at time, like some mouthbrooders and syngnathids (Kuwamura 1985; Okuda 2001; Foster & Vincent 2004; Kolm & Berglund 2004). In these species, males can devote all of their sperm during an entire brood cycle to just one predictable fertilization event.

In addition, we think it will be much less likely to find sperm depletion in species spawning in enclosed nests such as burrows, cavities, or shells, in which the exchange of water is limited. In addition to limited sperm dispersal, the nest surface often constitutes a limitation to the number of egg clutches a male may receive (e.g., Mazzoldi et al. 2002; Giacomello & Rasotto 2005). For a group like gobies, these factors combined with prolonged sperm release from sperm trails and the predictable and limited degree of polygyny makes sperm depletion unlikely.

For demersal spawners that lay eggs on open substrate, sperm limitation is more likely to occur, but only in some circumstances. If eggs are laid on a definite substrate, as is the case for most pomacentrid species in which males defend a substrate for egg deposition and perform parental care (Thresher 1984), a physical limitation on the number of egg clutches may still occur. In these species, we expect adaptations in the seminal fluid to reduce sperm dispersal, and we do not expect the occurrence of sperm depletion. The limited accounts for groups like pomacentrids suggest fertilization of clutches at or near 100% with little or no sperm limitation (Petersen & Warner 2002). Sperm limitation is most likely in species that have the potential for extended breeding cycles, with individual males spawning with multiple females and no mating constraints due to limited oviposition sites. In demersal spawners, this is most likely in species like the lemon tetra that scatter eggs on the open substrate and exhibit a mating system in which male mating success is not limited by nest size and paternal care is absent.

Fertilization in Internal Fertilizers

Internal fertilization has evolved independently in fishes a large number of times (Wourms 1981; Goodwin et al. 2002). Internal fertilization is less common than external fertilization in marine bony fish, occurring only in a few families spread over several orders: Atheriniformes, Beloniformes, Cyprinodontiformes, Ophidiiformes, Perciformes, and Scorpaeniformes. This mode of fertilization may be associated with viviparity, ovoviviparity, or oviparity. Usually, but not always, internal insemination implies the presence of a copulatory organ in males, devoted to sperm transfer, that is often constituted by a modification of the urogenital papilla to an intromittent organ (Breder & Rosen 1966). Internal fertilization is also associated with a major change in parental care patterns in fishes, with female care predominating whereas male care predominates in parental species with external fertilization (Gross & Shine 1981; Clutton-Brock 1991). With internal fertilization comes a number of changes in fertilization dynamics, including the physical environment at the time of fertilization and the degree or dynamics of sperm competition.

True internal fertilization implies the fusion of gamete nuclei within the female genital tract. However in the family Cottidae a peculiar form of internal insemination occurs, called internal gametic association (IGA). In several species belonging to this family, sperm are transferred to the female oviduct, then remain within the ovarian lumen where they associate with ovulated eggs, with one or more subsequently entering the micropyle (i.e. gametic association). However, penetration of the sperm into the ooplasm and fusion between gamete nuclei occur only after exposure to seawater when ova are released to the external environment (Munehara et al. 1989, 1991; see also Muñoz herein). An unusual plasticity in fertilization mode exists in this family, with species having both types of fertilization: the typical external fertilization and internal gametic association (Munehara 1988; Petersen et al. 2005). In *Alcichthys alcicornis*, a species with internal gametic association (Munehara et al. 1989), males copulate after females lay eggs. This behavior implies that the first egg batch of the season must be fertilized externally by sperm leaking from the females during and after copulation (Munehara 1988). In two other species, *Artedius fenestralis* and *A. lateralis*, although the most common fertilization mode is external, in some cases experimentally extruded clutches of eggs developed into embryos without the external addition of sperm (Petersen et al. 2005), implying internal insemination. While in species with internal gametic association the urogenital papilla is usually modified into a copulatory organ (Morris 1952, 1956; Ragland & Fisher 1987), in the two *Artedius* species mentioned above the urogenital papillae are quite small (Petersen et al. 2005). Although it has not been investigated how sperm are transferred to females in these two species, the possibility to have internal insemination without an obvious copulatory organ has been clearly found in the sculpins *Blepsias cirrhosus* (Munehara et al. 1991) and *Hemitripterus villosus* (Munehara 1996). In this last species, it has been observed that females actually evert the genital duct, producing a jellylike material in which sperm become embedded and which is then drawn back into the female reproductive tract (Munehara 1996).

While fertilization success has not been well investigated in internal fertilizers, it appears to be quite high, and some data exist suggesting long sperm lifetime within female genital tracts. In the cottid *Clinocottus analis*, females may store sperm for two months at least (Hubbs 1966), while in another scorpaeniform species, *Helicolenus dactylopterus dactylopterus*, sperm may be retained for 10 months; after that they are activated by a change in pH, from acid to basic, of the surrounding ovarian fluid (Munõz et al. 2002). In this last species, sperm are stored in crypts in the ovarian lumen that secrete polysaccharides that may provide nutrients for sperm (Munõz et al. 2002).

Postcopulatory sexual selection, consisting of sperm competition (Parker 1970, 1998) and/or cryptic female choice, occurring when female bias sperm use in favor of a certain male (Eberhard 1996), may occur in species with either internal fertilization or internal gametic association. In addition, copulations may be cooperative or coercive, as in the case of the well-studied poeciliids, a family of freshwater fish with internal fertilization and different degrees of coercive, sneaky copulations with respect to cooperative copulations (Constantz 1989; Houde 1997). In cooperative copulations of the guppy *Poecilia reticulata*, males may transfer larger amounts of sperm than during sneaky copulations (Pilastro & Bisazza 1999), suggesting that females may control the number of transferred sperm in at least some spawns and consequently exert cryptic mate choice (Pilastro et al. 2004). However, in several other poeciliid species, a mating advantage has been either shown or implied for small males in sneaky copulations (Bisazza & Pilastro 1997; Pilastro et al. 1997). The complex picture emerging from the well-studied poeciliids suggests that several aspects of postcopulatory sexual selection in marine internal fertilizers deserve greater attention.

EVOLUTION OF MALE EJACULATES

The male ejaculate includes sperm and seminal fluid. At both the interspecific and intraspecific levels, males may differ in total sperm production, sperm concentration, and sperm traits. Sperm traits analyzed in the light of their role in fertilization include morphology, in particular size, velocity, motility and longevity (lifespan), and adenosine triphosphate (ATP) content (reviewed by Snook 2005). Most of the work on variation in seminal fluid and sperm characteristics in fishes has been done on freshwater or anadromous (i.e., marine species that migrate to freshwater to spawn) fishes. Here we give an overview of data on sperm production, male ejaculates, and sperm characteristics in marine fishes, also including some examples from freshwater species when appropriate, with an emphasis on the role of life-history tradeoffs in shaping the high degree of variation in male ejaculates in fishes.

Sperm Production and Sperm Competition

In terms of sperm number and concentration, Stockley et al. (1997), Petersen and Warner (1998), and Taborsky (1998) reviewed male gonadal investment in fishes and found a strong, positive interspecific correlation between the degree of relative testis size, the standing crop of sperm, the volume of seminal fluid, and the estimated degree of sperm competition based on behavioral studies. Many authors have also shown that within species with multiple male mating tactics, males that experience higher levels of sperm competition have higher male allocation as measured by the GSI (e.g., Petersen & Warner 1998). To cope with the high level of sperm competition, males adopting alternative male mating tactics release larger amounts of sperm than do conspecifics that are exposed to lower levels of sperm competition, as predicted by theoretical models (Parker 1990), and this may be achieved by producing ejaculates of larger volumes or with more concentrated sperm.

In species with multiple male mating tactics, large territorial males often spend more time aggressively defending females or mating sites from potential competitors, and have reduced sperm output compared with non-territorial conspecifics. Sperm limitation appears to be more extreme in spawns of these pair-spawning, territorial males (e.g., Marconato et al. 1997), but females do not discriminate against them in favor of group spawns in species like bluehead wrasse. Even when supplemented with food, bluehead wrasse territorial males increase mating success, not fertilization success, apparently by devoting more time to male-male aggression and territorial defense (Warner et al. 1995). Similarly, when spawning in the presence of sneakers in the laboratory, neither territorial grass gobies nor black gobies (*Gobius niger*) increase their sperm release levels, but instead respond with increased aggression towards potential sperm competitors (Scaggiante et al. 2005). However, sneakers in both goby species do respond to differences in perceived sperm competition by changing the amount of sperm they release in a spawn. As the number of sneakers increases they first increase, then decrease the amount of sperm released per spawn (Pilastro et al. 2002), in agreement with the theoretical models for changes in sperm allocation with changes in the intensity of sperm competition (Parker et al. 1996).

In species not subjected to sperm competition and in which few sperm are needed to fertilize eggs, economy in sperm production may be obtained through a low rate of sperm maturation. In semi-cystic spermatogenesis, cysts open in the lumen of the testicular lobules before the completion of sperm maturation, releasing spermatids that complete their maturation along the reproductive duct system (Lahnsteiner et al. 1990; Manni & Rasotto 1997). This form of spermatogenesis causes an asynchronous maturation of the spermatids and, consequently, a low number of sperm are simultaneously mature. Semi-cystic spermatogenesis has been observed in species with demersal eggs having either a monogamous mating system (Rasotto et al. 1992; Marconato & Rasotto 1993; Mazzoldi 2001; Fishelson et al. 2006), or an enclosed nest with low numbers of eggs (Giacomello et al. 2008).

Sperm Production versus Production of Other Seminal Substances

The significance of sperm concentration in the seminal fluid of fishes is not well understood. It is not clear what the benefits are for having sperm concentrated in seminal fluid versus releasing a larger seminal volume to get the same number of sperm released. Interestingly, there is an emerging intraspecific pattern among teleosts of higher sperm concentration in the ejaculate of individuals that have higher sperm numbers. In three species, bluehead wrasse (Schärer & Robertson, 1999) and both black and grass gobies (Mazzoldi et al. 2000; Rasotto & Mazzoldi 2002), males that engage in chronic sperm competition had higher sperm concentrations in their ejaculates compared to males who experienced low levels of sperm competition. Schärer & Robertson (1999) proposed three nonexclusive hypotheses to explain this pattern: (1) that more concentrated sperm in individuals experiencing more intense sperm competition allows for the release of more sperm, faster; (2) milt may have different optimal characteristics (e.g., sperm concentration, viscosity) in pair versus group spawns; or (3) that by having more dilute sperm, males that release small amounts of sperm can have better control of the total amount of sperm released in a spawn. To date there have been no tests done to distinguish among these hypotheses in any fish species with this pattern.

Seminal fluid may include ions, proteins, polysaccharides, and other organic molecules. Seminal fluid may play a key role in shaping sperm performance, in particular prolonging sperm viability, and reducing sperm dispersal, as described in gobies (Marconato et al. 1996; Scaggiante et al. 1999), or in the rainbow trout, *Oncorynchus mykiss* (Lahnsteiner et al. 2004). In species with alternative mating tactics and accessory structures involved in seminal fluid production, intraspecific variability in their development has been found between territorial/parental males and sneaker males. In the studied species, parental males have well developed accessory structures while males that engage in alternative reproductive tactics (sneaking, streaking) have extremely reduced accessory structures (de Jonge et al. 1989; Ruchon et al. 1995; Scaggiante et al. 1999; Barni et al. 2001; Neat 2001; Rasotto & Mazzoldi 2002; Neat et al. 2003) and these males produce reduced amounts of mucins in their seminal fluid. For species that produce sperm trails, parental males produce trails that last for hours and slowly release sperm, while sneakers have trails that dissolve faster in seawater resulting in the release of a large amount of sperm that are immediately active (Scaggiante et al. 1999; Mazzoldi et al. 2000; Rasotto & Mazzoldi 2002). In the one study that performed a comparative analysis of these structures in gobies, however, the development of accessory structures in territorial males was positively correlated with the occurrence of polygynous mating systems, but not to the degree of sperm competition (Mazzoldi et al. 2005). The low number of species included in this latter study does not definitely rule out the possible additional influence of sperm competition, or of other factors, in the development of accessory structures.

Allocating energy away from sperm production and into the production of mucins may be differentially beneficial for territorial males in two ways. First, by allowing for a more constant release of sperm from a slowly dissolving sperm trail, males may be able to fertilize eggs with a lower total sperm production. Second, males may be freed to defend oviposition sites from potential sperm competitors while females are spawning, while still having sperm release taking place at the oviposition site from the sperm trail. For non-territorial males, the ubiquity of sperm competition probably puts a premium on sperm production, and the same accessory structures are reduced and/or used as sperm-storage organs (Scaggiante et al. 1999; Rasotto & Mazzoldi 2002).

In addition to differences in seminal fluid, the ejaculates of internal fertilizers can differ in how sperm are organized in the seminal fluid. In the transfer of sperm from male to female genital tracts sperm can be free in the seminal fluid or organized in encapsulated (spermatophores) or unencapsulated (spermatozeugmata) bundles (Grier 1981). The formation of sperm packets is hypothesized to improve sperm transfer to female genital tracts (Ginzburg 1968). Within bundles, sperm are specifically oriented with heads facing in the same direction, or either arranged around the periphery or the center of the bundle (Grier et al. 1978). Unpacked sperm have been observed in species, such as *Anableps anableps* (Anablepidae), which have a tubular gonopodium that can ensure an efficient transfer of sperm, even if they are not aggregated in bundles (Grier et al. 1981). This seminal fluid may also interact with the female genital tract and/or ejaculates from other males, opening the possibility for the rise of sexual conflict (Simmons 2001; Snook 2005).

The simple structure of the testis in most teleost species with pelagic eggs suggests that these species do not have as complex a seminal fluid as many species with demersal eggs.

Sperm Characteristics

Sperm morphology in fishes has been exhaustively reviewed in two very good books by Jamieson (1991, 2009). At the interspecific level, sperm morphology has been shown to be correlated with the mode of fertilization, with internal fertilizers having sperm with more elaborate, elongate heads (introsperm) than sperm from species with external fertilization that tend to have morphologically simple anacromsomal "aquasperm" (Jamieson 1991; Stockley et al. 1997). In some species, such as cardinalfish, batrachoids, and gobiesocids, sperm may be biflagellate; however the functional role of the presence of two flagella is not clear (Mattei 1988).

One prediction that follows from the level of gametic competition among males is that as the intensity of sperm competition increases in external fertilizers, there should be selection on sperm to increase speed, even if this incurs a cost in sperm longevity (Snook 2005). This idea is supported by studies such as those by Gage et al. (2004) in *Salmo salar* that show that the velocity of a male's sperm is the best predictor of his fertilization success in artificial, competitive spawnings. This has led several authors to look for a positive correlation between sperm competition intensity and sperm size, assuming that larger sperm will be faster swimmers, which appears to be the case in mammals (Gomendio & Roldan 1991). Although a review suggested that the relationship between sperm size and longevity or sperm swimming speed is not common in fishes (Snook 2005), a more recent paper found a strong interspecific relationship between sperm size and speed in a group of freshwater fishes (Fitzgerald et al. 2009). At the interspecific level, two studies have had opposite results, with sperm size negatively related with sperm competition intensity in a broad review of fishes (Stockley et al. 1997), and a positive relationship found among Lake Tanganyika cichlids (Fitzgerald et al. 2009).

At the intraspecific level, in most cases no differences in sperm size have been observed between males facing different levels of sperm competition (Gage et al. 1995; Schärer & Robertson 1999; Locatello et al. 2007), while in the freshwater sunfish *Lepomis macrochirus*, sneaker males had sperm with longer tails compared to sperm from males that defended nest sites (Burness et al. 2004).

Lifespan (the period of viability) of sperm released into saltwater appears to range from well under a minute in bluehead wrasse (Petersen et al. 1992) to days in herring (Ginzburg 1968). Some of this difference is probably due to the very different water temperatures experienced by marine species, with species in colder water having the greater potential for long-lived sperm.

The close juxtaposition of males and females during spawning and the synchrony of gamete release in most species should translate into a quickly diminishing probability for an individual sperm to fertilize an egg. As time from spawning increases, the number of eggs not fertilized from a spawn will decrease, and in a pelagically spawning species, the density of eggs will decrease as well. Given this, we might expect that sperm from species from demersal eggs will have higher longevity than sperm from pelagic species. Indeed, in some demersal spawners with an enclosed nest, prolonged egg deposition, and eggs that remain fertilizable for several hours, long sperm longevity has been recorded. For example, in the grass goby, *Zosterisessor ophiocephalus*, sperm released from trails can last for an average of 80 minutes (Scaggiante et al. 1999). In contrast, Petersen et al. (1992) found that artificial fertilization in the pelagic spawner *T. bifasciatum* was greatly reduced after sperm had spent just 15 seconds in seawater. In some species with pelagic eggs, like cod, sperm are relatively long lived and still have substantial fertilizing ability after one hour (Trippel & Morgan 1994). Species with pelagic eggs and spawning over an extended time in a restricted space may undergo selection for increased sperm longevity. This may help explain the long lifespan of sperm in species like herring, where spawning can occur over an extended time in an area. If fertilization is not simultaneous and immediate for all the eggs, sperm longevity can play an important role in the outcome of sperm competition (Ball & Parker 1996; Snook 2005).

In two species with alternative mating tactics, the grass goby, *Z. ophiocephalus*, and the black goby, *Gobius niger*, grass goby males performing different mating tactics did not differ in any of the studied sperm traits, while in the black goby, sneakers had faster sperm with higher viability and with more ATP content than territorial males (Locatello et al. 2007). These differences were not correlated with sperm size. Such differences between the two species may be due to the differences in nest type and sneaker behavior between the two species (Locatello et al. 2007). In the grass goby, the nest is an enclosed chamber where sneakers may hide and remain for extended periods (Mazzoldi et al. 2000), while in black gobies, the nest is more open, and sneakers are only able to enter for short time before being chased away (Mazzoldi & Rasotto 2002). In the grass goby, territorial males are exposed to prolonged sperm competition and may be forced to maintain as high a quality of sperm as sneakers in order to cope with the high level of sperm competition (Locatello et al. 2007). Differences in sperm quality, with sneakers having longer-lived sperm than guarding males, have also been found in the corkwing wrasse, *Symphodus melops*, another nesting species (Uglem et al. 2001), and in *Salmo salar* (Gage et al. 1995). In the freshwater species *Lepomis macrochirus*, however, sperm viability seems to trade off against speed, and sneakers have a higher proportion of motile sperm after activation, with faster initial swimming speeds but shorter longevity than parental males (Burness et al. 2004). In this species, it has been demonstrated that these differences imply a differential success in fertilization, with parental males having higher fertilization success late in the sperm activation cycle (Schulte-Hostedde & Burness 2005).

The presumed trade-off between sperm speed and longevity assumes a fixed investment per sperm, but at the level of the adult, allocation decisions may often involve tradeoffs between either quality versus number of sperm or investment in sperm production versus other allocations that could increase reproductive success. Thus, we may often find that there is either no correlation or a positive correlation among measures of sperm performance as might be expected when individual sperm differ in their initial energetic investment (Locatello et al. 2007). The most recent studies also suggest that measures of energetic investment in sperm such as ATP content may be a better metric of investment than morphological characteristics such as sperm size.

In another variation of sperm morphology and performance, in some species individual males produce two types of sperm, some of which are functionally able to fertilize (eusperm) and some that are morphologically different and cannot fertilize eggs (parasperm). These eusperm and parasperm have been observed in the sculpin *Hemilepidus gilberti*, an external fertilizer (Hayakawa et al. 2002b). In this species it has been demonstrated that parasperm may play two roles: they can reduce lateral dispersion of the ejaculate, increasing the distance that eusperm may travel (Hayakawa et al. 2002a); and they aggregate in lumps that might constitute a barrier for later arriving eusperm, such as those of sneaker males, thereby reducing the possibility of sperm competition (Hayakawa et al. 2002b).

A final consideration involves the role of ovarian fluid in fertilization. Besides cottid species, ovarian fluid has been demonstrated to influence sperm characteristics in terms of sperm longevity and velocity in species such as *Salmo trutta f. fario* (Lahnsteiner 2002), *Salvelinus alpinus* (Turner & Montgomerie 2002), *Gasterosteus aculeatus* (Elofsson et al. 2003), and *Gadus morhua* (Litvak & Trippel 1998). In *S. alpinus,* ovarian fluid from different females has differential effects on sperm, with ovarian fluid from some females enhancing sperm speed more than that of others. Even more interesting, sperm velocity was also found to vary depending on the individual male-female pair. This result opens the possibility, in species with sperm competition, for the occurrence of cryptic female choice, even in external fertilizers (Urbach et al. 2005).

HOW FERTILIZATION ECOLOGY INFORMS CONSERVATION BIOLOGY

Until very recently, fertilization success was not an explicit part of fisheries models, with the implicit assumption being that fertilization success was complete, or at least a constant, for a species. Among some commercially important species, the recent crashes of populations with very little subsequent recovery, and the documentation of populations with very low proportions of males, has heightened concerns about sperm limitation in exploited species and has led several authors to explicitly include fertilization success in their modeling of the population biology of exploited species. Two cases where the discussion of fertilization has been an explicit part of the conservation biology dialogue have been in Atlantic cod and in sex-changing fishes such as grouper. Both of these groups of fishes suffer from very high levels of exploitation, and both bring unique concerns for the effects of sperm limitation on population dynamics. Each of these two cases is reviewed in detail below.

Atlantic Cod (Gadus morhua)

In temperate marine fishes, the largest amount of work on fertilization ecology and reproductive behavior has been done by researchers on Atlantic cod (*Gadus morhua*). Atlantic cod, particularly off the Atlantic coast of Canada, have been severely depleted (Hutchings & Myers 1994; Myers et al. 1997), leading to severe restrictions of some fisheries in the Gulf of Maine, to complete closures of some fisheries in Atlantic Canada. The slow recovery of these species has led some to hypothesize that the decimation of these populations has led to an Allee effect or depensation, where populations at low densities suffer lower per capita growth rates, and that some of the failure of populations to rebound is caused by reduced fertilization due to reduced male numbers (Rowe and Hutchings 2003; Rowe et al. 2004). Although an interesting suggestion, the authors have made it clear that this is an untested hypothesis, with no empirical data to directly support depensation (Rowe & Hutchings 2003; Hutchings & Reynolds 2004).

Populations of cod have prolonged spawning periods of 6 to 12 weeks (Myers et al. 1993). Spawning in at least some populations has occurred at historically consistent locations, making these spawning aggregations vulnerable to overfishing (Ames 2004). Individuals appear to migrate to spawning sites where large numbers of males and females mate for several weeks (Hutchings et al. 1993; Morgan & Trippel 1996). Spawning occurs over the continental shelf, slightly off the bottom in 50 to 200m of water, where females tend to be found closer to the bottom than males. During the reproductive season, individual trawls typically have sex-biased catches, with a male-bias when individuals of both sexes are most reproductively active (Morgan & Trippel 1996). From these and other field collections, investigators have hypothesized that males form large spawning aggregations, while females visit these aggregations, spawn, and then return to their feeding grounds that in Canada appear to be in deeper and warmer water (Morgan & Trippel 1996).

Spawning in *G. morhua* has never been observed in the field. Despite this handicap, combining the field data with observations of spawning individuals in large tanks, several researchers have built a reasonable if slightly speculative scenario concerning spawning and fertilization ecology of *G. morhua* in the western Atlantic.

Descriptions of spawning from large tanks report very stereotyped pair-spawning behavior of individuals, where a male positions himself directly under a female and the two individuals swim slowly together while releasing gametes (Brawn 1961; Hutchings et al. 1999). However, Hutchings et al. (1999) did report satellite males joining in three spawning events in a large tank containing multiple males and females. Within observation tanks, males have been observed to act aggressively towards one other, and there appeared to be some size-assortative pairing in spawning partners (Bekkevold et al. 2002).

During the reproductive season, male Atlantic cod have relatively large testes (typically around 7% of their total body weight) that are similar in relative size to ovaries of females, implying a mating system with significant amounts of sperm competition (Cyr et al. 1998; Schwalme & Chouinard 1999; Rowe pers. comm.). Fertilization has been studied in a laboratory setting, and paternity of offspring in spawns has been determined using microsatellites as variable genetic markers. In artificial fertilizations, male size does not influence fertilization success (Rakitin et al. 1999). Fertilization in spawns in captivity averaged 91.5% in the one study where it was explicitly reported (Bekkevold et al. 2002), but fertilization was typically above 90% in spawns and only rarely below 80% in any of the reported spawns (see Figures 1 through 3 in Rowe et al. 2004). Based on genetic markers and using groups of eggs from a single female as a proxy for spawning, fertilization success increased when paternity increased from one to two males, but then appeared to level off for cases where more than two males successfully fertilized some of the eggs (Rakitin et al. 2001; Bekkevold et al. 2002; Rowe et al. 2004). In addition, in one of three studies the variance in fertilization success decreased with an increasing number of males in a spawning event. Thus, there may be a fertilization success increase with multiple males in spawns, although the increase appears to be less than 10% for eggs fertilized (Rowe et al. 2004). The arguments from several authors that there is an advantage in terms of genetic diversity to having multiple males in a spawn (cf. Rowe et al. 2004) appears to be minimized by the observation that these fish spawn multiple times in a season, almost undoubtedly with different partners.

In a more recent study, Rowe et al. (2007) showed that in large contained systems, mating success was positively correlated with partner size for both sexes by using genetic microsatellite markers to estimate the relative proportion of offspring produced by individuals in the tank. It was not clear if the increase in success for larger males was due to their higher fertilizing ability of clutches, or due to females releasing more eggs, or spawning more often, when paired with larger males.

Using these observations of fish in captivity to inform how fertilization success might change with increasing exploitation in this species is highly speculative. It is not clear at what point increasing the take of males either leads to sperm limitation directly, by limiting total sperm production in the population, or indirectly, by disturbing the social system in the field, or both. Although lab study results combined with population data in other species have shown the potential for substantial reductions in population growth rate due to decreases in fertilization success with fewer milt donors (Purchase et al. 2007), the application of these results to natural populations is not easily made, and other results using data from bluehead wrasse suggest that this effect will not be very strong under many circumstances (Petersen & Levitan 2001; Petersen & Warner 2002).

Sex Change, Spawning Aggregations, and Fertilization Success

One very simple question in fisheries is whether sex-changing species are more vulnerable to exploitation than gonochorisitc (separate-sexed) species. This is really a comparison of three different types of populations: protogynous (female-first) hermaphrodites, protandrous (male-first) hermaphrodites, and gonochoristic populations. Simultaneous hermaphroditism is rare in fishes and does not occur in any widely exploited fish species. The answer to this question depends on how we estimate the dynamics of fertilization and sex change within species.

Fisheries tend to differentially take larger, older individuals. The effects of fishing on egg production will be most strongly felt in protandrous species, followed by gonochores, followed by protogynous species. Thus, in the absence of any sperm limitation or behavioral disruption of spawning by a fishery, we would expect populations of protandrous species to be most affected by depletion due to overfishing.

Several authors have pointed out that any effect of differentially taking one sex in a fishery will be diluted by the rate at which individuals of the less-exploited sex change (Alonso & Mangel 2005; Molloy et al. 2007). Social control of sex change is known for many species of smaller reef fish (e.g., Robertson 1972; Shapiro 1980) and can occur in approximately two weeks in many of the species studied. In larger, exploited species, especially those that migrate to spawning aggregations and having limited spawning periods during the year, we expect that this compensation will be much slower. In groupers, limited evidence suggests that individuals change sex between spawning seasons (McGovern et al. 1998) or show little predictable temporal pattern for sex change with respect to spawning aggregation time (Shapiro 1987), so that any short-term changes in sex ratio on the spawning grounds would not be compensated for by immediate sex change. In addition, given that sex change may take several weeks, it might be disadvantageous for individuals to change sex in the middle of a short, intensive spawning season, with the cost of sex change including missing most of the reproductive season for a year. However, sex ratios or absolute numbers of males at spawning aggregations might influence the probability of sex change for the next season, which would increase the number of spawning males compared to a model of fixed size or age at sex change.

Using traditional population biology models, population growth is typically viewed as an exercise in modeling female growth, fecundity, and mortality in the absence of any paternal care (e.g., Wilson & Bossert 1971). If decreased male density or population size does not reduce the number or quality of successfully fertilized eggs, then any scenario that focuses fishing mortality on males will have less of an effect on population growth than scenarios where mortality is independent of sex or female-biased.

One concern about exploitation and fertilization success has been that in protogynous hermaphrodites, removal of the larger, older, and relatively rarer males will cause catastrophic reductions in fertilization success, so that protogynous species will be more vulnerable to exploitation and Allee effects (Smith 1982, as cited in Punt et al. 1993; Shapiro 1987; Petersen & Warner 2002; Alonso & Mangel 2004). In models where fertilization dynamics have been included, the impact on production of fertilized eggs for protogynous populations relative to gonochoristic populations depends on the relative intensity of fishing on males, the plasticity of sex change in the population, and on how fertilization is modeled with regard to either relative or absolute male numbers.

The most straightforward way to model fishing intensity would be to model effect of fishing mortality, *F*, on population structure and then apply a fertilization model to the population (Côté 2003). The effect on the male population will be particularly intense if fishing includes all size classes that include males (Alonso & Mangel 2004). Any model will be complicated by the size-selective nature of most fisheries, and will be sensitive to whether or not *F* should be a constant or size-class specific.

Modeling fertilization dynamics in exploited species to date has been a theoretical exercise. Several models use a relatively unrealistic assumption that fertilization success of eggs will be proportional either to the absolute or relative number of males (Bannerot et al. 1987; Huntsman & Schaaf 1994; Armsworth 2001; Côté 2003). More recent models have attempted to incorporate the asymptotic nature of the fertilization curve (Figure 7.1A)(Alonso & Mangel 2004; Heppel et al. 2006 for protogynous species; Molloy et al. 2007 for protandrous species). These latter models, although more realistic, still relate fertilization to total sperm production of the males in the population, not the amount of sperm released in a spawning event, and so miss most of the richness of the reproductive behavior in species in attempting to estimate the effects of sperm limitation on total fertilized egg production in populations. Some authors have picked two very different ways to model fertilization, hoping that their range of outcomes might include the true fertilization dynamics (Côté 2003; Heppel et al. 2006). All of the models to date show that under certain model parameters, sperm limitation can be a major factor influencing population recruitment and growth. However, until we can actually get accurate estimates of these fertilization parameters from the field, these results will be speculative.

In large species that have limited spawning times and migrate distances to spawn in large aggregations, the lack of some threshold number of males at a spawning site may cause females to abandon the site and search for a more populated locale to spawn. This problem is potentially more important than fertilization failure in these exploited species.

In protandrous (male-first) sequential hermaphrodites, several authors have concluded that populations run the risk of strong egg limitation when larger females are disproportionately taken in the fishery (Milton et al. 1998; Molloy et al. 2007). Sex change without quick replacement of taken females by smaller males leads to the largest declines in egg production in the population (Molloy et al. 2007), since female fecundity is directly correlated with body size. In protandrous species, fertilization success may decrease when populations are exploited, but the direct effects of exploitation on decreasing egg production are much stronger in limiting productivity of young in a population.

One problem with attempting to apply work on fertilization biology of fishes in the wild to conservation biology is that most conservation biology is focused on large, exploited species, while fertilization work has been focused on smaller, more tractable species that can be studied more easily (Vincent & Sadovy 1998). Generally, we can only guess how the results from these small species informs conservation biology of larger species.

The current evidence suggests that as the number or ratio of males in a local population decreases, sperm limitation will become more likely for the population, and to some extent it will compromise the embryo production of the population. Exploitation that reduces population size will have other potential negative impacts on populations tied to reproduction, such as the loss of traditional spawning sites. Until we know the real effect of these practices on fertilization success and successful recruitment, it is clearly in our best interest to take a precautionary approach to this problem and try to protect these populations both at spawning aggregations and at other places where impacts on population growth have the potential to severely deplete populations.

FERTILIZATION ECOLOGY IN FISHES AND MARINE INVERTEBRATES: IS THERE A DICHOTOMY?

There is currently substantial debate in the marine invertebrate literature on the importance of sperm limitation on the population dynamics and evolution of gametic and adult traits. Sedentary benthic marine invertebrates, ranging from attached species like corals, to slow moving species like sea urchins that have separate sexes and external fertilization, have the potential to be severely sperm limited, especially at low densities (e.g., Pennington 1985; Levitan & Petersen 1995). Alternatively, the limited data on externally fertilizing marine fishes suggests that sperm limitation makes a real but relatively small contribution to components of fitness in marine fishes (Levitan & Petersen 1995; Petersen & Warner 2002), probably due to the tight temporal and spatial synchrony of ova and sperm release (Petersen et al. 1992, 2001; Warner et al. 1995; Yund 2000).

One emerging view is that most animal taxa show evidence of sperm limitation in their evolutionary history, and that they have adaptations to reduce sperm limitation, including spawning synchronization and selection on gamete characteristics (Yund 2000). Invertebrate eggs have one additional problem that does not appear to be a major problem in bony fishes: polyspermy. At very high sperm concentrations, the percentage of eggs that successfully develop can actually decrease, due to developmental problems that result from polyspermy (Franke et al. 2002; Levitan et al. 2007). Thus in some invertebrate species, the probability of polyspermy in nature might be a stronger selective force for less permeable or fertilizable eggs compared to the selective force for ease of fertilization caused by sperm limitation.

Polyspermy does not appear to be a problem in the vast majority of bony fishes that have a single micropylar canal (Ginzburg 1968). This absence of polyspermy should push selection more towards ease of fertilization of fish eggs. This, along with behavioral synchrony of gamete release in time and space, should allow for high fertilization rates under most circumstances although there still may be predictable variation in fertilization in the wild that could be an evolutionary selective force.

Fertilization ecology and the potential for sperm limitation do appear to have different relative intensities between marine invertebrates and fishes, with sperm limitation more likely to be of greater concern in marine invertebrates. However, there will be variation in sperm limitation among species in both groups, and there is probably overlap in the levels of sperm limitation among these two groups, with some marine invertebrates having less sperm limitation than some fishes.

CONCLUSIONS: WHAT IS MISSING?

A large amount of research is being currently done on several aspects of fertilization, including the potential effects of limited fertilization in exploited species, methods to achieve high fertilization in aquaculture, and the evolution of gametic traits. In concluding, we would like to mention several areas that we believe are both currently understudied and would reward new research.

Measurements of Fertilization in Exploited Species

It is striking that despite extensive theoretical work by several research groups, there are no *in situ* measurements of fertilization success in the field for exploited species, especially for exploited tropical reef fishes such as snappers and groupers which are both currently overexploited, and have predictable spawning times and locations so that collecting eggs immediately post-spawning is possible.

Fertilization Dynamics in Group Spawners

Despite the growth of DNA fingerprinting techniques such as the use of hyper-variable microsatellite loci to determine paternity in freshwater fish, with the exception of Syngnathids (seahorses and pipefish)(reviewed in Avise et al. 2002) there has been very little work done on distribution of paternity in spawns of marine fishes, and no work that we are aware of for group spawners. By tagging females and taking small fin clips at the same time, females can be genotyped, and it would be possible to determine the distribution of paternity in that female's spawn in a group-spawning situation. Microsatellites have been isolated for *T. bifasciatum* (Wooninck et al. 1998) but have not been applied to this question. Currently, we do not know the distribution of reproductive success among males, or even the number of males that actually contribute paternity to an individual spawn in any group-spawning species. Such information would help us to better understand both the degree of sperm competition and behavioral tactics within group-spawning species. For example, although Shapiro et al. (1994) report the amount of sperm released in groups spawns of the bluehead wrasse, it is unknown how many males released this sperm.

Male Reproductive Apparatus and Fertilization Dynamics

Species belonging to several different families have modifications of the male reproductive apparatus. Such modifications can be in the form of accessory structures such as sperm duct glands, seminal vesicles or blind pouches, as in Gobiidae (Miller 1984; Fishelson 1991), Blennioidea (Rasotto 1995; Richtarski & Patzner 2000), or Batrachoididae (Barni et al. 2001). They can also be in the form of specializations of different parts of the sperm transport system for sperm storage and secretion of components of the seminal fluid, as, for example, in Blenniidae (Lahnsteiner & Patzner 1990), Cottidae (Petersen et al. 2005), or Batrachoididae (Barni et al. 2001); maturation of sperm, as in Blennioidea (Rasotto 1995; Richtarski & Patzner 2000; Giacomello et al. 2008); or the packaging of sperm in internal fertilizers, as in the Scorpaenidae (Muñoz et al. 2002) or several freshwater species (Grier et al. 1978; Burns et al. 1995). In addition, modifications related to reproduction have been observed in the male urinary system (Haemulidae: Rasotto & Sadovy 1995). The components secreted by the different parts of the male reproductive apparatus play an important role in fertilization dynamics as well as in sperm competition mechanisms, as highlighted in gobies and blennies (Scaggiante et al. 1999; Mazzoldi et al. 2005; Giacomello et al. 2008). An extended investigation of the different families having some modification of the male reproductive apparatus in the context of the relationship between morphology and fertilization dynamics and/ or sperm competition represents an interesting field of study.

In concluding, our understanding of fertilization in marine organisms has come a long way since the time when both field ecologists and theoretical population biologists assumed that fertilization was absolute and invariant in natural populations. We now have both theory that incorporates variable fertilization into population modeling, and direct measurements of fertilization *in situ* for a number of marine fishes. In order to determine if our theoretical work is adequate to describe the real world, we need to both expand our collection of data on fishes and collect data that will directly inform theory. This will not be easy, but it is clearly the next step if we are to use our increasing understanding to help manage and conserve marine fishes in both temperate and tropical oceans.

ACKNOWLEDGMENTS

S. Rowe and P. Molloy were very helpful in answering multiple questions about their work, R. Warner helped with his knowledge of how to best frame the interesting questions, and H. Hess and M. Rasotto reviewed the manuscript and provided many helpful comments that increased the clarity of the chapter. C.P. was partially supported by a grant from the David Rockefeller Foundation while working on this chapter.

REFERENCES

Ah-King M, Elofsson H, Kvarnemo C, Rosenqvist G, Berglund A (2006). Why is there no sperm competition in a pipefish with externally brooding males? Insights from sperm activation and morphology. Journal of Fish Biology 68: 958–962.

Alonso SH, Mangel M (2004). The effects of size-selective fisheries on the stock dynamics of and sperm limitation in sex-changing fish. Fishery Bulletin 102: 1–13.

Alonso SH, Mangel M (2005). Sex-change rules, stock dynamics, and the performance of spawning-per-recruit measures in protogynous stocks. Fishery Bulletin 103: 229–245.

Amanze D, Iyengar A (1990). The micropyle: a sperm guidance system in teleost fertilization. Development 109: 495–500.

Ames EP (2004). Atlantic cod stock structure in the Gulf of Maine. Fisheries 29: 10–28.

Armsworth PR (2001). Effects of fishing on a protogynous hermaphrodite. Canadian Journal of Fisheries and Aquatic Sciences 58: 568–578.

Avise JC, Jones AG, Walker D, DeWoody JA, collaborators (2002). Genetic mating systems and reproductive natural histories of fishes: lessons for ecology and evolution. Annual Review of Genetics 36: 19–45.

Ball MA, Parker GA (1996). Sperm competition games: external fertilization and "adaptive" infertility. Journal of Theoretical Biology 180: 141–150.

Bannerot SP, Fox WW Jr, Powers JE (1987). Reproductive strategies and the management of groupers and snappers in the Gulf of Mexico and the Caribbean. In: Polovina JJ, Ralston S (eds.), Tropical Snappers and Groupers: Biology and Fisheries Management. Westview Press, Boulder, Colorado, pp. 561–606.

Barni A, Mazzoldi C, Rasotto MB (2001). Reproductive apparatus and male accessory structures in two batrachoid species (Teleostei, Batrachoididae). Journal of Fish Biology 58: 1557–1569.

Baylis JR (1981). The evolution of parental care in fishes, with reference to Darwin's rule of male sexual selection. Environmental Biology of Fishes 6: 223–251.

Bekkevold D, Hansen MM, Loeschcke V (2002). Male reproductive competition in spawning aggregations of cod (Gadus morhua L.). Molecular Ecology 11: 91–102.

Bisazza A, Pilastro A (1997). Small male mating advantage and reversed size dimorphism in poeciliid fishes. Journal of Fish Biology 50: 397–406.

Blumer LS (1979). Male parental care in the bony fishes. Quarterly Review of Biology 54: 149–161.

Blumer LS (1982). A bibliography and categorization of bony fishes exhibiting parental care. Zoological Journal of the Linnean Society (London) 76: 1–22.

Brawn VM (1961). Reproductive behavior of the cod (Gadus callarias L.). Behaviour 18: 177–198.

Breder CM, Rosen DE (1966). Modes of Reproduction in Fishes. Natural History Press, Garden City, New York.

Burness G, Casselman SJ, Schulte-Hostedde AI, Moyes CD, Montgomerie R (2004). Sperm swimming speed and energetics vary with sperm competition risk in bluegill (*Lepomis macrochirus*). Behavioral Ecology and Sociobiology 56: 65–70.

Burns JR, Weitzman SH, Grier HJ, Menezes NA (1995). Internal fertilization, testis and sperm morphology in glandulocaudinae fishes (Teleostei: Characidae: Glandulocaudinae). Journal of Morphology 224: 131–145.

Clutton-Brock TH (1991). *The Evolution of Parental Care*. Princeton University Press, Princeton, New Jersey.

Colin PL (1983). Spawning and larval development of the hogfish, *Lachnolaimus maximus*. (Pisces: Labridae). Fishery Bulletin 80: 853–862.

Constantz GD (1989). Reproductive biology of poeciliid fishes. In: Meffe GK, Snelson FF (eds.), *Ecology and Evolution of Livebearing Fishes (Poeciliidae)*. Prentice Hall, Englewood Cliffs, New Jersey, pp. 33–50.

Cosson J, Groison A-L, Suquet M, Fauvel C, Dreanno C, Billard R (2008a). Marine fish spermatozoa: racing ephemeral swimmers. Reproduction 136: 277–294.

Cosson J, Groison A-L, Suquet M, Fauvel C, Dreanno C, Billard R (2008b). Studying sperm motility in marine fish: an overview on the state of the art. Journal of Applied Ichthyology 24: 460–486.

Côté IM (2003). Knowledge of reproductive behavior contributes to conservation programs. In: Festa-Bianchet M, Apollonio M (eds.), *Animal Behavior and Wildlife Conservation*. Island Press, Washington, DC, pp. 77–92.

Cyr DG, Idler DR, Audet C, McLeese JM, Eales JG (1998). Effects of long-term temperature acclimation on thyroid hormone deiodinase function, plasma thyroid hormone levels, growth, and reproductive status of male Atlantic Cod, *Gadus morhua*. General and Comparative Endocrinology 109: 24–36.

de Jonge J, Rutter AJH, Van den Hurk R (1989). Testis-testicular gland complex of two *Tripterygion* species (Blennioide, Teleostei): differences between territorial and nonterritorial males. Journal of Fish Biology 35: 497–508.

Eberhard WG (1996). *Female Control: Sexual Selection by Cryptic Female Choice*. Princeton University Press, Princeton, New Jersey.

Elofsson H, Mcallister BG, Kime DE, Mayer I, Borg B (2003). Long lasting stickleback sperm: is ovarian fluid a key to success in fresh water? Journal of Fish Biology 63: 240–253.

Fishelson L (1991). Comparative cytology and morphology of seminal vesicles in male gobiid fishes. Japanese Journal of Ichthyology 38: 17–30.

Fishelson L, Delarea Y, Gon O (2006). Testis structure, spermatogenesis, spermatocytogenesis, and sperm structure in cardinal fish (Apogonidae, Perciformes). Anatomy and Embryology 211: 31–46.

Fitzgerald JL, Montgomerie R, Desjardins JK, Stiver KA, Kolm N, Balshine S (2009). Female promiscuity promotes the evolution of faster sperm in cichlid fishes. Proceedings National Academy Sciences of the United States of America 106: 1128–1132.

Foster SJ, Vincent ACJ (2004). Life history and ecology of seahorses: implications for conservation and management. Journal of Fish Biology 65: 1–61

Franke ES, Babcock RS, Styan CA (2002). Sexual conflict and polyspermy under sperm-limited conditions: in situ evidence from field simulations with the free-spawning marine echinoid *Evechinus chlorotincus*. American Naturalist 160: 485–496.

Gage MJG, Stocley P, Parker GA (1995). Effects of alternative male mating strategies on characteristics of sperm production in the Atlantic salmon (*Salmo salar*). Philosophical Transactions: Biological Sciences 350: 391–399

Gage MJG, Macfarlane CP, Yeates S, Ward RG, Searle JB, Parker GA (2004). Spermatozoa traits and sperm competition in Atlantic salmon: relative sperm velocity is the primary determinant of fertilization success. Current Biology 14: 44–47.

Garnaud J (1950). La reproduction et l'incubation branchiale chez *Apogon imberbis* G. et L. Bulletin de l'Institut Océanographique, Monaco 977: 1–10.

Giacomello E, Rasotto MB (2005). Sexual dimorphism and male mating success in the tentacled blenny, *Parablennius tentacularis* (Teleostei: Blenniidae). Marine Biology 147: 1221–1228.

Giacomello E, Marchini D, Rasotto MB (2006). A male sexually dimorphic trait provides antimicrobials to eggs in blenny fish. Biology Letters 2: 330–333.

Giacomello E, Neat FC, Rasotto MB (2008). Mechanisms enabling sperm economy in blenniid fishes. Behavioral Ecology and Sociobiology 62: 671–680.

Ginzburg AS (1968). Fertilization in fishes and the problem of polyspermy. Translated from Russian by Israel Program for Scientific Translations, Jerusalem 1972.

Giulianini PG, Ota O, Marchesan M, Ferrero EA (2001). Can goby spermatozoa pass through the filament adhesion apparatus of laid eggs? Journal of Fish Biology 58: 1750–1752.

Gomendio M, Roldan ERS (1991). Sperm competition influences sperm size in mammals. Proceedings of the Royal Society of London B 243: 181–185.

Goodwin NB, Dulvy NK, Reynolds JD (2002). Life-history correlates of the evolution of live bearing in fishes. Philosophical Transactions: Biological Sciences 357: 259–267

Grier HJ (1981). Cellular organization of the testis and spermatogenesis in fishes. American Zoologist 21: 345–357.

Grier HJ, Fitzsimons JM, Linton JR (1978). Structure and ultrastructure of the testis and sperm formation in Goodeid teleosts. Journal of Morphology 156: 419–438.

Grier HJ, Burns JR, Flores JA (1981). Testis structure in three species of teleosts with tubular gonopodia. Copeia 1981: 797–801.

Gross, MR, Shine R (1981). Parental care and mode of fertilization in ectothermic vertebrates. Evolution 35: 775–793.

Hayakawa Y, Munehara H (1996). Non-copulatory spawning and female participation during early egg care in a marine sculpin *Hemilepidotus gilberti*. Ichthyological Research 43: 73–78.

Hayakawa Y, Munehara H (1998). Fertilization environment of the non-copulating marine sculpin, *Hemilepidotus gilberti*. Environmental Biology of Fishes 52: 181–186.

Hayakawa Y, Akiyama R, Munehara H, Komaru A (2002a). Dimorphic sperm influence semen distribution in a non-copulatory sculpin *Hemilepidotus gilberti*. Environmental Biology of Fishes 65: 311–317.

Hayakawa Y, Munehara H, Komaru A (2002b). Obstructive role of the dimorphic sperm in a non-copulatory marine sculpin, *Hemilepidotus gilberti*, to prevent other males' eusperm from fertilization. Environmental Biology of Fishes 64: 419–427.

Heppel SS, Heppel SA, Coleman FC, Koenig CC (2006). Models to compare management options for a protogynous fish. Ecological Applications 16: 238–249.

Hess HC (1993). Male mouthbrooding in jawfishes (Opistognathidae): constraints on polygyny. Bulletin of Marine Science 52: 806–818.

Houde AE (1997). *Sex, Color, and Mate Choice in Guppies*. Princeton University Press, Princeton, New Jersey.

Howell BR, Child AR, Houghton RG (1991). Fertilization rate in a natural population of the common sole, *Solea solea* (L.). ICES Journal of Marine Science 48: 53–59.

Hubbs C (1966). Fertilization, initiation of cleavage, and developmental temperature tolerance of the cottid fish, *Clinocottus analis*. Copeia 1966: 29–42.

Huntsman GR, Schaaf WE (1994). Simulation of the impact of fishing on reproduction of a protogynous grouper, the graysby. North American Journal Fisheries Management 14: 41–52.

Hutchings JA, Myers RA (1994). What can we learn from the collapse of a renewable resource? Atlantic cod, *Gadus morhua*, of Newfoundland and Labrador. Canadian Journal of Fisheries and Aquatic Sciences 51: 2126–2146.

Hutchings JA, Reynolds JD (2004). Marine fish population collapses: consequences for recovery and extinction risk. Bioscience 54: 297–309.

Hutchings JA, Myers RA, Lilly GR (1993). Geographic variation in the spawning of Atlantic cod, *Gadus morhua*, in the northwest Atlantic. Canadian Journal of Fisheries and Aquatic Sciences 50: 2457–2467.

Hutchings JA, Bishop TD, McGregor-Shaw CR (1999). Spawning behaviour of Atlantic cod, *Gadus morhua*: evidence of mate competition and mate choice in a broadcast spawner. Canadian Journal of Fisheries and Aquatic Sciences 56: 97–104.

Jamieson BGM (1991). *Fish Evolution and Systematics: Evidence from Spermatozoa*. Cambridge University Press, Cambridge and New York.

Jamieson BGM, ed. (2009). *Reproductive Biology and Phylogeny of Fishes (Agnathans and Bony Fishes): Phylogeny, Reproductive System, Viviparity, Spermatozoa*. Science Publishers, Enfield, New Hampshire.

Kiflawi M (2000). Adaptive gamete allocation when fertilization is external and sperm competition is absent: Optimization models and evaluation using coral reef fish. Evolutionary Ecology Research 2: 1045–1066.

Kiflawi M, Mazeroll AI, Goulet D (1998). Does mass spawning enhance fertilization in coral reef fish? A case study of the brown surgeonfish. Marine Ecology Progress Series 172: 107–114.

Kolm N, Berglund A (2004). Sex-specific territorial behaviour in the Banggai cardinalfish, *Pterapogon kauderni*. Environmental Biology of Fishes 70: 375–379

Kraak SBM (1996). A quantitative description of the reproductive biology of the Mediterranean blenny *Aidablennius sphynx* (Teleostei, Blenniidae) in its natural habitat. Environmental Biology of Fishes 46: 329–342.

Kuwamura T (1983). Spawning behavior and timing of fertilization in the mouthbrooding cardinalfish *Apogon notatus*. Japanese Journal of Ichthyology 30: 61–71.

Kuwamura T (1985). Social and reproductive behavior of three mouthbrooding cardinalfishes, *Apogon doederleini*, *A. niger*, and *A. notatus*. Environmental Biology of Fishes 13: 17–24.

Lahnsteiner F (2002). The influence of ovarian fluid on the gamete physiology in the Salmonidae. Fish Physiology and Biochemistry 27: 49–59.

Lahnsteiner F, Patzner R (1990). The spermatic duct of blenniid fish (Teleostei, Blenni-idae): fine structure, histochemistry and function. Zoomorphology 110: 63–73.

Lahnsteiner F, Richtarski U, Patzner RA (1990). Functions of the testicular gland in two blenniid fishes, *Salaria* (=*Blennius*) *pavo* and *Lipophrys* (=*Blennius*) *dalmatinus* (Blenni idae, Teleostei) as revealed by electron microscopy and enzyme histochemistry. Journal of Fish Biology 37: 85–97.

Lahnsteiner F, Mansour N, Berger B (2004). Seminal plasma proteins prolong the viability of rainbow trout (*Oncorynchus mykiss*) spermatozoa. Theriogenology 62: 801–808.

Levitan D, Petersen CW (1995). Sperm limitation in marine organisms. Trends in Ecology and Evolution 10: 228–231.

Levitan DR, Terhorst C.P, Fogarty ND (2007). The risk of polyspermy in three congeneric sea urchins and its implications for gametic incompatability and reproductive isolation. American Naturalist 61: 2007–2014.

Litvak MK, Trippel EA (1998). Sperm motility patterns of Atlantic cod (*Gadus morhua*) in relation to salinity: effects of ovarian fluid and egg presence. Canadian Journal of Fisheries and Aquatic Sciences 55: 1893–1898.

Locatello L, Pilastro A, Deana R, Zarpellon A, Rasotto MB (2007). Variation pattern of sperm quality traits in two gobies with alternative mating tactics. Functional Ecology 21: 975–981.

Manica A (2002). Filial cannibalism in teleost fish. Biological Review 77: 261–277.

Manni L, Rasotto MB (1997). Ultrastructure and histochemistry of the testicular efferent duct system and spermiogenesis in *Opistognathus whitehurstii* (Teleostei, Trachinoidei). Zoomorphology 117: 93–102.

Marconato A, Rasotto MB (1993). The reproductive biology of *Opistognathus whitehurstii* (Pisces, Opistognathidae). Biologia Marina Mediterranea, suppl. 1: 345–348.

Marconato A, Shapiro DY (1996). Sperm allocation, sperm production and fertilization rates in the bucktooth parrotfish. Animal Behaviour 52: 971–980.

Marconato A, Tessari V, Marin G (1995). The mating system of *Xyrichthys novacula*: sperm economy and fertilization success. Journal of Fish Biology 47: 292–301.

Marconato A, Rasotto MB, Mazzoldi C (1996). On the mechanism of sperm release in three gobiid fishes (Teleostei: Gobiidae). Environmental Biology of Fishes 46: 321–327.

Marconato A, Shapiro DY, Petersen CW, Warner RR, Yoshikawa T (1997). Methodological analysis of fertilization rate in the bluehead wrasse, *Thalassoma bifasciatum*: pair versus group spawns. Marine Ecology Progress Series 161: 61–70.

Markle DF, Waiwood KG (1985). Fertilization failure in gadids: aspects of its measurement. Journal of Northwest Atlantic Fishery Science 6: 87–93.

Mattei X (1988). The flagellar apparatus of spermatozoa in fish. Ultrastructure and evolution. Biology of the Cell 63: 151–158.

Mazzoldi C (2001). Reproductive apparatus and mating system in two tropical goby species (Teleostei, Gobiidae). Journal of Fish Biology 59: 1686–1691.

Mazzoldi C, Rasotto MB (2002). Alternative male mating tactics in *Gobius niger*. Journal of Fish Biology 61: 157–172.

Mazzoldi C, Scaggiante M, Ambrosin E, Rasotto MB (2000). Mating system and alternative male mating tactics in the grass goby, *Zosterisessor ophiocephalus* (Teleostei: Gobiidae). Marine Biology 137: 1041–1048.

Mazzoldi C, Poltronieri C, Rasotto MB (2002). Egg size variability and size-assortative mating in the marbled goby, *Pomatoschistus marmoratus* (Pisces, Gobiidae). Marine Ecology Progress Series 233: 231–239

Mazzoldi C, Petersen CW, Rasotto MB (2005). The influence of mating system on seminal vesicle variability among gobies (Teleostei: Gobiidae). Journal of Zoological Systematics and Evolutionary Research 43: 307–314.

Mazzoldi C, Randieri A, Mollica E, Rasotto MB (2008). Notes on the reproduction of the cardinalfish *Apogon imberbis* from Lachea Island, central Mediterranean, Sicily, Italy. Vie et Milieu 58: 63–66.

McGovern JC, Wyanski DM, Pashuk O, Manooch II CS, Seberry GR (1998). Changes in the sex ratio and size at maturity of gag, *Mycteroperca microlepis*, from the Atlantic coast of the southeastern United States during 1976–1995. Fisheries Bulletin 96: 797–807.

Miller PJ (1984). The tokology of gobioid fishes. In: Potts W, Wootton RJ (eds.), *Fish Reproduction: Strategies and Tactics*. Academic Press, London, pp. 119–153.

Milton DA, Die D, Tenakanai C, Swales S (1998). Selectivity for barramundi (*Lates calcarifer*) in the Fly River, Papua New Guinea: implications for managing gillnet fisheries on protandrous fishes. Marine and Freshwater Research 49: 499–506.

Molloy PP, Goodwin NB, Cote IM, Gage MJG, Reynolds JD (2007). Predicting the effects of exploitation on male-first sex-changing fish. Animal Conservation 10: 30–38.

Morgan MJ, Trippel EA (1996). Skewed sex ratios in spawning shoals of Atlantic cod (*Gadus morhua*). ICES Journal of Marine Science 53: 820–826.

Morris RW (1952). Spawning behavior of the cottid fish *Clinocottus recalvus* (Greeley). Pacific Science 6: 256–258

Morris RW (1956). Clasping mechanism of the cottid fish *Oligocottus synderi* Greeley. Pacific Science 10: 314–317.

Myers RA, Mertz G, Bishop CA (1993). Cod spawning in relation to physical and biological cycles of the northwest Atlantic. Fisheries Oceanography 2: 154–165.

Myers RA, Hutchings JA, Barrowman NJ (1997). Why do fish stocks collapse? The example of cod in Atlantic Canada. Ecological Applications 7: 91–106.

Munehara H (1988). Spawning and subsequent copulating behavior of the elkhorn sculpin *Alcichthys alcicornis* in an aquarium. Japanese Journal of Ichthyology 35: 358–364.

Munehara HK (1996). Sperm transfer during copulation in the marine sculpin *Hemitripterus villosus* (Pisces: Scorpaeniformes) by means of a retractable genital duct and ovarian secretion in females. Copeia 1996: 452–454.

Munehara H, Takano K, Koya Y (1989). Internal gamete association and external fertilization in the elkhorn sculpin, *Alcichthys alcicornis*. Copeia 1989: 673–678.

Munehara H, Takano K, Koya Y (1991). The little dragon sculpin *Blepsias cirrhosus*, another case of internal gamete association and external fertilization. Japanese Journal of Ichthyology 37: 391–394.

Munehara H, Koya Y, Hayakawa Y, Takano K (1997). Extracellular environments for the initiation of external fertilization and micropylar plug formation in a cottid species, *Hemitripterus villosus* (Pallas) (Scorpaeniformes) with internal insemination. Journal of Experimental Marine Biology and Ecology 211: 279–289

Munõz M, Koya Y, Casedevall M (2002). Histochemical analysis of sperm storage in *Helicolenus dactylopterus dactylopterus* (Teleostei: Scorpaenidae). Journal of Experimental Zoology 292: 156–164.

Nakatsuru K, Kramer DL (1982). Is sperm cheap? Limited male fertility and female choice in the lemon tetra (Pisces: Characidae). Science 216: 753–755.

Neat FC (2001). Male parasitic spawning in two species of the triplefin blenny (Tripterigiidae): contrasts in demography, behaviour and gonadal characteristics. Environmental Biology of Fishes 61: 57–64.

Neat FC, Locatello L, Rasotto MB (2003). Reproductive morphology in relation to alternative male reproductive tactics in *Scartella cristata*. Journal of Fish Biology 62: 1381–1391.

Okuda N (2001). The costs of reproduction to males and females of a paternal mouth-brooding cardinalfish *Apogon notatus*. Journal of Fish Biology 58: 776–787

Ota D, Marchesan M, Ferrero EA (1996). Sperm release behaviour and fertilization in the grass goby. Journal of Fish Biology 49: 246–256.

Parker GA (1970). Sperm competition and its evolutionary consequences in the insects. Biological Reviews 45: 525–567.

Parker GA (1990). Sperm competition games: raffles and roles. Proceedings of the Royal Society of London B 242: 120–126

Parker GA (1998). Sperm competition and the evolution of ejaculates: towards a theory base. In: Birkhead TR, Møller AP (eds.), *Sperm Competition and Sexual Selection*. Academic Press, London, pp. 3–54.

Parker GA, Ball MA, Stockley P, Gage MJG (1996). Sperm competition games: individual assessment of sperm competition intensity by group spawners. Proceedings of the Royal Society of London B 263: 1291–1297.

Pennington JT (1985). The ecology of fertilization of echioid eggs: the consequence of sperm dilution, adult aggregation, and synchronous spawning. Biological Bulletin 169: 417–430.

Petersen CW (1991). Variation in fertilization rate in tropical reef fish, *Halichoeres bivattatus*: correlates and implications. Biological Bulletin 181: 232–237.

Petersen CW, Levitan D (2001). The Allee effect: a barrier to recovery by exploited species. In: Reynolds JD, Mace GM, Redford KH, Robinson JG (eds.), *Conservation of Exploited Species*. Cambridge University Press, Cambridge, pp. 281–300.

Petersen CW, Warner RR (1998). Sperm competition in fishes. In: Birkhead TR, Møller AP (eds.), *Sperm Competition and Sexual Selection*. Academic Press, London, pp. 435–463.

Petersen CW, Warner RR (2002). The ecological context of reproductive behavior. In: Sale PF (ed.), *Dynamics and Diversity in a Complex Ecosystem*. Academic Press, San Diego, pp. 103–118.

Petersen CW, Warner RR, Cohen S, Hess H, Sewell A (1992). Variable pelagic fertilization success: implications for mate choice and spatial patterns of mating. Ecology 73: 391–401

Petersen CW, Warner RR, Shapiro DY, Marconato A (2001). Components of fertilization success in the bluehead wrasse, *Thalassoma bifasciatum*. Behavioral Ecology 12: 237–245.

Petersen CW, Mazzoldi C, Zarrella KA, Hale RB (2005). Fertilization mode, sperm characteristics, mate choice and parental care patterns in *Artedius spp.* (Cottidae). Journal of Fish Biology 67: 239–254.

Pilastro A, Bisazza A (1999). Insemination efficiency of two alternative male mating tactics in the guppy (*Poecilia reticulata*). Proceedings of the Royal Society of London B 266: 1887–1891.

Pilastro A, Giacomello E, Bisazza A (1997). Sexual selection for small size in male mosqui-tofish (*Gambusia holbrooki*). Proceedings of the Royal Society of London B 264: 1125–1129.

Pilastro A, Scaggiante M, Rasotto MB (2002). Individual adjustment of sperm expenditure accords with sperm competition theory. Proceeding of the National Academy of Sciences of the United States of America 99: 9913–9915.

Pilastro A, Simonato M, Bisazza A, Evans JP (2004). Cryptic female preference for colorful males in guppies. Evolution 58: 665–669.

Punt AE, Garratt PA, Govender A (1993). On an approach for applying per-recruit methods to a protogynous hermaphrodite, with an illustration for the slinger *Chrysoblephus puniceus* (Pisces:Sparidae). South African Journal of Marine Science 13: 109–119.

Purchase CF, Hasselman DJ, Weir LK (2007). Relationship between fertilization success and the number of milt donors in rainbow smelt *Osmerus mordax* (Mitchell): implications for population growth rate. Journal of Fish Biology 70: 934–946.

Ragland HC, Fisher EA (1987). Internal fertilization and male parental care in the scaly-head sculpin, *Artedius harringtoni*. Copeia 1987: 1059–1062.

Rakatin A, Ferguson MM, Trippel EA (1999). Sperm competition and fertilization success in Atlantic cod (*Gadus morhua*): effect of sire size and condition factor on gamete quality. Canadian Journal of Fisheries and Aquatic Sciences 56: 2315–2323.

Rakitin A, Ferguson MM, Trippel EA (2001). Male reproductive success and body size in Atlantic cod *Gadus morhua* L. Marine Biology 138: 1077–1085.

Rasotto MB (1995). Male reproductive apparatus of some blennioidei (Pisces: Teleostei). Copeia 1995: 907–914.

Rasotto MB, Mazzoldi C (2002). Male traits associated with alternative reproductive tactics in *Gobius niger*. Journal of Fish Biology 61: 173–184.

Rasotto MB, Sadovy Y (1995). Peculiarities of the male urogenital apparatus of two grunt species (Teleostei, Haemulidae). Journal of Fish Biology 46: 936–948.

Rasotto MB, Marconato A, Shapiro DY (1992). Reproductive apparatus of two jawfish species (Opistognathidae) with description of a juxtatesticular body. Copeia 1992: 1046–1053.

Richtarski U, Patzner RA (2000). Comparative morphology of male reproductive systems in Mediterranean blennies (Blennidae). Journal of Fish Biology 56: 22–36.

Robertson DR (1972). Social control of sex-reversal in a coral-reef fish. Science 177: 1007–1009.

Rowe S, Hutchings JA (2003). Mating systems and the conservation of commercially exploited marine fish. Trends in Ecology and Evolution 18: 567–572.

Rowe S, Hutchings JA, Bekkevold D, Rakitin A (2004). Depensation, probability of fertilization, and the mating system of Atlantic cod (*Gadus morhua* L.). ICES Journal of Marine Science 61: 1144–1150.

Rowe S, Hutchings JA, Skjæraasen JE (2007). Nonrandom mating in a broadcast spawner: mate size influences reproductive success in Atlantic cod (*Gadus morhua*). Canadian Journal of Fisheries and Aquatic Sciences 64: 219–226.

Ruchon F, Laugier T, Quignard JP (1995). Alternative male reproductive strategies in the peacock blenny. Journal of Fish Biology 47: 826–840.

Rurangwa E, Roelants I, Huyskens G, Ebrahimi M, Kime DE, Ollevier F (1998). The minimum effective spermatozoa: egg ratio for artificial insemination and the effects of mercury on sperm motility and fertilization ability in *Clarias gariepinus*. Journal of Fish Biology 53: 402–413.

Scaggiante M, Mazzoldi C, Petersen CW, Rasotto MB (1999). Sperm competition and mode of fertilization in the grass goby *Zosterisessor ophiocephalus* (Teleostei: Gobiidae). Journal of Experimental Zoology 283: 81–90.

Scaggiante M, Rasotto MB, Romvaldi C, Pilastro A (2005). Territorial male gobies respond aggressively to sneakers but do not adjust their sperm expenditure. Behavioral Ecology 16: 1001–1007.

Schärer L, Robertson DR (1999). Sperm and milt characteristics and male v. female gametic investment in the Caribbean reef fish, *Thalassoma bifasciatum*. Journal of Fish Biology 55: 329–343.

Schulte-Hostedde AI, Burness G (2005). Fertilization dynamics of sperm from different male mating tactics in bluegill (*Lepomis macrochirus*). Canadian Journal of Zoology 83: 1638–1642.

Schwalme K, Chouinard GA (1999). Seasonal dynamics in feeding, organ weights, and reproductive maturation of Atlantic cod (*Gadus morhua*) in the southern Gulf of St. Lawrence. ICES Journal of Marine Science 56: 303–319.

Shapiro DY (1980). Serial female changes after simultaneous removal of males from social groups of coral reef fish. Science 209: 1136–1137.

Shapiro DY (1987). Reproduction in groupers. In: Polovina JJ, Ralston S (eds.), *Tropical Snappers and Groupers: Biology and Fisheries Management*. Westview Press, Boulder, Colorado, pp. 295–327.

Shapiro DY, Giraldeau L-A (1996). Mating tactics in external fertilizers when sperm is limited. Behavioral Ecology 7: 19–23.

Shapiro DY, Marconato A, Yoshikawa T (1994). Sperm economy in a coral reef fish. Ecology 75: 1334–1344.

Simmons LW (2001). *Sperm Competition and its Evolutionary Consequences in the Insects*. Princeton University Press, Princeton, New Jersey.

Smith CL (1982). Patterns of reproduction in coral reef fishes. In: Huntsman GR, Nicholson WR, Fox WW Jr (eds.), The biological basis for reef fishery management. U.S. Department of Commerce, NOAA Tech. Memo. NMFS, NOAA-TM-NMFS-SEFC-80, pp. 49–66.

Snook RR (2005). Sperm in competition: not playing by the numbers. Trends in Ecology and Evolution 20: 46–53.

Stockley P, Gage MJG, Parker GA, Møller AP (1997). Sperm competition in fishes: the evolution of testis size and ejaculate characteristics. American Naturalist 149: 933–954.

Suquet M, Billard R, Cosson J, Normant Y, Fauvel C (1995). Artificial insemination in turbot (*Scophthalmus maximus*): determination of the optimal sperm per egg ratio and time of gamete contact. Aquaculture 133: 83–90.

Taborsky M (1998). Sperm competition in fish: "bourgeois" males and parasitic spawning. Trends in Ecology and Evolution 13: 222–227.

Thresher RE (1984). *Reproduction in Reef Fishes*. TFH Publications, Neptune City, New Jersey.

Trippel EA, Morgan MJ (1994). Sperm longevity in pelagic spawning cod (*Gadus morhua*). Copeia 1994: 1025–1029.

Trivers RL (1972). Parental investment and sexual selection. In: Campbell B (ed.), *Sexual Selection and the Descent of Man 1871–1971*. Aldine Press, Chicago, pp. 136–179.

Turner E, Montgomerie R (2002). Ovarian fluid enhances sperm movement in Arctic charr. Journal of Fish Biology 60: 1570–1579.

Uglem I, Galloway TF, Rosenqvist G, Folstad I (2001). Male dimorphism, sperm traits and immunology in the corkwing wrasse (*Symphodus melops* L.). Behavioral Ecology and Sociobiology 50: 511–518.

Urbach D, Folstad I, Rudolfsen G (2005). Effects of ovarian fluid on sperm velocity in Arctic charr (*Salvelinus alpinus*). Behavioral Ecology and Sociobiology 57: 438–444.

Vagelli A (1999). The reproductive biology and early ontogeny of the mouthbrooding Banggai cardinalfish, *Pterapogon kauderni* (Perciformes, Apogonidae). Environmental Biology of Fishes 56: 79–92.

Van Look KJW, Dzyuba B, Cliffe A, Koldewey HJ, Holt WV (2007). Dimorphic sperm and the unlikely route to fertilisation in the yellow seahorse. Journal of Experimental Biology 210: 432–437

Vincent ACJ, Sadovy Y (1998). Reproductive ecology in the conservation and management of fishes. In: Caro T (ed.), *Behavioral Ecology and Conservation Biology*. Oxford University Press, New York, pp. 209–245.

Warner RR, Shapiro DY, Marconato A, Petersen CW (1995). Sexual conflict: males with higher mating success convey the lowest fertilization benefits to females. Proceedings of the Royal Society of London B 262: 135–139.

Watanabe S, Hara M, Watanabe Y (2000). Male internal fertilization and introsperm-like sperm of the seaweed pipefish (*Syngnathus schlegeli*). Zoological Science 6: 759–767

Wilson EO, Bossert WH (1971). *A Primer of Population Biology*. Sinauer, Sunderland, Massachusetts.

Wooninck L, Strassman JE, Queller DC, Fleischer R, Warner RR (1998). Characterization of hypervariable microsatellite markers in the bluehead wrasse, *Thalassoma bifasciatum*. Molecular Ecology 7: 1613–1614.

Wourms JP (1981). Viviparity: the maternal-fetal relationship in fishes. American Zoologist 21: 473–515.

Yanagimachi R, Cherr GN, Pillai MC, Baldwin JD (1992). Factors controlling sperm entry into the micropyles of salmonid and herring eggs. Development Growth & Differentiation 34: 447–461.

Yund PO (2000). How severe is sperm limitation in natural populations of marine free-spawners? Trends in Ecology and Evolution 15: 10–13.

8

Bidirectional Sex Change
in Marine Fishes

Philip L. Munday, Tetsuo Kuwamura, and Frederieke J. Kroon

Sex change (sequential hermaphroditism) is well known in fishes, where its oc-currence and evolutionary advantage have been the focus of numerous reviews since the early 1960s (e.g., Atz 1964; Ghiselin 1969; Warner 1978, 1988; Kuwa-mura & Nakashima 1998; Munday et al. 2006a; Sadovy de Mitcheson & Liu 2008). Typically, individuals of sex-changing species either first function as fe-male and then change sex to male (protogynous sex change) or they first function as male and then change to female (protandrous sex change). Bidirectional sex change—where both males and females change sex in the same population—was not thought to occur, either because the conditions favoring sex change by both males and females did not exist within the same species, or because physiological constraints prevented individuals changing sex more than once. The discovery that individuals of some species can change sex more than once has overturned these assumptions and opened up a whole new area of research into the adaptive significance and proximate mechanisms of sex change in fishes (Kuwamura & Nakashima 1998; Munday et al. 2006a).

One of the earliest reports of bidirectional sex change in fishes involved ap-parent sex change by males of the protogynous grouper *Epinephalus akaara* when kept together in an aquarium (Tanaka et al. 1990). Subsequent experimen-tal manipulations with the hawkfish *Cirrhitichthys aureus* (Kobayashi & Suzuki 1992) and the goby *Trimma okinawae* (Sunobe & Nakazono 1993) confirmed that bidirectional sex change was possible, with both males and females of these species changing sex when kept in same-sex pairs. Bidirectional sex change was then confirmed in natural populations of the coral goby *Paragob-iodon echinocephalus* (Kuwamura et al. 1994a) and various species of *Gobiodon*

(Nakashima et al. 1996; Munday et al. 1998) by monitoring known-sex individuals in the field and by experimental manipulations of their social groups. The number of species reported to exhibit bidirectional sex change has continued to grow and although many cases are restricted to animals in captivity, there are also more confirmations that bidirectional sex change occurs in nature (e.g., Manabe et al. 2007a). The detection of bidirectional sex change in natural populations is important, because it demonstrates that this sexual pattern is not peculiar to fish in captivity and because it provides the opportunity to assess the adaptive significance of this mode of sex change by examining the correlates of sex change under natural conditions.

Bidirectional sex changers provide a unique opportunity to test theoretical explanations for the presence of sex change in animals, because the same species exhibits both protogynous and protandrous sex change and the same individual can change sex more than once. This extreme lability in sexual expression means that individuals are likely to be highly sensitive to the environmental conditions favoring either protogynous or protandrous sex change and it should be possible to test predictions of sex-change theory by altering those conditions to induce sex change in either direction (Munday 2002). Examining the social and environmental conditions under which sex change in each direction occurs in the same individual could provide a powerful test of sex allocation theory. Furthermore, some bidirectional sex changers have gonadal sex-cell allocation that is more similar to that of simultaneous hermaphrodites than it is to most sequential hermaphrodites (St. Mary 1993, 1996). Therefore, these species might also be useful for bridging the gap between sex allocation theory related to simultaneous hermaphrodites and theory related to sequential hermaphrodites (St. Mary 1997).

Most examples of bidirectional sex change involve repetitive or serial sex change, where adults change sex more than once, usually female–male–female. These species often appear to be fundamentally protogynous, with the exception that males sometimes revert to functional females. In addition to repetitive sex change by adults, some bidirectional sex changers are capable of maturing into either sex at maturation (Kuwamura et al. 1994a; Hobbs et al. 2004; Liu & Sadovy 2004). Furthermore, Kuwamura et al. (2007) found that primary males of a diandric protogynous wrasse can change sex to female. Therefore, even where alternative reproductive strategies develop early in life, there can remain the potential for sex change in each direction by adults. These examples demonstrate that bidirectional sex change may take a number of different forms and that lability in sexual expression may be present throughout much of an individual's life history.

Here we review the distribution of bidirectional sex change among teleost fishes and examine the patterns of sexual development and sexual expression that these species exhibit. We then use this information in conjunction with behavioral and ecological correlates to consider the adaptive significance of bidirectional sex change. We consider what bidirectional sex change tells us about the evolutionary advantage of sex change in general, and whether it is consistent with existing explanations for the presence of sex change in animals. Finally, we explore the proximate mechanisms controlling sex change in each direction and the physiological changes that occur in the brain, gonads, and endocrine system, which enable such extreme sexual lability to occur.

SEXUAL PATTERNS OF BIDIRECTIONAL SEX CHANGERS

Functional hermaphroditism has been confirmed in 27 families and 94 genera of teleost fishes, with a further 21 families and 31 genera containing unconfirmed examples (Sadovy de Mitcheson & Liu 2008). Many hundreds of species within these families are known to change sex. To date, 6 families, 12 genera, and 25 species are confirmed to be capable of bidirectional sex change (Table 8.1). A similar number of closely related species are likely to exhibit bidirectional sex change, based on the similarity of their ecologies and patterns of gonadal sex allocation with known bidirectional sex changers (Table 8.1). It is almost certain that many more fish species will be found to be bidirectional sex changers once the potential for this sexual pattern is tested further. The families where bidirectional sex change has so far been detected are commonly found on coral reefs and many of the species have a small body size and cryptic lifestyle. Bidirectional sex change seems to be particularly prevalent in the family Gobiidae and these small fishes offer an excellent opportunity to compare and contrast the conditions favoring sex change in each direction.

Bidirectional sex change is commonly detected using laboratory manipulations where pairs or groups of individuals of the same sex are kept together in aquariums. These experiments demonstrate that a species has the capacity for bidirectional sex change and can provide important information on the proximate mechanisms controlling sex change. However, they might not provide an accurate indication of the frequency of sex change in each direction in nature. For example, both male and female *Trimma okinawae* can be induced to change sex by keeping same-sex pairs together in aquariums (Sunobe & Nakazono 1993). However, monitoring of natural populations shows that sex change from male to female occurs less frequently than sex change from female to male (Manabe et al. 2007a). Therefore, even though both males and females have an equal capacity to change sex, this is not reflected in patterns of sex change in nature. Similarly, *Paragobiodon echinocephalus* can be induced to change sex from male to female by placing two males together on a coral head (Nakashima et al. 1995), but sex change by males in the natural population is much less frequent than sex change by females (Kuwamura et al. 1994a).

TABLE 8.1 Species confirmed or likely to exhibit bidirectional sex change

Family	Species	Data type	Habitat	Mating system	Spawning mode	Sexually dichromatic	Primary references
Gobiidae	Trimma okinawae	F & C	CR, cryptic	polygynous	demersal	N	Sunobe and Nakazono 1993; Manabe et al. 2007a
	T. grammistes	C	RR, cryptic	polygynous	demersal	N	Shiobara 2000
	T. kudoi	C	RR, cryptic	polygynous	demersal	N	Manabe et al. 2008
	T. yanagitai	C	RR	unknown	demersal	N	Sakurai et al. 2009
	Paragobiodon echinochephalus	F & C	CR, cryptic	monogamous	demersal	N	Kuwamura et al. 1994a; Nakashima et al. 1995
	Gobiodon histrio	F	CR, cryptic	monogamous	demersal	N	Munday et al. 1998; Munday 2002
	G. erythrospilus[a]	F & C	CR, cryptic	monogamous	demersal	N	Nakashima et al. 1996; Munday 2002
	G. micropus	C	CR, cryptic	monogamous	demersal	N	Nakashima et al. 1996
	G. sp.[b]	C	CR, cryptic	monogamous	demersal	N	Nakashima et al. 1996
	G. quinquestrigatus	C	CR, cryptic	monogamous	demersal	N	Nakashima et al. 1996
	Lythrypnus dalli	F & C	RR	polygynous	demersal	N	St. Mary 1993, 1996; Reavis & Grober 1999; Black et al. 2005a, b; Rodgers et al. 2007
Serranidae	Epinephelus akaara	C	RR	unknown	pelagic	N	Tanaka et al. 1990
	Cephalopholis boenak	C	CR	polygynous	pelagic	N	Liu & Sadovy 2004, 2005
Pseudochromidae	Pseudochromis flavivertex	C	CR, cryptic	pairs	demersal	N	Michael 2004; Wittenrich & Munday 2005
	P. aldabraensis	C	CR, cryptic	pairs	demersal	N	Michael 2004; Wittenrich & Munday 2005
	P. cyanotaenia	C	CR, cryptic	pairs	demersal	Y	Michael 2004; Wittenrich & Munday 2005
Pomacanthidae	Centropyge acanthops	C	CR	polygynous	pelagic	N	Hioki & Suzuki 1996
	C. ferrugata	C	CR	polygynous	pelagic	Y	Sakai et al. 2003
	C. fisheri	C	CR	polygynous	pelagic	N	Hioki & Suzuki 1996
	C. flavissimus	C	CR	polygynous	pelagic	N	Hioki & Suzuki 1996

Family	Species	F/C/H	Habitat	Mating system	Egg type	Bidirectional	Reference
Cirrhitidae	*Cirrhitichthys aureus*	C	CR	unknown	pelagic	N	Kobayashi & Suzuki 1992
	C. falco	F	CR	polygynous	pelagic	N	Kadota (2009)
Labridae	*Labroides dimidiatus*	C	CR	polygynous	pelagic	N	Kuwamura et al. 2002
	Halichoeres trimaculatus	F & C	CR	polygynous	pelagic	Y	Kuwamura et al. 2007
	Pseudolabrus sieboldi	C	RR	polygynous	pelagic	Y	Ohta et al. 2003
Proposed or likely							
Gobiidae	*Paragobiodon xanthosomus*	H	CR, cryptic	monogomous	demersal	N	Lassig 1977; Fishelson 1989
	Gobiodon okinawae	H	CR	monogamous	demersal	N	Cole & Hoese 2001
	G. citrinus	H	CR, cryptic	unknown	demersal	N	Fishelson 1989
	Eviota epiphanes	H	CR, cryptic	unknown	demersal	N	Cole 1990
	Lythrypnus zebra	H & C	RR	unknown	demersal	N	St. Mary 1993, 1996
	L. nesiotes	H	CR, RR	unknown	demersal	N	St. Mary 2000
	Bryaninops 4 species	H	CR, cryptic	monogamous	demersal	N	Fishelson 1989; Munday et al. 2002
	Priolepis 3 species	H	CR, cryptic	monogamous	demersal	N	Cole 1990; Sunobe & Nakazono 1999
	Trimma 3 species	H	CR, cryptic	polygynous	demersal	N	Cole 1990
Pseudochromidae	*Ogilbyina queenslandiae*	F	CR, cryptic	pairs	demersal	Y	Ferrell 1987
Pomacanthidae	*Apolemichthys trimaculatus*	C	CR	unknown	pelagic	N	Hioki & Suzuki 1995
Cirrhitidae	*Neocirrhites armatus*	H	CR, cryptic	polygynous	pelagic	N	Sadovy & Donaldson 1995
	Cirrhitichthys 3 species	H	CR, cryptic	unknown	pelagic	N	Kobayashi & Suzuki 1992; Sadovy & Donaldson 1995
	Cirrhitops hubbardi	H	CR	unknown	pelagic	N	Kobayashi & Suzuki 1992
	Cyprinocirrhites polyactis	H	CR	unknown	pelagic	N	Kobayashi & Suzuki 1992

NOTE: Bidirectional sex change is confirmed or deemed likely based on observational data in the field (F) or in captivity (C), or on gonadal histology (H). Habitat is classified as coral reef (CR) or rocky reef (RR).

[a] *G. rivulattus rivulattus* in Nakashima et al. 1996.

[b] *G. oculolineatus* in Nakashima et al. 1996.

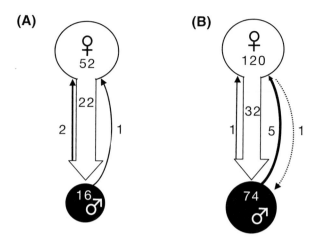

FIGURE 8.1. Frequency of sex change in each direction in natural populations of (A) *Trimma okinawae* and (B) *Paragobiodon echinocephalus*. Numbers of adult males and females in the study population are shown in the large circles. Arrows show the direction of sex change and the number of individuals changing sex. The thin, solid line to the left of the female-to-male sex change arrow indicates females that changed sex to male and then changed back to female during the course of each study. The dotted line in (B) indicates a male that changed sex to female and then back to male. Data from Manabe et al. 2007a and Kuwamura et al. 1994a.

Trimma okinawae and *P. echinocephalus* have been extensively studied and these two species serve as useful examples of different life histories exhibited by bidirectional sex changers. *Trimma okinawae* is a small polygynous goby that inhabits caves, holes and the undersides of corals. The most common social arrangement is a breeding group of one male and one to seven females (Sunobe & Nakazono 1990; Manabe et al. 2007a), although single males are common at the end of the breeding season. The male is usually the largest individual in a social group and protogynous sex change occurs if he disappears. In this circumstance the largest female within the group changes sex to male, or a large female from another social group immigrates and changes sex to male (Manabe et al. 2007a, b). Protogynous sex change also occurs when a female becomes single, either due to the loss of all other females in the group, or her movement from the group. Protandrous sex change only occurs when a solitary male enters a new social group that already contains a dominant male. Therefore, this species is basically protogynous, except that single males revert to female if they reenter a group and are smaller than the dominant male in the new group (Figure 8.1A).

Paragobiodon echinocephalus is a monogamous goby that lives among the branches of the coral *Stylophora pistillata*. The most common social arrangement is a breeding pair (Kuwamura et al. 1993, 1996). Any other individuals in the social group are juveniles. If one member of the breeding pair disappears, a new pair is formed through either (1) the maturation of a juvenile already present on the coral or the immigration and maturation of a juvenile from another coral, or (2) the immigration of an adult from another coral (Kuwamura et al. 1994a). Protogynous sex change occurs in two circumstances: when a single adult female changes sex and forms a pair with a juvenile that has matured as a female, or when adult immigration results in two females cohabiting a coral colony (one of them will change sex to male). In contrast, protandrous sex change only takes place when a male moves and forms a pair with another male - one of the two males will change sex to female. The narrower range of circumstances where males change sex compared to females means that male to female sex change tends to be much less frequent in the population than female to male sex change (Figure 8.1B).

In addition to bidirectional sex change as adults, juvenile coral-dwelling gobies (*Gobiodon* and *Paragobiodon* species) can mature into either sex depending on the sex of their future partner (Kuwamura et al. 1994a; Hobbs et al. 2004). Usually, a juvenile will mature as a female and form a pair with a single adult male or with an adult female that has changed sex to male. New pairs may also form by the maturation of two juveniles on a coral without an existing breeding pair. In this case, one of the juveniles matures as a female and the other as a male.

One of the most unexpected recent discoveries is that primary males of the diandric wrasse *Halichoeres trimaculatus* can change sex to female, and then back to male again (Kuwamura et al. 2007). In diandric species, males are derived either by sex change from female (secondary males) or by direct development before maturation (primary males). It has long been thought that primary males are gonochoristic and do not change sex. However, Kuwamura et al. (2007) observed sex change to female in a primary male in the field and induced sex change in primary males when they were kept together with other males and females in aquaria. This shows that fundamentally protogynous and protandrous life histories can occur within the same species.

In addition to well-described examples of bidirectional sex change in natural populations, such as those discussed above, there is a growing list of species where bidirectional sex change has been demonstrated in captivity (Table 8.1). Many of these species are known to be protogynous sex changers in natural populations, but it is not known if males change sex back to female, even though they clearly have the capacity to do so. The pygmy angelfishes, *Centropyge* species, are a good example. These fishes are haremic, protogynous sex changers (Sakai & Kohda 1997; Michael 2004) and the largest female in a group will change sex to male if the dominant male disappears. Laboratory manipulations of social groups have shown that males have the capacity to change sex back to female (Sakai et al. 2003), but whether they do so in nature is unknown.

Kuwamura et al. (2002) demonstrated the importance of both field and laboratory assessments of bidirectional sex change with the cleaner wrasse *Labroides dimidiatus*. This species is a haremic protogynous hermaphrodite where the dominant female changes sex to male following the loss of the harem male (Robertson 1972; Kuwamura 1984). Experiments in captivity revealed that the smaller male will change sex to female if two males are kept together in an aquarium. However, functional sex change by males could not be confirmed in nature. After removal of females in a low density population, single males formed pairs and exhibited spawning behavior for several days, but the pairs did not persist long enough for functional sex change to occur (Kuwamura et al. 2002). Determining if males of protogynous species known to be capable of sex change to female under laboratory conditions also exhibit reverse sex change in natural populations, and under what circumstances, is an important area for future research.

REPRODUCTIVE CHARACTERISTICS
Size and Age Structure

Signatures of protogynous or protandrous sex change are often present in the age- or size-frequency distribution of males and females (Sadovy & Shapiro 1987). The older age and size classes are expected to be dominated by males in protogynous sex changers. In contrast, older age and size classes are expected to be dominated by females in protandrous sex changers. These patterns are likely to break down in bidirectional sex changers, because larger and older individuals may revert to the original sex. Indeed, age and size distributions of males and females overlap substantially in some bidirectional sex changers (Munday et al. 1998; Manabe et al. 2008)(Figure 8.2A). In other bidirectional sex changers, such as *Trimma okinawae*, there is little overlap in the size-frequency distribution of males and females (Figure 8.2B). This occurs because only the largest individual in a social group becomes male, and males entering new groups change sex to female if they are smaller than the resident male (Manabe et al. 2007a). These different patterns show that size- or age-frequency distributions of the sexes do not always provide clear evidence for the presence or absence of bidirectional sex change.

(A)

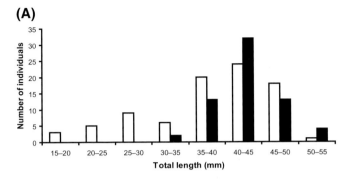

(B)

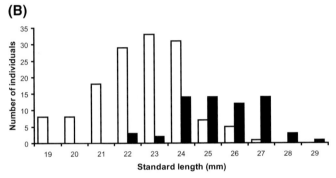

FIGURE 8.2. Size frequency distribution of male and female (A) *Gobiodon histrio* and (B) *Trimma okinawae*. White bars, female; black bars, male. Data from Munday et al. 1998 and Manabe et al. 2007a.

Sexual Dimorphism

Initial observations of bidirectional sex change mostly came from species where males and females had similar coloration and external morphology (except for the shape of the genital papillae, which often differs between males and females). It is easy to imagine that species exhibiting sex change in both directions might have similar male and female phenotypes, because this would reduce the morphological changes necessary to shift from one sexual phenotype to the other. However, sexual dimorphism does not preclude bidirectional sex change and a number of species in which males exhibit much brighter body coloration than females are capable of changing sex in each direction (Table 8.1). Changes in body coloration are closely linked to the timing of sex change in each direction in these species (Sakai et al. 2003; Wittenrich & Munday 2005; Kuwamura et al. 2007).

Gonadal Structure and Sex-Cell Allocation

Gonadal structure and patterns of sex allocation differ greatly among bidirectional sex-changing species. Some bidirectional species (e.g. *Trimma*) have delineated gonads with separate regions of ovarian and testicular tissue that proliferate or regress, depending on the functional sex of the individual (Table 8.2, Figure 8.3). The ovarian and testicular regions are often separated by a thin wall of connective tissue (Cole 1990; Sunobe & Nakazono 1993; Manabe et al. 2008). During sex change from female to male, the ovarian region contracts and ceases producing vitellogenic oocytes, and the testicular region expands and starts producing sperm. The opposite occurs during protandrous sex change (Sunobe & Nakazono 1993; Manabe et al. 2008). *Trimma* can change from one functional sex to the other in less than one week (Table 8.2), and it seems likely that the retention of a regressed gonadal region of either male or female tissue assists with this rapid transition in sexual function.

Other bidirectional sex-changing species do not have distinct separation of ovarian and testicular tissue within the gonad (Table 8.2, Figure 8.4), but tissue of the other sex is sometimes scattered throughout the functional ovary or testis. Testes in particular are likely to contain numerous previtellogenic oocytes. For example, there is no evidence of testicular tissue in mature ovaries of *Gobiodon* and *Paragobiodon*, but up to 20% of the testis can be taken up by previtellogenic oocytes (Cole 1990; Cole & Hoese 2001; Munday 2002)(Figure 8.4). Generally, the proportion of female tissue in the testis is greatest in newly sex-changed males and declines in males that have been in a breeding pair for an extended period (Munday 2002; Kroon et al. 2003). A similar pattern is seen in species of *Pseudochromis*; ovaries have no male tissue, but over 10% of the functional testes may be taken up by previtellogenic oocytes, especially after functional sex change (Wittenrich & Munday 2005). A common feature of all these species is that they do not have mature gametes of both sexes present in the gonad at the same time, nor do they retain regressed regions of ovarian or testicular tissue like that seen in *Trimma* species. During sex change, the reproductive tissue of one sex degenerates, and the reproductive tissue of the other sex develops throughout the gonad. Sex change in each direction often takes more than two weeks in these species (Table 8.2), probably because of the need to restructure the entire gonad.

Lythrypnus comprises an interesting group of hermaphroditic gobies because some species have gonadal sex-cell allocation resembling simultaneous hermaphrodites, even though individuals function as only one sex at time (St. Mary 1993, 1994, 1996, 2000). Gonads of these species can contain both vitellogenic oocytes and spermatozoa at the same time, although allocation to male and female sex cells is usually strongly biased to one sex or the other. More importantly, individuals function solely as male or solely as female over repeated breeding bouts.

TABLE 8.2 Reproductive characteristics of some bidirectional sex-changing fishes

| Family/Species | Gonad type | Female to male | | Male to female | | Primary references |
		Relative size	Min. time	Relative size	Min. time	
Gobiidae						
Trimma okinawae	delimited	L	6	S	4	Sunobe & Nakazono 1993
T. kudoi.	delimited	S	16	L	12	Manabe et al. 2008
Paragobiodon echinochephalus	non-delimited	L	27	S	24	Nakashima et al. 1995
Gobiodon histrio	non-delimited	L	<28	S	<28	Munday et al. 1998
G. okinawae	non-delimited	L	<21	S	>21	Cole & Hoese 2001
G. quinquestrigatus	non-delimited	L	30	S	23	Nakashima et al. 1996
Lythrypnus dalli	delimited	L	5–11	S	14	Reavis & Grober 1999; Black et al. 2005b
L. dalli		L	16	S	17	Rodgers et al. 2007
Pseudochromidae						
Pseudochromis flavivertex	non-delimited	L	28	S	52	Wittenrich & Munday 2005
P. aldabraensis	non-delimited	L	18	S	64	Wittenrich & Munday 2005
P. cyanotaenia	non-delimited	L	23	S	67	Wittenrich & Munday 2005
Pomacanthidae						
Centropyge acanthops	non-delimited	L	8	S	91	Hioki & Suzuki 1996
C. ferrugata	non-delimited	L	15	S	47	Sakai et al. 2003
C. fisheri	non-delimited	L	6	S	35	Hioki & Suzuki 1996
Labridae						
Labroides dimidiatus	non-delimited	L	14	S	53	Kuwamura et al. 2002

NOTE: Gonadal form, minimum recorded time to change sex in each direction, and the relative size of the individual(s) that change sex within same-sex groups are reported. Minimum time to sex change is based on the observation of fertilized egg clutches or complete functional sex change assessed by histological examination of gonads.

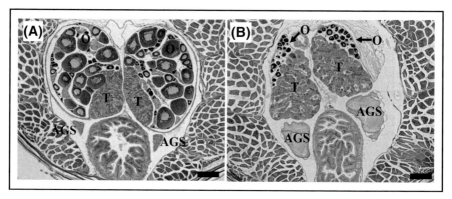

FIGURE 8.3. Gonadal structure of (A) functional female and (B) functional male *Trimma kudoi*. O = ovary. T = testis. AGS = accessory gonadal structure. Gonads of functional females contain vitellogenic oocytes but no spermatozoa in the testicular region and an inactive AGS. Gonads of functional males have spermatozoa and an active AGS, which is characteristic of functional males, but no vitellogenic oocytes. Adapted from Manabe et al. 2008.

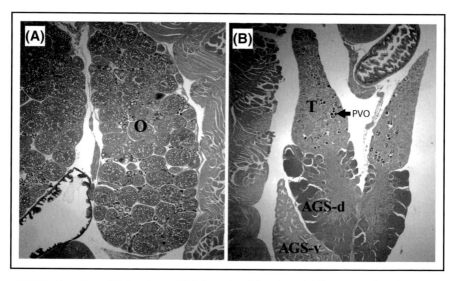

FIGURE 8.4. Gonadal structure of (A) functional female and (B) functional male *Gobiodon erythrospilus*. O = ovary. T = testis. AGS-d = dorsal accessory gonadal structure. AGS-v = ventral accessory gonadal structure. Active, secretory AGS-d is characteristic of a functional male. Females do not have secretory AGS-d. Note previtellogenic oocytes (PVO) scattered throughout the testis.

Therefore, from a functional perspective, these species are sequential hermaphrodites. *L. dalli* changes from one functional sex to the other and can appropriately be considered a bidirectional sex changer (Kuwamura & Nakashima 1998; Rodgers et al. 2007). All species of *Lythrypnus* have a unique gonadal structure with a central area of ovarian tissue between two or three peripheral regions of testicular tissue (St. Mary 1998). During sex change from functional female to functional male, the area of testicular tissue increases, and ovarian tissue declines. The opposite occurs during sex change from functional male to functional female.

Correlates of Gonadal Allocation and Duration of Sex Change

In general, differences in gonadal allocation among genera appear to be broadly related to the probability of unpredictable changes in social organization. The gonads of habitat-specialist species that are highly site attached and rarely move among social groups, such as *Gobiodon* and *Paragobiodon*, are largely dominated by either male or female tissue, and there are never mature gametes of both sexes present. Individuals of these species tend to retain the same partner for considerable periods of time and are therefore less likely to have the need for rapid or repeated sex change. In contrast, species that are less site attached and more likely to move between social groups, such as *Trimma* and *Lythrypnus*, exhibit either a greater allocation to both male and female tissue, or they continue to produce small numbers of mature gametes of the opposite sex, which might aid rapid sex change in each direction. Consequently, it seems that patterns of gonadal allocation among bidirectional sex changers are often associated with the predictability of their social environment.

The time required to change sex in each direction appears to be approximately equal for some species, but much slower from male to female in other species (Table 8.2). Species in which male to female sex change takes much longer than female to male sex change tend to be polygynous species that are known to exhibit protogynous sex change in nature, but where reverse sex change by males has so far not been observed. Strong dominance behaviors by harem or territorial males of these species may increase the time required to initiate sex change in subordinate males. For example, aggressive relationships between male *Centropyge ferrugata* can take several weeks to be settled, even when individuals are in continuous close contact (Sakai et al. 2003). In the field, these strong dominance behaviors may prevent subordinate males entering the territory or harem and thus limit the opportunities for male to female sex change.

There is also considerable variation among individuals in the time required for sex change and some of this variation is related to environmental conditions. For example, sex change in each direction takes approximately the same length of time in *L. dalli* when conditions are similar for groups of males and groups of females (Rodgers et al. 2007), but the time taken to change sex is influenced by temperature, social organization, and season (Black et al. 2005b; Lorenzi et al. 2006). Sex change is more rapid in warmer water (Black et al. 2005b), when dominance hierarchies have been established (Black ct al. 2005b; Lorenzi et al. 2006) and earlier in the breeding season (Lorenzi et al. 2006).

Individuals also adjust their allocation to male and female tissue depending on their current reproductive success and the certainty of mating opportunities. Male *L. dalli* that do not receive eggs in their nest retain higher levels of female tissue in their gonads than do males that have received eggs, possibly so that they can rapidly change sex back to female (St. Mary 1994). Similarly, female *L. dalli* delay sex change more near the end of the breeding season, perhaps because the cost of sex change could outweigh the benefits when breeding has nearly ceased (Lorenzi et al. 2006). Both of these observations suggest that individuals assess and adjust their gonadal sex allocation in relation to their expected reproductive success as either a male or a female.

ADAPTIVE SIGNIFICANCE
Bidirectional Sex Change and the Size-Advantage Hypothesis

The size-advantage hypothesis (SAH) predicts that sex change will be favored when the reproductive success of the sexes increases unequally with size, such that an individual reproduces more efficiently as one sex when small and more efficiently as the other sex when large (Ghiselin 1969; Warner 1975). The direction of sex change is often associated with the mating system: protogynous species typically exhibit a polygynous mating system, whereas protandrous species tend to be monogamous or random pair spawners (Munday et al. 2006a). The correlation between the mating system and the direction of sex change is consistent with expectations of the SAH, because male reproductive success tends to increase more steeply with size in polygynous mating systems, thereby favoring sex change from female to male (Figure 8.5A). In contrast, female reproductive success tends to increase more steeply with size in monogamous and random pair-spawning systems, thereby favoring sex change from male to female (Figure 8.5B). However, both polygynous and monogamous mating systems are associated in some instances with bidirectional sex change (Table 8.1), which raises the question of whether the SAH can explain sex change in each direction and, if it can, whether it is capable of providing an explanation for bidirectional sex change in all species.

Bidirectional sex change in the polygynous *T. okinawae* appears to be consistent with the SAH (Nakashima et al. 1995). This species is fundamentally a protogynous sex changer, except that males can change sex back to female. Individuals first breed as female and then change sex to male if they become large enough to control a harem of females (Sunobe & Nakazono 1990). Protogyny is favored

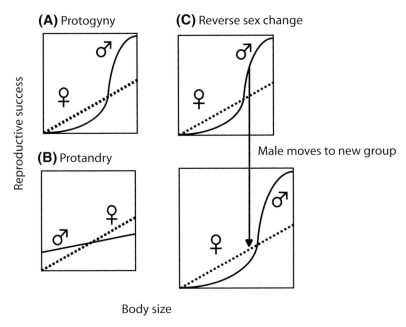

FIGURE 8.5.

A. Protogynous sex change can be favored in polygynous groups because male reproductive success (dark line) tends to increase more steeply with size than does female reproductive success (dotted line).

B. Protandrous sex change can be favored in monogamous groups or random pairing because female reproductive success tends to increases more steeply with size than does male reproductive success.

C. Repetitive sex change is favored if a male that changes sex from female moves to a new group where he is smaller than the resident male. In this case his reproductive success will be improved by changing sex back to female, because the resident male will prevent him breeding as a male. Adapted from Nakashima et al. 1995.

in haremic mating systems, because small males are excluded from breeding by the dominant male and thus have very low reproductive success. In contrast, large males have very high reproductive success because they mate with all the females in the harem. In polygynous societies, individuals can maximize their lifetime reproductive output by first reproducing as female and then changing sex to male when they reach a size large enough to defend a harem. As expected, the largest female in a *T. okinawae* harem changes sex following loss of the dominant male (Sunobe & Nakazono 1990; Manabe et al. 2007a, b). Females even move between social groups to improve their position in the size hierarchy and increase their chance of becoming the dominant female that changes sex following the loss of the male (Manabe et al. 2007b).

Reverse sex change in *T. okinawae* occurs if a single male enters an existing group where he is smaller than the resident male (Manabe et al. 2007a). The larger dominant male is likely to exclude him from reproducing as a male in the new group, but he could reproduce as a female. Therefore, his current reproductive success would be greater if he changed sex and functioned as a female. In effect, the male has slipped back down the size-fecundity slope to a position where his current size-related reproductive success is greater as a female than as a male (Figure 8.5C). As expected, he changes sex back to female. Bidirectional sex change in *T. okinawae* is an excellent test of the SAH, because it shows that females generally change sex when their reproductive success is higher as a male and revert to female if their reproductive success as a male falls below that of a similar sized female in the same social group.

An important question is why a male should enter an existing social group and change sex to female, instead of remaining male. Male *T. okinawae* only enter a new group and change sex to female if they are single (Manabe et al. 2007a). Because of their small size, most gobies are exposed to a very high risk of predation (Munday & Jones 1998) and consequently tend to have short life spans (Hernaman & Munday 2005; Depczynski & Bellwood 2006; Winterbottom & Southcott 2008). High and unpredictable rates of mortality mean that a male might unexpectedly lose all the females in his harem. The high risk of predation also means that a single male is likely to have a limited and uncertain period for reproduction available to him. Consequently, any delay in finding a breeding partner might seriously diminish his reproductive value (expected future reproductive success taking into account effects of growth and the probability of survival)(Munday et al. 2006a). The reproductive value of a single male may often be greater if he changes sex and breeds as a female in an existing group than if he remains male and waits for a new harem to develop.

Bidirectional Sex Change and Size-Fecundity Skew

Adjustment of functional sex in relation to reproductive value also seems to occur in *Trimma kudoi* (Manabe et al. 2008). This species appears to have a polygynous mating system, where males are larger than females and the sex ratio is highly skewed toward females. Therefore, we might expect the largest individual in a social group to always be male. However, Manabe et al. (2008) found that the second largest female usually changed sex to male when small groups of females were kept in aquariums. Muñoz & Warner (2003) showed that the largest female might not benefit from changing sex to male if the combined fecundity of all other females in the group (i.e., her prospective harem after sex change) was less than her existing fecundity. In this case, one of the smaller females may benefit most from changing sex to male. The patterns of sex change observed in *Trimma Kudoi* were broadly consistent with this prediction. Furthermore, when pairs of males or pairs of females were kept together, the larger one usually became/stayed female and the smaller stayed/became male (Manabe et al. 2008). This is exactly the social arrangement expected to maximize reproductive success in a breeding pair. Consequently, it seems that individuals of this species may adjust their sex to suit the precise social circumstances they encounter and it will not always be the largest individual that changes sex to male. Further analysis on the mating system of this species and a comparison of the size of males and females in groups of different sizes are needed to determine if individuals are indeed adjusting their sexual function in relation to fecundity relationships associated with different sized groups, or if there are other benefits to small male size.

Bidirectional Sex Change and the Cost of Movement

In contrast to species of *Trimma*, bidirectional sex change in coral-dwelling gobies (*Gobiodon* and *Paragobiodon*) is not consistent with the SAH, because there is no difference in the rate at which reproductive success of males and females increases with size (Kuwamura et al. 1993; Munday 2002). Coral-dwelling gobies are pair forming and monogamous. The reproductive success of a breeding pair depends on the size of both the male and the female (Kuwamura et al. 1993), and consequently, the male and female in a pair are approximately the same size (Kuwamura et al. 1993; Nakashima et al. 1996; Munday et al. 1998). Why reproductive success depends on the size of both sexes is uncertain, but it is likely that the fecundity of females increases with size and that the ability of males to care for the egg clutch also increases with size. Munday et al. (2006b) demonstrated that if one individual in a pair of *G. histrio* is smaller than the other, the smaller individual accelerates its growth and the larger individual slows its growth until the pair becomes size matched. This adjustment of growth by both individuals, regardless of sex, supports the notion that both male and female size are critical to the reproductive success of the pair.

The advantage of bidirectional sex change in coral-dwelling gobies is that they may need to move among hosts to find a new partner following the loss of a breeding partner, or the death of their host coral colony. Movement is likely to be risky for these small fishes. Furthermore, nearly all suitable coral colonies are occupied by a breeding pair and there are very few single adults in the population (Kuwamura et al. 1994a, b; Hobbs & Munday 2004). Being able to change sex in either direction enables an adult coral goby to mate with any other adult it encounters (Nakashima et al. 1995; Munday et al. 1998; Munday 2002). Nakashima et al. (1995) demonstrated that single *P. echinocephalus* adults prefer to pair with an adult of the same sex on a nearby coral rather than moving farther to find a single partner of the opposite sex. A similar pattern occurs with *G. histrio* and the closely related *G. erythrospilus* on the Great Barrier Reef (Munday unpublished data). Therefore, the benefit of changing sex in each direction appears to be that it reduces the risk of predation associated with searching for a new mate of the appropriate sex in a situation where there is low mate availability.

Juveniles reside either on the same corals as adult pairs (Kuwamura et al. 1994b, Thompson et al. 2007), or in corals that are too small for a breeding pair (Kuwamura et al. 1994a, 1996; Hobbs & Munday 2004). These juveniles will readily form a breeding pair with a single adult (Kuwamura et al. 1994a; Hobbs et al. 2004). Only protogynous sex change would be required if pair formation always occurred by this mechanism—a single female would change sex to male, and the juvenile would mature as a female to form a breeding pair. However, by pairing with a small partner an adult is likely to suffer a significant loss of reproductive success. Instead of forming a pair with a small juvenile, some adults move and pair with another adult (Kuwamura et al. 1994a; Nakashima et al. 1996; Munday et al. 1998; Munday 2002). Protogynous sex change occurs if two females end up cohabiting, and protandrous sex change occurs if two males end up cohabiting.

Coral-dwelling gobies would need to move and might form new partnerships if their host coral dies. Gobies might also move to secure more favorable habitat patches or larger partners. The size of coral-dwelling gobies is often correlated with the size of their host coral and the space between the coral branches. Small, tightly branched coral heads tend to contain small pairs, whereas, large, more openly branched coral heads tend to contain larger pairs (Kuwamura et al. 1994b; Munday 2001; Hobbs & Munday 2004). Because reproductive success of both males and females is size dependent, an individual of either sex might move from an existing partnership if a position becomes available in a superior coral. The benefits of moving to find a larger partner or a more favorable coral colony are, however, offset by the risk of predation involved in searching for a new partner or host coral. This trade-off probably explains why adults rarely move more than a few meters, even when superior breeding opportunities are available elsewhere (Nakashima et al. 1995).

Bidirectional Sex Change and Alternative Mating Strategies

Bidirectional sex change has recently been discovered in primary males of the diandric, protogynous wrasse *Halichoeres trimaculatus* (Kuwamura et al. 2007). Why primary males change sex has not been explicitly tested, but it might be associated with changes in the densities or proportions of different male strategies within the local population, which affect the success of these different strategies. Diandric protogynous hermaphrodites have alternative male mating strategies—individuals either mature as female and then change sex to become a large territorial male later in life, or they mature as a small primary male. In some species, the proportion of primary males in the population varies depending on the reproductive success likely to be associated with that strategy. For example, in the bluehead wrasse *Thalassoma bifasciatum*, there are few primary males on small reefs with small populations because territorial males can control most spawning events under these conditions, and thus primary males have low reproductive success (Warner & Hoffman 1980; Munday et al. 2006c). The number of primary males increases sharply on contiguous reefs with large populations, because primary males have high reproductive success under these conditions (Warner & Hoffman 1980). It is possible that sex change by primary males is associated with changes in local densities or sex ratios that alter the favorability of a primary male strategy. Primary males may change sex to female if social conditions change such that their reproductive success becomes higher as a female than as a primary male (Kuwamura et al. 2007).

Alternative male strategies have also been described in the bidirectional sex-changing goby *L. dalli* (Drilling & Grober 2005). This species could provide an excellent opportunity to test if: (1) the proportion of small sneaker males varies with male density or other components of the social environment that influence the mating success of this male strategy; and (2) if these sneaker males change sex to female when their reproductive success becomes seriously constrained by competition with larger males.

Toward a General Explanation for Bidirectional Sex Change

The unifying principal favoring bidirectional sex change in the previous examples is that it can be beneficial when social conditions experienced by males might change dramatically and unpredictably and when a delay in finding a new partner sex could result in a substantial loss of reproductive output. Bidirectional sex change in other small species, such as *Lythrypnus*, also appears to be related to unpredictable changes in social organization and the potential loss of reproductive output (St. Mary 1994). Bidirectional sex change is most prevalent among small coral reef fishes and is particularly well developed in gobies, many of which are known to experience high rates of mortality (Hernaman & Munday 2005). Bidirectional sex change is also common among habitat-specialist fishes where there may be few options to form new partnerships following mate loss. The advantage of bidirectional sex change in larger, habitat generalist species, such as serranids, remains uncertain.

In some instances, bidirectional sex change is clearly consistent with the SAH; in other cases, it is not. In general, however, sex change appears to occur when it is likely to increase an individual's reproductive value. Bidirectional sex change enables individuals to tailor their sexual function to suit unpredictable circumstances that have significant impacts on reproductive value. The fact that some individuals change sex more than once and that they do so when it is likely to increase their reproductive value suggests that individuals can assess their immediate environment to make decisions about the costs and benefits of changing sex, or not.

PROXIMATE MECHANISMS AND
PHYSIOLOGICAL CONTROL
Social Factors

The social environment has a strong influence on the timing of sex change in many hermaphroditic fishes (Shapiro 1984; Warner 1988; Ross 1990). A common observation is that the presence of a dominant male prevents females from changing sex in protogynous species, whereas the presence of a dominant female prevents males changing sex in protandrous species. Social conditions also influence the timing and direction of sex change in bidirectional sex changers, although not in a way consistent with a simple suppression model of sex change (Kuwamura & Nakashima 1998). In bidirectional sex changers, the presence of a large, dominant individual can either suppress or induce sex change in a smaller subordinate of the same sex. In most species studied to date, the larger individual changes sex to male when two or more females are kept together in a group. In contrast, one or more of the smaller individuals change sex to female when two or more males are kept together in a group (e.g., Sunobe & Nakazono 1993; Nakashima et al. 1995; Reavis & Grober 1999; Kuwamura et al. 2002; Munday 2002; Sakai et al. 2003; Wittenrich & Munday 2005; but see Manabe et al. 2008). This indicates that individuals adjust their sex according to their position in a social hierarchy.

In polygynous species the choice of male phenotype by the largest individual in a group and female phenotype by smaller individuals in the group is easily understood by the relative reproductive success of males and females of different sizes in this mating system—the largest individual has higher reproductive success as a male and smaller individuals have higher reproductive success as female. Rodgers et al. (2007) demonstrated that individuals of *L. dalli* determined their sexual phenotype based on a simple operational principle: be female if subordinate and male if dominant. This simple rule of thumb is likely to maximize individual reproductive success within a polygynous mating system, because large males have the highest reproductive success (St. Mary 1994). Dominance relationships are usually size based but may be related to other factors among similar-sized individuals. Consequently, a slightly smaller individual may change sex to male, or retain the dominant male position, if it has already established dominance within the group. The timing of sex change was also influenced by the strength of dominance relationships within groups. Sex change occurred rapidly when one individual was larger than the others and was therefore clearly dominant. Sex change took longer when individuals were of similar size and dominance relationships needed to be established independently of body size (Black et al. 2005b; Rodgers et al. 2007).

As observed in other species, the larger individual becomes/stays male and the smaller individual becomes/stays female when two coral-dwelling gobies of the same sex cohabit a coral colony (Kuwamura et al. 1994a; Nakashima et al. 1996; Munday 2002). In this case, however, males and females have similar size-related reproductive success and, therefore, larger individuals do not appear to choose the male phenotype simply because it increases their fertility. Single females always change sex to male (Kroon et al. 2005), which suggests that there might be some other benefit to adopting the male phenotype when dominant. For example, males might have lower mortality rates than females (Munday unpublished data). Pairs might also benefit from the larger individual being male and the smaller female because females tend to grow faster than males (Kuwamura et al. 1994a; Munday 2002). Both individuals in the pair would benefit by having the smaller partner adopt the faster-growing female phenotype because the pair will become size-matched more quickly (Kuwamura et al. 1994a; Munday et al. 2006b).

Interestingly, sex change does not occur in heterosexual sex pairs of coral-dwelling gobies, even if the male is smaller than the female (Kuwamura et al. 1994a; Munday 2002). This suggests that individuals refrain from changing sex when it is not necessary and the costs outweigh the benefits. In another exception to the common pattern of the larger individual changing sex to male, Manabe et al. (2008) found that it was usually the smaller individual that changed sex to male when two female *Trimma Kudoi* were kept together. Furthermore, an intermediate-sized individual usually changes sex to male in small groups of females (Manabe et al. 2008). These examples demonstrate that a simple suppression model of sex change based on dominant male behavior alone cannot explain the proximate control of sex change in all bidirectional sex changers. Individuals may often adjust their sexual function to suit the precise social conditions they experience and the proximate mechanisms that control sex change must therefore be sensitive to these conditions.

Linking Social Factors to Endocrine Control Mechanisms

Sexual development in teleost fishes is largely determined by reciprocal interactions in the brain-pituitary-gonadal (BPG) axis (Francis 1992; Perry & Grober 2003; Frisch 2004). In species with social control of sex change, such as bidirectional sex changers, the brain is hypothesized to determine the gonadal sex because social events can only affect the gonads through the brain (Kobayashi et al. 2009). The hormonal component of the BPG axis in the brain is gonadotropin releasing hormone (GnRH), which is synthesized primarily in the hypothalamus, preoptic area, and nervus terminalis. This hormone stimulates the release of pituitary gonadotropin (GtH) into the blood. GtH stimulates gametogenesis and steroidogenesis in the gonad. The gonadal steroid hormones, of which testosterone (T), 11-ketotestosterone (11-KT), and estradiol (E_2) are the most studied, are carried in the blood and play an important role in gametogenesis and in regulating reproductive behavior and development of secondary sexual characteristics (Fostier et al. 1983; Liley & Stacey 1983).

Kroon et al. (2003, 2005) demonstrated that a single enzymatic pathway can regulate both female and male sexual differentiation in the coral-dwelling goby *G. erythrospilus*. E_2 concentration in females was twice that in males, while concentrations of T did not differ between the sexes (Kroon et al. 2003). Manipulating E_2 levels via the aromatase (P450arom) pathway induced adult sex change in each direction under natural social conditions (Kroon et al. 2005). The presence and activity of P450arom controls the androgen/estrogen ratio by catalyzing the irreversible conversion of T into E_2. Specifically, an increase in E_2 resulted in protandrous sex change and a decrease in E_2 resulted in protogynous sex change (Kroon et al. 2005).

Gene isoforms for the cytochrome P450arom enzyme have been identified in ovarian (*CYP19A1*) and brain (*CYP19A2*) tissue of *G. histrio* (Gardner et al. 2003, 2005), further supporting a role for E_2 and the aromatase pathway in mediating sex change in each direction. Variations in levels of T and 11-KT do not appear to play a role in regulating sex change in *Gobiodon* species (Kroon et al. 2003, 2009). In fact, a lack of sex-specific differences in 11-KT concentrations may permit serial adult sex change in bidirectional sex-changing species, such as *Gobiodon* (Kroon et al. 2009).

At least in *Gobiodon* species, it seems likely that behavioral interactions between individuals could mediate sex change by the regulation of E_2 synthesis through the aromatase pathway (Kroon et al. 2005). This mechanism of socially controlled sex change could operate through behavioral modulation of cortisol concentrations and subsequent regulation of the glucocorticoid response element (GRE) on the *CYP19A1* isoform (Gardner et al. 2005). The patterns of sex change in this genus could thus be explained if exposure to male behavior activates cortisol synthesis, which in turn facilitates E_2 production via the GRE transcriptional factor on *CYP19A1*, suppressing protogynous sex change in females and inducing protandrous sex change in subordinate males. Conversely, the absence of male behavior would deactivate cortisol synthesis and reduce E_2 production, inducing protogynous sex change in dominant or single females. Further research is needed to link behavioral patterns in *Gobiodon* species to changes in steroid concentrations that could mediate sex change in each direction.

Gonadal steroidogenic pathways involved in bidirectional sex change have also been examined in *T. okinawae*. During sex change in either direction, three steroidogenic enzymes required for converting cholesterol into gonadal steroids (P450 cholesterol side-chain cleavage, P450scc; 3β-hydroxysteroid dehydrogenase, 3β-HSD; and P450arom) were detected in gonadal tissue (Sunobe et al. 2005a, 2005b). Sunobe et al. (2005a) hypothesized that the activity of the P450arom enzyme in the ovary, as well as of other enzymes involved in steroidogenesis, may mediate sex change in either direction. A transcription factor involved in the regulation of the three steroidogenic enzymes, Ad4-binding protein (Ad4BP)/

steroidogenic factor-1(SF-1), was found in ovarian, testicular, brain, and kidney tissue (Kobayashi et al. 2005). During adult serial sex change, expression of Ad4BP/SF-1 was observed in ovarian tissue but not in testicular tissue and was higher in females than in males, suggesting a direct relationship between Ad4BP/SF-1 expression and the female phase in *T. okinawae* (Kobayashi et al. 2005).

Gonadal steroids such as 11-KT and E_2 have been documented in *L. dalli* (Carlisle et al. 2000; Black et al. 2005b; Rodgers et al. 2006). In females undergoing protogynous sex change, 11-KT concentrations in urine samples were correlated with the percentage of testicular tissue, size of the accessory gonadal structure (AGS), and male behavior (Black et al. 2005b). Furthermore, female *L. dalli* implanted with 11-KT developed enlarged testicular tissue, regressed ovarian tissue, and active AGS (Carlisle et al. 2000). 11-KT concentrations and behavioral interactions were correlated, but it is unclear whether 11-KT concentrations influences behavior or vice versa (Black et al. 2005b). Relationships between E_2 concentrations and behavior and reproductive morphology were not presented.

The potential importance of the aromatase pathway in mediating protogynous sex change in *L. dalli* has been explored by Black et al. (2005a). Aromatase activity in both brain and gonadal tissues was significantly higher in females than in males. However, changes in aromatase activity in brain and gonadal tissues during the process of protogynous sex change were dissimilar, suggesting differential regulation of aromatase activity in these two tissues (see, for example, Gardner et al. 2005). Black et al. (2005a) hypothesize that changes in brain aromatase activity affect steroid concentrations, resulting in both behavioral and morphological sex change in *L. dalli*.

Overall, these studies suggest that changes in E_2 concentrations play a key role in mediating sexual function in bidirectional sex changers. Examination of gonadal steroids and steroidogenic pathways demonstrate that a single enzymatic pathway can regulate both female and male sexual differentiation (Kroon et al. 2005). Specifically, activation and deactivation of the P450arom pathway appears to initiate serial sex change in bidirectional sex-changing fish. It is likely that the activity of the aromatase pathway regulates sex change by increasing or decreasing the availability of E_2 precursors, such that these become available (or not) for androgen pathways such as 17β-hydroxysteroid dehydrogenase (Ohta et al. 2003). Further research is needed to understand how changes in social organization interact with the BPG axis in different species to influence the endocrine pathways mediating sex change in each direction.

CONCLUSIONS

Research on the reproductive strategies of hermaphroditic fishes over the past two decades has overturned the assumption that individuals change sex only once in their life and revealed a remarkable complexity and diversity of sexual strategies that fishes use to maximize their reproductive success (Kuwamura & Nakashima 1998; Munday et al. 2006a). It is now clear that a considerable number of tropical marine fishes are capable of bidirectional sex change and at least some of them exhibit this trait in nature. Bidirectional sex change is most prevalent among small coral-reef fishes, especially from the family Gobiidae (gobies). The unpredictability of their social circumstances, combined with a high risk of predation experienced due to their small body size, appears to favor bidirectional sex change in these species. The benefits of bidirectional sex change in larger species, such as some groupers, is uncertain.

Sex change in each direction appears to be consistent with the SAH for some polygynous species, but not for pair-forming species. In polygynous species, large females usually change sex to male when they have the opportunity to defend a harem. Males will change sex back to female if they move to a new group where they are smaller than the resident male. It seems that males will opt to join a new group and change sex to female in circumstances where they have low reproductive value as a male (e.g., if they are single). Interestingly, in at least one polygynous species, it is usually one of the smaller females that changes sex in pairs or small groups of females (Manabe et al. 2008). This suggests that the even among polygynous species the conditions favoring sex change in each direction may differ.

Bidirectional sex change among pair-forming gobies is not consistent with the SAH. In these species, it seems that the low density of available partners and the high risk of searching for a new partner favor the ability to change sex in either direction to facilitate the formation of new breeding pairs. A general explanation for all bidirectional sex-changing species is that individuals change sex when it is likely to increases their reproductive value (expected future reproductive success accounting for size-based fecundity, growth and mortality). At least some species appear to have evolved the capacity to change sex in each direction because their local environmental conditions can change dramatically and unpredictably in a way that favors repeated sex change.

The message for sex allocation theory in general is that very complex sexual patterns can evolve when they are favored by variable and unpredictable environmental conditions. Existing explanations for the evolution of sex change are generally sufficient to account for the presence of bidirectional sex change, but no single hypothesis (e.g., SAH) can account for all cases. The overarching principle is that individuals usually change sex when it increases their reproductive value and individuals of many species clearly have reliable mechanisms for assessing their reproductive value as either a male or a female, and adjusting their sexual function accordingly.

FUTURE RESEARCH AND DIRECTIONS

The capacity for bidirectional sex change has most often been demonstrated in laboratory experiments where pairs or small groups of males or females are kept together in aquariums. How often sex change in each direction occurs in nature is unknown for most species. Studying bidirectional sex change under natural conditions in the field must become a priority in order to properly document the occurrence of this sexual pattern and understand its adaptive significance.

Correlating ecological and environmental conditions with patterns of sex change within and among species will help assess the advantages of bidirectional sex change in fishes. More experimental manipulations are also needed to explicitly test specific hypotheses about the benefits of sex change in each direction. Further comparative analyses and experiments using species with highly labile sexual function, such as species of *Lythrypnus*, should be particularly promising because these species are likely to exhibit the greatest flexibility in sexual function in relation to environmental conditions. The recent discovery of sex change by primary males of a protogynous sex-changing wrasse opens up another new avenue of research into bidirectional sex change and indicates that sexual patterns in many fishes are likely to be even more flexible than currently appreciated.

The endocrine mechanisms responsible for translating environmental stimuli into functional sex change are still not fully understood in fishes. Bidirectional sex changers provide a unique opportunity to assess the biochemical pathways involved in sex change and recent research has pointed to a key role of the aromatase pathway as a primary means of regulating sex change in each direction. Although we are gaining a better understanding of how steroid hormones act to regulate gonadal sex change, we still lack a clear perspective on how social behavior and brain function interact with steroidal hormones to induce or prevent sex change in fishes. Linking behavior and brain function with steroidal pathways is a key challenge for understanding sex change in fishes, especially in light of the different social environments of bidirectional sex-changing species.

Hermaphrodites can be classified according to two different characters—anatomy or function. This duality in the way that hermaphrodites are diagnosed has sometime caused confusion about whether a species should be called a sequential or simultaneous hermaphrodite. It is clear that a gradation exists in patterns of gonadal sex allocation (anatomy), ranging from species whose gonads have only male or only female sex cells present at one time to species that have equal allocations of male and female sex-cells in the gonads at the same time. In some of these species with mixed gonadal allocation, there are only ever mature gametes of one sex present. Gonads of some other species, however, may contain mature gametes of both sexes, even though individuals only function as one sex at a time. This gradation in sex-cell allocation, which is not always closely linked to an individual's functional sex, means that gonadal allocation (anatomy) alone is not sufficient to describe a species as a sequential hermaphrodite or a simultaneous hermaphrodite. We encourage the use of direct observations of breeding behavior and sexual function in conjunction with assessments of gonadal sex-cell allocation to aid the description of sexual strategies in hermaphroditic fishes (see also Sadovy de Mitcheson & Liu 2008).

The capacity for individuals to change sex more than once and also in association with changes in the social environment demonstrates the remarkable flexibility in reproductive function that many fishes possess and that this flexibility is an adaptive response to variation in local environmental conditions. Determining the conditions under which sex change in each direction occurs and the mechanisms controlling sexual function in these species will continue to be an exciting area of research, with important implications for understanding the functional role and evolutionary advantage of sex change in general.

ACKNOWLEDGMENTS

We are grateful to Hisaya Manabe and Tomoki Sunobe for providing data and photomicrographs of *Trimma* species, Sue Riley for assistance with histology and photomicrographs of *Gobiodon* species, and Mathew Grober and Tatsuru Kadota for unpublished data on *Lythrypnus dalli* and *Cirrhitichthys falco*. Tamoki Sunobe and Marian Wong provided helpful comments on the manuscript.

REFERENCES

Atz JW (1964). Intersexuality in fishes. In: Armstrong CN, Marshall AJ, (eds.), *Intersexuality in Vertebrates Including Man*. Academic Press, London, pp. 145–232.

Black MP, Balthazart J, Baillien M, Grober MS (2005a). Socially induced and rapid increases in aggression are inversely related to brain aromatase activity in a sex-changing fish, *Lythrypnus dalli*. Proceedings of the Royal Society B 272: 2435–2440.

Black MP, Moore B, Canario AVM, Ford D, Reavis RH, Grober MS (2005b). Reproduction in context: field testing a laboratory model of socially controlled sex change in *Lythrypnus dalli* (Gilbert). Journal of Experimental Marine Biology and Ecology 318: 127–143.

Carlisle SL, Marxer-Miller SK, Canario AVM, Oliveira RF, Canario L, Grober MS (2000). Effects of 11-Ketotestosterone on genital papilla morphology in the sex changing fish *Lythrypnus dalli*. Journal of Fish Biology 57: 445–456.

Cole KS (1990). Patterns of gonad structure in hermaphroditic gobies (Teleostei: Gobiidae). Environmental Biology of Fishes 28: 125–142.

Cole KS, Hoese DF (2001). Gonad morphology, colony demography and evidence for hermahroditism in *Gobiodon okinawae* (Teleostei: Gobiidae). Environmental Biology of Fishes 61: 161–173.

Depczynski M, Bellwood DR (2005). Shortest recorded vertebrate lifespan found in a coral reef fish. Current Biology 15: R288–R289.

Drilling CC, Grober MS (2005). An initial description of alternative male reproductive phenotypes in the bluebanded goby, *Lythrypnus dalli* (Teleostei, Gobiidae). Environmental Biology of Fishes 72: 361–372.

Ferrell DG (1987). Population structure of *Ogilbyina queenslandiae* on One Tree Island. Master's thesis, Department of Marine Biology, Sydney University, Queensland, Australia.

Fishelson L (1989). Bisexuality and pedogenesis in gobies (Gobiidae: Teleostei) and other fish, or, why so many little fish in tropical seas? Senckenbergiana Maritima 20: 147–169.

Fostier EP, Jalabert B, Billard R, Breton B, Zohar Y (1983). The gonadal steroids. In: Hoar WS, Randall DJ, Donaldson EM (eds.), *Fish Physiology*, vol. 9A. Academic Press, London, pp. 277–372.

Francis RC (1992). Sexual lability in teleosts: developmental factors. The Quarterly Review of Biology 67: 1–18.

Frisch A (2004). Sex-change and gonadal steroids in sequentially hermaphroditic teleost fish. Reviews in Fish Biology and Fisheries 14: 481–499.

Gardner L, Anderson TA, Place AR, Elizur A (2003). Sex change strategy and the aromatase genes. Fish Physiology and Biochemistry 28: 147–148.

Gardner L, Anderson T, Place AR, Dixon B, Elizur A (2005). Sex change strategy and the aromatase genes. Journal of Steroid Biochemistry and Molecular Biology 94: 395–404.

Ghiselin MT (1969). The evolution of hermaphroditism among animals. The Quarterly Review of Biology 44: 189–208.

Hernaman V, Munday PL (2005). Life history characteristics of coral reef gobies I. Growth and lifespan. Marine Ecology Progress Series 290: 207–221.

Hioki S, Suzuki K (1995). Spawning behavior, eggs, larvae, and hermaphroditism of the angelfish, *Apolemichthys trimaculatus*, in captivity. Bulletin of the Institute of Oceanic Research & Development, Tokai University 16: 13–22 (in Japanese).

Hioki S, Suzuki K (1996). Sex changing from male to female on the way of protogynous process in three *Centropyge* angelfishes (Pomacanthidae: Teleostei). Bulletin of the Institute of Oceanic Research & Development, Tokai University 17: 27–34 (in Japanese).

Hobbs J-PA, Munday PL (2004). Intraspecific competition controls spatial distribution and social organisation of the coral dwelling goby, *Gobiodon histrio*. Marine Ecology Progress Series 278: 253–259.

Hobbs J-PA, Munday PL, Jones GP (2004). Social induction of maturation and sex determination in a coral reef fish. Proceedings of the Royal Society B 271: 2109–2114.

Kadota T (2009). Ecological study on the mating system and sexual pattern of hawkfishes (Pisces: Cirrhitidae) on reefs of Kuchierabu-jima Island, Southern Japan. Doctoral thesis, Hiroshima University, Hiroshima, Japan.

Kobayashi K, Suzuki K (1992). Hermaphroditism and sexual function in *Cirrhitichthys aureus* and other Japanses Hawkfishes (Cirrhitidae: Teleostei). Japanese Journal of Ichthyology 38: 397–410.

Kobayashi Y, Sunobe T, Kobayashi T, Nagahama Y, Nakamura M (2005). Promotor analysis of two aromatase genes in the serial-sex changing gobiid fish, *Trimma okinawae*. Fish Physiology and Biochemistry 31: 123–127.

Kobayashi Y, Nakamura M, Sunobe T, Usami T, Kobayashi T, Manabe H, Paul-Prasanth B, Suzuki N, Nagahama Y (2009). Sex-change in the gobiid fish is mediated through rapid switching of gonadotropin receptors from ovarian to testicular protion or viceversa. Endocrinology 150: 871–878.

Kroon FJ, Munday PL, Pankhurst NW (2003). Steroid hormone levels and bi-directional sex change in Gobiodon histrio. Journal of Fish Biology 62: 153–167.

Kroon FJ, Munday PL, Westcott DA, Hobbs, J-PA, Liley NR (2005). Aromatase pathway mediates sex change in each direction. Proceedings of the Royal Society B 272: 1399–1405.

Kroon FJ, Munday PL, Westcott DA (2009). Equivalent whole-body concentrations of 11-ketotestosterone in female and male coral goby (Gobiodon erythrospilus), a bi-directional sex-changing fish. Journal of Fish Biology 75: 685–692.

Kuwamura T (1984). Social structure of the protogynous fish Labroides dimidiatus. Publications of the Seto Marine Biological Laboratory 29: 117–177.

Kuwamura T, Nakashima Y (1998). New aspects of sex change among reef fishes: recent studies in Japan. Environmental Biology of Fishes 52: 125–135.

Kuwamura T, Yogo Y, Nakashima Y (1993). Size-assortative monogamy and paternal egg care in a coral goby Paragobiodon echinocephalus. Ethology 95: 65–75.

Kuwamura T, Nakashima Y, Yogo Y (1994a). Sex change in either direction by growth-rate advantage in the monogamous coral goby, Paragobiodon echinocephalus. Behavioral Ecology 5: 434–438.

Kuwamura T, Yogo Y, Nakashima Y (1994b). Population dynamics of goby Paragobiodon echinocephalus and host coral Stylophora pistillata. Marine Ecology Progress Series 103: 17–23.

Kuwamura T, Nakashima Y, Yogo Y (1996). Plasticity in size and age at maturity in a monogamous fish: effect of host coral size and frequency dependence. Behavioral Ecology and Sociobiology 38: 365–370.

Kuwamura T, Tanaka N, Nakashima Y, Karino K, Sakai Y (2002). Reversed sex-change in the protogynous reef fish, Labroides dimidiatus. Ethology 108: 443–450.

Kuwamura T, Suzuki S, Tanaka N, Ouchi E, Karino K, Nakashima Y (2007). Sex change of primary males in a diandric labrid Halichoeres trimaculatus: coexistence of protandry and protogyny within a species. Journal of Fish Biology 70: 1898–1906.

Lassig BR (1977). Socioecological strategies adopted by obligate coral-dwelling fishes. In: Taylor DL (ed.), Proceedings of the Third International Coral Reef Symposium. Vol. 1, Biology. Rosenstiel School of Marine and Atmospheric Science, Miami, Florida, pp. 566–570.

Liley N, Stacey NE (1983). Hormones, pheromones, and reproductive behaviour in fish. In: Hoar WS, Randall DJ (eds.), Fish Physiology, vol. 9A. Academic Press, New York, pp. 1–63.

Liu M, Sadovy Y (2004). The influence of social factors on adult sex change and juvenile sexual differentiation in a diandric, protogynous epinepheline, Cephalopholis boenak (Pisces, Serranidae). Journal of Zoology London 264: 239–248.

Liu M, Sadovy Y (2005). Habitat association and social structure of the chocolate hind, Cephalopholis boenak (Pisces: Serranidae: Epinephelinae), at Ping Chau Island, northeastern Hong Kong waters. Environmental Biology of Fishes 74: 9–18.

Lorenzi V, Earley RL, Grober MS (2006). Preventing behavioural interactions with a male facilitates sex change in female blueband gobies, Lythrypnus dalli. Behavioral Ecology and Sociobiology 59: 715–722.

Manabe H, Ishimura M, Shinomiya A, Sunobe T (2007a). Field evidence for bi-directional sex change in the polygynous gobiid fish *Trimma okinawae*. Journal of Fish Biology 70: 600–609.

Manabe H, Ishimura M, Shinomiya A, Sunobe T (2007b). Inter-group movement of females of the polygynous gobiid fish *Trimma okinawae* in relation to timing of protogynous sex change. Journal of Ethology 25: 133–137.

Manabe H, Matsuoko M, Goto K, Dewa S, Shinomiya A, Sakurai M, Sunobe T (2008). Bi-directional sex change in the gobiid fish *Trimma* sp.: does size-advantage exist? Behaviour 145: 99–113.

Michael SW (2004). *Basslets, Dottybacks and Hawkfishes*. TFH Publications, Neptune City, New Jersey.

Munday PL (2001). Fitness consequences of habitat selection and competition among coral-dwelling fish. Oecologia 128: 585–593.

Munday PL (2002). Bi-directional sex change: testing the growth-rate advantage model. Behavioral Ecology and Sociobiology 52: 247–254.

Munday PL, Jones GP (1998). The ecological implications of small body size among coral-reef fishes. Oceanography and Marine Biology: An Annual Review 36: 373–411.

Munday PL, Buston PM, Warner RR (2006a). Diversity and flexibility of sex-change strategies in animals. Trends in Ecology and Evolution 21: 89–95.

Munday PL, Cardoni AM, Syms C (2006b). Cooperative growth regulation in coral dwelling fishes. Biology Letters 2: 355–358.

Munday PL, White JW, Warner RR (2006c). A social basis for the development of primary males in a sex-changing fish. Proceedings of the Royal Society B 273: 2845–2851.

Muñoz RC, Warner RR (2003). A new version of the size-advantage hypothesis for sex change: incorporating sperm competition and size-fecundity skew. American Naturalist 161: 749–761.

Nakashima Y, Kuwamura T, Yogo Y (1995). Why be a both-ways sex changer. Ethology 101: 301–307.

Nakashima Y, Kuwamura T, Yogo Y (1996). Both-ways sex change in monogamous coral gobies, *Gobiodon* spp. Environmental Biology of Fishes 46: 281–288.

Ohta K, Sundaray JK, Okida T, Sakai M, Kitano T, Yamaguchi A, Takeda T, Matsuyama M (2003). Bi-directional sex change and its steroidogenesis in the wrasse, *Pseudolabrus sieboldi*. Fish Physiology and Biochemistry 28: 173–174.

Perry AN, Grober MS (2003). A model for social control of sex change: interactions of behaviour, neuropeptides, glucocorticoids, and sex steroids. Hormones and Behaviour 43: 32–38.

Reavis RH, Grober MS (1999). An integrative approach to sex change: social, behavioural and neurochemical changes in *Lythrypnus dalli* (Pisces). Acta Ethologica 2: 51–60.

Robertson DR (1972). Social control of sex reversal in a coral-reef fish. Science 177: 1007–1009.

Rodgers EW, Earley RL, Grober MS (2006). Elevated 11-ketotestosterone during paternal behavior in the Bluebanded goby (*Lythrypnus dalli*). Hormones and Behavior 49: 610–614.

Rodgers EW, Earley RL, Grober MS (2007). Social status determines sexual phenotype in the bi-directional sex changing blueband goby *Lythrypnus dalli*. Journal of Fish Biology 70: 1660–1668.

Ross RM (1990). The evolution of sex-change mechanisms in fishes. Environmental Biology of Fishes 29: 81–93.

Sadovy Y, Donaldson TJ (1995). Sexual pattern of *Neocirrhites armatus* (Cirrhitidae) with notes on other hawkfish species. Environmental Biology of Fishes 42: 143–150.

Sadovy Y, Shapiro DY (1987). Criteria for the diagnosis of hermaphroditism in fishes. Copeia 1987: 136–156.

Sadovy de Mitcheson Y, Liu M (2008). Functional hermaphroditism in teleosts. Fish and Fisheries 9: 1–43.

Sakai Y, Kohda M (1997). Harem structure of the protogynous angelfish, *Centropyge ferrugatus* (Pomacanthidae). Environmental Biology of Fishes 49: 333–339.

Sakai Y, Karino K, Kuwamura T, Nakashima Y, Maruo Y (2003). Sexually dichromatic protogynous angelfish *Centropyge ferrugata* (Pomacanthidae) males can change back to females. Zoological Science 20: 627–633.

Sakurai M, Nakakoji S, Manabe H, Dewa S, Shinomiya A, Sunobe T (2009). Bi-directional sex change and gonad structure in the gobiid fish *Trimma yanagitai*. Ichthyological Research 56: 82–86.

Shapiro DY (1984). Sex reversal and sociodemographic processes in coral reef fishes. In: Potts GW, Wootton RJ (eds.), *Fish Reproduction*. Academic Press, London, pp. 103–117.

Shiobara Y (2000). Reproduction and hermaphroditism of the gobiid fish, *Trimma grammistes*, from Suruga Bay, central Japan. Science Reports of the Museum, Tokai University 2: 19–30.

St. Mary CM (1993). Novel sexual patterns in two simultaneously hermaphroditic gobies, *Lythrypnus dalli* and *Lythrypnus zebra*. Copeia 1993: 1062–1072.

St. Mary CM (1994). Sex allocation in a simultaneous hermaphrodite, the blueband goby (*Lythrypnus dalli*): the effects of body size and behavioral gender and the consequences for reproduction. Behavioral Ecology 5: 304–313.

St. Mary CM (1996). Sex allocation in a simultaneous hermaphrodite, the zebra goby *Lythrypnus zebra*: insights gained through a comparison with its sympatric congener, *Lythrypnus dalli*. Environmental Biology of Fishes 45: 177–190.

St. Mary CM (1997). Sequential patterns of sex allocation in simultaneous hermaphrodites: do we need models that specifically incorporate this complexity? The American Naturalist 150: 73–97.

St. Mary CM (1998). Characteristic gonad structure in the gobiid genus *Lythrypnus* with comparisons to other hermaphroditic gobies. Copeia 1998: 720–724.

St. Mary CM (2000). Sex allocation in *Lythrypnus* (Gobiidae): variations on a hermaphroditic theme. Environmental Biology of Fishes 58: 321–333.

Sunobe T, Nakazono A (1990). Polygynous mating system of *Trimma okinawae* (Pisces: Gobiidae) at Kagoshima, Japan with a note on sex change. Ethology 84: 133–143.

Sunobe T, Nakazono A (1993). Sex change in both directions by alteration of social dominance in *Trimma okinawae* (Pisces: Gobiidae). Ethology 94: 339–345.

Sunobe T, Nakazono A (1999). Mating system and hermaphroditism in the gobiid fish, *Priolepis cincta*, at Kagoshima, Japan. Ichthyological Research 46: 103–105.

Sunobe T, Nakamura M, Kobayashi Y, Kobayashi T, Nagahama Y (2005a). Aromatase immunoreactivity and the role of enzymes in steroid pathways for inducing sex change in the hermaphrodite gobiid fish *Trimma okinawae*. Comparative Biochemistry and Physiology a-Molecular and Integrative Physiology 141: 54–59.

Sunobe T, Nakamura M, Kobayashi Y, Kobayashi T, Nagahama Y (2005b). Gonadal structure and P450scc and 3ß-Hsd immunoreactivity in the gobiid fish *Trimma okinawae* during bidirectional sex change. Ichthyological Research 52: 27–32.

Tanaka H, Hirose K, Nogami K, Hattori K, Ishibashi N (1990). Sexual maturation and sex reversal in red spotted grouper, *Epinephelus akaara*. Bulletin of the National Research Institute of Aquaculture 17: 1–15 (in Japanese).

Thompson VJ, Munday PL, Jones GP (2007). Habitat patch size and mating system as determinants of social group size in coral-dwelling fishes. Coral Reefs 26: 165–174.

Warner RR (1975). The adaptive significance of sequential hermaphroditism in animals. The American Naturalist 109: 61–82.

Warner RR (1978). The evolution of hermaphroditism and unisexuality in aquatic and terrestrial vertebrates. In: Reese ES, Lighter FJ (eds.), *Contrasts in Behaviour*. John Wiley & Sons, New York, pp. 78–101.

Warner RR (1988). Sex change and the size-advantage model. Trends in Ecology and Evolution 3: 133–136.

Warner RR, Hoffman SG (1980). Population density and the economics of territorial defense in a coral reef fish. Ecology 61: 772–780.

Winterbottom R, Southcott L (2008). Short lifespan and high mortality in the western Pacific coral reef goby *Trimma nasa*. Marine Ecology Progress Series 366: 203–208.

Wittenrich ML, Munday PL (2005). Labile sex allocation in three species of *Pseudochromis* (Pseudochromidae): an experimental evaluation. Zoological Science 22: 797–803.

Neuroendocrine Regulation of Sex Change and Alternate Sexual Phenotypes in Sex-Changing Reef Fishes

John Godwin

Our understanding of the diversity of sexual strategies occurring in nature has increased dramatically in the last 25 years. This is particularly true in the area of determination of an individual's sex by environmental signals. Progress in understanding environmental sex determination (ESD) has been greatest in the areas of temperature dependent sex determination in reptiles (Crews 2003) and social determination of sex and sexual expression in fishes, the primary topic of this chapter. Related to the question of how the same genotype may direct the development of different sexes in response to environmental signals is that of what physiological mechanisms generate discrete sexual phenotypes within a sex. Alternate male phenotypes are found in many marine fishes, and these males are typically "mosaics" of morphological and physiological features found in females and territorial male phenotypes. I will discuss physiological and neural mechanisms underlying the expression of alternate male phenotypes in sex-changing fishes here as well, both because these are closely related to those underlying sex change and because individual life histories in a number of species involve transitions both between sexes and between sexual phenotypes within a sex. Can study of physiological and neurobiological mechanisms inform our understanding of evolutionary patterns of sexual expression? Put another way, will "How" approaches inform "Why" questions? Although a definitive answer to this question is not yet possible, the strong conservation of basic mechanisms underlying sexual development argues that the answer is likely to be yes, and extremely useful from a practical standpoint for study. This conservation is also important because adaptations uncovered in "extreme" examples of environmental effects on reproductive physiology, such as socially mediated sex change, are likely to also yield insights into social influences on neuroendocrine systems subserving sexual expression more generally. This has already occurred to some extent thanks to advances in measurement and manipulation of both steroid hormone and neural signaling systems beginning in the late 1980s (e.g., Goodson & Bass 2000; Black et al. 2005). As genomic information and technologies become available for species that are not traditional biomedical models, the pace of such contributions is likely to accelerate.

This chapter is organized in a series of subsections intended to review what is known and what are promising areas for inquiry. First, I briefly review the vertebrate and teleost neuroendocrine axis as well as key steroid and neural signaling systems known to affect reproductive function, reproductive behavior, and aggression in fishes. Then, I review the known involvement of these systems in regulating sex change and sexual behavior for the best studied groups of tropical marine fishes in this respect: the gobies (Gobiidae); the basslets and groupers (Serranidae); and the wrasses, parrotfishes, and damselfishes (Labridae, Scaridae, and Pomacentridae). Finally, I will briefly examine the state of research in this area as well as prospects for future research.

INTEGRATING ENVIRONMENTAL INFORMATION: NEUROENDOCRINE AND NEURAL SIGNALING SYSTEMS IN FISHES

Both the overall organization and the functioning of the neuroendocrine system subserving reproduction are remarkably conserved across vertebrate animals (Figure 9.1). The nervous system is also the logical site of integration for social information, although direct environmental influences on the gonads are likely important for forms of ESD, such as temperature dependent sex determination (e.g., Crews 1993; Luckenbach 2005).

Across vertebrate animals, the endocrine control of reproduction centers on what is termed the hypothalamo-pituitary-gonadal (HPG) axis. Hypothalamic gonadotropin releasing hormone (GnRH) neurons integrate a variety of internal and environmental influences and control secretion of gonadotropins from the pituitary gland. Teleost fishes have three distinct types of GnRH, with the form expressed in the hypothalamus and controlling pituitary gonadotropin secretion being most similar to one originally described in chickens (chicken II GnRH). Other GnRH forms are expressed in the terminal nerve and tegmentum respectively, where they play neuromodulatory roles in neural processing (Soga et al. 2005; Maruska & Tricas 2007). Unlike tetrapods, the teleost pituitary is said to be hard-wired, with direct innervation of anterior pituitary target cells rather than release of hypothalamic releasing hormones into a portal system. As in tetrapods, teleosts have two gonadotropins (GtH I and GtH II) with functions very compa-

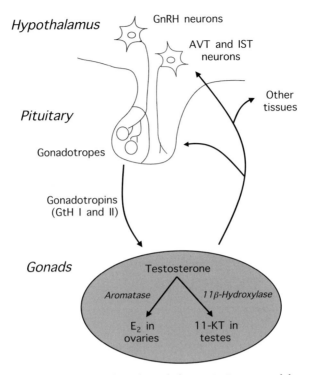

FIGURE 9.1. The teleost hypothalamo-pituitary-gonadal
(HPG) axis. Gonadotropin cells are found in the anterior
pituitary gland, and GnRH axons terminate at these cells
rather than at a portal system as in tetrapods. AVT and IST
neurons send processes to the posterior pituitary, but also
to other parts of the brain. Estrogen is synthesized through
aromatase activity in both the gonads and brain.

rable to follicle-stimulating hormone (FSH) and luteinizing hormone (LH) in
tetrapods, respectively. These gonadotropins regulate development and activity
of the gonads generally and steroid production and conversion, specifically.

The steroid hormones in fishes are generally similar to those of tetrapods but
also show important differences. Testosterone (T) is a major product of both the
ovaries and testes and functions both as an important androgenic signal and,
more importantly, as a prohormone in the biosynthesis of the predominant circulating estrogen in females, estradiol 17β (E_2), and of a key androgen, 11-
ketotestosterone (11-KT), in males (Borg 1994). Both E_2 and 11-KT have been
implicated in the control of gonadal sex differentiation and sexual behavior, and
control of the synthesis of these hormones appears likely to play a key role in the

process. The rate-limiting enzyme in estrogen synthesis is a member of the cytochrome p450 family of proteins and is most commonly referred to as aromatase. Aromatase enzymes catalyze the conversion of androgens to estrogens (Callard et al. 1990, 2001). As with a number of other important gene products relative to patterns in tetrapods, fishes produce two forms of aromatase that are distinct gene products, a gonadal form, termed gonadal aromatase, p450AromA, or cyp19A1; and a brain form, variously termed brain aromatase, p450AromB, and cyp19A2. The key synthetic enzyme regulating levels of 11-KT is 11β-hydroxylase. Unlike testosterone, 11-KT cannot be aromatized and this may contribute to androgenic effects as, at least in brain tissue, teleosts exhibit very high aromatase levels (Callard et al. 2001; Forlano et al. 2006).

In addition to studies of the HPG axis in sex-changing fishes, there is increasing interest in other neural and endocrine signaling systems that may influence both sexual expression and especially behavior. The endocrine stress system, mainly centered on the hypothalamo-pituitary-interrenal gland (HPI) axis, may play an important role in linking social behavior and interactions with gonadal function including sex change (Perry & Grober 2003). As with the HPG axis, this system is fundamentally similar to that found in tetrapods, while exhibiting some differences. Fishes do not have adrenal glands and the primary steroid hormone associated with stress responses in fishes, cortisol (chemically identical to that in humans), is produced by the interrenal gland. Cortisol secretion is stimulated by adrenocorticotropin (ACTH) from the anterior pituitary gland, as in tetrapods. ACTH secretion is in turn stimulated by corticotropin releasing hormone from the hypothalamus.

REEF FISH MODELS
OF SOCIALLY CONTROLLED SEX CHANGE

Hermaphroditism is exhibited in at least seven orders and 27 families of teleost fishes (Mank et al. 2006; Sadovy de Mitcheson & Liu 2008). A complete review of physiological correlates of sex change across teleosts is beyond the scope of this chapter, but excellent reviews of much of this literature have been previously published (Baroiller et al. 1999; Devlin & Nagahama 2002; Frisch 2004). Of the groups that exhibit sex change, however, relatively few are well studied at either the behavioral or the physiological level, and only four families of fishes have received significant attention at both levels. These are the primarily or commonly reef-associated gobies, basslets and groupers, wrasses, and parrotfishes (Labridae and Scaridae). Fortunately, for the goal of discerning general principles underlying sexual phenotype expression, these families exhibit some substantial and useful contrasts in body size, space use patterns, and mating systems. I review studies from these four families below. Gobies are covered first, followed by serranids, and then wrasses and parrotfishes. This sort of discussion is typically organized by physiological system rather than by taxonomic group. This chapter will present findings on physiological correlates and experimental manipulations of sex change within groups, with the goal of helping readers appreciate the integration of systems across physiological levels of organization within the same or similar species.

The Gobies

The gobies (family Gobiidae) are very common on both tropical and temperate reefs and have many features that make them attractive as models for both field and laboratory studies of sex change. These features include space use patterns often characterized by strong site fidelity and small territorial or home range areas, small body sizes, and high population densities that are advantageous in making statistically robust field experiments feasible. Gobies often show excellent adaptability to captivity, facilitating the study of their behavior and physiology under tightly controlled laboratory conditions. Finally, some goby species also display bidirectional sex change, allowing testing of hypothesized mechanisms of both protogynous and protandrous sex change in the same species.

The first goby species to be studied in detail with respect to sex change was the blackeye goby, *Coryphopterus nicholsi*. Cole described spawning behavior and reproductive success in *C. nicholsi* as well as identifying this species as a sex changer (1983). This initial work was followed with both ecological and physiological studies focused on steroid hormone metabolism. Kroon & Liley (2000) measured levels of E_2, testosterone, and 11-KT in whole-body extracts of mature males and females captured in the fall outside the summer breeding season. Testosterone and 11-ketotestosterone levels were significantly higher in males while estradiol levels were significantly higher in females. In order to test hypothesized roles for these steroids in mediating sexual phenotype and sex change, these authors treated females with slow-release elastomer implants containing 17α-methyltestosterone, 11-ketoadrenosterone, 11-ketotestosterone, or no hormone as a blank control treatment. Neither the control nor the 17α-methyltestosterone treatments induced gonadal changes. However, treatment with either of the 11-oxygenated androgens induced complete or nearly complete sex change over six weeks in all treated females. A second experiment exposed females to an aromatase inhibitor, fadrozole, and found a dose-response relationship where increasing concentrations of the drug produced increasing development of testicular morphology with the highest dose inducing testicular development in 87% of treated individuals.

Other goby species show similar variations in steroid metabolism and effects of estrogen synthesis on sexual development. Estradiol levels are higher in females than males in *Gobiodon histrio*, a species that exhibits bidirectional sex change, while testosterone levels were not different (Kroon et al. 2003). Levels of 11-KT were too low to permit measurement in most individuals of this small-bodied species and these authors suggest low 11-KT levels may be important in its ability to change sex in either direction. Experimental support for the role of estrogen synthesis in regulating sex change in *Gobiodon* was provided in a follow up study with *Gobiodon erythrospilus* (Kroon et al. 2005). In heterosexual experimental pairs, female *G. erythrospilus* treated with implants containing the aromatase inhibitor fadrozole changed sex to become male, while males treated with estradiol (the product of the aromatase enzyme) changed sex to become females. Conversely, sex change was not observed in this paired treatment for females treated with estrogen or males treated with the aromatase inhibitor. Unpaired individuals in this species become male, but estradiol treatment prevented this change in unpaired females. Unpaired males treated with estradiol changed sex to become female, while control males did not (Kroon et al. 2005). Unpaired females who were handled but not implanted did show sex change. These observations and those in *C. nicholsi* described above strongly implicate estradiol synthesis in the regulation of gonadal sex in gobies.

A series of studies in another gobiid implicates steroid hormone metabolism in controlling various aspects of sexual phenotype ranging from gonadal function to behavior. The blue-banded goby, *Lythrypnus dalli*, is native to warm, temperate regions of the eastern Pacific where it is found in relatively shallow, rocky areas associated with crevices or sometimes sea urchins for shelter. This species is a bidirectional sex changer that very interestingly displays shifts in allocation associated with social interactions. These shifts are associated with increases in dominance related behaviors, morphological changes including increases in body size, length of the dorsal fin, and changes in the genital papilla, in addition to the change in gonadal allocation between ovarian and testicular tissue (Carlisle et al. 2000). Individuals assume only one behavioral sex at a time with socially dominant individuals becoming males (St. Mary 1994; Rodgers et al. 2005; Lorenzi et al. 2006). At least some of these shifts are associated with changes in steroid hormone metabolism. Consistent with results for the bidirectionally changing *G. histrio* described above, comparisons of steroid levels excreted into holding water indicated a difference between male and female *L. dalli* in estradiol, although no differences were found between the sexes for testosterone, 11-ketotestosterone, or cortisol in this study (Lorenzi et al. 2008). As in some other sex changing species (see below), levels of 11-ketotesterone vary in male *L. dalli* with reproductive activity, being elevated in experienced brooding males (Rodgers et al. 2006). Treatment with this potent androgen causes the genital papilla to become more male-like in form (Carlisle et al. 2000). There also appears to be within-sex variation in reproductive tactics in male *L. dalli* (Drilling & Grober 2005), but endocrine correlates of this variation have not yet been explored.

All vertebrate animals produce or convert various types of steroid hormones in the central nervous system (Callard et al. 1990). In rats, testosterone masculinizes the brain around the time of birth, but only after conversion to estradiol by the enzyme aromatase (Clemens & Gladue 1978). Steroid hormone conversion by the brain also appears to play a critical role in controlling sex change and sexual phenotype development in fishes, but masculinization appears be blocked by estrogen synthesis rather than stimulated by it as in rats. Male removal from social groups in *L. dalli* induced the rapid development of a dominance-related behavior known as *displacement* in the largest female (Black et al. 2005). This increase in male-typical aggressive behavior was closely correlated with decreases in brain aromatase activity, suggesting an important functional link. Interestingly, while female *L. dalli* have higher aromatase activity in both the brain and gonads than males, alterations in these levels with assumption of social dominance were more rapid in the brain (Figure 9.2). This is consistent with social cues being the critical regulator of this process. What is as yet unknown for this system and other teleost systems are the mechanisms by which changes or differences in aromatase activity influence behavioral phenotype development. Two possibilities have been suggested (Schlinger et al. 1999; Black et al. 2005). First, aromatase in the brain may prevent masculinization by converting testosterone to estradiol and thereby preventing this hormone from acting as an androgen or, potentially, from being converted to the potent androgen 11-ketotestosterone. Alternatively, estradiol—produced either by the ovaries or in the brain through aromatization of testosterone—may inhibit male development and behavioral display. I return to this issue in the discussion of wrasses.

The biochemical regulation of steroid metabolism is beginning to be addressed in the bidirectionally sex changing goby *Trimma okinawae*. As in other teleosts, this species expresses two forms of the aromatase enzyme, cytochrome p450AromA predominantly in the gonads and p450AromB predominantly in the brain (Kobayashi et al. 2004). Immunoreactivity for the ovarian form has been found in the gonad, as predicted (Sunobe et al. 2005). The upstream promoter regulatory region has been examined for the gonadal form of aromatase (p450AromA) in *T. okinawae* and found to contain response elements for several key mediators, including several estrogen response elements, or EREs (Kobayashi et al. 2005). This finding is consistent with regulation of aromatase by estrogen and with the potential stimulation of aromatase expression and induction of male-to-female sex change in gobies as described for *G. erythrospilus* above, although this effect of exogenous estrogen has not been specifically tested at this writing. The promoter regions of both the ovarian and brain forms of aromatase were examined in *G. histrio* by Gardner et al. (2005). These authors, by contrast, identified putative EREs for the brain form and not the ovarian form. Interestingly, a response element for glucocorticoids (GRE), key mediators of the

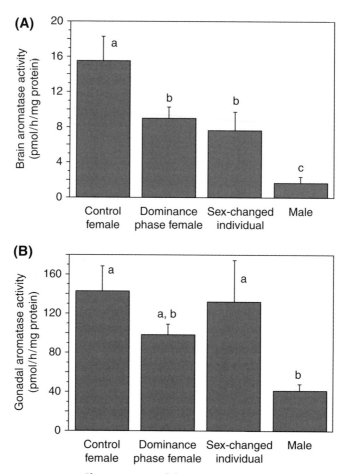

FIGURE 9.2. Changes in gonadal aromatase activity in brain and gonad between sexual phenotypes and during sex change in the blue-banded goby, *Lythrypnus dalli*. Groups designated with different letters over the bars are significantly different. Redrawn from Black et al. 2005.

endocrine stress response, was suggested for the promoter region of ovarian aromatase in *G. histrio*. These were not described in the other two species they examined (*Lates calcarifer* and *Cromileptes altivelis*), or for *T. okinawae*. This is potentially important, as glucocorticoid stress hormones have been proposed as important mediators of socially controlled sex change (Perry & Grober 2003).

What might be the consequences of these differences in steroid hormone influences on the neural substrates of reproductive function and behavior in gobies? Neuropeptide hormone systems have been the subject of intense research in the area of social neuroscience in recent years, and these signaling systems are implicated in key social behaviors in a number of mammalian, avian, and amphibian models (for recent reviews, see Goodson & Bass 2001; Rose & Moore 2002; De Vries & Panzica 2006). The neuropeptides arginine vasotocin (AVT) and isotocin (IST) have been the subject of substantial research in fishes, as have the homologous hormones in other vertebrate groups. This area is just beginning to be explored in gobies, but the extraordinary diversity found in this family suggests that it is likely to be a fruitful area of research.

Isotocin is the teleost homolog of oxytocin in mammals, which has a wide array of described functions, including a common association with female-typical sociosexual behaviors. Consistent with this overall pattern from mammals, female *L. dalli* show larger numbers of isotocin neurons than do males. By contrast, another bidirectionally sex-changing goby, *Trimma okinawae*, shows larger vasotocin neurons in male-phase than female-phase individuals (Grober & Sunobe 1996). Although not a sex-changing species, comparisons of AVT neurons in another gobiid species, the halfspotted goby (*Asterropteryx semipunctata*), indicated sex differences that are dependent on when sampling was performed (Maruska et al. 2007).

Gonadotropin-releasing hormone (GnRH) has been a focus of research in teleost reproduction, but it has not yet been well studied in sex-changing gobies. Studies in non-sex changing gobies suggest differences across sexual phenotypes, but with substantial variation in these patterns across species. In the study cited above on half spotted gobies, sex differences in GnRH neurons were evident and, as with AVT, these varied across sampling periods (Maruska et al. 2007). Scaggiante et al. (2006) studied GnRH neural phenotype in two European goby species, the grass goby (*Zosterisessor ophiocephalus*) and the black goby (*Gobius niger*), comparing sexual phenotypes and seasonal changes. As with the halfspotted goby, these authors found a complex pattern of differences, with grass gobies displaying dimorphism in forebrain GnRH expression both intrasexually across male reproductive tactics and intersexually. Black gobies, by contrast, displayed only intersexual differences. Interpretation of such divergence of among species is complicated by other potentially confounding differences (as noted by Scaggiante et al. 2006) and the lack of a comprehensive phylogenetic framework. Fortunately, the speciose nature of the Gobiidae and variation both within and among groups is favorable for this type of work going forward.

Basslets and Groupers

The groupers and basslets (family Serranidae) are the second of the groups of sex-changing species that has been well studied at both the behavioral and physiological levels. In addition to providing intriguing contrasts in body size and sexual pattern, including especially the presence of simultaneous hermaphroditism in the family, the serranids are ecologically and economically important because groupers support important fisheries in the tropics and subtropics. A better understanding of sexual function and sex change in groupers therefore has the strong potential of contributing to captive breeding and aquaculture efforts. Serranids are somewhat unusual in the context of this chapter because most of the behavioral work has focused on one part of the family, the basslets and hamlets, while most of the endocrine work to date has focused on the typically larger groupers. There are some exceptions and these will be highlighted, but it is also likely that there are strong similarities in mechanisms regulating both gonadal function and behavior across the family.

Much of the initial ethological study of hermaphroditism in the serranids focused on the basslet *Pseudanthias squamipinnis* (formerly *Anthias*, Shapiro, 1980, 1981). While this behavioral work has not been followed by physiological studies in *Pseudanthias*, it did help stimulate work in other small serannids, including studies of reproductive endocrinology. The belted sandbass, *Serranus subligarius*, is a simultaneous hermaphrodite native to the Gulf of Mexico. Despite having both functional ovarian and testicular tissue, individuals vary in their likelihood of spawning in the female or male role, with larger fish spawning more often as males (Oliver 1997). A follow-up study by the same researcher showed that this shift from predominantly female-role spawning to male-role spawning with increasing body size is mirrored by increasing plasma concentrations of both 11-KT and 20βS, a progestin-class steroid hormone that induces final oocyte maturation in some fishes (Cheek et al. 2000). Studies in other teleosts show that 20βS binds a G-protein coupled membrane steroid receptor (Zhu et al. 2003a, b), suggesting the possibility for rapid, non-genomic effects of this steroid on behavior.

Endocrine studies of gonadal function and gonadal sex change in serranids have focused primarily on groupers, especially members of the genus *Epinephelus*. This genus has a circumtropical distribution and extends into many warm temperate regions. *Epinephelus* species are the focus of a number of economically important fisheries and, increasingly, are of interest as potential aquaculture cultivars. These relatively large predators are often also very important ecologically and there is considerable interest in the potential of stock enhancement to replenish populations that have declined due to fishing pressure (Sadovy & Domeier 2005). These factors have provided considerable impetus to understanding reproductive endocrinology in groupers and substantial progress is being made.

The steroid hormone correlates of sexual phenotype have now been characterized for a number of protogynous groupers. The pattern of sexual development in groupers appears to be largely monandric, with males developing only from mature females, although there is at least one example of diandry (in which males may develop directly from juveniles or by sex change from females) from the

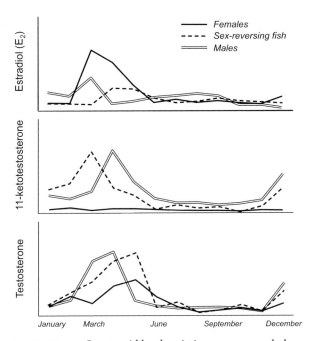

FIGURE 9.3. Sex steroid level variation across sexual phenotype and season in the grouper *Epinephelus akaara*. Redrawn from Li et al. 2007.

genus *Epinephelus* (Fennessy & Sadovy 2002). Females typically have higher plasma levels of E_2 and lower levels of 11-KT (Alam et al. 2006).

Plasma steroid profiles in male and female groupers have been investigated in five species, three in the genus *Epinephelus*, and two others. The consistent pattern in the breeding season is higher E_2 in females and higher 11-KT in males, with the predicted shifts in these levels in fish undergoing sex change (Figure 9.3). Plasma T (testosterone) levels do not show these consistent sex differences, possibly because T is the biochemical precursor for both E_2 and 11-KT. Higher estrogen levels for female groupers in the breeding season are reflected in, and likely a result of, higher aromatase expression as described in the red-spotted grouper, *Epinephelus akaara*, associated with both naturally occurring and hormonally induced sex change (Li et al. 2006a, b, 2007). Aromatase activity and mRNA levels were also reduced in the orange-spotted grouper with androgen-induced sex change (Zhang et al. 2007).

Male grouper show higher 11-KT synthetic capacity than females. Female honeycomb grouper (*Epinephelus merra*) have low 11-KT levels and some ovarian expression of the key enzyme in 11-KT synthesis, 11β-hydroxylase, which may be important in stimulating sex change as the process proceeds (Alam et al. 2006). Male honeycomb grouper have higher 11β-hydroxylase-like immunoreactivity in the gonads and significantly higher production of 11-KT from gonadal fragments in vitro.

As in the gobies discussed above and the wrasses and parrotfishes discussed in the next section, both steroid hormone manipulations—hormone implants and inhibitors of steroidogenesis—are effective in inducing sex change in groupers. Two groups have now described successful induction of protogynous sex change through inhibition of aromatase, specifically using the drug fadrozole, as in the goby studies referenced earlier (Bhandari et al. 2004, 2006; Li et al. 2006a, b). Several groups have also described successful induction of sex change with androgen implants in groupers and another large serranid (Yeh et al. 2003a, b; Benton & Berlinsky 2006; Li et al. 2006a; Sarter et al. 2006; Zhang et al. 2007). The initiating events of sex change have been difficult to discern because decreases in aromatase expression and E_2 production at the onset of the process are temporally confounded with increases in 11-KT. However, Bhandari et al. (2005) showed that coadministering E2 could prevent sex change that would otherwise be induced by inhibiting aromatase. These authors suggest that a decline in estrogen biosynthesis is the key event in the initiation of sex change and this hypothesis is consistent with findings and suggestions put forward for other fishes (Black et al. 2005; Kroon et al. 2005; Marsh 2007).

Little information is so far available regarding endocrine aspects of sexual function in other parts of the HPG axis, but this should change rapidly thanks to the development of a number of molecular tools for various grouper species. These include the molecular cloning of the different subunits of the gonadotropins (Shein et al. 2003; Li et al. 2005), a GnRH receptor from the orange-spotted grouper (He et al. 2006), and the brain form of aromatase (p450AromB)(Zhang et al. 2004).

The Labroidei (Wrasses, Parrotfishes, and Damselfishes)

Wrasses, parrotfishes, and damselfishes are conspicuous and ecologically important members of tropical and many temperate zone reef communities. These families are closely related (Kaufman & Liem 1982; see also Streelman & Karl 1997), and they are related to the cichlids of tropical fresh waters, which are the subject of considerable physiological research and a current genome sequencing effort. Another valuable feature of many wrasse and parrotfish species for exploring the physiological bases of sexual phenotype development is the presence of both functional protogynous sex change and discrete alternate male phenotypes. These alternate male phenotypes include typically large and colorful terminal phase (TP) males and smaller initial phase (IP) males that are often nearly indistinguishable externally from females (Warner 1984; Cardwell 1991a). This display of "three sexes" allows comparisons both across sexes and within a sex where behavioral phenotype differs strongly, but gonadal sex does not. The damselfishes (Pomacentridae) are useful models because both protogyny and protandry are exhibited in the family. This group is reviewed briefly at the end of the chapter, but it has received much less attention from a physiological standpoint than the wrasses and parrotfishes.

STEROID HORMONE CORRELATES
OF SEXUAL PHENOTYPE AND SEX CHANGE

Among the three main groups of sex changing reef fishes that are the focus of this chapter, steroid hormone correlates of sexual phenotype and sex change have been most extensively explored in the wrasses and parrotfishes. Reinboth & Becker (1984) focused on steroid hormone synthesis in studying testosterone conversion by the gonads of the Mediterranean wrasse *Coris julis*. A key finding of this study was that production of 11β-hydroxylated androgens by the gonads was largely restricted to secondary males. This finding is supported by a variety of other studies in wrasses and parrotfishes. Nakamura et al. (1989) explored differences in gonad structure and ultrastructure as well as circulating gonadal steroid levels in the Hawaiian saddleback wrasse, *Thalassoma duperrey*. Consistent with the findings of Reinboth & Becker (1984), terminal phase males had significantly greater circulating levels of 11-ketotestosterone than females (Figure 9.4). Conversely, females had higher circulating levels of E_2 and testosterone (likely related to testosterone's role as a substrate in E_2 synthesis). A follow-up study in *T. duperrey* found that 11-KT synthesis was greater *in vitro* by the testes of TP males than those of IP males and that circulating 11-KT levels were also higher in TP males. The saddleback wrasse has also been a very useful model in behavioral studies of sex change and in understanding monoamine neurotransmitter contributions to the process. We return to these findings below.

The bamboo wrasse, *Pseudolabrus seboldi*, exhibits sexual phenotype differences similar to those found in the *Thalassoma* species with both diandry and protogynous sex change. As in the saddleback wrasse, terminal phase male bamboo wrasses have higher plasma 11-KT levels than females overall, and levels within individuals are correlated with the degree of development of sexually dimorphic fin coloration (Ohta et al. 2008). Surprisingly, no differences were found in plasma E_2 levels in this study, but the authors suggest this may be attributable to sampling outside the spawning season.

The Caribbean stoplight parrotfish, *Sparisoma viride*, is another common and conspicuous species that exhibits both protogynous sex change and discrete alternate male phenotypes. Cardwell & Liley (1991a) compared circulating steroid levels between sexual phenotypes in *S. viride* using samples from field-caught

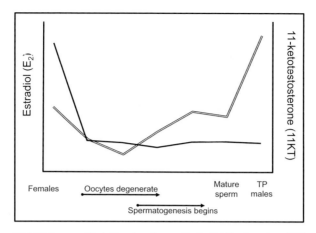

FIGURE 9.4. Variation in plasma E_2 (solid line) and 11-KT (double line) between females, TP males, and over the course of natural sex change in the saddleback wrasse, *Thalassoma duperrey*. Redrawn from Nakamura et al. 2005.

females, IP males, and TP males as well as some sex-changing individuals. As with saddleback wrasses, E_2 levels were higher in females, and 11-KT levels were elevated in TP males relative to both females and IP males. A follow-up study examined steroid hormone correlates of sexual phenotype and social status among males, finding that territorial TP males had elevated 11-KT levels relative to TP males that did not hold territories (Cardwell & Liley 1991a).

Little is known about potential differences in the expression of receptors for the key androgens and E_2. Kim et al. (2002) cloned portions of a nuclear androgen receptor (AR) and the α subtype of the estrogen receptor (ERα) in threespot wrasses (*H. trimaculatus*) and compared expression of these genes across sexual phenotypes using semi-quantitative RT-PCR (reverse transcription-polymerase chain reaction). No differences were found between females and terminal-phase males in ERα expression in either the gonads or brain, or in AR mRNA expression in the gonads. TP males did show higher AR mRNA expression in the brain suggesting potentially greater androgen sensitivity in this morph type. No information is available on other estrogen receptor subtypes known to be expressed in fishes (Hawkins et al. 2000, 2005). It is also worth noting that PCR-based techniques give little anatomical resolution, so sexual phenotype differences in more restricted regions of the gonads or brain remain to be critically examined.

As described above for gobies and groupers, estrogen synthesis through the activity of aromatase appears to be a key regulator of sex change in wrasses and parrotfish. Following up on the studies detailing differences in plasma concentrations of key gonadal steroids, immunocytochemistry (which localizes the enzyme proteins in tissues) was used to examine the expression of aromatase and the key enzyme in 11-KT synthesis, 11β-hydroxylase, across sexual phenotypes in the saddleback wrasse, *T. duperrey* (reviewed in Nakamura & Kobayashi 2005)(Figure 9.4). Aromatase expression was high in the ovary of *T. duperrey* and declined with sex change, while 11β-hydroxylase was expressed in the ovary, declined at the onset of sex change, and then steadily increased with testicular development. These changes in gonadal steroidogenic enzyme expression correlated well with concurrent changes in E_2 and 11-KT, respectively.

STEROID HORMONE CONTROL OF SEXUAL PHENOTYPE DIFFERENCES: MANIPULATIVE STUDIES

A number of studies in both wrasses and parrotfishes have taken a manipulative approach to addressing the role of gonadal steroid hormones in controlling sex change. A key emerging issue has been experimentally addressing the relative importance of estrogen inhibition and androgen stimulation in protogynous sex change.

The bluehead wrasse, *Thalassoma bifasciatum*, was the subject of a series of studies addressing androgen effects on sex change. Several authors reported that injections of androgens induced bluing of the head, a feature characteristic of terminal phase males, and some degree of gonadal sex change (Stoll 1955; Roede 1972; Reinboth 1975). In contrast, neither testosterone nor dihydrotestosterone implants administered to female bluehead wrasses induced testicular development in a later study, although the fish did exhibit discernible color changes within five days that progressed and "approached that which exists in the wild" (Kramer et al. 1988). It is noteworthy that this study was conducted with captive fish; the investigators were unable to assess the initial sex of treated individuals at the beginning of the experiments (female or initial phase male) and therefore inferred effects from sex ratios following sacrifice at the end of the study; and that T is a precursor for both E_2 and 11-KT. The last point complicates interpretation, because implanted T could act in at least three distinct ways: as an androgen through the nuclear androgen receptor as T or following conversion to 11-KT, or as an estrogen through one of the nuclear estrogen receptors following conversion by aromatase (biochemically distinct membrane receptors for steroids in teleosts add additional possibilities)(Thomas et al. 2006).

The non-aromatizable 11-KT does reliably induce sex change in the labroids in which this has been tested. Grober & Bass (1991) induced sex and color change in captive bluehead wrasses with 11-KT implants, and studies in the author's laboratory have replicated these results in free-living bluehead wrasses (Semsar & Godwin 2004; Austin et al. unpublished data)(Figure 9.5).

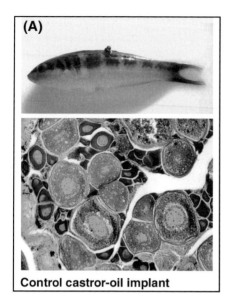
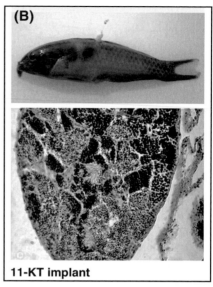

Control castror-oil implant   **11-KT implant**

FIGURE 9.5. Effects of 11-KT on body coloration and sexual development in the blue-head wrasse, *Thalassoma bifasciatum*. Females were implanted for two weeks in their natural habitat in the presence of dominant TP males, receiving either (A) a control castor oil implant or (B) an implant containing 11-KT dissolved in castor oil.

Behavioral sex change in the absence of gonads is not accompanied by permanent color changes, presumably because of a lack of endogenous 11-KT (Godwin et al. 1996; discussed below). Following their demonstration of sex differences in plasma 11-KT in stoplight parrotfish, Cardwell & Liley (1991a) were also able to induce sex change in females held in a reef enclosure with 11-KT injections. Control injections did not induce sex change. Feeding female threespot wrasses 11-KT induced complete sex change, but the aromatase inhibitor fadrozole used in goby and grouper studies referenced above was equally effective (Higa et al. 2003). An important and informative addition to these studies on threespot wrasses were treatments where E_2 was coadministered with either 11-KT or fadrozole. This coadministration of E_2 blocked the sex change that both 11-KT and fadrozole induced when administered alone. These results are consistent with those discussed previously for gobies and groupers, but the effects of estrogen supplementation suggest that estrogen inhibition may be more important than androgen stimulation in the initiation of sex change. It is also possible that a key action of 11-KT in inducing sex change is through inhibition of aromatase function, as has been demonstrated in another perciform teleost (Braun & Thomas 2003).

NEURAL CORRELATES OF SEXUAL PHENOTYPE
IN *THALASSOMA* WRASSES

Sex and role change involve widespread changes in sexual phenotype. This process is largely socially regulated in wrasses and parrotfishes, indicating that transduction of social cues must occur through the central nervous system. This is a complex problem that will be challenging to address, but progress is being made in understanding the neural correlates of sexual phenotype development.

The best-studied group of labroids in terms of linking brain and behavior are wrasses in the genus *Thalassoma*. This genus of approximately 30 species has a worldwide distribution in tropical and many warm temperate seas and members are often conspicuous components of the reef fish community where they occur. Members of this genus, especially the saddleback wrasse *T. duperrey* and bluehead wrasse *T. bifasciatum,* have also been well studied in terms of behavior and ecology (see Warner et al. 1975; Warner 1984; Ross 1986, 1987). This provides a rich context in which to interpret neuroendocrine and neurobiological patterns. The saddleback wrasse has proven amenable to studies of socially mediated sex change in captivity (Ross et al. 1983, 1990). The bluehead wrasse is well suited to manipulative studies of sex change under field conditions due to ease of capture, site attachment on small coral patch reefs that facilitates observations and recapture, and because the process is very rapid under field conditions with behavioral changes occurring almost immediately and full gonadal sex change being completed in 8 to 10 days (Warner & Swearer 1991; Godwin et al. 1996). Finally, the histological, ultrastructural, and endocrine correlates of gonadal function have been well studied in the saddleback wrasse as discussed above, and to a lesser extent in the bluehead wrasse (Nakamura et al. 1989; Hourigan et al. 1991; Shapiro & Rasotto 1993, 1998). This work provides critical background for understanding how neuropeptide and neurotransmitter systems contribute to sex and role change.

Following their study investigating the effects of T implants on sex change in bluehead wrasses, Kramer and colleagues tested the effects of manipulating the HPG axis at the pituitary and hypothalamic levels. The first of these experiments involved injecting human chorionic gonadotropin (hCG) at one of two dosages (20 or 40 international units/g body weight) either once or three times weekly or a saline control (Koulish & Kramer 1989). Fish were sacrificed at one, two, four, and six weeks after the initiation of treatments. Substantially higher proportions of individuals were found with both degenerating ovarian tissue and cysts of proliferating spermatogenic tissue in the low-dose hCG treatments than in the control treatment and few females remained, while there was a large number of females and no individuals undergoing sex change in the saline control group. Interestingly, the authors indicated that only about 40% of the individuals diagnosed as undergoing sex reversal showed evidence of permanent color change, but these individuals may have been very early on in the process. Pituitary gonadotropin secretion is primarily under the control of gonadotropin releasing hormone (GnRH), and the next study in this series addressed the effect of exogenous synthetic GnRH coadministered with the dopamine receptor antagonist domperidone (coadministered because dopamine antagonizes gonadotropin release in some teleosts and the authors wished to avoid this potential confound)(Kramer et al. 1993). After six weeks of treatment, 93% of treated females exhibited early signs of sex reversal, defined as the presence of spermatogenic-like cysts of cells, but more advanced sex change was not observed. The last in this series of studies addressed a potential role for the neuropeptide hormone NPY because of potential interactions with the GnRH system (Kramer & Imbriano 1997). As with the hCG and synthetic GnRH studies, NPY injections three times a week over eight weeks induced signs of sex change in approximately 82% of treated females. Also as in the previous studies, most of these sex-reversing individuals were in the early stages of the process as measured by spermatogenic tissue development.

This is a useful series of studies, but several points are noteworthy. First, the females were held individually in aquaria, so it is not known whether the treatments administered could overcome the social inhibition normally experienced by female bluehead wrasses in the wild. Second, if estrogenic inhibition is important as suggested by several studies, experiments under captive conditions may lower this inhibition if ovaries are regressed. Finally, while these experiments provided unambiguous evidence of spermatogenic tissue development in females, the time course was very slow relative to the eight to ten days required to complete sex change in field experiments (Warner & Swearer 1991). Nevertheless, the conclusions are consistent with a model where changes in gonadotropin production and release are critical for regulating sex change.

Do different sexual phenotypes in the bluehead wrasse exhibit differences in GnRH neural phenotype? This question was addressed in two studies where it was found that (i) TP male bluehead wrasses exhibited higher numbers of GnRH neurons in the preoptic area of the hypothalamus than either females or IP males, and (ii) a TP male-like GnRH neuronal phenotype could be induced in both females and IP males with 11-KT implants (Grober & Bass 1991; Grober et al. 1991). A similar pattern was described in the Ballan wrasse (*Labrus berggylta*), a monandric protogynous species in which males have larger numbers of GnRH neurons than do females (Elofsson et al. 1999). A recent study in saddleback wrasses adds to these results with demonstrations of extensive GnRH innervation well outside the hypothalamus, reflecting the variety of functions subserved by this hormone (Maruska & Tricas 2007). As with the effects of the manipulative studies described above, these results also point to a role for GnRH neurons in regulating sex and role change. More generally, such a role would also be consistent with the differences observed across sexual phenotypes in gonadal function and sex steroid profiles. Still lacking, unfortunately, is a detailed model of precisely how changes in GnRH neuron function could drive the sex change process. Detailed studies of production and release of GnRH as well as, ideally, GnRH receptor expression throughout the sex change process could be very valuable in this regard.

What is the relationship between gonadal and behavioral changes during sex change? One of the earliest descriptions of socially controlled sex change, in the cleaner wrasse *Labroides dimidiatus*, noted that behavioral changes in sex-changing females could occur in a matter of minutes. Warner & Swearer (1991) demonstrated socially controlled sex change in the bluehead wrasse and described a similar very rapid change in behavior following removal of dominant TP males. These observations call into question a role for gonadal hormones, and especially increases in plasma androgens, in driving at least the initial behavioral shifts. A gonadal role in behavioral changes is impossible to rule out in females with gonads. Therefore, working on patch reefs in the U.S. Virgin Islands, we surgically removed the ovaries in bluehead wrasse sex change candidates prior to TP male removal to test their necessity in the process (Godwin et al. 1996). We found that ovariectomized female bluehead wrasses can indeed exhibit complete behavioral sex change upon becoming behaviorally dominant and maintain that dominant status and associated territorial and courtship behaviors for at least several weeks. Behavioral profiles for these newly dominant ovariectomized females were not discernibly different from those of dominant sham controls, although permanent blue color development did not occur due presumably to the lack of testes and 11-KT.

What does mediate behavioral sex change? Based on the wealth of data implicating arginine vasotocin (AVT) in male-typical behaviors across vertebrates (see references above), we examined the expression of this neuropeptide across sexual phenotypes and sex change in bluehead wrasses. We found that AVT mRNA expression in the preoptic area of the hypothalamus was relatively low in females, high in TP males and intermediate in IP males (Godwin et al. 2000). Importantly, AVT mRNA abundances increased rapidly with the assumption of male behavior during sex change, consistent with a hypothesized role in the behavioral changes the fish were undergoing. Since expression of AVT and its mammalian homologue AVP are strongly androgen dependent in a number of species, it was unclear from these findings whether increases in AVT expression were related to the changing behavioral profile of sex changers or perhaps simply in response to the changing gonadal hormone environment over sex change. To address this, we compared AVT mRNA and AVT neuron size in females who were either ovariectomized or left intact (sham control) and either made socially dominant through TP males removal or remained in the presence of an aggressively dominant TP male (Semsar &

Godwin 2003). We found that AVT mRNA abundances were dependent on social status and that gonadal status had no effect (i.e., the presence of either an ovary in subordinate animals or an intersexual gonad in sham control dominants). Consistent with this lack of gonadal influence, we also found that neither castration of TP males or 11-KT implants in ovariectomized females affected hypothalamic AVT mRNA abundances.

The correlations between TP male-typical behavioral profiles and AVT expression are consistent with a key role for this neuropeptide in determining behavioral phenotype in bluehead wrasses. We next tested whether AVT was either necessary or sufficient for inducing the display of these behaviors in bluehead wrasses. On larger patch reefs in the U.S. Virgin Islands, approximately one-third to one-half of the TP males present are not territory holders (NT-TP). These individuals are typically larger than resident IP males and smaller than territory-holding TP males. When a territorial TP male (T-TP) disappears, an NT-TP male typically quickly takes over that territory. We found that NT-TP males showed increases in territorial aggression and courtship on days when they received an intraperitoneal injection of AVT in saline, but not on days when they received only the saline control (Semsar et al. 2001). Administering an AVT blocker to T-TP males reduced both their displays of territorial aggression and courtship, and it resulted in approximately half of these males abandoning their territories for that day's spawning period (Manning compound, an AVP V1 receptor antagonist, was used here). In order to test whether AVT was necessary for the assumption rather than simply maintenance of territorial status, we captured and injected NT-TP males with either the antagonist or a saline as a control and then captured T-TP males immediately before the daily spawning period, opening their territories for occupancy by the treated NT-TP males (Semsar & Godwin 2004). NT-TP males treated with saline all successfully occupied territories while only 25% of the NT-TPs treated with the receptor antagonist did. Finally, in order to test the role of AVT in mediating behavioral transitions during behavioral sex change, we treated the largest females in social groups on small reefs with either saline or the AVT receptor antagonist and then created a social environment permissive to sex change by removing TP males. As with the NT-TP males, saline-treated females responded to this social "opportunity" by exhibiting behavioral sex change, while females treated with the AVT receptor antagonist did not.

Do steroid hormones play a role in determining behavioral phenotypes in bluehead wrasses? Several lines of evidence now suggest they do. One intriguing aspect of the AVT manipulation experiments described above was that while we could induce territorial behavior in NT-TP males with AVT injections and reduce or block it in T-TP males, NT-TP males, and female sex change candidates with an AVT receptor antagonist, we could not induce TP male-typical behaviors in a socially inhibitory environment in either females or IP males with exogenous

AVT. This finding is consistent with those from some other species (e.g., Goodson & Bass 2000) but raised the question of how sensitivity to AVT is mediated. Hypothesizing that 11-KT might increase sensitivity to AVT in TP males, we implanted ovariectomized females with 11-KT and compared their behavioral responses to exogenous AVT with those of ovariectomized females receiving blank implants (Semsar & Godwin 2004). The 11-KT implants induced full color change, but did not induce contesting or defense of territories or increase the behavioral responsiveness to AVT. Interestingly however, 11-KT implants did increase the display of *opportunistic* courtship behavior, as seen when implanted fish would encounter gravid females away from established spawning sites and exhibit TP male-typical courtship displays directed towards these females. Blank-implanted females did not display any courtship behavior. This finding suggests that 11-KT may mediate development of some components of a TP male behavioral phenotype (such as courtship), but is not responsible for the development of aggressive territoriality.

As with gonadal change, it appears that estrogenic inhibition is also critical in regulating behavioral aspects of sex change. The brain form of aromatase is strongly expressed in the preoptic area of the hypothalamus in bluehead wrasses, with aromatase-immunoreactive glial cells in very close proximity to both AVT neurons and tyrosine hydroxylase-immunoreactive neurons (putatively dopaminergic, Marsh et al. 2006). Cloning of a portion of the brain form of aromatase from bluehead wrasses allowed localization and quantification of aromatase mRNA through in situ hybridization. This work localized aromatase mRNA to the preoptic area of the hypothalamus and showed that expression was higher in females than in TP males, with IP males displaying intermediate values (Marsh 2007; Marsh et al. under review). Finally, we found that estradiol implants both increased aromatase mRNA abundances in the preoptic area, as assessed by *in situ* hybridization, and effectively blocked behavioral sex change in female bluehead wrasses under socially permissive conditions, while blank-implanted females did exhibit complete behavioral sex change.

Evidence for estrogen and AVT influences on TP male behavior and changes in these systems during sex change lead logically to questions about how perception of the social environment is transduced into changes in neuroendocrine phenotype. This area is still poorly explored, but some progress has been made. The monoamine neurotransmitters play important roles in sociosexual behavior and neuroendocrine function in fishes as in other vertebrates (e.g., Summers & Winberg 2006; Nelson & Trainor 2007). Working with saddleback wrasses undergoing sex change in experimental pens, Larson et al. (2003a) documented changes in serotonergic, noradrenergic, and dopaminergic metabolism over a number of brain areas. These changes were most pronounced during the first week of sex reversal, and a decline in serotonergic activity was mirrored by an increase in noradrenergic activity in the preoptic area of the hypothalamus. These reciprocal changes in this key brain region for the regulation of reproductive function and sexual behavior were suggested to be particularly important for initiating gonadal sex reversal. A second study employed a variety of pharmacological agents to either interfere with or augment the actions of the serotonergic, dopaminergic, and noradrenergic monoamine neurotransmitter systems (Larson et al. 2003b). These agents were administered under experimental environments that were either socially permissive or socially inhibitory for sex change. Briefly summarized, the conclusions from this study suggested that both dopamine and serotonin (5-hydroxytryptamine, or 5-HT) are important influences inhibiting females from entering into the sex reversal process while serotonin also inhibits the completion of sex reversal. By contrast, the results suggest that noradrenergic influences stimulate both phases of sex change. These saddleback wrasse experiments were performed in floating 1-m^3 pens, a design previously used very successfully to study sex change in this species (e.g., Ross et al. 1983). In a preliminary study with bluehead wrasses, our laboratory implanted the same dopaminergic inhibitor used by Larson and colleagues, haloperidol—a nonselective dopamine receptor antagonist—into free-living females on coral patch reefs and found that this treatment could stimulate sex change in an inhibitory social environment in the wild as well.

Serotonergic metabolism also affects at least male-typical aggression in bluehead wrasses. Fluoxetine administered either acutely in the field or chronically in the laboratory decreases aggression against territorial intruders by TP males (Perreault et al. 2003). Fluoxetine (trade name: Prozac) is a selective serotonin reuptake inhibitor that should increase serotonergic signaling and so these behavioral results are consistent with a general pattern of serotonergic inhibition of aggression in fishes (Winberg & Nilsson 1993). However, perhaps somewhat surprisingly, the mechanisms of action of this drug are not completely understood even in well-studied mammalian models. The inhibition of aggression in TP male bluehead wrasses was accompanied by a decrease in AVT mRNA abundances in the preoptic area of the hypothalamus, which could also account for the inhibition of aggression in this experiment (Semsar et al. 2004). It is also possible that this type of fluoxetine effect is due to changes in neural synthesis of steroid hormones and indirect effects on signaling through the gamma-aminobutyric acid (GABA) neurotransmitter system rather than changes in serotonin signaling (discussed further in Semsar et al. 2004; also see Pinna et al. 2003).

Experimental results with saddleback wrasses suggest that further characterization of monoamine neurotransmitter effects is likely to be a fruitful line of investigation. Distributions of the rate-limiting enzyme in dopamine synthesis, tyrosine hydroxylase, were described for the brain of the bluehead wrasse (Marsh et al. 2006). However, little is otherwise known about innervation patterns of other key monoaminergic systems (e.g., see Khan & Thomas 1993), and non-aminergic neurotransmitter systems likely to be important influences on reproductive function and behavior (especially the GABAergic and glutamatergic systems) or distributions of receptors for each.

THE POMACENTRIDAE
(*DASCYLLUS* AND *AMPHIPRION*)

The gobies have been excellent models in part because of the bidirectionality of sex change in a number of species, enabling the study of sex change in both directions. While this degree of plasticity in a single species is not known or well characterized in other groups currently, the damselfishes (Pomacentridae) present opportunities here because protogyny is observed in the genus *Dascyllus* (reviewed in Godwin 1995) and protandry in the genus *Amphiprion* (Miura et al. 2008). Species in these genera are useful models because they are common on many west Pacific reefs, typically very site-attached and easily captured (facilitating field studies), relatively small bodied and adapt well to captivity, and because this family is the sister taxon to the well-studied cichlids that are focus of a current genome sequencing effort. Sexual patterns in the genus *Dascyllus* have been very carefully explored in a series of studies by K. Asoh (e.g., Asoh 2003, 2005), setting the stage very well for physiological work.

Amphiprion are developmentally protogynous, but functionally protandrous, as juvenile animals display an immature ovarian morphology, males possess an ovotestis with immature ovarian tissue and mature spermatogenic tissue, and females possess only ovarian tissue (Reinboth 1980; Godwin 1994b; Miura et al. 2008). Godwin & Thomas (1993) described increases in E_2 and decreases in 11-KT with protandrous sex change in *Amphiprion melanopus*. Levels of T and androstenedione followed a similar pattern to that of E_2 and, significantly, decreased during gonadal sex change before rising again in females. Overall, androgen levels were not strongly correlated with the display of aggressive behavior, declining over the course of sex change while the fish became much more aggressive (Godwin 1994a). Miura and coworkers found greater numbers of cells immunoreactive for the steroidogenic p450 cholesterol side-change cleavage enzyme in *Amphiprion clarkii* at the ovarian stage relative to individuals with spermatogenic tissue, which is potentially consistent with the higher E_2 levels and trend toward higher T and androstenedione found by Godwin & Thomas (1993). The only study to examine neural differences in *Amphiprion* found greater numbers of GnRH neurons in males than in females (Elofsson et al. 1997), a result consistent with that found in wrasses, despite the opposite direction of sex change exhibited. The damselfishes are labroids like the wrasses and parrotfishes, but relatively little work has been done with them.

CONCLUSIONS AND DIRECTIONS

In a 1980 review of the environmental control of sex in fishes, Reinboth remarked, "The term 'social control' is nothing better than a 'black box'" (Reinboth 1980, p. 54). The box remains pretty dark, but substantial progress has been made in the last two decades. The findings described above for three divergent groups of coral reef fishes exhibiting socially mediated sex change show some remarkable consistencies. Estrogens in general and E_2 in particular appear likely to play a controlling role in the onset of sex change with E_2 levels being dependent on the expression and activity of the aromatase enzymes in the ovaries and brain. Research in several species also suggests regulation of these changes in estrogen metabolism occurs through gonadotropin signaling, with gonadotropes being under the control of GnRH neurons in the preoptic area of the hypothalamus. Despite these advances, a number of key questions remain to be addressed.

Prominent among these questions is the precise mechanism by which a change in GnRH and gonadotropin signaling could lead to sex change. The rapid degeneration of more advanced oocytes at the initiation of protogynous sex change suggests a loss of gonadotropin support for the ovary. The observation that sex change is more common in the nonbreeding season in at least some species also suggests that the differentiation of testicular tissue in the ovary may be more likely when gonadotropin and estradiol levels are low. Beyond these observations, however, detailed models for how gonadotropic mediation of sex change might work are still lacking.

The mechanisms by which social information is transduced into neural and the neuroendocrine events that underlie changes in reproductive physiology and behavior also remain very poorly understood in both sex-changing and gonochoristic species. This is a challenging problem, but also a very important one, as many of the mechanisms are likely conserved across both fishes and vertebrates more generally. Sex-changing species provide favorable systems for addressing it because of the dramatic and often very manipulatable nature of the transformation, because the process is usually relatively rapid, and because it can be experimentally studied in an adult animal. The relationship between monoamine metabolism in the brain and social dominance as well as the documented effects of monoamine manipulations on sex change in saddleback wrasses (Larson et al. 2003b) suggest these neurotransmitter systems are likely to be an important part of this puzzle. The support for dopaminergic innervation of AVT neurons in bluehead wrasses (Marsh et al. 2006) and serotonergic innervation of GnRH neurons in a gonochoristic teleost, the Atlantic croaker, *Micropogonias undulatus* (Khan & Thomas 1993), are consistent with such a role but much more work needs to be done in this area. The neuroanatomy of these systems in the teleost brain presents some logistical advantages because neuropeptidergic neurons are distributed periventricularly in the preoptic area of the hypothalamus. This feature has been exploited in elegant studies of AVT and isotocin neurons in trout (Saito & Urano 2001; Saito et al. 2004), but so far, it has not been examined in any sex-changing species.

Another area that should be fruitful for further inquiry is the relationship between social stress, stress-related hormones, and gonadotropin signaling. Perry & Grober (2003) developed a detailed model of how glucocorticoid hormones might control sexual phenotype in the bluehead wrasse with applicability to sex-changing fishes more generally. Briefly, they proposed that chronic social stress produces elevated glucocorticoid levels in subordinate individuals and that these elevated glucocorticoids may inhibit processes necessary for sex and/or role change at several levels, including the sorts of direct interactions with the HPG axis that have been described in other species, inhibition of AVT expression, and reductions in 11-KT levels through competitive inhibition of enzymatic reactions critical to 11-KT synthesis. Few data are available to assess the model to date. Godwin & Thomas (1993) found elevated cortisol levels during protandrous sex change in *A. melanopus*, but this result is not inconsistent with Perry and Grober's model since *A. melanopus* is protandrous rather than the protogynous case the model addresses. Contrary to the predictions of this model, cortisol implants in female sandperch (*Parapercis cylindrica*) did not inhibit sex change (Frisch et al. 2007). This model and other potential links between glucocorticoid metabolism and sex change nevertheless deserve further study both because of the potential complexity of the links between cortisol and social interactions (see Abbott et al. 2003 for an example from primates) and a large literature describing effects of stress on reproduction.

The next five to ten years should see a substantial increase in our understanding of socially controlled sex change. A number of gobies, wrasses, and groupers have now been established as excellent laboratory models and an understanding of their basic reproductive biology is in place. Advances in molecular endocrinology, neurobiology, and genomics will greatly facilitate investigations and studies in these different systems should continue to aid in discerning general principles. Progress in our understanding of sex change will be important for insights into a basic problem in reproductive biology. These advances will also be of practical value in aquaculture, and potentially in stock enhancement efforts, because many ecologically and economically important reef species are hermaphrodites.

REFERENCES

Abbott DH, Keverne EB, Bercovitch FB, Shively CA, Medoza SP, Saltzman W, Snowdon CT, Ziegler TE, Banjevic M, Garland T Jr, Sapolsky RM (2003). Are subordinates always stressed? A comparative analysis of rank differences in cortisol levels among primates. Hormones and Behavior 43: 67–82.

Alam MA, Bhandari RK, Kobayashi Y, Nakamura S, Soyano K, Nakamura M (2006). Changes in androgen-producing cell size and circulating 11-ketotestosterone level during female-male sex change of honeycomb grouper *Epinephelus merra*. Molecular Reproduction and Development 73: 206–214.

Asoh K (2003). Reproductive parameters of female Hawaiian damselfish *Dascyllus albisella* with comparison to other tropical and subtropical damselfishes. Marine Biology 143(4): 803–810.

Asoh K (2005). Gonadal development and diandric protogyny in two populations of *Dascyllus reticulatus* from Madang, Papua New Guinea. Journal of Fish Biology 66(4): 1127–1148.

Baroiller JF, Guigen Y, Fostier A (1999). Endocrine and environmental aspects of sex differentiation in fish. Cellular and Molecular Life Sciences 55(6–7): 910–931.

Benton CB, Berlinsky DL (2006). Induced sex change in black sea bass. Journal of Fish Biology 69(5): 1491–1503.

Bhandari RK, Higa M, Nakamura S, Nakamura M (2004). Aromatase inhibitor induces complete sex change in the protogynous honeycomb grouper (*Epinephelus merra*). Molecular Reproduction and Development 67(3): 303–307.

Bhandari RK, Alam MA, Higa M, Soyano K, Nakamura M (2005). Evidence that estrogen regulates the sex change of honeycomb grouper (*Epinephelus merra*), a protogynous hermaphrodite fish. Journal of Experimental Zoology A 303A(6): 497–503.

Bhandari RK, Alam MA, Soyano K, Nakamura M (2006). Induction of female-to-male sex change in the honeycomb grouper (*Epinephelus merra*) by 11-ketotestosterone treatments. Zoological Science 23(1): 65–69.

Black MP, Reavis RH, Grober MS (2004). Socially induced sex change regulates forebrain isotocin in *Lythrypnus dalli*. Neuroreport 15: 185–189.

Black MP, Balthazart J, Baillien M, Grober MS (2005). Socially induced and rapid increases in aggression are inversely related to brain aromatase activity in a sex-changing fish, *Lythrypnus dalli*. Proceedings of the Royal Society B 272: 2435–2440.

Borg B (1994). Androgens in teleost fishes. Comparative Biochemistry and Physiology C 109(3): 219–245.

Braun AM, Thomas P (2003). Androgens inhibit estradiol-17beta synthesis in Atlantic croaker (*Micropogonias undulatus*) ovaries by a nongenomic mechanism initiated at the cell surface. Biology of Reproduction 69(5): 1642–1650.

Callard G, Schlinger B, Pasmanik M, Corina K (1990). Aromatization and estrogen action in brain. Progress in Clinical and Biological Research 342: 105–111.

Callard GV, Tchoudakova AV, Kishida M, Wood E (2001). Differential tissue distribution, developmental programming, estrogen regulation and promoter characteristics of cyp19 genes in teleost fish. Journal of Steroid Biochemistry and Molecular Biology 79(1–5): 305–314.

Cardwell JR, Liley NR (1991a). Androgen control of social-status in males of a wild population of stoplight parrotfish, *Sparisoma viride* (Scaridae). Hormones and Behavior 25(1): 1–18.

Cardwell JR, Liley NR (1991b). Hormonal-control of sex and color-change in the stoplight parrotfish, *Sparisoma viride*. General and Comparative Endocrinology 81(1): 7–20.

Carlisle SL, Marxer-Miller SK, Canario AVM, Oliveira RF, Carneiro L, Grober MS (2000). Effects of 11-ketotestosterone on genital papilla morphology in the sex changing fish *Lythrypnus dalli*. Journal of Fish Biology 57: 445–456.

Cheek AO, Thomas P, Sullivan CV (2000). Sex steroids relative to alternative mating behaviors in the simultaneous hermaphrodite *Serranus subligarius* (Perciformes: Serranidae). Hormones and Behavior 37(3): 198–211.

Clemens LG, Gladue BA (1978). Feminine sexual behavior in rats enhanced by prenatal inhibition of androgen aromatization. Hormones and Behavior 11(2): 190–201.

Cole KS (1983). Protogynous hermaphroditism in a temperate zone territorial marine goby, *Coryphopterus nicholsi*. Copeia 1983(3): 809–812.

Crews D (1993). The organizational concept and vertebrates without sex chromosomes. Brain, Behavior and Evolution 42(4–5): 202–214.

Crews D (2003). Sex determination: where environment and genetics meet. Evolution and Development 5(1): 50–55.

Devlin RH, Nagahama Y (2002). Sex determination and sex differentiation in fish: an overview of genetic, physiological, and environmental influences. Aquaculture 208: 191–364.

De Vries GJ, Panzica GC (2006). Sexual differentiation of central vasopressin and vasotocin systems in vertebrates: different mechanisms, similar endpoints. Neuroscience 138(3): 947–955.

Drilling CC, Grober MS (2005). An initial description of alternative male reproductive phenotypes in the bluebanded goby, *Lythrypnus dalli* (Teleostei: Gobiidae). Environmental Biology of Fishes 72: 361–372.

Elofsson U, Winberg S, Francis RC (1997). Number of preoptic GnRH-immunoreactive cells correlates with sexual phase in a protandrously hermaphroditic fish, the dusky anemonefish (*Amphiprion melanopus*). Journal of Comparative Physiology A 181(5): 484–492.

Elofsson UO, Winberg S, Nilsson GE (1999). Relationships between sex and the size and number of forebrain gonadotropin-releasing hormone-immunoreactive neurones in the Ballan wrasse (*Labrus berggylta*), a protogynous hermaphrodite. The Journal of Comparative Neurology 410(1): 158–170.

Fennessy ST, Sadovy Y (2002). Reproductive biology of a diandric protogynous hermaphrodite, the serranid *Epinephelus andersoni*. Marine and Freshwater Research 53(2): 147–158.

Forlano PM, Schlinger BA, Bass AH (2006). Brain aromatase: new lessons from nonmammalian model systems. Frontiers in Neuroendocrinology 27(3): 247–274.

Frisch A (2004). Sex-change and gonadal steroids in sequentially-hermaphroditic teleost fish. Reviews in Fish Biology and Fisheries 14(4): 481–499.

Frisch AJ, McCormick MI, Pankhurst NW (2007a). Reproductive periodicity and steroid hormone profiles in the sex-changing coral-reef fish, *Plectropomus leopardus*. Coral Reefs 26(1): 189–197.

Frisch AJ, Walker SPW, McCormick ML, Solomon-Lane TK (2007b). Regulation of protogynous sex change by competition between corticosteroids and androgens: an experimental test using sandperch, *Parapercis cylindrica*. Hormones and Behavior 52(4): 540–545.

Gardner L, Anderson T, Place AR, Dixon B, Elizur A (2005). Sex change strategy and the aromatase genes. Journal of Steroid Biochemistry and Molecular Biology 94(5): 395–404.

Godwin J (1994a). Behavioural aspects of protandrous sex change in the anemonefish, *Amphiprion melanopus*, and endocrine correlates. Animal Behaviour 48: 551–567.

Godwin J (1994b). Histological aspects of protandrous sex-change in the anemonefish *Amphiprion melanopus* (Pomacentridae, Teleostei). Journal of Zoology 232: 199–213.

Godwin J (1995). Phylogenetic and habitat influences on mating system structure in the humbug damselfishes (*Dascyllus*, Pomacentridae). Bulletin of Marine Science 57(3): 637–652.

Godwin J, Crews D, Warner RR (1996). Behavioural sex change in the absence of gonads in a coral reef fish. Proceedings of the Royal Society of London Series B 263(1377): 1683–1688.

Godwin J, Sawby R, Warner RR, Crews D, Grober MS (2000). Hypothalamic arginine vasotocin mRNA abundance variation across sexes and with sex change in a coral reef fish. Brain Behavior and Evolution 55(2): 77–84.

Godwin JR, Thomas P (1993). Sex change and steroid profiles in the protandrous anemonefish, *Amphiprion melanopus* (Pomacentridae, Teleostei). Endocrinology 91: 144–157.

Goodson JL, Bass AH (2000). Forebrain peptides modulate sexually polymorphic vocal circuitry. Nature 403(6771): 769–772.

Goodson JL, Bass AH (2001). Social behavior functions and related anatomical characteristics of vasotocin/vasopressin systems in vertebrates. Brain Research Reviews 35(3): 246–265.

Grober MS, Bass AH (1991). Neuronal correlates of sex/role change in labrid fishes: LHRH-like immunoreactivity. Brain, Behavior and Evolution 38(6): 302–312.

Grober MS, Sunobe T (1996). Serial adult sex change involves rapid and reversible changes in forebrain neurochemistry. Neuroreport 7(18): 2945–2949.

Grober MS, Jackson IMD, Bass AH (1991). Gonadal steroids affect LHRH preoptic cell number in sex/role changing fish. Journal of Neurobiology 22(7): 734–741.

Hawkins MB, Thornton JW, Crews D, Skipper JK, Dotte A, Thomas P (2000). Identification of a third distinct estrogen receptor and reclassification of estrogen receptors in teleosts. Proceedings of the National Academy of Sciences of the United States of America 97(20): 10751–10107.

Hawkins MB, Godwin J, Crews D, Thomas, P (2005). The distributions of the duplicate oestrogen receptors ER-beta a and ER-beta b in the forebrain of the Atlantic croaker (*Micropogonias undulatus*): evidence for subfunctionalization after gene duplication. Proceedings of the Royal Society B 272(1563): 633–641.

He Q, Li W, Lin H (2006). Molecular cloning and functional characterization of the gonadotropin-releasing hormone receptor in orange-spotted grouper, *Epinephelus coioides*. Journal of Experimental Zoology A 305A(2): 132.

Higa M, Ogasawara K, Sakaguchi A, Nagahama Y, Nakamura M (2003). Role of steroid hormones in sex change of protogynous wrasse. Fish Physiology and Biochemistry 28(1–4): 149–150.

Hourigan TF, Nakamura M, Nagahama Y, Yamauchi K, Grau EG (1991). Histology, ultrastructure, and *in vitro* steroidogenesis of the testes of two male phenotypes of the protogynous fish, *Thalassoma duperrey* (Labridae). General and Comparative Endocrinology 83: 193–217.

Kaufman LS, Liem KF (1982). Fishes of the suborder Labroidei (Pisces: Perciformes): phylogeny, ecology and evolutionary significance. Brevortia 472: 1–19.

Khan IA, Thomas P (1993). Immunocytochemical localization of serotonin and gonadotropin-releasing-hormone in the brain and pituitary gland of the Atlantic croaker *Micropogonias undulatus*. General and Comparative Endocrinology 91(2): 167–180.

Kim SJ, Ogasawara K, Park JG, Takemura A, Nakamura M (2002). Sequence and expression of androgen receptor and estrogen receptor gene in the sex types of protogynous wrasse, *Halichoeres trimaculatus*. General and Comparative Endocrinology 127(2): 165–173.

Kobayashi Y, Kobayashi T, Nakamura M, Sunobe T, Morrey CE, Suzuki N, Nagahama Y (2004). Characterization of two types of cytochrome P450 aromatase in the serial-sex changing gobiid fish, *Trimma okinawae*. Zoological Science 21(4): 417–425.

Kobayashi Y, Sunobe T, Kobayashi T, Nagahama Y, Nakamura M (2005). Promoter analysis of two aromatase genes in the serial-sex changing gobiid fish, *Trimma okinawae*. Fish Physiology and Biochemistry 31(2–3): 123–127.

Koulish S, Kramer CR (1989). Human chorionic-gonadotropin (hcg) induces gonad reversal in a protogynous fish, the bluehead wrasse, *Thalassoma bifasciatum* (Teleostei: Labridae). Journal of Experimental Zoology 252(2): 156–168.

Kramer CR, Imbriano MA (1997). Neuropeptide Y (NPY) induces gonad reversal in the protogynous bluehead wrasse, *Thalassoma bifasciatum* (Teleostei: Labridae). Journal of Experimental Zoology A 279: 133–144.

Kramer CR, Koulish S, Bertacchi PL (1988). The effects of testosterone implants on ovarian morphology in the bluehead wrasse, *Thalassoma bifasciatum* (Bloch) (Teleostei: Labridae). Journal of Fish Biology 32: 397–407.

Kramer CR, Caddell, MT, Bubenheimerlivolsi, L (1993). SGnRH-A [(D-Arg6,Pro9,net-) LHRH] in combination with domperidone induces gonad reversal in a protogynous fish, the bluehead wrasse, *Thalassoma bifasciatum*. Journal of Fish Biology 42(2): 185–195.

Kroon FJ, Liley NR (2000). The role of steroid hormones in protogynous sex change in the blackeye goby, *Coryphopterus nicholsii* (Teleostei: Gobiidae). General and Comparative Endocrinology 118(2): 273–283.

Kroon FJ, Munday PL, Pankhurst NW (2003). Steroid hormone levels and bi-directional sex change in *Gobiodon histrio*. Journal of Fish Biology 62(1): 153–167.

Kroon FJ, Munday PL, Westcott DA, Hobbs JPA, Liley NR (2005). Aromatase pathway mediates sex change in each direction. Proceedings of the Royal Society B 272(1570): 1399–1405.

Larson ET, Norris DO, Grau EG, Summers CH (2003a). Monoamines stimulate sex reversal in the saddleback wrasse. General and Comparative Endocrinology 130(3): 289–298.

Larson ET, Norris DO, Summers CH (2003b). Monoaminergic changes associated with socially induced sex reversal in the saddleback wrasse. Neuroscience 119(1): 251–263.

Li CJ, Zhou L, Wang Y, Hong YH, Gui JF (2005). Molecular and expression characterization of three gonadotropin subunits common alpha, FSH beta and LH beta in groupers. Molecular and Cellular Endocrinology 233(1–2): 33–46.

Li GL, Liu XC, Lin HR (2006a). Effects of aromatizable and nonaromatizable androgens on the sex inversion of red-spotted grouper (*Epinephelus akaara*). Fish Physiology and Biochemistry 32(1): 25–33.

Li GL, Liu XC, Zhang Y, Lin HR (2006b). Gonadal development, aromatase activity and P450 aromatase gene expression during sex inversion of protogynous red-spotted grouper *Epinephelus akaara* (Temminck and Schlegel) after implantation of the aromatase inhibitor, fadrozole. Aquaculture Research 37(5): 484–491.

Li GL, Liu XC, Lin HR (2007). Seasonal changes of serum sex steroids concentration and aromatase activity of gonad and brain in red-spotted grouper (*Epinephelus akaara*). Animal Reproduction Science 99(1–2): 156–166.

Lorenzi V, Earley RL, Grober MS (2006). Preventing behavioural interactions with a male facilitates sex change in female bluebanded gobies, *Lythrypnus dalli*. Behavioral Ecology and Sociobiology 59(6): 715–722.

Lorenzi V, Earley RL, Rodgers EW, Pepper DR, Grober MS (2008). Diurnal patterns and sex differences in cortisol, 11-ketotestosterone, testosterone, and 17 beta-estradiol in the bluebanded goby (*Lythrypnus dalli*). General and Comparative Endocrinology 155(2): 438–446.

Luckenbach JA, Godwin J, Daniels HV, Borski RJ (2003). Gonadal differentiation and effects of temperature on sex determination in southern flounder (*Paralichthys lethostigma*). Aquaculture 216(1–4): 315–327.

Luckenbach JA, Early LW, Rowe AH, Borski RJ, Daniels HV, Godwin J (2005). Aromatase Cytochrome P450: cloning, intron variation, and ontogeny of gene expression in southern flounder (*Paralichthys lethostigma*). Journal of Experimental Zoology Part A: Comparative Experimental Biology 303: 643–656.

Mank JE, Promislow DEL, Avise JC (2006). Evolution of alternative sex-determining mechanisms in teleost fishes. Biological Journal of the Linnean Society 87(1): 83–93.

Marsh KE (2007). Neuroendocrine transduction of social cues in the bluehead wrasse, *Thalassoma bifasciatum*. Ph.D. dissertation, North Carolina State University, Raleigh.

Marsh KE, Creutz LM, Hawkins MB, Godwin J (2006). Aromatase immunoreactivity in the bluehead wrasse brain, *Thalassoma bifasciatum*: immunolocalization and co-regionalization with arginine vasotocin and tyrosine hydroxylase. Brain Research 1126(1): 91–101.

Maruska KP, Tricas TC (2007). Gonadotropin-releasing hormone and receptor distributions in the visual processing regions of four coral reef fishes. Brain, Behavior and Evolution 70(1): 40–56.

Maruska KP, Mizobe MH, Tricas TC (2007). Sex and seasonal co-variation of arginine vasotocin (AVT) and gonadotropin-releasing hormone (GnRH) neurons in the brain of the halfspotted goby. Comparative Biochemistry and Physiology A 147(1): 129–144.

Miura S, Nakamura S, Kobayashi Y, Piferrer F, Nakamura M (2008). Differentiation of ambisexual gonads and immunohistochemical localization of P450 cholesterol side-chain cleavage enzyme during gonadal sex differentiation in the protandrous anemonefish, *Amphiprion clarkii*. Comparative Biochemistry and Physiology B 149(1): 29–37.

Nakamura M, Kobayashi Y (2005). Sex change in coral reef fish. Fish Physiology and Biochemistry 31(2–3): 117–122.

Nakamura M, Hourigan TF, Yamauchi K, Nagahama Y, Grau EG (1989). Histological and ultrastructural evidence for the role of gonadal steroid hormones in sex change in the protogynous wrasse *Thalassoma duperrey*. Environmental Biology of Fishes, 24(2): 117–136.

Nelson RJ, Trainor BC (2007). Neural mechanisms of aggression. Nature Reviews Neuroscience 8(7): 536–546.

Ohta K, Hirano M, Mine T, Mizutani H, Yamaguchi A, Matsuyama M (2008). Body color change and serum steroid hormone levels throughout the process of sex change in the adult wrasse, *Pseudolabrus sieboldi*. Marine Biology 153(5): 843–852.

Oliver AS (1997). Size and density dependent mating tactics in the simultaneously hermaphroditic seabass *Serranus subligarius* (Cope, 1870). Behaviour 134: 563–594.

Perreault HA, Semsar K, Godwin J (2003). Fluoxetine treatment decreases territorial aggression in a coral reef fish. Physiology and Behavior 79(4–5): 719–724.

Perry AN, Grober MS (2003). A model for social control of sex change: interactions of behavior, neuropeptides, glucocorticoids, and sex steroids. Hormones and Behavior 43(1): 31–38.

Pinna G, Dong E, Matsumoto K, Costa E, Guidotti A (2003). In socially isolated mice, the reversal of brain allopregnanolone down-regulation mediates the anti-aggressive action of fluoxetine. Proceedings of the National Academy of Sciences of the United States of America 100(4): 2035–2040.

Rasotto MB, Shapiro DY (1998). Morphology of gonoducts and male genital papilla, in the bluehead wrasse: implications and correlates on the control of gamete release. Journal of Fish Biology 52(4): 716–725.

Reinboth R (1975). Spontaneous and hormone-induced sex-inversion in wrasses (Labridae). Publications Stazione Zoologie Napoli 39: 550–573.

Reinboth R (1980). Can sex inversion be environmentally induced? Biology of Reproduction 22(1): 49–59.

Reinboth R, Becker B (1984). In vitro studies on steroid metabolism by gonadal tissues from ambisexual teleosts. I. conversion of [14C]testosterone by males and females of the protogynous wrasse *Coris julis* L. General and Comparative Endocrinology 55(2): 245–250.

Rodgers EW, Drane S, Grober MS (2005). Sex reversal in pairs of *Lythrypnus dalli*: behavioral and morphological changes. Biological Bulletin 208(2): 120–126.

Rodgers EW, Earley RL, Grober MS (2006). Elevated 11-ketotestosterone during paternal behavior in the bluebanded goby (*Lythrypnus dalli*). Hormones and Behavior 49(5): 610–614.

Roede MJ (1972). Color as related to size, sex, and behaviour in seven Caribbean labrid fish species (genera *Thalassoma, Halichoeres, Hemipteronotus*). Studies of the Fauna of Curacao and other Caribbean Islands XLII: 1–264.

Rose JD, Moore FL (2002). Behavioral neuroendocrinology of vasotocin and vasopressin and the sensorimotor processing hypothesis. Frontiers in Neuroendocrinology 23(4): 317–341.

Ross RM (1986). Social organization and mating system of the Hawaiian reef fish *Thalassoma duperrey* (Labridae). In: Uyeno T, Arai R, Taniuchi T, Matsuura K (eds.), Indo-Pacific Fish

Biology. Proceedings of the International Conference on Indo-Pacific Fishes. Ichthyological Society of Japan, Tokyo, pp. 794–802.

Ross RM (1987). Sex-change linked growth acceleration in a coral-reef fish, *Thalassoma duperrey*. Journal of Experimental Zoology 244(3): 455–461.

Ross RM, Losey GS, Diamond M (1983). Sex change in a coral-reef fish: dependence of stimulation and inhibition on relative size. Science 221(4610): 574–575.

Ross RM, Hourigan TF, Lutnesky MMF, Singh I (1990). Multiple simultaneous sex-changes in social groups of a coral reef fish. Copeia 1990 (2): 427–433.

Sadovy Y, Domeier M (2005). Are aggregation-fisheries sustainable? Reef fish fisheries as a case study. Coral Reefs 24(2): 254–262.

Sadovy de Mitcheson Y, Liu M (2008). Functional hermaphroditism in teleosts. Fish and Fisheries 9(1): 1–43.

Saito D, Urano A (2001). Synchronized periodic Ca^{2+} pulses define neurosecretory activities in magnocellular vasotocin and isotocin neurons. Journal of Neuroscience 21(RC178): 1–6.

Saito D, Komatsuda M, Urano A (2004). Functional organization of preoptic vasotocin and isotocin neurons in the brain of rainbow trout: central and neurohypophysial projections of single neurons. Neuroscience 124(4): 973–984.

Sarter K, Papadaki M, Zanuy S, Mylonas CC (2006). Permanent sex inversion in 1-year-old juveniles of the protogynous dusky grouper (*Epinephelus marginatus*) using controlled-release 17 alpha-methyltestosterone implants. Aquaculture 256(1–4): 443–456.

Scaggiante M, Grober MS, Lorenzi V, Rasotto MB (2006). Variability of GnRH secretion in two goby species with socially controlled alternative male mating tactics. Hormones and Behavior 50(1): 107–117.

Schlinger BA, Creco C, Bass AH (1999). Aromatase activity in the hindbrain vocal control region of a teleost fish: divergence among males with alternative reproductive tactics. Proceedings of the Royal Society of London Series B 266(1415): 131–136.

Semsar K, Godwin J (2003). Social influences on the arginine vasotocin system are independent of gonads in a sex-changing fish. Journal of Neuroscience 23(10): 4386–4393.

Semsar K, Godwin J (2004). Multiple mechanisms of phenotype development in the bluehead wrasse. Hormones and Behavior 45(5): 345–353.

Semsar K, Kandel FLM, Godwin J (2001). Manipulations of the AVT system shift social status and related courtship and aggressive behavior in the bluehead wrasse. Hormones and Behavior 40(1): 21–31.

Semsar K, Perreault HA, Godwin J (2004). Fluoxetine-treated male wrasses exhibit low AVT expression. Brain Research 1029(2): 141–147.

Shapiro DY (1980). Serial female sex changes after simultaneous removal of males from social groups of a coral reef fish. Science 209: 1136–1137.

Shapiro DY (1981). Intragroup behavioural changes and the initiation of sex reversal in a coral reef fish in the laboratory. Animal Behaviour 29: 1199–1212.

Shapiro DY, Rasotto MB (1993). Sex-differentiation and gonadal development in the diandric, protogynous wrasse, *Thalassoma bifasciatum* (Pisces, Labridae). Journal of Zoology 230: 231–245.

Shein NL, Takushima M, Nagae M, Chuda H, Soyano K (2003). Molecular cloning of go-nadotropin cDNA in sevenband grouper, *Epinephelus septemfasciatus*. Fish Physiology and Biochemistry 28(1–4): 107–108.

Soga T, Ogawa S, Millar RP, Sakuma Y, Parhar IS (2005). Localization of the three GnRH types and GnRH receptors in the brain of a cichlid fish: insights into their neuroen-docrine and neuromodulator functions. Journal of Comparative Neurology 487(1): 28–41.

St. Mary CM (1994). Sex allocation in a simultaneous hermaphrodite, the blue banded goby (*Lythrypnus dalli*): the effect of body size and behavioral gender and the conse-quences for reproduction. Behavioral Ecology 5: 304–313.

Stoll LM (1955). Hormonal control of the sexually dimorphic pigmentation of *Thalassoma bifasciatum*. Zoologica 40: 125–131.

Summers CH, Winberg S (2006). Interactions between the neural regulation of stress and aggression. The Journal of Experimental Biology 209: 4581–4589.

Streelman JT, and Karl SA (1997). Reconstructing labroid evolution with single-copy nu-clear DNA. Proceedings of the Royal Society of London B 264: 1011–1020.

Sunobe T, Nakamura M, Kobayashi Y, Kobayashi T, Nagahama Y (2005). Aromatase im-munoreactivity and the role of enzymes in steroid pathways for inducing sex change in the hermaphrodite gobiid fish *Trimma okinawae*. Comparative Biochemistry and Physiology A 141: 54–59.

Thomas P, Dressing G, Pang YF, Berg H, Tubbs C, Benninghoff A, Doughty K (2006). Progestin, estrogen and androgen G-protein coupled receptors in fish gonads. Steroids 71(4): 310–316.

Warner RR (1984). Mating behavior and hermaphroditism in coral-reef fishes. American Scientist 72(2): 128–136.

Warner RR, Swearer SE (1991). Social-control of sex-change in the bluehead wrasse, *Tha-lassoma bifasciatum* (Pisces, Labridae). Biological Bulletin 181(2): 199–204.

Warner RR, Robertson DR, Leigh EG (1975). Sex change and sexual selection. Science 190(4215): 633–638.

Winberg S, Nilsson GE (1993). Roles of brain monoamine neurotransmitters in agonistic behavior and stress reactions, with particular reference to fish. Comparative Biochem-istry and Physiology C 106(3): 597–614.

Yeh SL, Kuo CM, Ting YY, Chang CF (2003a). Androgens stimulate sex change in protog-ynous grouper, *Epinephelus coioides*: spawning performance in sex-changed males. Comparative Biochemistry and Physiology C 135: 375–382.

Yeh SL, Kuo CM, Ting YY, Chang CF (2003b). The effects of exogenous androgens on ovarian development and sex change in female orange-spotted protogynous grouper, *Epinephelus coioides*. Aquaculture 218: 729–739.

Zhang WM, Zhang Y, Zhang LH, Zhao HH, Li X, Huang H (2007). The mRNA expression of P450 aromatase, gonadotropin beta-subunits and FTZ-F1 in the orange-spotted grouper (*Epinephelus coioides*) during 17 alpha-methyltestosterone-induced preco-cious sex change. Molecular Reproduction and Development 74: 665–673.

Zhang Y, Zhang WM, Zhang LH, Zhu TY, Tian J, Li X (2004). Two distinct cytochrome P450 aromatases in the orange-spotted grouper (*Epinephelus coioides*): cDNA cloning and differential mRNA expression. Journal of Steroid Biochemistry and Molecular Biology 92(1–2): 39–50.

Zhu Y, Bond J, Thomas P (2003a). Identification, classification, and partial characterization of genes in humans and other vertebrates homologous to a fish membrane progestin receptor. Proceedings of the National Academy of Sciences of the United States of America 100: 2237–2242.

Zhu Y, Rice CD, Pang YF, Pace M, Thomas P (2003b). Cloning, expression, and characterization of a membrane progestin receptor and evidence it is an intermediary in meiotic maturation of fish oocytes. Proceedings of the National Academy of Sciences of the United States of America 100: 2231–2236.

Acoustical Behavior
of Coral Reef Fishes

Phillip S. Lobel, Ingrid M. Kaatz, and Aaron N. Rice

The soundscapes of the ocean have been underappreciated for far too long. The notion that the sea was a silent world was conveyed early in the history of scuba diving (Cousteau & Dumas 1953), and the idea has persisted. This perspective was reinforced by the fact that human hearing is poor underwater and that the sounds of many fishes are not easily heard. Scuba divers are especially at a disadvantage for hearing underwater because of the near constant stream of noisy bubbles running over their ears. Exhaled bubbles and boat noise can often mask our being able to hear sound-producing fishes (Lobel 2001b, 2005; Radford et al. 2005).

Many reef fishes are acoustic, but in most cases, this is not yet a particularly well studied aspect of their behavior. The obstacle to studying underwater bioacoustics has been a combination of technology limitations for underwater recording and the fact that many reef fishes appear to be very discrete about where and when they produce sounds. For these reasons, until recently, underwater acoustic ecology has been largely overlooked. Advances in scuba technologies such as closed-circuit re-breathers newly expose divers to experience with increased awareness the natural structure and tempo of the ambient acoustic world underwater (Lobel 2001b).

There is now an emerging awareness that many fishes produce specific courtship and spawning sounds (e.g., Lobel 1992, 2001a, 2002) and that a coral reef is also a "choral" reef. Research on underwater sound and its ecological role has accelerated in recent years as the result of several scientific and technical developments. First, new technology in the form of camcorders, hydrophones, and computers has made the task of recording and analyzing underwater animal sounds and behavior much easier (Lobel 2001b, 2005). Second, discoveries that fishes produce species-specific courtship and spawning sounds opened the feasibility for the development of passive acoustic monitoring for documenting reproductive patterns (Lobel 1992, 2001b, 2005; Mann & Lobel 1995; Rountree et al. 2006; Luczkovich et al. 2008a). Third, loud noises from ships, sonar, seismic surveys, and global climate experiments such as ATOC (Acoustic Thermometry of Ocean Climate, http://atoc.ucsd .edu) have raised real concern about potential adverse impacts of loud underwater sounds on marine animals (McCauley et al. 2003; Popper 2003; Popper et al. 2003b; Vasconcelos et al. 2007; Popper & Hastings 2009). Last, new research is showing that larval reef fishes may be using the sounds emanating from coral reefs to navigate during their migration from the open ocean to benthic habitat (Simpson et al. 2004; Leis & Lockett 2005; Mann et al. 2007; Radford et al. 2008b). All of this demonstrates that underwater acoustic ecology is important to know in order to better manage ocean resources and for better understanding of how acoustics influences marine animal behavior, ecology, and evolution.

Sound production by fishes is most often associated with two behavioral contexts: reproduction and aggression. Sound production is typically more intense during the breeding season (Bass & McKibben 2003). Even so, the courtship and mating behaviors of many fishes have been elusive, and consequently, their acoustic behavior has been poorly known. Acoustic behavior is often aimed discretely at nearby prospective mates. Some of the quietest sounds are produced by carapids (pearlfishes, which are internal symbionts of sea cucumbers), syngnathids (seahorses), and gobiids (gobies). Only a few fishes make sounds loud enough to be easily heard by a diver, and it is these loudest of the reef fishes that have been the focus of most studies. These notably include the pomacentrids (damselfish), holocentrids (squirrelfish), sciaenids (drums), and batrachoidids (toadfish). Other fishes, such as scarids, can produce audible adventitious sounds while feeding (parrotfish; Sartori & Bright 1973; Takemura et al. 1988). A few fish have been found to also produce sounds specifically associated with the mating act (i.e., gamete release, Lobel 2002). The emerging pattern is that many fishes are sound producers, although the exact role of this behavior for mate selection and in predator-prey interactions is still being explored.

Hearing in fishes is an early evolutionary development in vertebrates and most likely preceded active acoustic behavior (Fay & Popper 2000; Ladich 2000; Bass et al. 2008). Investigations of the fish auditory system and their hearing abilities have been conducted for well over a century, including early detailed studies of the inner ear anatomy and physiology (e.g., Parker 1903; Marage 1906; Lafite-Dupont 1907; Bernoulli 1910; Bierbaum 1914; Warner 1932), clearly demonstrating behavioral and neurophysiological responses of fishes to acoustic stimuli. These studies were a prelude to the famous work on fish hearing by Karl von Frisch (1936, 1938), which led to general acceptance of the belief that fish can hear. However, the level at which fish communicate using acoustic signals is still relatively unknown and is still actively debated.

The inner ear morphological structure of three semicircular ear canals and basic sensitivity to a range of low to mid frequency sounds is an ancestral evolutionary innovation that is a shared character in gnathostomes (Lauder & Liem 1983). The emerging notion is that hearing evolved primarily as a mechanism for monitoring the ambient acoustic soundscape with particular regard to detecting predators or potential prey (Ladich 2000). Some species with advanced hearing specializations are particularly vulnerable prey species, such as freshwater ostariophysians (Ladich 2000) and marine clupeids (Mann et al. 1997). Other advanced taxa have also independently expanded their hearing range beyond low- to mid-range frequencies, evolving high-frequency hearing sensitivity (Braun & Grande 2008). While all living fishes, so far as known, maintain their hearing abilities, there are many examples of fishes that have lost their sight, suggesting the overall adaptive significance of the auditory sense.

Sound producing mechanisms in fishes are highly varied and derived from diverse morphological adaptations. However, not all fish families with acoustic species share sound producing abilities. Some fish apparently remain mute (Hawkins & Myrberg 1983; Chen & Mok 1988; Ladich 2000). Fish will also become momentarily silent if threatened. Sound production may attract predators, and some species have been found to go immediately silent when potential predators are detected (Luczkovich et al. 2000; Remage-Healey et al. 2006). The pattern of sound production by fishes in general is not at all clear. Surveys to date have found that some groups of fishes have widespread occurrence of sound production throughout the family (e.g., batrachoidids, pomacentrids, and sciaenids), while other sympatric families make sounds very sparingly. Other fish families include species that appear to have secondarily lost acoustic ability entirely while related fishes still make sounds. These patterns point to an unknown underlying complexity at the core of the evolution of acoustic communication in fishes in general, including coral reef fishes.

This review was developed to provide a summary guide to the literature of shallow, tropical marine (i.e., coral reef) fish bioacoustics and to outline the fish families known for sound production. The hope is that this status report will encourage further research in fish acoustic communication and underwater acoustic ecology. As the reader will note in this chapter, the findings so far indicate that many coral reef fishes are most acoustically active during reproduction. It seems that some species produce sounds only when courting and mating and not at all during other times.

BRIEF HISTORY OF ACOUSTICAL OUTPUT IN FISH

Reports that fishes produce sounds date back to Aristotle 350 BCE, who observed that fishes "emit certain inarticulate sounds and squeaks." Aristotle also wrote that "the apparent voice in all these fishes is a sound caused in some cases by a rubbing motion of their gills, which by the way are prickly, or in other cases by internal parts about their bellies; for they all have air or wind inside them, by rubbing and moving which they produce the sounds" (Aristotle 1910, Book 4, Part 9).

Darwin was also keenly aware of fish sounds, known to him primarily from the work of Dufossé (1862, 1874a, b; cited in Pauly 2004). Dufossé reported that some fish sounds could be voluntarily produced (by pharyngeal bones and swim bladder vibration)(Dufossé 1874a, b). Darwin noted that in fish, as in insects, these sounds could play a role in sexual selection (Pauly 2004).

One of the earliest scientific reports of sound from a tropical reef fish appears to be Burkenroad (1930) describing the sounds of grunts (Haemulidae) in the Caribbean. Advanced research on the sounds of wild fishes was initiated after WWII from the need of the U.S. Navy to understand ambient ocean sounds. The Navy's task was to detect the sounds from enemy ships when sonar became an operational technology (Marshall 1962). The early studies by Fish (1948; Fish et al. 1952, 1954), Griffin (1950), Moulton (1958), and Tavolga (1960) grew out of this effort and established the foundations for modern fish bioacoustics. The specific study of reef fishes in their natural environment was pioneered in the 1960s at the Lerner Marine Laboratory and later, in the underwater habitat, Tektite (e.g., Bright 1972; Bright & Sartori 1972; Collette & Earle 1972; Sartori & Bright 1973).

In 1963, a camera and hydrophone system was deployed on the reef at about 20 m depth off the Lerner Lab on Bimini Island, Bahamas. The system was linked by cable to the shore lab where a room full of electronics was required at the time to process the audio-video signals (see photos in Kronengold et al. 1964). This setup did record a variety of sounds, but it was frustrating because the fixed camera usually did not catch the sound producer (Kumpf 1964). It did, however, document that there were temporal patterns to distinctive marine animal sounds (Cummings et al. 1964). A few years later, experiments were conducted using playback of sounds to test attraction to bony fishes and sharks (Richard 1968; Myrberg et al. 1969). Myrberg initiated his acoustic study of damselfishes at the Lerner Lab (Myrberg 1980, 1996). He and his colleagues continued the study of pomacentrid acoustic behavior and established the importance of pulse-repetition rate as a basis for interspecies recognition (Myrberg & Riggio 1985; Myrberg 1997a). Myrberg also led the development of the "model bottle" technique to elicit sounds and other agonistic behavioral responses from territorial fishes (Myrberg & Thresher 1974), and this simple technique is still a powerful method for experimentally inducing fishes to vocalize (Santangelo & Bass 2006; Tricas et al. 2006).

In 1968, Charles Breder wrote that "very little work on the sonic ecology and its relation to the life history and behavior of any species has been reported." Most astutely, Breder commented that study of fish behavior "has usually been treated as though fishes were both deaf and mute" (Breder 1968, p. 329). Breder's message

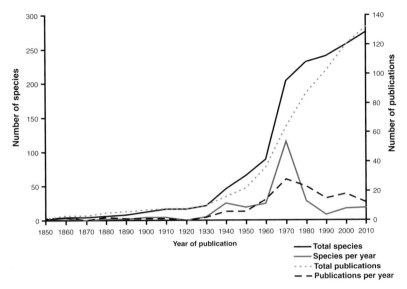

FIGURE 10.1. Number of sonic reef fish species (solid lines) described in scientific publications (dashed lines) in recent history.

is worth repeating today, as little has changed after 40 years. Many papers are still published describing fish behaviors that ignore the potential occurrence or role of sounds. This is not entirely due to neglect; recording and analyzing underwater sounds has been nontrivial. However, there has been a steady increase in fish acoustic studies over the years. To date, fewer than 300 coral reef species have been reported on in about 130 publications (Figure 10.1).

The Tektite program in 1969 was the first to use divers to record fishes. The Tektite scientific divers used Navy diving rebreathers so that scuba bubbles were not an acoustic interference. They customized an underwater housing for an 8-mm movie camera in tandem with a tape recorder and hydrophone. The camera and tape recorder were operated independently but simultaneously. The benefits of using a rebreather to record the sounds of fishes were clearly noted by Bright (1972). The Tektite report (Collette & Earle 1972) was also notable, because it contained a small, flexible 33-RPM record of the marine animal recordings.

In spite of a history of scientific observations and interest, fish acoustic behavior has been a difficult topic to accurately evaluate. This is mainly due to the fact that scuba divers can only hear the loudest of sound producing fishes such as damselfish (Pomacentridae), toadfish (Batrachoididae), groupers (Serranidae), and drums (Sciaenidae). Other fishes that produce sound are relatively quiet and not easily audible without the aid of a hydrophone (Lobel 1992). The challenge has been to clearly record fish sounds, to correlate these sounds to specific individuals and to discriminate responsive behaviors. New technologies for silent diving and underwater video-acoustic synchronous recording has helped overcome past difficulties (Lobel 2001b). Another significant historical problem has been the technical analysis of the sounds. This has evolved rapidly in the last few years. At present, there are a number of software programs that make it easy to do the acoustical analyses on ever more powerful and inexpensive computers. One of the most accessible software programs made especially for scientific analysis of animal sounds is Raven, produced by the Cornell Laboratory of Ornithology (Charif et al. 2008).

Today it is mostly a matter of a scientific diver's skill (and some luck) when making underwater observations, than it is the recording technology, to be successful at obtaining good acoustic recordings from wild fishes (Lobel 2003a, b, 2005). Of course, the alternative to the study of fishes in the wild is in an aquarium. Small aquariums do create acoustic problems, but if the aquarium is large enough and appropriately insulated from ambient noises, quality recordings are possible (Parvulescu 1967; Akamatsu et al. 2002; Okumura et al. 2002). The problem associated with captive fish studies concerns mostly the issue of understanding the full interaction of acoustic fishes in their natural acoustic landscape, including the presence of predators.

RESEARCH OBJECTIVES

The following basic research questions are the main issues in the study of the acoustical ecology of fishes:

- What is the pattern of sound production and associated behavior (especially in a reproductive context)? Are specific sounds repeatedly associated with specific behavior (e.g., courtship and the mating act)? Can we elicit reactions from fishes in response to specific call playbacks (such as attracting mates to a spawning site)?
- How similar are fish sounds among sympatric species, specifically the male courtship-associated sounds? The test is to determine if species will respond differently to playback of conspecific verses sibling species sounds. Differences between species or individuals would indicate that sound display could play an important role in assortative mating, female mate choice, and reproductive isolation of populations based on species-specific sound signals.
- What is the functional morphology of sound production, and how does it affect the acoustic signal?

Environmental background sounds can be both biologically and ecologically meaningful (Simpson et al. 2005; Mann et al. 2007; Radford et al. 2008b). Background noises also create the ambient interference that can limit a fish's ability to discriminate sounds. Hydrodynamic sounds of fishes swimming can be detected by conspecifics and by potential predators (Moulton 1960). The mechanical sounds of marine animals disturbing substrate could contribute to the acoustic features characterizing specific coastal habitats and are hypothesized as cues to larval fishes for finding suitable settlement locations (Radford et al. 2008a). Adventitious sounds, such as scarids grinding food, can signal competitors that there is a food source available (Sartori & Bright 1973) and in pufferfishes these sounds attract conspecifics (Breder & Clark 1947). The ecology of sound has ramifications in how fishes behaviorally use it. The key issue here is the balance between the need to communicate and the risk of being overheard by a predator or a competitor (Myrberg et al. 1969; Myrberg 1981; Luczkovich et al. 2000; Gannon et al. 2005; Remage-Healey et al. 2006).

One important practical application for using fish sound is for tracking where and when fish spawn (Mann & Lobel 1995; Luczkovich et al. 1999, 2008b). The scientific and technical challenge has been to develop methods that allow measurement of fish reproduction synchronously with time-series measurement of temperature, salinity, and other physical oceanographic variables that are easily recorded using modern devices (Mann & Grothues 2009). If we can associate specific sound patterns that are exclusively correlated with specific fish species and behaviors (such as the courtship call of a damselfish or the mating sound of the hamletfish), then we can develop listening devices to document their occurrence in time and space (Lobel 2001b, 2002; Lammers et al. 2008). A passive acoustic detection device that is programmed to monitor fish courtship and mating sounds becomes a "spawn-o-meter" that records data in a way that is comparable to that from other meters (e.g., a current meter, conductivity-temperature-depth meter, and temperature logger) at the same site (Mann & Lobel 1995; Lobel 2001b, 2005). The acoustical information thus generated can be used to evaluate how climate change (sea temperature, salinity, flow, etc.) may offset the timing and location(s) of fish reproduction. Overall, it is clear that being able to monitor fish mating activities is an essential tool for the successful management of fisheries and for associated conservation efforts (Rountree et al. 2006). The application of a spawn-o-meter is that such a device could be used to: (1) define important breeding habitats relevant to establishing protected areas; (2) establish existing relationships between physical oceanography and the timing of fish reproduction; and (3) define a critical endpoint measurement in pollution studies where the courtship vigor of a fish can be monitored and related to its health and fitness (Lobel 2001b).

REVIEW OF REVIEWS: AN ANNOTATED GUIDE

There have been a series of excellent reviews of fish behavior and sound production over the past several decades, and none are obsolete. The most recent update with an overview discussion of sound production mechanisms and sound structure is by Kasumyan (2008). It is detailed and complete and is thus a great introduction. Moreover, predecessor reviews all offer important insights as well as collated information cataloging the diversity of sounds and proposed sound producing mechanisms. Rather than repeat this information, we outline the most significant of these reviews, especially if they refer directly to coral reef fishes in particular. Our chapter is slanted particularly toward reproductive aspects and therefore fills a gap in current acoustic review papers. These review books and papers serve as the foundations for underwater bioacoustics as a science and thus are required reading for everyone interested in this field. Collectively, the reviews listed below summarize the many descriptive studies of individual fish sounds and associated behaviors. A chronological reading of this literature provides a perspective of how the field has developed, how fish produce sounds mechanistically, the diversity of hearing sensitivities and the relationship between sounds and behavior. The fundamental question concerning the role of sound in a fish's behavior is a core theme throughout these publications. It is important to note the date of publications as technology of the day limited what was achievable scientifically at the time.

The first series of papers that defined fish bioacoustics as a research field and raised the scientific awareness concerning the importance of underwater acoustic ecology appeared between 1960 and 1964. Tavolga's 1960 seminal paper reviewed sound production and underwater communication in fishes (Tavolga 1960). This paper was followed by reviews by Marshall (1962) and Moulton (1963, 1964a, b). Collectively, these papers provided the first detailed inventory and assessment of widespread acoustic behavior in fishes, with an emphasis on marine species. They raised the questions of how important sound is in fish behavior and the role of acoustics in animal ecology. The first broad synthesis of marine bioacoustics was published from the proceedings of a 1963 symposium held at the Lerner Marine Laboratory, Bimini, Bahamas (Tavolga 1964). These early studies are remarkable as the scientists were not only working in a new environment—underwater— but also adapting large and cumbersome electronics of the day to record a new source of sounds.

The encyclopedic compendium of fish sounds by Fish & Mowbray (1970) was a landmark publication. They reviewed the acoustic abilities of 220 fishes in 59 families from along the Atlantic coast and Caribbean. It was a dramatic display of the broad range of fishes capable of sound production and many were the first examples for the species. They illustrated the sounds using 160 spectrographs and 329 oscillographs for 153 species in 36 families of fishes. In terms of primary research and recordings, no subsequent work has been able to repeat the sheer diversity and number of fishes examined, and despite being almost 40 years old, *Sounds of the Fishes of the Western North Atlantic* is still an indispensable reference.

The review by Demski et al. (1973) delved into the mechanisms of sound production in fishes. They defined the three categories of sound producing mechanisms as: (1) hydrodynamic sounds from swimming, (2) stridulatory mechanisms of hard structures rubbing, and (3) swimbladder sounds produced by muscle contraction. The field of fish bioacoustics was still in its infancy at the time of their paper. They reported that although sound production has been reported in a number of diverse fishes, the biological significance was known only in a few examples. They concluded at the time that it was possible that many sounds produced by fishes "may have no biological significance but may be incidental to other aspects of the fish's behavior" (p. 1142). Their paper clearly set forth the criteria for research to not only identify the sounds being made but also how such sounds may or may not be directly a part of the fish's behavior.

In terms of sheer comprehensiveness, the seminal review by Fine et al. (1977) is still the most valuable starting point for a student of fish bioacoustics. Simply titled "Communication in fishes," it was published as a chapter in the massive tome edited by Sebeok (1977) titled *How Animals Communicate*. They emphasized all the modalities that could be involved in fish communication, including chemical, visual, and behavioral. Their table on message and modulation of fish vocalization and that from Fish et al. (1952) were the models for our updated table describing all reported occurrences of sounds in coral reef fishes (see Table 10.1 at end of chapter). The Fine et al. (1977) review was comprehensive and accurately established the bioacoustics research agenda that is still appropriate today. The synthesis chapter by Fine et al. (1977) was complimented by the publication of two volumes that collated a series of the most influential primary research papers on sound production and reception in fishes up to that time (Tavolga 1976, 1977).

The review by Myrberg et al. (1978) clearly focused on the issue of communication and proposed that potential information content in fish sounds was determined by signal timing. Based upon extensive field studies of pomacentrids, the authors proposed that the pulsed patterns of fish sounds contain temporal information (i.e., pulse interval and pulse number) that is likely used by these fishes for species identification.

Tavolga et al. (1981) brought together the next major synthesis volume on hearing and communication in fishes. In his review in this book, Myrberg (1981) expanded on his view of how to test the concepts of communication in fishes. He defined how communication in fishes could be observed and he provided a framework for analyzing interactions. He also introduced the concept of acoustic interception, where an unintended recipient receives the information. Interception can be used by potential competitors and by predators. This chapter was followed by Hawkins & Myrberg (1983) and Hawkins (1986), both of which review the physical aspects of underwater sound and how these special conditions influence the way fishes can acoustically communicate. Schwarz (1985) included in her review an emphasis on the underwater environmental noises as they may affect fish behavior. She also concluded that for purposes of communication, fishes should use pulsed signal patterns rather than continuous sounds or varying frequencies. Bass & Clark (2003) present the most recent updated review covering the physical acoustic properties of underwater sound as basis for better understanding how sound communication by fishes can function in water.

In 1997, the journal *Marine and Freshwater Behaviour and Physiology* issued a volume dedicated to different aspects of underwater bioacoustics, with many papers focusing on fishes. Myrberg (1997b) updated earlier reviews with a decade of new data and reaffirmed many of the hypotheses regarding pulse timing as the key informational cue and the behavioral role of overhearing signals by predators. Ladich (1997) focused his review on the role of sound in the agonistic behavior of fishes. Agonistic vocalizations between aggressive fishes are easier to elicit experimentally than are courtship or mating sounds. Ladich noted that during agonistic interactions, male fish are often more vocal than females, with some exceptions. The pattern that male fish are the main sound producers in most species is emerging as a general trend. Bass (1997) reviewed the central and nervous system components regulating the fish vocal/sonic motor system, and Fine (1997) discussed how different hormones influence fish behavior and the production of sounds mediating those behaviors.

The new millennium transitioned from a largely descriptive phase to a more ethological and ecological one. Several publications updated earlier research findings of fish sensory abilities, with an emphasis on communication, especially the behavioral role of sounds. Myrberg (2001) presented a synthesis of the acoustical biology of elasmobranchs. One important conclusion was that several species of sharks were attracted to low frequency pulsed sounds such as typically produced by many fishes during aggression or courtship. Myrberg & Fuiman (2002) reviewed the multiple senses of reef fishes in the context of communication. This was followed next by Collin & Marshall's (2003) edited volume on sensory processing in aquatic environments. This book is notable for the new information it presented on color vision and communication in fishes as well as updated reviews on the mechanisms of hearing and sound production in fishes (Ladich & Bass 2003; Popper et al. 2003a). Bass & McKibben (2003) examined fish acoustic behavior from a neural mechanism perspective. The review by Rosenthal & Lobel (2005) reemphasized that sounds, color, and action patterns all function in concert to transmit elements of communication in fishes. They defined the structure of a pulsed fish sound and illustrated different types of fish mating sounds with sonograms.

Lobel (2001b) drew attention to the possibility of using fish sounds for monitoring fish reproduction by listening for species-specific mating sounds (also Lobel

2002). A symposium was held in 2002 that addressed how science could now apply acoustic technology to fisheries issues based on the fact that a variety of fish species produced distinguishable sounds (Rountree et al. 2003). The theme of this meeting was to review the accumulating evidence that species-specific sounds could be used by passive acoustic detection for monitoring fish behavior. The overall conclusion was that many fish species produce identifiable sounds that can be detected by passive acoustic devices (Rountree et al. 2006).

Two books were recently published that were entirely on fish communication with a significant emphasis on acoustics. Ladich et al. (2006) published a two-volume set entitled *Communication in Fishes*. This book has several chapters on fish acoustic communication including a review of sound generating mechanisms (Ladich & Fine 2006), swimbladder sound mechanisms (Parmentier & Diogo 2006), diversity of fish sounds (Amorim 2006), propagation of fish sounds (Mann 2006), agonistic sounds (Ladich & Myrberg 2006), and reproductive sounds (Myrberg & Lugli 2006). The second book, edited by Webb et al. (2008) was titled *Fish Bioacoustics*. The content is centered on the neurological and sensory aspects of how fishes sense vibrations, water movement, and sounds. The chapter in this book by Bass & Ladich (2008) considers the neural basis for fish communication. They bring forward Myrberg's hypothesis (Myrberg et al. 1978) for the temporal coding of signals by fishes and add new data to support this concept.

Finally, the most recent review of examples of fish sounds and sound producing mechanisms is by Kasumyan (2008). It is detailed and includes many illustrations of different types of sound-producing morphologies and fish sounds. Given this recent publication, we decided not to repeat the same material. The reader is encouraged to read this rich literature, especially the major reviews cited above. These papers do very well in describing the current state of knowledge about fish sound producing mechanisms, hearing, diversity of sounds produced, and how acoustics plays a role in the behavior of fishes.

BEHAVIORAL CONTEXTS FOR SOUND PRODUCTION IN REEF FISHES

Of the more than 179 families of fishes inhabiting coral reefs, and the nearshore tropical marine environment (Choat & Bellwood 1991; Lieske & Myers 1999), 48 families represented by 273 species in 137 genera are currently known as sound producing and hypothesized to use signaling in communication (see Table 10.1). Of these, surprisingly few have had sounds recorded and statistically described in undisturbed, intraspecific social contexts, especially reproduction. Reef fishes produce sounds in the same behavioral contexts as other marine and freshwater fishes (Amorim 2006): disturbance and predator defense (Fish & Mowbray 1970), agonism (e.g., Ladich 1997; Ladich & Myrberg 2006), and reproduction (e.g.,

Myrberg & Lugli 2006). Following below, we review the spectrographic properties of sounds produced by tropical fishes, many associated with reefs, and the behavioral contexts with which they are associated (see Table 10.1) and discuss these aspects of their acoustic biology. Five families, Aploactinidae (Matsubara 1934), Sillaginidae (Walls 1964), Synanceidae (Walls 1964), Tetrarogidae (Walls 1964), and Triglidae (e.g., Uchida 1934; Rauther 1945; Evans 1969, 1970), are known to produce patterned sounds, but both their spectrographic characteristics and details of the behavioral contexts in which they are produced have not been further pursued.

Twenty families of reef fishes produce some kind of agonistic sound. Agonistic encounters included competitive feeding, intraspecific and interspecific chase, territory defense, feeding competition, threat and attack, fights or combat, and interactions with potential predators that involve sound production when either fleeing from or confronting and sometimes attacking the predator. As in other fishes, sounds of tropical marine species play an important role in retreat defense. The pomacentrid, *Stegastes partitus*, has been described as producing a "keep-out" signal (Myrberg 1997a). This species guards a small patch of algae within its territory and uses these sounds to ward off intruders (Myrberg 1972a, b). The acoustic signature of these territorial sounds also communicates an individual's identity to conspecific neighbors (Myrberg & Riggio 1985; Myrberg et al. 1993).

Many of the territorial conflicts and especially male to male combat occur in direct association with the breeding season, although many species that maintain territories all year will continue to vocalize outside the breeding season (Gray & Winn 1961; Miyagawa & Takemura 1986; Ladich 1997). Territory maintenance correlates strongly with the presence of an acoustic signaling system. The selective advantage of the acoustic communication modality as opposed to other categories of signals in aggression is that sounds can enhance signals as they can correlate with individual body size and therefore provide an honest indicator of the likely winner for the outcome of a fight (Ladich 1990; Myrberg et al. 1993). The most recent study to demonstrate this in a common reef fish genus, *Amphiprion*, further supports the common trend for the dominant frequency of male fish agonistic sounds to correlate with body size; smaller males produce sounds with higher dominant frequencies (Colleye et al. 2009). This study has additionally identified pulse duration as correlating with body size. Significantly, this study has also shown that agonistic sounds may be important to both sexes, unlike in reproductive contexts where females are silent or may produce much lower amplitude sounds (Ladich 2007).

Fourteen reef fish families have been demonstrated to produce sounds during the breeding season (see Table 10.1). These reproductive sounds are commonly associated with courtship displays. In some of these species, particularly blenniids (de Jong et al. 2007), gobiids (Malavasi et al. 2003; Amorim & Neves 2007), and pomacentrids (e.g., Myrberg 1972a; Avidor 1974; Lobel & Mann 1995a; Lobel & Kerr 1999), sounds are part of a more elaborate courtship behavior with both acoustic and visual signals functioning to attract females to the territory.

While it is most common for the male to vocalize to attract females, there are examples of males and females exchanging calls during spawning. A case of male and female sound exchanges, or duets, has been observed in a syngnathid (Fish 1953), and a holocentrid (Herald & Dempster 1957). In the hermaphroditic *Hypoplectrus unicolor* (Serranidae), individuals alternate vocalizations while alternating spawning roles (Lobel 1992). Chaetodontid individuals have also been observed to exchange sounds between paired males and females that are hypothesized as mate alert or contact calls (Tricas et al. 2006).

Although the majority of acoustic fish families produce sounds in intraspecific contexts, many also produce disturbance sounds, which may perform a means of communicating interspecifically. Many fishes that produce disturbance sounds also produce sounds in undisturbed behavioral contexts, and therefore, the presence of disturbance sounds is often an indicator that the fish has the capacity to produce sounds for communication (Fish & Mowbray 1970; Lin et al. 2007), hence the purpose for emphasizing the "disturbance sound context" as evidence for potential sound signal production in our review of reef fishes. However, the absence of disturbance sounds in a species does not necessarily indicate total silence, since some acoustic fishes do not produce any kind of sounds when disturbed. In some marine taxa, disturbance sounds are directly associated with defensive weapon displays and are suggestive of acoustic aposematism or an acoustic warning of the fish's ability to damage a predator during a prey attack. Evidence that supports this hypothesis includes the observation that these sounds are produced by structures independent of the defense mechanism itself, hence not incidental noise. In tetraodontids (Sörensen 1894–1895) and diodontids (Burkenroad 1931), sounds occur during defensive displays of body inflation, suggesting a possible signal function in warning potential predators of their ability to defend. Other families erect spines as defensive structures, and these groups do produce sounds directly associated with the weaponized (often venom deployment capable) structures themselves, such as the pectoral fin spines of ariids (Tavolga 1962). Fourteen families have thus far only been reported to produce sounds during disturbance (see Table 10.1). Three of these families—Dactylopteridae (Müller 1857; Sörensen 1894–1895; Fish 1948; Fish & Mowbray 1970), Priacanthidae (Salmon & Winn 1966), and Pempheridae (Takayama et al. 2003)—have specialized acoustic muscles associated with the swimbladder, strongly suggesting that sounds are likely produced in other undisturbed social contexts yet to be observed (Fish & Mowbray 1970).

Fewer than half of the acoustic reef fish families cited in this review have been monitored with hydrophones during reproductive behaviors. Since many recently discovered acoustic fish species are now known to produce sounds inaudible to a casual human observer without the use of an amplified hydro-acoustic monitoring system, we cannot assume any particular taxonomic group is silent simply because we cannot easily hear them produce sounds. Clues to the potential for sound production in monacanthids are reported in a more recent study (Kawase 2005), which observed that males vibrate their dorsal spine rapidly as a common component of their courtship display but the researchers did not use a hydrophone in their study. Early reports on disturbance sounds in this family sometimes describe "creaking" sounds produced by the spines of species in this family. Only acoustic recording concurrent with natural behavior can verify if sounds are indeed generated during these and other species' courtship displays.

During their acoustic monitoring survey of marine fishes, Fish and Mowbray (1970) identified 14 families (Ammodytidae, Antennariidae, Atherinidae, Bothidae, Cyclopteridae, Echeneidae, Lophiidae, Mugilidae, Ogcocephalidae, Pleuronectidae, Soleidae, Stromateidae, Uranoscopidae, and Zoarchidae) as "silent" (i.e., not producing significant patterned sounds). However, even these families were not monitored specifically during reproductive activities. Therefore, we do not assume that they are completely silent, as an absence of evidence in this case does not equal evidence of absence. For example, sounds have been reported from *Uranoscopus scaber*, which is a member of a supposedly "silent" family (Mikhailenko 1973), and the detailed description of the acoustic apparatus of species belonging to numerous families in the order Scorpaeniformes, including some reef species, have only recently been followed up by actual recordings of sounds in undisturbed behavioral contexts (Širović & Demer 2009). It would therefore be difficult to draw broader conclusions about the difference between silent and acoustic reef fish taxa based on our current state of knowledge.

Three additional families (Aulostomidae, Lethrinidae, and Sphyraenidae) were found to produce only noises during swimming but other contexts of behavior have not been acoustically monitored (Fish & Mowbray 1970). Hydrodynamic sounds in general have been recorded in association with stereotypical agonistic and reproductive behaviors in chaetodontids, scarids, and labrids and are described as possible acoustic signals (Lobel 1992; Boyle & Tricas 2006; Tricas et al. 2006). While fishes may produce sounds as a by-product of swimming (Moulton 1960), the breadth of functional significance of swimming sounds is not currently certain. In addition to incidental sounds in fishes, the functional importance of the interception of signals is an area open for study (Myrberg 1981, 1997b). As an example, Steinberg et al. (1965) describe the dramatic sand diving behavior of a labrid (wrasse) in response to its common predator's swimming noises.

SOUND PRODUCTION AND BEHAVIOR
IN POMACENTRIDS (DAMSELFISHES)

The damselfishes (Pomacentridae) are one of the most thoroughly investigated and best understood family of acoustic reef fishes. This is in large part due to their conspicuous presence and abundance in coral reef communities, their demersal and often territorial behavior, and most notably, the sheer volume loudness of their sounds. Scuba divers can easily hear damselfish sounds without the aid of a hydrophone, particularly when a male is aggressively defending his territory. These features of pomacentrid acoustic behavior make them easily accessible to bioacoustic study.

Damselfishes are a diverse and speciose group (e.g., Quenouille et al. 2004; Cooper et al. 2009), and they play a dominant role in coral reef ecosystems worldwide (Bellwood & Hughes 2001). As of this writing, sounds have been recorded from 36 species (Tables 10.1 and 10.2 at end of chapter), representing four of the five subfamilies: Stegastinae, Chrominae, Abudefdufinae, and Pomacentrinae (following the topology and classification of Cooper et al. 2009; the Amphiprioninae, often considered a subfamily, are nested within the Pomacentrinae). The only pomacentrid subfamily from which sounds have not been recorded is the monotypic Lepidozyginae containing *Lepidozygus tapeinosoma*. Given the widespread occurrence of sound production throughout the family, the damselfishes may provide one of the first examples of sounds being a behavioral character uniting the entire family. If so, for any taxa that do not vocalize, this lack of an ability to produce sounds may represent its secondary loss. Damselfish sounds are distinctive among fishes in that they not only have highly repeatable patterned pulses and interpulse intervals in the basic sound display, the "chirp," but they also repeat the "chirp" call type at regular intervals presenting a complex acoustic display with two orders of temporal information, referred to as a call bout (Figure 10.2).

As with many fishes, pomacentrids produce sounds in two main behavioral contexts: aggression and courtship. Aggressive sounds are produced by males defending territories, doing so most fiercely when guarding their demersal eggs. These sounds are of short duration and broadband, and are often produced while resident fish are chasing or biting at conspecific or interspecific intruders (e.g., Mann & Lobel 1998). Agonistic sounds recorded from 26 species show a low mean number of pulses and maximum frequencies often above 1,000 Hz (Parmentier et al. 2006b). The higher-frequency component of the aggressive sound may increase detectability of the call (Fine & Lenhardt 1983; Mann & Lobel 1997; Bass & Clark 2003; Mann 2006) and thereby serve as a warning to other potential intruders.

During courtship displays, many damselfishes combine their repeated, pulsed vocalizations with a prominent visual display, the signal jump (Myrberg 1972a;

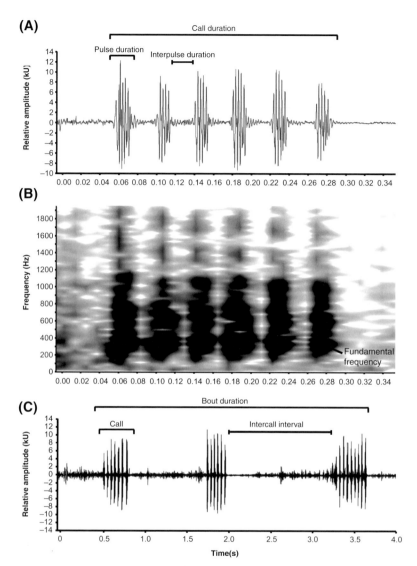

FIGURE 10.2. Representative call from the damselfish *Dascyllus albisella*, recorded from Johnston Atoll. The sounds are represented two ways: (A) the waveform, which shows relative amplitude, or sound pressure, versus time and (B) the spectrogram or sonogram, which shows the frequency content of the call versus time. This example is a single call from *D. albisella* comprised of six pulses. These different views can be used to reveal different temporal and spectral features of an individual sound or series of sounds. (C) Waveform of a calling bout from *D. albisella*, comprised of three calls, shows the broader time duration between calls and pulses.

Avidor 1974; Lobel & Mann 1995b; Mann & Lobel 1998; Parmentier et al. 2009). In the signal jump, fish rise up into the water column and then rapidly swim downwards while vocalizing before returning to the initial position and repeating the pattern. These displaying fish can often be seen and heard from quite a distance. Courtship sounds have been reported from 11 species within the family, but not enough acoustic parameters have been described to enable any broad quantitative analysis of taxon-specific features of courtship sounds.

The specific anatomy involved in sound production in damselfishes has been the subject of speculation for quite some time (Freytag 1968; Myrberg 1972b; Rice & Lobel 2003). Because damselfish sounds exhibit both harmonic and broadband characteristics, it seems likely that the sound-producing mechanism involves muscular and stridulatory elements. Also, given the loud nature of the sound, the swimbladder seems likely to be involved as a resonating device. Thus, the pharyngeal jaw apparatus has been suggested as a possible sound production mechanism (reviewed in Rice & Lobel 2003). Pomacentrids possess well-developed and highly mobile pharyngeal jaws (Galis & Snelderwaard 1997) and it is possible that they have been co-opted for use in sound production (Rice & Lobel 2003).

An alternative hypothesis was proposed from recent work on anemonefish that suggests that the oral jaws are involved in sound production (Parmentier et al. 2007), at least within the genus *Amphiprion*. *Amphiprion clarkii* is able to rapidly close its lower jaw with a novel ligament connecting the ceratohyal and coronoid process of the mandible. The sounds result from the occlusion of the upper and lower jaw teeth, and the jaws themselves are suggested to serve as the source of sound radiation (Parmentier et al. 2007). This work is particularly exciting, since the species-specific sounds produced by *Amphiprion* may correlate with interspecific differences in tooth morphology, suggesting exaptation and perhaps coevolution of feeding and acoustic behaviors (Chen & Mok 1988; Parmentier et al. 2007). Though this acoustic ligament has been suggested to be homologous among pomacentrids (Stiassny & Jensen 1987; Parmentier et al. 2007), its role in sound production across the family remains to be investigated.

FISH SOUNDS: TERMINOLOGY AND CLASSIFICATION

Fish sounds are complex signals and have a diverse combination of different components (Figure 10.2); one or more classes of these different parameters often vary among closely related taxa. Fish sounds have been classified in different ways, usually according to the following criteria: (1) phonetic/onomatopoeia, (2) behavioral context, (3) adaptive or hypothesized function, (4) morphological nature of mechanism, (5) specific acoustic parameters (amplitude or loudness, temporal and frequency), and (6) temporal duration categories (Rountree et al. 2006). Human

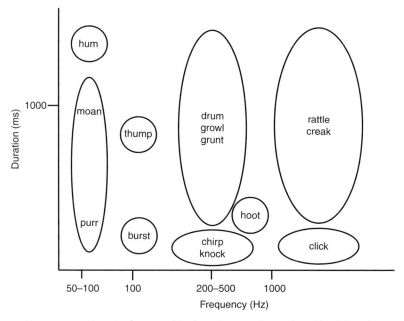

FIGURE 10.3. Terminology used to describe sounds produced by fishes. See Table 10.1 for a listing of fishes and acoustic characteristics on which this figure is based.

appellations for fish sounds— onomatopoeia, or the use of words that imitate the associated sound—commonly capture the temporal and frequency components of a sound (see Figure 10.3). They are widely used for all acoustic animals and are analogous to common names for describing species in addition to a genus and species designation. As observed by Fish & Mowbray (1970), certain general sound terms relate to the types of sound producing mechanisms fish employ. Creaks or clicks are typically higher and broadband frequency stridulation sounds, while the lower frequency sounds (<1,000 Hz) referred to by the greatest diversity of sound terms are typically produced by swimbladder-associated muscles (Figure 10.3). However, onomatopoeia does not provide an absolute, systematic way to differentiate between all sounds. For example, the usefulness of this approach to categorize fish sounds breaks down when onomatopoeia is described in a foreign language or when patterns become more complex than simple time and frequency characteristics. Fish sounds are also often referred to interchangeably as sounds, calls, or signals. These terms are not necessarily always interchangeable and it is likely that further criteria for distinguishing them will follow as we further examine the role of sounds in communication versus noise production.

There have been a number of suggestions for a rigorous and consistent consensus terminology for fish sounds and their components (Winn 1964; Fine et al. 1977; Kihslinger & Klimley 2002)(see Figure 10.2). Fine et al. (1977) provided a classification scheme for fishes that focused on acoustic parameters, specifically temporal patterns of sounds. Such a framework provides a statistically testable system, while a naming system based only on inferred or expected function may result in frequent name changes with new studies. It is important to note that if we can specify what acoustic parameters are significant to the fish, then naming sounds according to only those acoustic parameters that are meaningful will add power to this type of classification scheme.

Marshall (1962) observed that fish sounds produced by different mechanisms sound different to the human observer. He also summarized phonetic descriptions of sounds produced by fish with different mechanisms and classified them into two major categories: stridulation and swimbladder sounds. It is useful when describing a new fish sound to classify it according to the sound production mechanism (SPM), because different types of acoustic mechanisms often are acoustically constrained; that is, they produce sounds that differ in frequency or temporal pattern (e.g., Walls 1964; Myrberg 1972a; Demski et al. 1973). Identifying structures of a likely acoustic mechanism in a museum preparation can provide information about its likely signal characteristics, many fishes are known only from their preserved materials. Inversely, having spectrographic information about a sound signal can provide a clue to identifying a yet unknown acoustic mechanism in a newly discovered acoustic fish species (Rice & Lobel 2002, 2003).

Behaviors are also useful for classifying fish sounds. Naming fish sounds on the basis of their behavioral context or the specific motor patterns with which they occur may involve the use of some of the following terms: male courtship dip display, spawning, nest brooding, agonistic, or schooling sounds. When sounds are additionally described on the basis of their hypothesized function, terms such as appeasement, dominance, mate attraction, fright, or alarm are appended to other descriptions of the sound. The behavioral context description is most valuable as it is purely descriptive and does not imply any function, which can only be determined through experimentation. Naming a fish sound by its presumed function should be carefully qualified as a hypothesis. The use of a strict context or physical activity for naming a fish sound is the better choice as it provides accurate information about the association of a particular behavior with sound(s), without making assumptions about sound function. The advantage of using behavioral context is that it is consistent. A sound produced during courtship alone and named as such will provide a reliable means for categorizing that sound. The disadvantage of using context as a naming device is that a particular sound may be used in more than one context. In such a case, this system does not provide an exclusive naming system. In naming a fish sound, it is therefore useful to ongoing research in the field to describe as many known aspects of the sound as possible, but to treat all such terms as working hypotheses subject to further study.

SPECTROGRAPHIC PROPERTIES
OF REEF FISH SOUNDS

Frequency

Frequency ranges for most fish sounds are broadly overlapping but fall into two general categories: those predominantly below 1,000 Hz in dominant frequency with narrower band frequency overall; and those with broad band frequency ranging up to 8 kHz depending on the mechanism involved (Demski et al. 1973; Ladich & Fine 2006). The tropical reef fish sound spectrum is currently known to extend from below 100 Hz up to 8,000 Hz and is the same as found in many other well-known sound producing fishes. Other frequency indicators that may be more informative regarding biologically significant and evolutionarily selected traits, such as dominant frequency that could indicate age or size (Myrberg et al. 1993; Lobel & Mann 1995b), were not consistently reported for many fish species. The relationship between the spectral properties of the sound and the physical condition of the signaler remains a productive avenue for future research, in essence allowing us to address what properties of the signal reveal about the sender.

Duration

The duration of the basic sound unit of an acoustic display is one measure of temporal patterns that can indicate communicative content in the sounds of fishes in general (McKibben & Bass 1998). Durations for the basic sound unit of reef fishes ranged from 10 ms to just over 6 seconds across acoustic reef fish families (see Table 10.2), similar to the range for fishes found in all other aquatic habitats. The longest acoustic displays known are associated with courtship and spawning among fishes in general (Amorim 2006), where these sounds serve as an advertisement signal to attract females. Sounds with the greatest number of pulses that also had regularly spaced interpulse intervals were most commonly associated with reproductive context calling. Reef fish families with basic sound units of the longest duration, greater than one second, included balistids, batrachoidids, carangids, chaetodontids, holocentrids, monacanthids, pomacentrids, sciaenids, and tetraodontids. A sound display incorporating a series of several different call types by a chorusing tropical sciaenid male, *Johnius macrorhynus*, lasted for 143 minutes (Lin et al. 2007). In some temperate batrachoidids, the basic sound unit of a male reproductive call of an individual fish may last for seconds to minutes, and the call displays continue for up to one hour (Ibara et al. 1983; Brantley & Bass 1994; Rice & Bass 2009).

SPECTRAL PATTERNS:
PULSED VERSUS TONAL SIGNALS

The sounds of many acoustic fishes for which only spectrograms are available are sometimes difficult to classify as either pulsed or non-pulsed, since the waveforms are not always expanded to reveal the presence or absence of interpulse intervals. We provide a conservative classification of sound types for each marine species (Table 10.1), restricting our designation of pulsed, tonal or other call characteristics to those specifically described as such by the authors whose publications we had access to. Many species of sound producing fishes have not had their sounds spectrographically analyzed.

The sounds produced by most fishes in disturbance and escape contexts appear to be short in duration (<500 ms in duration) and have irregular interpulse (i.e., variable interval)(Winn 1972) durations and could be considered simple single pulse displays, although their selective advantage in these contexts remains elusive beyond proposed hypotheses. These sounds could simply be distress noises or a release of sounds produced during other contexts, or they may play a role in a prey species communicating its ability to escape or defend itself. Predator defense weapons, such as the abduction and adduction of venomous pectoral spines, can produce stridulation sounds. In marine catfishes, these sounds are broadband in frequency range and occur in pairs, each consisting of a series of pulses with interpulse intervals that are produced in sound bouts of irregular intervals and thus could be a form of acoustic aposematism.

The basic sound described for many tropical marine fishes in agonistic and reproductive contexts commonly consists of a single pulse or multiple pulses. Comparing the duration of the agonistic and reproductive sounds for our acoustic fish sample we found that the longest duration sounds were produced in association with reproductive contexts, while agonistic sounds were shorter in duration. Multiple pulses consist of regular repeating patterns of interpulse intervals, or off times, between pulses. Basic sound units may be repeated in bouts, which are highly patterned or regular in some damselfishes (*Stegastes*). Sound displays consisting of patterned pulses with stereotypical interpulse off-time durations have been statistically described for members of several families (i.e., Carapidae, Chaetodontidae, Gobiidae, Holocentridae, Pempheridae, Pomacanthidae, Pomacentridae, Sciaenidae, Serranidae, and Terapontidae) and are most commonly associated with male courtship displays. Other families with regularly spaced pulsed waveforms that are agonistic or disturbance sounds, but which have not been statistically described, include Ariidae, Balistidae, Diodontidae, Haemulidae, Ostraciidae, and Priacanthidae.

The most uncommon spectrographic sound type pattern among reef fishes (and all fishes in general) is tonal, that is, sounds that exhibit pure tone frequencies. Of the 48 social sound producing tropical families, only batrachoidids and ostraciids have so far been reported to produce purely tonal sounds. Among tropical batrachoidids, two species in the genus *Opsanus,* and *Batrachomoeus trispinosus,* are known to produce a tonal component to the male courtship display (e.g., Amorim 2006; Rice & Bass 2009). In the ostraciid family *Ostracion meleagris,* males produce tonal sounds during spawning (Lobel 1996). Tonal sounds are produced by the fastest rates of muscle contraction and are therefore extremely physiologically demanding, often requiring specialized muscles to create these sounds (e.g., Rome et al. 1996; Rome 2006). They are temporally indicative of the highest repetition rate for a call, pulses are repeated so rapidly that they are not separated by pulse intervals, and could convey a message of male vigor, and therefore be a male fitness indicator, to females. Tonal sounds are equally rare for other fish families from temperate marine and freshwaters. In these taxa, they are also found as one of multiple call types associated with a male courtship display. In temperate batrachoidids, females are not known to produce tonal sounds, and the sounds they do produce in agonistic contexts are typically single pulse sounds with irregular intervals between successive pulses.

FUNCTIONAL SIGNIFICANCE OF SOUNDS: MALE FITNESS AND FEMALE MATE CHOICE

The hypothesized functional significance of tropical fish sounds is the same as that for other vocal animals (Table 10.3): mate localization; individual discrimination (age, sex, aggressive strength); an indicator of mate fitness (size and vigor or rate of display); species discrimination; and gamete release synchronization.

There are often striking sexual differences in fish acoustic displays indicating the possibility that many fishes can identify the sex of a caller by their sound characteristics. In some species, females lack the major structures involved in sound production, produce quieter sounds or are silent due to the atrophy of their swimbladder drumming muscles in the breeding season, suggesting other physiological priorities over sound communication (Nguyen et al. 2008). There are differences in sounds between sexes in carapid reef fishes. Carapid females, *Carapus boraborensis,* produce longer pulses (Lagardère et al. 2005). In temperate sciaenids, sex differences in sound production, including fundamental frequency, interpulse interval, and number of pulses per call, have been found in several species (Takemura et al. 1978; Ueng et al. 2007).

The evolutionary significance of reproductive sound signaling in fishes, differences in the sounds of species and the ability of individuals to discriminate was first clearly demonstrated in marine fishes for damselfishes. Male display in damselfishes is considered an advertisement signal (Kenyon 1994) and its potential role as an indicator of male fitness and female choice has been proposed (Myrberg et al. 1993). Individual recognition is accomplished by male pomacentrids who can distinguish their neighbors on nearby territories (Myrberg & Riggio 1985). Within marine fish genera, species recognition (i.e., the ability of an individual fish to recognize when another is or is not a member of their own species) that is based on sound production has only been experimentally demonstrated in damselfishes (Myrberg et al. 1986). This was shown by choice experiments in four *Stegastes* species where females preferred male sounds whose pulse numbers matched their own species, thereby allowing for the distinction of conspecifics from heterospecifics. Recent work in acoustic neurophysiology of a damselfish demonstrated that auditory neurons are indeed sensitive to the pulsed temporal components of their own sounds (Maruska & Tricas 2009). Courtship sounds of male *Stegastes* species differ in unit rate, pulse number, frequency, pulse duration, and pulse interval (Myrberg et al. 1978). The role of acoustic parameters other than pulse number for species recognition remains to be tested within this family. Species differences in acoustic male courtship displays underscore its possible significance in reproductive isolation since damselfish females prefer the pulse number totals of their own species. Dialects, or the geographic variation in the male calling display of damselfishes, further support the hypothesis that fish species may diverge on the basis of reproductive-context call characteristics (Parmentier et al. 2005). Congeners of other tropical marine families differ in the acoustic properties of their sounds (Table 10.4). Other spectrographic parameters that vary among reproductive courtship displays of species in the same genus, all of which are also sympatric, include pulse repetition rate in tropical sciaenids (Lin et al. 2007), pulse number, duration, and interpulse interval in pomacentrids (Maruska et al. 2007), number of sound pulses per display in batrachoidids (Fish & Mowbray 1959), and amplitude and duration in gobiids (Stadler 2002). While temporal call differences have been behaviorally demonstrated to provide information to fishes in various communication contexts among damselfishes, other call parameters such as amplitude or frequency may also provide acoustic clues to listeners of other acoustic fish families. Male fitness discrimination by choosey females is hypothesized based on the honest signaling potential of the pomacentrid acoustic system, where a relationship between body size, swimbladder volume, and call dominant frequency exists (Myrberg et al. 1993). Increased body size directly correlating with lower dominant call frequency for male reproductive acoustic display has also been determined for other temperate marine fishes, in particular gobies (Malavasi et al. 2003). In contrast to frequency characteristics, female plainfin midshipmen are attracted to and prefer playbacks of tonal overpulsed male acoustic display components (McKibben & Bass 1998), suggesting that an acoustic feature other than size may be the basis for female choice in this species. This other feature could be male vigor, evidenced by a faster calling rate for tonal versus pulsed sounds. However, further work to determine if and how females choose mates on the basis of these varied male acoustic characteristics is needed.

In fishes with external fertilization, the importance of spawning synchronization cues could be very important. The scarid (*Scarusiseri,* formerly *iserti*) forms spawning aggregations and produces hydrodynamic sounds when groups of individuals rush up in the water column and release gametes (Lobel 1992). These sounds are broadband and adventitious to the swimming movements. Research from several acoustic fish groups, and reef families in particular, have recorded patterned sounds associated with spawning (Lobel 1992). It is presumed that it is mainly for reproduction when groups of individuals are calling together in one specific locality. However, not all fish species producing sounds in choruses have yet been identified as specifically engaging in reproductive behaviors. While closer detailed observations of individual behaviors in these groups are essential, they have been difficult to obtain in the field.

CHORUSING SOUNDS
AND BREEDING AGGREGATIONS

From early hydrophone monitoring, coral reefs were found to be very noisy soundscapes. The sounds noted by the earliest reef fish acoustics researchers were typically highly audible and widely propagating. Reefs can be noisy due to the chorusing behavior of breeding reef fishes (e.g., Cato 1976, 1978; McCauley & Cato 2000). Numerous marine fishes form spawning aggregations (see Knudsen et al. 1948a; Takemura et al. 1978) that occur over specific diel patterns (Breder 1968; Cato 1976, 1978; McCauley & Cato 2000). Most of these species have peaks in their acoustic chorus activities nocturnally with some activity peaks under low light conditions, dusk or dawn. Pomacentrids are notably active predominantly during the day under lighted conditions. Many of these reef sounds appear to be primarily the result of the reproductive activities of pomacentrid, sciaenid, serranid, and batrachoidid species, while the crepuscular calling peaks of holocentrids are due solely to agonistic sounds (Figure 10.4).

SONIC INTERACTIONS

Predators seem to place major selection constraints on fish sound signaling (Nottestad 1998; Luczkovich et al. 2000; Wahlberg & Westerberg 2003; Remage-Healey et al. 2006). Although this work has been demonstrated only in temperate and subtropical marine fishes to date, these species all belong to families that include tropical reef species. Predators elicit a reaction from a temperate toadfish, whose family has representatives in tropical habitats as well. These temperate batrachoidids reduce their calling rate in response to playbacks of dolphin sounds,

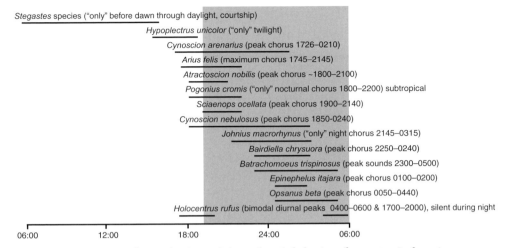

Stegastes species ("only" before dawn through daylight, courtship)

Hypoplectrus unicolor ("only" twilight)

Cynoscion arenarius (peak chorus 1726–0210)

Arius felis (maximum chorus 1745–2145)

Atractoscion nobilis (peak chorus ~1800–2100)

Pogonius cromis ("only" nocturnal chorus 1800–2200) subtropical

Sciaenops ocellata (peak chorus 1900–2140)

Cynoscion nebulosus (peak chorus 1850-0240)

Johnius macrorhynus ("only" night chorus 2145–0315)

Bairdiella chrysoura (peak chorus 2250–0240)

Batrachomoeus trispinosus (peak sounds 2300–0500)

Epinephelus itajara (peak chorus 0100–0200)

Opsanus beta (peak chorus 0050–0440)

Holocentrus rufus (bimodal diurnal peaks 0400–0600 & 1700–2000), silent during night

06:00   12:00   18:00   24:00   06:00

FIGURE 10.4. Diel reproductive activity and sonic behavior of some tropical marine species show three different temporal patterns of acoustic chorusing: diurnal, nocturnal, and crepuscular. Gray shaded area represents night.

indicating that calling in sonic fishes bears risks from intercepting predators (Remage-Healey et al. 2006). It has been proposed that predatory dolphins intercept fish sounds when hunting clupeids, batrachoidids, and sciaenids (Luczkovich et al. 2000; Gannon et al. 2005). On the other hand, an increase in acoustic activity has been reported for the tropical squirrelfish, *Holocentrus adscensionis*, which has been observed confronting predators with pulsed sound bouts and engaging in mobbing behavior as a predator deterrent (Winn et al. 1964).

The timing of chorusing behavior in predominantly nocturnal breeding aggregations of reef fishes may be greatly influenced by the threat to adults of predator interception of the sounds, as well as the threat to freshly fertilized eggs released into the open water in a concentrated area. Calling and spawning at night is hypothesized as a diurnal predator evasion strategy for both adults and spawned eggs. Research on sciaenids supports the notion that cetacean predators can intercept sciaenid sounds (Gannon et al. 2005). Experimental work has demonstrated that concentrations of eggs are under increased predation pressure, indicating that night spawning would result in greater dispersion of eggs by the time visual predators become active the next day (Holt et al. 1985).

These observations raise questions about the evolutionary role of predators in influencing the acoustic displays in fishes. If acoustic calling poses a sufficient risk, then a reduction in the amplitude of acoustic displays is likely. Such adverse selection could even lead to the elimination of sound by previously acoustic species. Evolutionary secondary loss of acoustic activity is a likely scenario given that the homology of neural development of the acoustic motor nucleus indicates an ancestral ability for acoustic communication in vertebrates (Bass et al. 2008).

CONCLUSIONS AND FUTURE DIRECTIONS

The diversity found among coral reef fishes makes them a fascinating study group for scientists in many fields; the field of sound production in reef fishes represents the intersection of these different interests and perspectives. The fact that reef fishes live in warm, clear waters is conducive to underwater study by scuba divers. Reef fish bioacoustics is frequently overlooked in studies of fish behavior, but it offers the potential for major advances in the study of animal communication. Tropical coral reefs around the world are home to more than 4,000 species of fishes (Lieske & Myers 1999; Bellwood & Hughes 2001), and in over 100 years of study, fewer than 10% of taxa have been reported as producing sounds. Given the widespread taxonomic occurrence of sounds in fishes (e.g., Amorim 2006; Bass & Ladich 2008; Fay 2009), and the evidence that all vertebrates share similar brain mechanisms responsible for producing these sounds (Bass et al. 2008), it is clear that bioacoustic signaling is a modality that can no longer be ignored or overlooked in behavioral studies of any fish. For far too long, studies have reported on the courtship or territorial behavior of reef fish groups, with neither mention nor apparent awareness of the possibility that the focal taxon may be using sounds to communicate. Scientific studies of either communication or intraspecific interaction in other (non-fish) animals would be deemed at best incomplete and at worst unacceptable if potential vocalizations were not accounted for. Yet this has been the case for the majority of research on fishes (imagine studying courtship in passerine birds without reporting on the role of song). We raise this issue to serve as encouragement to researchers of coral reef fishes to include the study of sounds as a vital component of behavioral research.

The majority of publications on fish sounds have primarily focused on their temporal occurrence or acoustical characteristics, but the specific behavioral function of such sounds is still relatively understudied. As evidenced by the large and diverse body of work on the bioacoustics of damselfishes described here, understanding how sounds function in behavior requires knowing the diversity of the vocal repertoire, the behavioral response that particular sounds elicit, the hearing range of the receiver, and the acoustic features of the signal to which conspecifics pay attention. These topics have been addressed in only a few fishes (e.g., damselfishes, gobies, and toadfishes). The opportunity to study these components in other taxa is wide open. As Karl von Frisch wrote in 1938, after realizing the co-occurrence of fish sound production and their hearing ability: "There may be much to discover in the future about the language of fishes" (von Frisch 1938, p. 11). His words still hold true today.

ACKNOWLEDGMENTS

Our research on the sounds of coral reef fishes was supported by grants from the Army Research Office (DAAG55-98-1-0304, DAAD19-02-1-0218), Office of Naval Research (N00014-19-J1519, N00014-92-J-1969 and N00014-95-1-1324), the DoD Legacy Resource Management Program (DAMD-17-93-J-3052, DADA87-00-H-0021, DACA87-01-H-0013, W912D4-06-2-0017) and NOAA Seagrant (NA90-AA-D-SG535, NA86-AA-D-SG090, NOAA/NURC-FDU 89-09-NA88A-H-URD20).

REFERENCES

Aalbers SA, Drawbridge MA (2008). White seabass spawning behavior and sound production. Transactions of the American Fisheries Society 137: 542–550.

Akamatsu T, Okumura T, Novarini N, Yan HY (2002). Empirical refinements applicable to the recording of fish sounds in small tanks. Journal of the Acoustic Society of America 112: 3073–3082.

Albrecht H (1981). Aspects of sound communication in some Caribbean reef fishes (*Eupomacentrus* Spec, Pisces, Pomacentridae). Bijdragen tot de Dierkunde 51: 70–80.

Albrecht H (1984). Harmonics in courtship sounds of four Caribbean reef fish species of the genus *Eupomacentrus* (Pomacentridae). Bijdragen tot de Dierkunde 54: 169–177.

Allen GR (1972). *The Anemonefishes: Their Classification and Biology.* TFH Publications, Neptune City, New Jersey.

Amorim MCP (1996a). Acoustic communication in triglids and other fishes. M.Phil. thesis, University of Leicester, Leicester, UK.

Amorim MCP (1996b). Sound production in the blue-green damselfish, *Chromis viridis* (Cuvier, 1830) (Pomacentridae). Bioacoustics 6: 265–272.

Amorim MCP (2006). Diversity of sound production in fish. In: Ladich F, Collin SP, Moller P, Kapoor BG (eds.), *Communication in Fishes*, vol. 1, *Acoustic and Chemical Communication.* Science Publishers, Enfield, New Hampshire, pp. 71–105.

Amorim MCP, Neves ASM (2007). Acoustic signalling during courtship in the painted goby, *Pomatoschistus pictus*. Journal of the Marine Biological Association of the United Kingdom 87: 1017–1023.

Aristotle (1910). *Historia animalium* (translated by DA Thompson). The Internet Classics Archive http://classics.mit.edu//Aristotle/history_anim.html (accessed Feb. 15, 2010).

Avidor A (1974). The signal jump and its associated sound in fish of the genus *Dascyllus* from the Gulf of Eilat. Master's thesis, Tel Aviv University.

Bass AH (1997). Comparative neurobiology of vocal behaviour in teleost fishes. Marine and Freshwater Behaviour and Physiology 29: 47–63.

Bass AH, Clark CW (2003). The physical acoustics of underwater sound communication. In: Simmons AM, Fay RR, Popper AN (eds.), *Acoustic Communication.* Springer, New York, pp. 15–64.

Bass AH, Ladich F (2008). Vocal-acoustic communication: from neurons to behavior. In: Webb JF, Fay RR, Popper AN (eds.), *Fish Bioacoustics.* Springer, New York, pp. 253–278.

Bass AH, McKibben JR (2003). Neural mechanisms and behaviors for acoustic communication in teleost fish. Progress in Neurobiology 69: 1–26.

Bass AH, Gilland EH, Baker R (2008). Evolutionary origins for social vocalization in a vertebrate hindbrain-spinal compartment. Science 321: 417–421.

Bellwood DR, Hughes TP (2001). Regional-scale assembly rules and biodiversity of coral reefs. Science 292: 1532–1535.

Bernoulli AL (1910). Zur frage des hörvermögens der fishce. Pflugers Archiv für die Gesamte Physiologie des Menschen und der Tiere 134: 633–644.

Bierbaum G (1914). Examinations on the structure of the auditory organs of deep sea fish. Zeitschrift für Wissenschaftliche Zoologie 111: 281–380.

Board PA (1956). The feeding mechanism of the fish *Sparisoma cretense* (Linné). Proceedings of the Zoological Society of London 127: 59–77.

Boyle KS, Tricas TC (2006). Sound communication by the forceps fish, *Forcipiger flavissimus* (Chaetodontidae). Journal of the Acoustical Society of America 120: 3104.

Brantley RK, Bass AH (1994). Alternative male spawning tactics and acoustic signals in the plainfin midshipman fish *Porichthys notatus* Girard (Teleostei, Batrachoididae). Ethology 96: 213–232.

Braun CB, Grande T (2008). Evolution of peripheral mechanisms for the enhancement of sound reception. In: Webb JF, Fay RR, Popper AN (eds.), *Fish Bioacoustics*. Springer, New York, pp. 99–144.

Breder CM, Clark E (1947). A contribution to the visceral anatomy, development, and relationships of the Plectognathi. Bulletin of the American Museum of Natural History 88: 293–319.

Breder CM Jr (1968). Seasonal and diurnal occurrences of fish sounds in a small Florida bay. Bulletin of the American Museum of Natural History 138: 327–378.

Bridge TW (1904). Fishes. In: Farmer SF, Shipley AE (eds.), *Cambridge Natural History*. MacMillan, London, pp. 139–537.

Bright CM (1972). Bio-acoustic studies on reef organisms. In: Collette BB, Earle SA (eds.), Results of the tektite program: ecology of coral reef fishes. Science Bulletin 14, Natural History Museum of Los Angeles County, pp. 45–69.

Bright TJ, Sartori JD (1972). Sound production by the reef fishes *Holocentrus coruscus, Holocentrus rufus* and *Myripristis jacobus*, Family Holocentridae. Hydro-Lab Journal 1: 11–20.

Burgess WE (1989). *An Atlas of Freshwater and Marine Catfishes: A Preliminary Survey of the Siluriformes*. TFH Publications, Neptune City, New Jersey.

Burke TE, Bright TJ (1972). Sound production and color changes in the dusky damselfish. Hydro-Lab Journal 1: 21–29.

Burkenroad MD (1930). Sound production in the Haemulidae. Copeia 1930: 17–18.

Burkenroad MD (1931). Notes on the sound-producing marine fishes of Louisiana. Copeia 1931: 20–28.

Caldwell DK, Caldwell MC (1967). Underwater sounds associated with aggressive behavior in defense of territory by the pinfish, *Lagodon rhomboides*. Bulletin of the Southern California Academy of Sciences 66: 69–75.

Carlson BA, Bass AH (2000). Sonic/vocal motor pathways in squirrelfish (Teleostei, Holocentridae). Brain, Behavior and Evolution 56: 14–28.

Cato DH (1976). Ambient sea noise in waters near Australia. Journal of the Acoustical Society of America 60: 320–328.

Cato DH (1978). Marine biological choruses observed in tropical waters near Australia. Journal of the Acoustical Society of America 64: 736–743.

Charif RA, Waack AM, Strickman LM (2008). *Raven Pro 1.4 User's Manual*. Cornell Laboratory of Ornithology, Ithaca, New York.

Chen KC, Mok HK (1988). Sound production in the anemonefishes, *Amphiprion clarkii* and *A. frenatus* (Pomacentridae), in captivity. Japanese Journal of Ichthyology 35: 90–97.

Choat JH, Bellwood DR (1991). Reef fishes: their history and evolution. In: Sale PF (ed.), *The Ecology of Fishes on Coral Reefs*. Academic Press, San Diego, pp. 39–66.

Collette BB, Earle SA, eds. (1972). Results of the Tektite program ecology of coral reef fishes. Science Bulletin 14, Natural History Museum of Los Angeles County.

Colleye O, Frederich B, Vandewalle P, Casadevall M, Parmentier E (2009). Agonistic sounds in the skunk clownfish *Amphiprion akallopisos*: size-related variation in acoustic features. Journal of Fish Biology 75: 908–916.

Collin SP, Marshall NJ (2003). *Sensory Processing in Aquatic Environments*. Springer-Verlag, New York.

Colson DJ, Patek SN, Brainerd EL, Lewis SM (1998). Sound production during feeding in *Hippocampus* seahorses (Syngnathidae). Environmental Biology of Fishes 51: 221–229.

Connaughton MA, Fine ML, Taylor MH (2002). Weakfish sonic muscle: influence of size, temperature and season. Journal of Experimental Biology 205: 2183–2188.

Cooper WJ, Smith LL, Westneat MW (2009). Exploring the radiation of a diverse reef fish family: phylogenetics of the damselfishes (Pomacentridae), with new classifications based on molecular analyses of all genera. Molecular Phylogenetics and Evolution 52: 1–16.

Courtenay WR Jr, McKittrick FA (1970). Sound-producing mechanisms in carapid fishes, with notes on phylogenetic implications. Marine Biology 7: 131–137.

Cousteau JY, Dumas F (1953). *The Silent World*. Harper & Brothers, New York.

Cummings WC, Brahy BD, Herrnkind WF (1964). The occurence of underwater sounds of biological origin off the west coast of Bimini, Bahamas. In: Tavolga WN (ed.), *Marine Bio-acoustics*. Pergamon Press, New York, pp. 27–43.

Cummings WC, Brahy BD, Spire JY (1966). Sound production, schooling, and feeding habits of the margate, *Haemulon album* Cuvier, off North Bimini, Bahamas. Bulletin of Marine Science 16: 626–240.

de Jong K, Bouton N, Slabbekoorn H (2007). Azorean rock-pool blennies produce size-dependent calls in a courtship context. Animal Behaviour 74: 1285–1292.

Demski LS, Gerald JW, Popper AN (1973). Central and peripheral mechanisms of teleost sound production. American Zoologist 13: 1141–1167.

Dobrin MB (1947). Measurements of underwater noise produced by marine life. Science 105: 19–23.

Dobrin MB, Loomis WE (1943). Acoustic measurements at the John G. Shedd Aquarium, Chicago, Illinois. Naval Ordnance Laboratory Memorandum 3416: 1–17.

Dufossé L (1858a). De l'ichthyopsophie, ou des différents phénomènes physiologiques nommés voix des poissons (deuxième partie). Comptes Rendus Hebdomadaires des Séances de l'Académie des Sciences 46: 916.

Dufossé L (1858b). Des différents phénomènes physiologiques nommés voix des poissons. Comptes Rendus Hebdomadaires des Séances de l'Académie des Sciences 46: 352–356.

Dufossé L (1862). Sur les différents phénomènes physiologiques nommés voix des poissons, ou sur l'ichthyopsophose (troisième partie). Comptes Rendus Hebdomadaires des Séances de l'Académie des Sciences 54: 393–395.

Dufossé L (1874a). Recherches sur les bruits et les sons expressifs que font entendre les poissons d'Europe et sur les organes producteurs de ces phénomènes acoustiques ainsi que sur, les appareils de l'audtion de plusieurs de ces animaux. Première partie. Annales des Sciences Naturelles Cinquième Série: Zoologie et Paléontologie 19: 1–53.

Dufossé L (1874b). Recherches sur les bruits et les sons expressifs que font entendre les Poissons d'Europe et sur les organes producteurs de ces phenomenes acoustiques ainsi que sur les appareils de l'audtion de plusieurs de ces animaux. Annales des Sciences Naturelles Cinquième Série: Zoologie et Paléontologie 20: 1–134.

Emery AR (1973). Comparative ecology and functional osteology of fourteen species of damselfish (Pisces: Pomacentridae) at Alligator Reef, Florida Keys. Bulletin of Marine Science 23: 649–770.

Evans RR (1969). Phylogenetic significance of sound producing mechanisms of Western Atlantic fishes of the family Triglidae and Peristediidae. Ph.D. dissertation, Department of Zoology, Boston University, Ann Arbor, Michigan.

Evans RR (1970). Phylogenetic significance of teleost sound producing mechanisms. Journal of the Colorado-Wyoming Academy of Science 7: 9–10.

Fay RR (2009). Fish bioacoustics. In: Havelock D, Kuwano S, Vorländer M (eds.), *Handbook of Signal Processing in Acoustics*. Springer, New York, pp. 1851–1860

Fay RR, Popper AN (2000). Evolution of hearing in vertebrates: the inner ears and processing. Hearing Research 149: 1–10.

Fine ML (1997). Endocrinology of sound production in fishes. Marine and Freshwater Behavior and Physiology 29: 23–45

Fine ML, Lenhardt ML (1983). Shallow-water propagation of the toadfish mating call. Comparative Biochemistry and Physiology A 76A: 225–231.

Fine ML, Winn HE, Olla BL (1977). Communication in fishes. In: Sebeok TA (ed.), *How Animals Communicate*. Indiana University Press, Bloomington, pp. 472–518.

Fish JF, Cummings WC (1972). A 50-dB increase in sustained ambient noise from fish (*Cynoscion xanthulus*). Journal of the Acoustical Society of America 52: 1266–1270.

Fish MP (1948). *Sonic Fishes of the Pacific*. Woods Hole Oceanographic Institution, Woods Hole, Massachussetts.

Fish MP (1953). The production of underwater sound by the northern seahorse, *Hippocampus hudsonius*. Copeia 1953: 98–99.

Fish MP (1954). The character and significance of sound production among fishes of the western North Atlantic. Bulletin of the Bingham Oceanographic Collection 14: 1–109.

Fish MP, Mowbray WH (1959). The production of underwater sound by *Opsanus* sp., a new toadfish from Bimini, Bahamas. Zoologica 44: 71–79.

Fish MP, Mowbray WH (1970). *Sounds of the Western North Atlantic Fishes*. Johns Hopkins University Press, Baltimore.

Fish MP, Kelsey AS, Mowbray WH (1952). Studies on the production of underwater sound by North Atlantic coastal fishes. Journal of Marine Research 11: 180–193.

Fourmanoir P, Laboute P (1976). *Poissons des mers Tropicales: Nouvelle Calédonie, Nouvelles Hébrides*. Hachette, Tahiti.

Freytag G (1968). Ergebnisse zur marinen bioakustik. Protokolle zur Fischereitechnik 11: 252–352.

Gainer H, Kusano K, Mathewson RF (1965). Electrophysiological and mechanical properties of squirrelfish sound-producing muscle. Comparative Biochemistry and Physiology 14: 661–671.

Galis F, Snelderwàárd P (1997). A novel biting mechanism in damselfishes (Pomacentridae): the pushing up of the lower pharyngeal jaw by the pectoral girdle. Netherlands Journal of Zoology 47: 405–410.

Gannon DP, Barros NB, Nowacek DP, Read AJ, Waples DM, Wells RS (2005). Prey detection by bottlenose dolphins, *Tursiops truncatus*: an experimental test of the passive listening hypothesis. Animal Behaviour 69: 709–720.

Gilmore RG (2003). Sound production and communication in the spotted seatrout. In: Bortone SA (ed.), *Biology of the Spotted Sea Trout*. CRC Press, Boca Raton, Florida, pp. 177–195.

Graham R (1992). Sounds fishy. Australia's Geographic Magazine 14: 76–83.

Gray GA, Winn HE (1961). Reproductive ecology and sound production of the toadfish, *Opsanus tau*. Ecology 42: 274–282.

Griffin DR (1950). Underwater sounds and the orientation of marine animals, a preliminary survey. Cornell University Project NR 162-429, Contract N.6 ONR. 264 t.o.9. between the Office of Naval Research and Cornell University, Technical Report 3.

Guest WC, Lasswell JL (1978). A note on courtship behavior and sound production of red drum. Copeia 1978: 337–338.

Hardenberg JDF (1934). Ein Töne erzeugender Fisch. Zoologischer Anzeiger 108: 224–227.

Hawkins AD (1986). Underwater sound and fish behavior. In: Pitcher TJ (ed.), *The Behaviour of Teleost Fishes*. Chapman & Hall, London, pp. 129–169.

Hawkins AD, Myrberg AA, Jr. (1983). Hearing and sound communication under water. In: Lewis B (ed.), *Bioacoustics: A Comparative Approach*. Academic Press, London, pp. 347–405.

Herald ES, Dempster RP (1957). Courting activity in the white-lipped squirrelfish. Aquarium Journal 28: 43–44.

Holt GJ, Holt SA, Arnold CR (1985). Diel periodicity of spawning in sciaenids. Marine Ecology Progress Series 27: 1–7.

Holt SA (2002). Intra- and inter-day variability in sound production by red drum (Sciaenidae) at a spawning site. Bioacoustics 12: 227–229.

Holzberg S (1973). Beobachtungen zur oekologie und zum socialverhalten des korallenbarsches *Dascyllus marginatus* Rueppell (Pisces: Pomacentridae). Zeitschrift für Tierpsychologie 33: 492–513.

Horch K, Salmon M (1973). Adaptations to the acoustic environment by the squirrelfishes *Myripristis violaceus* and *M. pralinius*. Marine Behaviour and Physiology 2: 121–139.

Ibara RM, Penny LT, Ebeling AW, van Dykhuizen G, Cailliet G (1983). The mating call of the plainfin midshipman fish, *Porichthys notatus*. In: Noakes DLG, Lindquist DG, Helfman GS, Ward JA (eds.), *Predators and Prey in Fishes*. Dr. W. Junk Publishers, The Hague, pp. 205–212.

James PL, Heck KL (1994). The effects of habitat complexity and light intensity on ambush predation within a simulated seagrass habitat. Journal of Experimental Marine Biology and Ecology 176: 187–200.

Jordan DS, Richardson RE (1907). Fishes from the islands of the Philippine Archipelago. Bulletin of the Bureau of Fisheries 27: 233–295.

Kasumyan AO (2008). Sounds and sound production in fishes. Journal of Ichthyology 48: 981–1030.

Kawase H (2005). Spawning behavior of the pygmy leatherjacket *Brachaluteres jacksonianus* (Monacanthidae) in southeastern Australia. Ichthyological Research 52: 194–197.

Kenyon TN (1994). The significance of sound interception to males of the bicolor damselfish, *Pomacentrus partitus*, during courtship. Environmental Biology of Fishes 40: 391–405.

Kihslinger RL, Klimley AP (2002). Species identity and the temporal characteristics of fish acoustic signals. Journal of Comparative Psychology 116: 210–214.

Kim SH (1977). Sound production and phonotactic behaviour of the yellowtail, *Seriola quinqueradiata* Temminck et Schlegel. Bulletin of the National Fisheries University, Busan (Natural Sciences) 17: 17–25.

Knudsen VO, Alford RS, Emling JW (1948a). Survey of Underwater Sound. Report No. 3: Ambient Noise. Office of Scientific Research and Development, National Defense Research Committee, Washington, DC.

Knudsen VO, Alford RS, Emling JW (1948b). Underwater ambient noise. Journal of Marine Research 7: 410–429.

Koenig O (1957). Erfahrungen mit korallenfischen. Aquarien und Terrarien Zeitschrift 10: 154–156.

Kronengold M, Dann R, Green WC, Loewenstein JM (1964). Description of the system. In: Tavolga WN (ed.), *Marine Bio-acoustics*. Pergamon Press, New York, pp. 11–26.

Kumpf HE (1964). Use of underwater television in bioacoustic research. In: Tavolga WN (ed.), *Marine Bio-acoustics*. Pergamon Press, New York, pp. 45–57.

Ladich F (1990). Vocalization during agonistic behaviour in *Cottus gobio* L. (Cottidae): an acoustic threat display. Ethology 84: 193–201.

Ladich F (1997). Agonistic behaviour and significance of sounds in vocalizing fish. Marine and Freshwater Behaviour and Physiology 29: 87–108.

Ladich F (2000). Acoustic communication and the evolution of hearing in fishes. Philosophical Transactions of the Royal Society of London B 355: 1285–1288.

Ladich F (2007). Females whisper briefly during sex: context- and sex-specific differences in sounds made by croaking gouramis. Animal Behaviour 73: 379–387.

Ladich F, Bass AH (2003). Underwater sound generation and acoustic reception in fishes with some notes on frogs. In: Collin SP, Marshall NJ (eds.), *Sensory Processing in Aquatic Environments*. Springer-Verlag, New York, pp. 173–193.

Ladich F, Fine ML (2006). Sound-generating mechanisms in fishes: a unique diversity in vertebrates. In: Ladich F, Collin SP, Moller P, Kapoor BG (eds.), *Communication in Fishes, Vol. 1. Acoustic and Chemical Communication*. Science Publishers, Enfield, New Hampshire, pp. 3–43.

Ladich F, Myrberg AA Jr. (2006). Agonistic behavior and acoustic communication. In: Ladich F, Collin SP, Moller P, Kapoor BG (eds.), *Communication in Fishes, Vol. 1. Acoustic and Chemical Communication*. Science Publishers, Enfield, New Hampshire, pp. 121–148.

Ladich F, Collin SP, Moller P, Kapoor BG (2006). *Communication in Fishes*. Science Publishers, Inc., Enfield, New Hampshire.

Lafite-Dupont JA (1907). Recherches sur l'audition des poissons. Comptes Rendus Des Séances de la Société de Biologie et de ses Filiales 63: 710–711.

Lagardère JP, Fonteneau G, Mariani A, Morinière P (2003). Les émissions sonores du poisson-clown mouffette *Amphiprion akallopisos*, Bleeker 1853 (Pomacentridae), enregistrées dans l'aquarium de la Rochelle. Annales de la Société des Sciences Naturelles de la Charente-Maritime 9: 281–288.

Lagardère JP, Millot S, Parmentier E (2005). Aspects of sound communication in the pearlfish *Carapus boraborensis* and *Carapus homei* (Carapidae). Journal of Experimental Zoology 303A: 1066–1074.

Lammers MO, Brainard RE, Au WWL, Mooney TA, Wong KB (2008). An ecological acoustic recorder (EAR) for long-term monitoring of biological and anthropogenic sounds on coral reefs and other marine habitats. Journal of the Acoustical Society of America 123(3): 1720–1728.

Lauder GV, Liem KF (1983). The evolution and interrelationships of the actinopterygian fishes. Bulletin of the Museum of Comparative Zoology 150: 95–197.

Leis JM, Lockett MM (2005). Localization of reef sounds by settlement-stage larvae of coral-reef fishes (Pomacentridae). Bulletin of Marine Science 76: 715–724.

Lieske E, Myers R (1999). *Coral Reef Fishes*. Princeton University Press, Princeton, New Jersey.

Limbaugh C (1964). Notes on the life history of two California pomacentrids: Garibaldis, *Hypsypops rubicunda* (Girard), and blacksmiths, *Chromis punctipinnis* (Cooper). Pacific Science 28: 41–50.

Lin YC, Mok HK, Huang BQ (2007). Sound characteristics of big-snout croaker, *Johnius macrorhynus* (Sciaenidae). Journal of the Acoustical Society of America 121: 586–593.

Lobel PS (1978). Diel, lunar, and seasonal periodicity in the reproductive behavior of the pomacanthid fish, *Centropyge potteri*, and some other reef fishes in Hawaii. Pacific Science 32: 193–207.

Lobel PS (1992). Sounds produced by spawning fishes. Environmental Biology of Fishes 33: 351–358.

Lobel PS (1996). Spawning sound of the trunkfish, *Ostracion meleagris* (Ostraciidae). Biological Bulletin 191: 308–309.

Lobel PS (2001a). Acoustic behavior of cichlid fishes. Journal of Aquariculture and Aquatic Sciences 9: 89–108.

Lobel PS (2001b). Fish bioacoustics and behavior: passive acoustic detection and the application of a closed-circuit rebreather for field study. Marine Technology Society Journal 35: 19–28.

Lobel PS (2002). Diversity of fish spawning sounds and the application of acoustic monitoring. Bioacoustics 12: 286–289.

Lobel PS (2003a). Fish courtship and mating sounds: unique signals for acoustic monitoring. In: Rountree RA, Goudey CA, Hawkins AD (eds.), *Listening to Fish: Passive*

Acoustic Applications in Marine Fisheries. Proceedings from an International Workshop in Passive Acoustics. MIT Press, Cambridge, Massachussetts, pp. 54–58

Lobel PS (2003b). Synchronized underwater audio-video recording. In: Rountree RA, Goudey CA, Hawkins AD (eds.), *Listening to Fish: Passive Acoustic Applications in Marine Fisheries. Proceedings from an International Workshop in Passive Acoustics.* MIT Press, Cambridge, Massachussetts, pp. 127–130.

Lobel PS (2005). Scuba bubble noise and fish behavior: a rationale for silent diving technology. Proceedings of the American Academy of Underwater Sciences Symposium, University of Connecticut at Avery Point, Groton, Connecticut, pp. 49–59.

Lobel PS, Kerr LM (1999). Courtship sounds of the Pacific Damselfish, *Abudefduf sordidus* (Pomacentridae). Biological Bulletin 197: 242–244.

Lobel PS, Mann DA (1995a). Courtship and mating sounds of *Dascyllus albisella* (Pomacentridae). Bulletin of Marine Science 57: 705.

Lobel PS, Mann DA (1995b). Spawning sounds of the damselfish, *Dascyllus albisella* (Pomacentridae), and relationship to male size. Bioacoustics 6: 187–198.

Locascio JV, Mann DA (2008). Diel periodicity of fish sound production in Charlotte Harbor, Florida. Transactions of the American Fisheries Society 137: 606–615.

Luczkovich JJ, Sprague MW, Johnsen SE, Pullinger RC (1999). Delimiting spawning areas of weakfish, *Cynoscion regalis* (Family Sciaenidae) in Pamlico Sound, North Carolina using passive hydroacoustic surveys. Bioacoustics 10: 143–160.

Luczkovich JJ, Daniel HJ, Hutchinson M, Jenkins T, Johnson SE, Pullinger RC, Sprague MW (2000). Sounds of sex and death in the sea: bottlenose dolphin whistles silence mating choruses of silver perch. Bioacoustics 10: 323–334.

Luczkovich JJ, Mann DA, Rountree RA (2008a). Passive acoustics as a tool in fisheries science. Transactions of the American Fisheries Society 137: 533–541.

Luczkovich JJ, Pullinger RC, Johnson SE, Sprague MW (2008b). Identifying sciaenid critical spawning habitats by the use of passive acoustics. Transactions of the American Fisheries Society 137: 576–605.

Luh HK, Mok HK (1986). Sound production in the domino damselfish, *Dascyllus trimaculatus* (Pomacentridae) under laboratory conditions. Japanese Journal of Ichthyology 33: 70–74.

Malavasi S, Torricelli P, Lugli M, Pranovi F, Mainardi D (2003). Male courtship sounds in a teleost with alternative reproductive tactics, the grass goby, *Zosterisessor ophiocephalus*. Environmental Biology of Fishes 66: 231–236.

Mann DA (2006). Propagation of fish sounds. In: Ladich F, Collin SP, Moller P, Kapoor BG (eds.), *Communication in Fishes, Vol. 1. Acoustic and Chemical Communication.* Science Publishers, Enfield, New Hampshire, pp. 107–120.

Mann DA, Grothues TM (2009). Short-term upwelling events modulate fish sound production at a mid-Atlantic Ocean observatory. Marine Ecology Progress Series 375: 65–71.

Mann DA, Lobel PS (1995). Passive acoustic detection of spawning sounds produced by the damselfish, *Dascyllus albisella* (Pomacentridae). Bioacoustics 6: 199–213.

Mann DA, Lobel PS (1997). Propogation of damselfish (Pomacentridae) courtship sounds. Journal of the Acoustic Society of America 101: 3783–3791.

Mann DA, Lobel PS (1998). Acoustic behavior of the damselfish *Dascyllus albisella*: behavioral and geographic variation. Environmental Biology of Fishes 51: 421–428.

Mann DA, Lu Z, Popper AN (1997). A clupeid fish can detect ultrasound. Nature 389: 341.

Mann DA, Casper BM, Boyle KS, Tricas TC (2007). On the attraction of larval fishes to reef sounds. Marine Ecology Progress Series 338: 307–310.

Mann DA, Locascio JV, Coleman FC, Koenig CC (2009). Goliath grouper *Epinephelus itajara* sound production and movement patterns on aggregation sites. Endangered Species Research 7: 229–236.

Marage L (1906). Contribution à l'étude de l'audition des poissons. Comptes Rendus Hebdomadaires des Séances de l'Académie des Sciences 143: 852–853.

Marshall NB (1962). The biology of sound-producing fishes. Symposia of the Zoological Society of London 7: 45–60.

Maruska KP, Tricas TT (2009). Encoding properties of auditory neurons in the brain of a soniferous damselfish: response to simple tones and complex conspecific signals. Journal of Comparative Physiology A 195: 1071–1088.

Maruska KP, Boyle KS, Dewan LR, Tricas TC (2007). Sound production and spectral hearing sensitivity in the Hawaiian sergeant damselfish, *Abudefduf abdominalis*. Journal of Experimental Biology 210: 3990–4004.

Matsubara K (1934). Studies on the Scorpaenoid fishes of Japan. I. Descriptions of one new genus and five new species. Journal of the Imperial Fisheries Institute of Tokyo 80: 199–210.

Matsuno Y, Hujieda S, Chung YJ, Yamanaka Y (1994). Underwater sound in the net pen at the culture grounds in the innermost area of Kagoshima Bay. Bulletin of the Japanese Society of Fisheries Oceanography 58: 11–20.

McCauley RD, Cato DH (2000). Patterns of fish calling in a nearshore environment in the Great Barrier Reef. Philosophical Transactions of the Royal Society of London B 355: 1289–1293.

McCauley RD, Fewtrell J, Popper AN (2003). High intensity anthropogenic sound damages fish ears. Journal of the Acoustical Society of America 113: 638–642.

McKibben JR, Bass AH (1998). Behavioral assessment of acoustic parameters relevant to signal recognition and preference in a vocal fish. Journal of the Acoustical Society of America 104: 3520–3533.

Mikhailenko NA (1973). Organ of sound formation and electro generation in the Black Sea stargazer *Uranoscopus scaber* (Uranoscopidae). Zoologicheskii Zhurnal 52: 1353–1359.

Miyagawa M, Takemura A (1986). Acoustical behaviour of the scorpaenoid fish *Sebasticus marmoratus*. Bulletin of the Japanese Society of Scientific Fisheries 52: 411–415.

Möbius K (1889). *Balistes aculeatus*, ein trommelnder Fisch. Sitzungsberichte der Preussischen Akademie der Wissenschaften 46: 999–1006.

Moulton JM (1958). The acoustical behavior of some fishes in the Bimini area. Biological Bulletin 114: 357–374.

Moulton JM (1960). Swimming sounds and the schooling of fishes. Biological Bulletin 119: 210–223.

Moulton JM (1962). Marine animal sounds of the Queensland coast. American Zoologist 2: 542.

Moulton JM (1963). Acoustic behaviour of fishes. In: Busnel RG (ed.), *Acoustic Behaviour of Animals*. Elsevier, Amsterdam, pp. 655–685.

Moulton JM (1964a). Acoustic behaviour of fishes. In: Busnel RG (ed.), *Acoustic Behaviour of Animals*. Elsevier, New York, pp. 655–693.

Moulton JM (1964b). Underwater sound: biological aspects. Oceangraphy and Marine Biology Annual Review 2: 425–454.

Moulton JM (1969). The classification of acoustic communicative behavior among teleost fishes. In: Sebeok TA, Ramsay A (eds.), *Approaches to Animal Communication*. Mouton & Co. N.V., The Hague, pp. 146–178.

Moyer JT (1975). Reproductive behavior of the damselfish *Pomacentrus nagasakiensis* at Miyake-jima, Japan. Japanese Journal of Ichthyology 22: 151–163.

Moyer JT (1979). Mating strategies and reproductive behavior of ostraciid fishes at Miyake-jima, Japan. Japanese Journal of Ichthyology 26: 148–160.

Moyer JT, Thresher RE, Collin PL (1983). Courtship, spawning and inferred social organization of American angelfishes (genera *Pomacanthus*, *Holacanthus* and *Centropyge*; *Pomacanthidae*). Environmental Biology of Fishes 9: 25–39.

Müller J (1857). Über die Fische, welche Töne von sich geben, und die Entstehung dieser Töne. Archiv für Anatomie, Physiologie und wissenschaftliche Medicin: 249–279.

Myrberg AA, Jr. (1972a). Ethology of the bicolor damselfish, *Eupomacentrus partitus* (Pisces: Pomacentridae): a comparison of laboratory and field behaviour. Animal Behaviour Monographs 5: 199–283.

Myrberg AA Jr (1972b). Social dominance and territoriality in bicolor damselfish, *Eupomacentrus partitus* (Poey) (Pisces: Pomacentridae). Behaviour 41: 207–230.

Myrberg AA Jr (1980). Fish bio-acoustics: its relevance to the "not so silent world." Environmental Biology of Fishes 5: 297–304.

Myrberg AA Jr (1981). Sound communication and interception in fishes. In: Tavolga WN, Popper AN, Fay RR (eds.), *Hearing and Sound Communication in Fishes*. Springer-Verlag, New York, pp. 395–426.

Myrberg AA Jr (1996). Fish bioacoustics: serendipity in research. Bioacoustics 7: 143–150.

Myrberg AA Jr. (1997a). Sound production by a coral reef fish (*Pomacentrus partitus*): evidence for a vocal, territorial "keep-out" signal. Bulletin of Marine Science 60: 1017–1025.

Myrberg AA Jr (1997b). Underwater sound: its relevance to behavioral functions among fishes and marine mammals. Marine and Freshwater Behavior and Physiology 29: 3–21.

Myrberg AA Jr (2001). The acoustical biology of elasmobranchs. Environmental Biology of Fishes 60: 31–45.

Myrberg AA Jr, Fuiman LA (2002). The sensory world of coral reef fishes. In: Sale PF (ed.), *Coral Reef Fishes: Dynamics and Diversity in a Complex Ecosystem*. Elsevier Academic Press, San Diego, pp. 123–148.

Myrberg AA Jr, Lugli M (2006). Reproductive behavior and acoustical interactions. In: Ladich F, Collin SP, Moller P, Kapoor BG (eds.), *Communication in Fishes, Vol. 1. Acoustic and Chemical Communication*. Science Publishers, Enfield, New Hampshire, pp. 149–176.

Myrberg AA Jr, Riggio RJ (1985). Acoustically mediated individual recognition by a coral reef fish (*Pomacentrus partitus*). Animal Behaviour 33: 411–416.

Myrberg AA Jr, Spires JY (1972). Sound discrimination by the bicolor damselfish, *Eupomacentrus partitus*. Journal of Experimental Biology 57: 727–735.

Myrberg AA Jr, Stadler JH (2002). The significance of the sounds by male gobies (Gobiidae) to conspecific females: similar findings to a study made long ago. Bioacoustics 12: 255–257.

Myrberg AA Jr, Thresher RE (1974). Interspecific aggression and its relevance to the concept of territoriality in reef fishes. American Zoologist 14: 81–96.

Myrberg AA Jr, Banner A, Richard JD (1969). Shark attraction using a video-acoustic system. Marine Biology 2: 264–376.

Myrberg AA Jr, Spanier E, Ha SJ (1978). Temporal patterning in acoustical communication. In: Reese ES, Lighter FJ (eds.), Contrasts in Behavior. Wiley Interscience, New York, pp. 137–179.

Myrberg AA Jr, Mohler M, Catala JD (1986). Sound production by males of a coral reef fish (Pomacentrus partitus): its significance to females. Animal Behaviour 34: 913–923.

Myrberg AA Jr, Ha SJ, Shamblott MJ (1993). The sounds of bicolor damselfish (Pomacentrus partitus): predictors of body size and a spectral basis for individual recognition and assessment. Journal of the Acoustical Society of America 94: 3067–3070.

Nakazato M, Takemura A (1987). Acoustical behavior of Japanese parrot fish Oplenathus [sic] fasciatus. Nippon Suisan Gakkaishi 53: 967–973.

Nelson EM (1955). The morphology of the swim bladder and auditory bulla in the Holocentridae. Fieldiana: Zoology 37: 121–130.

Nguyen TK, Lin H, Parmentier E, Fine ML (2008). Seasonal variation in sonic muscles in the fawn cusk-eel Lepophidium profundorum. Biology Letters 4: 707–710.

Nottestad L (1998). Extensive gas bubble release in Norwegian spring-spawning herring (Clupea harengus) during predator avoidance. ICES Journal of Marine Science 55: 1133–1140.

Okumura T, Akamatsu T, Yan HY (2002). Analyses of small tank acoustics: empirical and theoretical approaches. Bioacoustics 12: 330–332.

Oliver SJ (2001). Mate choice and sexual selection in domino damselfish, Dascyllus albisella. Ph.D. dissertation, Boston University, Boston, Massachussetts.

Onuki A, Somiya H (2007). Innervation of sonic muscles in teleosts: occipital vs. spinal nerves. Brain, Behavior and Evolution 69: 132–141.

Pappe L (1853). Synopsis of the Edible Fishes at the Cape of Good Hope. Van de Sandt de Villiers & Tier, Capetown.

Parker GH (1903). The sense of hearing in fishes. American Naturalist 37: 185–204.

Parmentier E, Diogo R (2006). Evolutionary trends of swimbladder sound mechanisms in some teleost fishes. In: Ladich F, Collin SP, Moller P, Kapoor BG (eds.), Communication in Fishes, Vol. 1. Acoustic and Chemical Communication. Science Publishers, Enfield, New Hampshire, pp. 45–70.

Parmentier E, Vandewalle P, Lagardère JP (2003). Sound-producing mechanisms and recordings in Carapini species (Teleostei, Pisces). Journal of Comparative Physiology A 189: 283–292.

Parmentier E, Lagardère JP, Vandewalle P, Fine ML (2005). Geographical variation in sound production in the anemonefish Amphiprion akallopisos. Proceedings of the Royal Society of London B 272: 1697–1703.

Parmentier E, Fine M, Vandewalle P, Ducamp J-J, Lagardère J-P (2006a). Sound production in two carapids (Carapus acus and C. mourlani) and through the sea cucumber tegument. Acta Zoologica 87: 113–119.

Parmentier E, Lagardere J-P, Braquegnier J-B, Vandewalle P, Fine ML (2006b). Sound production mechanism in carapid fish: first example with a slow sonic muscle. Journal of Experimental Biology 209: 2952–2960.

Parmentier E, Vandewalle P, Frédérich B, Fine ML (2006c). Sound production in two species of damselfishes (Pomacentridae): *Plectroglyphidodon lacrymatus* and *Dascyllus aruanus*. Journal of Fish Biology 69: 491–503.

Parmentier E, Colleye O, Fine ML, Frédérich B, Vandewalle P, Herrel A (2007). Sound production in the clownfish *Amphiprion clarkii*. Science 316: 1006.

Parmentier E, Lecchini D, Frederich B, Brie C, Mann D (2009). Sound production in four damselfish (*Dascyllus*) species: phyletic relationships? Biological Journal of the Linnean Society 97: 928–940.

Parvulescu A (1967). The acoustics of small tanks. In: Tavolga WN (ed.), *Marine Bioacoustics*. Pergamon Press, Oxford, pp. 7–14.

Pauly D (2004). *Darwin's Fishes: An Encyclopedia of Ichthyology, Ecology and Evolution*. Cambridge University Press, Cambridge.

Picciulin M, Costantini M, Hawkins AD, Ferrero EA (2002). Sound emissions of the Mediterranean damselfish *Chromis chromis* (Pomacentridae). Bioacoustics 12: 236–238.

Popper AN (2003). Effects of anthropogenic noise on fishes. Fisheries 28: 24–31.

Popper AN, Hastings MC (2009). The effects of human-generated sound on fish. Integrative Zoology 4: 43–52.

Popper AN, Salmon M, Parvulescu A (1973). Sound localization by the Hawaiian squirrelfishes *Myripristis berndti* and *M. argyromus*. Animal Behaviour 21: 86–97.

Popper AN, Fay RR, Platt C, Sand O (2003a). Sound detection mechanisms and capabilities of teleost fishes. In: Collin SP, Marshall NJ (eds.), *Sensory Processing in Aquatic Environments*. Springer-Verlag, New York, pp. 3–38.

Popper AN, Fewtrell J, Smith ME, McCauley RD (2003b). Anthropogenic sound: effects on the behavior and physiology of fishes. Marine Technology Society Journal 37: 35–40.

Quenouille B, Bermingham E, Planes S (2004). Molecular systematics of the damselfishes (Teleostei: Pomacentridae): Bayesian phylogenetic analyses of mitochondrial and nuclear DNA sequences. Molecular Phylogenetics and Evolution 31: 66–88.

Radford CA, Jeffs AG, Tindle CT, Cole RG, Montgomery JC (2005). Bubbled waters: the noise generated by underwater breathing apparatus. Marine and Freshwater Behaviour and Physiology 38: 259–267.

Radford C, Jeffs A, Tindle C, Montgomery JC (2008a). Resonating sea urchin skeletons create coastal choruses. Marine Ecology Progress Series 362: 37–43.

Radford CA, Jeffs AG, Tindle CT, Montgomery JC (2008b). Temporal patterns in ambient noise of biological origin from a shallow water temperate reef. Oecologia 156: 921–929.

Ramcharitar J, Gannon DP, Popper AN (2006). Bioacoustics of fishes of the family Sciaenidae (croakers and drums). Transactions of the American Fisheries Society 135: 1409–1431.

Rauther M (1945). Uber die schwimmblase und die zu ihr in beziehung tretenden somatischen muskeln bei den Triglidae und anderen Scleroparei. Zoologische Jahrbucher 69: 159–250.

Remage-Healey L, Nowacek DP, Bass AH (2006). Dolphin foraging sounds suppress calling and elevate stress hormone levels in a prey species, the Gulf toadfish. Journal of Experimental Biology 209: 4444–4451.

Rice AN, Bass AH (2009). Novel vocal repertoire and paired swimbladders of the three-spined toadfish, *Batrachomoeus trispinosus*: insights into the diversity of the Batrachoididae. Journal of Experimental Biology 212: 1377–1391.

Rice AN, Lobel PS (2002). Enzyme activities of pharyngeal jaw musculature in the cichlid *Tramitichromis intermedius*: implications for sound production in cichlid fishes. Journal of Experimental Biology 205: 3519–3523.

Rice AN, Lobel PS (2003). The pharyngeal jaw apparatus of the Cichlidae and Pomacentridae (Teleostei: Labroidei): function in feeding and sound production. Reviews in Fish Biology and Fisheries 13: 433–444.

Richard JD (1968). Fish attraction with pulsed low frequency sound. Journal of the Fisheries Research Board of Canada 25: 1441–1452.

Ripley JL, Foran CM (2007). Influence of estuarine hypoxia on feeding and sound production by two sympatric pipefish species (Syngnathidae). Marine Environmental Research 63: 350–367.

Rome LC (2006). Design and function of superfast muscles: new insights into the physiology of skeletal muscle. Annual Review of Physiology 68: 193–221.

Rome LC, Syme DA, Hollingworth S, Lindstedt SL, Baylor SM (1996). The whistle and the rattle: the design of sound producing muscles. Proceedings of the National Academy of Sciences of the United States of America 93: 8095–8100.

Rosenthal GG, Lobel PS (2005). Communication. In: Sloman KA, Wilson RW, Balshine S (eds.), *Behaviour and Physiology of Fish*. Fish Physiology series, vol. 24. Academic Press, San Diego, pp. 39–78.

Rountree RA, Goudey CA, Hawkins AD, Luczkovich JJ, Mann DA (2003). Listening to fish: passive acoustic applications in marine fisheries. Massachusetts Institute of Technology, Sea Grant Digital Oceans, Cambridge. MITSG 0301 http://web.mit.edu/seagrant/digitalocean/listening.pdf.

Rountree RA, Gilmore RG, Goudey CA, Hawkins AD, Luczkovich JJ, Mann DA (2006). Listening to fish: applications of passive acoustics to fisheries science. Fisheries 31: 433–446.

Sadovy de Mitcheson Y, Liu M (2008). Functional hermaphroditism in teleosts. Fish and Fisheries 9: 1–43.

Salmon M (1967). Acoustical behavior of the menpachi, *Myripristis berndti*, in Hawaii. Pacific Science 21: 364–381.

Salmon M, Winn HE (1966). Sound production by priacanthid fishes. Copeia 1966: 869–872.

Salmon M, Winn HE, Sorgente N (1968). Sound production and associated behavior in triggerfishes. Pacific Science 22: 11–20.

Santangelo N, Bass AH (2006). New insights into neuropeptide modulation of aggression: field studies of arginine vasotocin in a territorial tropical damselfish. Proceedings of the Royal Society of London B 273: 3085–3092.

Santiago JA, Castro JJ (1997). Acoustic behaviour of *Abudefduf luridus*. Journal of Fish Biology 51: 952–959.

Sartori JD, Bright TJ (1973). Hydrophonic study of the feeding activities of certain Bahamian parrot fishes, family Scaridae. Hydro-Lab Journal 2: 25–56.

Schneider H (1961). Neuere ergebnisse de lautforschung bei fischen. Naturwissenschaften 48: 512–518.

Schneider H (1964a). Bioakustische untersuchungen an anemonenfischen der gattung *Amphiprion* (Pisces). Zeitschrift für Morphologie und Ökologie der Tiere 53: 453–474.

Schneider H (1964b). Physiologische und morphologie untersuchungen zur bioakustik der tigerfische (Pisces, Theraponidae). Zeitschrift für Vergleichende Physiologie 47: 493–558.

Schneider H, Hasler AD (1960). Laute und lauterzeugung bein suesswassertrommler *Aplodinotus grunniens* Rafinesque (Sciaenidae, Pisces). Zeitschrift für Vergleichende Physiologie 43: 499–517.

Schwarz AL (1985). The behavior of fishes in their acoustic environment. Environmental Biology of Fishes 13: 3–15.

Sebeok TA (1977). *How Animals Communicate.* Indiana University Press, Bloomington

Shishkova EV (1958a). Concerning the reactions of fish to sounds and the spectrum of trawler noise. Rybnoye Khozyaystvo 34: 33–39.

Shishkova EV (1958b). Recordings and analysis of noise made by fish. Trudy Vsesoiuznyi Nauchno-Isseledovatel'skii Institut Morskogo Rybnogo Khoziaistva i Okeanografii 36: 280–294.

Simpson SD, Meekan MG, McCauley RD, Jeffs A (2004). Attraction of settlement-stage coral reef fishes to reef noise. Marine Ecology Progress Series 276: 263–268.

Simpson SD, Meekan M, Montgomery J, McCauley R, Jeffs A (2005). Homeward sound. Science 308: 221.

Širović A, Demer DA (2009). Sounds of captive rockfishes. Copeia 2009: 502–509.

Sörensen W (1894–1895). Are the extrinsic muscles of the air-bladder in some Siluroidae and the "elastic spring"' apparatus of others subordinate to the voluntary production of sounds? What is, according to our present knowledge, the function of the weberian ossicles? A contribution to the biology of fishes. Journal of Anatomy and Physiology 29: 109–139; 205–229; 399–423; 518–552.

Spanier E (1970). Analysis of sounds and associated behavior of domino damselfish *Dascyllus trimaculatus* (Rueppell, 1828). (Pomacentridae). Master's thesis, Tel-Aviv University.

Spanier E (1979). Aspects of species recognition by sound in four species of damselfishes, genus *Eupomacentrus* (Pisces: Pomacentridae). Zeitschrift für Tierpsychologie 51: 301–316.

Stadler JH (2002). Evidence for hydrodynamic mechanism of sound production by courting males of the notchtongue goby *Bathygobius curacao* (Metzelaar). Bioacoustics 13: 145–152.

Steinberg JC, Cummings WC, Brahy BD, Spires JYM (1965). Further bioacoustic studies off the west coast of North Bimini, Bahamas. Bulletin of Marine Science 15: 942–963.

Stiassny MLJ, Jensen JS (1987). Labroid intrarelationships revisited: morphological complexity, key innovations, and the study of comparative diversity. Bulletin of the Museum of Comparative Zoology 151: 269–319.

Takayama M, Onuki A, Yosino T, Yoshimoto M, Ito H, Kohbara J, Somiya H (2003). Sound characteristics and the sound producing system in silver sweeper, *Pempheris schwenkii* (Perciformes: Pempheridae). Journal of the Marine Biological Association of the United Kingdom 83: 1317–1320.

Takemura A (1983). Studies on the underwater sound. VIII. Acoustical behaviour of clownfishes (*Amphirion* spp.). Bulletin of the Faculty of Fisheries Nagasaki University 54: 21–27.

Takemura A, Takita T, Mizue K (1978). Studies on the underwater sound. VII. Underwater calls of the Japanese marine drum fishes (Sciaenidae). Bulletin of the Japanese Society of Scientific Fisheries 44 (2): 121–125.

Takemura A, Nishida N, Kobayashi Y (1988). The attraction effect of natural feeding sound in fish. Nagasaki Daigaku Suisangakauba (Sasebo Japan) Kenkyu Hokoku 63: 1–4.

Tavolga WN (1958a). The significance of underater sounds produced by males of the gobiid fish, *Bathygobius soporator*. Physiological Zoology 31: 259–271.

Tavolga WN (1958b). Underwater sounds produced by two species of toadfish, *Opsanus tau* and *Opsanus beta*. Bulletin of Marine Science of the Gulf and Caribbean 8: 278–284.

Tavolga WN (1960). Sound production and underwater communication in fishes. In: Lanyon WE, Tavolga W (eds.), *Animal Sounds and Communication*. American Institute of Biological Sciences, Washington, DC, pp. 93–136.

Tavolga WN (1962). Mechanisms of sound production in the Ariid catfishes *Galeichthys* and *Bagre*. Bulletin of the American Museum of Natural History 124: 1–30

Tavolga WN (1964). *Marine Bio-acoustics*. Pergamon Press, New York.

Tavolga WN (1968). Fishes. In: Sebeok TA (ed.), *Animal Communication: Technique of Study and Results of Research*. Indiana University Press, Bloomington, pp. 271–288.

Tavolga WN (1976). *Sound Reception in Fishes*. Dowden, Hutchinson & Ross, Stroudsburg, Pennsylvania.

Tavolga WN (1977). *Sound Production in Fishes*. Dowden, Hutchinson & Ross, Stroudsburg, Pennsylvania.

Tavolga WN, Popper AN, Fay RR (1981). *Hearing and Sound Communication in Fishes*. Springer-Verlag, New York, pp. 608.

Taylor M, Mansueti RJ (1960). Sounds produced by very young crevalle jack, *Caranx hippos*, from the Maryland seaside. Chesapeake Science 1: 115–116.

Thorson RF, Fine ML (2002a). Acoustic competition in the gulf toadfish *Opsanus beta*: acoustic tagging. Journal of the Acoustical Society of America 111: 2302–2307.

Thorson RF, Fine ML (2002b). Crepuscular changes in emission rate and parameters of this boatwhistle advertisement call of the gulf toadfish, *Opsanus beta*. Environmental Biology of Fishes 63: 321–331.

Thresher RE (1982). Courtship and spawning in the emperor angelfish *Pomacanthus imperator*, with comments on reproduction by other pomacanthid fishes. Marine Biology 70: 149–156.

Tricas TC, Boyle K (2009). Sound production and hearing in coral reef butterflyfishes. Journal of the Acoustical Society of America 125: 2487.

Tricas TC, Kajiura SM, Kosaki RK (2006). Acoustic communication in territorial butterflyfish: test of the sound production hypothesis. Journal of Experimental Biology 209: 4994–5004.

Uchida K (1934). Sound producing fishes of Japan. Report of Japan Science Association 9: 369–375.

Ueng J-P, Huang B-Q, Mok H-K (2007). Sexual differences in the spawning sounds of the Japanese croaker, *Argyrosomus japonicus* (Sciaenidae). Zoological Studies 46: 103–110.

Vasconcelos RO, Amorim MCP, Ladich F (2007). Effects of ship noise on the detectability of communication signals in the Lusitanian toadfish. Journal of Experimental Biology 210: 2104–2112.

Verwey J (1930). Coral reef studies. I. The symbiosis between damselfishes and sea anemones in Batavia Bay. Treubia 12: 305–355.

von Frisch K (1936). About the sense of hearing in fish. Biological Reviews of the Cambridge Philosophical Society 11: 210–246.

von Frisch K (1938). The sense of hearing in fish. Nature 141: 8–11.

Wahlberg M, Westerberg H (2003). Sounds produced by herring (*Clupea harengus*) bubble release. Aquatic Living Resources 16: 271–275

Walls PD (1964). The anatomy of the sound producing apparatus of some Australian teleosts. Honors thesis, Bowdoin College, Brunswick, Maine.

Warner LH (1932). The sensitivity of fishes to sound and to other mechanical stimulation. Quarterly Review of Biology 7: 326–339.

Webb JF, Fay RR, Popper AN (2008). *Fish Bioacoustics.* Springer, New York.

Whitley GP (1957). A kennel of frogfishes. Australian Museum Magazine 12: 139–142

Winn HE (1964). The biological significance of fish sounds. In: Tavolga WN (ed.), *Marine Bio-acoustics.* Pergamon Press, New York, pp. 213–231.

Winn HE (1972). Acoustic discrimination by the toadfish with comments on signal systems. In: Winn HE, Olla BL (eds.), *Behavior of Marine Animals: Current Perspectives in Research.* Vol. 2, Vertebrates. Plenum Press, New York, pp. 361–385.

Winn HE, Marshall JD (1963). Sound-producing organ of the squirrelfish, *Holocentrus rufus.* Physiological Zoology 36: 34–44.

Winn HE, Marshall JD, Hazlett B (1964). Behavior, diel activities, and stimuli that elicit sound production, and reaction to sounds in the longspine squirrelfish. Copeia 1964: 413–425.

Yokoyama K, Kamei Y, Toda M, Hirano K, Iwatsuki Y (1994). Reproductive behavior, eggs, and larvae of a caesionine fish, *Pterocaesio digramma*, observed in an aquarium. Japanese Journal of Ichthyology 41: 261–274.

TABLE 10.1. Catalog of reef fish sounds and behaviors.

Species are included for which any information or mention (even anecdotal) of the occurrence of sound production in coral reef fishes is reported.

Family/species	Sound pattern	No. sound types	No. pulses	Frequency range (hz)	Sound duration (ms)	Behavioral contexts	References
ACANTHURIDAE (4 species)							
Acanthurus bahianus	–	–	–	150–4,700	100	chase conspecific, hydrodynamic sound	Steinberg et al. 1965
A. bahianus	–	2	–	–	–	disturbance	Fish & Mowbray 1970
A. chirurgus	–	–	–	–	–	disturbance, escape	Fish & Mowbray 1970
A. coeruleus	–	3	–	–	–	disturbance, escape	Fish & Mowbray 1970
Paracanthurus hepatus	–	–	–	–	–	disturbance*	Fish 1948
APLOACTINIDAE (1 species)							
Paraploactis trachyderma	–	–	–	–	–	unknown	Walls 1964
ARIIDAE (2 species)							
Bagre marinus	short pulse series	3	–	–	~200	chorus of individuals	Tavolga 1960
B. marinus	descending frequency	–	–	400–850	110–200	spontaneous in social groups	Tavolga 1960
B. marinus	descending frequency	–	–	350–275	420–550	spontaneous in social groups	Tavolga 1960
Arius felis	–	3	–	low < 100	10	disturbance	Tavolga 1962
A. felis	–	–	–	low 300–450	45	disturbance	Tavolga 1962
A. felis	–	–	–	high 2000	30–50	disturbance	Tavolga 1962
A. felis	–	2	–	–	–	disturbance*	Burkenroad 1931
A. felis	–	3	–	~100–500	~75–180	swimming social groups	Tavolga 1960
A. felis	broadband frequency	–	–	harmonics to 4,000	30–50	disturbance: fishing line caught	Tavolga 1960

(continued)

TABLE 10.1. (continued)

Family/species	Sound pattern	No. sound types	No. pulses	Frequency range (hz)	Sound duration (ms)	Behavioral contexts	References
Arius felis	—	—	—	—	—	nocturnal chorus, schooling individuals	Tavolga 1960
A. felis	—	—	—	—	—	chorus of seasonal aggregations	Breder 1968
A. felis	—	—	—	—	—	disturbance	Fish & Mowbray 1970
AULOSTOMIDAE (1 species)							
Aulostomus maculatus	harmonic intervals	—	—	—	—	lunge at prey, hydrodynamic swimming noise	Bright 1972
BALISTIDAE (14 species)							
Balistes sp.	—	—	—	—	—	sonic morphology	Fish 1948
B. sp.	—	—	—	—	—	sonic morphology	Bridge 1904; Fish 1948
B. sp.	—	—	—	—	—	sounds reported	Fish 1948
B. (= Sufflamen) bursa	—	—	—	75–9,600	—	disturbance	Salmon et al. 1968
B. capriscus	—	—	—	—	—	interspecific agonism, disturbance	Fish 1948
B. capriscus	—	3	—	—	—	intraspecific agonism, escape	Fish & Mowbray 1970
B. capriscus	—	2	—	—	—	escape	Fish 1954
B. capistrattus	—	—	—	75–9,600	—	disturbance	Salmon et al. 1968
Balistapus undulatus	—	—	—	—	—	sonic morphology	Fish 1948
B. vetula	—	—	—	—	—	sonic morphology	Möbius 1889; Sörensen 1894–1895

Species					Behavioral context	Reference
B. vetula	–	–	0–5,800	30	disturbance in air	Moulton 1958
B. vetula	–	–	600–2,900	150	free swimming during feeding in fish pen	Moulton 1958
B. vetula	multipulsed	≤11	50–2,000	1,410–2,400	attack territory intruders	Steinberg et al. 1965
B. vetula	–	–	1,000–2,350	100	feeding	Steinberg et al. 1965
B. vetula	–	–	–	–	feeding	Tavolga 1968
B. vetula	–	–	–	–	chase intraspecific	Salmon et al. 1968
B. vetula	–	2	–	–	disturbance, feeding	Fish & Mowbray 1970
B. vetula	–	–	75–9,600	99 ±19	disturbance	Salmon et al. 1968
B. vetula	–	–	–	–	chase conspecific	Salmon et al. 1968
Canthidermis sufflamen	–	4	–	–	competitive feeding, disturbance, spine raising	Fish & Mowbray 1970
Melichthys buniva	–	–	75–9,600	–	disturbance	Salmon et al. 1968
M. niger	–	–	–	–	sound reported	Uchida 1934
M. niger	–	–	–	–	feeding	Moulton 1958
M. niger	multipulsed	3	100–350	100–300	disturbance defense "trigger spine raised"	Fish & Mowbray 1970
M. niger	–	–	–	–	territory chase intraspecific, disturbance	Salmon et al. 1968
M. piceus (=niger)	–	–	0–8,000	60–100	disturbance in air	Moulton 1958
M. piceus (=niger)	–	–	0–8,000	20–40	disturbance in air	Moulton 1958
M. piceus (=niger)	–	–	75–9,600	212 ±92	disturbance	Salmon et al. 1968
M. vidua	pulse groups	–	–	–	disturbance	Salmon et al. 1968
Odonus niger	–	2	–	–	sonic morphology	Schneider 1961
Rhinecanthus aculeatus	–	–	–	–	sonic morphology	Fish 1948
R. aculeatus	–	–	–	–	sonic morphology	Möbius 1889
R. aculeatus	–	–	–	–	sonic morphology	Sörensen 1894–1895
R. rectangulus	–	–	75–9,600	180 (mean)	disturbance	Salmon et al. 1968
R. rectangulus	–	–	150–1,200	100–200	disturbance	Salmon et al. 1968
Sufflamen bursa	–	–	–	–	chase, intraspecific agonism, disturbance	Salmon et al. 1968
S. frenatum	–	–	–	–	disturbance	Salmon et al. 1968

(continued)

TABLE 10.1. *(continued)*

Family/species	Sound pattern	No. sound types	No. pulses	Frequency range (hz)	Sound duration (ms)	Behavioral contexts	References
BATRACHOIDIDAE (4 species)							
Batrachomoeus trispinosus	long sound	4	–	–	285–6,077	undisturbed in aquarium	Rice & Bass 2009
B. trispinosus	short sound	–	–	–	276 (mean)	undisturbed in aquarium	Rice & Bass 2009
B. trispinosus	series of short sounds	–	–	–	28 per series (mean)	undisturbed in aquarium	Rice & Bass 2009
B. trispinosus	acoustic beats	–	–	–	147 (mean)	disturbance, undisturbed in aquarium	Rice & Bass 2009
Halophryne diemensis	–	–	–	low 85	1,000–3,000	disturbance	Whitley 1957
H.diemensis	–	–	–	–	–	sounds reported	Walls 1964
Opsanus beta	single pulses in series	2	–	100–1,800	30–70	reproductive	Tavolga 1958b
O. beta	tonal	–	–	200–2,100	160–410	reproductive	Fish & Mowbray 1959
O. beta	multi-note: pulsed & tonal	–	–	~200–900	214–1,409 (mean)	male-male agonism, male display on nest	Thorson & Fine 2002a
O. beta	single & double pulsed	–	–	–	–	reproductive	Thorson & Fine 2002b
O. beta	single-note tonal	–	–	~200–900	201–506 (mean)	male-male agonism, male display on nest	Tavolga 1958b
O. phobetron	multiple pulse series	–	–	~50–800	–	reproductive	Fish & Mowbray 1959, 1970
O. phobetron	pulsed & tonal	–	–	–	–	disturbance	Fish & Mowbray 1970

Species	(sound description)						Context	Reference
BLENNIIDAE (1 species) Hypsoblennius hentz	–	–	–	150–1,000	150–350		male courtship	Tavolga 1960
CAESIONIDAE (1 species) Pterocaesio digramma	–	–	–	–	–		pre-reproductive swimming aggregation	Yokoyama et al. 1994
CAPROIDAE (1 species) Capros aper	–	–	–	–	–		disturbance	Fish 1948
CARAPIDAE (7 species) Carapus acus	pulse bursts	–	–	1.7–22k	600–7,600 (sequence)		interaction inside holothurian host	Parmentier et al. 2003
C. acus	12–13 peaks/ sound	–	–	250–1600	35 (mean)		silent inside sea star host, solitary spontaneous swim outside host	Parmentier et al. 2006a, c
C. mourlani	11–20 peaks/ sound	–	–	570–100	16–30		compete for entrance into sea star	Parmentier et al. 2006c
C. boraborensis	10–28 sounds/ sequence	3	–	55–800	83 (mean)		agonism,* social context inside sea cucumber	Lagardère et al. 2005
C. boraborensis	16–83 sounds/ sequence	–	–	55–800	136 (mean)		agonism,* social context inside sea cucumber	Lagardère et al. 2005
C. boraborensis	11–30 pulses/ sound	–	–	80–800	25–30 seconds		interaction inside holothurian host	Parmentier et al. 2003
C. homei	10 sounds / sequence	–	–	90–4,450	218 (mean)		agonism,* social context inside sea cucumber	Lagardère et al. 2005
C. homei	–	–	–	90–>10,000	262 (mean)		interaction inside holothurian host	Parmentier et al. 2003
Encheliophis gracilis	single beat	–	–	<600	362 (mean)		interaction inside holothurian host	Parmentier et al. 2003
E. gracilis	sequence	–	–	<600	<1,000		interaction inside holothurian host	Parmentier et al. 2003

(continued)

TABLE 10.1. (continued)

Family/species	Sound pattern	No. sound types	No. pulses	Frequency range (hz)	Sound duration (ms)	Behavioral contexts	References
Onuxodon margaritiferae	–	–	–	–	–	sonic morphology	Courtenay & McKittrick 1970
O. parvibrachium	–	–	–	–	–	sonic morphology	Courtenay & McKittrick 1970
CARANGIDAE (24 species)							
Alectis ciliaris	–	–	–	–	–	disturbance, escape	Fish 1954
A. crinitis	–	2	–	~400–1,500	~30–80	disturbance, escape	Fish & Mowbray 1970
Carangoides bartholomaei	–	2	–	–	–	electric stimulation only	Fish & Mowbray 1970
C. equula	–	–	–	–	–	disturbance	Uchida 1934
C. ruber	–	–	–	–	–	swimming	Moulton 1960
C. ruber	–	–	–	10–500	700	swimming	Cummings et al. 1964
C. ruber	–	–	–	–	–	disturbance	Fish & Mowbray 1970
Caranx crysos	–	–	–	–	–	disturbance	Moulton 1960
C. crysos	–	–	–	–	–	chase prey as a group, schooling group	Steinberg et al. 1965
C. crysos	–	2	–	~100–600	~100–120	disturbance, escape	Fish & Mowbray 1970
C. hippos	–	–	–	–	–	feeding	Fish 1948
C. hippos	–	–	–	–	–	disturbance	Burkenroad 1931
C. hippos	–	–	–	0–8,000	60	disturbance	Moulton 1958
C. hippos	–	–	–	–	–	disturbance, spontaneous solitary	Taylor & Mansueti 1960

Species			Behavior			Reference
C. hippos	–	–	disturbance	~100–2,000	~60–80	Fish & Mowbray 1970
C. latus	–	–	disturbance	–	–	Fish 1954
C. latus	–	–	swimming	–	–	Moulton 1960
C. latus	regular pattern	–	disturbance, escape, feeding	~100–1,200	~100	Fish & Mowbray 1970
Chloroscombrus chrysurus	–	–	disturbance	–	–	Fish 1954
C. chrysurus	regular pattern	–	disturbance	~150–1,500	~400–600	Fish & Mowbray 1970
Elagatis bipinnulata	–	–	escape response to sharks	–	–	Fish & Mowbray 1970
Oligoplites saurus	–	–	escape	~100–600	~100–200	Fish & Mowbray 1970
Selar crumenophthalmus	regular pattern	–	disturbance hook & line	~400–1,600	~60–100	Fish & Mowbray 1970
Selene brevoortii	–	–	disturbance	–	–	Fish 1948
S. declavifrons	–	–	spontaneous, continuous	–	–	Fish 1948
S. vomer	–	–	disturbance	–	–	Fish 1948, 1954
S. vomer	–	–	disturbance	–	–	Fish & Mowbray 1970
S. setipinnis	–	–	disturbance	–	–	Fish 1948, 1954
S. setipinnis	–	–	disturbance	~100–1,500	~600–1,300	Fish & Mowbray 1970
Seriola sp.	–	–	disturbance "speared"	–	–	Steinberg et al. 1965
Seriola dumerili	–	–	feeding	–	–	Matsuno et al. 1994
S. dumerili	–	–	feeding competition	~60–240	~100–200	Fish & Mowbray 1970
S. quinqueradiata	–	–	feeding	–	–	Kim 1977
S. zonata	–	–	disturbance, escape	–	–	Fish 1954
S. zonata	–	–	disturbance	~50–180	~300–800	Fish & Mowbray 1970
Trachinotus falcatus	–	–	escape, flee predator	–	–	Fish & Mowbray 1970
T. ovatus	–	–	disturbance	–	–	Fish 1954
T. ovatus	–	–	escape, feeding	–	–	Fish & Mowbray 1970
T. paitensis	–	–	dorsal fin display	–	–	Knudsen et al. 1948b

(*continued*)

TABLE 10.1. (continued)

Family/species	Sound pattern	No. sound types	No. pulses	Frequency range (hz)	Sound duration (ms)	Behavioral contexts	References
Trachinotus paitensis	–	–	–	–	–	sound recorded	Fish 1948
T. paitensis	–	–	–	–	–	swimming	Moulton 1960
Trachurus japonicus	–	–	–	–	–	feeding	Uchica 1934
T. trachurus	–	–	–	–	–	schooling	Shishkova 1958a, b
CHAETODONTIDAE (7 species)							
Chaetodon multicinctus	hydrodynamic	6	1	40–98	154 (mean)	resident aggressive	Tricas et al. 2006
C. multicinctus	single pulse	–	1	2449–5,190	10 (mean)	resident aggressive	Tricas et al. 2006
C. multicinctus	multipulsed	–	6	346–593	300 (mean)	resident aggressive	Tricas et al. 2006
C. multicinctus	single pulse	–	1	179–260	17 (mean)	resident & bottled intruder	Tricas et al. 2006
C. multicinctus	single pulse	–	1	113–137	115 (mean)	resident aggressive	Tricas et al. 2006
C. multicinctus	multipulsed	–	17	132–228	5,700 (mean)	agonism, mated pairs "alert call"*	Tricas et al. 2006
C. auriga	–	–	–	–	–	pairing behavior	Tricas & Boyle 2009
C. ocellatus	–	–	–	–	–	electric stimulation only	Fish & Mowbray 1970
C. ornatissimus	–	–	–	–	–	pairing behavior	Tricas & Boyle 2009
C. striatus	–	–	–	–	–	sonic morphology	Sörensen 1894–1895
C. striatus	–	–	–	–	–	electric stimulation only	Fish & Mowbray 1970
C. ulietensis	–	–	–	–	–	spontaneous in loose school	Lobel pers. comm.
Forcipiger flavissimus	single pulse	3	–	318 (peak)	21	head movement	Boyle & Tricas 2006
F. flavissimus	low-frequency pulse	–	–	41 (peak)	9	hydrodynamic fin movement	Boyle & Tricas 2006

	broadband frequency				
F. flavissimus	–	7,924 (peak)	3	hydrodynamic tail slap	Boyle & Tricas 2006
F. flavissimus	–	–	–	pairing behavior	Tricas & Boyle 2009
DACTYLOPTERIDAE (2 species)					
Dactyloptena orientalis	–	–	–	sonic morphology	Müller 1857
D. orientalis	–	–	–	sonic morphology	Bridge 1904; Fish 1948
D. orientalis	–	–	–	sonic morphology	Sörensen 1894–1895
D. orientalis	–	–	–	sonic morphology	Jordan & Richardson 1907; Fish 1948
Dactylopterus volitans	–	~100–800	~80–120	disturbance	Fish & Mowbray 1970
DIODONTIDAE (7 species)					
Chilomycterus atringa	multipulsed	–	–	disturbance defense inflation	Fish & Mowbray 1970
C. schoepfii	–	–	–	sonic morphology	Sörensen 1894–1895
C. schoepfii	–	–	–	feeding competition, disturbance defense inflation	Fish 1954
C. schoepfii	–	~100–1,500	~60–80	disturbance defense inflation	Fish & Mowbray 1970
C. spinosus	–	–	–	disturbance defense inflation	Burkenroad 1931
Dicotolichthys punctulatus	–	–	–	defense, feeding	Graham 1992
D. hystrix	–	–	–	disturbance defense inflation & non-air sound	Sörensen 1894–1895

(continued)

TABLE 10.1. (*continued*)

Family/species	Sound pattern	No. sound types	No. pulses	Frequency range (hz)	Sound duration (ms)	Behavioral contexts	References
Dicotolichthys hystrix	–	–	–	–	–	disturbance defense inflation	Uchida 1934; Fish 1948
D. hystrix	–	–	–	0–8,000	90	disturbance defense inflation, feeding	Moulton 1958
D. hystrix	–	–	–	~50–5,000	~30–50	disturbance defense inflation, feeding	Fish & Mowbray 1970
Diodon holocanthus	–	–	–	–	–	disturbance defense inflation	Uchida 1934; Fish 1948
Tragulichthys jaculiferus	–	–	–	–	–	sounds reported	Walls 1964
ENOPLOSIDAE (1 species)							
Enoplosus armatus	–	–	–	–	–	teeth grinding during normal activities	Graham 1992
EPHIPPIDAE (2 species)							
Chaetodipterus faber	–	2	–	–	–	disturbance	Burkenroad 1931
C. faber	–	–	–	220	150	in aquarium	Knudsen et al. 1948b
C. faber	–	2	–	75–150	–	free swimming in aquarium	Fish et al. 1952
C. faber	–	2	–	–	–	competitive feeding, escape	Fish & Mowbray 1970
C. ocellatus	–	2	–	–	–	electrical stimulation only	Fish & Mowbray 1970
GERREIDAE (2 species)							
Eucinostomus gula	–	–	–	–	–	disturbance in net	Fish & Mowbray 1970
Gerres cinereus	–	–	–	–	–	disturbance	Fish & Mowbray 1970

GOBIIDAE (2 species)						
Bathygobius curacao						
B. curacao	broadband	2	–	–	courting male	Stadler 2002
B. curacao	–	–	100–1,500	50	courting male	Myrberg & Stadler 2002
B. curacao	multipulsed	≤19	100–200 peak	35 per pulse	courting male	Myrberg & Stadler 2002
B. soporator	nonharmonic	–	100–500	150–350	courting male	Tavolga 1958a
HAEMULIDAE (14 species)						
Anisotremus surinamensis	–	1	–	–	disturbance	Fish & Mowbray 1970
A. virginicus	–	1	~100–600	60–100	disturbance	Fish & Mowbray 1970
Haemulon album	multipulsed	–	–	–	feeding competition, disturbance, schools spontaneous	Fish & Mowbray 1970
H. album	burst feeding stridulation	–	50–1,600	–	feeding	Cummings et al. 1964; Kumpf 1964; Cummings et al. 1966
H. album	plankton feeding noise	–	20–700	–	feeding	Cummings et al. 1964; Kumpf 1964; Cummings et al. 1966
H. album	hydrodynamic swimming noise	–	10–500	–	swimming	Cummings et al. 1964; Kumpf 1964; Cummings et al. 1966
H. aurolineatum	multipulsed	–	~100–1,500	50–100	disturbance	Fish & Mowbray 1970
H. carbonarium	multipulsed	–	~100–1,000	30–80	disturbance	Fish & Mowbray 1970
H. flavolineatum	multipulsed	–			disturbance "mild annoyance" & netted	Fish & Mowbray 1970

(continued)

TABLE 10.1. (continued)

Family/species	Sound pattern	No. sound types	No. pulses	Frequency range (hz)	Sound duration (ms)	Behavioral contexts	References
Haemulon flavolineatum	–	1	–	–	–	disturbance, feeding	Moulton 1958
H. macrostomum	multipulsed	–	–	~100–600	~50–150	disturbance, escape	Fish & Mowbray 1970
H. melanurum	–	–	–	–	–	swimming	Cummings et al. 1964
H. melanurum	multipulsed	–	–	~50–900	~50–100	feeding competition, disturbance, school escape	Fish & Mowbray 1970
H. parra	multipulsed	–	–	–	–	disturbance	Fish & Mowbray 1970
H. plumierii	–	–	–	–	–	disturbance	Burkenroad 1930
H. plumierii	multipulsed	–	–	~100–1,200	~60–100	disturbance	Graham 1992
H. sciurus	–	–	–	–	–	disturbance	Burkenroad 1930
H. sciurus	rasp pulses	–	–	0–8,000	20–100	disturbance	Moulton 1958
H. sciurus	multipulsed	–	–	~100–1,100	80–150	disturbance, escape	Fish & Mowbray 1970
H. striatum	–	–	–	–	–	disturbance, escape	Fish & Mowbray 1970
Plectorhincus sp.	–	–	–	–	–	sounds reported	Fish 1948
Pomadasys maculata (=mauclatus)	–	–	–	–	–	sounds reported and recorded	Walls 1964
HEMIRAMPHIDAE (1 species)							
Hyporhamphus unifasciatus	–	–	–	–	–	disturbance	Burkenroad 1931
HOLOCENTRIDAE (12 species)							
Holocentrus adscensionis	–	–	–	–	–	sonic morphology	Fish 1948
H. adscensionis	–	–	–	–	–	sonic morphology	Myrberg & Stadler 2002
H. adscensionis	–	2	–	0–4,000	40–100	hydrophone attacked, disturbance, escape	Moulton 1958

Species						Context	Reference
H. adscensionis	–	–	–	–	–	sonic morphology	Winn & Marshall 1963
H. adscensionis	–	2	–	–	–	mobbing, crevice territory defense	Winn et al. 1964
H. adscensionis	multipulsed	–	–	–	–	agonism intraspecific, disturbance, escape	Fish & Mowbray 1970
H. adscensionis	–	3	–	–	–	–	Bright 1972
H. rufus	–	1	–	–	–	–	Winn & Marshall 1963
H. rufus	multipulsed	–	2–5	85–4,500	–	disturbance	Winn & Marshall 1963
H. rufus	–	2	–	–	22–72	chase, territorial, intra- & interspecific, disturbance, chorus	Winn et al. 1964
H. rufus	–	–	–	–	–	sonic morphology	Gainer et al. 1965
H. rufus	–	–	–	–	–	chase, territorial, intra- & interspecific	Salmon 1967
H. rufus	multipulsed	–	2–10	500	–	–	Bright & Sartori 1972
Myripristis amaena	–	–	–	–	–	sonic morphology	Carlson & Bass 2000
M. amaena	–	–	–	–	–	sonic morphology	Nelson 1955
M. amaena	–	4	–	–	–	chasing, nonterritorial schools, chorus	Salmon 1967
M. berndti	–	–	–	–	–	predator alarm calls	Popper et al. 1973
M. berndti	–	–	–	>3,000	–	agonism, congeners school over reefs	Salmon 1967
M. berndti	–	–	–	–	–	at predator (moray), disturbance	Salmon 1967

(continued)

TABLE 10.1. *(continued)*

Family/species	Sound pattern	No. sound types	No. pulses	Frequency range (hz)	Sound duration (ms)	Behavioral contexts	References
Myripristis berndti	–	–	–	–	10	chase small fish	Salmon 1967
M. berndti	–	–	–	–	–	disturbed by predator	Salmon 1967
M. berndti	multipulsed	–	7–10	75–4,800	80–118	disturbance	Salmon 1967
M. berndti	–	–	–	–	–	predator alarm calls	Popper et al. 1973
M. jacobus	–	–	–	–	–	sounds reported	Winn 1964
M. jacobus	multipulsed	–	3–5	–	–	disturbance	Fish & Mowbray 1970
M. jacobus	multipulsed	–	1–2	150–500	80–100	chase, intra- & interspecific, disturbance, chorus	Bright & Sartori 1972
M. jacobus	hydrodynamic	–	–	–	–	territorial defense	Bright 1972
M. pralinia	–	4	–	–	–	disturbance	Horch & Salmon 1973
M. violacea	–	–	–	–	–	agonism: circle, tail beat, chase, disturbance	Horch & Salmon 1973
M. violacea	multipulsed	–	many	–	–	agonism, disturbance: response to diver	Horch & Salmon 1973
M. violacea	3–7 groups	–	–	–	–	–	Horch & Salmon 1973
M. violacea	up to 10 groups	–	–	–	300–2,000	–	Horch & Salmon 1973
Neoniphon sammara	–	–	–	–	–	sonic morphology	Carlson & Bass 2000
Sargocentron cornutum	–	–	–	–	–	sonic morphology	Carlson & Bass 2000
S. coruscus	–	2	–	450–1,500	–	agonism, intra- & interspecific, chorus	Bright & Sartori 1972
S. coruscus	–	–	–	–	–	disturbance	Bright 1972
S. coruscus	–	3	–	–	–	agonism	Winn 1964
S. seychellense	–	–	–	–	–	sonic morphology	Carlson & Bass 2000
S. xantherythrum	–	–	2–9	–	–	courtship duet	Herald & Dempster 1957

					Sounds reported	Reference
KYPHOSIDAE (2 species)						
Atypichthys strigatus	–	–	–	–		Graham 1992
Kyphosus sectator	–	3	~50–250	~20	disturbance, spontaneous, two fish in tank	Fish & Mowbray 1970
LABRIDAE (4 species)						
Choerodon venustus	pulse series	–	–	–	swimming noise	Moulton 1964b
Halichoeres bivittatus	–	–	50–2,400	200 (series 3,000)	feeding	Steinberg et al. 1965
H. bivittatus	–	–	~100–300	~100–200	electrical stimulation only	Fish & Mowbray 1970
H. radiatus	–	–	–	–	feeding noises	Fish & Mowbray 1970
Lachnolaimus maximus	–	–	~100–200	~100	disturbance "body twist"	Fish & Mowbray 1970
LETHRINIDAE (1 species)						
Gymnocranius audleyi			none	none	swimming noises only	Moulton 1964b
LUTJANIDAE (7 species)						
Lutjanus analis	–	–	–	–	electrical stimulation only	Fish & Mowbray 1970
L. apodus	–	–	–	–	disturbance	Fish & Mowbray 1970
L. apodus	–	–	~100–400	~100–150	escape	Fish & Mowbray 1970
L. griseus	–	–	~50–100	500	disturbance = in nets	Fish & Mowbray 1970
L. griseus	–	3	~100–300	~100–200	disturbance = in nets	Fish & Mowbray 1970
L. jocu	–	–	–	~500	escape	Fish & Mowbray 1970
L. synagris	–	–	~50–200	~100–190	disturbance	Fish & Mowbray 1970
Ocyurus chrysurus	–	–	~80–300	~200–300	competitive feeding	Fish & Mowbray 1970
O. chrysurus	–	–	–	–	escape	Fish & Mowbray 1970
Rhomboplites aurorubens	–	2	–	–	electrical stimulation only	Fish & Mowbray 1970
MONACANTHIDAE (8 species)						
Aluterus scripta	–	–	–	–	disturbance	Fish & Mowbray 1970
A. shoepfi	–	–	~200–1,000	~80–1,200	competitive feeding, spontaneous	Fish & Mowbray 1970

(continued)

TABLE 10.1. (continued)

Family/species	Sound pattern	No. sound types	No. pulses	Frequency range (hz)	Sound duration (ms)	Behavioral contexts	References
Aluterus shoepfi	–	–	–	~200–500	~100	disturbance	Fish & Mowbray 1970
A. shoepfi	–	1	–	–	–	feeding competition, escape	Fish 1954
A. shoepfi	–	–	–	50–4,800	–	feeding	Fish et al. 1952
Cantherhines pardalus	–	–	–	–	–	sonic morphology	Sörensen 1894–1895
C. pullus	–	–	–	–	–	defensive trigger raised	Fish & Mowbray 1970
Monacanthus filicauda	–	–	–	–	–	sounds recorded	Walls 1964
Paramonacathus oblongus	–	–	–	–	–	sounds recorded	Walls 1964
Stephanolepis cirrhifer	–	–	–	–	–	disturbance, swimming, feeding	Fish 1948
S. hispidus	–	–	–	–	–	disturbance	Burkenroad 1931
S. hispidus	–	2	–	–	–	disturbance, defense, spine raising	Fish & Mowbray 1970
S. hispidus	–	–	–	–	–	feeding noise	Fish & Mowbray 1970
S. hispidus	–	2	–	–	–	feeding competition, disturbance, escape	Fish 1954
MONOCENTRIDAE (1 species)							
Monocentris japonica	–	–	–	100–600	–	disturbance	Onuki & Somiya 2007
MULLIDAE (2 species)							
Mulloidichthys martinicus	–	–	–	~50–450	~100	disturbance	Fish & Mowbray 1970
M. martinicus	–	–	–	–	–	feeding noises very low intensity	Bright 1972

Species	Sound type		Frequency range (Hz)	Peak/dominant (Hz)	Sound context	Reference
Pseudopeneus maculatus	–	–	–	–	feeding noises	Bright 1972
P. maculatus	–	–	~50–200	~100	disturbance	Fish & Mowbray 1970
OPHICHTHYIDAE						
Ophichthys spp.	–	–	–	–	disturbance & threat: "opercular vibrations"	Carlson & Bass 2000
OPLEGNATHIDAE (1 species)						
Oplegnathus fasciatus	–	–	160	13–20	territorial, chase (reproductive season), chorus reported	Nakazato & Takemura 1987
O. fasciatus	–	–	–	–	sound reported	Uchida 1934
OSTRACIIDAE (9 species)						
Acanthostracion quadricornis	multipulsed	–	1,000–3,400	80 and 140	chorus: multiple calls from sea grass beds most common	Steinberg et al. 1965
A. quadricornis	–	–	~50–350	~100	disturbance	Fish & Mowbray 1970
Lactophrys bicaudalis	–	–	–	–	feeding noises	Fish & Mowbray 1970
L. triqueter	–	–	–	–	disturbance	Fish & Mowbray 1970
L. triqueter	–	–	–	–	chewing food	Fish & Mowbray 1970
L. triqueter	–	–	–	–	swimming	Bright 1972
L. trigonus	–	–	–	–	disturbance*	Fish 1948
L. trigonus	–	–	~100–200	~300–700	disturbance, swimming noise	Fish & Mowbray 1970
Lactoria fornasini	–	–	–	–	spawning chants	Moyer 1979
Ostracion immaculatus	–	–	–	–	–	Uchida 1934
O. meleagris	tonal, frequency modulation	–	100–300	300	interspecific w/damselfish	Lobel 1996
O. meleagris	tonal & broadband	–	–	–	agonism	Lobel 1998

(*continued*)

TABLE 10.1. (continued)

Family/species	Sound pattern	No. sound types	No. pulses	Frequency range (hz)	Sound duration (ms)	Behavioral contexts	References
Ostracion meleagris	broadband	–	–	<4,000	9.9–10.6	combat: two males head-butting	Lobel 1996
O. meleagris	–	–	–	<1,000	130–209	male interrupt mating, disturbance	Lobel 1996
O. meleagris	tonal	–	–	<500	–	spawning sound	Lobel 1996
O. meleagris	low vibration	–	–	–	–	–	Pappe 1853
O. cubicus	–	–	–	–	–	swimming noise	Moulton 1964b
O. cubicus	–	–	–	–	–	sonic morphology	Sörensen 1894–1895
O. cubicus	–	–	–	–	–	sounds recorded	Walls 1964
Tetrosomus reipublicae	low frequency	–	–	–	–	sound reported	Graham 1992
PEMPHERIDAE (2 species)							
Pempheris japonica	–	–	–	–	–	disturbance	Uchida 1934; Fish 1948
P. japonica	–	–	–	–	–	sounds reported	Uchida 1934; Fish 1948
P. schwenkii	multipulsed	–	2–7	100–300	56 (mean)	disturbance: while schooling near diver	Takayama et al. 2003
P. schwenkii	–	–	–	100–300	60,75, 75	disturbance	Onuki & Somiya 2007
POLYNEMIDAE (1 species)							
Polydactylus virginicus	–	–	–	~100–500	~10–20	escape	Fish & Mowbray 1970
PLOTOSIDAE (1 species)							
Plotosus lineatus	–	–	–	–	–	sounds reported	Uchida 1934; Fish 1948
P. lineatus	–	–	–	–	–	disturbance	Burgess 1989

Species					Behavior context	Reference
POMACANTHIDAE (7 species)						
Centropyge potteri	–	–	–	–	sounds reported	Lobel 1978
Holacanthus ciliaris	2	–	100–200	~100	electric stimulation only "body twist"	Fish & Mowbray 1970
H. ciliaris	–	–	100–400	~100	electric stimulation only	Fish & Mowbray 1970
H. ciliaris	–	–	<500	60–100	free in sea tank	Moulton 1958
H. isabelita	–	–	~50–300	~200	disturbance	Fish & Mowbray 1970
H. tricolor	–	–	~100–400	~100	escape	Fish & Mowbray 1970
Pomacanthus arcuatus	–	–	–	–	field monitoring	Fish & Mowbray 1970
P. arcuatus	–	–	<500	40–200	pair near hydrophone, feeding, startled, free in sea tank	Moulton 1958
P. arcuatus	–	–	–	–	interspecific "butting" by pair	Moulton 1969
P. arcuatus	–	–	–	200	pair call to each other	Moulton 1969
P. arcuatus	–	–	~100–300	~200	escape	Fish & Mowbray 1970
P. arcuatus	–	–	–	–	courtship	Moyer et al. 1983
P. paru	–	–	~100–400	~100	escape, feeding	Fish & Mowbray 1970
P. imperator	–	–	–	–	agonistic	Fourmanoir & Laboute 1976
P. imperator	–	–	–	–	male chase female after spawn	Thresher 1982
P. imperator	multipulsed	3–12	101–3,778	30.8–128.3 per phrase	heterospecific chase, approach, lateral display	Amorim 1996a
POMACENTRIDAE (36 species)						
Abudefduf abdominalis	multipulsed	11 (mean)	–	1,793 (mean)	male courtship	Maruska et al. 2007
A. abdominalis	multipulsed	1–2	90–380	161 (mean)	aggressive, hydrodynamic quick body moves	Maruska et al. 2007
A. abdominalis	–	3–13	–	1,013 (mean)	aggressive	Maruska et al. 2007
A. abdominalis	–	6 (mean)	–	1,425 (mean)	male nest prep.	Maruska et al. 2007

(continued)

TABLE 10.1. (continued)

Family/species	Sound pattern	No. sound types	No. pulses	Frequency range (hz)	Sound duration (ms)	Behavioral contexts	References
Abudefduf abdominalis	–	–	6 (mean)	–	949 (mean)	male looping female	Maruska et al. 2007
A. abdominalis	–	–	1 (mean)	–	1,133 (mean)	male mouth-pushing in nest	Maruska et al. 2007
A. luridus	pulse series	–	2	–	64–82	agonism	Santiago & Castro 1997
A. luridus	pulse series	–	–	–	700–1,000	agonism	Santiago & Castro 1997
A. luridus	multipulsed	–	15–20	–	15–20	agonism	Santiago & Castro 1997
A. saxatilis	–	–	–	–	–	feeding	Fish & Mowbray 1970
A. saxatilis	–	2	–	–	–	escape	Fish & Mowbray 1970
A. sordidus	multipulsed	–	5 (mean)	–	620 (mean)	agonism	Lobel & Kerr 1999
Amphiprion akallopisos (Madag.)	pulsed chirp	4	8 (mean)	665 (mean)	89 (train mean)	territory defense	Parmentier et al. 2005
A. akallopisos (Madag.)	single pulse	–	1	1,097 (mean peak)	8 (mean)	territory defense	Parmentier et al. 2005
A. akallopisos (Madag.)	single pulse	–	1	896 (mean peak)	13.3 (mean)	territory defense	Parmentier et al. 2005
A. akallopisos (Madag.)	single pulse	–	1	724 (mean peak	12.8 (mean)	territory defense	Parmentier et al. 2005
A. akallopisos (Indon.)	single pulse	3	1	1,088 (mean peak)	7.4 (mean)	territory defense	Parmentier et al. 2005
A. akallopisos (Indon.)	single pulse	–	1	655 (mean peak)	11.7 (mean)	territory defense	Parmentier et al. 2005

		1	572 (mean peak)	12.7 (mean)	territory defense	Parmentier et al. 2005
A. akallopisos (Indon.)	single pulse	–	572 (mean peak)	12.7 (mean)	territory defense	Parmentier et al. 2005
A. akallopisos	multipulsed	7–11	–	–	agonism	Lagardère et al. 2003
A. akallopisos	–	–	–	–	sounds reported	Verwey 1930
A. (=Premnas) biaculeatus	–	–	.	–	sounds reported	Takemura 1983
A. bincinctus	–	–	–	–	sounds reported	Schneider 1964a
A. bincinctus	–	–	–	–	sounds reported	Chen & Mok 1988
A. chrysopterus	–	1	–	35–45	agonism: threat attack, submission	Onuki & Somiya 2007
A. chrysopterus	–	–	–	–	sounds reported	Fish & Mowbray 1970
A. clarkii	multipulsed train	1–8	450–800	26 (mean)	conspecific approaches territory	Parmentier et al. 2007
A. clarkii	–	3	500	45–60	fight	Burgess 1989
A. clarkii	–	–	500	250–400	agonism "shake"	Schneider 1964a
A. clarkii	–	–	600	25–30	threat	Schneider 1964a
A. clarkii	single pulse	1 pulse	–	–	agonism	Takemura 1983
A. clarkii	multipulsed	pulse series	–	–	agonism	Takemura 1983
A. clarkii	multipulsed	1–17	1,000–1,500	–	agonism	Chen & Mok 1988
A. clarkii	multipulsed	1–2	1,000–2,000	–	agonism	Chen & Mok 1988
A. clarkii	single pulse	1 pulse	–	–	agonism	Takemura 1983
A. frenatus	–	–	5,000–6,000	–	agonism	Takemura 1983
A. frenatus	–	–	200–600	–	agonism	Takemura 1983
A. frenatus	multipulsed	2	–	–	sounds reported	Fish 1948
A. frenatus	single pulse	1	–	56	agonism	Takemura 1983
A. frenatus	–	–	–	45–6	"fighting sound"	Schneider 1964a
A. frenatus	multipulsed	1–2	–	50	agonism	Chen & Mok 1988
A. frenatus	multipulsed	1–7	–	50	agonism	Chen & Mok 1988
A. melanopus	–	–	up to 8,000	–	agonism	Takemura 1983
A. melanopus	–	–	250–500	–	agonism	Takemura 1983

(continued)

TABLE 10.1. *(continued)*

Family/species	Sound pattern	No. sound types	No. pulses	Frequency range (hz)	Sound duration (ms)	Behavioral contexts	References
Amphiprion melanopus	single pulse	–	1	–	64	agonism	Takemura 1983
A. ocellaris	–	–	–	1.25–2.8 k	–	agonism	Takemura 1983
A. ocellaris	–	–	–	<2,500	–	agonism	Takemura 1983
A. ocellaris	multipulsed series	–	–	>3,000	–	agonism	Takemura 1983
A. ocellaris	single pulse	–	1	–	–	agonism	Takemura 1983
A. percula	–	–	–	–	–	threat, fight, shake, feeding	Schneider 1964a
A. perideraion	–	–	–	–	100	threat attack, submission	Allen 1972
A. perideraion	–	–	–	–	–	intraspecific agonism	Chen & Mok 1988
A. polymnus	–	–	–	–	–	sounds reported	Verwey 1930
A. polymnus	–	–	–	–	–	threat, fight, attack, feeding	Schneider 1964a
A. polymnus	–	–	–	–	–	agonism	Takemura 1983
A. polymnus	multipulsed	–	4–5	2.5–5 k	–	agonism	Takemura 1983
A. polymnus	single pulse	–	1	4,000	–	agonism	Takemura 1983
A. polymnus	single pulse	–	1	>8,000	–	agonism	Takemura 1983
A. sandaracinos	single pulse	–	1	200–3,500	–	agonism	Takemura 1983
A. sandaracinos	multipulsed	–	<3	200–3,500	–	agonism	Takemura 1983
A. sandaracinos	–	–	–	–	–	agonism	Takemura 1983
Chromis viridis	multipulsed	–	1–5	500–2,000	4.9–20.8	conspecific agonism	Amorim 1996b
C. chromis	single pulse	–	1	max. 340–1420	–	agonism, courtship	Picciulin et al. 2002
Chrysiptera leucopoma	–	–	–	–	–	sounds reported	Graham 1992
Dascyllus albisella	–	2	–	–	–	sounds reported	Fish 1948
D. albisella	multipulsed	–	1–14	–	4–25 per pulse	courtship	Oliver 2001

Species	Sound type		Pulse number	Frequency	Duration	Context	Reference
D. albisella	multipulsed	–	6 (mean)	–	262	courtship	Lobel & Mann 1995a
D. albisella	multipulsed	–	3 (mean)	–	127	mating	Lobel & Mann 1995a
D. albisella	multipulsed	–	1–2	–	17	agonism	Mann & Lobel 1998
D. albisella	multipulsed	–	3–11	–	16	agonism	Mann & Lobel 1998
D. albisella	multipulsed	–	5 (mean)	–	–	courtship	Mann & Lobel 1998
D. albisella	multipulsed	–	–	–	–	agonism only, female sound	Mann & Lobel 1998
D. albisella	multipulsed	–	–	–	–	male courtship	Mann & Lobel 1997
D. albisella	multipulsed	–	3–10	–	–	courtship	Schneider 1964a
D. albisella	multipulsed	–	–	401±4	45.6±0.4	courtship	Parmentier et al. 2009
D. aruanus	–	–	–	–	–	sounds reported	Avidor 1974
D. aruanus	–	–	–	–	–	sounds reported	Graham 1992
D. aruanus	single pulse	–	1	>4,000	6.4	agonism	Parmentier et al. 2009
D. aruanus	multipulsed	–	12–42	–	0.8	agonism	Parmentier et al. 2006a
D. aruanus	multipulsed	–	3–9	474 (max mean)	<400	courtship	Parmentier et al. 2006a
D. aruanus	–	–	–	466±4	30±0.3	courtship	Parmentier et al. 2009
D. carneus	–	–	–	–	–	sounds reported	Koenig 1957
D. flavicaudus	multipulsed	–	3–10	348±2	48±0.4	courtship	Parmentier et al. 2009
D. marginatus	–	–	–	–	–	signal jump courtship reproductive*	Avidor 1974
D. marginatus	–	–	–	–	–	sounds reported	Holzberg 1973
D. trimaculatus	–	–	–	–	–	sounds reported	Fish 1948
D. trimaculatus	–	–	–	–	–	sounds reported	Spanier 1970
D. trimaculatus	single pulse	–	1	up to 10000	13–55	agonism only, none	Luh & Mok 1986
D. trimaculatus	multipulsed	–	3–6	up to 10000	13–55	agonism only, none	Luh & Mok 1986
D. trimaculatus	multipulsed	–	3–6	up to 10000	13–55	agonism only, none	Luh & Mok 1986
D. trimaculatus	multipulsed	–	3–11	465±5	49±1	courtship	Parmentier et al. 2009
Hypsypops rubicundus	–	–	–	7,400	11	sounds reported	Knudsen et al. 1948b
H. rubicundus	–	–	–	75–100	–	adult group in an aquarium	Dobrin 1947
H. rubicundus	–	–	–	–	–	reported sounds	Fish 1948

(continued)

TABLE 10.1. *(continued)*

Family/species	Sound pattern	No. sound types	No. pulses	Frequency range (hz)	Sound duration (ms)	Behavioral contexts	References
Hypsypops rubicundus	–	–	–	–	–	reported sounds	Limbaugh 1964
H. rubicundus	–	3	–	–	–	competitive feeding	Fish & Mowbray 1970
Microspathodon chrysurus	–	–	–	–	–	disturbance	Emery 1973
Plectroglyphidodon lacrymatus	multipulsed	–	2–5	100–1,000	56	agonism	Parmentier et al. 2006a
Pomacentrus nagasakiensis	–	–	–	–	–	enticement	Moyer 1975
Premnas biaculeatus	–	–	–	–	–	territorial, intraspecific agonism	Takemura 1983
Stegastes dorsopunicans (=*adustus*)	–	3	–	–	–	territorial defense	Burke & Bright 1972
S. dorsopunicans (=*adustus*)	multipulsed	–	3–9	–	–	male courtship	Spanier 1979
S. dorsopunicans (=*adustus*)	multipulsed	–	–	–	–	male courtship	Albrecht 1981
S. dorsopunicans (=*adustus*)	–	–	–	–	–	male courtship	Albrecht 1984
S. fuscus	–	–	–	–	–	male courtship display	Dobrin & Loomis 1943
S. fuscus	–	–	–	–	–	sounds reported	Myrberg 1972a
S. leucostictus	–	–	–	0–1,500	20	male pursue/chase others	Moulton 1958
S. leucostictus	–	–	–	–	–	chase, competitive feeding	Fish & Mowbray 1970
S. leucostictus	multipulsed	–	2–6	–	–	male courtship	Spanier 1979
S. leucostictus	multipulsed	–	–	–	–	male courtship	Albrecht 1981
S. leucostictus	–	–	–	–	–	male courtship	Albrecht 1984
S. leucostictus	14-chirp series	–	–	50–2,000	150	chase	Steinberg et al. 1965
S. leucostictus	multipulsed	–	4	–	7–10	agonism	Myrberg & Spires 1972

Species									Reference
S. partitus	–	–	–	–	–	–	–	male courtship	Myrberg & Spires 1972
S. partitus	single pulse	–	1	–	–	10–40	–	agonism	Myrberg 1972a
S. partitus	multipulsed	–	3–6	–	–	8–15	–	agonism	Myrberg & Spires 1972
S. partitus	multipulsed	–	3	–	<50–2,000	10–20 (120–240 sequence)	–	colony of individuals	Myrberg 1972a
S. partitus	multipulsed	–	4–6	–	<50–2,000	10–20 (160–500 sequence)	–	colony of individuals	Myrberg 1972a
S. partitus	–	–	variable	–	<50–1,300	10–20	–	colony of individuals	Myrberg 1972a
S. partitus	multipulsed	–	8–12	–	350–1,000	20–30	–	colony of individuals	Myrberg 1972a
S. partitus	single pulse	–	1	–	<50–2,000	10–30	–	colony of individuals	Myrberg 1972a
S. partitus	variable	–	variable	–	<50–10,000	20–30	–	colony of individuals	Myrberg 1972a
S. partitus	–	–	–	–	–	–	–	male courtship	Graham 1992
S. partitus	multipulsed	–	1–4	–	–	–	–	male courtship	Spanier 1979
S. partitus	multipulsed	–	–	–	–	–	–	male courtship	Albrecht 1981
S. partitus	–	–	–	–	–	–	–	male courtship	Albrecht 1984
S. partitus	–	–	–	–	–	–	–	territorial display, chasing, male courtship	Myrberg & Riggio 1985
S. partitus	multipulsed	–	3	–	–	–	–	male courtship	Myrberg & Riggio 1985
S. partitus	–	–	–	–	–	–	–	male courtship	Myrberg et al. 1986
S. partitus	–	–	–	–	–	–	–	male courtship	Myrberg et al. 1993
S. partitus	–	–	2	–	–	–	–	courtship, pre-mating	Kenyon 1994
S. partitus	–	–	–	–	–	–	–	territory "keep-out" signal	Myrberg 1997a
S. planifrons	multipulsed	–	–	–	–	–	–	male courtship	Albrecht 1981
S. planifrons	–	–	–	–	–	–	–	male courtship	Albrecht 1984
S. planifrons	multipulsed	–	2–6	–	–	–	–	male courtship	Spanier 1979

(continued)

TABLE 10.1. *(continued)*

Family/species	Sound pattern	No. sound types	No. pulses	Frequency range (hz)	Sound duration (ms)	Behavioral contexts	References
Stegastes planifrons	multipulsed	–	4	–	7–12	agonism	Myrberg & Spires 1972
S. variabilis	–	several	–	–	–	male courtship dip	Myrberg & Spires 1972
PRIACANTHIDAE (3 species)							
Heteropriacanthus							
cruentatus	multipulsed	–	–	75–1,200	76–839	chased; 6–10 in caves, disturbance	Salmon & Winn 1966
Priacanthus meeki	multipulsed	–	–	–	64–318	chased; 6–10 in caves, disturbance	Salmon & Winn 1966
P. macracanthus	–	–	–	–	–	unknown	Moulton 1962
P. macracanthus	–	–	–	–	–	sonic morphology	Walls 1964
SCARIDAE (11 species)							
Scarus coeruleus	–	–	–	–	~100	escape	Fish & Mowbray 1970
S. coelestinus	–	–	–	–	–	escape when prodded	Fish & Mowbray 1970
S. guacamaia	–	–	–	~100–600	~100–200	disturbance	Fish & Mowbray 1970
S. iseri	–	–	–	–	–	escape held by tail	Fish & Mowbray 1970
S. iseri	hydrodynamic	–	–	30–1,200	750	mating sound (= noise), schools spawning noise	Lobel 1992
S. vetula	–	–	–	–	–	escape fast turn in field pen, feeding noise	Fish & Mowbray 1970
Sparisoma aurofrenatum	–	–	–	–	–	disturbance, feeding noise	Fish & Mowbray 1970
S. cretense	–	–	–	–	–	feeding noises	Board 1956

Species						
S. chrysopterum	–	–	–	–	escape	Fish & Mowbray 1970
S. radians	–	–	–	–	spontaneous, solitary individual	Fish & Mowbray 1970
S. rubripinne	–	–	–	–	disturbance, feeding noises	Fish & Mowbray 1970
Sparisoma viride	–	–	–	–	escape, feeding	Fish & Mowbray 1970
SCIAENIDAE (17 species)						
Atractoscion nobilis	sound series	–	–	7–55 sec	spawning chants	Aalbers & Drawbridge 2008
A. nobilis	multipulsed	–	–	473 (mean)	courtship	Aalbers & Drawbridge 2008
A. nobilis	pulsed series	–	–	697–1450 (mean)	courtship	Aalbers & Drawbridge 2008
A. nobilis	multipulsed	–	–	230–360	spawning	Aalbers & Drawbridge 2008
A. nobilis	non-pulsed	–	–	200–310	spawning	Aalbers & Drawbridge 2008
A. nobilis	non-pulsed	–	13–450	–	spawning, burst swimming	Aalbers & Drawbridge 2008
A. nobilis	sound series	–	–	5–45 sec	–	Aalbers & Drawbridge 2008
Bairdiella chrysoura	–	–	–	–	reproductive aggregations	Locascio & Mann 2008
Cynoscion arenarius	multipulsed	2–12	~200–500	235±93 (mean ± SD)	chorusing	Locascio & Mann 2008
C. nebulosus	multipulsed	2	100–1,150	140–210	courtship, spawning	Gilmore 2003
C. nebulosus	multipulsed	3–5	100–1,150	140–450	courtship, spawning	Gilmore 2003
C. nebulosus	single pulse	1	90–1,150	175–367	courtship, spawning	Gilmore 2003
C. nebulosus	multipulsed	>16	30–1,300	822.5	courtship, spawning	Gilmore 2003
C. nebulosus	–	–	–	–	reproductive aggregations	Locascio & Mann 2008

(continued)

TABLE 10.1. (continued)

Family/species	Sound pattern	No. sound types	No. pulses	Frequency range (hz)	Sound duration (ms)	Behavioral contexts	References
Cynoscion regalis	multipulsed	–	6–10	–	–	disturbance	Connaughton et al. 2002
C. xanthulus	multipulsed	–	4–13	400–1,200	~50	reproductive aggregations	Fish & Cummings 1972
Equetus lanceolatus	–	–	–	–	–	sonic morphology	Schneider & Hasler 1960
Johnius australis	–	–	–	–	–	sounds recorded	Walls 1964
J. belengerii	–	–	–	–	–	disturbance	Lin et al. 2007
J. macrorhynus	multipulsed	–	8–28	–	111–281 (143 min display)	disturbance, field recordings	Lin et al. 2007
J. macrorhynus	multipulsed	–	2	–	46 (mean)	disturbance, field recordings	Lin et al. 2007
J. tingi	–	–	–	–	–	disturbance	Lin et al. 2007
Odontoscion dentex	–	–	–	–	–	escape	Fish & Mowbray 1970
Otolithes ruber	–	–	–	–	–	disturbance	Lin et al. 2007
Pareques acuminatus	–	2	–	–	–	disturbance	Fish & Mowbray 1970
Pennahia macrocephalus	–	–	–	–	–	disturbance	Lin et al. 2007
P. pawak	–	–	–	–	–	disturbance	Lin et al. 2007
Sciaenops ocellata	–	–	–	–	–	male courtship display, chorus	Guest & Lasswell 1978
S. ocellata	–	–	–	240–1,000	–	courtship, spawning	Holt 2002
S. ocellata	–	2	–	–	–	disturbance	Fish & Mowbray 1970

SCORPAENIDAE (2 species)					
Scorpaena plumieri	–	–	–	heterospecific in cave territory	Fish & Mowbray 1970
Scorpaenopsis gibbosa	–	–	–	sounds reported	Fish & Mowbray 1970
SEBASTIDAE (1 species)					
Sebastiscus marmoratus	1	85–125	100–160	agonism	Miyagawa & Takemura 1986
S. marmoratus	multiple	–	–	agonism	Miyagawa & Takemura 1986
SERRANIDAE (18 species)					
Alphestes afer	2	–	–	disturbance, escape	Fish & Mowbray 1970
Cephalopholis fulva	2	–	–	disturbance, escape	Fish & Mowbray 1970
C. cruentata	–	–	–	chase heterospecific	Bright 1972
C. cruentata	2	–	–	electrical stimulation only	Fish & Mowbray 1970
Diplectrum formosum	2	–	–	disturbance, escape	Fish & Mowbray 1970
Epinephelus adscensionis	2	–	–	feeding competition, disturbance, escape	Fish & Mowbray 1970
E. adscensionis	2	<900	40–100	retreat from hydrophone, disturbance, swimming accompanying feeding	Moulton 1958
E. drummondhayi	–	–	–	feeding competition, flee predator, escape	Fish & Mowbray 1970
E. guttatus	–	–	–	feeding competition interspecific, disturbance	Fish & Mowbray 1970
E. itajara	single pulse	–	132 (mean)	spawning aggregations	Mann et al. 2008
E. itajara	–	–	–	disturbance, flee predator	Fish & Mowbray 1970
E. morio	–	–	–	feeding competition	Fish & Mowbray 1970
E. nigritus	2	–	–	disturbance, escape	Fish & Mowbray 1970
E. striatus	3	–	–	feeding competition, feeding	Fish et al. 1952

(continued)

TABLE 10.1. (continued)

Family/species	Sound pattern	No. sound types	No. pulses	Frequency range (hz)	Sound duration (ms)	Behavioral contexts	References
Epinephelus striatus	—	1	—	0–2,000	100–200	retreat from hydrophore, quickened swimming accompanying feeding	Moulton 1958
E. striatus	sound series	—	—	—	—	unknown	Moulton 1958
E. striatus	—	—	—	—	—	disturbance	Moulton 1958
E. striatus	—	—	—	—	—	feeding competition	Fish & Mowbray 1970
E. striatus	—	—	—	—	—	escape (fleeing predator)	Bright 1972
E. striatus	—	—	—	low <600	50–125	agonism, disturbance	Moulton 1958
Hypoplectrus unicolor	multipulsed	3	—	500	200–1,500	courtship	Lobel 1992
H. unicolor	frequency modulated	—	—	600–200	150	mating sound	Lobel 1992
H. unicolor	broadband	—	—	350–1,650	1,250	mating (gamete release)	Lobel 1992
Mycteroperca bonaci	multipulsed	—	—	—	—	disturbance	–
M. bonaci	multipulsed	—	4–5	100–400	~150	territorial;* arrids swim by cave, disturbance	Tavolga 1960
M. bonaci	multipulsed	—	4–6	~40–100	~500	disturbance, escape, spontaneous	Fish & Mowbray 1970
M. microlepis	—	—	—	—	—	electrical stimulation only	Fish & Mowbray 1970
M. venenosa	—	—	—	—	—	disturbance, feeding	Fish & Mowbray 1970
Rypticus bistrispinus	—	—	—	—	—	electrical stimulation only	Fish & Mowbray 1970
R. saponaceus	—	—	—	—	—	electrical stimulation only	Fish & Mowbray 1970
Serranus tigrinus	—	—	—	—	—	electrical stimulation only	Fish & Mowbray 1970
SILLAGINIDAE (1 species)							
Sillago maculata	—	—	—	—	—	sounds recorded	Walls 1964

Taxon						Behavior	Reference
SPARIDAE (8 species)							
Archosargus sp.	–	–	–	5,800	26	feeding noise*	Knudsen et al. 1948a
A. probatocephalus	–	–	–	–	–	feeding noise	Fish & Mowbray 1970
A. rhomboidalis	–	–	–	–	–	escape	Fish & Mowbray 1970
Calamus bajonad	–	–	–	~50–400	~100	escape	Fish & Mowbray 1970
C. calamus	–	–	–	~100–400	~50–100	escape	Fish & Mowbray 1970
C. calamus	–	–	–	–	–	disturbance in net	Fish & Mowbray 1970
C. penna	–	2	–	–	–	escape	Fish & Mowbray 1970
Diplodus argenteus	–	–	–	–	–	disturbance, escape	Fish & Mowbray 1970
Lagodon rhomboides	–	–	–	2,000–3,000	50	chase intraspecific	Caldwell & Caldwell 1967
SPHYRAENIDAE (1 species)							
Sphyraena barracuda	–	2	–	–	–	swimming	Fish & Mowbray 1970
SYNANCEIDAE (1 species)							
Erosa erosa	–	–	–	–	–	sound recorded	Walls 1964
SYNGNATHIDAE (4 species)							
Hippocampus erectus	–	–	–	–	–	male-female duet breeding	Dufossé 1874
H. erectus	–	–	–	–	–	feeding noise	Colson et al. 1998
H. erectus	–	–	–	–	–	feeding noise	James & Heck 1994
H. erectus	–	–	–	<50–4,800	–	spontaneous new surroundings	Fish 1953
H. erectus	single pulse	–	–	<50–4,800	–	unknown	Fish 1954
H. erectus	pulse series	–	2–5	50–4,800	–	spontaneous, solitary individual	Fish 1954
H. erectus	pulse series	–	2–5	<50–1,600	–	unknown	Fish et al. 1952
H. erectus	–	–	–	~100–1,200	~200	male-female duet, explore new surroundings "orientation"	Fish & Mowbray 1970

(*continued*)

TABLE 10.1. (*continued*)

Family/species	Sound pattern	No. sound types	No. pulses	Frequency range (hz)	Sound duration (ms)	Behavioral contexts	References
Hippocampus zostera	–	–	–	2,650–3,430 peak	–	feeding noise	Colson et al. 1998
Syngnathus floridae	–	–	–	–	–	feeding chorus	Ripley & Foran 2007
S. acus	–	–	–	–	–	disturbance*	Burkenroad 1931
TERAPONTIDAE (4 species)							
Pelates quadrilineatus	–	–	–	–	–	sound reported	Moulton 1964b
P. quadrilineatus	–	–	–	–	–	sound reported	Graham 1992
Therapon (=*Terapon*) *jarbua*	multipulsed	–	3–30	800	10, 60–150	agonism	Schneider 1964b
T. (=*Terapon*) *jarbua*	sound series	–	–	–	5,000–10,000 sec	agonism	Schneider 1964b
T. puta	–	–	–	–	–	sound recorded	Walls 1964
T. theraps	–	–	–	–	–	chase	Hardenberg 1934
T. theraps	multipulsed	–	9–12	–	79–105	free-ranging in ocean	McCauley & Cato 2000
T. theraps	–	–	–	–	7	fight	Schneider 1964b

TETRAODONTIDAE (6 species)

Species				Behavior			Reference
Amblyrhynchotes honckenii	–	–	–	disturbance defense inflation	–	–	Pappe 1853
Canthigaster rivulata	–	–	–	sound reported	–	–	Uchida 1934
Lagocephalus sceleratus	–	–	–	sonic morphology	–	–	Moulton 1964b
Sphoeroides nephelus	–	–	–	defense inflation (during & after)	–	–	Burkenroad 1931
S. spengleri	–	–	–	defense inflation (during & after)	–	–	Fish 1948
S. spengleri	–	–	–	defense inflation	–	–	Fish & Mowbray 1970
S. spengleri	–	–	–	disturbance	0–8,000	70	Moulton 1958
S. testudineus	–	–	–	defense inflation	~40–6,000	~80–1,100	Fish & Mowbray 1970
TETRAROGIDAE (2 species)							
Centropogon australis	–	–	–	sounds recorded	–	–	Walls 1964
C. marmoratus	–	–	–	sounds recorded	–	–	Walls 1964
TRIGLIDAE (1 species)							
Lepidotrigla argus	–	–	–	sounds recorded	–	–	Walls 1964

* Based on authors' interpretation of the published data.

TABLE 10.2 Interspecific and intraspecific acoustic properties of tropical fish sounds

Family	No. species recorded	Frequency range (hz)	Sound duration (ms)	Behavioral contexts
Acanthuridae	1	150–4,700	100	agonism
Ariidae	2	100–4,000	10–550	disturbance, schooling chorus
Balistidae	7	50–9,600	20–2,400	disturbance, defense, feeding competition, territoriality
Batrachoididae	4	50–2,100	30–6,077	disturbance, agonism, reproduction
Blenniidae	1	150–1,000	150–350	reproduction
Carangidae	11	10–8,000	30–1,300	disturbance, escape, feeding competition
Carapidae	5	55–4,450	16–362	agonism hypothesized
Chaetodontidae	2	40–5,190	3–5,700	agonism, reproduction
Dactylopteridae	2	~100–800	~80–120	disturbance
Diodontidae	2	50–8,000	30–90	disturbance defense display
Ephippidae	1	75–220	150	disturbance, spontaneous in aquarium
Gobiidae	2	100–1,500	35–350	reproduction
Haemulidae	8	~50–8,000	20–200	disturbance, escape, feeding competition, schooling
Holocentridae	8	75–4,800	10–3,000	disturbance agonism, reproduction
Kyphosidae	1	50–250	20	"spontaneous" in social group
Labridae	2	~100–300 [50–2,400]	~100–200 [200]	escape, [feeding noise]
Lutjanidae	10	~50–400	~100–500	escape, feeding competition
Monacanthidae	1	200–1,000	~80–1,200	disturbance, feeding competition,
Monocentridae	1	100–600	unknown	disturbance
Mullidae	2	~50–450	~100	escape
Oplegnathidae	1	160	13–20	agonism, reproductive chorus
Ostraciidae	3	~50–4,000	10–700	disturbance, agonism, spawning, chorus
Pempheridae	1	100–300	56–75	disturbance, agonism
Polynemidae	1	~100–500	~10–20	escape
Pomacanthidae	6	100–3,800	31–200	escape, agonism, reproduction
Pomacentridae	23	200–7,400	7–1,793	agonism, reproduction
Priacanthidae	2	75–1,200	64–839	disturbance, agonism
Scaridae	3	30–1200	~100–750	disturbance, escape, spawning
Sciaenidae	7	13–1,300	5–1,450	disturbance, escape, reproductive chorus aggregation
Sebastidae	1	85–125	100–160	agonism
Serranidae	5	~40–2,000	40–200	disturbance, agonism, chorus spawning

TABLE 10.2 *(continued)*

Family	No. species recorded	Frequency range (hz)	Basic sound unit duration (ms)	Behavioral contexts
Sparidae	4	~50–5,800	26–100	escape, agonism
Syngnathidae	2	100–4,800 [2.6–3.4k]	~200 [5–20]	reproduction "duet," solitary [feeding noise]
Terapontidae	2	200–1,500	7–105	agonism, spontaneous in ocean
Tetraodontidae	2	40–8,000	70–1,100	disturbance, defense display

Approximations "~" are from Fish & Mowbray (1970) spectrograms when no other data was available. Square brackets "[ ]" indicate feeding noise data. "Disturbance" in this table refers only to artificially manipulated or restrained specimens. Only contexts with recorded data are noted.

TABLE 10.3 Possible information included in fish acoustic signals, in order of increasing complexity of signal interpretation

Message	Acoustic clue
Mate location	Sound occurrence
Readiness to spawn Synchronization of gamete release (= Mating or spawning sound)	Sound occurrence
Vigor/aggressiveness	Duration of call and/or call repetition rate
Individual size	Dominant frequency
Species identity	Variation in pulse repetition rate in a call, number of pulses in a call, variation in pulse amplitude, call duration, plus color patterns and behavior
Individual identity	Combination of all above clues, plus other features of behavior

TABLE 10.4 Coral reef fish congeners whose sounds have been recorded and for which comparisons of temporal patterns and frequency can be made

Family/ genus	No. species	Species	Behavioral contexts	Species sounds differed in . . .
Balistidae (Salmon et al. 1968)				
Melichthys	3	*buniva, niger, vidua*	agonism & disturbance	waveform
Balistes	3	*bursa, capistratus, vetula*	agonism & disturbance	waveform
Batrachoididae (Fish & Mowbray 1959)				
Opsanus	2	*beta, phobetron*	reproductive	sound pulse number per display
Carapidae (Courtenay & McKittrick 1970; Lagardère et al. 2005; Parmentier et al. 2006b)				
Carapus	4	*acus, boraborensis, mourlani, homei*	agonism?	pulse duration, interpulse interval
Gobiidae (Stadler 2002)				
Bathygobius	2	*curacao, soporator*	male courtship display	amplitude, duration
Holocentridae (Winn et al. 1964; Bright & Sartori 1972; Popper et al. 1973)				
Holocentrus	2	*adscensionis, rufus*	disturbance	sounds similar
Myripristis	3	*brendti, jacobus, violacea*	agonism	sounds similar
Pomacanthidae (Thresher 1982; Moyer et al. 1983; Amorim 1996a)				
Pomacanthus	2	*arcuatus, imperator*	agonism, pair interactions	duration
Pomacentridae (e.g., Parmentier et al. 2006a; Maruska et al. 2007; Parmentier et al. 2009)				
Abudefduf	3	*abdominalis, luridus, sordidus*	male courtship	pulse number, duration
Amphiprion	8	*alkallopisos, chrysopterus, clarkii, frenatus, melanopus, ocellaris, polymnus, sandaracinos*	agonism	sound similar
Chromis	2	*viridis, chromis*	agonism, male courtship	frequency
Dascyllus	4	*albisella, aruanus, flavicaudus, trimaculatus*	agonism, male courtship	pulse number & interval, duration

(continued)

TABLE 10.4 *(continued)*

Family/ genus	No. species	Species	Behavioral contexts	Species sounds differed in . . .
Stegastes	4	*dorsopunicans, leucostictus, partitus, planifrons*	male courtship display	pulse number & interval, duration
Sciaenidae (Ramcharitar et al. 2006; Lin et al. 2007; Locascio & Mann 2008)				
Cynoscion	2	*arenarius, nebulosus*	courtship, spawning	pulse repetition rate
Johnius	3	*belangeri, macrorhynus, tingi*	disturbance	pulse repetition rate

At its inception, this volume was envisaged as an opportunity to shine a spotlight on a number of topics associated with reproductive biology among marine fishes. Many of the topics have either received scant coverage in the past or were ready for a comprehensive and updated treatment. Accordingly, contributions to the volume were chosen to fill in previous gaps in our knowledge, to present new approaches to existing problems, and to generate new testable models for questions related to the evolution of reproductive and sexual biology in marine fishes.

As a topic, the biology of vertebrate reproduction encompasses a wide variety of subdisciplines ranging from the study of molecules, cells, tissues, and organ systems to that of individuals, populations, metapopulations, and species. Among a considerable number of marine fish taxa, an additional (and unusual, for vertebrates) feature is that phenotypic sexuality is not always dictated by genotype. In these cases, sexual function involves the strategic apportionment of ova and sperm production within a single individual, and the nature of expressed sexual patterns reflects the combined influences of social system, reproductive mode, and reproductive advantage. Sexuality, instead of being fixed, is labile, and sexual patterns are characterized by functional hermaphroditism. Not surprisingly, labile sexual patterns found among marine fish taxa are inextricably intertwined with their reproductive biology. When viewed from several different perspectives as provided by a number of chapters within this volume, it becomes clear that understanding the interrelationships between reproduction and sexuality is central to understanding the significant evolutionary and adaptive success of a number of functionally hermaphroditic marine fish taxa.

This volume also brings a new focus to some relatively small-sized and inconspicuous marine fish taxa. There has always been a fascination with the classical archetype of a coral reef fish comprising an exotic body shape and brilliant poster coloration. This is reflected in the many early studies of reproductive biology that focused on some of the more conspicuous fish species occupying accessible marine environments. Recently however, there has been increasing recognition that a significant portion of biodiversity, biomass, trophic cycling, and energy flow within complex marine fish communities is linked to small, and typically cryptic, fishes. These fishes—which are usually either underrepresented in, or entirely excluded from, fish surveys—constitute a hidden underworld, the reproductive biology of which remains predominantly unknown. Accordingly, this volume highlights a number of aspects of the reproductive biology and sexuality found among some of the smallest and least conspicuous of marine fish taxa, the blennioids and gobiids.

A recurring theme provides a subtext for many of the included chapters: What is the present state of our ocean environments, and how will marine fishes fare with possible changes to the ocean environments of tomorrow? A number of chapters are particularly timely in this regard. Increasing fishing pressure is raising concerns regarding the sustainability of commercially important species at present harvesting rates. Anthropogenic influences on marine environments are increasingly becoming associated with physiological and behavioral abnormalities among marine community inhabitants. The steadily increasing wealth of data documenting substantial changes in saltwater environments in terms of pH, salinity, CO_2 levels, and temperatures—the latter at all depths from sea surface to bottom water—signal significant ongoing changes in our oceans. And yet, with a few exceptions, we know very little regarding the biology, and particularly the reproductive biology, of most marine fishes.

As our awareness of marine environments has grown over the last several decades, it is evident that our preconceptions as to the constancy and apparent invulnerability of these aquatic regions have been misplaced. Marine environments are changing, and the distribution and abundance of marine organisms are undergoing changes as well. Our ability to make effective decisions regarding local and global issues that bear directly on the health and sustainability of marine environments and their resident communities depends directly on our ability to make informed choices. And that ability rests on having a sound understanding of the biological interrelationships within and among marine habitats and marine communities.

Collectively, the chapters included here offer new insights into patterns and processes of reproduction and sexuality among marine fishes. The contents, in providing the latest information available in the covered topics, hold the promise of suggesting new approaches to existing problems and point the way for future research. It is hoped that the efforts of the contributing authors to produce this volume will not only advance our knowledge of reproductive biology among marine fishes, but will also move us a step closer to the optimistic goal of ensuring a future for all marine fishes.

Kathleen S. Cole, editor

INDEX

Citations ending with a "t" indicate a table; those with an "f" indicate a figure.